Discovering Leadership

Second Edition

SAGE PUBLISHING: OUR STORY

We believe in creating fresh, cutting-edge content that helps you prepare your students to make an impact in today's ever-chang business world. Founded in 1965 by 24-year-old entrepreneur Sara Miller McCune, SAGE continues its legacy of equipping instruc with the tools and resources necessary to develop the next generation of business leaders.

- We invest in the right **authors** who distill the best available research into practical applications.
- We offer intuitive **digital solutions** at student-friendly prices.
- We remain permanently independent and fiercely committed to **quality, innovation, and learning**.

Discovering Leadership

Designing Your Success

Second Edition

Anthony Middlebrooks
University of Florida

Scott J. Allen
John Carroll University

Mindy S. McNutt
Wright State University

James L. Morrison
University of Delaware

Los Angeles | London | New Delhi
Singapore | Washington DC | Melbourne

FOR INFORMATION:

SAGE Publications, Inc.
2455 Teller Road
Thousand Oaks, California 91320
E-mail: order@sagepub.com

SAGE Publications Ltd.
1 Oliver's Yard
55 City Road
London, EC1Y 1SP
United Kingdom

SAGE Publications India Pvt. Ltd.
Unit No. 323-333, Third Floor, F-Block
International Trade Tower
Nehru Place, New Delhi 110 019
India

SAGE Publications Asia-Pacific Pte. Ltd.
18 Cross Street #10-10/11/12
China Square Central
Singapore 048423

Acquisitions Editor: Lily Norton

Content Development Editor: Darcy Scelsi

Production Editor: Astha Jaiswal

Copy Editor: Karin Rathert

Typesetter: diacriTech

Cover Designer: Janet Kiesel

Marketing Manager: Jennifer Haldeman

Copyright © 2024 by SAGE Publications, Inc.

All rights reserved. Except as permitted by U.S. copyright law, no part of this work may be reproduced or distributed in any form or by any means, or stored in a database or retrieval system, without permission in writing from the publisher.

All third-party trademarks referenced or depicted herein are included solely for the purpose of illustration and are the property of their respective owners. Reference to these trademarks in no way indicates any relationship with, or endorsement by, the trademark owner.

Printed in [the United States of America / Canada]

Paperback ISBN: 9781071866986

Loose-leaf ISBN: 9781071904107

This book is printed on acid-free paper.

23 24 25 26 27 10 9 8 7 6 5 4 3 2 1

BRIEF CONTENTS

Foreword	**xxi**
Preface to the Second Edition	**xxiii**
Prologue	**xxv**
Teaching Resources	**xxxvii**
Acknowledgments	**xxxix**
About the Authors	**xli**

Introduction and Foundations		1
Chapter 1	A Framework for Leadership Success: Design and Your CORE™	15

MODULE 1　DESIGN LEADERSHIP SELF　47

Chapter 2	Designing Your Perceptions of Leaders and Leadership	49
Chapter 3	Designing Your Leadership Capacity	79
Chapter 4	Your Why and What for Leading	121

MODULE 2　DESIGN LEADERSHIP RELATIONSHIPS　147

Chapter 5	Your Values and Ethical Actions	149
Chapter 6	Decision-Making	181
Chapter 7	Influence, Power, and Motivation	209

MODULE 3　DESIGN OTHERS' SUCCESS　237

Chapter 8	Creativity, Problem-Solving, and Idea-Generating	239
Chapter 9	Effective Practices for Leading Others to Success	273
Chapter 10	Utilizing Change Processes Effectively	307

MODULE 4　DESIGN CULTURE AND COMMUNITY　335

Chapter 11	Culture	337
Chapter 12	Leading a Team	369
Chapter 13	Designing a Culture That Cares	399

MODULE 5 DESIGN THE FUTURE — 429

Chapter 14	Creating a Culture of Innovation	431
Chapter 15	Entrepreneurial Leadership	461
Chapter 16	Systems and Sustainability	489

Glossary	515
Notes	523
Index	559

DETAILED CONTENTS

Foreword	xxi
Preface to the Second Edition	xxiii
Prologue	xxv
Teaching Resources	xxxvii
Acknowledgments	xxxix
About the Authors	xli

Introduction and Foundations	**1**
Leadership Matters	1
Organization of This Textbook: The Leadership by Design Framework	3
Content: Topics and Special Features	5
Leadership by Design Model	6
Leadership That Makes a Difference	6
Leadership by Design	7
DEI by Design	8
Myth or Reality?	9
Experts Beyond the Text: Insightful Leaders Know About _____	10
Moments of Awareness	10
CORE™ Attribute Builders	11
Skill Builder Activities	12
Chapter Summary	13
Key Terms	14
Chapter 1 A Framework for Leadership Success: Design and Your CORE™	**15**
Introduction	15
Designing Your Leadership	18
Design Process as a Creative Problem-Solving Process: Understand, Imagine, Implement, and Iterate	18
Design as a Mental Habit: Design Thinking	20
Design Principles: Rules You Can Apply to Design Your Leadership	22
Designing Your Leadership by Building Your Core™	24
Confidence	25
Optimism	28
Resilience	29
Engagement	33
DEI by Design	36
Designing Your Leadership—First Step: Your Goals	37
Purposeful, Present, Planning: 3 Ps for Your Leadership Journey	38

Chapter Summary	39
Key Terms	40
CORE™ Attribute Builders: Build Now for Future Leadership Challenges	40
Challenge Yourself	41
Skill Builder Activity	44

MODULE 1   DESIGN LEADERSHIP SELF   47

Chapter 2   Designing Your Perceptions of Leaders and Leadership   49

Introduction	49
You: Student and Designer of Your Own Leadership	51
Learning Leadership	51
What to Expect as You Learn Leadership	52
Your Brain Is a Lean, Mean, Pattern-Making Machine: You Construct Your World	54
Misconceptions About Leaders and Leadership	56
Leadership Is . . . a Process	57
Misconception: Leaders Are Born	59
Misconception: Leaders Need to Have a Specific Set of Traits, Particularly Extroversion	59
Leadership Is . . . a Process of Influencing	59
Misconception: Leaders Do the Talking and Take Charge	59
Misconception: Leaders Do the Influencing	60
Leadership Is . . . a Process of Influencing Others	60
Misconception: There Is Only One Specific Way to Be an Effective Leader	60
Misconception: A Leader Cannot Be Friends With Their Followers	60
Leadership Is . . . a Process of Influencing Others Toward	61
Misconception: Effective Leaders Are Always Collaborative	61
Leadership Is . . . a Process of Influencing Others Toward a Common	61
Misconception: Confident Leaders Who Celebrate Their Success Are Arrogant and Selfish	61
Misconception: Explaining the Vision More Clearly Is the Best Way to Acquire Follower Support	62
Leadership Is . . . a Process of Influencing Others Toward a Common Vision	62
Misconception: Leadership Education Is Not Really Applicable to the Real World	62
Effective Leaders Are Like _____: Characteristics and Traits	65
Effective Leaders Can Do _____: Skills, Practices, and Expertise	68
In Competency Terms	68
Management? Leadership? Both	69
The Expert Leader	69
The Credible Leader	71
DEI by Design	74
Chapter Summary	75
Key Terms	75
CORE™ Attribute Builders: Build Now for Future Leadership Challenges	76
CORE™ Attribute Builders: Build Now for Future Leadership Challenges	76
Skill Builder Activity	77
Skill Builder Activity	78

Detailed Contents   **ix**

Chapter 3   Designing Your Leadership Capacity   79

Introduction   79

Assess to Better Know Yourself: Does It Matter That You Are a Gold-Red Kangaroo Triangle Guardian?   81

Designing Your Capacity: Three Foundational Mindsets   82
     Growth Mindset   82
     Process-Oriented Mindset   83
     Strengths-Based Mindset   83

Design Thinking for Your Leadership Toolbox   85
     Explorative and User-Centered to Better Understand   88
        Explorative   88
        User-Centered   89
        Empathy: User-Centeredness at the Deep End of the Pool   91
     Divergent and Multidisciplinary to Better Imagine   92
        Divergent   92
        Multidisciplinary   93
     Integrative and Iterative to Better Implement   96
        Integrative   96
        Iterative   97
     Assess Your Design Thinking, Then Design Leadership Relationships   98

New Challenges . . . Need New Leadership . . . Need You   101
     Risk-Taking Replaces Status Quo   101
     Workspace Transforms the Workplace   102
     Streamlined Organizational Structure Displaces the Hierarchy   102
        Diverse, Inclusive, and Equitable Workplaces Expected   103
     Business Values Synchronizing With Cultural Expectations   104
     Humans Compete With Technology   104
     Disruption Interrupts Normalcy   105

New Leadership Skills in Demand   106
     Exhibit Empathy by Engaging in Candid Discussions   106
     Engage Digital Transformation   108
     Empower an Inclusive and Collaborative Work Culture   109
     Extend Capacity With Stretch Assignments   111
     Enrich the Leadership Capacity of Others   112

DEI by Design   113

Capacity Capstone: Commit to the Journey   114

Chapter Summary   116

Key Terms   117

Skill Builder Activity   117

CORE™ Attribute Builders: Build Now for Future Leadership Challenges   118

Chapter 4   Your Why and What for Leading   121

Introduction   121

Why Do You Want to Lead?   124
     Finding Purpose in Challenge   125
     Finding Purpose in Personal Meaning   126

DEI by Design—Recognizing Who You Are   126

x   Discovering Leadership

Your Purpose: Charisms and Flow   130

   Identify Your Charisms   130

   Finding Your Flow   131

      From Being to Doing: TJ Watt   132

Learning From Shadows   133

   Understanding the Shadow: Hardship and Tough Life Lessons Can Bring Clarity to Purpose   133

   Exploring the Shadow to Find the Stretch   134

The Process of Influencing Others . . . for What?   135

   What Does the World Need? Nisha Ligon   138

What Purpose Deserves You?   140

   Every Purpose Impacts Individuals   141

   Activate Your Purpose   141

Chapter Summary   142

Key Terms   143

Skill Builder Activity   143

CORE™ Attribute Builders: Build Now for Future Leadership Challenges   145

CORE™ Attribute Builders: Build Now for Future Leadership Challenges   145

MODULE 2   DESIGN LEADERSHIP RELATIONSHIPS   **147**

Chapter 5   Your Values and Ethical Actions   **149**

Introduction   149

Getting Leadership Right   150

Ethical Issues and the Student Experience   151

Ethics—The Key Concepts   154

   Ethics/Code of Ethics   154

   Laws   154

   Moral Principles   154

   Personal Values   155

   Virtues and Thoughtful Intentionality   155

   Character   158

   Integrity   158

The Roots of Moral Development   160

The Ethical Challenges of Leadership   161

   Ethical Issues in Five Domains   162

   Why Individuals Fail to Behave Ethically   163

   Toxic and Bad Leaders and Leadership   165

   Courageous Followers and Dissent   168

DEI by Design   170

Designing Your Ethical Leadership   171

   Ethical Decision-Making   171

   The BASE Model   172

      Begin With You   172

      Assess   173

      Seek Options   173

      Elect and Evaluate   175

Detailed Contents   **xi**

Chapter Summary	175
Key Terms	176
CORE™ Attribute Builders: Build Now for Future Leadership Challenges	176
Skill Builder Activity	177

Chapter 6   Decision-Making   181

Introduction	181
Decisions, Decisions, Decisions in Leadership	183
Defining Decision-Making	185
Levels of Decision-Making	185
Types of Decision-Making	186
Technical or Adaptive? Types of Problems Leaders Face	188
Technical or Tame Problems	188
Adaptive Challenges/Wicked Problems/Ill-Defined Problems	188
In Leadership, Decision-Making Is a Team Sport (Much of the Time)	190
Align Your Decision-Making Style	191
Design Your Decision-Making Style	192
Designing Your Approach to Decision-Making: The SOLVE Model of Decision-Making	193
Set Roles	193
Common Pitfalls at This Stage	193
Outline the Problem and Decision Criteria	194
Common Pitfalls at This Stage	194
List Multiple Strategies	195
Common Pitfalls at This Stage	195
Veer Toward Consensus	196
Common Pitfalls at This Stage	196
Evaluate Decision and Process	197
Common Pitfalls at This Stage	197
SOLVE in Action: Designing (and Deciding) How the Team Will Work	198
How Did We Get Here? This Was Not the Plan: Barriers to Decision-Making	198
Cognitive Biases That Hinder Decision-Making	199
Confirmation Bias	199
One-Right-Answer Thinking	199
Groupthink	199
Framing Effect	199
Overconfidence Effect	200
Law of Triviality	200
Illusion of Control	200
Ways You Could Be the Barrier to Effective Decision-Making	201
Ways Others Could Be the Barrier to Effective Decision-Making	203
Other Factors That Impede Effective Decision-Making	204
DEI by Design	205
Chapter Summary	206
Key Terms	206
CORE™ Attribute Builders	206
Skill Builder Activity	207

xii Discovering Leadership

Chapter 7 Influence, Power, and Motivation — 209

Introduction	209
Influence is (mostly) Not About You	211
The Path to the Goal and Your Style	212
Forms of Influence	213
The Difference Between Influence and Authority	215
The Difference Between Influence and Manipulation	216
DEI by Design	216
Designing Your Influence with Individuals and Team	217
Influence Tactics for Leaders	218
Involve Others/Consulting	218
Facts/Logic/Rational Persuasion	219
Relationships	219
Lead a Coalition	219
Emphasize win-win	219
Create Positive Energy	219
Inspirational Appeal	219
Negotiation/Bargaining/Exchange	220
Personal Appeal	220
Pressure/Coercion	221
Ingratiation	221
Gaining Power in Groups and Organizations	222
Sources of Power: Personal and Positional Power	222
Reward Power	222
Personal Charisma/Referent Power	223
Outmatched Effort	223
Wealth/Resource	223
Expertise	224
Relevance	224
Visibility	224
Network	225
Legitimacy	225
Legitimate Power	226
Motivation	227
Intrinsic and Extrinsic Motivation	227
Sources of Intrinsic and Extrinsic Motivation	228
Financial Compensation	228
Alignment With Values	228
Meaning	229
Showing Appreciation	229
Reward and Recognize	229
Empowerment	230
Belonging	230
Achievement/Success/Competence	230
Fairness	230
Autonomy	231
Feedback/Coaching	231
Flexibility/Freedom	231
Career pathing	232
Psychological Safety	232

Detailed Contents **xiii**

The Leadership Challenge: Designing Leadership Relationships 233

Chapter Summary 234

Key Terms 235

CORE™ Attribute Builders: Build Now for Future Leadership Challenges 235

Skill Builder Activity 236

MODULE 3 DESIGN OTHERS' SUCCESS 237

Chapter 8 Creativity, Problem-Solving, and Idea-Generating 239

Introduction 239

Yes, You Really Are Creative 241

DEI by Design 245

Moving From Reactive Problems to Proactive Opportunities 246

Algorithm, Heuristic, and the Important Thing 247

Yes, Creativity Will Help (a Lot) 248

Product: Unique and Valuable 248

Person: Divergent Thinking, Open-Mindedness, and Creative Confidence 249

Press: Context and Culture 252

Process: Understand, Imagine, Implement, and Iterate Revisited 252

Yes, You Can Generate Many, Many Ideas 255

Divergent Thinking Techniques 256

Problem Analysis Techniques 257

Visualization Techniques 258

Play and Build Techniques 260

Senses and Emotions 260

Incubation Techniques 262

Alternative Perspective Techniques 262

Yes, You Can Find Many, Many Ideas 263

Inspiration and Exploration Techniques 263

No, You Are Not "Done": Iteration, Convergence, and Assurance 268

Chapter Summary 270

Key Terms 270

CORE™ Attribute Builders: Build Now for Future Leadership Challenges 271

Skill Builder Activity 271

Skill Builder Activity 271

Skill Builder Activity 272

Chapter 9 Effective Practices for Leading Others to Success 273

Introduction 273

DEI by Design 275

Practices for Your Follower's Brain 276

Brain Leading in Six Dimensions 277

Physiological, Emotional, and Social Dimensions 278

Reflective, Constructive, and Dispositional 281

Effective Leadership: Creating Conditions Using Dimensions of the Brain 284

xiv   Discovering Leadership

Practices for Followers' Needs and Motivation	285
Know What Followers Need to Succeed	286
Followers Need the Freedom to Raise Issues	286
Followers Need to Be Believed In	286
Followers Need to Possess Cutting-Edge Job Skills	286
Followers Need Time to Think Creatively	286
Followers Need to Capitalize on Their Strengths	287
Followers Want to Have Impact	289
Mastery of Problem-Solving Skills	289
Membership Through Community Solidarity	289
Meaning by Focusing Upon the Big Picture	289
Practice Leadership and Management: When Multitasking Really Matters	291
IGNITE as a Leader	292
Instill a Culture That Despises Complacency	292
Grow Engagement and Innovation With Compassion	292
Note and Study Your Competitors and Collaborators	293
Invest in Real-Time, Data-Driven Decision-Making	294
Tackle Candid Conversations	294
Ensure a Clear Vision to Make It Happen	294
DELIVER as a Manager	296
Designate One Individual Who Will Have Responsibility Over the Implementation Process	296
Empower Followers to Make Thoughtful Decisions by Delineating Clear Lines for the Scope of Their Authority	296
List What Is Unique About Each Person, Then Capitalize on It	296
Initiate a Risk Response Team to Assist Those Being Subjected to Significant Obstacles and Possible Failure	297
Verify Progress by Establishing Checkpoints for Accomplishments	297
Encourage and Exhibit Calm When Under Fire	298
Redesign Work Patterns and Assignments so They Are Cross-Functional	298
Design Others' Success With a Situational Leadership Approach	299
Situational Leadership: Adapt to the Capacity of Followers to Perform	300
Understand the (New) Rules of Engagement	302
Chapter Summary	303
Key Terms	303
CORE™ Attribute Builders: Build Now for Future Leadership Challenges	303
Skill Builder Activity—Go Do Some Leadership!	305
Chapter 10 Utilizing Change Processes Effectively	**307**
Introduction	307
Identify Levels of Change	309
Initiate Individual Change (Level 1)	310
Support Change at the Project Level (Level 2)	310
Generating a Change Culture at the Enterprise Level (Level 3)	311
Change Yourself Before You Can Change Others	311
Individual Change in Stages	312
Change Directly Affects Your Capacity to Lead Effectively	314
Be Reactive or Proactive	314

Gain or Lose Control Over Work Life 316
Adjust or Reject a Set of New Organizational Core Values 317
Transform How Careers Evolve 317

Transformational Versus Transactional Leadership 318

Barriers to Change 319
Thinking Rationally About Change May Not Work 320
Not All Opportunities for Change Are Worth Taking 320
Someone Will Resist the Change 321

Leading Change 321
Preparing to Execute Change 322
Executing Change for Others' Success 324
Justify an Opportunity to Act by Creating an Urgency for Change 324
Collaborate With Those Affected by Forming a Coalition 325
Ideate and Communicate Possibilities Through a Clear Vision for Change 325
Prove the Change Is Acceptable 326
Empower Others to Implement and Build 326
Sustain Momentum and Resilience After Change Is Implemented 327
Implementing Positive Organizational Scholarship as a Basis for Performing 328

DEI by Design 329

Chapter Summary 330

Key Terms 331

CORE™ Attribute Builders: Build Now for Future Leadership Challenges 331

Skill Builder Activity 332

Skill Builder Activity 332

Skill Builder Activity 332

MODULE 4 DESIGN CULTURE AND COMMUNITY 335

Chapter 11 Culture 337

Introduction 337

The Way We Do Things Around Here: Understanding Culture 340

Understanding Organizational Culture 341

Culture at the Societal Level 343
Understanding the Iceberg 344
The GLOBE Study 345

The Leader's Role and Organizational Culture 348
Personal Values—Forming and Informing Organizational Culture 348
Do Your Values Align With the Organization's Values? Ensuring Fit 349
Vision, Mission, and Values in Organizational Culture 350

Contemporary Approaches to Organizational Culture 351
The Great Pandemic 352

DEI by Design 353

Designing Culture 354
Tools to Facilitate Culture Change 355
Appreciative Inquiry 356
Strategic Planning Toward Culture Change 358

Chapter Summary	364
Key Terms	364
CORE™ Attribute Builders: Build Now for Future Leadership Challenges	365
CORE™ Attribute Builders: Build Now for Future Leadership Challenges	365
Skill Builder Activity	366

Chapter 12 Leading a Team — 369

Introduction	369
Just What Is a Team?	371
Teams Versus Groups	373
Types of Teams	374
Envisioning a Great Team	375
How Do Teams Come Together, and What Makes Them Excellent?	376
Shared Vision, Values, and Culture—Key to Team Success	379
Team Charter: Agreeing on the Basics	381
DEI by Design	382
From Group to Team: Stages of Development	383
Tuckman's Stages of Group Development	383
Leading and Being a Team	385
Models of Team Leadership	385
Your and Others' Role on the Team: What Makes a Good Team Member?	387
What Strengths Do I Bring to This Group?	388
When Teams Go Wrong	388
Reasons Teams Fail	388
Abilene Paradox	389
Groupthink	389
Dysfunctional Teams	390
How to Fix It When Things Go Wrong?	392
Chapter Summary	393
Key Terms	394
CORE™ Attribute Builders: Build Now for Future Leadership Challenges	394
CORE™ Attribute Builders: Build Now for Future Leadership Challenges	395
Skill Builder	395
Skill Builder	397

Chapter 13 Designing a Culture That Cares — 399

Introduction	399
A Culture That Cares	401
Values and Intention	402
Care, Empathy, and Compassion	403
Vulnerability	403
Motivation and Maslow's Hierarchy of Needs	404
Leading With Service	407
Servant Leadership and the Servant Leader	408
Empathy	409
Community building	409
Organizational Benefits of Servant Leadership	409

Detailed Contents   **xvii**

DEI by Design	412
Make a Difference: Designing a Culture That Cares	413
Social Change Model of Leadership Development	415
Individual Values	416
Group Values	416
Community Values	417
Making a Difference Now and Later: Opportunities and Actions	417
Service to Others in College	418
Types of College Service	419
Service Outside College	419
Service Within the Organization	420
Service Outside the Organization	420
Chapter Summary	422
Key Terms	422
CORE™ Attribute Builders: Build Now for Future Leadership Challenges	422
CORE™ Attribute Builders: Build Now for Future Leadership Challenges	423
Skill Builder Activity	424

MODULE 5 DESIGN THE FUTURE — **429**

Chapter 14 Creating a Culture of Innovation — **431**

Introduction	431
Why Innovate? Designing the Future	433
Drivers of Innovation	435
Innovation From Needs	435
Innovation From Desires	435
Innovation From Advances	435
Understanding Innovation	436
Collaborative Process	437
Defining a Problem	437
Translating Ideas	438
Translating Ideas Into Something of Value	439
Diverge for Creativity, Converge for Innovation	441
Benchmarking	441
How? Now, Wow!	442
Force Field Analysis	443
The $100 Test	443
Creating a Culture of Innovation With Design Thinking	444
DEI by Design	448
Creating a Climate of Innovation With the Dimensions of the Brain	449
Social Dimension: Collaboration and Community	450
Constructive Dimension: Seeking and Seeing Different	451
Reflective Dimension: Time, Space, and Structure	453
Chapter Summary	456
Key Terms	457
CORE™ Attribute Builders: Build Now for Future Leadership Challenges	457
CORE™ Attribute Builders: Build Now for Future Leadership Challenges	457

Skill Builder Activity	458
Skill Builder Activity	459

Chapter 15 Entrepreneurial Leadership — 461

Introduction	461
Entrepreneurship: Re-envisioning Leadership	464
Defining Entrepreneurship	464
Entrepreneurship Is a Process	464
Entrepreneurship Involves Pursuing Opportunity	464
Conception, Validation, and Launch of New Ideas	465
Into the Marketplace	465
The Broad Domain of Entrepreneurship	466
Entrepreneurship and Leadership	466
Design Revisited	467
The Entrepreneurial Mindset	468
See More Opportunity: Mindful, Observant, and Open to New Ideas	469
See Differently: Reframing Problems as Opportunities	470
See More Answers: Ideation, Effectuation, and Resourcefulness	471
See It Started: Predilection for Action . . . and Reflection	472
See It Through: Remembering Your Purpose	473
DEI by Design	475
Leading the Entrepreneurial Process	476
Impact Modeling	477
Lean Startup Methods	478
Customer Discovery Interviewing	478
Prototyping Minimum Viable Products	479
The Evolving Role of the Entrepreneurial Leader	479
The Founder	480
The Innovator	480
The Team Builder	481
The Chief Executive	481
The Leadership Challenge: From Founder to Chief Executive	482
Chief Engagement Officer: Entrepreneurial Leadership at Every Level	483
Chapter Summary	484
Key Terms	485
CORE™ Attribute Builders: Build Now for Future Leadership Challenges	485
CORE™ Attribute Builders: Build Now for Future Leadership Challenges	486
Skill Builder Activity	486
Skill Builder Activity	487

Chapter 16 Systems and Sustainability — 489

Introduction	489
Systems and Systems Thinking	493
Seeing Interconnections	494
Where's the Energy in the System?	496
The Learning Organization	497
DEI by Design	498

Design for Sustainability 499
 The Sustainable Culture 500
 Environmental Sustainability 500
 Sustaining Creativity and Innovation 501
 Ethical Sustainability 502
 Economic Sustainability 503
 Sustainable Learning and Development 503
 Sustainable Results 505

Sustainable You: Mindfulness and Personal Growth 506

Sustainable Leadership—Authentic Leadership 507

Chapter Summary 510

Key Terms 510

CORE™ Attribute Builders: Build Now for Future Leadership Challenges 511

Skill Builder Activity 511

My Leadership Design™ Begins and Continues With This Summary Page . . . 511

Glossary **515**

Notes **523**

Index **559**

FOREWORD

When is the last time you read one foreword by two people? Probably never! Even more unusual, we are best known for our work on followership rather than leadership. Yet we have been invited by the authors of *Discovering Leadership* to set the stage for this new edition. We believe our presence to be emblematic of the authorial team's bold and iconoclastic approach to learning and perhaps to living as well. And so, it is with excitement and a bit of intellectual mischief that we proceed in welcoming you, the adventurous reader, to this work of self-discovery.

We know the authors of *Discovering Leadership: Designing Your Success* to be teachers who dare to remove the wall between an educator and their students and who continually seek new paths between a student's absorption of information and its application to their lives. They are also scholars with an insatiable curiosity to know more about leadership from widely diverse thinkers both inside and outside the field.

Leadership is a relational practice, and for that reason, it is continually evolving. The principles of design thinking introduced in this textbook provide scaffolding for you to likewise change and evolve in your own leadership. The authors guide you through an interdisciplinary discovery process, and crucially, they help you do something that is all too rare: conceive of leading and following as a dance of equally strong and graceful partners.

Just as a "design thinker" begins by considering the needs and desires of their product's end user, a "design leader" begins by asking, "Who is being led, to what goal, and in what context?" In the beginning, the person you are leading—and therefore following—may be yourself. Later, you will lead others; you'll lead teams; you'll lead organizations, movements, maybe even cultures. While leading in all these contexts, we urge you to remain keenly aware of who is following and how and why they are willing to follow. That will make you an extraordinary leader.

Deep respect for those you lead instantly transforms what leadership is and can be. It makes it more inventive, more agile, more specific, more compassionate, and ultimately, more effective. Through curated methods of design thinking, this textbook prepares you to embrace the leader-follower relationship as an ongoing, co-creative dynamic. In designing leadership, pause from time to time to turn the telescope around by reflecting on the follower perspective, first in yourself, then in others with whom you interact. How do you become a leader that others want to follow, particularly those who share your interests and passions? By challenging you to design leadership as an expression of core values, this book helps you wrestle with the question of how to wield power ethically in partnership with those you hope to lead.

As you journey through these pages, highlighter in hand, you may realize that even while internalizing its simple and elegant definition of leadership—**the process of influencing others toward a common vision**—you are also beginning to understand how you, in turn, are influenced by those you lead. You may be surprised and slightly disoriented as you notice how those you lead, also, in some ways, seem to lead you!

Can you be a leader who also follows? Indeed, you can. You must! Otherwise, you become a blind-sided authoritarian rather than a dynamic leader. Like the ancient Chinese principle of yin and yang, harmony comes from knowing that within a healthy and sustainable leadership practice, there remains the potent essence of a followership practice, and vice versa. In an organization of any size, you will shift between leading and following. The power of design in this course will help you discover and elegantly develop each role so that you can learn, practice, and perform both stunningly well.

Ira Chaleff & Sharna Fabiano

October 2021

PREFACE TO THE SECOND EDITION

The world has become a very different place since the last edition of this text. But then, the world is constantly changing and, with change, the demands on leaders and the individuals and organizations with whom they work. The past years have seen extraordinary technological innovations continue accelerating—the practical, material, and human application of scientific knowledge. This has made the world more wealthy, humane, and creative. And yet, with this complexity has come a widening divide across many realms, most notably in politics and prosperity. Increasingly individualized platforms for communication, messaging, and services have facilitated a shared vision but as contentious tribalism rife with confirmation bias and inflamed self-righteousness. Trickled down to specific individuals and organizations, these trends have manifested in considerable challenges to fundamental leadership and management activities. These trends informed the revisions of this second edition.

Significant changes that exemplify the second edition seek to expand awareness and the ability to see and maximize value:

Broadening Voices and Perspectives: The text is revised throughout to increase the breadth of perspectives and greater diversity, with more examples of leaders representing multiple differences. A new section entitled *DEI by Design* was created for every chapter, introducing concepts relevant and vital to the respective chapters that simultaneously are key to leading with and enhancing one or more of diversity, equity, and inclusion.

Clarifying Purpose: We created a new chapter to prompt students to consider their reasons for leading (their "why") and identify the world in which they want to lead (their "what"), together which make up their purpose.

Expanding Capacity and Practices: Extensive updates referencing classic and current research add further venues to explore for readers. In addition, we've added new topics and tools to address current issues, such as compassion, empathy, mindfulness, identity, vulnerability, both/and thinking, and crisis leadership.

Leadership scholars Ira Chaleff and Sharna Fabiano open the text with a wonderfully insightful foreword emphasizing the relational nature of leadership. They reinforce the idea that leadership and followership are integrated, reciprocal processes that can only succeed with each other. The following section describes the text's overall themes and organizational structure, including the unique approach and content, explanation of features, and chapter-by-chapter overview.

PROLOGUE

One way or another, we are all impacted by leaders and leadership. Individuals in leadership influence our lives every day by the decisions they make, the behaviors they model and encourage, how they influence others, the values, and vision they hold, and the culture they foster. These leadership activities can be positive, supportive, life-affirming, negative, repressive, selfish, or anything in between. Within this incredibly complex, interconnected world, those leader behaviors, directly and indirectly, impact our life, perspective, and aspirations. Leadership matters, and a leader's behavior is both impactful and far-reaching.

Leadership matters. Leadership educators know this and so do experienced leaders. Traditional leadership education has become considerably more interactive and experiential in and out of the classroom. Yet students often struggle to organize the many pieces of leadership knowledge, overlook key lessons from experience, and default to prior patterns of behavior they rationalize as leadership. Out of the classroom, talented individuals are promoted to leadership positions where they are surprised to find that they are facing an entirely different set of challenges . . . and they too do not know where to begin learning about leadership.

Discovering Leadership: Designing Your Success provides a practical, engaging foundation and framework for individuals to design leadership purposefully. It is a core textbook for undergraduate or graduate students from any discipline seeking a framework and foundation upon which to build as their experience and future leadership learning continue. The book is also ideal for aspiring or new leaders outside the classroom—those who have found themselves with a real, immediate need to understand and apply leadership in their context.

What does one need to know, be able to do, or be like to engage in leadership effectively? The answer to that question highlights the most significant challenge to leadership educators. Effective leadership is complex and situational—it depends on the specific person serving as the positional leader—their strengths, tendencies, style, perspective, values, and reputation, and how others perceive them. Effective leadership depends on the followers and their characteristics; on the specific organization and its vision, mission, and culture; on the particular challenges currently facing the organization; on the distinct social and political culture within which the organization must operate; and on the norms, values, and tools of the current times.

Discovering Leadership: Designing Your Success uses a simple, powerful leadership definition as the backbone of the entire textbook—*the process of influencing others toward a common vision*. Each element of this definition drives the purposeful design of leadership. Many existing sources offer valuable insights relative to these many variables influencing leadership. A seemingly endless stream of leadership books, courses, consultants, coaches, workshops, blogs, and other sources provide a wide array of good advice. However, these valuable resources can be overwhelming without a foundation and framework. When people are overwhelmed, they default to established patterns, try to simplify, or walk away.

OUR VISION: DESIGNING LEADERSHIP, BUILDING CORE™

Our vision in writing this book was to create a tool that could serve as *the one thing* that a new leader would need, and later, it could provide a foundational framework that students could continuously add to as they learn and experience more. Some students may currently be in a leadership position, others aspire to one, and many will one day find themselves in that position. All individuals, however, will experience the impact of leadership. We want students to understand that leadership matters, that it is much more complex than a position, and most importantly, that they can do things now to prepare for the challenges ahead. Two unique themes are emphasized across all chapters of this book: the purposeful design of leadership and developing core capacities to face an unpredictable future.

Designing Leadership

Discovering Leadership: Designing Your Success applies a uniquely useful design framework and engages students in the purposeful design of their leadership. Design is the process of originating and developing a plan. This design approach organizes leadership into five significant design challenges, each comprising a distinct and separate module aligned with the core components of the leadership definition. This starts with the students' design of *themselves*. Each chapter begins with the framework shown that follows, highlighting the critical question for that design challenge.

The design approach also offers new ways of seeing and engaging challenges. The tools and perspectives from the design field are used to help leaders see differently as they solve problems, make decisions, navigate and build relationships, and find innovative ways to address challenges. Specific chapters focus on the design process and design thinking, significantly enhancing creative problem-solving and innovation. And the Leadership by Design feature throughout the book asks students to apply design principles to different aspects of leadership, helping them see their leadership activities in new ways.

Module	Leadership Design Challenge (and Module Title)	Leadership Definition	Key Question
1	Design Leadership of Self	Leadership	How can I design myself as a leader?
2	Design Leadership Relationships	Is a process of influencing	As a leader, how can I design my relationships with others?
3	Design Others' Success	Others	As a leader, how can I design success for others?
4	Design Culture and Community	Toward a common	As a leader, how can I design the culture of my organization?
5	Design the Future	Vision	As a leader, how can I innovate?

Building CORE™

Many professionals try to predict the future so they are adequately prepared and positioned for success. Unfortunately, the future is constantly surprising everyone. While leaders cannot predict the future, they can prepare for it by building capacities that could be flexibly applied to various challenges. Leaders cannot know what specific knowledge, skills, or experiences will be needed. This is particularly true for students. However, some core capabilities will help leaders navigate any future challenge and effectively facilitate the process of influencing others toward a common vision, also known as leadership. Just as an athlete exercises to build the physical core that will improve performance, so must leaders develop their psycho-social-emotional CORE™—an acronym for *confidence, optimism, resilience,* and *engagement*. With a strong CORE™, students are better prepared for the unpredictable future.

Discovering Leadership: Designing Your Success starts with the individuals designing themselves. However, individual leadership development is a continuous, life-long process. The goals for any student of leadership are emphasized throughout the book and include the following:

Find your leadership self, identify as a leader, and recognize your potential.

Change how you look at leaders and leadership, develop a clear foundation from which to see the field more broadly and note the complexities.

Develop your leadership dispositions—the mental habits you use to see, think about, and respond to the world.

Build your leadership CORE™—confidence, optimism, resilience, and engagement—personal attributes that will enhance your leadership now and long into the future.

Acquire a road map and a toolkit to effectively design your leadership into the future.

The information and insights within each chapter provide an essential foundation for any individual seeking to make sense of this complicated field. The ideas and activities in this text have been used with college students, adult professionals aspiring to leadership positions, new leaders and managers in many areas and organizations, co-curricular college leadership programs, and leaders of student organizations.

UNIQUE APPROACH

Conceived and designed by experienced, engaged leadership educators and generations of their students, *Discovering Leadership: Designing Your Success* provides a unique approach that will maximize student engagement and retention.

Interactive and engaging: As leadership educators, we strive to bring information and ideas to life. Learning is a process of codesign, and this textbook is structured in that manner. The action-oriented design approach makes leadership learning a purposeful activity. The variety of special features appeals to new leaders, enhance the breadth and depth of the topic, and provide instructors with additional learning tools.

Flexible: The entire textbook is divided into five modules focusing on a different aspect of designing your leadership, all within a more significant, connected logic. This allows professors and other trainers the maximum amount of flexibility to fit chapters and modules into their existing courses and curriculum to best meet the current needs of students and faculty expertise.

Accessible: The language of professions can discourage newcomers. This text clearly and simply defines the terms students will need in a way understandable to those with limited to no experience in leadership or with leadership studies/terminology. Organized within an easily understood framework, the content connects to the limited experiences of the new or aspiring leader.

Practical: The textbook starts with useful definitions and examples highlighting perceptions and misperceptions about leaders and leadership. The text balances leadership theories and research with lessons from experienced leaders and applied tools. Content is filled with real-world activities, skill-building exercises, and effective practices in leadership and its related disciplines (i.e., collaboration, conflict resolution, team management, etc.).

Distinctively focused on future success: While much leadership wisdom focuses on helping students meet current challenges, this text also focuses on assisting students to meet the unknown future. We focus on topics that help students build capacity, such as change management, creativity, design thinking, innovation processes, culture design, entrepreneurship, systems and sustainability, and building personal CORE™.

Inspiring and aspirational: As leadership educators, we want nothing more than for students to be inspired to learn more and then make a difference in whatever world they choose. This text seeks to inspire students to be the individuals and leaders others want to follow and be like and assures them that every leader has a first time.

Sustainable: This is one of the few texts that students will want to keep for their college career and beyond, to refer to repeatedly. With every reading, they will find new aspects of themselves and their leadership to learn and explore further.

UNIQUE CONTENT

In addition to the design framework and emphasis on developing CORE™, *Discovering Leadership: Designing Your Success* offers an array of unique content amidst the important, more commonly found topics.

Instructors are provided with **interactive and experiential learning activities** to use inside and outside the classroom, including specific activities to develop confidence, optimism, resilience, and engagement.

Unique sections on **design thinking and brain learning** help students understand critical mental attributes and habits they can apply now and develop over time.

Invaluable **innovation tools** throughout unique sections on creativity, idea generation, problem-solving, and leading innovation.

Unique section on **designing the future**, introducing cutting-edge topics such as fostering a culture of innovation, entrepreneurial leadership, and seeing the long-term and big picture with sustainability and systems.

Perceptions and **misconceptions of leaders and leadership**—in the words of new leaders, often overlooked in textbooks—including a Myth or Reality? feature using research to address common questions.

Content **designed to maximize learning** by reinforcing and integrating concepts throughout multiple chapters, including an early section on what to expect when learning leadership.

Leadership is a very complex, multidisciplinary subject that is often field-specific. Many important leadership topics are not part of this textbook, such as an in-depth examination of leadership research and different leadership theories, the historical development of leadership, various philosophies of leadership, and leadership in specific contexts or with particular populations. This book prepares students to explore and learn more about this fascinating world. Your expertise and interests as a leadership educator enhance and continue that journey.

FEATURES

At the start of each chapter, **Leadership That Makes a Difference** profiles a leader, leaders, or leadership that had an impact. Many subjects are unexpected, as this feature is designed to broaden students' conception of who is a leader and what it means to make a difference. For example, Chapter 14 highlights three women who successfully created cultures of innovation within predominantly male fields.

Leadership by Design introduces students to different design principles—rules that designers use to enhance their products. These rules can often be applied to leaders and leadership to encourage exploration, discussion, and new ways of thinking. For example, the principles of balance and repetition are fundamental to visual design. Applied to leadership, what are the many things that leaders need to balance? Where might repetition be necessary in leadership? Can you have both?

The **DEI by Design** sections in each chapter invites the reader into the discussion to consider the broadest range of ideas for advancing their individual leadership journey and practice. Overall, the new feature endeavors to

a. Be as inclusive as possible, which sometimes translates into more accessible language for those who are not yet familiar with different topics

b. Reach the broadest audience, which sometimes translates into using more descriptive words instead of technical terms to open dialogues with those who might initially shut down

c. Integrate these concepts into effective leadership practices – which may appear to lessen the moral and ethical implications (it does not)

d. Expand beyond the Western European and U.S. cultural view of leadership to allow for the broadest possible understanding of the value and applicability of the concepts

e. Emphasize the value of these ideas to individuals who want to make a practical difference, which may appear to minimize the theoretical depth and implications (it should not)

The **Myth or Reality?** feature examines commonly held beliefs through established research and practice. For example, the feature in Chapter 5, "Values," asserts, "I don't have a title, I can't make a difference." Experienced leaders know the answer, but new, young, or entry-level leaders wonder if this is true.

Experts Beyond the Text: Insightful Leaders Know About . . . Invited experts provide a brief introduction to a topic beyond the scope of this introductory text, yet students should be aware that it is an important topic. New to this edition, expert Nyasha GuramatunhuCooper shares important work on identity and leadership (Chapter 4), expert Wendy Smith talks about the value of paradoxical thinking (Chapter 6), expert Ralph Gigliotti discusses crises and opportunity (Chapter 10), and Reo Watanabe explains leadership vis-à-vis Japanese culture (Chapter 11).

For every leader, there are **Moments of Awareness**—critical decision-making, ethical challenges, or difficult truths. This feature shares short quotes and stories of the most challenging self-reflection with which aspiring leaders must grapple. For example, in the "Introductions and Foundations" chapter, one undergraduate student realizes that one of her most important jobs as a leader is to create opportunities for others to lead.

CORE™ Attribute Builders at the end of every chapter comprise engaging activities that emphasize one or more of confidence, optimism, resilience, and engagement. These activities ask students to actively work to develop their CORE™. In contrast, **Skill Builder Activities** at the end of each chapter are self-directed activities, tested for learning success in and out of real classrooms, in which students can develop essential skills and gain a richer understanding of specific concepts.

Reflection Questions throughout the features and the text prompt deeper thinking and discussion about the topics. And **Chapter Summaries** and **Key Terms** at the end of each chapter highlight important points, reinforce learning, and provide guidance for studying and instructor assessment.

CONTENT AND ORGANIZATION

Discovering Leadership: Designing Your Success comprises 16 chapters within five modules. The "Introductions and Foundations" chapter provides a detailed overview of the logic and framework and previews the many features found in each chapter. Note that even in the features "preview," there are valuable lessons for students. Each module begins with a brief introduction of the design focus of that module and foreshadows the chapters within that section.

Introduction and Foundations

This important chapter includes some of the most essential things instructors and students need to know, including the definition of leadership, overall logic and framework, organization and features of the text, and some fun and interesting examples.

The two major themes of the text are elaborated in this chapter: designing your leadership and building your CORE™. Here the tools of design are distinguished between the design process, design thinking, and the unique lens of design principles. Likewise, the elements of CORE™ are clarified along with suggested activities for further development.

Chapter 1: A Framework for Leadership Success: Design and Your CORE™

Module 1: Design Leadership Self

Module 1 begins where all leadership starts—with the individual, the leader. The more you know about yourself, the more effective you can be as a leader, and the more likely you will find the best fit for your leadership. Understanding a leader starts with how one perceives leaders and leadership. Everyone has had various experiences with leaders—parents/guardians, teachers, coaches, siblings, friends, bosses—and those experiences form values, expectations, assumptions, and behaviors as leaders. Some of those personal characteristics and mental habits are very effective for leadership, but unfortunately, many are not. The chapters in this section explore perceptions and personal attributes that characterize effective leaders, provide tools for enriching leadership capacity, and provoke reflection on your reasons for leading.

Chapter 2: Designing Your Perceptions of Leaders and Leadership

Chapter 3: Designing Your Leadership Capacity

Chapter 4: Your Why and What for Leading

Module 2: Design Leadership Relationships

Module 2 focuses on designing relationships with others. An amusing old leadership saying goes, "If you think you are leading, you might want to turn around and see if anyone is following." Without followers, there is no leadership. The nature of the relationships leaders design with followers and other stakeholders will greatly determine leadership success. The chapters in this section examine the foundations of powerful and influential leader-follower connections and guide students through the design of relationships.

Chapter 5: Your Values and Ethical Actions

Chapter 6: Decision-Making

Chapter 7: Influence, Power, and Motivation

Module 3: Design Others' Success

Module 3 shifts focus to the success of others. If the first rule of leadership is *It's about you*, the second rule is *It's not about you*. We all want to feel successful. One's ability as a leader to facilitate learning and development in others is critical to the organization and achieving the vision. The chapters in this section examine what a leader needs to know to design others' success, beginning with expanding the capacity to generate ways to do so creatively.

Chapter 8: Creativity, Problem-Solving, and Idea-Generating

Chapter 9: Effective Practices for Leading Others to Success

Chapter 10: Utilizing Change Processes Effectively

Module 4: Design Culture and Community

Module 4 expands the leadership lens to focus on designing culture. Simply put, culture is the way we do things around here. All groups have a culture—teams, organizations, communities—a visible and invisible set of rules that defines the group. Culture happens, but a good leader designs the culture to influence others toward a common vision. The chapters in this section guide the design of culture, with particular emphasis on leading effective teams and fostering an ethic of care.

Chapter 11: Culture

Chapter 12: Leading a Team

Chapter 13: Designing a Culture That Cares

Module 5: Design the Future

Module 5 applies students' growing leadership capacity to ensuring future success, focusing on perspectives and tools that develop the ability to see the big picture and long term. The inevitability of change, unpredictable future, and interconnected nature of individuals and ideas require leaders who can innovate and maximize the value of their ideas. Leaders need to foster this capacity in others to sustain success. The chapters in this section guide efforts to design the future by introducing new ways of seeing, taking the initiative, and understanding the interconnected systems that comprise sustainable organizations, communities, and the world.

Chapter 14: Creating a Culture of Innovation

Chapter 15: Entrepreneurial Leadership

Chapter 16: Systems and Sustainability

NEW TO THIS EDITION

Introduction and Foundations

Limited changes to this foundational chapter. Changes include foreshadowing and explaining the addition of the new DEI by Design section in each chapter, including an explanation of benefits, opportunities created, and problems avoided by learning more about these topics. A new table was also added that clarifies the chapters where readers can find key leadership theories/approaches.

Chapter 1

Minimal changes to this foundational chapter. Addition of DEI by Design section defining terms and framing the importance of diversity, equity, and inclusion as an explanation for section inclusion in all chapters.

References updated and expanded approximately 40%.

Chapter 2

Limited changes to this foundational chapter. New DEI by Design section highlighting key characteristics of identity relative to how leadership is perceived.

References updated and expanded approximately 40%.

Chapter 3

Major changes to this chapter, including the following:

- Addition of sections introducing growth mindset, process orientation, and strengths-based mindset
- Integration of design thinking mental habits, reframed as capacity-building (previously in Chapter 5)
- Updated and additional "new challenges" and "new skills" for leaders

New DEI by Design section focused on the role of power relative to one's leadership capacities References updated and expanded approximately 70%.

Chapter 4

New chapter focused on helping aspiring leaders understand (and begin to consider) the importance of their purpose—described as an integration of their "why" and their "for what" (versus the "how to" that comprises much of the rest of the text).

The chapter also includes a new Experts Beyond the Text guest feature focused on how aspects of your identity influence your purpose, as well as a related DEI by Design feature with a model of the Cycle of Socialization.

The chapter concludes with a model prompting students to develop their Greater Purpose Statement.

All content and references are new to this textbook.

Chapter 5

Minimal changes to this chapter. Reorganization of sections within Ethics: The Key Concepts for greater clarity. Updated Experts Beyond the Text feature on Followership.

New DEI by Design section focused on the cycle of liberation, raising awareness of leadership ethics issues.

Updated and expanded references 35%.

Chapter 6

Minor changes to chapter focused on new examples to broaden range of perspectives.

New Experts Beyond the Text feature focused on Paradoxical Leadership.

New DEI by Design section focused on key decision-making pitfalls.

Updated and expanded references 40%.

Chapter 7

New DEI by Design section focused on forms of bias and how these impacts influence.

Added and expanded the Leadership Challenge content as applied to designing relationships.

Updated and expanded references 50%.

Chapter 8

New DEI by Design section focused on fragility and vulnerability relative to creative confidence.

Updated and expanded references 30%.

Chapter 9

Significant expansion of effective practices for leadership, which includes a new first half of the chapter on understanding brain characteristics that impact individual perception and performance.

New Leadership That Makes a Difference feature previewing the IGNITE practices outlined later in the chapter.

Updated Experts Beyond the Text feature on Women and Leadership.

More current issues and research introduced in subsections of IGNITE as a Leader and DELIVER as a Manager.

New DEI by Design section focused on social dynamics that might impact leadership practices.

Updated and expanded references 100%.

Chapter 10

New Experts Beyond the Text feature on Crisis Leadership.

New DEI by Design section focused on activism and advocacy as tools for change.

Updated and expanded references 30%.

Chapter 11

New Experts Beyond the Text feature on Leadership in Japan.

Expanded Contemporary Approaches to Organizational Culture section highlighting organizations dealing with current challenges.

New DEI by Design section focused on the 8 Scales of Culture Map.

New section on Strategic Planning Toward Culture Change with practical tools, including a new Cultural Values Assessment tool.

Updated and expanded references 40%.

Chapter 12

New DEI by Design section focused on intergroup dialogue techniques.

New tools for creating a team charter and running effective team meetings. Updated and expanded references 25%.

Chapter 13

New section on Care, Empathy, and Compassion; section on vulnerability, and updated Experts Beyond the Text feature on Spiritual Capital.

New DEI by Design section focused on radical empathy.

Updated and expanded references 35%.

Chapter 14

New introduction to module and chapter.

Added new DEI by Design section focused on cultivating and harvesting diversity to foster innovation.

Updated and expanded references 35%.

Chapter 15

New section revisiting/reminding students about the design framework: process, principles, and design thinking mental habits.

New DEI by Design section focused on social entrepreneurship.

New Leadership That Makes a Difference feature and new section on chief engagement officer.

Updated and expanded references 60%.

Chapter 16

New Leadership That Makes a Difference feature.

New DEI by Design section focused on generativity and identity for sustaining your leadership impact.

New section on Sustainable You: Mindfulness and Personal Growth, and a summary Skill Builder: Leadership Best Fit and Beliefs.

Updated and expanded references 70%.

Starting Your Journey

As leadership educators, we have heard many experienced leaders and experts assert various qualifiers to those aspiring to lead: *You must go through the crucible of experience! You need to study the leaders of the past. You must carefully study leadership theory. You are too young. You are not skilled enough.* This is good advice and certainly crucial to becoming an experienced and wise leader. But individuals—even you, perhaps—are assuming leadership positions right now, with or without the prerequisites the experts recommend. Understanding the influence, impact, and importance of leadership, as well as a bit of how-to knowledge, is just the start any student needs. We, the authors, want your students to be successful, facilitate the success of others, and make a difference. We have designed this textbook to that end.

Tony Middlebrooks, PhD

On behalf of the author team

TEACHING RESOURCES

This text includes an array of instructor teaching materials designed to save you time and to help you keep students engaged. To learn more, visit **sagepub.com** or contact your SAGE representative at sagepub.com/findmyrep.

ACKNOWLEDGMENTS

Leadership and the success of a project require that different individuals take initiative, but the reality of any accomplishment lies hidden under the vast array of interconnected influences, quiet contributions, and culture of support. This text is no different. I, Dr. Tony Middlebrooks, am grateful for the many individuals and teams that both purposefully and unknowingly influenced my development as a leadership educator, as well as to those contributing to the achievement of designing and crafting this textbook. Thank you to the generations of students, colleagues, family, friends, and mentors who have graciously shared both their triumphs and challenges as leaders, educators, and humans. This book is for all of us.

A very special thank you to those directly involved with this second edition of the text—it was an absolute pleasure to work with them all. Our great thanks for the gracious and insightful contributions of guest authors: Foreword by Ira Chaleff and Sharna Fabiano; chapter authors Ingrid Richter, Eliane Ubalijoro, and Jules Bruck; guest expert authors Ralph Gigliotti, Nyasha M. GuramatunhuCooper, Wendy Smith, and Reo Watanabe. And, a special thanks to Courtney Mainwaring for her meticulous work digging through databases to help us find the most current leadership research. It is an honor to have your respective wisdom as part of this textbook.

For this edition of the textbook, we purposefully sought to diversify voices and perspectives, as well as create a more inclusive learning tool. To that end, we invited Susamma Seeley to scan chapters for inclusivity blind spots and presumptive language. We invited Susamma because we wanted to learn from both her lived experience and her expertise. Her attention to detail, honest and open communication, and thoughtful guidance informed this new edition.

Relatedly, we owe tremendous thanks to Vivechkanand "V" Sewcharran Chunoo for his foundational work in conceptualizing and drafting the DEI by Design sections for all chapters. His expertise laid the foundation for helping communicate the significant impact of diversity, equity, and inclusion on a broad array of leadership topics.

Great thanks to the supportive teams at SAGE for another round of guiding, educating, and supporting a bunch of professors through the professional publishing process. I would specifically like to thank Maggie Stanley and Lily Norton, our acquisitions editors, and Darcy Scelsi, our development editor for their confidence, optimism, resilience and engagement (yes . . . that's CORE™).

Finally, my thanks to those developing leaders in my life who share with me their challenges and triumphs: Jakob, Hannah, Sydney, and Stefan. And my greatest thanks to my amazing wife, partner, collaborator, friend, and (when requested) critic, Dr. Jules Bruck. Thank you for your incredibly generous support, encouragement, and insights. Your exemplary leadership in your world inspires me to work harder in mine.

Dr. Scott Allen would like to thank five key individuals in his growth and development—they were there when he needed sound role models and leadership: Chris Whritenour, John Dailey, Nan Corwin, Dennis Pluth, and Scott Smith.

Dr. Mindy McNutt would like to thank her daughter Alexis and mother Penny for their support, patience, and encouragement.

Dr. James Morrison would like to thank Dr. Pamela Porter Morrison for her insight and passion in suggesting innovative strategies resulting in a highly interactive textbook. Her expertise in the field of communication was most helpful in designing a unique writing style for having students be continually engaged as they read each chapter.

SAGE would like to thank the following reviewers:

Amy Davis, Pima Community College
Erin Elliott, Portland State University
Amy L. Everitt, Salem State University
Samuel S. Hemby, Southeastern University
John C. Hill, University of Kentucky
Stephen Hill, Nazareth College
Jenny Kuzmic, Ohio State University
Dr. Gregory Warren, Chapman University
Cris Wells, Arizona State University

Reviewers of the First Edition

Kris L. Baack, University of Nebraska
Cheryl B. Baker, Plymouth State University
Tondalaya O. Carroll, Lincoln University
Robert Dibie, Indiana University Kokomo
Linette P. Fox, Johnson C. Smith University
Megan W. Gerhardt, Miami University
Michele Goins, Santa Clara University
Madinah F. Hamidullah, Rutgers University–Newark
Kimberly A. Hunley, Northern Arizona University
Chris Hutchison, Chapman University
Daniel M. Jenkins, University of Southern Maine
DeNisha McCollum, John Brown University
Patricia Mitchell, University of San Francisco
Don Mulvaney, Auburn University
Kerry Priest, Kansas State University
Kirk A. Randazzo, University of South Carolina
Julie K. Roosa, Des Moines Area Community College
Rian Satterwhite, University of Nevada, Las Vegas
John Silveria, Suffolk University
Nicole LP Stedman, University of Florida
Ramon Tejada, California State University Channel Islands
Joshua H. Truitt, University of Central Florida
Pamela R. Van Dyke, Southern Methodist University
Heather A. Vilhauer, California State University, East Bay
Ellen J. West, California University of Pennsylvania
Tara Widner-Edberg, Iowa State University
Michael A. Williams, Thomas Edison State University
Patricia Wilson, Otterbein University

ABOUT THE AUTHORS

Tony Middlebrooks, PhD, creates programs and tools, teaches, and explores at the intersection of leadership, innovation, creativity, and design. He is Clinical Full Professor of Leadership in the Warrington College of Business at the University of Florida. An award-winning professor, he has created and taught more than 35 different courses for all collegiate levels, as well as numerous experiential abroad programs. He presently teaches courses in leadership theory and practice and creativity and innovation.

Previously, Dr. Middlebrooks served as director of the Siegfried Leadership Initiative for Horn Entrepreneurship at the University of Delaware. He codeveloped the undergraduate Leadership program at UD and the doctoral program in leadership as a professor at Cardinal Stritch University, all after ten years prior in nonprofit leadership positions.

Dr. Middlebrooks has published numerous articles and book chapters and has delivered hundreds of presentations. He is co-author of *Public Sector Leadership* and co-creator of the *Idea Fan Deck* and *Design Thinking Cards* and has served as Symposium Editor for the *Journal of Leadership Studies* from 2011–2021.

A firm believer that leadership learning can benefit everyone and every field, Dr. Middlebrooks consults and facilitates workshops for a wide variety of organizations and audiences. His current scholarly interests focus on methods of leadership education and the integration of leadership, creativity, and design thinking. Dr. Middlebrooks has a PhD in Educational Psychology from the University of Wisconsin–Madison. He resides in Gainesville, Florida, with his wife and collaborator Dr. Jules Bruck.

Scott J. Allen, PhD, is the Standard Products—Dr. James S. Reid Chair in Management at John Carroll University. Allen is an associate professor and teaches courses in leadership, future of work, and executive communication. He's an award-winning professor passionate about working with learners of all ages.

Scott has published more than 60 book chapters and peer-reviewed journal articles. He is the co-author of *The Little Book of Leadership Development: 50 Ways to Bring Out the Leader in Every Employee*, *Emotionally Intelligent Leadership: A Guide for College Students*, and *Captovation: Online Presentations by Design*. He is also the host of two podcasts: *The Captovation Podcast* and *Phronesis: Practical Wisdom for Leaders*.

In addition to writing and teaching, Scott consults, facilitates workshops, and leads retreats across industries. Scott co-founded Captovation, a services firm dedicated to "Presentation Coaching for the Digital Age." He is also the co-founder and Board Chair of the Collegiate Leadership Competition. He has served on the board of the International Leadership Association, Association of Leadership Educators, and Management and Organizational Behavior Teaching Society. Allen was named an ILA Fellow by the International Leadership Association in 2021. He resides in Chagrin Falls, Ohio, with his wife, Jessica, and three children, Will, Kate & Emily.

Mindy S. McNutt, PhD, is an Associate Professor of Leadership at Wright State University in Dayton, Ohio. Currently, she teaches in all three leadership programs at Wright State: the undergraduate program in Organizational Leadership, the master of science in Leadership Development, and the doctorate in Organizational Studies, and has received both the teaching and research excellence awards for her college.

Dr. McNutt has engaged in leadership curriculum development for over 30 years for high school youth and undergraduate curricular and extracurricular programs, and most recently, she served with several faculty colleagues to write the proposal for the doctorate in Organizational Studies. At Wright State and at several area community colleges, she has held a variety of leadership positions, including, among others, academic vice president, campus dean, and dean of student services and institutional advancement. Additionally, Dr. McNutt is or has been involved in a number of boards and committees at the local, state, and national levels.

Among her varied research interests are leadership education, transformational leadership, women in leadership, leader values, and examining the relationship between values and organizational culture. She has been involved in several projects of significance: serving as an associate editor of the International Leadership Association Building Leadership Bridges book entitled *LEADERSHIP 2050: Contextualizing Global Leadership Processes for the Future* and collaborating with a nationwide team to create and serve as faculty for the international Leadership Education Academy. Most importantly, she is currently researching the life and legacy of Dr. Warren Bennis, considered to be the father of leadership.

James L. Morrison, PhD, is currently a Professor of Leadership in the School of Urban Affairs and Public Policy at the University of Delaware in Newark, Delaware. His research interest focuses on issues surrounding senior leadership accountability. Currently, he is researching whether any discrimination exists in terms of the roles of and input from female administrators during the planning process when preparing for a natural disaster. He has published two books and over 82 manuscripts in a variety of professional journals. In addition, Dr. Morrison has presented over 91 papers at regional, national, and international conferences. He is currently serving on three refereed editorial boards for academic journals and also holds the position of executive editor of the *Journal of Education for Business*. He has been the recipient of seven outstanding teaching awards in the College of Education and the College of Human Resources at the University of Delaware. Within the leadership major at the University of Delaware, his teaching focuses on preparing future leaders to initiate change within organizations by adopting a new set of principles and practices that have emerged in recent years.

INTRODUCTION AND FOUNDATIONS

LEARNING OBJECTIVES

Upon completion of this introduction, the reader should be able to

0.1   State the definition of leadership and summarize why leadership matters

0.2   Explain the big picture of how to design your leadership (and how the textbook is organized)

0.3   Recognize special features of the textbook that will enhance your learning and leadership design

LEADERSHIP MATTERS

LEARNING OBJECTIVE

0.1   State the definition of leadership and summarize why leadership matters.

This is not your typical textbook because you do not want to be a typical leader. You want to be uniquely extraordinary—a leader who inspires others, a leader whom others remember and aspire to become, and a leader who seeks to make a positive difference. In whatever world you choose to work or operate, no matter the size or scope, you can be that effective leader who impacts others. You can *design* your leadership.

Leadership is the process of influencing others toward a common vision.[1]

There are many definitions and ways to explain leadership, and all offer some interesting and valuable insight into this complicated, dynamic activity.[2] But when you are trying to observe leadership, practice leadership, explain leadership, or further develop your leadership, you are going to want a simple, meaningful definition. So right here in the introduction is your first and perhaps most important assignment. Memorize this simple definition—*Leadership is the process of influencing others toward a common vision.* You will see this definition many more times throughout this text, and the components serve as a framework for assessing (and improving) your leadership. Chapter 2 further explains each component: process, influence, others, toward, common, and vision. However, take note that there is a big difference between the *leader* (that's you—a person, possibly with a position), *leadership* (a process in which you may or may not be "in charge"), and *leading* (a description of activity or comparative position). These distinctions are often overlooked or confused. Back to the definition: Do you have it memorized? Try again—say it out loud, say it to a friend, write it down—*Leadership is the process of influencing others toward a common vision.*

1

The importance and consequences of leadership are evident throughout the news. The world is full of complex challenges and wicked problems.[3] Yet addressing those global issues can begin at any level, even one relationship at a time. Along your leadership learning journey, you may hear "experts" telling you the only path to leadership is years of experience and extensive knowledge. You will certainly hear that you are too _____ to make a difference. In reality, individuals are put into leader positions every day, all over the world . . . with no formal leadership training. Those persons are influential, for better or worse. You are influential.

Leadership feels most important when it is personal. When you think about the best leaders with whom you have interacted (parents, coaches, teachers, bosses), many of the things you liked felt like the characteristics of a good friend—they had your back, were honest, a good listener, celebrated your wins, and shared in your struggles—someone who wanted you to succeed. On the other hand, you may have experienced a bad leader, someone in charge who was less than effective. Do you wish that person would have had some training in how to be a better leader? If you do not believe your own answer, ask a few others.[4] While everyone has their own definition of bad, the reality is that everyone has *felt* the impact of leadership. When you are part of an organization, those feelings matter. Those relationships matter. Leadership matters. An effective leader can mean greater productivity, efficiency, innovation, satisfaction, retention, and a host of other personal, organizational, and cultural benefits.[5]

Leadership is an extraordinarily powerful practice that can be used to advance a variety of values and ends through many means. Wielding influence comes with great responsibility to carefully consider what you are doing, to whom, how, to what end, and so much more. And an ineffective leader or, worse, a bad leader, can destroy an organization, poison a culture, and negatively impact lives—with lasting effects long after the bad leader departs. There is a considerable and important difference, however, between an ineffective leader (i.e., someone who is just not good at influencing others toward a common goal) and a bad or toxic leader (i.e., someone who is unethical, immoral, or otherwise intent on harm). Many definitions of leadership include an ethical dimension, and there certainly is a good reason to advocate for that kind of *good* in leaders.

So why doesn't the definition used in this text specify that leadership must be *good* in the moral sense? Because with a value-free definition, *you* must be thoughtful and consider all the distinctions and perspectives of how and to what end you practice leadership. Leadership is always a specific, value-laden activity because everyone brings their values, ethics, norms, and experiences to the group. An effective leader recognizes that the situation, persons, context, culture, time, and more help define what kind of leadership is most ethical, most preferred, and most effective. A really effective leader realizes they may not have the complete picture and will consequently exercise the humility to keep learning.

Fortunately, few individuals try to be either ineffective or bad leaders. Rather, most poor leadership results from lack of action, specifically the failure of individuals to think carefully and strategically about themselves as leaders, the individuals they are leading, and the culture required for success. And sometimes, poor leadership is not as bad as you think. Each of us has unconscious assumptions of what constitutes an "effective" or "ineffective" leader (or leadership). You may value someone of great integrity and a noble vision, while your classmate may value entirely different qualities in a leader. These may be personality traits, behaviors, or other attributes that impact our perceptions of people engaging in the activity of leadership. These qualities or personal characteristics constitute our "implicit leadership theories."[6] The word implicit means that your understanding of effective leadership may not be easily communicated—similar to personal attraction, you know it when you feel it, even if you may not consciously understand all the variables of why you think the way you do.

In essence, these implicit theories are based on the "subjective perception of everyday life."[7] However, they have a very real impact on how you experience leaders and leadership—how you make sense of the phenomenon and how you judge the effectiveness of an individual's efforts. One immediate goal as you explore this text is for you to become clearer on what *you* value in a leader and why. By making implicit leadership theories explicit, you will better understand (a) the leader you hope to be and (b) why you experience some individuals as great leaders and others as less than effective. Perhaps most importantly, you can critically reflect on assumptions that may no longer be useful as you look to the future, helping you to overcome the biases that serve in certain situations but limit in others.

The goal of this text, however, is to move your explicit understanding of leader and leadership to a mindful, purposeful decision about what kind of leader you choose to be. In other words, you have a choice: You can consciously *design* your leadership, or you can just act (or react), see what happens, and hope for the best.

This introductory text to leadership engages you in the design of leadership over the course of five distinct modules, starting with your design of you.

ORGANIZATION OF THIS TEXTBOOK: THE LEADERSHIP BY DESIGN FRAMEWORK

LEARNING OBJECTIVE
0.2 Explain the big picture of how to design your leadership (and how the textbook is organized).

Leadership is the process of influencing others toward a common vision. Within this definition lay the most important elements of leadership *and* the organizing structure of this text. Look at that definition in a slightly different way (**Leadership extended** definition):

Leadership comprises your perceptions, strengths, style, skills, and the way you make decisions and solve problems, including how you persuade, guide, teach, and build relationships with others. But leadership goes beyond you—it is also how you help others succeed and create a culture of success so you, your followers, your organization, and your society can make a positive difference in the world.

That definition sounds a bit more complicated. Table 0.1 shows how it aligns with the simple definition.

TABLE 0.1 ■ Alignment of the Definition of Leadership to Elements of Leadership	
Leadership	Your leadership comprises your perceptions, strengths, style, skills, and . . .
is a process	the way you make decisions and solve problems, including . . .
of influencing	how you persuade, guide, teach, and . . .
others	build relationships with others. But leadership goes beyond you—how do you help others succeed . . .
toward a common	and create a culture of success so that you, your followers, your organization, and your society . . .
vision.	can make a positive difference in the world?

Design is the process of originating and developing a plan. This textbook guides you through the process of designing your leadership, focusing on practical skills and valuable attributes that will maximize your leadership success now and into the future.

Each of the major components of the leadership definition can be mindfully considered and *purposefully* planned and developed (i.e., designed). The framework for this textbook takes a design approach, organizing a leadership design process into five major design challenges: (1) design yourself as a leader, (2) design your relationships with others, (3) design others' success, (4) design your culture and community, and (5) design the future. This framework is outlined at the start of each chapter throughout the textbook, highlighting the section you are reading. Table 0.2 lays out this framework.

| | **Leadership Design Challenge (and** | **Leadership** | |
Module	**Module Title)**	**Definition**	**Definition Explained**
1	Design Leadership Self	Leadership	Your leadership comprises your perceptions, strengths, style, skills, and . . .
2	Design Leadership Relationships	is a process	the way you make decisions and solve problems, including . . .
		of influencing	how you persuade, guide, teach, and . . .
3	Design Others' Success	others	build relationships with others. But leadership goes beyond you—how do you help others succeed . . .
4	Design Culture and Community	toward a common	and create a culture of success so that you, your followers, your organization, and your society . . .
5	Design the Future	vision.	can make a positive difference in the world?

TABLE 0.2 ■ Leadership by Design Framework Modules

Designing your leadership is different from learning *about* leadership or learning *to lead*. If you were to visit your local bookstore (virtual or real) and look at all the books on leadership, you might conclude that either (a) leadership is anything and everything or (b) learning leadership is simply too big of a task. The truth is every one of those books is both correct and incorrect, depending on the individual leader. To you, some books will be filled with wisdom and insight, while those same books will strike others as not useful. You can and will learn a great deal about leadership from many sources. But then you must decide what is and is not relevant to you— what works for you and how—and what does not.

Leadership is such a personal, subjective, situational, and context-based endeavor that individuals often simply default to acting and reacting based on their prior experiences and then explaining it as leadership (often because they occupy a leadership position). Do not be that person. Instead, purposefully *design your leadership*. Read, observe, interview, discuss, interact, engage as much as you can with people, organizations, and leadership. Fill your toolbox of knowledge, skills, and experiences and then draw from it to design who you will be as a leader and how you will execute the process of leadership.

Introduction and Foundations **5**

CONTENT: TOPICS AND SPECIAL FEATURES

LEARNING OBJECTIVE
0.3   Recognize special features of the textbook that will enhance your learning and leadership design.

What does it take to practice leadership? This should be an easy answer after having memorized the definition. Leadership requires engaging in and facilitating the process of influencing others and progressing toward achieving a vision you have crafted with followers. Sounds simple. But as many have noted, leadership would be simple if it were not for the people.

Central to every design project is the end user or client—the human element. Excellent design begins with a human problem, focuses on human feelings and perceptions, and ends with human assessment. Even for folks who design toasters or buildings or websites—the user is central. Designing your leadership is no different. The content of this text focuses on the heart of leadership—the individuals involved in leading and following—starting with you, the leader, and expanding outward. Chapters comprise topics and information you can use now and long into the future as your leadership journey unfolds. Table 0.3 reiterates the Leadership by Design framework, listing the chapter titles as they align with the definition.

TABLE 0.3 ■ Leadership by Design Chapters			
Module	**Leadership Design Challenge (and Module Title)**	**Leadership Definition**	**Chapters**
Intro	A Framework for Your Success		Chapter 1: A Framework for Leadership Success: Design and Your CORE™
1	Design Leadership Self	Leadership	Chapter 2: Designing Your Perceptions of Leaders and Leadership Chapter 3: Designing Your Leadership Capacity Chapter 4: Leadership for What?
2	Design Leadership Relationships	is a process	Chapter 5: Your Values and Ethical Actions Chapter 6: Decision-Making
		of influencing	Chapter 7: Influence, Power, and Motivation
3	Design Others' Success	others	Chapter 8: Creativity, Problem-Solving, and Idea-Generating Chapter 9: Effective Practices for Leading Others to Success Chapter 10: Utilizing Change Processes Effectively

6 Discovering Leadership

TABLE 0.3 ■ Leadership by Design Chapters			
Module	Leadership Design Challenge (and Module Title)	Leadership Definition	Chapters
4	Design Culture and Community	toward a common	Chapter 11: Culture Chapter 12: Leading a Team Chapter 13: Designing a Culture That Cares
5	Design the Future	vision.	Chapter 14: Creating a Culture of Innovation Chapter 15: Entrepreneurial Leadership Chapter 16: Systems and Sustainability

As you work through this textbook, there are also many special features included to enhance your learning. The features are designed to highlight the focus of each chapter and expand your understanding, often by introducing alternative perspectives or stories from real students. Read the special features, think about them, and engage in any activity they prompt. Many of the features will also pose questions for reflection and discussion. While the special features are valuable in and of themselves, they also serve as a model for how you can pursue additional learning outside the classroom.

This section profiles each of the special features you will find within each chapter. Each special feature is explained, followed by an example of that feature focused around one of the most common misconceptions about leadership—that leadership is all about the leader (hint: it is not).

Leadership by Design Model

Each chapter begins with what you will learn (learning objectives) and the Leadership by Design Model highlighting the design focus (module) of the current chapter. The key question within each module should prompt and focus your thinking as you read the chapters of that module.

Design Self (Module 1)
How can I design myself as a leader?

Design Relationships (Module 2)
As a leader, how can I design my relationships with others?

Design Others' Success (Module 3)
As a leader, how can I design success for others?

Design Culture (Module 4)
As a leader, how can I design the culture of my organization?

Design Future (Module 5)
As a leader, how can I innovate?

Leadership That Makes a Difference

This special feature, found near the start of each chapter, highlights leaders and leadership that played a role in addressing social problems and improving social well-being. This feature will

Introduction and Foundations **7**

help you visualize the broader implications and applications of leadership activity, including those skills and characteristics used by successful social entrepreneurs and leaders. Across the entire textbook, you will see the wide variety of individuals who apply leadership and the even wider variety of forms effective leadership can take. Here is an example of a Leadership That Makes a Difference feature.

Leadership That Makes a Difference

There are a good many stories about leaders who make a positive difference addressing the big challenges of our world, and you will read about many of these individuals throughout this text. Did you ever ask yourself where that leader was *before* they made a big impact or became a story? The following story highlights one of the key attributes of leadership that makes a big difference . . . and it all starts with how you define *difference* as a descriptor of leadership impact.

When I was in high school, I participated in a charitable event. The president of our club put the entire event together and did a lot of hard work. At the event, another girl was taking all the credit for the event in front of the retirement community for whom the event was organized. My friend and I were so confused and honestly, kind of upset for the president, who put it all together. We did not understand why someone else would think it was okay to take all of the credit when they did not do anything. I wanted to say something and then asked the president about it. She said, "It doesn't bother me. The event was a success, and all of the houses that needed work got done, and look at how happy it made all of these people! That's all that matters." I was humbled by the president's positivity and realized how amazing a leader she was and how big her heart was. She did not care about any of the credit, just that the job got done. Real leaders want the best for their followers and whomever else they are helping or contributing toward; they do not care about their personal success or gains. Since that day, I have been inspired to help and lead others without expecting anything in return.

—Brooke Hoffman, Undergraduate

Making a positive difference on a large scale begins with doing so on a small scale or even observing and learning from someone doing so. Effective leaders know that there is no small scale, only small attitudes.

Reflection QuestionsRemember, *you* are designing *your* leadership. What difference would you like to make? What local actions can you take now that will prepare you?

Leadership by Design

Throughout the textbook, you will find many examples of how you can apply lessons from other design worlds that will be very helpful to designing leadership. Here is an example: Designers follow rules, which they call principles. Following the right rules makes a design effective. This is true for leadership design as well. Within the overall model of this text, the Leadership by Design feature highlights these design rules and translates them into insights and applications for leaders. How can various design principles (rules) used in the design world be applied to effective leadership practice? Here is an example of a Leadership by Design feature.

Leadership by Design

Design Principle: Visibility

Definition: "The usability of a system is improved when its status and methods of use are clearly visible."[8]

In Other Words: Designs that enable you to see what is going on, what to do next, or what will happen if you do something are more useful.

For Example: The battery icon on your cell phone that tells you how much charge you have left makes the phone much more useful. Without that little image, you would not know when the phone might shut off.

For Leaders: Leaders can use the design principle of visibility by considering what important systems, behaviors, or activities they could make more visible—not only as a matter of transparency but as a mechanism of feedback regarding the status of those things. If you are a more introverted leader who tends to process information in your head, visibility is a key design principle to consider. What would followers need to know about you at a given moment to make you more useful as a leader? Your mood? Your credibility? Your decision-making process? How could you design yourself to enhance visibility?

DEI by Design

Diversity, equity, and inclusion (DEI) comprise three related concepts with the potential to considerably enhance your leadership. You are likely familiar with those terms but may not think of them as critical to organizational success. Ethically, your purposeful efforts to translate and implement diversity, equity, and inclusion into action reflects what you and the organization value. Practically, the DEI by Design segment in each chapter highlights important concepts that enable you to see more fully and strategically enhance work activities and systems.

The benefits of carefully considering the DEI by Design segments enable you to

Understand yourself more fully—including how identity matters in context and culture and how you influence and are influenced

Engage in the discussion of ideas and practices by having some familiarity with the terms and concepts

See more and see different—perspectives, ideas, decision options, vision aspirations, potentials and possibilities

Maximize the value and potential each person brings by more accurately seeing who brings what and who needs what

Capture organizational advantages, some of which are summed in Table 0.4

TABLE 0.4 ■ Some Organizational Advantages of Integrating Diversity, Equity, and Inclusion.[9]			
This Characteristic	**Creates This Opportunity**	**With This Benefit**	**Helping to Avoid This Outcome**
Diversity the pursuit, presence, and appreciation of differences	Expanded perspectives, interconnections, and pathways to growth	More options, ideas, and possibilities for success Better decision-making, problem-solving, and creativity	Missed opportunities
Equity just and fair systems of distributing benefits and burdens	Fair and just relationships, policies, practices, culture, and systems	Greater engagement and more resilient, sustainable success	Disengagement, reputational damage, liability, and systemic instability
Inclusion individually considered and welcome access to resources and opportunities	Individual consideration, authenticity, and opportunity for individuals to develop personally and professionally	Maximizing the value of each person's contribution Increased satisfaction and continued engagement in a healthy climate and culture	Overlooking valuable contributors and their potential

Myth or Reality?

Leadership is filled with myths and misconceptions, many of which will be addressed in Chapter 2 as you design your leadership self. The Myth or Reality? feature simply and directly addresses the common misconceptions about chapter topics. Here is an example of a Myth or Reality? Feature.

MYTH OR REALITY?

The leader is the one who takes charge and does most of the talking.

Myth . . . and Reality. Leaders come in all shapes and sizes (and volume levels). Just because someone "takes charge" or talks first, doesn't mean they are facilitating *the process of influencing others toward a common vision*. Some leaders do influence others through charismatic speeches where all eyes are on them, much like depicted in the movies. But other leaders influence by quietly listening, building relationships, and creating space and opportunity for others to shine and take charge.

Reflection Question

Now that you know a definition of leadership and the distinction between leader, leadership, and taking the lead, describe one of your initial misconceptions about leadership. How did you come to understand it differently?

Experts Beyond the Text: Insightful Leaders Know About _____

Understanding and effectively practicing leadership is a complex, life-long learning adventure. Insightful leaders understand what they know about leadership today is only one part of this developing and dynamic field. This textbook facilitates your efforts to design your leadership, yet there are many important topics that expert leadership researchers and practitioners continue to think about, explore, and test. This special feature briefly highlights an area of leadership study that you will find more extensively outside the textbook. As your leadership knowledge grows, you will encounter these topics in more depth. This feature will give you a brief familiarity now to prepare you for later learning.

There are many, many experts beyond this text that have brought forth invaluable ideas for advancing leadership from their research, practice, teaching, and thinking. At the end of the textbook, you will find a glossary of key terms as well as extensive notes that can further inform your explorations and learning. Within the design framework that organizes this text are essential overviews of many of the most-referenced broad leadership approaches. Table 0.5 provides a quick reference for where to find some of those key perspectives.

TABLE 0.5 ■ Mapping the Leadership Approaches	
Key Leadership Approaches	**Can Be Found In**
Traits & skills	Chapter 2
Strengths-based	Chapter 3
Leader-member exchange	Mod 2 Intro
Followership	Chapter 5
Path-goal	Chapter 7
Situational	Chapter 9
Transformational	Chapter 10
Servant	Chapter 13
Entrepreneurial	Chapter 15
Authentic	Chapter 16
Design	ALL Chapters
Your best fit leadership	YOU! . . . and your context and your followers[10]

Moments of Awareness

For every leader, there are moments of critical decision-making, ethical challenges, and difficult truths. These short quotes and stories highlight some of the most challenging self-reflections with which aspiring leaders must grapple. This feature may also highlight ethical issues relevant to each chapter, as ethical issues permeate leadership practice. Here is an example of a Moment of Awareness feature.

Introduction and Foundations   **11**

MOMENT OF AWARENESS

Leaders create opportunities for others to lead.

When I thought of a leader, I thought of someone who was tough, hands on, loud, and asser-tive. Leadership style really depends on the followers and the overall situation, not neces-sarily the leader themselves. A leader I valued was my campus minister. She developed personal relationships with the young women at my school and inspired us to be confident, giving, respectful, and patient. I volunteered to go to nursing homes, help with the retreat, and go to soup kitchens under her leadership. She set up so many opportunities for the stu-dents to better themselves and offered her genuine experiences to girls in need. She talked about coming into her own and growing into the person she is today. She led by example in terms of giving to those in need, being available, and being a leader for the good of the community. —Morgan Smith, Undergraduate

Reflection Question

Describe a Moment of Awareness that you have had as a leader. What was the *big* lesson that you will not soon forget?

CORE™ Attribute Builders

When are you going to be serving as a leader? What challenges will you face? How can you know what personal abilities you will need when you do not even know the followers, context, or situation? The best thing you can do right now is to develop the personal characteristics or attributes that will come in handy when facing that future leadership challenge—building your CORE™—*confidence, optimism, resilience,* and *engagement.*

Chapter 1 discusses the importance of these CORE™ attributes, and at the end of each chap-ter, you will find brief lessons and activities designed to develop those dispositions. With strong confidence, an optimistic mindset, significant resilience, and full engagement, you will be ready to effectively lead across multiple situations and challenges. Here is an example of a CORE™ Attribute Builder feature.

CORE™ Attribute Builders—Build Now for Future Leadership Challenges

Attribute: Engagement

Builder: Moment of Awareness

You will not learn unless you engage. You will not lead unless you are present. Consider what happens when your mind is occupied with something other than what you are cur-rently doing. You look up and wonder what happened, the events have little meaning, and you do not really remember much. If that happens while you are in a leadership position (or in class), you will miss valuable learning opportunities. To raise your level of engagement, take a Moment of Awareness (you might also see this called a Mindful Moment). A Moment of Awareness, as you read about in the special feature example, raises your awareness of important aspects of a context or situation. The greater your awareness, the more likely you will not miss something and consequently make a not-so-great decision. Here are two cards that you can copy, cut out, and reference to take a Moment of Awareness. Keep the cards with you—they will fit into your pocket or behind your phone. One is for decision-making and the other for general leadership moments. Practicing both will build your engagement.

Moment of Awareness (MoA) for Decisions

1. What is happening *right now*?
   a. What am I doing?
   b. What am I feeling?
   c. What am I thinking?

2. What do I want right now?

3. What am I doing right now to prevent myself from getting what I want?

4. **Make a decision/choice.**

5. And move on!

Source: Senge, P. M. (1994). *The fifth discipline fieldbook.*[11]

MoA: Critical Reflection for Leadership

1. What is happening? Describe it.

2. What am I thinking and feeling?

3. What is important to others in this situation?

4. What is important about the context?

5. What information or perspectives could I be missing? How might I be wrong?

6. What is the goal or desired outcome?

7. Have I experienced something similar? How can I apply what I already do well—my strengths? What leadership theory/practices apply?

8. **What did I learn?**

Credit: ©Middlebrooks, 2021[12] (tmiddleb@udel.edu)

Skill Builder Activities

Effective leaders know things, but they can also do certain things (i.e., have skills). At the end of each chapter, you will also find some self-directed activities, tested for learning success in and out of real classrooms, in which you can engage to develop important skills, gain richer understanding of specific concepts, and move your ideas forward. Make a promise to yourself that you will take at least one idea from the end of each chapter and apply it to your leadership practice. Here is an example of a Skill Builder Activity feature.

Introduction and Foundations **13**

Skill Builder Activity

Get ready to design your leadership. Think about who through your life has served as a model of leadership for you. Identify one individual from your past or present. Consider each of the facets of the leadership by design framework:

One of the best leaders I have experienced:_____		
Key Question	Design Level	Describe the Person You Identified Based on Each Question
What great strengths did they exhibit?	**Design Self**	
What made them easy to relate to?	**Design Relationships**	
What did they do to help others be successful?	**Design Others' Success**	
What kind of an impact did they have on the larger team or group?	**Design Culture**	
What positive difference did they seek to make?	**Design Future**	

You might consider calling them to find out more about how they lead.

When you have some answers, pick one of their skills that you would like to develop in yourself and try it out for a day.

CHAPTER SUMMARY

Leadership is the process of influencing others toward a common vision. Leadership matters for individuals, teams, organizations, communities, and the world. Leader differs from leadership, and both differ from being in the lead. Effective leaders mindfully and purposefully design their leadership.

Design is the process of originating and developing a plan. The organization for this textbook aligns important elements of the leadership definition with the different aspects of designing your leadership: yourself, your relationships with followers, others' success, culture, and the future. And because your learning will come from many different sources, the text provides lots of interesting special features that reinforce and extend the main ideas: Leadership That Makes a Difference, Leadership by Design, Myth or Reality? DEI by Design, CORE™ Attribute Builders, and Skill Builder Activities.

Leaders learn in a variety of ways—from the models they observe, their experiences, what they read, the conversations they have, and their own reflections. You will get the most out of each of these engagements if you are observant at the time, reflective after, and open to changing your own concepts.

KEY TERMS

Design (p. 4)

Leadership (p. 1)

Leadership (extended) (p. 3)

1

A FRAMEWORK FOR LEADERSHIP SUCCESS: DESIGN AND YOUR CORE™

LEARNING OBJECTIVES

Upon completion of this chapter, the reader should be able to

1.1   Interpret leadership as a design process, enriched with design principles and advanced by design thinking

1.2   Assemble a plan for each attribute of CORE™ (confidence, optimism, resilience, engagement) to design your CORE™ attributes

1.3   Recognize the concepts of diversity, equity, and inclusion as part of your framework for leadership success

1.4   Create your initial leadership development goals

Leadership by Design Model

Design Self
How can I design myself as a leader?

Design Relationships
As a leader, how can I design my relationships with others?

Design Others' Success
As a leader, how can I design success for others?

Design Culture
As a leader, how can I design the culture of my organization?

Design Future
As a leader, how can I innovate?

INTRODUCTION

Leadership is the process of influencing others toward a common vision. Do you have a plan for your leadership? Have you created a design for yourself as a leader? A design (noun) can be defined as a proposed plan, solution, or product. You likely have many thoughts about who you are and what you are good at as a leader. That is a great start. Leadership, as the definition states, is a *process*. That means that your design *should be* a work in progress. Designing (verb) your leadership means *the process of originating and developing a plan*. This textbook aims to facilitate your design-centered activity—that is, to help you develop the characteristics of thinking and activities that improve or enhance your leadership.

> *Design is the process of originating and developing a plan.*

Designing your leadership is about *mindfully engaging*. **Mindfulness** simply means being aware of both your internal state and external context. What are you doing right now? Presumably, you are reading this textbook. What else are you doing or thinking about? What are you feeling right now? What are you thinking, and more importantly, *how* are you thinking? Mindfulness in the broadest sense has been described as awakening to experiences.[1] When you are more aware, you see more, learn more, and are better able to make effective decisions about your learning and your leadership. You also become more aware of others, how they might be thinking and feeling, and how you are influential. There are many advantages to becoming more mindful.[2] Mindfulness also includes numerous practices that help develop both your mindfulness capability and your overall wellness. You can read more about sustaining yourself using this powerful concept in Chapter 16. Utilizing the Moments of Awareness questions from the end of the previous chapter (Introduction and Foundations) can enhance your general mindfulness. For now, remember that when you mindfully design your leadership, you are the leader of your own learning and behavior.

The aim of this textbook is to enable you to design your leadership in a mindfully engaging manner. This chapter introduces two elements that will frame your work throughout the text and likely long into the future: Design and CORE™. The design frame provides both the mindset (purposeful and present) and the organizing model explained in the previous chapter (and summed up in the Leadership by Design Model box at the start of each chapter). The design frame also contributes processes, principles, and unique ways of thinking that will greatly enhance your leadership. The other frame, CORE™, will help build your **leadership capacity**— your fundamental attributes that can be applied to any leadership challenge in the future. Recall that CORE™ stands for your *confidence, optimism, resilience,* and *engagement*. Strengthen your CORE™, improve your future performance.

Leadership That Makes a Difference

Imagine for a moment that you can look back across the history of humankind and survey everyone who held a leadership position, from the earliest tribal leaders to military generals to presidents, business executives, and community organizers. From your observations and discussions with those leaders, what matters most? What were each of those leaders ultimately striving for: fame, causes they believed in, fortune, survival of their people, happiness, legacy, representation, human rights, self-fulfillment? And how did they assert and maintain their leadership? What were they like? Whose leadership made a big difference? What did others (or perhaps you) learn from their challenges?

In 1978, a political science professor and historian named James MacGregor Burns wrote a book entitled *Leadership*, and with it, he officially started the field of leadership studies.[3] Of course, leadership as a practice existed long before that book. James MacGregor Burns drew upon that long history of leadership activity, including his own experiences as a combat historian in the Pacific Ocean theater during World War II, to frame his initial impressions. When individuals talk about leaders and leadership, they refer to those in a position of power and authority. Unfortunately, that authority also decides who represents a leader, which considerably limited the diversity of leaders and breadth of leadership activities actually happening across the world and through history. So there are significant limits when you ask, how can others do what great leaders do? The answer had always been to look at what those great leaders knew, could do, or were like, such as their characteristics and their charisma. But James MacGregor Burns saw leadership in a broader sense, as an interconnected system of situations and relationships over time—a process. "Leadership is an aspect of power, but it is also a separate and vital process in itself," he wrote.[4]

Even more important, James MacGregor Burns recognized that *power over* is less effective than *power with*. As he explains,

> The crucial variable is *purpose*. Some define leadership as leaders making followers do what *followers* would not otherwise do, or as leaders making followers do what the *leaders* want them to do; I define leadership as leaders inducing followers to act for certain goals that represent the values and the motivations—the wants and needs, the aspirations and expectations—of *both leaders and followers*. And the genius of leadership lies in the way leaders see and act on their own and their followers' values and motivations.[5]

For James MacGregor Burns, there was a difference between leadership as a transaction (you work for me, I pay you) and leadership as a transformation (together, you and I can do great things). Transforming leadership, he explains, "occurs when one or more persons *engage* with others in such a way that leaders and followers raise one another to higher levels of motivation and morality."[6]

That is a tall order. How can a leader have such an impact on others? For James MacGregor Burns, the answer lies in carefully understanding yourself, your followers and their motivations, the goals, and the obstacles to those goals. "Essentially the leader's task is consciousness-raising on a wide plane,"[7] but he advises, "In real life the most practical advice for leaders is not to treat pawns like pawns, nor princes like princes, but all persons like *persons*."[8] This advice has only grown more powerful with deeper knowledge of what equitable and inclusive treatment of persons looks like.

Jame MacGregor Burns pioneered a new way of defining and looking at leaders.

AP Photo/Nathaniel Brooks

You took this class or picked up this book because you want to be a better leader, because you want to make a big difference. At the start of each chapter of this text, you will read about a leader who made a big difference. Some of these leaders will look like you or share your background; others will not. But every individual has a story, and those who have served in leadership roles have lessons to share. What will your big difference look like? Start your leadership journey with a charge from the individual who made leadership studies possible, James MacGregor Burns: "Decide on whether we are really trying to lead anyone but ourselves, and what part of ourselves, and where, and for what purposes."[9]

REFLECTION QUESTIONS

Who are some of the leaders you look to for guidance and inspiration? Take a closer look at their story. What were they striving to accomplish? How did they engage with others over time and across contexts? Then find someone leading who is very different from yourself. How does their story compare?

DESIGNING YOUR LEADERSHIP

LEARNING OBJECTIVE

1.1 Interpret leadership as a design process, enriched with design principles and advanced by design thinking

Design comprises a broad variety of fields, many of which we equate to products like chairs and buildings. Take a moment to look around the room. What in the room has been designed? As you look around, you might immediately notice the wide range of products that have been designed: the furniture, carpet, light fixtures, your pen, computer, even this textbook. You might also notice the less obvious: haircuts, room layout, architecture of the building, heating and cooling system. Those things were also designed.

Design also includes things you cannot see; things you can only feel or experience. For example, the class or meeting you may be sitting in right now was *designed*. In the case of a class, the instructor considered the learning goals they wanted to meet and then carefully created a plan to help the students learn. In other words, the instructor went through a process of planning your *experience*. The instructor could have also designed the *climate* of the classroom, focusing on how the experience feels. This is a field called instructional design. Organizational design does the same thing but for employees—who does what, when, why, reporting to whom—designing the experience of working at an organization.

Design Process as a Creative Problem-Solving Process: Understand, Imagine, Implement, and Iterate

For well over a decade savvy organizations have realized that leaders need to solve problems and designers can help them do so more creatively. Heather Winkle, Head of Design at Capital

Chapter 1 ● A Framework for Leadership Success: Design and Your CORE™   19

One, says, "When decision-makers are able to connect these [design and business leaders'] perspectives as a unified force, and do it in a way that rises above organizational constructs, that's when innovation really flourishes."[10] Designers are problem solvers, and they follow a problem-solving process. Design professionals write up a design brief outlining the problem and the parameters based on what the client wants, such as a more efficient toaster, a faster bike, a bee-friendly landscape, a more challenging golf course, or a more appealing website. At the university, the problem might be a more secure dorm or a healthier menu at the dining hall. Finding and identifying the problem is the start of the process, which designers then continue to originate and develop a plan to solve. Many design-related processes have been created, varying in length, specificity, and emphasis. A quick web search under design process, problem-solving process, creative problem-solving process, or innovation process yields hundreds of processes ranging from well-established to homemade and from general use to organization specific.

Despite this broad and lengthy list of processes, *all* of them can be mapped onto a general **design process** consisting of three major phases: *understand, imagine, and implement*. Each phase defines a significant step in the design process. Understand—what do we know about the problem, context, stakeholders, history, and so on? Imagine—what are the most creative ideas we can generate for addressing the problem? Implement—what activities, resources, and timelines are necessary to bring the idea to reality?[11] A fourth phase runs throughout the process: *iterate*. Iteration is the action of trying things out and changing (often improving) the design based on feedback.

1. *Understand*. When you look around at all the things that were designed, it is not always clear what the original problem entailed. A pen that feels good in your hand may have been designed to solve the problem of cost-effectiveness or reliable ink transfer. Nevertheless, the designer had to *understand* the problem and all its variables to move forward, otherwise the designer is solving the wrong problem. Now look at your phone. What kinds of problems was the design team trying to solve? What did they need to understand before they could solve each problem?

2. *Imagine*: The pen in your hand may not have been the only idea to solve that problem. In the *imagine* phase, the designer generates many, many ideas; this is the most creative part of the process. Problem solvers find a solution, but creative problem solvers *do not stop* with the first good idea, they keep coming up with ideas to find that *great* idea.

3. *Implement*. Returning to the pen example, once that solution was chosen, what did it take to get the pen from idea to production to retail store and into your hand? The designer—or likely others in a collaborative team—needed to address all the facets of *implementation*.

4. *Iterate*. Lastly, throughout the process, the designer needed to **iterate**, thoughtfully (and willingly) backtracking in the process as new information and ideas came to light, until the final solution was ready. Iteration is an important activity that happens throughout all three phases. For example, as you generate ideas, you may realize that you are not really solving the right problem, which sends you back to understand more. Or as you implement an idea, you realize the technology does not yet exist, so you need to return to the imagine phase and come up with more ideas. At any point in the process, how might your current progress make you rethink or redesign? Figure 1.1 illustrates the general steps in the design process.

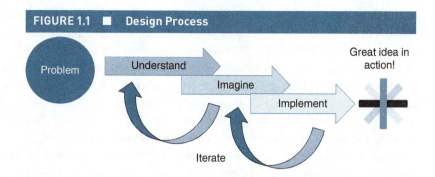

FIGURE 1.1 ■ Design Process

You are going to design something much more complicated than a pen. Designing your leadership comprises a wide menu of problems. The Leadership by Design framework helps organize those problems. Following a process will greatly enhance both your innovation and your success. For example, to design yourself as a leader:

- First, *understand* many things about yourself. For instance, what are your strengths, values, biases, assumptions, and goals?

- Then, as you grow in that understanding, you need to *imagine* the possibilities for yourself. Who will you become? What characteristics and attributes should you acquire and develop?

- From there you must *implement*—how will you learn and develop? What resources do you need to acquire? How will you make those lessons stay with you over time?

- Finally, you will *iterate* by assessing yourself in a variety of ways and then changing directions, altering your plans, dropping some solutions for others, but overall improving.

Understand, imagine, implement, and iterate: Attending to the full process will help you design your most effective and innovative leadership. But the design process is only part of the picture. How you think, see, and process information makes a big difference in how effectively you utilize each part of the process. That is called *design thinking*.

Design as a Mental Habit: Design Thinking

Designers follow a process (understand, imagine, implement, iterate), *and* they have specific habitual ways of thinking that help them see the world, enhance their process, and address their design challenge in a unique way. This set of dispositions is called **design thinking**. A **disposition** is defined as habits of mind that are often seen as tendencies or characteristics. Design thinking has taken on different forms as it has been applied and further developed.[12]

Design thinking is often described as a process—a set of steps to enhance problem-solving and innovation by applying some of the tools used by designers. These processes have proven very effective for many non-design fields, including business, education, health care, and social innovation generally.[13,14] Indeed, co-founder Tim Brown from the design firm IDEO, which has played a key role in advancing design thinking, describes the method as "an approach to innovation that is powerful, effective, and broadly accessible . . . that individuals and teams can use to generate breakthrough ideas that are implemented and that therefore have an impact."[15]

While IDEO elaborates on what a design-thinking *approach* might entail, the important part of design thinking is about your *thinking habits*: "Thinking like a designer can transform the way organizations develop products, services, processes, and strategy,"[16] Bruck and Middlebrooks provide the following definition: Design thinking is a cognitive approach to engaging problems that embodies a specific mindset that is (a) user-centered, (b) explorative, (c) divergent, (d) multidisciplinary, (e) iterative, and (f) integrative—striving for feasibility, viability, desirability.[17] Engaging and developing these habits of mind enables you to more successfully and creatively work through ill-defined and dynamic problems, such as the kind you find in leadership and certainly the type of problems you will face in designing your leadership. Table 1.1 aligns the design thinking dispositions within the understand, imagine, implement, iterate problem-solving process to better illustrate how design thinking helps each phase.

TABLE 1.1 ■ Design Thinking Dispositions by Creative Problem-Solving Phase
Design thinking is a cognitive approach to engaging problems that embodies a specific mindset that is:
Understand
User-centered: mindset that focuses on the user and how they experience and feel
Explorative: mindset that assumes purposeful ambiguity and curiosity
Imagine
Divergent: mindset of generating many, many ideas for a single problem
Multidisciplinary: mindset that engages many minds and pursues multiple areas of expertise
Implement and Iterate
Iterative: mindset of always seeing solutions in process—assessing and improving
Integrative: mindset of attending to and balancing multiple and contrasting variables and creatively resolving the tensions between them

As you design your leadership, the important aspect of the process lies with the ability to think like a designer, adopting the mental habits that will maximize each phase of the process. For example, in your effort to understand your strengths as a leader, you might take many self-assessments. Considering the design-thinking disposition of user-centeredness, you might add interviews of your followers to your exploration, asking them about how it feels to be led by you; or perhaps, spend a day in their role to better understand their context. Developing your individual capacity to think like a designer ultimately helps you solve complex problems in more creative ways. Design thinking as a leadership tool is more extensively explained in Chapter 3: Designing Your Leadership Capacity.

If you were the leader of a group, how could you use each of the design-thinking habits to help you influence others toward a common vision? Here is an example for each disposition to get you started:

- **User-centered:** Ask members: Put yourself in the shoes of new students to recruit—who feels included and welcomed, and who does not? Who is sure about how to connect with your group and who is unsure? Create fun new officer names and positions based on member strengths and interests

- **Explorative:** Ask every member to generate a question about the history and practices of the group and to think about perspectives the group is missing.

- **Divergent:** Challenge the group to generate 100 different ways you could raise funds.

- **Multidisciplinary:** Invite members from 10 very different groups to talk about how they would approach a problem your group is working on.

- **Iterative:** Try out a new activity with a few members and improve it before introducing it to the whole group.

- **Integrative:** Create numerous ways to assess the success of a new group activity, not just if people like it.

Design Principles: Rules You Can Apply to Design Your Leadership

Designers follow rules, which they call **design principles**. Designers apply these rules to whatever they are designing to help the design better meet its goals. For example, the goal of a poster design might be to clearly communicate an event or to advocate for a cause. A product design might strive for easy use or greater durability. The goal of a building design might be to encourage people to talk with one another or, by contrast, to focus on their individual work. Following the right rules helps a design more effectively meet its goals.

There are hundreds of design principles, and they focus on both tangible design fields (i.e., fields that produce a product, such as industrial design, architecture, graphic design) as well as those fields that design things you cannot touch (i.e., experiences, services, systems). Over the course of this text, you will see a feature called Leadership by Design. This feature highlights the insights leaders can draw from design. How might various design principles used in the design world be applied to effective leadership practice? Following is another example of what a Leadership by Design feature looks like using the most basic visual design principles: balance, focal point, contrast, repetition, proportion, and unity.

Could you draw a picture of your leadership? What if your leadership was a painting or photo? As you thought about the design of you as a leader, what would be most important? What rules might help you design? The main principles of visual design provide a very useful metaphor for guiding the design of your leadership self. The questions that emerge from these design principles are critical to your success, and because of that importance, you will see them again and again throughout this text.

Leadership by Design

Design Principles: Visual Design Principles: Balance, Focal Point, Contrast, Repetition, Proportion, Unity

   Definitions: Explained from an artist perspective, "The elements and principles of design are the building blocks used to create a work of art. The elements of design can be thought of as the things that make up a painting, drawing, design, and so forth. The principles of design can be thought of as what we do to the elements of design. How we apply the principles of design determines how successful we are in creating a work of art."[18]

Balance—a sense of equilibrium
Focal point—an area of emphasis that draws attention
Contrast—the notable or opposing difference between elements
Repetition—repeated elements that reinforce a theme

Proportion—a sense of order among elements
Unity—the relationship among elements that gives a sense of oneness

Balance and repetition

Balance and Focal Point

In Other Words: When the designer wants to convey a specific visual message, the preceding visual design principles can be applied to emphasize that message.

For Example: The first photo here illustrates *balance* and *repetition*, while the second photo shows an interesting *contrast* between the formal jacket and informal shorts, and clearly, those Bermuda socks are the *focal point*.

For Leaders: This segment of the feature is important for you as the designer of your leadership. This is the part that helps you apply the design principle to your leadership. The visual design principles hold many important implications and applications. Table 1.2 notes the fundamental application of each principle in the form of a prompting question for you to consider. Take a moment to note how each of these principles could be applied to your current context.

TABLE 1.2 ■ Reflection Questions

You Might Apply This Design Principle	By Asking Yourself This Key Question
Balance	Am I seeing all perspectives? Is my approach balanced? What counterbalances what I am doing?
Focal Point	What needs to be highlighted? What needs to be the focus?
Contrast	What distinctions need to be drawn between things to highlight and clarify?
Repetition	What could be better learned, retained, or highlighted through consistency or repetition?

You Might Apply This Design Principle	By Asking Yourself This Key Question
Proportion	What needs to be prioritized? Am I spending the right amount of time and energy on things relative to their importance?
Unity	Do all the things I am doing align with the vision?

DESIGNING YOUR LEADERSHIP BY BUILDING YOUR CORE™

LEARNING OBJECTIVE
1.2   Assemble a plan for each attribute of CORE™ (confidence, optimism, resilience, engagement) to design your CORE™ attributes.

"Who looks outside, dreams. Who looks inside, awakens." —Carl Jung[19]

Life is challenging, and leadership often more so. Humans become frightened, intimidated, tired, discouraged, distracted, saddened, overwhelmed, burned out, bitter, and disengaged. How can you prepare yourself for all the situations you cannot see or even imagine now and stay positive and engaged as a leader through it all? Just as you can develop your core strength for physical activities, you can also develop your internal CORE™: confidence, optimism, resilience, and engagement. This section introduces these four elements and explains how you can develop each as a central part of designing your leadership.

Building your CORE™ is about developing the mental habits that will help you excel when things are going well and sustain you when things are most challenging. Your brain is a lean, mean, pattern-making machine; when you repeat patterns of thinking over and over, they become habits. Like all habits, thinking habits can hinder your leadership and the success of others (like biases and stereotyping), while some can advance your leadership (like being inquisitive and empathetic). In this case, you want mental habits that will bolster your *future* leadership through unknown challenges. The foundation of CORE™ is rooted in positive psychology and the construct known as psychological capital, or PsyCap. **PsyCap** has been defined as "an individual's positive psychological state of development and is characterized by (a) having **confidence** (self-efficacy) to take on and put in the necessary effort to succeed at challenging tasks; (b) making a positive attribution (**optimism**) about succeeding now and in the future; (c) persevering toward goals and, when necessary, redirecting paths to goals (hope) in order to succeed; and (d) when beset by problems and adversity, sustaining and bouncing back and even beyond (**resilience**) to attain success."[20] Meta-analysis of the research finds that high levels of psychological capital are associated with job satisfaction, positive attitude, performance, and organizational citizenship behavior among employees.[21]

The CORE™ elements work together in a complementary and reinforcing way. When you are confident, you see the world and your success in more positive terms (optimism).[22] When you are optimistic, you are more likely to bounce back from setbacks (resilience).[23] When you are more resilient, every time you pick yourself up and try again, it builds your confidence.[24]

And driving the growth of all of this is positive engagement. The more you are engaged, the more you experience, the more you learn, and the more opportunities open up to you for further engagement.[25] The model illustrating the interrelationship between the elements of confidence, optimism, resilience, and engagement is shown in Figure 1.2.

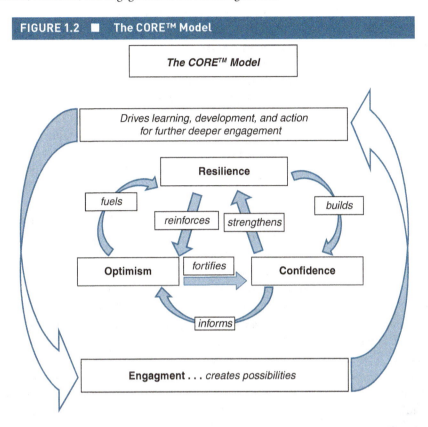

FIGURE 1.2 ■ The CORE™ Model

Confidence

Confidence as part of leadership CORE™ underpins your ability to learn, adapt, and succeed. You may have also heard the terms self-efficacy, self-confidence, assurance, self-esteem, or simply belief in yourself. But the key to confidence lies in its Latin root *con+fidere*, which means with intense trust. Trust in yourself. Consider what it means to intensely trust yourself. What would you do? How would you act? You would believe your ideas are correct, be willing to take risks and make mistakes, be open to learning new things and hearing other perspectives (even ones that contradict or challenge your own), and likely feel very good about yourself. When you trust in yourself—who you are and what you think and do—you leave behind all the fear, doubt, self-consciousness, anxiety, and hesitation that limits your thinking and ultimately your success.

REFLECTION QUESTIONS

When have you felt confident, and when have you not? Compare those situations. In what ways did you trust yourself? In situations in which you did not feel confident, what did you fear?

Your confidence as a leader has significant effects on you, your followers, and the organization. With great confidence, you can focus on others and the organization rather than yourself. For you as a leader, confidence results in greater influence with followers.[26] Followers are influenced by a leader they find credible, and when you trust in yourself, followers trust in you, too. Confident leaders also take the initiative to meet followers and build relationships, hear and discuss alternative perspectives, try new things regardless of who contributed the idea, and facilitate the success of others. When you are confident, you are not fearful that other perspectives will undermine your leadership; you do not need to take credit for new ideas or be the sole font of information.

Confident leaders maximize the value that followers can offer, which in turn results in everyone's success. Building the confidence of your followers and fostering a culture of confidence has been described as the most important challenge for leaders.[27] Leadership guru Rosabeth Moss Kanter writes, "One difference between winners and losers is how they handle losing."[28] She explains that every organization, no matter how successful, faces setbacks and unexpected problems. But knowing that leadership is a process, she states, "Anything can look like failure in the middle." Confidence, along with the other elements of CORE™, can ensure you successfully move through those failures. And that is the capacity your confidence will build in your followers and into the culture of the organization. In Chapter 11, you will learn more about the nature and nurture of culture and how to specifically utilize your CORE™ to shape it.

There are many ways that you can work on building your confidence, and all of them center around the sources of information you use to change your mindset and to increase your trust in yourself.[29] Self-efficacy researchers note there are four main sources that inform beliefs about self: enactive mastery experiences, vicarious experiences, social influences, and emotional states.[30] Enactive mastery experiences are activities in which you directly participate and achieve small wins, which propels further performance. These experiences are the most influential because they are the most authentic. When you engage and succeed, it builds confidence. The sources informing self-efficacy can best be understood by thinking about an activity for which you feel great confidence. Perhaps you are a really confident public speaker. Your path to confidence was likely informed by observing others successfully speak and get positive feedback (vicarious experiences), supportive friends or perhaps a class where everyone was learning (social influences), a series of progressively more challenging experiences that started with small, safe audiences (enactive mastery), and a safe space with encouragement (emotional states). The path to confidence can be followed again and again when you engage. And when you engage and succeed over and over again, especially if you had to overcome setbacks, you develop a resilient confidence and an optimistic view of your success in future activities.

Again, note how the CORE™ elements work together (see Figure 1.2). Confidence strengthens resilience and informs optimism. Resilient activities build confidence, while optimism reinforces that confidence.

REFLECTION QUESTIONS

Consider an activity you feel confident about. Can you recall your early successes and small wins? How many times did you need to succeed before you felt generally confident?

Other ways to build confidence include observing what others do to succeed (vicarious experiences), receiving evaluative feedback that highlights your capabilities (social influences), and a wide variety of activities that impact physical wellness, including exercise, diet, and grooming.

Chapter 1 ● A Framework for Leadership Success: Design and Your CORE™   **27**

There is increasing evidence illustrating the connection between what you do physically and how you think about yourself and the world. This is obvious when you think about things like sleep and caffeine. You can even physically assume what social psychologist Amy Cuddy calls high- and low-power body positions that can change your brain chemistry and how others perceive you.[31] At the end of this chapter, you will find the CORE™ Adventure, which is a series of activities outside the classroom that will help you identify what aspects of your CORE™ need work and help jump-start your development of these capacities.

MOMENT OF AWARENESS

One of the most influential factors in who I am as a leader, and the most overlooked, is my failures. Often in our society so much stress is placed on our successes, but little is put into our shortcomings. I feel that I have had enough of both to recognize that they both have played a lasting role in my leadership. I have been captain of sports teams and a leader in academic organizations . . . and I have been denied those positions. I have lived up to my potential in some regards, and I also have been a huge flop at times. I believe that being a good leader is not dependent on where you are at that certain point, but rather when you look back and consider the question: Did I make a positive difference? Would things be different if I wasn't there? Am I happy with what I provided?
—Benjamin Mergenthaler, Undergraduate

There are many assessments available online that you can utilize to assess your confidence and raise your awareness of the areas in which you are more and less confident.[32] However, as you plan for designing your leadership self and your confidence, there is a dark side you must consider. Confidence is not arrogance. Trusting in yourself to the point of excluding other perspectives, and others generally, results in a dangerous level of overconfidence. Overconfidence has been described in three ways: "*overestimation*: thinking that you're better than you actually are . . . *overplacement*: thinking that you're better than others when you are not . . . (and) *overprecision*: being too sure you know the truth."[33] Overconfidence as a leader can result in poor decisions, failing to see deficiencies accurately, impractical goals, and disenchanted followers that soon become alienated.[34] In other words, you will make unnecessary mistakes that may irreparably harm others, your organization, and your credibility. Overconfidence can also spread to others, it is easily transmissible between individuals in a group.[35]

Here are some suggestions for avoiding overconfidence: (a) question whether you are overlooking something, especially if performance feels too easy; (b) understand there are many variables that account for outcomes and you are only one of those variables; (c) seek out contrary and external perspectives, especially those that are the least noticed; and (d) back up your claims and your confidence with evidence. *Fake it until you make it* is a fine strategy for facing fears and building confidence, but it can quickly turn to outright falsehoods and deception, even deceiving yourself. And, after you "make it," researchers note the higher your social or professional "rank," the more susceptible you are to overconfidence.[36]

Within every experience lies the chance to build your CORE™ if you take the time to think about that experience and ask the right questions (remember the Moments of Awareness from the introduction). At the end of this section, you will find Table 1.3 called "CORE™: Assessing Leadership Challenges." This table poses a few key questions you can ask yourself during that moment of awareness, during or right after a leadership experience you felt was probably impactful. Here are the questions related to building confidence:

- Did I put in my best effort?

- Did fear influence my effort?

- Did I take initiative?

- Did I focus and dedicate my attention to the effort?

Optimism

Optimism is the ability and tendency to see the positive, both now and into the future. You likely know people who you would describe as upbeat, positive, and always seeing the glass half full (and a host of other metaphors). But the key to optimism lies in its Latin root *optimus*, which means *the best*. What does it mean to see the best in yourself, others, and every situation? How would you act? You would likely work to try and bring out that best in yourself and others, which of course would feel great. As leadership scholars James Kouzes and Barry Posner note in their book *Encouraging the Heart*, people want to be in a relationship with someone who makes them feel good and brings out their best.[37] Optimism is your tool for building those great relationships. Of course, when you can see your best, you become more confident.

Optimism can be a purposefully acquired mental habit, culturally transmitted, or a characteristic you can inherit from your parents. When people call someone an optimist, it sounds like part of who they are that cannot be changed. It has even been referred to as a core personality trait of managers.[38] You will read more about traits in the next chapter. But optimism can be learned, practiced, developed, and used by anyone. So when you read *optimist*, it refers to someone with that ability and tendency to see the best, regardless of how they came to be an optimist.

A good deal of research has been done on the relationship between optimism and a variety of leadership variables. Greater optimism predicts greater career succes, better social relations, better health, and greater engagement in pursuit of desired goals.[39] Optimists are perceived by supervisors as having leadership potential and being better able to cope with stressors.[40] Most importantly, focusing on the best things results in greater performance. The previous section noted that confident leaders maximize the value that followers can offer. Optimism enables leaders to *see* that positive value so they can capitalize on it.

REFLECTION QUESTIONS

How optimistic are those with whom you associate? Make a quick list of family and friends and order them according to how you perceive their ability and tendency to see the best. Compare and contrast the most and least optimistic. In what ways do you think their level of optimism has affected their life?

While optimism is a personal attribute, it is not necessarily an individual endeavor. If you have ever been part of a great team, you know how powerful and motivating a culture of optimism can feel. As each teammate communicates their positive perspective, the capacity of the entire team to see and strive for the best increases exponentially. Setbacks become opportunities for improvement. Problems become challenges. Achievements become affirmations of effort

Chapter 1 • A Framework for Leadership Success: Design and Your CORE™   29

and capability. Groups that are highly optimistic experience heightened positive emotions when they are interacting with each other and, ultimately, operate as cohesive, high-performing work units. In what researchers call positive contagion theory, individual members of a group that have higher dispositional optimism impact outcomes for the group at large.[41]

"I think I can, I think I can. I think I can. I know I can," wrote Watty Piper in *The Little Engine That Could*. Are you like the little engine, rooting your effort in a firm vision of your best? If not, you may want to very seriously consider developing your optimism. Optimism is a reinforcing cycle between what you highlight in the world and what you believe. The more opportunities you create to highlight the positive and the possible, the stronger you will make your mental habit of searching out those best elements in any situation. Try some of these ideas to build your optimism (or go online to find many more)[42]:

1. *Seek* positive perspectives, positive people, multiple perspectives, and upbeat words. Try responding to others' comments with "yes, and . . ." rather than "but . . ." even when you may disagree.

2. *Reframe* negative phrases, complaining, griping, and negative environments. Seek to identify and address the underlyling problem.

3. *Engage* in recognizing what is going well and what is going great; practice thinking about what could be; encourage open dialog and collaborate to build a compelling vision that inspires others.

4. *Celebrate* to reinforce optimistic habits. When was the last time you celebrated a small win, learning something new, another person who did something well, or a moment of awareness of all that is going pretty well for you? Even small celebrations make a big impact.

Optimism is not about pretending everything is happy and perfect. Nor do optimists avoid challenges and difficult people and situations. An optimistic approach is often rejected by those claiming they are realists and their perspective is more accurate. Do not be fooled or dissuaded into thinking another person's assessment of reality is more important than your own. You can have a full understanding and acceptance of the real *and* still strive to see the positive and the potential. Within the CORE™ Model, optimism reinforces confidence and fuels resilience. If you can see the best and believe it is possible, then you will move forward without fear and keep moving forward even with setbacks.

See Table 1.3, at the end of this section ("CORE™: Assessing Leadership Challenges") that poses key questions you can ask yourself, this time related to building optimism:

- Did I feel I would succeed?

- Was my success due to my effort and skill?

- Did I need to redirect my efforts?

Resilience

Resilience is your ability to withstand and recover from difficulties. You may also have heard the terms *hardiness, grit, stick-to-itiveness,* and *gutsiness.* Once again, the Latin root captures the essence of the concept, in this case *resilire,* which means to *spring back.* Consider what it means to spring back. First, something must have pushed you over. A life without setbacks leaves no opportunity to display or build resilience. Second, there must be some initial resistance to the setback. A flower blown back by the wind started with enough resistance to stand upright in the first place. Third, there must be some energy to spring back, energy that exists before the setback, built in preparation for the challenge. Finally, there is a positive energy to springing back. You do not crawl, limp, hobble, or scrape your way back, you spring.[43] Funto Boroffice is the founder and CEO of award-winning Chanja Datti, Ltd. She is a Nigerian entrepreneur who has navigated several headwinds in a male-dominated society and industry of recycling/waste management. However, she has remained resilient and is making a significant difference. In her words "let's her results speak for themselves."

REFLECTION QUESTIONS

Think about the last time you experienced a setback. How many times did you try again? What helped you to try again, and/or what kept you from doing so?

Once again, your mental habit-forming lean, mean, pattern-making machine of a brain can work with you or against you when it comes to resilience. The founder of positive psychology, Martin Seligman, and other researchers have summed up the mental habits you need. When something in your life goes wrong (or right), how do you explain it?[44]

1. Do you think problems happen for many reasons, or do problems happen because you are incapable, incompetent, and other bad things?

2. Do you see adversity as a challenge or chance to learn, or do you see it as a threat?

3. Do you see the problem as one specific thing or just another indication that your whole life is problematic?

4. Do you see difficulties as permanent situations or as something you can address or change?

5. Are *you* in control of the outcome, or is it out of your hands with nothing you can do about it?

For each of these questions, thinking and seeing as described in the first half of the question lead to very different outcomes than in the second. Resilient individuals and leaders work to develop psychologically positive mental habits.

Resilience in leadership goes beyond personal well-being, although it is critically important to the individual leader. A resilient leader not only springs back but also leaps forward by displaying a willingness to be coached and change, using the setback to advance themselves and the organization.[45] The cliché of seeing every challenge as an opportunity reflects the interplay of optimism and resilience and has been embraced by innovators and entrepreneurs as the power of failure.[46] Although no one wants to fail, those moments hold great value for individual learning and group modeling. Leaders who model resilience help create a resilient culture. Looking beyond the single moments of failure to the broader pattern of shortcomings brings even greater insights. In other words, sometimes many little failures are all hints at a more fundamental problem—a problem you would not see otherwise, or worse, one that would build into a large problem.[47]

Great resilience does not come easily nor without considerable emotional consequences. Challenges and setbacks are exactly that; they are challenging and set you back. They are painful, disheartening, annoying, disorienting, and extraordinarily frustrating. The level, amount, and duration of these feelings varies, and what constitutes a challenge to one person may not be so to another. As a leader, you must understand the level of understanding for each follower. This means you must understand how others feel, which is part of a concept called emotional intelligence. **Emotional intelligence** is a person's ability to know and regulate their own feelings, perceive and understand the feelings of others, and effectively work between their own and others' feelings (see the Experts Beyond the Text: Insightful Leaders Know About . . . Emotional Intelligence feature at the end of this section).[48]

Resilience is not something one is born with, nor can you afford to purposefully engage in failure to build your resilience . . . or can you? The effort to develop resilience goes back to antiquity. Lucius Annaeus Seneca (4BC–AD65) was a Roman philosopher who, among his many wise letters, advised a friend on how to build resilience:

Set aside a certain number of days, during which you shall be content with the scantiest and cheapest fare, with coarse and rough dress, saying to yourself the while: 'Is this the condition that I feared?' It is precisely in times of immunity from care that the soul should toughen itself beforehand for occasions of greater stress . . . If you would not have a man flinch when the crisis comes, train him before it comes.

In modern times, author Jia Jiang took on 100 different challenges, one each day, that purposefully set him up for rejection in order to build his resilience. His challenges included activities that forced him to do something he feared or in which he would likely experience rejection, such as "Borrow $100 from a stranger," and "Get a live interview on radio."[49] Not surprisingly, Seneca also noted this activity for building resilience also provided insight that brought empathy (and emotional intelligence): "There is no reason, however, why you should think that you are doing anything great; for you will merely be doing what many thousands of slaves and many thousands of poor men are doing every day."[50]

REFLECTION QUESTIONS

Try holding your arms straight out away from your body for three minutes. As it starts to hurt, push through the pain. Keep them up. Were you able to keep your arms up for the full time? Why did you keep going (or why did you quit)? What did it feel like once you dropped your arms? What could you do without for a time that would build your resilience . . . and your appreciation?

Fortunately, there are many other ways to build resilience besides diving into failure. Developing your resilience as a leader depends upon engaging in experiences and mindfully learning from them. Here are a few suggestions based on attending to different kinds of health:[51]

1. Attend to your physical health: exercise, sleep, eat well, and destress

2. Attend to your mental and emotional health: take time for yourself, develop your confidence, laugh

3. Attend to your social health: connect with others, foster relationships with family and friends, build your support system, ask advice

32   Discovering Leadership

4. Attend to your attitude health: practice optimism, see problems as experiences you can learn from, put problems into perspective

5. Attend to your aspirational health: identify big and little goals for yourself, commit to them, act to move toward achieving them

Take a second look at the summary of resilience-building activities. Note that all five start with the idea that you must *attend to* these aspects of your health. There is a strong connection between mindfulness and resilience-related outcomes.[52] If you are feeling good, have a great support system, see the bigger picture, and know leadership is a process, your capacity for resilience will grow. What one thing can you do today to start building your capacity to spring back?[53]

Refer to Table 1.3, at the end of this section ("CORE™: Assessing Leadership Challenges") that poses key questions you can ask yourself, this time related to building resilience:

- Did I encounter setbacks or significant challenges?

- Did setbacks discourage my efforts?

- Did I confront problems directly?

- Did problems make me question my ability?

Experts Beyond the Text

INSIGHTFUL LEADERS KNOW ABOUT . . . EMOTIONAL INTELLIGENCE

The Role of Emotional Intelligence in Leadership

By Scott Allen

The topic of emotions is central to leadership. After all, a central activity of leadership is engaging, inspiring, and motivating others to work above and beyond toward the goal or objective—all of which engages emotions. Likewise, because of the nature of leadership work, leaders must navigate any number of stressors, such as interpersonal conflicts, issue conflicts, rapid change, and organizational bureaucracy. The heightened levels of stress that come with leadership mean leaders must be acutely aware of their emotional state and that of others. In essence, leaders need to be *intelligent* about emotions and understand how emotions can influence themselves and others.

There are a number of different ways to make sense of emotional intelligence (EI). Some scholars feel that EI is a form of intelligence,[54] and others believe it is simply a constellation of personality traits.[55] The most well-known model of EI explores the concept as a series of competencies.[56] Researcher Daniel Goleman provides a definition that nicely captures all three general approaches:

Emotional intelligence, at the most general level, refers to the abilities to recognize and regulate emotions in ourselves and in others.[57]

As you look at the definition, note that having EI means an individual *recognizes* their emotions and can *regulate* them as appropriate. This does not mean they *stuff away* their feelings; it simply means they are more aware of their emotional state in the face of a challenging situation. They can intentionally regulate their emotional state in an effort to move

Chapter 1 ● A Framework for Leadership Success: Design and Your CORE™ **33**

forward toward the end objective—aware of their emotions as they arise or are *triggered* by the various stressors. Individuals who are more easily triggered will often react in ways that diminish trust and credibility. A second important highlight of the definition is the term *others*. The leader is responsible for awareness and regulation of both their own emotions and those of their colleagues. This means leaders with EI can read the emotional state of the group and regulate that emotional state (e.g., pick them up during a difficult time).

Who in your life best maintains emotional intelligence when triggered by the various stressors that accompany their role? Who struggles to do so? What is the impact on the group?

Scholars have made positive associations that underscore the importance of leadership and EI. Here are several examples of what scholars from different paradigms have found based on their research.

- "The high EI individual, most centrally, can better perceive emotions, use them in thought, understand their meanings, and manage emotions better than others. . . . The person also tends to be somewhat higher in verbal, social, and other intelligences, particularly if the individual scored higher in the understanding emotions portion of EI. The individual tends to be more open and agreeable than others. The high EI person is drawn to occupations involving social interactions, such as teaching and counseling, more so than to occupations involving clerical or administrative tasks."[58]
- "Both emotional and social competencies and personality traits are valuable predictors of job performance."[59]
- "Experienced partners in a multinational consulting firm were assessed on the EI competencies plus three others. Partners who scored above the median on 9 or more of the 20 competencies delivered $1.2 million more profit from their accounts than did other partners—a 139 percent incremental gain."[60]
- "In a national insurance company, insurance sales agents who were weak in emotional competencies such as self-confidence, initiative, and empathy sold policies with an average premium of $54,000. Those who were very strong in at least 5 of 8 key emotional competencies sold policies worth $114,000."[61]

While some might minimize emotions as a fuzzy or *soft* topic, research suggests that EI helps individuals succeed. Effective leaders understand emotional intelligence and strive to develop this key capacity.

Engagement

What grabs your full attention or your involvement? How often do you choose to observe, take notes, inquire further, learn more, or pursue an activity? If you have ever been talking with someone while they look at their phone or around the room, mumbling an occasional "uh huh," then you know engagement is key to connecting with others. But engagement extends beyond the interpersonal to encompass your connection with the world. For instance, Dr. Sara Safari, climbs the world's tallest mountains to help marginalized women around the world. She is deeply engaged in this work; it's a part of her identity as a human being. The worst result of disengagement is the missed opportunities to learn, to connect, and to discover new ideas and possibilities.

Engagement is one of the most powerful tools in your leadership toolbox. The origin of the word *engage* comes from the Old French *engagier*, meaning bind by promise or pledge. For example, engagement to a person means you pledge a binding promise to marry. Engaging the enemy binds you to the promise of conflict. For leaders, engagement promises the binding of your attention and involvement. **Engagement** is the degree of individual involvement, investment, and enthusiasm within and for a specific context or situation.

REFLECTIVE QUESTIONS

Are you involved? Invested? Do you notice the world around you? Do you actively listen to others and seek to discover more about them? How often would your friends say you are truly present?

If you are not paying attention to the things you are experiencing, or simply not involved enough to have a wide range of experiences, then you shortchange your chances for learning and growth. For effective leadership, engagement needs to add value, that is to say, it needs to be *positive*. **Positive engagement** means you initiate and participate in ways that add value in a reflective and mindful manner, critically and carefully integrating new information into your understanding. *Your most valuable internal asset is your positive engagement.* Engaged leaders are perceived as more charismatic, and they inspire performance and commitment.[62]

Increasing your own engagement is a choice, but it is also a mental and behavioral habit. The best way to develop a habit is, of course, to repeat a behavior over and over again. Here are a few ideas for how you can increase your engagement:

- Take a leisurely walk and purposefully look up.

- Eat with your eyes closed and focus on the flavors.

- Unplug—set a time and time limit for dealing with social media.

- Meet someone new and learn about their world.

- Meet someone who you think is very different from you.

- Meet someone you already know—interview them and get to know them better.

- Learn to do something new in your leadership setting and beyond—learn to tie knots, learn a specific dance, cook a meal, identify trees.

- Try sketching, even if you do not think you can—it forces you to really look at something.

- Identify one activity that you would really like to do but never seem to have the time—commit to doing that activity every day for 30 days (and start by watching the Matt Cutts TED Talk for inspiration: Go to www.ted.com, then search for Matt Cutts, Watch *Try Something New for 30 Days*).

Similar to confidence, optimism, and resilience, engagement rubs off on others. Leaders model engaged behavior, and in turn, they become engaging. If you consistently positively engage—in any role, in any situation, in any context—you will ultimately find success. And here at the end of this section is Table 1.3 ("CORE™: Assessing Leadership Challenges"), which poses key questions that you can ask yourself. The questions related to building engagement are as follows:

- Did I reflect and learn from the experience?

- Did I integrate this new knowledge into prior?

One of the best ways to build your entire CORE™ is to raise your awareness of what is happening, what you are doing, how you are feeling, and what you could have done better. Using Table 1.3 create an index card containing the attributes and their prompting questions. Use the prompting questions on the cards to enhance your self-awareness as you engage in any leadership challenge.

TABLE 1.3 ■ CORE™ Card: Assessing Leadership Challenges

CORE™: Assessing Leadership Challenges

1. **Confidence:** self-efficacy and effort

   Did I put in my best effort?

   Did fear influence my effort?

   Did I take initiative?

   Did I focus and dedicate my attention to the effort?

2. **Optimism:** positive about success

   Did I feel I would succeed?

   Was my success due to my effort and skill?

   Did I need to redirect my efforts?

3. **Resilience:** perseverance and flexibility, using setbacks as set-forwards

   Did I encounter setbacks or significant challenges?

   Did setbacks discourage my efforts?

   Did I confront problems directly?

   Did problems make me question my ability?

4. **Engagement:** reflective and mindful

   Did I reflect and learn from the experience?

   Did I integrate this new knowledge into prior?

MYTH OR REALITY?

Without mobile phones and social media, individuals are more engaged.

Myth . . . and Reality. A recent study asked a thousand students in ten different countries to go without all media for one full day. The resulting reactions, observations, and insights indicate that media use is more than a habit, rather, it is "essential to the way they construct and manage their friendships and social lives," and it is critically useful for both practical performance and psychological and emotional security.[63] On the other hand, "Many students, from all continents, literally couldn't imagine how to fill up their empty hours without media" and limited their news and awareness to the brief and simplified media worlds in which they operate.

Could you go without media for 24 hours? Try it and note your observations.

36   Discovering Leadership

"A well-designed product does not equal a well-designed business."[64] Likewise, a well-designed leader does not equal well-designed leadership . . . but it is a necessary start. This chapter focused on your perceptions and the task of designing your leadership self. Acquiring a thorough and continually reviewed understanding of yourself will prove to be one of your most valuable assets as a leader. But as you know, leadership as a process extends far beyond your role, beliefs, values, and capabilities. Well-designed leadership must address the broader system and each of its component parts—and in the organizational structure of this text, well-designed leadership must address self, relationships, others' success, culture, and the future.

DEI BY DESIGN

LEARNING OBJECTIVE
1.3   Recognize the concepts of diversity, equity, and inclusion as part of your framework for leadership success.

Leadership always involves *others*, and the framework for your leadership success is incomplete without considering that key component. Diversity, equity, and inclusion (DEI) comprise one important frame that has great influence on your confidence, optimism, resilience, and engagement. Likewise, DEI provides a powerful frame for applying your CORE™ toward personal, follower, and organizational success. As an individual, you no doubt want these things for yourself. You will certainly want these conditions for your organization because they lead to considerable and significant practical success.[65] A greater challenge and the one that will maximize value to all involves seeing how these conditions can and should apply to those different than yourself. And then, purposefully designing your leadership to pursue them.

Diversity, equity, and inclusion encompass a wide range of ideas and actions, many of which will be introduced throughout the text. For now, you need some key definitions. **Diversity** can be defined as a state characterized by the pursuit, presence, and appreciation of differences. **Equity** is likewise a state, but a state of just and fair systems of distributing benefits and burdens. **Inclusion** comprises the continuous process of individual consideration and welcome access to resources and opportunities. As you might imagine, there is a great deal of explanation behind these definitions. Take another moment to go back and re-read the definitions. How do they differ from your initial thoughts? Can you imagine what it would be like to *not* have a diverse and equitable context that is inclusive for yourself?

Before concluding this introduction to DEI, you should note two important distinctions that are often confused. First, diversity is often thought of in the context of extending participation to persons from specific groups—ethnic, racial, religious, differently abled, to name but a few. And indeed, that is a key aspect. However, many of these groups are marginalized, which means they lack access or have been denied power. In this context, diversity is intertwined with **social justice,** and many people may even use these two terms interchangeably. "Social justice is both a goal and a process. The *goal* of social justice is full and equitable participation of people from all social identity groups in a society that is mutually shaped to meet their needs. The *process* for attaining the goal of social justice should also be democratic and participatory, respectful of human diversity and group differences, and inclusive and affirming of human agency and capacity for working collaboratively with others to create change."[66]

A second important distinction is that between equity and equality. Put simply, **equality** means everyone gets treated the same, regardless of social standing. Equity, by contrast, means everyone gets treated in accordance with how they are located within society (or within an organization). Equality is important, for example, when considering consistent protection under federal, state, and local laws. Equity is essential when considering who has access to what opportunities and which factors impact favorable outcomes. In the broader society, this could include such things as reliable health care, well-paying jobs, affordable housing, and access to safe water and food.

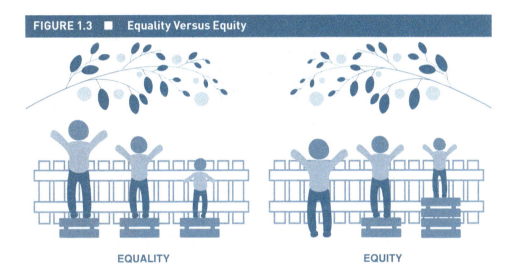

FIGURE 1.3 ■ Equality Versus Equity

EQUALITY   EQUITY

Mindful, purposeful leadership includes consideration of these elements: diversity, social justice, equity, equality, and inclusion. As Ming-Ka Chan, M.D., suggests, "It's really hard to be well if you've never felt welcome."[67] The elements we've highlighted can be leveraged to lead in equitable, respectful, and inclusive ways. Imagine how they might be used to bring the best to your organization and to bring out the best in each individual. You may want to go back and take a quick look at the overview of the DEI by Design segment in the Introduction and Foundations chapter so that you can fully achieve and benefit from these ideas.

DESIGNING YOUR LEADERSHIP—FIRST STEP: YOUR GOALS

LEARNING OBJECTIVE
1.4   Create your initial leadership development goals.

How rich are you? This is a more complicated question than you might initially think. Wealth in the form of money or valuable possessions is the typical measure of value. But consider what other forms of capital you can use to measure your wealth. For example, how positive and widely known is your reputation? How many friends do you have in the virtual world? How many friends do you have in the real world? How many different perspectives and voices are represented across those you know, collaborate with, or know you? How many connections do your friends have in their networks? All of these are measures of your **social capital**—the value created through common and stable individual relationships. A leader rich in social capital is likely to wield greater influence. This is one of many forms of value you can build as a leader.

Learning and designing your leadership builds your **human capital**—the value you bring from your knowledge, skills, experiences, and dispositions. Even though designing your leadership will be a collaborative endeavor, *you* must be the designer of your own growth. How rich do you want to be? You can start to address that question by setting your goals as a student of leadership.

One way to better understand these concepts is to explore a case study. Use your favorite search engine to explore the work of Dr. Sara Khurram. She is the co-founder and CEO of Sehat Kahani, an organization that is bringing telemedicine to people in need across her country. Another fun and effective way to better understand your capital is to explore where your assets came from in the history of you. You have identified many things about yourself: strengths, traits, skills, values, and more. All of these are you, but only some of them are *very* consequential and *very* foundational to you as a leader. Try this exercise:

1. Take a moment to gather or write out many of the single words or phrases that describe you. Ask for input from friends or family if you like.

2. Now picture yourself in a leadership position. What are you doing? For whom or what are you responsible? How are you influencing others? What are others looking to you for?

3. Looking back at the list you wrote, circle the words about you that are *most* important for your leadership success.

4. Now choose *one word*—a value, a skill, an attitude, a strength—and *write the story* of where that personal attribute came from. How and when did you acquire it? From where or whom? What event or experience highlighted the importance of that attribute? And how will you continue to apply and develop the attribute?

5. Be prepared to share the story with others in a compelling manner (i.e., in a way that helps us understand the full importance of that attribute to you as a leader).

Purposeful, Present, Planning: 3 Ps for Your Leadership Journey

This chapter introduced the essential framework for your leadership success: purposeful leadership design and foundational CORE™. Leadership is truly a life-long journey. That is not cliché or trite, but it is a fact to which every single experienced leader will attest. With such a long and winding journey, the best thing you can do to prepare for a lifetime of challenges and learning consists of 3 Ps: purposeful, present, planning.

- *Purposeful*: As noted earlier, as a leader you can make conscious, mindful decisions about what you do or simply be a nonparticipant and let things happen.

- *Present*: Mindful leaders are present and aware of the context, situation, individuals, relationships, and themselves. And if they are ill-informed, they get informed.

- *Planning*: Effective leaders design their leadership; they originate and develop a plan for themselves, their followers, their relationships, the culture, and the future of the venture.

Utilizing design process, design thinking, and design principles (3D) and focusing on building your confidence, optimism, resilience, and engagement (CORE™) will greatly enhance your abilities as a purposeful, present, and plan-oriented leader (3D + CORE™ = 3P for the math inclined). This textbook aims to help you achieve those goals and more. Some additional important leadership learning goals are listed next. Take a moment to consider how each of these goals fits into your understanding and your plan for developing. Then, *you* need to identify some personal goals for yourself.*

Goal 1. Find my leadership—begin to identify as a leader and recognize my potential.

Goal 2. Explore new leadership ideas and diverse leaders; allow myself to see the field more broadly and note the complexities.

Goal 3. Develop my leadership dispositions—the mental habits I use to see, think about, and respond to the world.

Goal 4. Build my leadership CORE™—personal attributes that will enhance my leadership now and long into the future.

Goal 5. Provide both a road map and a toolkit to effectively design my leadership.

Additional Goals. As the designer of my own leadership, I will set additional goals by asking myself some of the following questions:

a. An immediate practical goal for me as leader is _____ _____.

b. The *best* leader I ever saw or worked with did this: _____ _____.

c. Other goals I have for designing myself as a leader are _____.

d. One thing I can do this week to become a more effective leader is _____. (Hint: What could you explore, learn, develop, do, or whom could you meet?)

*Reread all the goals and put a *large star* by the one that most appeals to you. Then, rewrite that goal here in your own words. This will help make it stick and help you stay focused on what is most important to you: _____.

The next chapter continues your design of leadership self, starting with how you learn leadership and clarifying important aspects of leadership that are often misconceived.

CHAPTER SUMMARY

Leadership is the process of influencing others toward a common vision. Leadership matters for individuals, teams, organizations, communities, and the world. Effective leaders consciously design their leadership and strive to be as mindful as possible.

The framework of this textbook emphasizes your purposeful design of your leadership and consistently working to build your CORE™—confidence, optimism, resilience, and engagement.

Design is the process of originating and developing a plan. Designers are problem solvers, and a complete design process will include understanding, imagining, and implementing.

The design process is enhanced by specific ways of thinking—design thinking—dispositions that include user centered, explorative, divergent, multidisciplinary, iterative, and integrative. Developing design-thinking habits makes you a more effective problem solver and will result in a better design; in this case, that design is you and your leadership.

Leaders who develop deep, foundational capabilities are able to excel when faced with new challenges. Confidence, optimism, resilience, and engagement (CORE™) provide individuals with the capacity to lead now and into the future. The elements of CORE™ influence the development of each other, and there are very concrete activities that will build your CORE™. Leaders are only as successful as those they lead—identifying and bringing forth the value of each follower. You can mindfully, purposefully design this capacity through your awareness and pursuit of diverse, equitable, and inclusive conditions.

Finally, keep the goals of this text and your own personal goals in mind as you move forward and experience your own *aha* moments.

KEY TERMS

Confidence (p. 24)	Integrative (p. 22)
Design principle (p. 22)	Iterate (p. 19)
Design process (p. 19)	Iterative (p. 22)
Design thinking (p. 20)	Leadership capacity (p. 16)
Disposition (p. 20)	Mindfulness (p. 16)
Divergent (p. 22)	Multidisciplinary (p. 22)
Diversity (p. 36)	Optimism (p. 24)
Emotional intelligence (p. 31)	Positive engagement (p. 34)
Engagement (p. 34)	PsyCap (p. 24)
Equality (p. 37)	Resilience (p. 24)
Equity (p. 36)	Social capital (p. 38)
Explorative (p. 22)	Social justice (p. 36)
Human capital (p. 38)	User-centered (p. 21)
Inclusion (p. 36)	

CORE™ ATTRIBUTE BUILDERS: BUILD NOW FOR
FUTURE LEADERSHIP CHALLENGES

Attribute: Confidence, Optimism, Resilience, and Engagement

Builder: CORE™ adventure

Complete the CORE™ development tasks following.. For added fun, complete these as a group, with each group member taking on *one* of the four CORE™ challenges: **confidence, optimism, resilience, engagement.**

Although each team member has a set of tasks, you must work as a team, observing the completion of each task and supporting each member.

Chapter 1 • A Framework for Leadership Success: Design and Your CORE™   41

CHALLENGE YOURSELF

This adventure is designed to be a learning experience . . . but only if you really strive to make it so. Any of the tasks can be completed with minimal effort and zero learning; however, as aspiring leaders, you will want to fully engage the tasks, take some uncomfortable risks, question your assumptions, and reflect on the learning and development that each task has the potential to offer. Good luck and have fun!

Confidence

- Enter **two** establishments. Assuming your neutral face, ask the individual behind the counter to assess your confidence (circle their answer):

  Not Confident *Very* Confident

  0   1   3   5   7   9   10

  0   1   3   5   7   9   10

- Enter **two other** establishments, this time assuming a *big* smile, shoulders back, and with eye contact, clear voice, and power pose, ask the individual behind the counter to assess your confidence (circle their answer):

  Not Confident *Very* Confident

  0   1   3   5   7   9   10

  0   1   3   5   7   9   10

  What did you observe?

  _____

  _____

  _____

- Take a risk—try something new.

  What did you try?

  _____

  _____

  _____

- Assume an attitude of gratitude—write a thank you note to someone who deserves your thanks.

  To whom did you write? For what did you thank them?

  _____

  _____

  _____

- List out 10 great things about *you*.

  1. _____
  2. _____
  3. _____
  4. _____
  5. _____
  6. _____
  7. _____
  8. _____

42   Discovering Leadership

    9. _____

  10. _____

- Ask each person in your group to add one.

    1. _____

    2. _____

    3. _____

    4. _____

    5. _____

    6. _____

    7. _____

    8. _____

    9. _____

  10. _____

Optimism ☺

- Name two establishments that you really do not like. ☹
  - _____

  Reframe those by naming *five* things about *each* that are positive.
  - _____
  - _____
  - _____
  - _____
  - _____

- Ask three individuals that you do not know to share a joke with you (and be sure to thank them).
  - What joke was your favorite?

  _____
  _____

  - What did you observe?

  _____
  _____

- Do *one* spontaneous thing.
  - What did you try?

  _____
  _____

- Encourage your team to complete their tasks.
  - Ask them to rate your optimism:

  Not Optimistic   Very Optimistic

  0   1   3   5   7   9   10

Chapter 1 ● A Framework for Leadership Success: Design and Your CORE™   **43**

- Influence five separate groups of individuals to *smile*.
  - List out all of the things you did to make them smile:

_____

_____

_____

Resilience

- For every decision your group makes, take a moment for *you* to *decide* what *you* want and assert *yes* or *no*.
  This does not mean you get to decide, nor that you will always get your way. Just make sure you get your *say*.
  - At the end of the adventure, have your group assess your assertiveness:
    Not Assertive   *Very* Assertive
       0 1 3 5 7 9 10
  What did you observe?

_____

_____

_____

- Make a request from someone where you will likely be rejected (nothing illegal or unethical).

- Make the request again from a different person.

- Make the request a third time from yet a different person and ask them to sign affirming that you did so:

_____

_____

_____

_____

What did you feel?

_____

_____

What did you observe?

_____

_____

- Apologize to someone to whom you owe an apology.
  What did you apologize for?

_____

_____

- And ask each person in your group to share one (or more) things they admire about you.
  Write them here:

_____

_____

44   Discovering Leadership

_____
_____
_____
_____

Engagement

- Keep your team engaged and on task. Help them succeed.
  Ask them to rate your ability to encourage their engagement:
  Not Helpful *Very* Helpful
  0   1   3   5   7   9   10
  What did you observe?

  _____
  _____
  _____

- Ask three individuals that you do not know to share a grand vision of excellence about themselves—who do they want to be, where do they want to go, and so forth (and be sure to thank them).
  What were some of those grand visions?

  _____
  _____
  _____
  _____
  _____

- Build a bridge—find two individuals that YOU know—connect them with someone in your group.
  How did you connect them?

  _____
  _____
  _____

  What did you observe?

  _____
  _____
  _____

- Recognize a great performance in EACH of your group members and reward it.
  - What did they do?   And how did you reward them?

  _____
  _____
  _____
  _____
  _____

SKILL BUILDER ACTIVITY

Build Your Design Process: Explore Understand—Imagine—Implement

Design thinking involves building specific mental habits that enhance your process.

Design principles comprise rules you apply that also enhance your process.

Chapter 1 ● A Framework for Leadership Success: Design and Your CORE™   45

So you need to have a process, and there are many from which to choose.

1. *Find a creative problem-solving process, innovation process, or design process* that tells you step-by-step how to go from zero to innovative idea or product. The process you find can be from a specific model, researcher, or company. Consider searching in a field of interest to you. Design happens in every field.

2. The process you find should be a *process* (first do this, then do that). And it should be a generalized process (i.e., follow these steps to solve a problem or generate an innovation in any context; not specific instructions on how to do something). For example, Arek Dvornechcuck at Ebaqdesign uses these steps in his logo design process: discover, research, brainstorm, sketch, design, present, deliver.[68]

3. Examine the steps of the process you found and note which steps fit within each of the three general phases: understand, imagine, and implement. Are there any steps that prompt iteration? Which phase(s) is (are) overlooked or over-emphasized? Are there any steps that cross stages or help you move from one to the next?

4. Compare the process you found with those found by your classmates. What process steps seem particularly interesting and/or useful to creatively solve problems?

Note that every process provides useful tools to design your leadership. Explore processes, familiarize yourself with their tools, and utilize them to design your leadership. Most importantly, use a process.

DESIGN LEADERSHIP SELF

MODULE

1

Chapter 2	Designing Your Perceptions of Leaders and Leadership	49
Chapter 3	Designing Your Leadership Capacity	79
Chapter 4	Your Why and What for Leading	121

Module 1 begins where all leadership begins—with you, the leader. There is a lot to know about you. And like all subjects, the more you know, the more effective you will be. Understanding yourself as a leader starts with how you perceive leaders and leadership. Everyone has had a variety of experiences with leaders—parents, teachers, coaches, siblings, friends, bosses—and those experiences form your values, expectations, assumptions, and behaviors as leaders. Some of the personal characteristics modeled by your early leaders are very effective for leadership, but unfortunately, many are not.

The chapters in this section explore those personal attributes that characterize effective leaders, with a focus on understanding yourself—how you see leaders and leadership, your strengths and style, and the values and ethics that will shape your decisions. As you work your way through the three chapters of the Design Leadership Self module, keep the key question in mind: *How can I design myself as a leader?* Purposeful attention to *you* will be the most useful guide through the process of applying what you learn to your growing leadership capacity.

2

DESIGNING YOUR PERCEPTIONS OF LEADERS AND LEADERSHIP

LEARNING OBJECTIVES

Upon completion of this chapter, the reader should be able to

2.1 State your expectations for learning about leadership

2.2 Explain how conceptions and perceptions guide leaders

2.3 Identify common misconceptions about leaders and leadership

2.4 Critique the characteristics of leaders based on research and your perceptions

2.5 Contrast leadership skills with management, expertise, and established competencies

2.6 Appraise your leadership credibility

2.7 Interpret identity as an often-hidden variable in how you perceive leaders and leadership

Leadership by Design Model

Design Self
HOW CAN I DESIGN MYSELF AS A LEADER?

Design Relationships
As leader, how can I design my relationship with others?

Design Others' Success
As a leader, how can I design success for others?

Design Culture
As a leader, how can I design the culture of my organization?

Design Future
As a leader, how can I innovate?

INTRODUCTION

This chapter, *Designing Your Perceptions of Leaders and Leadership*, introduces the notion of leader and leadership by exploring *your* ideas and experiences with leadership, and it examines what others have thought and found about the leader in leadership. As a leader, you have a choice: You can act as a leader in whatever way *feels* right and then try to explain why you did what you did later, or you can understand your options for action *before* you act, using your leadership knowledge to *design* your leadership activity.

49

Leadership That Makes a Difference

When you think of great leaders, those who make a *big* difference, the names that arise are usually famous politicians, military or business leaders, or maybe social entrepreneurs. This chapter is all about perceptions and misconceptions, and what counts as a *big* difference may not be very accurate. Yes, there are indeed many individual leaders who have famously influenced broadly. The missed conception, in this case, lies in the considerable (a.k.a. big) difference made by tens of thousands of leaders at the local level. Indeed, when asked to describe who has most influenced their idea of leadership, nearly all students described parents, colleagues, teammates, coaches, or immediate supervisors. Why? Because leadership is the process of influencing others toward a common vision—not just *any* others—but others with whom you have built a relationship. Those individuals are the most influential in your life. So, cumulatively, the big difference in leadership is made by a sea of individualized relationships that impact who you are and how you see the world. The following student example could likely be anyone's story:

> The best leader I have ever had is my grandfather. He taught me virtues through his stories and showed me the compassion and empathy needed to be a good leader. My grandfather truly had a love for all of those around him and wanted to see and help others to succeed. My grandfather saw potential that I could not see myself, and he taught me that anything less than my best is simply cheating myself. As a man who worked his way out of poverty, served in World War II, and became a successful entrepreneur, he had more to teach me about resilience and work ethic than anyone else I have met. He taught me never to quit and to set my goals high. He has helped me to understand how to have a vision and follow it, and I would not be the person or leader that I am today without him. —Matthew Divis, Undergraduate

Take a moment to consider who you would identify as a leader who has made a big difference. What matters most about that difference—how broadly it influences others or how deeply it influences a few? Both matter, just in different ways.

Some of your first lessons on leadership will come from members of your own family.
©iStockphoto.com/SDI Productions

Chapter 2 • Designing Your Perceptions of Leaders and Leadership   51

YOU: STUDENT AND DESIGNER OF YOUR OWN LEADERSHIP

LEARNING OBJECTIVE
2.1   State your expectations for learning about leadership.

Leadership is a dynamic, personal, situation-specific, context-dependent, multidisciplinary process. With so many variables, learning leadership requires a more carefully considered, reflective, individualized approach. As the designer of yourself, you will be the designer of your own learning. Before you continue your leadership journey, there are a few things you should know about your own learning.

Learning Leadership

What did you learn today? Most people would answer that question by recalling some new bit of information or new skill they acquired, but what they are really describing is new information they were exposed to. *Exposure* to a new idea is only the starting point of learning, and that exposure quickly fades unless revisited and reinforced. The acquisition of new knowledge happens as you engage with information over and over again. Remember the leadership definition introduced a few pages back? You read: *leadership is the process of influencing others toward a common vision.* And then you read it again and again. Every single time you interact with information, you reinforce your recall (and often enhance your understanding) of that information. Designing your leadership learning means *thinking* about and *planning* all the various ways in which you can engage with the topic, each time reinforcing and refining your understanding.

Right now, you have some knowledge about leadership and leaders. You also may have some experience serving in a leadership position. How did you learn to do that? Most likely, you learned by watching others who were in leadership positions or some position of power and authority. Think back on all those in leadership positions with whom you may have interacted—parents or guardians, grandparents, teachers, coaches, priests or pastors, club/organization leaders, managers or bosses, or perhaps a babysitter. Whether they had formal training or not, they did their best to fulfill the position, and in the meantime, they unknowingly served as a role model for you. That is how most individuals initially learn leadership—by interacting with and observing others.

REFLECTION QUESTIONS

Who were your leadership models? Does your approach to leadership look like any of theirs?

The second way many learn leadership is through experience—by serving as a formal or an informal leader. Generally, without any notion of what leadership is or entails, individuals are tasked with a position that requires influencing others toward a goal such that the organization succeeds. If you have had a leadership position, you undoubtedly learned a lot. If you had some significant challenges that you had to work through while in that position, then you learned even more. Bennis and Thomas (2002) called this a **crucible of leadership**.[1] A crucible is a vessel used to subject substances to extreme heat in order to fundamentally change them. You might have heard the term used to describe medieval alchemists trying to transform metal into gold. For a leader, the analogy describes a difficult challenge that has the potential to transform their values, assumptions, and future capabilities. As Bennis and Thomas (2002) explained, "The crucible experience was a trial and a test, a point of deep self-reflection that forced them to question who they were and what mattered to them."[2] As you focus on designing yourself as a leader, we will find out from Bennis and Thomas what leadership skills help you learn the most from a crucible experience.

REFLECTION QUESTIONS

Learning through experience is of great value but only if you reflect on the experience and are aware of the impacts and outcomes. What leadership experiences have you had? What were some of the greatest challenges? How did those experiences change your leadership and self-perception?

Of course, there are also many leadership courses, programs, and workshops—all purporting to impart the knowledge and skills that will make you the successful leader of tomorrow. Learning leadership is partly about knowledge and skills, but it is more so about developing dispositions—defined as habits of mind that are often seen as tendencies or characteristics, even a personality. As introduced in the previous chapter, both design thinking and CORE™ are great examples of dispositions. Optimism and pessimism are very clear examples of dispositions you see every day. Some of your peers habitually see situations as positive and possible, while others see the pitfalls and worst-case scenarios. For leaders, another useful disposition might be the tendency to empathize (i.e., to habitually consider the perspective of your followers). You will learn even more about dispositions in Chapter 3 on building your leadership capacities.

Learning comes with every encounter you have with information. Consider the full range of where your learning can come from and how you can access those sources. Sometimes, that information comes in the form of a professor or a textbook, and more often, information comes in the form of engaging with others—discussing ideas, internships, student organizations, asking questions, interviewing leaders, and working through problems together. Information also comes from observing role models and the experiences of others. But that is just the start. Insight and consequent learning come from your *reflection* and taking the time to integrate that information into your current understanding. For example, researchers have found that reading about leaders in action *and then* critically reflecting on the events, causes, and perspectives in the story helped participants formulate stronger leadership visions.[3] To that end, a word of encouragement and caution from economist John Kenneth Galbraith: "Faced with the choice between changing one's mind and proving that there is no need to do so, almost everyone gets busy on the proof."[4] As you learn more about leadership you will be asked to change—change your behavior, change your mindset, change your understanding. Change is at the heart of learning. In Chapter 10, you will learn more about change as you design others' success (facilitating the learning of your followers).

What to Expect as You Learn Leadership

As you learn leadership and discuss your learning with your peers, you will find that everyone has their own unique significant learning moments—events or situations when a big insight changes the way you see the world. While the moment is unique, there are some common themes and lessons that developing leaders tend to experience. Here are some insights you might encounter

Chapter 2 • Designing Your Perceptions of Leaders and Leadership   53

while learning leadership. Of course, they will not seem as consequential to you now just reading them, but seeing them will prime your brain to spot these lessons in action later. Here are six very important lessons (Figure 2.1), shared by leadership students in their own words, which you can expect to learn again and again:

1. **Leaders develop real relationships with each individual.**

   There was a specific point in my life when I took a step back and saw the person in everyone. I was home during vacation when my mom walked into the room. She started talking about why she was stressed and how it was affecting her, and for the first time, I looked at her and didn't see my mom. I saw who she was, and I responded how I would if a friend had come to me in a bad place . . . I don't know why it took so long for me to notice everyone individually and the importance of taking into account the personal thoughts, experiences, and feelings of every person . . . —Daniel Clark, Undergraduate

2. **There are many ways to solve a problem.**

   There are so many different ways of tackling an issue . . . think of ways that are different and something that you'd never expect to do. —Tyler Saltiel, Undergraduate

3. **Leadership and the concepts and aspects of the process are deeper and broader than you think.** You will find that some things you do well, that you seem to do naturally, are actually explained by leadership theory and best practices. Learning more about leadership concepts will help you use those strengths more effectively.

   For a long time, I have led best by seeking to help those struggling around me and have found it to be incredibly rewarding. It was not until we learned about empathy's role in leadership, however, that I realized it was what I had been doing and found so rewarding. . . . Only after learning about it, did I realize that I could reflect on, and improve, my empathy for others. —Matthew Divis, Undergraduate

4. **The leader and the followers are both important.**

   The greatest "aha" moment for me in learning about leadership was learning that the leader is no more important than his or her followers. When learning this, it really made me stop and think. People have been subconsciously trained to believe that the most important person in a situation is the leader. A leader wouldn't get anything done without loyal followers. If Abraham Lincoln didn't have any followers, he would not have won the presidency or gone on to be one of the greatest leaders of all time. Yes, Abraham Lincoln is the big name, but he is no more important than his followers. They are the ones that made his successes possible. —Marina Wells, Undergraduate

5. **Anyone can be a leader.**

   My greatest "aha" moment in learning about leadership came from a seven-year-old at a day camp. This boy was one of my campers, and he wanted to win Color Wars (the day camp version of the Olympics) extremely badly because he didn't win the past two summers. Formally, his role was very small because there were more than 100 campers on our team ranging from three to twelve years old; however, he was a leader and motivator. Throughout the week, he was involved and got others who were sitting out of activities to participate. He would strategize activities, including who would go in the front during tug of war and who would be better in the back. He screamed his head off (spirit points were considered the highest point bracket) the whole week, and I was not surprised when he had no voice during the last week of camp. In Color Wars, he was a true leader. I realized that anyone can be a leader and at any age. He was passionate about the activities, and I could see how his passion rubbed off on my other campers. He led for a reason, and I realized that anyone (even a seven-year-old) could influence others toward a common vision. —Daniel Auerbach, Undergraduate

6. Even quiet people can lead. Leadership starts from within.

For me, the greatest "aha" moment was when I realized that you don't need to be loud or extroverted to be a leader. I am not a loud person whatsoever and used to be extremely small. This discouraged me, but when we talked about creativity and resilience, it made me realize that the power comes from within, not the physical presence. Leaders come in all shapes and sizes; it's the influence you hold from the traits and skills you obtain. —Maxwell Gold, Undergraduate

The examples are just a few of the more common themes that you can expect to encounter as you design your leadership. Earlier, you were introduced to the notion of mindfulness—the concept of being as fully aware of your present learning and moment as possible. Did you notice a common theme across the six lessons you just read? They all required the developing leader pay attention to what was happening. These students needed to pay attention to their context, the situation, the interactions between individuals, and the personal characteristics of everyone. The most important thing they needed to be mindful of, however, was their own understanding of leaders and leadership. If you don't know what you know, how will you learn what you do not know? You should probably read that sentence again—it is a bit confusing, but it is very important.

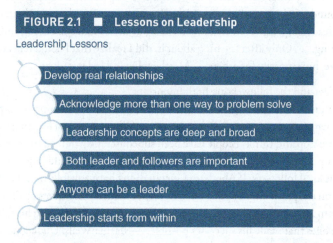

FIGURE 2.1 ■ Lessons on Leadership

Leadership Lessons
- Develop real relationships
- Acknowledge more than one way to problem solve
- Leadership concepts are deep and broad
- Both leader and followers are important
- Anyone can be a leader
- Leadership starts from within

YOUR BRAIN IS A LEAN, MEAN, PATTERN-MAKING MACHINE: YOU CONSTRUCT YOUR WORLD

LEARNING OBJECTIVE

2.2 Explain how conceptions and perceptions guide leaders.

Have you ever kept doing the same wrong thing over and over? How did you know when to make an adjustment in your thinking and behavior? In the introduction chapter, you learned about the concept of mindfulness—being aware of the full, present moment, and you learned about the importance of taking moments of awareness and being mindfully engaged. However, there is more to mindfulness if you are going to design your leadership, it will require disrupting your way of thinking. Behaviors are repeated, even when there is an awareness of them, because "it's a habit." Peter Bregman, author of *Four Seconds*, notes, "It doesn't take long to change a habit, but it's hard. Really hard."[5] Bregman writes, "we have no hope of changing anything that we're not aware we're doing. A moment of awareness allows us to pause (that's the four-second part of *Four Seconds*)." You will see this valuable technique employed again in Chapter 6 as it relates to decision-making and emotional intelligence.[6]

Your brain is a lean, mean, pattern-making machine.[7] Do you remember where you read that funny phrase earlier in the text? Repeat it a few more times: My brain is a lean, mean, pattern-making machine. Can you feel the pattern forming? Every interaction you have with the world influences the connections your brain has made about the world, culminating in your mental model. A **mental model** is your mental representation of things in the world—not just the picture in your head but how you understand things and even how you process information. Your mental model guides your behavior and your thinking. For example, everyone *knows* what a classroom looks like, right? But what if you attended a nature-based school where every class was held in the forest? Or what if you were part of a culture that educated their young through apprenticeships without formal schools? Or perhaps your grandchildren will meet their classmates in a virtual space. These conceptions of classroom are formed by experiencing something over and over.[8]

Have you ever heard traditional Hawaiian folk music? Surely a rush of images just filled your head as your mental models about Hawaii were triggered. If you have never been to Hawaii, then your mental model is likely filled with clichés from media—palm trees, hula dancers with grass skirts, coconuts to hold your drink, beaches. This is the case for everyone who has limited experience and/or exposure to a phenomenon. But if you have lived in Hawaii, those mental models are far more detailed and accurate. More interesting, mental models built from first-hand experience go beyond information and visuals and include multiple senses and emotions. For example, when you think about *home*—whatever that might mean to you—your mind fills with far more than just an image. That is the power and strength of mental models—a strength you must both recognize and utilize. The legendary Hawaiian folk singer Israel "Iz" Kaʻanoʻi Kamakawiwoʻole created a record entitled *Facing Future*. For the aspiring leader, facing the future means addressing the mental models built from the past—mental models in the deeper sense—models of feeling and reacting, habits of perceiving and processing others and the world, and the personal challenges interwoven with your sense of self.

Mental models are very useful—they help you remember details, categorize new information, and generally navigate the world effectively and efficiently. But that construction comes with two great cautionary warnings: (a) the illusion of validity (My ideas about the world are true.) and (b) the illusion of verification (What *I see* in the world is true.). Mental models are constructed from your experience, and that experience may or may not be accurate, complete, or even true. In many ways, they are like an illusion, *your* illusion of the world. The only way to know if your conception of the world is accurate is to first be aware of your conception and then to question, test, and revise that model. The second caution is that mental models influence *what you see* in the world. If you conceive that all leaders are out to get you, then you will perceive leaders through that lens, interpreting a leader's behaviors as somehow negative and nefarious and emphasizing negative outcomes, while overlooking anything to the contrary. What you see includes *who you see* (and how you see them). That is how your brain works—how you think about the world primes and influences what you see in the world, which reinforces how you think about the world.[9] The model in Figure 2.2 illustrates this reinforcing relationship and how it ultimately influences your conception.

For aspiring leaders, the key question is how to continue growing in your conception of the world versus narrowing to a rigid, single-view perception of the world. The answer: Leaders must understand that their brain constructs and interprets the world, and then knowing, this they must explore and verify their conceptions (and misconceptions). The next section explores the common misconceptions about leaders and leadership. As you work your way through the next section, keep your lean, mean, pattern-making machine of a brain in mind and be open to exploring new ways of thinking about leadership.

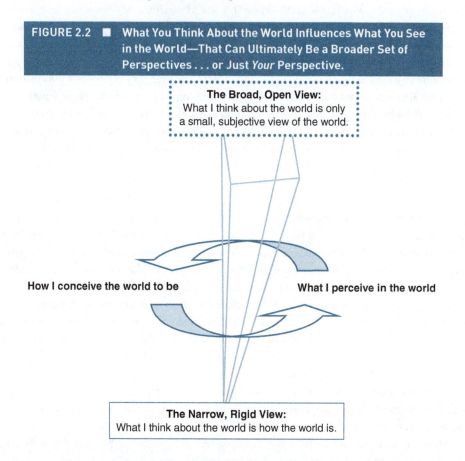

FIGURE 2.2 ■ What You Think About the World Influences What You See in the World—That Can Ultimately Be a Broader Set of Perspectives . . . or Just *Your* Perspective.

MISCONCEPTIONS ABOUT LEADERS AND LEADERSHIP

LEARNING OBJECTIVE

2.3 Identify common misconceptions about leaders and leadership.

You already have a mental model of leadership, one that you have built from all your interactions with the world—leaders you have observed, worked with and for, heard about, seen on television and the Internet, and even your experience and feedback from being the leader. Perhaps the accompanying image represents your idea of leadership—the conquering hero, the individual at the top, perhaps inducing fear or asserting dominance, receiving accolades for victories that many others worked hard to achieve. Who looks like a leader within your mental model? How do they act? How should they be treated? Start with your mental model and then look outside that model to see who and what you are missing.

Once again, recall the definition of leadership from the introduction chapter—the process of influencing others toward a common vision. It should sound more and more familiar because you continue to repeat it, forming and reinforcing that connection. Using the definition of leadership, this section introduces important distinctions in leadership by exploring common misconceptions. As you make your way through this textbook, you will find that many of the most common leadership theories and approaches explain away these misconceptions. However, for now, the focus is on expanding the definition. As you learn more about leadership, the terms within the definition will take on greater meaning for you—that is you building a mental model about leadership.

Heroic leadership and the many faces of followers

Pablo Nicolás Taibi Cicare via Flickr.com/CC BY 2.0 https://creativecommons.org/licenses/by/2.0/legalcode

REFLECTION QUESTIONS

What terms from the leadership definition can you identify in the image of the heroic leader statue? What could the leader do to more effectively influence each of the other individuals in this photo?

Leadership Is . . . a Process

The *leader* is a person. The person has characteristics you can identify, which may or may not be effective in each situation and may change but only with time. *Leadership*, on the other hand, is a process. A process consists of a series of steps or activities over time. When you consider leadership as a process, many possibilities emerge. First, the positional leader becomes the facilitator of the process versus the person in charge. Thus, the task of moving the individuals and organization toward the goal is more accurately seen as a dynamic, situational, and context-dependent adventure. Second, leadership as a process means that mistakes can be made, and that is okay. Too often, leaders believe any mistake is a setback. In fact, making minor mistakes helps the organization learn and better orient toward the goal relative to the ever-changing context. Third, the person in the leadership position does not always need to be (nor should be) the person taking the lead. Quite often, there are others within the organization that are better suited, better skilled, or simply available to take the lead for a time or for a specific project.

Although leadership is a process, there are still individuals who hold the responsibility to facilitate that process. For those individual leaders, there are two simple rules:

Rule #1: It's about you.

Rule #2: It's not about you.

The first rule is clear to most aspiring leaders. *It's about you* means you have the responsibility and accountability for the success of the organization and its followers. But it also refers to your designing your leadership self. Leaders must know about themselves, and the more they know, the more effectively they can respond to situations, facilitate the process, and further design their leadership.

The second rule is a little less obvious, particularly given the assumptions many have about leadership. *It's not about you* means exactly that; the activities of leadership should be focused on the success of the organization and the followers, they should not be focused on calming *your* fears, addressing *your* needs, or pumping up *your* ego. Making leadership not about you when you are in the leader position is more difficult than you might think, but the benefits are extraordinary. "What the research shows consistently is that leaders who are secure enough in their strengths to admit their weaknesses and vulnerabilities actually get better ideas from the people around them, they learn more, and that ultimately enables them to lead more effectively. I think the balance of confidence and humility is to say: These are not opposite ends of a see-saw. These are actually states that can go hand-in-hand. Confidence is believing that you can do great things. Humility is knowing that you don't always have the knowledge and skills to do them yourself."[10] You might call this the paradox of confidence: Effective leaders must simultaneously be confident and humble. Yet that pairing is not as contradictory as it may first appear. A most compelling illustration of the idea that true confidence results in humility is captured by the many stories of leadership guru Jim Collins.[11]

The pinnacle of leadership development found in Collins' research, which he calls **Level 5 leadership**, consists of high-level resolve coupled with compelling personal humility. In other words, leaders who are so confident in their abilities and sense of self are more interested in putting all their focus on the success of the organization and its people. You can be a highly capable individual (Level 1 in Collins' model) all the way up to an effective leader (Level 4), but to move from *good to great* (the title of his book), you need to get your own ego out of the way. Humility—making it not about you—is the true measure of confidence and can build confidence.

If you are still doubtful about this connection, try the following: The next time you have to give a presentation, write yourself a large prompting sign and place it where you can see it often while you speak. The prompt should say, "Do they get it?" You will find that when you shift your focus from how *you* feel about your presentation (Did *I* say that right? Do *I* sound ok?) to how well the audience understands your message (Do *they* get it? What more do *they* need to know?), you not only feel more confident, you perform the task far better, which was to help the audience learn in the first place. Confidence with humility; it's about you; it's not about you.

These rules will be revisited throughout the text, just as you should revisit them throughout your leadership journey as they underpin numerous misconceptions about the individual leader. Throughout this section, you can read the voices of students as they debunk these mistaken assumptions.

Chapter 2 ● Designing Your Perceptions of Leaders and Leadership   **59**

Misconception: Leaders Are Born

Well, technically everyone is born. And yes, there are obvious differences between persons. But the reality is that most of those differences were developed over time and can be altered if so desired.[12]

> One of my biggest misconceptions about leadership is that people are born to be leaders. Ever since I was a little girl, I have always heard people say "so and so is a born leader," and to me that meant that I could only be a leader if I was born to do so. However, after growing up and taking a few leadership courses (I realized) that you do not have to be a born leader or that is even a real thing. Sure there are qualities that a leader possesses, but more often than not, these traits are acquired. I have learned that people can be successful leaders if they are good people and have the ability to understand what people want and need. —Aubrey Seeley, Undergraduate

Misconception: Leaders Need to Have a Specific Set of Traits, Particularly Extroversion

Some traits are pretty much always helpful to leaders, while other traits are helpful in some circumstances. But there is no specific set of traits. What is a trait anyway? You will learn more about traits later in the chapter, but for now, **traits** can be defined as well-habituated, stable, and consistent personal characteristics.

> I always thought leaders needed to be extroverts. However, learning about the trait theory, one of its weaknesses is that there is not a specific set of traits that qualifies someone to be a good leader. You need different types of leaders for the different types of situations. —Melissa Cabrero, Undergraduate

Leadership Is . . . a Process of Influencing

Leaders influence others in a variety of ways. The most important thing to understand is *how you* most effectively influence others and *with whom* you are most influential, under what conditions, or in what situations. Sometimes influence is grandly inspirational, and other times it is simple and subtle to the point of being nearly invisible. There are a great many techniques and tools that leaders can learn to influence others—build your influence toolbox. Consider a few more misconceptions.

Misconception: Leaders Do the Talking and Take Charge

Sometimes leaders influence by taking charge, and acting in a directive manner is necessary, but sometimes listening and observing are more effective. And, yes, even introverts can be effective leaders.[13, 14] Your strengths and style, explored in Chapter 3, are adaptable enough to address a variety of needs.

> I always thought that the leader leads the discussion and comments on everything. A leader should be aware of everything around them and put the pieces together without saying a word. A leader who listens gains credibility and trust because they give a fair chance for everyone to share their thoughts and feel they are in a safe environment. —Brandon Bellina, Undergraduate

> A big misconception that I held about leadership was that to be an effective leader you only had to be able to "take charge" of a group. I viewed it as a very individualistic

concept, but I now know that leadership goes far beyond having authority within a group or team setting. It requires a willingness to motivate/inspire followers to the point where you're not just making the plan, delegating tasks, and telling them what they have to do but instead working collaboratively to come to the best solution. —Jamie Fisher, Undergraduate

Misconception: Leaders Do the Influencing

Every human interaction results in reciprocal influence, and leaders are no exception. As a leader, you are constantly influenced by many things, particularly your followers. For example, consider a time you presented to a group. As you noticed the reaction of the audience to your talk, did you find yourself making slight changes in your delivery or explanation? You are in a constant process of interacting with your world, constructing and reconstructing your understanding, and reacting accordingly. Acknowledging the influences around you is both honest and accurate. So while you are building your influence toolbox, note also what influences you and how.

> Growing up you are constantly surrounded by leadership figures such as your teachers, but you never hear about who helped them get there. For me, that realization came with maturing and realizing that everyone, even the leaders throughout your life, are just people. —Daniel Clark, Undergraduate

Leadership Is . . . a Process of Influencing Others

At the heart of all leadership lies the relationship between leader and follower. If there are no *others*, then you are not leading but simply acting alone. Considering the individual followers is critical to how effectively you are able to influence and move them and the organization toward the common vision.

Misconception: There Is Only One Specific Way to Be an Effective Leader

Your leadership approach may be consistent at this stage in your leadership design, but expert leaders can shift their style to complement and meet the needs of different followers.

> A misconception about leadership is that there is one way to be a good leader. What I learned is that there are so many ways to be an effective leader. It all depends on who you are leading and what they react to positively. —Trevor Cox, Undergraduate

Misconception: A Leader Cannot Be Friends With Their Followers

This misconception might really surprise you. After all, how can you tell a friend what to do? How can you be their boss? (Are you seeing all the misconceptions in those questions already?) There has been a lot of research on the leader–follower relationship, called leader–member exchange (LMX), which will be explained more fully in the Intro to Module 2, when you focus on designing your leadership relationships. The truth is that close relationships, even friendships, generally enhance the organization.[15] Consider this . . . would you work harder and be more committed to the success of a friend or a stranger? Researcher Adam Grant explains, "When friends work together, they're more trusting and committed to one another's success. That means they share more information and spend more time helping—and as long as they don't hold back on constructive criticism out of politeness, they make better choices and get more done."[16] While it might seem difficult to supervise a friend, especially if you must assess them or be critical, the benefits of building strong relationships far outweigh that possible momentary discomfort.

Chapter 2 ● Designing Your Perceptions of Leaders and Leadership   61

Leadership Is . . . a Process of Influencing Others Toward

Leaders move their organization toward success. They do not influence others to keep the status quo, do nothing special, stay the course, or just live with it. Leadership dynamically advances the organization.

Misconception: Effective Leaders Are Always Collaborative

After reading all the previous misconceptions, you are likely noticing a pattern: As a facilitator of the leadership process, leaders need to effectively navigate the ever-changing sea filled with unique waves, weather, sea creatures, and crew. In other words, the dynamic nature of leadership requires that leaders be equally flexible to meet needs as they arise, whether predictable or not. Sometimes, the best approach is collaborative, and sometimes, it is directive, and sometimes, it will be entirely different. This student sums it up well:

> One of my greatest misconceptions about leadership was that leaders had to pick only one leadership style/concept to stick with to live and lead by. For example, while I was leading in my roles and facilitating meetings, I am naturally transformational, support-ive, and understanding; however, there were some moments where it was necessary to be more firm and structured, and it was essential to assign due dates and specific assign-ments or roles. —Brooke Hofmann, Undergraduate

Whatever set of behaviors, skills, and actions moves your organization toward the vision is ultimately the right set of leadership tools for the job (provided they are ethical, of course). As you design your leadership, you will find a number of tools that can do more than one job, such as con-fidence, optimism, resilience, and engagement—the CORE™ attributes. Remember to utilize the CORE™ Attribute Builder activities at the end of each chapter to build your most versatile tools.

Leadership Is . . . a Process of Influencing Others Toward a Common

Rule #2 states that leadership is not about you. The vision of your organization will be most suc-cessful if you craft a *common* vision. Not common in the sense of indistinguishable, but common in that everyone has a stake in and supports the vision.

Misconception: Confident Leaders Who Celebrate Their Success Are Arrogant and Selfish

Maybe, but probably not. Quite often, you see leaders taking credit for the success of their orga-nizations, but what you do not see are the relationships and interactions between the leader and followers—celebrating individual and organizational success, passing along acknowledgments and words of thanks, and continuing to inspire others around the common vision.

> I always thought leaders were cocky/over-confident. I have learned that as a leader you can acknowledge your success to a point without being greedy. It's important to be able to pat yourself on the back because you need to congratulate yourself at times—you earned it. I learned the difference between confidence and arrogance. It's vital to have confidence so that you believe in your abilities. I found this quote, "Confidence isn't walking into a room with your nose in the air and thinking you're better than everyone else. It's walking into a room and not having to compare yourself to anyone in the first place." —Erin Grady, Undergraduate

Yes, some may mistakenly see arrogance in your confidence, but that is not a reason to dis-count accomplishment or discontinue celebration for yourself and your followers.

Misconception: Explaining the Vision More Clearly Is the Best Way to Acquire Follower Support

The power of a common vision lies in the connections between leader and follower. While the elements of the leadership definition can be independently explained, those elements work together. For example, in this case, how you—as a leader—influence others will determine the extent to which followers feel part of the vision. Influencing others through intimidation, reasoned argument, or appeal to your position of authority is far less effective than connecting with followers' emotions, values, and their stake in the vision.

> A misconception I had about leadership is that the leaders are the boss and the system is a hierarchy. However, I learned that there are leaders who influence followers to accomplish more by being concerned with followers' emotions and values. The leader serves to help their followers grow. —Becca Estes, Undergraduate

A common vision entails more than general agreement on the vision; rather, it requires a sense of shared contribution and emotional connection. Leaders skilled in emotional intelligence, discussed back in Chapter 1, excel at designing relationships.

Leadership Is . . . a Process of Influencing Others Toward a Common Vision

Extensive research on the nature and power of goals positions this element of the leadership definition as perhaps the most powerful.[17] If you do not know where you are going, what are you facilitating? How can you influence others toward nothing? More than simply a goal, a **vision** is a picture of the future you seek to create.[18] The organizational vision serves many purposes and has great power. A vision can be inspirational, aspirational, a means by which individuals in the organization connect, a way of assessing progress, and a guiding light for leaders and followers to navigate the day-to-day challenges without getting sidetracked. A common vision provides meaning and purpose to the work of the organization, and ultimately, it reflects the values of those sharing the vision. Highly effective leaders utilize the power of the common vision.

Misconception: Leadership Education Is Not Really Applicable to the Real World

The benefits of learning leadership and designing your leadership are often difficult to measure and may in some cases be more long term than immediate. This often results in the final misconception of this section, namely, the usefulness of learning leadership in the face of so many ineffective leaders. The real misconception, in this case, is that individuals in leadership positions believe they are effective leaders simply by holding the position or title. Typically, individuals are promoted to leadership positions because they excel in the technical aspects of their job (e.g., you are an excellent accountant, so you are now promoted to manager). This is the equivalent of saying, "Hey, you're really good at fixing cars, so you are now promoted to quarterback for the football team." Huh? Exactly. Leadership is an entirely different field of expertise, requiring specific knowledge, skills, and abilities. And that is primarily why so many leaders are ineffective if not downright detrimental to the organization.

> I think one of the greatest misconceptions about leadership is that people always wonder why it is a college major and how learning about leadership can help you later in life. I agree; when I first enrolled in a leadership class I wasn't really sure what to make of it, it made me think differently and how there was often no single right answer. Now to me

Chapter 2 • Designing Your Perceptions of Leaders and Leadership 63

this kind of sounded like a joke, but I was entirely wrong. Over the last two years, I have learned so much about leadership and that in the future when you have an "adult job" (is how I put it) being a leader and knowing how to influence others to reach a common goal is very beneficial. You are considered a trusted individual, and you understand the way people think and what they need to succeed. My respect for leadership as a study has changed dramatically, and I believe those lucky enough to learn about it will be better off in their futures. —Jessica Szymanski, Undergraduate

Table 2.1 provides a summary of the misconceptions discussed in this section but stated as a more accurate conception for your use in (re)designing your leadership self.

TABLE 2.1 ■ Summary of Misconceptions	
Misconception	Instead . . . Consider That
Leaders are those who have the position or title of leader.	You are a leader when you influence others toward a common vision, which does not necessarily require a title or position.
Leaders are born.	You can learn the skills and habits of effective leadership.
Leaders need to have a specific set of traits, particularly extroversion.	Leadership is dynamic and situational—your characteristics may be effective in some cases and not in others.
Leaders do the talking and take charge.	Leaders need to sometimes talk and sometimes listen, sometimes take charge and sometimes observe or encourage others to take charge.
Leaders do the influencing.	Leaders are also influenced.
There is only one specific way to be an effective leader.	There are many different ways to influence others toward a common vision.
A leader cannot be friends with their followers.	A leader depends on close, authentic relationships, and that often defines friendship.
Effective leaders are always collaborative.	Effective leaders are sometimes collaborative, sometimes directive, and sometimes other behaviors are necessary.
Confident leaders who celebrate their success are arrogant and selfish.	Confidence is not arrogance, and celebrating success is key to effective leadership.
Explaining the vision more clearly is the best way to acquire follower support.	Followers, like all people, are driven more by their values and their emotions than a rational argument.
Leadership education is not really applicable to the real world.	Leadership is a distinct field of study, and applying it in the real world makes a big difference.

This chapter began with explaining how you construct ideas with your lean, mean, pattern-making machine brain and then examined many of the most common misconceptions about leaders and leadership. At this point in the chapter, you should feel a little skeptical about what you thought you knew about leadership, and you should be ready to dig deeper into what makes an effective leader. Before you continue, revisit the definition of leadership as seen on the card in Figure 2.3 Make a copy of this card, cut it out, and put it in your phone case or workbag so you have a ready reference and reminder to access when you are facing a leadership challenge.

FIGURE 2.3 ■ Leadership Definition Reference Card

Leadership is . . .

Process . . . beyond person, over time, dynamic`

Influencing . . . explicit and implicit, ethical

Others . . . building and developing relationships

Toward . . . advancing and improving

Common . . . socially just, all voices heard

Vision . . . creative, clear, shared, sustainable

Rule #1: It's about you.

Rule #2: It's not about you.

Leadership by Design

Design Principle: **Comparison**

Definition: A method of illustrating relationships and patterns in system behaviors by representing two or more system variables *in a controlled way*.[19]

In Other Words: To accurately understand and assess something, you must look at it next to things that relate.

For Example: If you want to assess the quality of an apple, what you use for comparison must be related to what you want to assess. An apple is great as a healthy food compared to a donut. An apple is not so great as a weapon compared to a spear.

For Leaders: To what do you compare aspects of your leadership? How can you use an appropriate comparison that makes it easier for others to understand? Think about ways to highlight different parts of your leadership compared to others. Leaders can use comparisons to illustrate relationships between values, between different people, or between themselves and others by presenting information in a controlled way. What do you want at this moment or for the organization . . . compared to what?

©iStock.com/xavierarnau

Who in the photo is the happiest? Are these individuals friends? Without being able to compare this moment to other times, you can only guess. What else would you want to know before you made any deductions?

EFFECTIVE LEADERS ARE LIKE _____: CHARACTERISTICS AND TRAITS

LEARNING OBJECTIVE
2.4 Critique the characteristics of leaders based on research and your perceptions.

When you read the title of the section, what word did you want to put into the blank space? Early leadership researchers asked that same question, seeking those individuals in leadership positions whose organizations were successful or who appeared to emerge as leaders in groups. Effective leaders are tall, imaginative, and agreeable. Maybe some individuals fitting that description are indeed effective . . . in some contexts . . . in some situations. But so too are others with different characteristics.[20]

The trait approach to leadership asserts that a specific set of personal attributes (initially including physical characteristics) enable and explain effective leadership. Recall, traits can be defined as well-habituated, stable, and consistent personal characteristics. At first glance, this appears to make sense—everyone can describe leaders with whom they've worked, and there seem to be similarities between effective and ineffective leaders. Not only did researchers agree and pursue many studies trying to identify those specific traits, but other researchers studied those studies (this is called a meta-analysis, and it provides a big summary of many prior related studies). A scholar named Ralph Stogdill did a meta-analysis on leadership traits—twice.[21] His latest, in 1974, looked at 163 different trait studies. Table 2.2 displays the common traits he found, but after all that research, even Stogdill said there is no evidence for a single set of effective leader traits.

TABLE 2.2 ■ Common Traits and Skills From Stogdill's Meta-Analysis—Which Ones Do You Have?	
Traits	**Skills**
• Adaptable to situations	• Clever (intelligent)
• Alert to social environment	• Conceptually skilled
• Ambitious and achievement orientated	• Creative
• Assertive	• Diplomatic and tactful
• Cooperative	• Fluent in speaking
• Decisive	• Knowledgeable about group task
• Dependable	• Organized (administrative ability)
• Dominant (desire to influence others)	• Persuasive
• Energetic (high activity level)	• Socially skilled
• Persistent	
• Self-confident	
• Tolerant of stress	
• Willing to assume responsibility	

REFLECTION QUESTIONS

The list of traits and skills noted by Stogdill in Table 2.2 are from the period 1949–1974. A lot has changed in the world since then—in how people communicate, structure of organizations, and view of leaders and leadership. What traits and skills from the list seem relevant today? Which ones feel outdated? What might you add?

Presently, five major traits have been highlighted as those most closely tied to effective leadership: intelligence, determination, sociability, self-confidence, and integrity.[22] You probably have a few questions right at this moment:

- *If I possess all five, will I be an effective leader?*

- *If I lack all five, does that mean I will never be an effective leader?*

- *I have lots of other great things about me—a good sense of humor, outgoing, creative, focused—do these not count for anything in leadership?*

Maybe; no; and yes, are the answers to the three questions. Trait approaches provide valuable information about the range of attributes you can draw from, develop, and highlight as situations or context requires. The five traits noted also provide insight on what you should consistently work to develop in yourself and in your followers (because followers today will be the leaders tomorrow—it's your job to help them get there).

Leadership is a process, and traits, like all useful tools, must be used for the right project in the right setting. What traits do you possess? You likely could describe yourself pretty well, but you are far more complex than you realize. That complexity takes time and tools to understand. The Skill Builder Activity at the end of this chapter prompts you to discover more about your traits and attributes.

The traits you possess are like a set of tools. They are only as handy as your ability to use them. Sometimes, you have tools buried in the toolbox that you discover later. Sometimes, other people give you new tools by modeling their use or direct instruction. And sometimes, you focus on a single tool just because you're good at using it. As the common saying goes, everything looks like a nail to the person holding a hammer. Here are some suggestions as you design your leadership:

1. Identify your traits and learn about them

2. Find out what others see as your traits

3. Consider what contexts and situations best fit your traits

4. Note traits you aspire to acquire and then create opportunities to do so

5. Know that traits are quite stable, so it takes time and effort to change them

One trait often associated with leaders is charisma. **Charisma** can be defined as the personal quality that commands attention, respect, and attraction. Charismatic leaders are described as inspiring, charming, and confident—powerfully alluring to their followers. Charisma would seem to be the ultimate trait to possess, yet an elusive treasure for most. And indeed, it is a

Chapter 2 • Designing Your Perceptions of Leaders and Leadership **67**

powerful tool.[23] However, the charisma tool can be misused if, for example, the leader inspires followers in the wrong direction or toward unethical ends.[24] The leader must also possess the competence to back up their charismatic approach—even though the lure of appearance is so strong.[25] The following story illustrates this phenomenon:

> Who is the leader? That was the question we asked the group. We had been together as a group for only a short time—three orientation meetings, each a couple hours long. Now we were three days into a month-long study abroad trip. There were 30 students on this trip, all focused on leadership and creativity but coming from a variety of majors. While all were highly engaged, some were clearly more outgoing and charismatic than others. But one stood above the rest—literally and in personality. Jake was tall, dark, and handsome with a constant, winning smile and nonstop energy to talk, explore, and meet people. He was the personification of charisma, and the students loved him. So, it was no surprise when we asked our question (write your answer in confidentially and anonymously) that Jake was deemed the leader. But an interesting thing happened over the course of a month together. At the end of the trip, we asked the group to again write down on a slip of paper who they thought of as the leader of the group. Jake's name was nowhere to be found among the votes. Instead, the group deemed another student the leader—a student who had a valued set of traits and skills and had used those tools to build relationships and facilitate others toward the common vision of the trip. For this leader, charisma was not part of their leadership toolbox but that just meant taking a bit more time. As for Jake, he didn't change a thing, and was still the happy, charismatic person throughout the trip; but he did realize the limits of charisma for leaders. —Tony Middlebrooks, Leadership Professor

Charisma used well and appropriately is a very useful trait to cultivate, although perhaps it needs to be reframed to focus on its great value as *initiating*—the very important person with the courage, tenacity, enthusiasm, willingness, and wherewithal to start something that others look to and follow. Sounds like leadership. But before you get carried away with the charismatic excitement, remember that leadership is a process. Jim Collins asks with what do we replace the charismatic leader because organizations are not sustainable long term when they are based on an individual. In other words, once you and your charisma and competence as a leader are gone, will the organization survive and thrive without you? Collins notes,

> Building mechanisms is one of the CEO's most powerful but least understood and most rarely employed tools. Along with figuring out what the company stands for and pushing it to understand what it's really good at, building mechanisms is the CEO's role—the leader as architect.[26]

The skill of building mechanisms and systems transitions the design of leadership self from what leaders *are* to what leaders *can do*—what skills do effective leaders wield to success?

REFLECTION QUESTIONS

Many would argue that organizations and history are shaped by a few extraordinary individuals. Do you agree or disagree that this was the case? Should it be the model in the future? What are the advantages and disadvantages of having a *hero* as leader?

EFFECTIVE LEADERS CAN DO _____:
SKILLS, PRACTICES, AND EXPERTISE

LEARNING OBJECTIVE
2.5   Contrast leadership skills with management, expertise, and established competencies.

The skills approach to leadership focuses on what leaders can do—their competencies. Unlike traits, skills can be more readily acquired and in turn seem to be more teachable. Similar to traits, the list of important, useful, and relevant skills is very long. One early attempt to simplify skills that has stood the test of time is Katz's three-level model of skills focus.[27] The three-level approach categorizes skills into technical skills, human skills, and conceptual skills. As individuals move up in an organization, the requisite skills needed shift accordingly. For example, imagine you are a skilled portrait artist recently hired by a company that does just that—produces high-quality portraits for customers. On the job, you are judged on your technical skills, in this case, your ability to paint the portrait. There are likely some human skills needed as well—working with clients and colleagues—and at some point, perhaps mentoring new artists. Over time, the boss notes what an excellent artist you are, and so you are promoted to division manager, overseeing the portrait making of ten other artists. With this change in role comes a change in skills. Now, the big focus is on human skills—motivating, inspiring, solving conflicts, training, communicating, recruiting, and retaining. Your technical skills still come in handy for training others, but you simply don't have time to do portraits. At this level, you also start to consider the success of the overall organization but mostly as it intersects with your artists. Finally, after many successful years as division manager, you become the big boss, the CEO. Now, the success of the organization as a whole—big picture, long term—is your focus, and you need conceptual skills, such as strategic planning, market forecasting, and fostering innovation. You clearly will need those human skills you have developed, but you are now far removed from needing to know how to paint a portrait.

Katz's model of shifting technical, human, and conceptual skills is an important moment for all individuals within an organization as it explains why certain roles focus on what they need to, as well as what specific skills need emphasis and development (and which can and should be ignored, which is no small thing given that you can't focus on everything). More important, this model exemplifies that skills, while specific in practice, need to be considered categorically when applied to developing leaders. In other words, many specific skills represent human skills—you can acquire some and not others and still have human skills. This notion is of great importance as the field of leadership matures and is tempted to frame itself too constrictively with required competencies.

In Competency Terms

As you design your leadership and others' success in future chapters, it is tempting to grab for a set of very concrete competencies—easy to list out, easy to measure and assess, but not necessarily appropriate or mindful. In an analysis of leadership models and competency frameworks, the Center for Leadership Studies stated the following about competencies:

> The "leader" (as post holder) is thus promoted as the sole source of "leadership." . . .
> Fewer than half of the frameworks cited refer directly to the leaders' ability to respond

Chapter 2 ● Designing Your Perceptions of Leaders and Leadership   69

and adapt their style to different circumstances. . . . This almost evangelistic notion of the leader as a multi-talented individual with diverse skills, personal qualities and a large social conscience, however, poses a number of difficulties. Firstly, it represents almost a return to the trait theory of leadership, just with a wider range of attributes. Secondly, when you attempt to combine attributes from across the range of frameworks, the result is an unwieldy, almost over-powering list of qualities. . . . Personal qualities of the leader are undoubtedly important but are unlikely to be sufficient in themselves for the emergence and exercise of leadership.[28]

Although dated, the ideas critical of competencies are timeless, just as the call for an easy-to-assess checklist persists to this day. An organized list of attributes and skills can be useful as a menu from which to identify useful and necessary characteristics as well as provide guidance for further development. But recall the two rules from earlier in the chapter: Leadership is about you, and leadership is not about you. As a process (and as Kellerman argues, a system[29]), leadership goes beyond you to include followers and context. Developing and applying your leadership based solely on a checklist of competencies is contrary to mindful leadership design.

Management? Leadership? Both

You have no doubt heard leader and manager used synonymously, likewise leadership and management. The good news is that the person in the position must be both leader and manager and consequently possess (or develop) some of the skills for both. The better news is that a skilled leader and manager will know how to discern and address leadership problems with leadership and management problems with management. The concepts are separate but complementary—like eating and drinking—same players, same ends; different means, different processes; and some overlap, which is what everyone argues about.

Leadership is the process of influencing others toward a common vision. Classic **management** activities include forecasting, planning, organizing, commanding, coordinating, and controlling.[30] Many leadership scholars have weighed in on the distinction between leadership and management, with Jon Kotter providing one of the most prevalent distinctions: Management produces order and consistency, while leadership produces change and movement.[31] You will find there are many quick and quirky ways to differentiate the two concepts, generally making management and the manager appear to be the less appealing role (e.g., The manager is the classic good soldier; the leader is their own person.[32] Who would *not* want to be their own person?).

The practical reality is there are a variety of activities, skills, and roles necessary for an organization to succeed. Some organizations are highly complex and require a great deal of organization and coordination, while others may be more dynamic and require adaptability and continual strategy readjustment. This situational and contextual nature means that sometimes you need leadership skills and activities, and sometimes you need management, and usually, it is a combination of both. The flexible leadership model proposed by Yukl and Lepsinger outlines a number of critical activities where leadership behaviors and management programs and systems must work together.[33, 34]

The Expert Leader

The ultimate end of any skill development effort is to achieve expert status. Expertise has been carefully studied much the way leadership has—find experts, observe them, interview them, identify what makes them experts (and others not). Experts—in chess, tennis, firefighting, and so forth—are characterized by how they think and what they perceive. Table 2.3 lists the characteristics of experts found by two researchers.

TABLE 2.3 ■ Characteristics of Expertise	
Bransford, J., National Research Council. (2000). *How people learn: Brain, mind, experience and school.*[35]	Klein, G. (1998). *Sources of power: How people make decisions.*[36]
• Notice features and meaningful patterns of information not noticed by novices • Have acquired a great deal of content knowledge that is organized in ways that reflect a deep understanding of their subject • Knowledge that reflects contexts of applicability, not just simple facts • Ability to flexibly retrieve important aspects of their knowledge with little attentional effort • Possess varying levels of flexibility in their approach to new situations	• Notice patterns that novices do not notice • Notice anomalies—events that did *not* happen and other violations of expectancies • See the big picture—context and situation • Understand the way things work • Notice opportunities and can improvise • See differences that are too small for novices to detect • Deeply understand their own limitations

Based on the dynamic, situational, and context-based nature of leadership, the idea of an expert leader seems implausible.[37] How could you possibly know/be able to do/be like every known trait and skill related to effective leadership? Take another look at the characteristics of experts noted in the table. Positional leaders who have mindfully practiced their role for many years display these abilities. As a developing leader, you can benefit from knowing what you do not know as well as the *how to* of what you do not know. In a dynamic field like leadership, expertise may be rooted in one's ability to excel adaptably. For example

- Recognizing other people's emotions and regulating your own

- Connecting and working with a wide diversity of individuals

- Seeing the big picture of how things interact and impact a situation

- Learning new things and adjusting how you learn to meet new conditions

- Generating unique ideas that are of value and facilitating others to do the same

What other skills or capacities will enhance your leadership no matter what the context or situation?

As you design your leadership, the skills you choose to develop will often overlap and work in a complementary way. For example, skills as a systems thinker enable you to see underlying variables, which will enhance your ability to solve conflicts. Thinking creatively enhances your ability to make great decisions by helping you see more options, which would also help solve conflicts (more ideas for compromise).

REFLECTION QUESTIONS

If you could possess one extraordinary trait, what would it be and why? Have you ever met someone with a trait you thought could never be useful and then were surprised when that person proved you wrong?

Chapter 2 • Designing Your Perceptions of Leaders and Leadership   71

THE CREDIBLE LEADER

LEARNING OBJECTIVE
2.6   Appraise your leadership credibility.

The broad palette of traits and skills offer you many possible design options. Yet underlying every effective leader is an effective person, regardless of what combination of skills and traits they possess. The effective person can be seen from two perspectives: internally and externally; it's about you, and it's not about you. Internally, effective individuals have developed a strong CORE™—confidence, optimism, resilience, and engagement—attributes that work in unison to maximize success in any situation. Externally, you are only as effective as others perceive you to be. For some, this effectiveness is initially rooted, in charisma. For all, effectiveness is known as your credibility and reputation.[38] *Your reputation as credible is your most valuable external asset.*

Credibility is the quality of being believed and, in practice, doing what you say you are going to do. Kouzes and Posner consider credibility as the foundation of leadership and fundamental to their First Law of Leadership: "If you don't believe in the messenger, you won't believe the message."[39] Without credibility, a leader has no positive relationship with followers, and without a positive relationship, there is no positive influence. "When people perceive their *immediate* manager to have high credibility, they're significantly more likely to: be proud to tell others they're part of the organization, feel a strong sense of team spirit, see their own personal values as consistent with those of the organization, feel attached and committed to the organization, (and) have a sense of ownership of the organization."[40]

Credibility comprises the foundational external attribute for a leader—external because it is based on the perceptions of followers. You cannot possess credibility without the approval of others. You cannot develop it within yourself. You can, however, learn ways to build your credibility—a task that must begin the very moment you meet a follower, if not before by reputation. Research has found that individuals judge you within microseconds. And knowing that people construct knowledge and form mental models, your first impression (no matter how professional, humble, relatable, and so forth) may run headfirst into followers' past negative mental models of leaders. So step 1 of establishing your credibility is simple—talk to followers, find out what they know, want, need, aspire to, enjoy—and do so with genuine interest and enthusiasm.

What would you "most look for and admire in a leader, someone whose direction (you) would *willingly* follow?" asked Kouzes and Posner.[41] According to their research, individuals noted four characteristics: honest, competent, inspiring, and forward-looking. Now turn the question around: Why should anyone be led by you? That is the question Goffee and Jones posed, highlighting four qualities effective leaders employ: showing their humanity, intuitively sensing timing and actions, managing with empathy, and capitalizing on their uniqueness as the leader.[42] The Graham Jones Credibility Pyramid indicates that 50 percent of a leader's credibility comes from the perception that they care (and another 25 percent is—based on their enthusiasm about the organization and its people). Together these studies highlight the key to credibility: building a trusting relationship—one where followers believe you can and will facilitate success.

Focus on small wins because people pay attention to the little things, especially when it directly relates to them. The perception of leaders and leadership brings forth what you might call the gray matter. Not the stuff between your ears, although directly relevant, but rather the situation where ambiguity lies. Many things in leadership are rife with those "it depends" situations. This includes your credibility as a leader. When there is no clear black and white, when the answer is not readily apparent, then you are in gray territory. And when it comes to gray matters, the little things matter because followers are still trying to decide your credibility. "Respect is carried not in great, bold proclamations, but in small moments of surprising intimacy and empathy."[43]

Table 2.4 lists a number of other actions you can take to establish and build your credibility. Consider each one and the actions you might take to display these attributes.

TABLE 2.4 ■ Credibility Actions	
How you treat people	With respect, honesty, and accountability
	Trust in follower capability and intentions
	Staying loyal to followers and backing their success
	Seeking to inspire
	With humility, gratitude, and confidence
	Celebrating and recognizing others' strengths and accomplishments
How you treat the job	Staying focused on goals and vision
	Fully engaging and leading by example
	Bringing current expertise to the table
	Admitting what you need to learn more about
How you treat yourself	Authentically—be true to your genuine self
	With respect and honesty
	Continuing to learn and grow
	Seeing mistakes as learning opportunities
	Being resilient in the face of critics and setbacks

Leaders need to understand more about why people work, what matters to them, how they can support them more effectively, and what might motivate them to perform better. Credibility with followers means connecting with followers, and the nature and means of connecting will continue to change with evolving technology, organizational structures, and conceptions of leadership and work by new generations: "Many firms are moving toward a coaching model in which managers facilitate problem solving and encourage employees' development by asking questions and offering support and guidance rather than giving orders and making judgments."[44]

Just as important as knowing how to build your credibility, you must also be aware of what will tarnish, if not destroy, it. Not doing something you said you were going to do, without explanation or apology, will crush your credibility. Withholding information and not being transparent in your decisions and actions communicates to others that they don't matter, that they are unimportant, and that you don't care. When followers ask themselves whether they can trust you, the answer is a deafening no. Even if a leader is a brilliant expert and wildly successful, followers will know they are working *for* a leader, not *with* and will invest themselves accordingly.

Other ways a leader can diminish or destroy their credibility include trying to fake any credibility-building activity, all of which then appears dishonest. Leaders who try to earn *likes* rather than respect and demand respect because of their position (versus through building a relationship and demonstrating care and expertise) also risk loss of credibility. Lastly, many leaders continue to operate under a top-down, hierarchical mindset. When a problem occurs, the top blames the next level down, who blames the next level, and so on to the bottom. Credible leaders accept personal responsibility and build that mindset into the organization. When a problem occurs, the first questions at the top should be the following: How have I created the conditions such that this problem occurred? Did I not train someone effectively? Did I delegate too much, too quickly? Did I not provide sufficient resources? There certainly are times when a problem lies with a follower, but far more often, leaders inadvertently set others up for that problem. The credible leader admits mistakes, learns from them, and is willing to say, "I don't know."

How, then, can you become someone others desire to follow? Establishing your credibility in a specific leadership role or context is critical to your success, and it is something you will need to attend to every time, all the time. The next chapter continues your design of leadership self, looking at the dynamic needs of tomorrow's leaders and how you can build the capacity to meet those unknown challenges.

Leadership by Design

Design Principle: **Closure**

Definition: "The principle of closure applies when we tend to see complete figures even when part of the information is missing."[45]

In Other Words: What you do not show people, they will make up on their own.

For Example: Skimming a chapter that is due tomorrow (although not recommended) can be beneficial if you are already familiar with the material because you will automatically fill in missing information in order to understand something.

For Leaders: Use closure to think about how you can best design yourself as a leader and what might be missing. What is lacking from your personal leadership brand that your followers will have to fill in for themselves? Are you being clear with your goals, values, and expectations or leaving room for interpretation? Are there facets about yourself that you *do not* want perceived as a single element, which you would rather stand alone? When conveying a vision, use closure to reduce complexity and increase interest—let groups fill in the gaps that lead up to the common goal.

The streams of water in this photo that you perceive as fluid are simply many tiny droplets, but you subconsciously use closure to make them seem like one cohesive element.

Many or one?
©iStock.com/Imgorthand

DEI BY DESIGN

LEARNING OBJECTIVE
2.7 Interpret identity as an often-hidden variable in how you perceive leaders and leadership.

This chapter began by considering your mental model of leaders and leadership. In developing perceptions of leadership and what it means to lead, consider the role of identity in leadership. What are your perceptions of *you* as a leader? Conceptually, **identity** is the mental picture of yourself that you carry with and update as you change and grow.[46] However, this self-portrait is made up of a variety of different elements. Parts of your identity are individually unique to you—your **personal identity**. Personal identities might include coffee-drinker, board game enthusiast, stamp collector, amateur podcaster, or aspiring magician. Conversely, **social identities** are human-made groupings based on shared characteristics. For example, your race, gender, ethnicity, sexual orientation, and religious affiliation are all forms of social identities. One interesting menu of identity elements is captured by the Four Layers of Diversity model, which extends out from the self, starting with personality (openness, agreeableness, etc.), to internal dimensions (physical ability, age, gender, race), to external dimensions (income, religion, educational background), to organizational dimensions (such as seniority, work location, union affiliation).[47]

Right now, inside of you and everyone else lies a multitude of personal and social identities. How do different parts of your identity help or hinder you to do or achieve specific things? For example, what parts of your identity help you connect with new people? You will get to explore this further with an activity in Chapter 4. The impacts of those identities are not seen or felt at the same time or in identical ways. As your awareness is drawn to how your various identities help and harm you across interactions with others, their relative prominence, or salience, changes. For example, your identity as someone in a leadership role might help you connect with other leaders but might harm you in connecting with, say, workers who distrust their boss. Usually, multiple social identities are salient at the same time. This crossroads of identity elements, where different identity elements are relevant all at the same time, is referred to as **intersectionality**.[48] Each person brings their intersectional identities to leadership. These overlapping and intersecting identity elements constitute the foundation upon which you build your perceptions of yourself and others as leaders, attitudes and behaviors of leading, and the social and emotional processes of leadership.

Consider a group with which you associate. Who in your group is the most trusted? Who would you guess will be successful? To what extent are your answers influenced by a shared or favored identity? Society and thus organizations are built on social dynamics that advantage some members at the cost of others. These advantages and disadvantages are bestowed, in large measure, based on intersectional social identities. **Agentic identities** are based on factors you share with others that reward you with unearned privileges based on membership in those groups.[49] **Targeted identities**, by contrast, result in arbitrary challenges for belonging to certain groups.[50] The prizes or penalties you accrue may not be the result of your efforts but rather from the hidden influence of the unique constellation of agentic and targeted identities you embody. This is called your **positionality**.[51]

Your identity as a leader both impacts and is impacted by other intersectional identities. In some cases, positionality will grant special leadership advantages, while in others, it will hinder the ability to lead. Take some time to consider the following:

Chapter 2 • Designing Your Perceptions of Leaders and Leadership **75**

1. What are all the different ways you would describe yourself? Distinguish between personal and social identity elements.

2. Which identity elements do you tend to emphasize with others (salience)?

3. How do some of your identity elements relate? Do they overlap in some cases?

4. For each identity element, consider if (and with whom) it buys you privileges (agentic) or results in burdens (targeted).

CHAPTER SUMMARY

Your brain is a lean, mean, pattern-making machine that loves to construct mental models of the world as you interact with the world. Those interactions and experiences have helped form your conception of leaders and leadership . . . some of which might be mistaken. But the more you become aware of your own conceptions, the more broadly you can perceive the world, including leadership.

Misconceptions about leaders and leadership can be more easily understood within the framework of the definition: Process of influencing others toward a common vision. Rule #1 (It's about you.) and Rule #2 (It's not about you.) provide additional guidance.

Effective leaders possess specific traits—the challenge lies in identifying what specific traits fit a specific situation, context, challenge, and group of followers. Nonetheless, as you design your leadership, it is important to know what traits you possess, where they are best utilized, and what traits you aspire to develop.

Likewise, effective leaders have a menu of skills that can be learned and developed as tools for a variety of leadership activities—influencing others, developing relationships, crafting vision, facilitating others' success, and so forth. Skills can be very specific or fall into general categories. One helpful way of organizing skills is by technical, human, and conceptual skills. Leaders need to shift their emphasis to different skills as they move to different roles and levels within an organization.

The list of what effective leaders could or should know, be able to do, or be like is quite vast. Some have tried to make sense of these by creating competencies, distinguishing between leadership and management, and envisioning what an expert leader might look like. Your personal and social identity informs and influences your efficacy, through both internal and external forces. Whatever combination of personal attributes you possess, developing your credibility and CORE™ provide you with transferable assets for effective leadership.

KEY TERMS

Agentic identity (p. 74)

Charisma (p. 66)

Closure (p. 73)

Comparison (p. 64)

Credibility (p. 71)

Crucible (of leadership) (p. 51)

Identity (p. 74)

Intersectionality (p. 74)

Level 5 leadership (p. 58)

Management (p. 69)

Mental model (p. 55)

Personal identity (p. 74)

Positionality (p. 74)
Skills (p. 68)
Social identity (p. 74)

Targeted identity (p. 74)
Traits (p. 59)
Vision (p. 62)

CORE™ ATTRIBUTE BUILDERS: BUILD NOW FOR FUTURE LEADERSHIP CHALLENGES

Attribute: Optimism

Builder: Send a thank you

Studies have shown that expressing gratitude increases happiness and optimism.[52] Take a moment right now to consider someone you could thank for something. The something could be big (thanks for helping me get into college) or small (thanks for showing me how to solve that math problem). Send that someone a thank you right now. You could simply email a thank you, but to get the maximum impact—for them and yourself—try writing and sending a note. Try doing this on a regular basis. Not only will you build your optimism, but you will further develop relationships that may someday be helpful.

CORE™ ATTRIBUTE BUILDERS: BUILD NOW FOR FUTURE LEADERSHIP CHALLENGES

Attribute: Confidence

Builder: Reflected Best Self

This activity is based on the Reflected Best Self (RBS) exercise out of the Ross School of Business at the University of Michigan. Utilizing the idea that self-awareness and focusing on your strengths are two very important facets of your development as a leader, the RBS seeks to provide you with a more objective sense of what your *best* self entails. Here is your task:

1. Identify five to eight individuals who know you very well. Consider who will provide honest feedback for you and who will take the time to provide a thoughtful answer.

2. Email those individuals and tell them you are taking a class that requires you to find out more about yourself and your potential as a leader. Ask them to provide three examples of when they have seen you at your best. Ask them to think carefully, provide you with a detailed answer, and then thank them.

3. Ask those individuals to complete the following:
    a. One thing you (the student) do very well, one of your most valuable attributes is
        i. For example, the time you:
    b. One situation that really brings out the best in you is
        ii. For example, the time you:
    c. One way that you add value/make an important contribution is
        iii. For example, the time you:

Chapter 2 • Designing Your Perceptions of Leaders and Leadership   **77**

4. Create a table with the following categories:

Best Attributes	Example Noted	My Interpretation
EXAMPLE 1. Honest	1. Found and returned that big pile-o-cash	I am very empathetic to how others feel, and my honesty follows from that perspective.

5. Using the data from the table, craft a single page (1-page) summary portrait of your Reflected Best Self—reflected from others and reflected upon by you.

SKILL BUILDER ACTIVITY

Leadership Either/Or

How do you perceive leaders and leadership?

Following you will find some contrasting choices. Pick the one with which you most agree. No, you cannot say *both*, even if that is what you think.

Then choose the other option and try to justify your (second) choice to a friend.

A leader

1. Is inspirational   or   instructional

2. Is a model   or   a teammate

3. Is a friend   or   a boss

4. Is an expert   or   a good problem solver

5. Knows themselves   or   knows their followers

6. Is born   or   learns and develops

7. Has fun   or   assumes responsibility

8. Dresses to impress   or   dresses to fit in

9. Produces winners   or   wins

10. Makes it happen   or   facilitates a process

11. Challenges and critiques   or   maintains the current success

12. Decides based on their values or   decides based on others' values

13. Achieves through their own initiative   or   achieves through creating conditions for others to succeed

14. Motivates others   or   removes barriers to allow others to pursue their motivation

15. Creates vision   or   allows vision to emerge

SKILL BUILDER ACTIVITY

Who Are You?

Understanding yourself is key to leadership. There are many ways to describe oneself, some of which are very specific to an individual and others that describe general traits and tendencies shared by many. Many self-assessments have been created to help define you. None of them are the full picture, but *all* of them provide some interesting insights for you. Find a few new ways to describe yourself and how that personal insight relates to you as a leader. Here is the assignment:

1. Start a new folder or file that is all about you. Have you previously taken any personality or other assessments, such as Myers-Briggs or True Colors? Find those results and revisit them.

2. Find three other personal assessments online (or elsewhere) and assess yourself (take the test, etc.). You might start with a general search, but dig a little deeper and find some interesting aspects that you assess about yourself.

3. Using the results from #1 and #2, answer the following—in a personal journal or in a conversation with a friend

    a. Describe your assessments: What did they measure? What are the different ways in which the assessments describe people? What are the different categories or types of people described by each assessment?

    b. Describe *your* results: What characteristics would you describe as defining you (based on these assessments)? What characteristics are definitely not you?

    c. Explain two things you need to know about yourself as a leader based on the results of these assessments.

3

DESIGNING YOUR LEADERSHIP CAPACITY

LEARNING OBJECTIVES

Upon completion of this chapter, the reader should be able to

3.1   Assess your current personal attributes for leadership success

3.2   Revise your leadership capacity based on a growth mindset, process-orientation, and strengths-based approach

3.3   Apply design thinking mental habits to enhance your capacity to address challenges

3.4   Describe important new challenges of leadership in a changing workplace

3.5   Identify cutting-edge skills for leaders now in demand

3.6   Recognize the role of power, privilege, and oppression in capacity-building

3.7   Commit to begin a new journey that will accelerate your career

Leadership by Design Model

Design Self
HOW CAN I DESIGN MYSELF AS A LEADER?

Design Relationships
As a leader, how can I design my relationships with others?

Design Others' Success
As a leader, how can I design success for others?

Design Culture
As a leader, how can I design the culture of my organization?

Design Future
As a leader, how can I innovate?

INTRODUCTION

Every individual has the capacity to positively impact someone else's life. You also have the ability to live a different kind of life from those who choose to follow someone else's lead. What kind of person do you need to be in order to take the lead? What personal strengths do you need to adopt to become a person of influence? What will you draw upon to effectively facilitate the process of influencing others toward a common vision?

80 Module 1 ● Design Leadership Self

Designing your leadership self starts with identifying individual attributes that can be developed into effective leadership tools. Designing your leadership *capacity* builds on those attributes so you are better prepared to take on unforeseeable future challenges. Some leadership capacities are useful in all situations and contexts, such as the CORE™ (confidence, optimism, resilience, engagement) capacities. However, others are particularly effective in certain situations or contexts.

This chapter introduces three foundational mindsets (growth, process, and strengths-based) that complement your CORE™ capacities and then elaborates on the mental habits of design thinking that will supercharge your capacity to solve problems and innovate in the face of tomorrow's changing world and workplace. The second part of the chapter explores some of the challenges you will face as a leader and then profiles skills you will need to meet those challenges.

Leadership That Makes a Difference

One never knows when a moment will arise that will change one's life forever. Your awareness of your capacity to lead may become evident when least expected. Put yourself in the position of a 15-year-old girl living in Pakistan. She is attending a public school in your hometown. She gets on a bus to go home at the end of the day. On the way home, her bus is stopped by two young men who are specifically searching for her because she had previously spoken in public about how she wanted to be educated and become someone special. At that moment, she is shot in the head. This is a day that not only changed this 15-year-old's life but also that of a country and eventually the world. This individual endures several operations, suffers from partial paralysis on one side of her face, and is without a country in which to reside. However, her confidence, resilience, and vision for change continues with her as she has a desire to take on leading a movement that is not expected of any 15-year-old. With the assistance of a global press, she gains the world's attention through her courageous attempts to spread the word of not only her own plight but those of millions of other children around the world. Remarkably at age 17, she stands before officials in the United Nations in New York City, thousands of miles from her home country, and addresses a global audience about the plight of over 60 million children who are deprived of an education, some deprived of equal opportunity with their male counterparts, and others deprived of any opportunity to engage in employment outside of the home. The story continues. In 2014, at 17 years old, she receives the Nobel Peace Prize for leading a movement to end the suppression of children's rights to receive an education. This is a remarkable accomplishment of a young person that began at age 11, when she took the initiative to influence others to allow girls to have an education; in just six years, she has demonstrated leadership in a movement to change the lives of millions of others. Now her vision for change has spread to every corner of the world. Who is this individual?

The moment to assume leadership often comes quickly and perhaps unexpectedly. In this instance, a 15-year-old faces that moment, and she rises to meet the challenge. In five short years, she had made a significant impact on world opinion, both in terms of how the world sees residents of Pakistan, as well as the challenge to eliminate extreme poverty and to improve the future for over 60 million young people. Her name is Malala Yousafzai. This extraordinary young woman experienced the worst and best of humanity. One moment can change your whole life. Will you be ready for that moment when you have the opportunity to assume leadership that can make a difference?

One moment can change your life; Malala Yousafzai became a voice and leader for equity in education in Pakistan.

Photo by Nigel Waldron/Getty Images

ASSESS TO BETTER KNOW YOURSELF: DOES IT MATTER THAT YOU ARE A GOLD-RED KANGAROO TRIANGLE GUARDIAN?

LEARNING OBJECTIVE

3.1 Assess your current personal attributes for leadership success.

You have undoubtedly taken some self-assessments or personality tests (as the Skill Builder at the end of Chapter 2 asked you to do). What did you conclude from your self-assessment results? In the last chapter, you learned about some things effective leaders needed: accurate conceptions, specific traits and skills, aspects of expertise and credibility, and some understanding of who you are—your identity. So does it matter if an assessment labels you a giver or taker,[1] an introverted-intuitive-thinking-judge,[2] a partner–follower,[3] or a Gold-Red Kangaroo? The label does not matter, but the insights about yourself across many of these self-assessments (and assessments by others) will be key to you designing you.

How much do you know about you? Try this: Can you list five things you are really good at when working on a project? Maybe considering these seven categories could help: (1) values, (2) passions, (3) aspirations, (4) fit, (5) patterns of thinking, (6) reactions or (7) the effect you have on others. These "Seven Pillars of Insight" have been linked to very successful individuals and comprise both how aware you are of yourself and your awareness of how others see you. Remember the person profiled at the start of this textbook—James MacGregor Burns?[4] In his seminal book on leadership development, he introduced the notion that individuals initially must learn to lead themselves before they can lead others. This crucial step involves analyzing our existing personal strengths through a thoughtful self-awareness process. Many sections of this text ask that you assess and know different aspects of yourself, all of which should help you design your leadership and identify your best fit. Clearly understanding yourself enriches and enhances many aspects of leadership, including greater confidence.[5] Unfortunately, most individuals think they are more self-aware than they actually are.[6] Your purposeful pursuit of greater self-awareness will help you articulate your value and stand out as a leader.

DESIGNING YOUR CAPACITY: THREE FOUNDATIONAL MINDSETS

LEARNING OBJECTIVE
3.2   Revise your leadership capacity based on a growth mindset, process-orientation, and strengths-based approach.

Designing your leadership begins with you. In the first chapters of this textbook, you began to explore your perceptions and some of the CORE™ capacities required for effective leadership. This section illuminates three significant mindsets, or ways of thinking, that will catalyze your efforts to build your leadership capacity: cultivating a growth mindset, adopting a process-orientation, and engaging a strengths-based approach.

Growth Mindset

At what age or under what circumstances do you stop learning? Chances are pretty good that if you are reading this textbook, you are doing so because you believe you can learn, at any age, under many circumstances, because that is your mindset. The **growth mindset** is your belief that you can acquire and develop new abilities and that your capacity is only limited by your effort.[7] There are, unfortunately, individuals for whom circumstances lead them to believe their abilities are set and there is no chance for growth. These individuals approach the world and themselves with a **fixed mindset,** wherein you see your abilities and capacity as a change agent as set traits— they are what they are.

Upon first read, you probably thought, "Of course I have a growth mindset!" But a fixed mindset can sneak up on you and stifle your growth, decision-making, optimism, and willingness to take risks (and make mistakes) on the road to learning. Do you shy away from challenges and opportunities to grow because you do not want to "look bad," change activities when your immediate success is not assured, or label yourself as not good at something when you first try it and fail? Would you follow a leader who did those things? Everyone is susceptible to the fixed mindset because it feels good to do things well and protect your ego. As a leader, there is great pressure to have the answers and do things right. But leadership is a process, and a growth mindset enables that process to succeed. The good news is you can engage in a variety of activities to develop and reinforce a growth mindset, many of which are aligned with effective leadership.[8,9] Which of the following could you try in order to develop or reinforce your growth mindset?

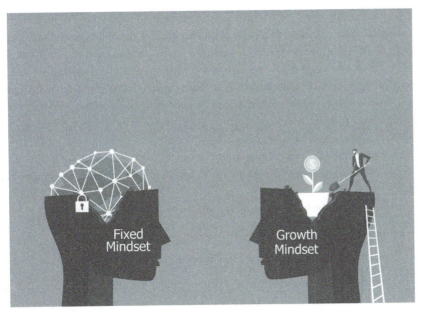

Take a risk and grow. Cultivate a growth mindset and know your learning is limitless.
©iStockphoto.com/useng

1. Add the word "yet" to the end of your self-assessments: "I am not a good writer . . . yet."
2. Take a small risk in front of others (and be OK with a mistake).
3. Give up a label—what you "are" is fixed; what you can know, do, or be like is able to grow.
4. Reflect on what you learned today . . . and every day.
5. Reframe failing as learning and criticism as advice—better still, ask for advice.[10]

Process-Oriented Mindset

Individuals with a growth mindset also see projects, challenges, and their own learning as a *process*. When your interest is primarily on achieving outcomes, then your framework reflects getting tasks done in an efficient and orderly fashion. Of course, this is necessary and valuable. However, many outcomes, particularly those that are highly innovative, synergistic, or sustainable, require processes that purposefully include multiple perspectives, testing and improvement, and systems that will sustain long-term projects. In an organizations, this is called a business process orientation and results in a positive climate.[11,12] For individual leaders, a process-orientation honors the long-term and big-picture possibilities. A process-orientation will still have achievement goals, but it is more relational and collaborative in order to create an environment where people and teamwork are valued.[13,14] Consider your current orientation—is it outcomes or process-oriented?

Strengths-Based Mindset

What if you simply ignored things you were not very good at? What if you focused on improving things you were already doing well? In fact, that is what most people generally do . . . except at work. Think about the things you like to do in your free time. Do you play a sport, have a hobby, dominate online games, or play a musical instrument? You are probably pretty good at the things you like to do. Would you take up a sport or hobby you are not so good at, much less perform terribly? You probably would not. It would take significant interest (and resilience) to stick with it. So why in the work setting do leaders focus more on the things you must improve instead of those things at which you are already good? Development and growth do not need to mean fixing weaknesses, they can mean building on strengths. The main premise of **strengths-based leadership** is an emphasis on what you do well—your strengths.

Research conducted by Gallup International identified 34 common strengths that individuals possessed to varying degrees.[15] Here are a few examples of strengths researchers identified:

- *Activator*—the ability to make things happen, turning thoughts into action

- *Strategic*—the ability to create alternative ways to proceed

- *Command*—the ability to take control of a situation and make decisions

- *Individualization*—the ability to identify the unique qualities of each person and help different individuals work well together

- *Maximizer*—the ability to stimulate individual and group excellence—always seeking to transform something from great to super great.[16]

Do you see yourself possessing any of these strengths? Researchers subsequently developed a tool to identify an individual's top strengths, enabling leaders and followers alike to strategically focus their performance on their already established strengths. You may already be familiar or have even taken the StrengthsFinder™ Assessment. Great! Go revisit your strengths right now.

Leaders who focus on enhancing individual strengths find greater engagement and innovation than attempting to eliminate weaknesses of followers (such as through training programs).[17] In their book *Strengths Based Leadership*, Tom Rath and Barry Conchie defend the position that there is no one strength that all successful leaders possess.[18] Most effective leaders are *not* well-rounded, but instead, they are acutely aware of their own talents and use them to their best advantage—that is, their best fit. Based on in-depth interviews with leaders around the world, they found that when leaders in an organization focus on the strengths of their employees, more effective work teams are formed, and productivity and employee engagement in decision-making increase substantially.

MYTH OR REALITY?

People who use their strengths in the workplace are likely to have better health over their careers.

Reality. According to a Gallup Poll, employees who apply their strengths in the workplace tend to be much more engaged. Engaged employees lead healthier lives. And engaged employees will also likely reap two other benefits, which include higher income and higher job satisfaction. Relatedly, learning to use your strengths in the workplace in a leadership role requires you also to build trust, compassion, stability, and hope among your followers.[19] These four aspects of work generally create an environment that is conducive to generating collegiality, which reduces stress and conflict, leading ultimately to better health.

Chapter 3 ● Designing Your Leadership Capacity   **85**

The bottom line is that people who are aware of their strengths are likely to reap a competitive advantage that continues to grow over a lifetime. These outcomes highlight the value of leaders knowing their own strengths and also reveal how important it is for leaders to help others uncover their strengths as early as possible.

REFLECTION QUESTIONS

Think about a time in the past when you assumed a leadership role, whether at work, for a charity, or for a community organization. How would you rate your performance in terms of influencing others, executing responsibilities, building relationships, and following through on strategic thinking? Which skills were you most efficient at carrying out? What specific strengths made the difference in your performance?

DESIGN THINKING FOR YOUR LEADERSHIP TOOLBOX

LEARNING OBJECTIVE

3.3   Apply design thinking mental habits to enhance your capacity to address challenges.

Why would you want to think like a designer? Shouldn't you want to think like a leader? At this point in your textbook, you should have some ideas about what leadership is (and is not) and what effective leaders know, do, and are like. Designing your capacity as a leader requires a more unique set of tools—tools that will facilitate your explorations, help you generate innovative ideas, and generally make you a more creative problem solver, better decision maker, and effective leader. The world of design has developed some extraordinarily useful tools in the form of design thinking. **Design thinking** is a cognitive approach to engaging problems that embody a specific mindset that is

- *Explorative*
- *User-centered*
- *Divergent*
- *Multidisciplinary*
- *Integrative*
- *Iterative*

The *way* people think determines the way people behave, as this text has often noted. If you have taken a philosophy course, you know people have been trying to understand their own thinking for quite a long time, both generally and within fields of practice. Designers too have long discussed what a *designerly* way of thinking looks like.[20] Emanating from efforts to understand how designers give "form, organization, and order to physical things," designers have moved to apply this to human action, specifically to give form to "a desired state of affairs."[21] In other words, how does one design an experience that results in specific outcomes?

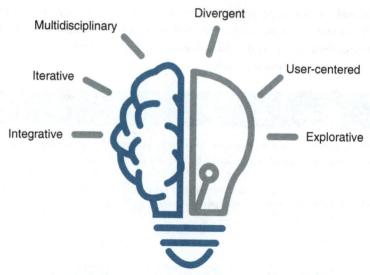

Light up your brain for maximum innovation with design thinking.
©iStockphoto.com/PeterSnow

Design thinking provides a unique problem-solving methodology and mindset that is particularly well-suited to the wicked problems and ambiguous challenges of leadership, focusing on *what ought to be* (innovation) versus *what is* (analysis).[22, 23] Picture yourself working on a group project with some classmates. You are all meeting about the project and trying to address the problem at hand. Can you envision the typical conversation? "Ok, what do we need to do?" "Anyone know anything about this problem?" "Anyone have any ideas?" "What if we do this?" And the conversation continues as it usually does—sometimes with innovative, excellent results, but most often, not so much.

But what if you were a design thinker? What if *you* were the person in the group who raised a question that was so unique it guided the group in a more fruitful direction? That is what design thinking is and does. Take a moment to examine the key questions in Table 3.1. Imagine yourself raising each of these questions.

Design thinking is often used synonymously with design process, particularly as it has been applied to business settings.[24] You will read more about design process as creative problem-solving in Chapter 8 when you are designing others' success. However, although *doing* certain things when you solve a problem may influence your thinking, it does not entail a *thinking habit*. One of the best ways to distinguish design thinking from the activity of a design process lies in what and how a design thinker would think that is different from any other smart problem solver. Take another look at Table 3.1, this time focusing on the definitions of each of the dispositions. To what extent do you think like this, in each of these ways? Assess yourself on each of the design-thinking dispositions, and note which one/s are strengths for you and which one/s you need to further develop.

Design thinking can be applied to any problem, but it is uniquely suited to addressing complex, ambiguous, wicked problems. A **wicked problem** is a problem that is difficult or impossible to solve because of incomplete information, multiple perspectives, dynamic variables, and interconnections with other problems.[25] Because of this complexity, wicked problems resist solution, and solutions that are applied often result in additional problems. Social problems often

TABLE 3.1 ■ Design Thinking Dispositions and Key Questions		
Design Thinking **. . . Is a Cognitive Approach to Engaging Problems That Embodies a Specific Mindset That Is**	**What if I Was the Person in the Room Who Asks . . .**	**How Likely Am I to Raise That Question?** (0 = not to 10 = very)
Explorative Mindset that assumes purposeful ambiguity and curiosity	What if everything we know about this problem is wrong or untrue?	
User-centered Mindset that focuses on the user and how they experience and feel	How would the user view this problem? How would they feel? What user information do we need?	
Divergent Mindset of generating many, many ideas for a single problem	What processes can we use to generate many, many ideas?	
Multidisciplinary Mindset that engages many minds and pursues multiple areas of expertise	What other perspectives and expertise could inform? What less obvious fields might offer new perspectives? In what ways could we engage others in the process?	
Integrative Mindset of attending to and balancing multiple and contrasting variables and creatively resolving the tensions between them	What are the various goals, issues, and stakeholders that we must consider? How could we increase solution viability, feasibility, and desirability?	
Iterative Mindset of always seeing solutions in process—assessing and improving	How can we assess and improve this solution? Can we build a prototype or pilot test?	

comprise wicked problems—issues like poverty, homelessness, drug abuse, obesity, and . . . effective leadership. Wicked problems cannot be fixed or solved, but they can be incrementally and systematically improved. Design thinking, effective leadership, and you can help make that difference.

The next section of this chapter explores each of the six design-thinking dispositions, briefly (re)introducing each with a definition and key question, followed by how that design-thinking disposition applies to designing your leadership capacity. More importantly, this section offers ideas and activities for developing each of the design-thinking dispositions (remember, these are mental habits). One helpful way to remember and apply the design-thinking dispositions is by embedding them into the design process: understand, imagine, and implement. When this process was introduced in Chapter 1, it was noted that you would be designing something much more complicated than a pen and that attending to the full process would be critical. Add design thinking to following a full design process to greatly enhance your design capability and, more importantly, your leadership capacity.

Explorative and User-Centered to Better Understand

One of the greatest challenges in working with others is not their misunderstanding but rather their conviction that their current misunderstanding is actually correct. They are unconsciously incompetent. This notion has been captured in a model of learning called the Four Stages for Learning Any New Skill.[26] In brief, when you learn something, you go through four stages. First, you are unconsciously incompetent—you are so clueless that you do not even realize how clueless you are. Ouch. But it gets worse. The next stage is consciously incompetent, which means you now have a clue . . . but still limited skill. From there, you slowly move into conscious competence—you know what you know and can do, and you can do it. Here is where things get a little strange. The final stage is unconscious competence. This is where you are so skilled and so experienced that you do not even have to think about what you are doing—you just do it and do it well. If you have a skill-based hobby, play a sport, or drive a car, you might have a sense of this. You cannot really explain how to do it anymore because those details have become second nature—you just do them.

Knowing that your brain constructs conceptions and habits, this model should be no surprise. However, this model helps you realize there is more to learning than just the acquisition of skill or knowledge—that there are limitations to your awareness through the process. Possessing the metacognitive capacity to recognize this lack of awareness will give you a more accurate indication of where you are on your way to really understanding something. That is only half of the challenge. Ability is one thing, willingness yet another. As you grow in your confidence, experience, and expertise, you will be increasingly looked to for answers. Your expectations of yourself as an expert who has answers will reinforce your desire to find the simple explanation. And you will be more likely to develop a deadly disorder: The God complex. Tim Harford describes the origins of this notion and describes the symptoms of the God complex: "No matter how complicated the problem, you have an absolutely overwhelming belief that you are infallibly right in your solution."[27] Recognizing, accepting, and acting on the idea that you might be mistaken—in the way you see a situation, your understanding of the problem or context, or in the solution you propose—is absolutely critical to designing your leadership capacity and ultimately successful leadership. The explorative and user-centered design-thinking habits help you do just that.

Explorative

The explorative mindset assumes purposeful ambiguity and curiosity, and it asks, What if everything we know about this problem is wrong or untrue?

Have you ever felt really stupid? Of course you have—we all have—and surprisingly we should strive to feel that more often. But why? The explorative disposition highlights the importance of being *productively stupid*. "I'm not talking about 'relative stupidity,' in which the other students in the class actually read the material, think about it, and ace the exam, whereas you don't. I'm also not talking about bright people who might be working in areas that don't match their talents," explains Martin Schwartz in *The Importance of Stupidity in Scientific Research*.[28] Productive stupidity means questioning and pushing your understanding and seeking out and allowing others to do so. "The more comfortable we become with being stupid, the deeper we will wade into the unknown and the more likely we are to make big discoveries."[29]

Chapter 3 ● Designing Your Leadership Capacity   **89**

REFLECTION QUESTION

What CORE™ (confidence, optimism, resilience, engagement) capacities are necessary for you to comfortably pursue productive stupidity?

The explorative disposition can best be described as a combination of curiosity and **inquisitiveness,** which is an inclination to ask questions, seek information, or otherwise inquire.[30] Curiosity piques your interest, but inquisitiveness puts that intrigue into explorative action. There are two facets to the explorative pursuit—one focused on a specific problem or a general, non-specific approach. When focusing on a single problem, the explorative disposition pushes you to find both the deep and the broad regarding that problem. The broad dimension of the problem includes understanding things like the context, history, other solutions that have been tried (and why and how they did and did not work), the range of stakeholders, and so forth. The deep dimension asks that you dig down to find the root of the issue or problem. For example, finding the more basic, underlying dynamics within a relationship will help you focus on the most impactful solution. The skill builder activity at the end of this chapter called Relationship Designer provides a checklist of activities covering the full design process and engaging all of the design-thinking dispositions, in this case, focused on your capacity to build relationships with your followers.

In a group or work setting, the explorative disposition can be the most aggravating. Imagine having someone in your group who is persistent in questioning the group's understanding of things. However, this level of questioning, even when there is no *problem*, underpins innovation and continuous improvement.[31] As a leader, you can build a culture of inquisitiveness, curiosity, and questioning. One fun approach is by encouraging yourself and your followers to be *explorers of the world*, as author Keri Smith encourages. She offers some advice to help prompt your capacity to see things through new eyes like an explorer.

1. Always be looking. (Notice the ground beneath your feet.)

2. Everything is interesting. Look closer.

3. Alter your course often.

4. Observe for long durations (and short ones).

5. Notice the stories going on around you.

6. Notice patterns. Make connections.

7. Observe movement.

8. Trace things back to their origins.

9. Use all of the senses in your investigations.[32]

Exploratory activities can give you and your team a playful yet important start to observing more, seeing differently, and understanding more deeply.

User-Centered

The **user-centered** mindset focuses on the user and how they experience and feel, and it asks, How would the user view this problem? How would they feel? What user information do we need?

What is it like to be you? What do you do all day? How do you feel? With whom do you interact and why and how? What spaces do you occupy during the day and night? What do you have in those spaces? User-centeredness has become an increasingly used design perspective because it seeks to deeply and authentically understand those individuals who will be affected by the design. More importantly, understanding the user will make it more likely the design will be accepted and used. For example, Christopher Charles was a Canadian student working in Cambodia to address anemia. He knew anemia was caused by low levels of iron in the blood and that iron levels could be raised by simply putting a block of iron into the pots Cambodian families were using to cook food. After explaining this to families and distributing iron blocks, the families simply did not want to use the blocks because they were ugly and scratched up their pans. But in a stroke of user-centeredness, he researched his users and came upon the idea of combining the iron block with the Cambodian cultural reverence of fish. Shaping the iron into a fish made putting the lucky iron fish in cookpots very desirable. And consequently, anemia levels dropped substantially.[33]

What is the lucky iron fish for your design—the form that users will embrace?
By LIFEintern—Own work, CC BY-SA 4.0, https://commons.wikimedia.org/w/index.php?curid=90968232

Developing a user-centered disposition starts with respecting the perspectives of others and then seeking to discover what that perspective entails. But how do you find out what others think, feel, and see? Answering the question of how to get inside someone else's head is perhaps the most interesting and challenging facet of design thinking. How do you develop that level of empathy? Asking questions is a good start, maybe doing some observing or perhaps a formal interview. Luckily, many additional methods have been developed to help discover and discern the user perspective. The design firm IDEO incorporates user-centeredness as a core phase in their process. In a particularly poignant user-centered example, the team at IDEO is asked to redesign the emergency room experience at a large hospital. They decide to capture the patient

Chapter 3 • Designing Your Leadership Capacity   **91**

experience by putting one of their team through the emergency room while toting a large video camera to capture the experience. What they got back, to the surprise of the hospital leaders, is an extended video of ceiling tiles and lights. That is what it looks and feels like to be a patient in the hospital.

What does it feel like to be led by you? To work in your organization? To interact with you on a regular basis as a follower? These are the questions you need to answer as you design your leadership. As noted, there are many tools for acquiring user-centered information, including two developed by IDEO: The Field Guide to Human-Centered Design and design Method Cards.[34] Each card in the method deck highlights a way of acquiring and interpreting others. Here are some excellent examples—try these with one of your friends and see what new things you learn about them:

- *Behavioral archaeology*—*look for the evidence of people's activities inherent in the placement, wear patterns, and organization of places and things—how do artifacts and environments figure in people's lives and highlight aspects of their lifestyle, habits, priorities, and values?*

- *Activity analysis*—*list or represent in detail all tasks, actions, objects, performers, and interactions involved in a process.*

- *Guided tours*—*accompany participants on a guided tour of the project-relevant spaces and activities they experience.*[35]

Right now, this generation of leaders—employers, managers, salespersons, teachers, clergy— is working hard to figure out how the next generation thinks. What do new employees value? How do they like to work? What will inspire them? In what settings and culture do they achieve? At one point, the buzz centered around millennials seeking jobs that offer a better quality of life rather than greater compensation.[36] What will be the driving force for your generation—climate change? Racial equity? Global conflict or cooperation? More important, what will drive the generation after you—the individuals with whom you will be striving to design leadership futures? A user-centered disposition will ensure that you pursue activities to really find out.

Empathy: User-Centeredness at the Deep End of the Pool[37]

Designing your leadership must incorporate user-centeredness. Without this information and perspective, you are stuck at Rule #1 (It's about you). When followers perceive that your actions do not include them, they are unlikely to see their place in the organization and vision. "Humans react to emotional probes—solicited or not—that are often accompanied by emotional assurances rather than logic, reason, or dispassion. I call these 'emosurances.'"[38] What would you need to know from your leader in order to feel *emotionally* assured?

From the designing leadership relationships perspective, you are seeking much more than a deep and accurate understanding of your followers. Rather, you are seeking a level of trust and authenticity that only comes with a connection built with true empathy. Empathy is emotionally putting yourself in someone else's position—to share and understand their feelings, needs, concerns, and emotional state. Empathy only fully exists when you have experienced the same situation; and even then, you are not the same person who brings the same background, mental models, and dispositions to the situation. Nonetheless, the ability to emotionally and personally understand the needs of each follower can improve both culture and performance.[39]

What is the difference between your teacher and this textbook or the difference between you as a leader and an employee handbook that outlines all activities? That difference comprises the distinctly *human* part of leadership, and it matters. Consider some of the best relationships you have. They are generally based on a feeling that the other person really understands and can relate to you. Empathy builds trust, provides support and stability, communicates acceptance and authenticity, opens communication, and generally fosters a positive culture. "'You can't hate someone whose story you know.' You don't have to like the story, or even the person telling you their story. But listening creates a relationship."[40] Like all mental habits, engaging in user-centered and empathic practices again and again will develop this disposition over time. Table 3.2 lists some suggested activities that will further develop these two design thinking dispositions.

TABLE 3.2 ■ Activities to develop Your Explorative and User-Centered dispositions	
To Develop This Design-Thinking Disposition . . .	I Could Try These Activities
Explorative	Relook to find the more basic, underlying problem Engage pre-flection and reflection on your process Choose an unrelated field and force a solution
User-Centered	Visualize the problem or solution from the user point of view Spend a day in the life of the user (or an hour) Interview, observe, interview, observe Try to replace as many functions as possible with what a computer could do—what is left? Visualize the problem or solution void of all technology Research and engage in emotional intelligence and empathy building

Divergent and Multidisciplinary to Better Imagine

In what ways might we . . . ? What would happen if . . . ? What are all the different ways we could . . . ? After working to understand your problem to the extent possible, it is time to shift to a period of imagining. Many leaders come up with a solution that seems workable and then head to implementation. This is called **satisficing**, which is a process of *satisfying* minimal criteria with a solution that will *suffice*. Design thinkers utilize two habits of mind that help maximize their idea-generating capability—divergent thinking and multidisciplinary thinking. While all the design-thinking dispositions help leaders to see differently, these two are particularly suited to the imagine phase, and in turn, they will help you generate many possible ideas for designing your leadership relationships.

Divergent

The divergent mindset generates many, many ideas for a single problem, and it asks, What processes can we use to generate many, many ideas?

Right now, can you set this textbook aside and write down 20 different uses for a pencil besides writing? Go ahead and try it. You probably came up with things such as something to poke someone with, a chopstick, a conductor's baton, a hair tie, a back scratcher, and maybe even something a bit odd like a crutch for a wounded squirrel. Now, imagine trying to generate 50 uses or 100—probably feels impossible, right? Wrong. This is what divergent thinkers do—and

Chapter 3 • Designing Your Leadership Capacity   93

you can do it too. The immediate problem is that you have been trained in school for many years to be a convergent thinker. *Convergent* thinkers take lots of information and converge it into a single essay or test answer or model. By contrast, **divergent** thinking is the process of generating many ideas from a single problem, much like the multiple uses challenge, which is a classic creativity assessment.

Divergent thinking underpins creativity, and it is key to generating ideas. But while generating ideas implies something of value, divergent thinking is really about quantity—coming up with as many answers as possible. Developing a divergent-thinking disposition requires confidence, comfort with ambiguity, a tolerance for intellectual risk-taking, and the mental habit of making distant connections, all without self-judging or self-editing. This challenging set of characteristics is why most individuals and groups satisfice, even when they say they are *brainstorming*. Brainstorming actually has strict rules that include going for quantity and no judgments, which are intended to facilitate divergent thinking. Chapter 8: "Creativity, Problem-Solving, and Idea-Generating" examines this concept and many other methods for generating ideas, in great detail.

Building your divergent-thinking disposition requires engaging in any activities where you need to generate many ideas from a single problem. Here are some fun examples:

- Choose an item from your pocket or purse or bag—list as many professions or roles that could use that item (and how).

- You are the dictator with great power. Think of as many ways as you can to control people.

- Alpha doodle—using a single letter, doodle as many different pictures as you can using that letter as the basis.

- Think of as many business ideas based on a childhood hobby or experience or toy. And then, think of all the worst business ideas . . . ever.

Divergent thinking seems like all fun, and in fact, there is no reason why developing this disposition need not be fun. Unfortunately, the fun aspect often works against bringing divergent thinking into serious organizations because of two fears. The first of these fears lies in management believing that if followers are encouraged to think divergently and engage in this kind of go-for-quantity/no self-editing behavior, it will open up the gates of craziness and never end. This fear is easily remedied with a little management of the process, simply indicating when, where, and within what parameters the group will engage divergent thinking. And of course, making very clear when it will end and when the process will move forward to implementation.

The second fear is that the activity will be a waste of time, generating nothing but silly answers with no useful applications. This may be true . . . sort of. Any time invested in facilitating divergent thinking will be one step toward developing this disposition in yourself and others. So at a minimum, the activity has that benefit. Realistically, however, the more ideas that are generated, the more likely that innovative ideas will surface. There is no doubt the odds are in your favor when you generate 100 ideas for raising workplace happiness than if you generate five. Do not, however, expect those innovative ideas to be perfect and polished. Limited self-editing means you are looking for rough diamonds—the spark of an idea that will lead to the great innovation.

Multidisciplinary

The **multidisciplinary** mindset engages many minds and pursues multiple areas of expertise, and it asks, What other perspectives and expertise could inform? What less obvious fields might offer new perspectives?

"It was six men of Indostan, to learning much inclined, who went to see the elephant, (though all of them were blind)."[41] Thus begins the poem by John Godfrey Saxe based on an ancient Chinese story about how each of six blind men touched a different part of the elephant and individually (and mistakenly) assumed what was in front of them. You can find the full poem in Chapter 16 on Systems. The man who touched the tail thought he had a rope, the one who touched the tusk thought he had a spear. In the end, the poem highlights their great dispute, rooted in their own conceptualization. How often have you worked with a group where everyone thought they had a grasp of the situation, yet each person had a different concept of the situation? And if you have ever worked with students majoring in fields different from yours, the differences are even greater. As the poem about the blind men and the elephant sums, "Though each was partly right, all were in the wrong."

The fact is, encyclopedic knowledge is in the crowd, and specialized knowledge will rest with the individual. The leaders and experts of tomorrow have to be either polymaths (deep multidomain experts), curators (those who collect or collate different domains), polyglots (the overlay and meaning makers), or all three.[42]

Engage with other disciplines to see the bigger picture and generate more innovative ideas.
©iStockphoto.com/Prostock-Studio

A multidisciplinary disposition can also be described with the idea of the **T-shaped person**. This metaphor has been used since the early 1990s to describe a certain set of skills that were sought after in the design and technology fields.[43] The stem of the T represents an individual's depth of knowledge in their own field, while the cross of the T models an individual's capacity to collaborate and work with other disciplines.[44] Researchers and practitioners continue to define the skills and experiences that enable one to effectively communicate their expertise to other fields and, in turn, hear and incorporate expertise from other fields. These include things you would expect, such as oral and written communication, exposure to other fields, and emotional intelligence in working with those of different perspectives. None of these skills will matter, however, if you do not have the disposition to value, seek out, and work to interpret the connections across disciplines.

Developing a multidisciplinary disposition merely requires that you purposefully and frequently engage with very different perspectives. With whom can you engage this week to begin to develop your multidisciplinary design-thinking disposition? In addition to building a uniquely valuable network, this will significantly broaden your ability to lead and innovate. A common way to accomplish this in a more organized manner is to put together a personal board of directors. Just like organizations have a group of individuals providing guidance, each of whom brings a unique expertise, you too can thoughtfully put together a diverse group with whom you informally consult when wrestling with problems or simply thinking about future directions.

Design-thinking dispositions intertwine and work in a complementary manner. For example, the multidisciplinary mindset can function as a way to categorize user-centered information and further enhance divergent thinking. Taking a broader definition of discipline, you can construct a list of general person types or needs. If you were tasked to design a new park for your community, you might imagine a list of persons as follows:

- I need a place to reflect on big problems.

- My arthritic knees feel better when I can take a walk.

- I need to entertain my toddler safely.

- I like to attend outdoor concerts.

- I need a place to meet and impress important visitors.

- I need a place where my sports team can practice.

- I like to watch birds and identify new ones.

- I want to have a picnic with my family.

- I need a place to run my environmental research studies.

If you put yourself in each of these roles, what do you envision yourself doing? In what kind of space do you envision yourself doing it? Adopting multiple perspectives is another idea-generating technique that will be further explored in Chapter 8 on creative problem-solving. The ability to consider these multiple and competing demands illustrates the next design-thinking disposition: integrative thinking. Table 3.3 lists some suggested activities that will further develop your divergent and multidisciplinary design thinking dispositions.

TABLE 3.3 ■ Activities to Develop Your Divergent and Multidisciplinary Dispositions	
To Develop This Design-Thinking Disposition...	**I Could Try These Activities**
Divergent	Find 50 uses for an object; find 100 uses . . . Engage "What if" . . . current solutions were not possible Reverse the problem and brainstorm; then un-reverse solutions
Multidisciplinary	Engage and interview experts in other fields Visualize your problem in another context Bring together diverse groups to discuss a problem Incorporate and build off the ideas of others Work in codesign and team-based projects Engage others to play devil's advocate and strive for consensus

Integrative and Iterative to Better Implement

The explorative and user-centered dispositions help you better understand others and your relationship with them. Divergent and multidisciplinary dispositions help you generate many ideas and approaches to building those relationships. The final two design-thinking dispositions help your leadership process. Integrative thinking enables you to see multiple and competing facets of a situation or decision, while iterative thinking prompts you to continuously assess and improve those situations.

Integrative

The **integrative** mindset attends to and balances multiple criteria, particularly viability, feasibility, and desirability, and it asks, What are the various goals, issues, and stakeholders that we must consider? How could we increase solution viability, feasibility, and desirability?

Have you ever tried to juggle? Juggling a single ball is easy; in fact, it really isn't juggling. Your sole focus is on the one and only ball. Add a second and third ball and things get a bit more interesting, but now you are doing something different—you are juggling. Add a fourth and fifth ball . . . and eat a sandwich . . . and text your friend, and your mind is racing to track and shift across many foci. At this point in life, you should know that multitasking is a myth; in reality, you are rapidly shifting your attention from task to task, and your activity has again become (lots of) separate things. Your brain is pretty nimble, and shifting focus is an early acquired mental habit that has been well developed such that we seem to balance multiple thoughts in our head—a pretty handy skill for any complex endeavor, such as driving a car, cooking a meal, or leading an organization.

Are you attending to each ball, or did you integrate them into the act of juggling?
©iStockphoto.com/FilippoBacci

Integrative thinking represents the mental habit that brings those different thoughts together. Management thinker Roger Martin interviewed over 50 successful leaders and found they shared a somewhat unusual trait: "The ability to face constructively the tension of opposing

Chapter 3 • Designing Your Leadership Capacity **97**

models and instead of choosing one at the expense of the other, to generate a creative resolution of the tension in the form of a new model that contains elements of the individual models but is superior to each."[45]

Martin further explains integrative thinking in the context of decision-making, clarifying that the uniqueness of the integrative thinker lies in how they approach and work through each step. Of course, that is a disposition by definition—a habitual way of thinking.

Interestingly, the disposition of an integrative thinker sounds similar to some of the characteristics of an expert as described in Chapter 1 and the both/and mindset from Chapter 2 (see the Experts feature). Martin contrasts conventional decision-making with that of an integrative thinker by highlighting their tendency to seek, consider, and conceptualize more broadly and systemically. Likewise, experts are able to notice features and patterns that nonexperts miss, and experts conceptualize content in a more complex and integrated manner. This is important to note because you may need to acquire a level of expertise before or while you fully develop your integrative-thinking disposition.

There are still facets of integrative thinking you can develop even if you are not an expert, and you can certainly put this thinking to use. Integrative thinkers recognize their own mental models and are both capable and comfortable considering information contrary to that model. Martin explains that "great integrative thinkers are fairly rare . . . because putting it to work makes us anxious. Most of us avoid complexity and ambiguity and seek out the comfort of simplicity and clarity."

The willingness to see complexity captures the great utility of integrative thinking. A leader with this disposition excels in identifying the broad range of variables and the systems they comprise. For example, designing productive leader–follower relationships often depends on how well you can balance a variety of competing and contrasting aspects, as well as how you can creatively resolve those tensions. An incompetent follower today will likely become competent over time. An employee you know to be skilled is having an *off* day. In one context, your follower shines—but not so much in another context. A personal characteristic considered troublesome may have some uniquely positive applications in the eyes of an integrative-thinking leader.

Iterative

The **iterative** mindset always sees solutions in process—assessing and improving—and it asks, How can we assess and improve this solution? Can we build a prototype or pilot test?

If you have ever watched an infant go from crawling to walking, you have seen them pull up, wobble, fall, and repeat. Each time may be only marginally better, but after what seems like thousands of falls, they become a toddler, then a walker, runner, and more. When *you* try something and fail, how many times do you typically try again? Two? Three? Although a toddler's degree of resilience and grit is admirable, the fascinating aspect is that humans seem to be hardwired with the *try-fail-improve-try-again* cycle. In other words, you are a natural at iteration. So why is iteration so often left out of the problem-solving process?

Purposeful iteration is the process of revising based on feedback. As a disposition of design thinking, iteration requires both practice and the development of numerous supporting personal characteristics. Examine the list that follows. Which of the following do you find easy and which rather difficult?

- Willingness to change your idea and openness to being uncertain or wrong
- Critical-thinking ability to see shortcomings

- Creative-thinking ability to see potential

- Comfort with trying imperfect ideas

- Confidence enough to fail and see it as informative

- Resilient enough to try again

- Optimistic enough to know there's a better idea out there

- Purposeful trial and error, allowing you to make mistakes in the right direction and continuously improve

The iterative disposition is of great importance to every aspect of designing your leadership. An iterative leader constantly assesses and improves themselves, their performance, and their organization. Even though this activity may seem obvious, it is too often one of the last considerations in leadership. As a regular activity, iteration results in keeping up with current changes in market, users, and context; innovative ideas and possible new directions; and an accurate understanding of organizational quality. As a disposition applied to leadership, iterative thinking communicates accountability, care, and reciprocal credibility. In other words, your attention and follow-through as a leader help build your credibility, and your work with followers to understand their performance and facilitate their improvement builds their credibility in your eyes. Table 3.4 lists some suggested activities that will further develop your integrative and iterative design thinking dispositions.

TABLE 3.4 ■ Activities to Develop Your Integrative and Iterative Dispositions	
To Develop This Design-Thinking Disposition . . .	**I Could Try These Activities**
Integrative	Assess your solution for viability, feasibility, and desirability . . . improve each Consider two competing interests . . . generate creative solutions to resolve . . . repeat Again, identify a conflict . . . find an alternative perspective . . . find another
Iterative	Force yourself to revise a solution . . . five times . . . ten times . . . Assess anything and then generate ideas to make it better Discard your current solution and start anew

Assess Your Design Thinking, Then Design Leadership Relationships

Applying the design-thinking dispositions to designing leadership can begin immediately. These ways of thinking can be used as purposeful tools now. The more you actively use them, the sooner they will become habits. And the more practice you get with each disposition, the more specific uses you will uncover. You can revisit the summary tables at the end of each prior section and commit to engaging in different activities to build your design-thinking habits. The Design Thinking Assessment in Table 3.5 can better guide which dispositions you already tend to use and which could be further developed.

Chapter 3 • Designing Your Leadership Capacity 99

TABLE 3.5 ■ Design Thinking Assessment

Instructions: Following are statements that describe how you may think during and about your own problem-solving. For each statement, please check one of the following: always, almost always, more often than not, sometimes, not very often, never.

	SCORE	6	5	4	3	2	1
	Statement about your problem-solving	Always	Almost always	More often than not	Sometimes	Not very often	Never
1	When solving problems, I set aside time to imagine *crazy* ideas						
2	I research the history of the problem						
3	I think about how making my idea more affordable might make it less effective						
4	I establish written criteria for my solution						
5	I solicit ideas or feedback from others outside my field of practice/ study						
6	I avoid viewing the problem through the eyes of those directly affected by it						
7	Setting aside the problem criteria for a time, I will generate at least 20 ideas for solving a problem before choosing one						
8	I make sure I am aware of nearly all the previous solution ideas to a problem						
9	I strive for excellence in meeting one goal (versus balance in meeting multiple goals)						

(Continued)

100   Module 1 ● Design Leadership Self

TABLE 3.5 ■ Design Thinking Assessment (*Continued*)							
SCORE		**6**	**5**	**4**	**3**	**2**	**1**
Statement about your problem-solving		**Always**	**Almost always**	**More often than not**	**Sometimes**	**Not very often**	**Never**
10	I am willing to start over on a problem						
11	I take time to explore how other fields have addressed my problem						
12	I note how individuals interact with the problem						
13	I utilize specific techniques (besides *brainstorming*) to come up with ideas						
14	In my problem-solving process, I purposefully set aside my initial ideas						
15	I note the competing needs of a problem						
16	I build and test prototypes of my solution						
17	I purposefully avoid *whacky* perspectives						
18	I take time to collect information about the user of the solution						
19	I will move forward with a good idea as soon as I find it						

Throughout your problem-solving process, from start to finish, estimate the percentage of time you spend on each of the phases listed:

Researching and focusing the problem	Researching the users	Generating ideas	Assessing and prototyping solution	Revising solution	Implementing solution

| Scoring Key | | | |
| Questions 1–19 are organized as follows: | | | |
Design Thinking Disposition	Questions	Notes	Score Total
Divergent—generating many, many ideas for a single problem	1, 7, 13, 19	Q19 is reverse scored	(out of 24)
Explorative—assuming purposeful ambiguity and curiosity	2, 8, 14		(out of 18)
Integrative—attending to and balancing multiple criteria, particularly viability, feasibility, and desirability	3, 9, 15		(out of 18)
Iterative—always seeing solutions in process—assessing and improving	4, 10, 16		(out of 18)
Multidisciplinary—engaging many minds and pursuing multiple areas of expertise	5, 11, 17	Q17 is reverse scored	(out of 18)
User-centered—focused on the user and how they experience and feel	6, 12, 18	Q6 is reverse scored	(out of 18)
Reflections and Insights			

NEW CHALLENGES . . . NEED NEW LEADERSHIP . . . NEED YOU

LEARNING OBJECTIVE
3.4 Describe important new challenges of leadership in a changing workplace.

Leadership is for someone else, not me. The initial feeling that often arises when facing a difficult challenge or thinking about the complicated, messy problems of the world is one of skepticism. However, by stretching your perspective to broaden an awareness of your own capabilities, you can change both that feeling and mindset—and much can be accomplished. The question that underlies a hesitant leader is, *Do I have the capacity to lead others?* Purposefully and mindfully designing your CORE™, foundational mindsets, and design thinking mental habits will allow you to push your boundaries, embrace the excitement of a new challenge, bring forth the courage to take it on, and display the ability to facilitate the process.

You are living in a world that is changing as you read this text. Not only is the structure of institutions and organizations changing but also the nature of leadership. There are numerous opportunities to assume leadership roles all around you—not just in the workplace. Leadership can be applied to almost any situation, whether at home, socially, or professionally.

Risk-Taking Replaces Status Quo

There is an extraordinary opportunity accessible to each of you. The need to remain competitive in a global economy has resulted in rethinking leadership roles in the private sector as well as in the nonprofit and public sectors.[46] Leadership is the process of influencing others toward a common vision. For the moment, consider what leadership looks like when that process is *inspiring others to want to achieve something special.*

Risk-taking requires *imagination*. It was the imagination of Steven Jobs at Apple that drove his passion, which evolved into a new wave of creativity and produced the iPad and the iPhone. Risk-taking requires **perseverance**—the steady persistence in a course of action in spite of unexpected delays. It was the attribute of perseverance of Helen Clark, former prime minister of New Zealand, that enabled her to become the first female director of the United Nations Development Group in 2009. And risk-taking requires *passion*. It was the passion of Madeline Bell of Children's Hospital of the University of Pennsylvania that invigorated new approaches for treating childhood diseases through family-centered care programs. History has witnessed these individuals coming out of nowhere to lead a decade of progress. These individuals were like you in that they had a dream but also acted to see their dream become a reality. They are part of a new cadre of leaders that challenged themselves and at the same time conquered their fears. The word *can't* was not in their vocabulary.

Workspace Transforms the Workplace

Leadership is not about assembling individuals into a *workplace* but rather creating a work*space* for others to thrive. Advanced technology has enabled individuals to achieve outcomes that were never considered a reality. And following the pandemic, individuals have had to reconceptualize the spaces where connections and work happen.[47] Accordingly, working environments have become more virtual, dynamic, and digital. Technology has enabled individuals to form innovative, collaborative work teams that are more capable of taking on the challenges of a global economy. For example, the emergence of freelance workers enables organizations to flatten their hierarchies by requiring smaller physical facilities for fewer managers and operatives. A more virtual workspace is not only more cost efficient to organizations, but it also allows for developing partnerships with those with the specific skills required. Crowdsourcing is an example of how structures are changing to accommodate a dynamic working environment. This is the process of getting work performed or generating new ways of doing things, usually online, from a crowd of people. The idea is to enhance productivity by outsourcing it to a crowd of independent workers. It has had considerable impact on the way work is accomplished in retailing and food services. For example, companies such as Samsung, Lays Potato Chips, Starbucks, and Legos have taken advantage of crowdsourcing to bolster operations.[48] As the future continues to unfold, consider that work will be less defined by physical space and more so by how you can and/or choose to perform your work.[49]

Streamlined Organizational Structure Displaces the Hierarchy

The opportunity now exists for a new generation of leaders to take the successes of the past to a new level, one beyond the development of the Internet, a variety of social media, and digital networks. According to Colvin, every aspect of organizational structure is about to change.[50] The context for how we organize ourselves and inspire others to accomplish a shared vision is in transition. For example, traditionally, leadership has been based on one's position or title, such as president or CEO of an organization, in an environment of command and control over others from the top down. This organization reflects a hierarchy where individuals are closely supervised by someone above them. However, other organizational structures such as matrix, team, network, and virtual are being considered for what best fits the mission, values, and culture of a specific organization. Alternative organizational structures also change the way leaders communicate with and influence followers, make decisions, and facilitate success. For example, at the world-famous Longwood Gardens, Director Paul Redman uses strategic planning and a collaborative process to emphasize broad buy-in across all levels of the organization. By including as many stakeholders as possible in the vision-crafting process and then identifying and allowing experts to make that vision happen, Longwood is able to streamline activities and build an inclusive culture.[51]

World famous Longwood Gardens requires many experts and services. A collaborative organizational structure brings about a shared vision across diverse areas.

©iStockphoto.com/Kirkikis

Diverse, Inclusive, and Equitable Workplaces Expected

With different generations come different expectations for what is and is not acceptable in the workplace. Those expectations translate into ethics and morals, as you will read more about in Chapter 5. When leaders meet or exceed expectations, followers are satisfied, engaged, and perform. For some time, both research and practice have recognized the multiple advantages of creating a diverse, inclusive, and equitable workplace.[52] Relatedly, a consistent stream of information clearly highlighting the explicit, implicit, and often systemic ways in which individual differences are marginalized has resulted in young professionals demanding diverse and inclusive workplaces.[53]

Instituting policies and practices that both reflect and intentionally pursue fairness, inclusion, and diversity is a complex issue that will require your full leadership design attention.[54,55] Fortunately, there are many resources to help you bring these values into real experiences, with concrete actions that include steps like regularly assessing DEI, building DEI into the systems and strategic vision of the organization, and holding leaders accountable for advancing outcomes.[56] And of course, all of these activities involve facilitating the advancement of all individuals, whether broadening perspectives or expanding opportunities.

Leadership is a process, and your success will depend on your ability and willingness to engage and continue learning. Like the larger societal culture, the culture within an organization may be comprised of a wide range of perspectives, with those veteran participants more likely to embrace an embedded tradition. A diverse, inclusive, and equitable workplace will require careful and frequent consideration of what traditions are consistent with DEI values and activities and then purposefully, mindfully designing yourself, your relationships, other's success, culture, and the future position of your organization.[57]

Business Values Synchronizing With Cultural Expectations

Culture is defined as shared values and assumptions by organizational (or group) members; it is the way we do things around here. Like culture at the societal level, an organization's culture often silently communicates what is valued and believed and how members should behave. Chapter 11, entitled "Culture," examines how leaders can purposefully design this important and powerful aspect of their leadership.

Another current challenge comprises how leaders must navigate the intersection and integration of cultural values with business values, relative to followers and the overall organization. Societal-level culture is often divided into smaller, more localized cultures that, by definition, share values, beliefs, and customs, regardless of other organizational cultures with which they engage. While societal values such as honesty, ethics, social welfare, or respect may provide the foundation for how citizens relate, these values also provide guidelines for leaders to design relationships, make decisions, solve problems, and collaborate. Simultaneously, the declared core values of an organization, often unique to that organization, generally set parameters for growing the work culture. These values also become criteria used for hiring, developing, and assessing employees. The once-discrete separation between cultural expectations and business practices has blended and blurred, requiring leaders to consider both the organizational and cultural values. Examples of these include protection of the environment, optimization of product safety standards, and securing organizational liability.[58] For instance, Patagonia's mission statement reflects the intersection of cultural and societal values: "Build the best product, cause no unnecessary harm, use business to protect nature, and not bound by convention."[59] This mission statement allows both employees and the general public to understand that the company values intersect with societal values, for the benefit of society as a whole. In our immediate future, the challenge is how to motivate each employee to align an organization's core values with general societal cultural expectations. This is where leadership comes into play.

Humans Compete With Technology

Another intriguing aspect of the future is how humans will continue to add value to the workplace as technology intervenes in almost every aspect. Advances in artificial intelligence, which have resulted in an explosion of new applications for technology in the workplace through big data analytics, social media, and robotics, may replace decision makers at various levels in the future. Although the fear of technological unemployment remains a concern, the good news is that humans will be needed to think through the consequences of our decisions, something that machines are unable to do effectively. Decisions about values, ethics, civil rights, and social welfare will require human assessment.[60] "In this blur of fast-moving transformation, it would be easy to chart the adoption of technology, tools, and services, while missing the more significant business evolution, so let's make it clear: Digital transformation is, at its core, human transformation. No matter how sophisticated they become, tools need humans, and as new tools have become necessary, we humans have adapted rapidly. So much so, in fact, that it is fair to say that we are entering a new economic era, the Human Capital Era."[61]

The conflict between technology and human values is currently being played out in the field of artificial intelligence (AI) whereby decisions and everyday work tasks are controlled by machines. Imagine your job as a health care technician, insurance agent, human resources manager, or accountant is replaced by a machine. Replacing human intelligence with machines will not only change the nature of work but may also result in massive job losses and more severe income inequality.[62] In addition, researchers suggest that algorithm-based decision-making by

Chapter 3 • Designing Your Leadership Capacity   105

large corporate entities can inadvertently result in bias and discriminatory practices. Examples are Facebook and Twitter with their practices of screening commentary of contributors, thus reflecting a form of influence at best and thought control at worst. In addition, the expansion of data collection with corporate ownership can threaten the right to privacy. For example, considerable data is collected on patients in health care, consumers in banking and finance, and on citizens by government officials. Thus, our human values of fairness, equity, and inclusion may be compromised as the capabilities of technology take on a larger share of decision-making and control that traditionally lay in the hands of humans.

Disruption Interrupts Normalcy

With the emergence of Covid-19 and its impact upon the capacity of organizations to continue producing their products and services following traditional work practices, the ability to return to normalcy becomes a challenge. Other disruptions are likely to emerge with tornadoes, hurricanes, wildfires, and floods adding to disrupting traditional workplace practices. In this regard, disruptions to workflow are unpredictable as well as tragic in many cases. Failing to put strategies in place to not only *be prepared* for such catastrophic events can lead to severe repercussions.

The challenge here is for those leaders in the private, nonprofit, and public sectors to join together in designing systematic approaches that not only protect specific facilities and infrastructure from destruction but also those citizens in communities in which that organization exists. Having input from not only organizational leaders but also those to be most affected is vital if coworkers are going to have confidence in their leadership. Accordingly, the challenge here is to recognize that disruptions to normalcy are part of everyday operations—and the capacity to continue operations as normal requires careful planning

Leadership by Design

Design Principle: Form follows function

Definition: Beauty in design results when it is designed to function well. "A thing is defined by its essence. In order to design it so that it functions well—a receptacle, a chair, a house—its essence must first be explored; it should serve its purpose perfectly, that is, fulfill its function practically and be durable, inexpensive and 'beautiful.'"[63]

In Other Words: The shape of something is determined by what it needs to actually do.

For Example: Your resume is an example of form following its function—the point is to provide a brief summary of your skills, abilities, and accomplishments. The function of a resume is not to tell a life story, mystify with intrigue, lull others to sleep—if it were any of the latter, its form would be different. The simpler and more succinct it is in form, the more usable it is perceived to be from an employer's perspective.

For Leaders: What form does your leadership need to take? That depends on what you need your leadership to actually do. Leadership can be applied to almost any situation, whether at home, socially, or professionally. Start with the functional question: What actually needs to be done here? Then form your leadership—your method of influence, your style, strengths you apply—to the required function. Do you lead differently depending on the environment? The constituency? Form follows function reminds designers to be as usable as possible in order to best serve a need—one way in which a leader can mimic that idea is to develop a repertoire of varying leadership styles and be familiar with when to use each one.

106 Module 1 ● Design Leadership Self

REFLECTION QUESTIONS

Can you think of at least three challenges that you as a future leader are likely to face? Have you faced similar challenges in your past work experience? How do you expect to face the challenge of technology possibly taking your career from you? List your perceived challenges here by degree of severity in terms of impacting your future.

1. _____ (Most Severe)

2. _____

3. _____ (Least Severe)

NEW LEADERSHIP SKILLS IN DEMAND

LEARNING OBJECTIVE

3.5   Identify cutting-edge skills for leaders now in demand.

New challenges could be the mantra for leadership. Facilitating the process of influencing others toward a common vision will always bring forth new challenges. You will need skills to navigate the dynamic, changing world (imagination, perseverance, problem-solving); the changing nature of organizational structure (changing from workplace to workspace); and the paradox of balancing the human factor in the face of continuously increasing technological advances.[64] The unique contexts in which you will someday lead require additional skills to fully design your leadership (the **Five Es**):

1. Exhibit empathy

2. Engage digital transformation and competence

3. Empower organizational culture building (inclusivity and collaboration)

4. Extend capacity with stretch assignments

5. Enrich the leadership capacity of others (social intelligence to bring out the best in your peers and the person leading you).

As you read about each of these skills, which one would you identify as the most critical leadership skill for the 21st century and beyond? The skills required for 21st-century leadership will help you design yourself, your relationships, others' success, culture, and the future.

Exhibit Empathy by Engaging in Candid Discussions

To Meg Bear, vice president at Oracle,[65] the new leadership skill for the 21st century is that of becoming more socially sensitive to the feelings of others in a more encroaching scientific workspace. You may be surprised that feeling empathy is a cutting-edge skill for our future leaders, but in fact it ranks as one of the most important, especially during challenges.[66] Pat Summit, former basketball coach for 38 seasons at the University of Tennessee with eight national titles, was

Chapter 3 ● Designing Your Leadership Capacity   **107**

demanding of her players. But she also showed a caring respect by ensuring they all graduated from college while participating in the sport. Being demanding and caring at the same time may be unusual, but achieving excellence in what you do relies on setting high standards and fostering the success of each person. Thus, an important aspect to exhibiting empathy is encouraging candid conversations on difficult issues, such as workplace bullying, discrimination, favoritism, inclusion, or diversity.

What is empathy and how is it defined? Empathy is about caring about others. It is symbolic of your *heart*, which generally implies a sense of love or respect toward another. In this regard, **empathy** is defined as the ability to sense the feelings of others with the capacity to detect another's mindset. Empathy is one aspect of your emotional intelligence that you read about in Chapter 1 and is a very important tool you will need for design thinking in Chapter 5.

Why is empathy important to leadership? Empathy is considered the basis for forming a trustful relationship with others, and trust is the foundation of credibility. When you feel that someone truly understands your perspective, you feel heard and considered. Also, empathy is a key building block of morality since it places you in the shoes of another. It becomes a key component for building quality relationships.[67] Consequently, empathy also reduces implicit bias, which can lead to prejudice, bullying, and inequality in the workplace.[68]

How well have you developed empathy? Most individuals already possess elements of empathy. Suppose you enrolled in a university course and volunteered to work on a team project with five others. One person in the group is from Italy and learned English as a second language. Your Italian team member has difficulty understanding the nuances of the English language and is often confused about what is happening at meetings. You had a similar experience when you took a course in China, when you had difficulty understanding the native language during class. You remember being confused about what was going on in class and when interacting with your classmates. If you had to select an action based in empathy, which of the following would you do to prepare your Italian classmate to participate in a team presentation? You can only select one action, so this may be challenging. What would an effective and empathetic leader do?

Choose One

____**1.** You would suggest they enroll in an English Language Institute immediately to help refine their English language skills.

____**2.** You would give them an easy part of the project to do so they can get it done.

____**3.** You would isolate them from the others and have someone help them after the meetings.

____**4.** You would match up with them during the project and concentrate on listening to them.

____**5.** You would match them with another foreign student on the team so they could support one another.

____**6.** You would choose a different course of action from the above options. Explain:

Each of the above alternatives is intriguing. Which one did you select and why? Are there other things (Option #6) you could do to show empathy? One important point is to separate having sympathy (feeling sorry for) and/or acting in a condescending manner from exhibiting empathy. Demonstrating empathy also helps when assisting others to gain confidence through active listening and equitable action. The other alternatives are more about having sympathy by removing yourself from the issue while having someone else assist. In this instance, Option #4 is perhaps most empathetic since you took the step to take on a personal relationship with your classmate from Italy and devoted time to listening to their suggestions, points of view, and concerns. You were attempting to identify with their feelings about the project.

What can you do to further develop empathy? Here are some specific practices you can implement to take your own empathy to a higher sense of awareness.[69]

- First, concentrate on becoming an active listener. By demonstrating to others that you are interested in what they are saying, an open dialogue can be generated that enables individuals to express their feelings as well as their ideas.

- Second, list what you have in common with your coworkers. Since you are likely to be working with someone who is very different from you—maybe with age, nationality, or gender difference—identifying what you have in common with others may reduce the stress of the unknown.

- Third, use your imagination to visualize what the other person may be experiencing at the time. This practice will likely get you to focus on the other person more than yourself.

These are just a few but important things you can do immediately to bring empathy totally into your life.

Engage Digital Transformation

Another skill set that continues to grow exponentially in importance relates to a leader's ability to digitally engage—not just employees and customers, but "getting our heads around the many new ways of doing things, new business models, new ways of working and new ways of delivering our services."[70] Imagine yourself living in a digital workplace where you are connected to hundreds of coworkers anytime you need to no matter where or when needed—regardless of location, device, or time zone. By putting workers at the center of design, it becomes possible to create a digital workplace that transforms how people collaborate, get work done, and ultimately do business.[71] Consider work life before computers, cell phones, email, and the Internet. Think of how much has changed because of all those things. Technology always changes, and those changes impact how work happens and how leaders can and should lead.

Digital transformation comprises a broad array of activities and approaches that utilize digital technology to see, operate, and solve problems in new ways. This may involve having a set of skills, attitudes, and/or abilities that enables an individual to use a variety of technical tools (the Internet, platforms, mobile tools, and computers, etc.) when seeking, gathering, and analyzing data and communicating findings to others. Being digitally competent requires an individual to understand how information and communications technology (ICT) interact for creating a real-time office space where immediate access to information is expected by employees.

Digital transformation is critical to leadership because it enables leaders to both do more and see more possibilities.[72] Competence utilizing technology can enhance employee productivity considerably, manage time more efficiently, and improve worker capacity to become more creative and innovative.[73] When tools change, the possibilities change, and so too do expectations. In what ways will future leaders inspire followers, usher them outside their comfort zone, or catalyze them to generate new products and services using less time and resources? New leadership roles will reflect digital engagement, collaboration, and accountability at a different level.

What will digital competence include for your future work?
©iStockphoto.com/metamorworks

You will likely be transcending physical boundaries to incorporate a blend of in-person, online, and other virtual forms of smart technology when leading others into action. The cloud-based operating system, MindSphere enables coworkers to connect their machines to a cloud for data collection and analysis or even the designing of a new operational model.[74] For example, imagine yourself in a worldwide network focused on designing a smart city where a new infrastructure is being developed for supplying energy, water, electricity, and mobility for creating an environmentally secure city. In this system, your decisions are arrived at in real time, your involvement is apparent to all, and you help shape the way we will live in the future.

How well have you developed digital competence? You are working for the local community branch of the Alzheimer's Association designing a packet of materials seeking contributions from potential donors. You need to somehow communicate and distribute these materials. Do you simply put together an effective letter to go with the package? Other volunteers basically work out of their homes. What digital tools would you use to design the letter and funding package collaboratively with five other volunteers? Now, you realize that you need to be adept at performing in a virtual workspace using digital technology. Accessing real-time databases, digital documents, images, and motion video to produce a shared outcome with individuals situated in different locations is part of the operational style of this organization. Does this sound familiar? What aspects of digital literacy do you need to develop? Could you form a team of users at work and meet regularly to discuss how new forms of digital technology can transform a current workplace practice into a more dynamic operation?

Empower an Inclusive and Collaborative Work Culture

What is collaborative work culture and how is it defined? Organizational culture is defined as shared values and assumptions by organizational members. These shared understandings—things that are learned and developed over time—become a way of life for a group of individuals. In an organization, culture is cultivated through learned beliefs, values, customs, and norms established over time by those in leadership roles. In this regard, individuals in the workplace are programmed with a mindset that distinguishes the organization from others. (You will explore the concept of designing culture more fully in Chapter 11.)

Why is collaborative work culture important to leadership? An organizational culture that rewards change reflects a working environment where success and failure are treated as part of the process. The ability to generate teams of workers that can collaborate—that is, gather and share information with others, elaborate on ideas, coordinate the work of many, and create harmony among workers with different views—requires leaders who can rally others around a single cause.[75] Your capacity to encourage others to nurture unorthodox thinking that unleashes the talent of coworkers forms the foundation for generating a culture of innovation. Think about it. Would we have a company called Tesla that produces totally electric automobiles if a team of workers did not take a risk and present the idea? This openness is based on the fundamental belief that ideas for new products and services can come from anyone, anywhere, and at any time. Promoting risk-taking as a norm requires a collaborative culture.

How well have you developed the ability to foster a collaborative work culture? Imagine that you are employed in an organization where 20% of your time may be spent beyond performing normal routines to devising new ways to accomplish your job or to produce a new product or service. The expectation is that this discretionary time provided during a typical workweek will result in something special. The goal of leadership in this case is to create new markets rather than fighting competitors for existing market share.[76] In this instance, you and your employer realize that it will require a new work culture to take current products and services to a higher order of quality, usefulness, and cost-effectiveness.

As a future leader, establishing an organizational culture that includes input from employees at varying levels of management for collaborative decision-making presents an intriguing challenge. One strategy for achieving this objective is to search for existing organizations that have done just that. In this instance, Pfizer, a leading pharmaceutical company, is one organization that is considered a leader in the industry for creating a more diverse, equitable, and inclusive workforce.[77] Visualize yourself as an undergraduate at a university in your state. As an individual who has worked exceptionally hard in your major to achieve something special, you are invited to participate in a 10-week internship with Pfizer. At the conclusion, you will be eligible for immediate employment with Pfizer. In addition, after 2 years of employment, Pfizer will pay your tuition if you complete an MBA or other degree in health care. The target population for the program is students of color and Indigenous and Latino/Hispanic students who desire to flourish in collaborative efforts to advance health care efforts. The overall goal of Pfizer is to increase representation of these working groups to at least a third of their entire workforce, up from the current 5.1%. Thus, the strategy is about putting people first in terms of providing collaborative support and opportunities to grow and become a significant part of the future leadership.

Ask yourself, to what degree have you developed a capacity to motivate others to use different work patterns, such as the preceding one, for producing results?

___1. Do you accept risk-taking as a personal social norm?

___2. Do you encourage those around you to nurture unorthodox thinking?

___3. Do you motivate people around you to create a shared work culture?

___4. Do you generate an environment of trust around you?

___5. Do you use your own discretionary time to think outside your comfort zone?

If you responded *yes* to at least three of these items, you may already possess a great deal of organizational awareness.

Chapter 3 • Designing Your Leadership Capacity   111

What can you do to develop collaborative work culture? At first, one way to create a collaborative work culture is to have a clear vision of purpose. This vision will set the stage for how individuals set their own work goals and perceive your leadership. Second, establish clearly stated organizational values that blend with operational practices in that organization. Third, building an open organizational culture requires hiring individuals who will accept risk-taking as an organizational norm. Individuals generally stick with a culture they like, which brings some stability to the workforce. Finally, design an open architecture workspace where walls do not keep people apart. Placing individuals in spaces that encourage collaboration, communication, and camaraderie will go a long way toward establishing a culture of trust, respect, and collegiality.

Promote the narrative of the organization, the individuals, and its purpose. Most organizations have a heritage or tradition that illustrates past successes and milestones. This is a powerful way to carry on an organization's culture with a new generation of workers. Examples of organizations with a strong narrative are Coca-Cola with its World of Coke narrative, Apple with its fascination with small digital components, and Gore Industries with its legacy of people-centered operations. As you read further in this textbook, you will focus on designing various facets and types of culture, from organizational (Chapter 11) and team (Chapter 12), to designing a culture that cares (Chapter 13) and one that fosters innovation (Chapter 14).

Extend Capacity With Stretch Assignments

An intriguing aspect to leadership is the ability to customize work patterns that enable others to test their capacity and accomplish tasks beyond their own expectations. Challenging others to undertake a task beyond their current knowledge or skill set, known as stretching, puts into motion opportunities to enhance personal learning and growth and maybe even results in significant accomplishments previously thought unreachable. This strategy also encourages employees who may be pondering their future to challenge themselves, go beyond current constraints, and consider a new endeavor that may result in extraordinary economic and intrinsic rewards. Stretch assignments can also build confidence, camaraderie, and collaboration as individuals take on the risks associated with entering the unknown. As a leader, providing stretch assignments may help individuals distinguish themselves, fulfill their passion to succeed, or simply expand their perspective.

Take a moment to consider a personal stretch experience you have undertaken in your past by answering each of the following questions:

1. When is the last time you took on a new venture or project outside your comfort zone?

2. How did that venture work out?

3. What did you learn about yourself as a result of this new venture?

4. How did your leader help you achieve success in this new venture?

5. What would you have done differently if you had the opportunity to redo?

Of course, those in leadership roles need to make sure those taking on a new task are adequately supported and equipped with appropriate resources. An example of entering the unknown is the recent July 2021 flight into space sponsored by Jeff Bezos of Amazon.com. Blue Origin, a privately owned company, was initially created in 2020 with the objective to design a reusable space cabin for the average person. By providing the resources needed to complete the project, many career paths were changed during the experiment.[78] This stretch assignment generated excitement, commitment, and a passion to achieve a remarkable outcome. Leaders who assume success, even with a stretch assignment, create trust and respect. This contributes to an environment where pushing for high achievement is an organizational priority and personal growth becomes a primary driver to engage in new ventures that may spawn new products and services never thought possible. ***A passion to enter into the unknown is what leadership is all about!***

Enrich the Leadership Capacity of Others

Another useful skill for those assuming leadership roles is that of exhibiting social intelligence by enriching others, especially those in a workplace that is quite diverse.[79] Social intelligence reflects your pattern for working with others in an effort to achieve something special. The ability to enrich others (including those above you in rank) and to not create excessive conflict results in building trust, an outcome vital to effective leadership.

Social enrichment is basically engaging others to establish effective interactive networks. Specifically, it is defined here as the ability to get along well with others by getting them to collaborate and eventually partner with you for achieving a specific result. While the importance of social intelligence in leadership has been known for some time, its importance and practical application has grown stronger as work cultures have grown more collaborative.[80]

Why is social enrichment important to leadership? Social enrichment-oriented leaders are more empathetic, more capable of influencing and inspiring others, and better able to bring out the best in a team.[81] In a leadership role, your social intelligence will help build quality relationships and ultimately enhance your credibility and effectiveness. Socially intelligent leaders are also better able to help others work through conflicts and challenges, as well as be more creative.[82] This means leaders have the capacity to help people feel valued, respected, encouraged, and even competent. The skill of enriching the leadership capacity of that individual who is above you in rank and to whom you report will differentiate you from the norm. For example, if your organizational leader is somewhat strong handed and dominates decision-making, knowing how to change that behavior to a more collegial style can result in increased productivity among all. This skill may be noteworthy in the private and nonprofit sectors but also the public sector.

How well have you developed social enrichment skills? Imagine you are working in the public sector in the mayor's office of your hometown. Your constituents are quite diverse but also vocal. A current issue concerning school budgeting has come forth. You anticipate the mayor to be confrontational and stern when interacting with community residents. You need to assist the mayor by getting her to become less demonstrative and forceful and more open to alternatives. You need to read a situation as it unfolds, consider the appropriate ways to respond, and select an alternative that will yield the best result for all involved. The subset skills required for effective leadership are exhibiting active listening, utilizing a strong command of conversational language, differentiating cultural cues, reading subtle facial expressions, and negotiating. To what degree have you already developed this attribute yourself? This job is very political in nature, so think about how you would perform in this situation.

Yes/No?

___**1.** When others disagree with you, do you manage conflict well?

___**2.** Can you build partnerships (quality relationships) quickly?

Chapter 3 • Designing Your Leadership Capacity   113

___**3.** Can you negotiate common ground from cultural differences?

___**4.** Can you interpret cues (facial expressions) of others accurately?

___**5.** Do you know the impression you send of yourself to others?

If you responded *yes* to at least three of these items, you may already possess a great deal of the capacity to assist others in becoming more effective. What can you do to individually develop the capacity to make those above you more effective as a leader? There are several practices you can adopt that will enable you to intelligently create quality relationships with others. At the beginning, it is important to be perceived as acting with ethical motives that align with your personal values. In this regard, having authenticity is the foundation for creating collaborative work styles. Secondly, begin paying more attention to those in leadership roles that surround you. Work on becoming a conversationalist—not only with friends but with strangers also. For example, during social gatherings, being proactive by carrying on conversations with a variety of individuals will demonstrate your confidence in yourself. Greeting and being tactful with those in leadership roles above your rank reflects an individual at ease with going outside their social comfort zone. Finally, become comfortable playing different social roles with individuals with different expectations. When there is a conflict among ideas, become an active listener by reflecting back on what you believe the speaker said. In other words, being capable of understanding what the other person is thinking or feeling is basic to reading the situation that you are in. People tend to make inferences about your competence based on the behavior they observe.

REFLECTION QUESTIONS

Can you recall the five Es that describe the complementary skills required for future cadres of leaders? List them below for your future reference. Circle the one skill that will challenge you the most and indicate why. What can you do to enhance your capacity to perform each of these skills?

1. E _____

2. E _____

3. E _____

4. E _____

5. E _____

DEI BY DESIGN

LEARNING OBJECTIVES

3.6   Recognize the role of power, privilege, and oppression in capacity-building.

Building your leadership capacity also means enhancing your ability to see things that may otherwise be invisible. You may have identified your strengths, incorporated design thinking, and embraced some of the most in-demand leadership skills. But there may be some less obvious things holding you back, and until you notice them, you may be inadvertently holding others back, too. Your capacities for leadership are affected by your access to power and how that power may be unfairly applied—often called forms of privilege and oppression. Power is having the ability to make others behave as you would like,[83] and you will explore power more fully in Chapter 7. There are many forms of power within personal, relational, and organizational settings, however, leaders need to consider civic power: "where power means getting a community to make the choices and to take the actions that you want."[84] Civic power comes from six primary sources: physical force; monetary pressure (or wealth); governmental forces (or state actions); social influences, such as group and community norms; intellectual forces, like creativity and innovation; and numerical force, or the power of the crowd. Many individuals seek to wield civic power, but often this power is built into the laws, institutions, and norms of a society. A savvy leader seeks to understand power dynamics, so they are aware of who is influencing whom (and how and why). Mapping power also helps leaders learn to impact the flow of power through relationships, organizations, and communities.

Power is not always earned, and it can be unevenly distributed among members of society, which is then often mirrored in organizations. **Privilege** occurs when unearned power is unequally distributed by social structures and systems.[85] When this happens, these structural power inequalities result in various forms of unjust treatment called **oppression**—where people with power systematically treat those without power in unfair ways. As a leader, these forces and their related outcomes require both your awareness and ability to address and dismantle.

When power is awarded differentially among social groupings in society, various forms of identity-based privileges emerge. You may know these as racism, sexism, heterosexism, classism, ableism, and ageism, among others. In an organization, establishing a common vision and facilitating success becomes very difficult when some followers get unmerited, unearned advantages and others do not. Revisit your personal and social identities from Chapter 2 and now this information about power differences. These influences impact leadership. Are there unspoken, assumed advantages you may be enjoying? Are there some advantages others are receiving that you are not—only because for your general identity it is the way things are done. Currently, in this country, white privilege, male privilege, heterosexual privilege, and able-bodied privilege, (just to name a few) impact individual opportunity. Intentionally design your leadership capacity toward being a socially responsible cartographer and author of power by understanding and seeing power, privilege, and oppression.

CAPACITY CAPSTONE: COMMIT TO THE JOURNEY

LEARNING OBJECTIVES
3.7   Commit to begin a new journey that will accelerate your career.

Perhaps the greatest capacity you can build is your commitment to the continuous journey of exploring, learning, and designing your leadership. Convincing yourself that you can develop into an effective leader is essential to staying on track for accomplishing great things personally and professionally. Now is the time to begin thinking about generating a personal commitment that results in a strategy for becoming an effective leader. Twenty years ago, Jim Collins, author of the book *Good to Great*, pointed out that with rapid changes in work styles and expectations of the younger workforce entering the market, the need for different kinds of leaders is on the rise.[86] That idea seems almost quaint given the extraordinarily different technological and cultural

Chapter 3 • Designing Your Leadership Capacity 115

shifts that have greeted subsequent generations. Moreover, global and instant communications, dynamic markets, and consumers demanding individualized, instant, and innovative products and services means leaders now need to be more versatile by changing strategies quickly. You can be the leader that meets these emerging challenges.

Now that you have completed this chapter, you are ready to sign a letter of commitment. This acclamation on your part is the first step of your journey to become part of something new and exciting. Designing your leadership self means taking charge of your own destiny rather than letting someone else do it. Using the template provided in this exercise, put together a commitment letter, sign it, and give it to your instructor.

Example

Exercise: Make a Commitment to Undertake the Leadership Journey

Directions: Fill in the blanks below to reflect your personal commitment to learning about leadership and submit your commitment letter to your instructor.

Dear _____:

Re: Commitment to Leadership

I am making a pledge to begin my journey of learning and designing my leadership. My commitment shall entail learning how to use my present strengths to enhance my capacity to lead and make a positive difference.

My *three most significant current strengths* to be used in this endeavor are

- _____
- _____
- _____

I commit to building my leadership capacity: My CORE™, mental models, and design thinking. In this regard, I pledge to make considerable effort to *further develop two capacities*. They are

- _____
- _____

I also commit to learning additional skills that will support my future leadership success. In this regard, I pledge to make considerable effort to *learn three new leadership skills* for the 21st century. They are

- _____
- _____
- _____

My overall objective is to be a _____ leader who can be used in a(n) _____ organization.

I want to be known for being _____ so I can deliver _____.

I understand this letter constitutes a voluntary commitment to my future.

Sincerely,

(Your Signature)

Now you have an initial direction to designing your leadership self. But it is not enough to have a plan; you have to act on it. Your commitment letter is the vision you have designed for yourself. It reflects a promise to yourself and a reference point as your design develops. Keep this commitment letter nearby and refer to it as you proceed further.

REFLECTION QUESTIONS

Now that you have composed a commitment to leadership letter, what part separates you from all the other people you know—what makes you unique? Identify at least three aspects of your commitment that distinguish you. What will give you a competitive advantage as you prepare for taking an important step to enhance your career?

As you continue your journey and build your capacity, keep in mind that a good deal of leadership is about the heart, and it is often a process of caring about others as organizational goals are met. Leaders who genuinely lead with their heart—not just their head—are more equipped to connect with the emotional needs of others. They understand that people need to be valued, respected, listened to, and involved. Carol Burnett, a television icon from the 1960s to the 1990s, had a highly successful career in show business and is a perfect example of a leader with heart.[87] She never criticized employees or appeared demanding. When she needed something done, she would simply ask for help with the task required. This leadership approach shows her respect for the abilities of her subordinates. By acknowledging and honoring the human aspect of leadership, the heart-centered leader enhances the quality of work life for both themselves and for all those surrounding them. Do you know leaders like this? Do you want to be this kind of leader? Read on as the next chapters focus on designing your leadership relationships.

CHAPTER SUMMARY

The challenges you will face in the coming decades are only now providing hints at the skills and strengths future leaders will need. Changes in the nature of work, technology, and personal and organizational values are altering what works in leadership. This chapter outlined the mental habits you will need to succeed: self-awareness, growth mindset, process-orientation, and a strengths-based approach. Developing these habits deepens and broadens what you think about and how you see the world. Some mental habits are most useful in helping you see and solve problems. Collectively, these dispositions are called design thinking, and they include the following: explorative, user-centered, divergent, multidisciplinary, integrative, and iterative. Each of these mindsets provides unique and valuable tools as you design your leadership.

Preparing yourself also means attending to trending challenges in individuals, organizations, and society. Some of those challenges are discussed in this chapter, followed by some of the newly relevant skills that future leaders will need. These new skills can be summed with **five "Es"**:

- *Exhibit* empathy

- *Engage* digital transformation

- *Empower* an inclusive and collaborative work culture

- *Extend* and stretch capacity

- *Enrich* others with social intelligence

The most applicable strengths and skills of a leader may change somewhat over time, but the need for human intervention remains critical. The changes demanded of each of you will reflect a more dynamic approach to learning leadership that is somewhat different from the

Chapter 3 • Designing Your Leadership Capacity   117

past. Committing to the continuous journey of learning leadership may be the most important capacity you can build. Keep your commitment letter where you can refer to it as you proceed in this text.

KEY TERMS

Culture (p. 104)
Design thinking (p. 85)
Digital transformation (p. 108)
Divergent (p. 93)
Empathy (p. 107)
Explorative (p. 88)
Five Es (p. 106)
Fixed mindset (p. 82)
Growth mindset (p. 82)
Inquisitiveness (p. 89)
Integrative (p. 96)
Iterative (p. 97)

Multidisciplinary (p. 93)
Oppression (p. 114)
Organizational culture (p. 109)
Perseverance (p. 102)
Privilege (p. 114)
Satisficing (p. 92)
Social enrichment (p. 112)
Strengths-based leadership (p. 84)
T-shaped person (p. 94)
User-centered (p. 89)
Wicked problem (p. 86)

SKILL BUILDER ACTIVITY

Relationship Designer—You can use design thinking dispositions to enhance the design of any aspect of your leadership. In this activity, use design thinking to better design your relationships. Follow and complete the different assignment/prompts in the first column to facilitate your relationship design. Note how the different design-thinking dispositions enhance the overall process.

	Assignment/Prompt	Design-Thinking Disposition	Design Process Phase
1	Consider relationships of interest to you—which ones do you want to know more about and make a difference regarding?	Explorative	Understand
2	Write a brief history of specific relationships—both a professional history and your personal history.	Explorative	Understand
3	Create a visual model to better understand different aspects of the relationship—for example, a mental map or a systems diagram.	Explorative	Understand
4	Write the *story* of solutions as it regards these relationships and highlight *best practices*—when was the relationship at its best?	Explorative	Understand
5	Engage user-centered methods to collect information, identifying the stakeholders. Consider what kind of relationship you want with each individual.	User-centered	Understand

(Continued)

	Assignment/Prompt	Design-Thinking Disposition	Design Process Phase
6	Envision the ideal solutions and/or outcomes—what would/could it look like and how?	Divergent	Understand imagine
7	Generate many, many, many ideas for *solving* your issue or achieving your ideal.	Divergent	Imagine
8	Examine multiple views and perspectives on both your specific relationships as well as those of other leaders.	Multidisciplinary	Imagine
9	Research and establish criteria by which you will judge the success of your solution. Create metrics as applicable.	Iterative	Implement
10	Craft a strategic implementation plan to develop your relationships. What different demands do you need to balance?	Integrative	Implement
11	Consider and plan possible collaborations. Who could help you advance your relationships?	Collaborative	Implement
12	Consider unintended consequences, worst cases, and ethical issues arising from your envisioned plan.	Iterative	Implement

CORE™ ATTRIBUTE BUILDERS: BUILD NOW FOR FUTURE LEADERSHIP CHALLENGES

Attribute: Engagement

Builder: Exploring Cutting-Edge Challenges, Cutting-Edge Skills

What challenges lie ahead for leaders and followers? Often small annoyances (and small tips) hint at larger trends to come. Check out some of the websites that follow to explore what's next. Note five (5) great cutting-edge trends to watch out for OR new ideas/tips that you could use today . . . and likely tomorrow.

Website #1: Dan Pink's Pinkcast—simple solutions and ideas in very brief videos: https://www.danpink.com/pinkcast/

Website #2: Center for Creative Leadership Insights: https://www.ccl.org/categories/

Website #3: Gallup Workplace Insights: https://www.gallup.com/workplace/insights.aspx

Website #4: International Institute for Management Development insights: https://www.imd.org/imd-reflections/reflection-page/leadership-skills/

Website #5: McKinsey & Company Featured Insights: https://www.mckinsey.com/featured-insights

Bonus: Darden Business School at UVA's Ideas to Action: https://ideas.darden.virginia.edu/leadership-in-2022

Chapter 3 • Designing Your Leadership Capacity   119

New Challenges	New Skills

4

YOUR WHY AND WHAT FOR LEADING

By Ingrid Richter and Eliane Ubalijoro

LEARNING OBJECTIVES

Upon completion of this chapter, the reader should be able to

4.1 Discuss the importance of *why* in designing your leadership

4.2 Examine how socialization and identity inform purpose

4.3 Recognize the important aspects of your charisms and flow

4.4 Translate your shadow experiences into leadership lessons for purpose

4.5 Appraise the range of worlds that might need your leadership

4.6 Distinguish what purpose deserves you through creating a Greater Purpose Statement

Leadership by Design Model

Design Self
HOW CAN I DESIGN MYSELF AS A LEADER?

Design Relationships
As a leader, how can I design my relationships with others?

Design Others' Success
As a leader, how can I design success for others?

Design Culture
As a leader, how can I design the culture of my organization?

Design Future
As a leader, how can I innovate?

INTRODUCTION

Congratulations! It's not every day that a distinguished leader such as yourself gets to celebrate their 100th birthday. For this momentous occasion, a leading historian has gathered comments about you and your accomplishments from colleagues, collaborators, friends, and family. She has prepared a summary that will be read at your celebration.

What do you hope will be said about you as you near the end of your leadership efforts? Individuals often refer to the memorable, mentionable summary as their "legacy," but they really don't consider legacy until toward the end of their role in a specific context. What if you started thinking about your legacy now? Better still, what if you used your vision of that 100th birthday summary as a roadmap and action plan for the present?

When you tell others you are learning leadership, their likely response is something like: So *how* can someone be an effective leader? This question probably prompted you to dig into this textbook and learn more. Great design, however, is guided by two more profound questions: why and for what? You can see that impact reflected in every design, including how organizations design their products or services. Simon Sinek refers to this distinction as the "golden circle"—three concentric circles like a target, with "why" as the bullseye and moving outward to "how" and "what." (see Figure 4.1)[1] Sinek explains that a strong purpose connects with others and is more profoundly influential than explaining how one does something or what one does. He further asserts that those organizations that have established and communicated a clear, strong purpose (their why) are more appealing to customers. Likewise, leaders with a clear *why* behind their actions find greater follower engagement.

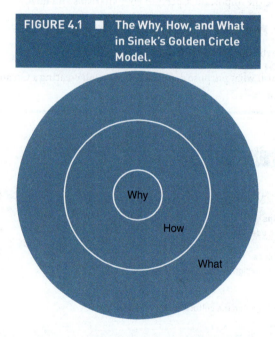

FIGURE 4.1 ■ The Why, How, and What in Sinek's Golden Circle Model.

The most significant aspect of designing your leadership and finding your best fit requires a much deeper, personal exploration—the reflective work to find your internal "why" and your external "for what." Together, your what and why will form your purpose for leading, which will be critical as you transition from the internal work of designing your leadership self to the external engagement of designing relationships, others, culture, and the future. This chapter will first guide you through key considerations intended to prompt your answer: Why do you want to serve as a leader? You will then consider the possible world or context in which you might bring your purpose to life—the needs that will drive your efforts to make a difference. Finally, you will combine both why and what to craft a Greater Purpose Statement—your GPS, a purposeful metaphor for guiding you to what you ultimately wish for on that 100th birthday.

Chapter 4 ● Your Why and What for Leading   123

Leadership That Makes a Difference

Eliane Ubalijoro: Confronting the Shadow

I was born in one of the most densely populated countries in Africa. My birthplace is also called the land of a thousand hills. From a young age, I felt deeply connected with the farmers who cultivated this land and decided to study agriculture to support their work. The issues of hunger, malnutrition and sustainable development have always attracted me. My plan was to study agriculture in Canada and return home after my studies to support subsistence farmers—those who cultivate enough to feed their families and have enough product to sell in markets.

What I didn't expect that summer of 1990 was to witness (from afar) the beginnings of a civil war at home. The following year, I spent part of my summer working in Rwanda with an international development agency studying grasses for feedstock and novel crop varieties that could increase local food production. My time at home also involved navigating a country at war, with checkpoints operated by armed military men. Special passes required me to travel from province to province to discuss research findings. I realized that summer that my peaceful dream of working with smallholder farmers in Rwanda would involve risks I had never imagined. My desire to serve the world in one way was confronted with the very real danger of working in a country at war.

While writing my thesis in 1994, close to a million people from my homeland were killed (in about 100 days). The 1994 Genocide Against the Tutsis challenged me in a way nothing else has. I was a 22-year-old living more than 7,000 miles away. I watched my country ignite with violence in the most visceral way. This was the first time I started thinking about the *power of purpose*—of leadership for evil or good, and how both involved telling stories that influenced and changed others in massive ways.

I wondered: If such evil could be accomplished with machetes in 100 days, what could *contagious good* do over a year? Or ten? or 100? However, I was trained as a scientist, not a manager or leader. I was an African female scientist leading a team of molecular genetics and bioinformaticians in Canada doing work that could support food safety and bioterrorism monitoring across the globe.

Nobody looked like me . . . at my level or among the senior ranks. I often felt isolated and wanted to feel a sense of belonging. I loved the work but was challenged by the relational part of leading a team—negotiating boundaries and expectations of my team with those of the chief executive officer (CEO) and the board.

I know that to be a force for good, we need to understand evil. We need to explore our individual and collective shadows among the forces that have defined and shaped who we are consciously and unconsciously.

I see my work as an opportunity to improve those things that break my heart open: global hunger, racism, genocide, climate crisis, and biodiversity loss. I do all I can to learn how exploitative paradigms can be shifted to regenerative ones. Paul Hawken defines regeneration as a *"means [of] restoring our relationship to the planet by restoring our relationships with one another."*[2] I see leadership as doing all we can to contribute to this healing.

AP Photo/Muhizi Olivier

WHY DO YOU WANT TO LEAD?

LEARNING OBJECTIVE

4.1 Discuss the importance of *why* in designing your leadership.

Why do you want to lead? The answer to that question may bind together both your internal reasons (your why) and your external pursuits to impact a specific world (your what). As noted in the introduction, together, these elements comprise what you might describe as your **purpose**. With any answer, you are likely following the intrinsic path that has become the mindset of life success: Do-Have-Be. For example, generally

1. DO: Work hard as diligently as possible
2. HAVE: If you work hard, you will have lots of money or things you want
3. BE: If you work hard, you will have what you want, and then you will BE happy

Many people approach life this way, work hard for many years and perhaps have some success but do not feel happy. It is a delayed life plan. It implies that you fulfill all kinds of criteria to get the payoff—being happy. But, in the authors' experience working with leaders from around the world, a better version of this formula starts with BEING. If you are using your gifts and strengths in the best possible ways, showing up authentically at your best, then the world rewards you with opportunities to "DO" more and "HAVE" various rewards and recognition. Entrepreneurs, as you will read in Chapter 15, use effectual thinking to start with HAVE. In other contexts, such as community engagement, leaders often start with BE. All these processes

Chapter 4 ● Your Why and What for Leading   125

address *how* to achieve a specific end. The missing answer addresses *why*: Why do you want to BE a certain way? In the words of Mark Twain, *"The two most important days in your life are the day you are born and the day you find out why."*[3]

Do you feel you have a strong sense of purpose, or are you just "going along" from need to need, challenge to challenge, position to position? As noted earlier, many people are promoted to leadership positions because they do great work in their field or domain and need to learn a new set of skills and ideas, namely leadership and management. But there is perhaps a more salient consequence. Once promoted, individuals may start to feel removed from the aspects of their work that gave them a sense of meaning and purpose. Based on the authors' work with hundreds of leaders, many feel far away from the "front lines" or the "real work." They often feel "cut off" or "adrift" and lacking connection with the fundamental work of the organization.

At the same time, some leaders make the transition more successfully by reflecting on and realizing that they can have a much broader impact by using their deep understanding of the work to support greater effectiveness across the organization. They are still deeply committed to the mission of the organization, but they also understand they are serving the organization and its mission in a different way. They draw a clear connection between their role and the purpose and impact of the organization—even if it is no longer at the "front lines."

Purpose can be considered at multiple levels of analysis. A sense of purpose is an important driver of human motivation and inspires excellence in all domains and all types of endeavors— from profit, nonprofit, and government sectors through to science, religion, and service to all of society's haves and have-nots.[4] At the organizational level, purpose often drives activity, albeit implicitly within descriptions of mission, vision, and objectives.[5] A strongly felt sense of purpose is also linked to the experiences of happiness and contentment. American social scientist and Harvard professor Arthur C. Brooks argues that finding purpose or meaning in life is required for you to be a happy person.[6] Happiness, he explains, is like a meal with three macronutrients— protein, carbohydrates, and fat. The three macronutrients of happiness he identifies are enjoyment, satisfaction, and purpose.

Finding Purpose in Challenge

But how do you really "know" or discover what your purpose is? Many struggle with this question, while others just seem to step into their purpose with grace and ease. For those who struggle, there is an important clue in the podcast conversation Brooks has with physician and professor B. J. Miller. Through his life experiences and his research, Miller has discovered an interesting paradox: When people are asked what helped them understand their life's purpose, they talk about *periods of unhappiness.* According to several "happiness" scholars,[7] to be happy, you need purpose. And to find purpose, you need unhappiness. You need some pain. You need some sacrifice.

This insight is similar to that of psychiatrist and holocaust survivor Viktor Frankl. In his profoundly wise book, *Man's Search for Meaning*[8] he describes the horrific conditions of the concentration camps where he was held captive. In reflecting on his experiences under these horrific conditions, he developed the extraordinary insight that those who fiercely focused on their deeply felt sense of purpose and meaning were more likely to survive. In his words, "everything can be taken from a man but one thing: the last of the human freedoms—to choose one's attitude in any given set of circumstances."[9]

What experiences have informed your sense of purpose? Perhaps some of them were difficult or even painful. How did those challenging experiences also ignite a passion for change, leadership, or for engagement in a particular vocation?

Finding Purpose in Personal Meaning

What do you currently do that you find satisfying and meaningful? Why is this so meaningful for you? Simon Sinek suggests in his widely popular TED talk, *How Great Leaders Inspire Action*, and book *Start with Why*, if you explore what is most meaningful to you, you can pinpoint your *why*—the purpose, cause, or belief that is foundational to you. As noted in the Introduction, your *why* deeply informs your *what* (the work you engage in) and your *how* (the way you go about it).[10]

The following sections guide you through perspectives and questions designed to help you articulate your unique "why" and, ultimately, your purpose. It is likely that your "why" and purpose will shift, evolve, or change dramatically over the years. That iterative engagement is both natural and desirable in the process of designing your leadership. Most important is that you continually situate and ground yourself and your work in these questions. Pay close attention to your answers. There is important data for you (and perhaps the world) in your answers.

Leadership by Design

Design Principle: Affordance

Definition: The perceived and actual properties of a thing, particularly the properties that determine how something can be used.[11]

In Other Words: The physical actions you can do with an object (throw it, eat it, write on it) are its affordances.

For Example: If you have ever pulled the door handle of a door that needed to be pushed (and wondered why someone put a pull handle on a push door!), you have experienced a poor application of affordance. The physical shape of a pull handle affords pulling, not pushing. Poor design often feels awkward.

For Leaders: What is your intended function as a leader? In the words of this text: What is your best fit? Your purpose should guide your answer. Do you have the affordances (e.g., knowledge, skills, dispositions, capacity, will) to function as you intend? As necessary, do others perceive those affordances in you? For example, if you intend to help followers recognize their strengths, you need to purposefully highlight them, intentionally focus on them, strategically utilize them, and so forth. When the affordance of an object or environment (or leader) corresponds to its envisioned role, the design is more efficient and effective. Some might even call this a sweet spot or a purpose that deserves you. Followers' perceptions of you as a leader should match your intent, leadership style, and capabilities. Design things the way you want people to use them, which means designing your leadership the way you want others to see and utilize your capabilities.

DEI BY DESIGN—RECOGNIZING WHO YOU ARE

LEARNING OBJECTIVE

4.2 Examine how socialization and identity inform purpose.

As you start to think about your reasons for leading—your purpose comprised of why and what—understanding yourself once again plays a key role. Your experiences relating to others socializes you to those purposes you deem of value. Socialization is described as systematic training about how to live according to your configuration of social identities, and this process is often described as a *cycle of socialization* (see Figure 4.2).[12] The cycle of socialization is just one way of detailing how socialization happens, where it comes from, how it impacts your life, and how it continues from generation to generation. The parts of this cycle are omnipresent, patterned, coordinated, predictable, self-sufficient, self-perpetuating, and often invisible.[13] Despite their ubiquitous nature, the socialization cycle is also extremely effective in keeping you unaware of how you are influenced; subtly driving you toward specific and often unequal roles in society.[14]

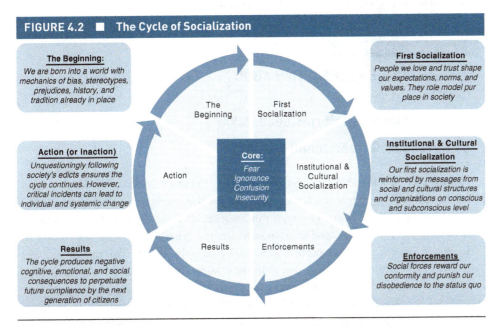

FIGURE 4.2 ■ The Cycle of Socialization

The Beginning: We are born into a world with mechanics of bias, stereotypes, prejudices, history, and tradition already in place

First Socialization: People we love and trust shape our expectations, norms, and values. They role model our place in society

Institutional & Cultural Socialization: Our first socialization is reinforced by messages from social and cultural structures and organizations on conscious and subconscious level

Enforcements: Social forces reward our conformity and punish our disobedience to the status quo

Results: The cycle produces negative cognitive, emotional, and social consequences to perpetuate future compliance by the next generation of citizens

Action (or Inaction): Unquestioningly following society's edicts ensures the cycle continues. However, critical incidents can lead to individual and systemic change

Core: Fear, Ignorance, Confusion, Insecurity

Source: adapted by V. Chunoo based on the model by Harro, B. (2000a). The cycle of socialization.

At the beginning of the cycle, you are born into a world where the mechanics of inequity are already in place. Your first socialization occurs when you come into contact with the adults responsible for raising you and bestow upon you the assumptions they carry with them. As your social life extends beyond your family of origin, the messages you receive are initially reinforced by social structures and aided by your natural psychological inclination to believe information supporting your preexisting ideas and rejecting evidence that refutes our prior notions—that is, your confirmation bias, which is explained more fully in Chapter 6 as a decision-making trap. These conformity pressures increase based on which and how many social structures you encounter. If you belong to social groups that benefit from the socialization process, you are less likely to notice it is there at all. However, when you retain membership in groups that are marginalized or oppressed by society's rules, socialization pressures become harder to ignore. The longer you unquestioningly stay in the cycle, the more likely you are to identify with it (i.e., "that's just the way it is"), perpetuate it yourself, and become a person who embodies its core of ignorance, insecurity, confusion, obliviousness, and fear.[15, 16]

Fortunately, you are not doomed to such a tragic fate! At any point in the cycle, you can encounter *critical incidents* or experiences that force you to confront these systems and strive toward change. Your response to such an incident determines what happens next: If you do not resist the influences of the socialization cycle, you become part of the force that keeps it going. However, when you do something other than what the cycle would have you do, you can avoid the consequences of compliance and begin a new way of being—the *cycle of liberation*.[17] When you choose to ignore potential critical incidents, implicitly or explicitly, you volunteer to perpetuate the socialization cycle. However, by reaching out to others, building community, seeking opportunities for change, and dedicating your leadership to transforming institutions, surrounding communities, and society-at-large, you cultivate the values at the liberation cycle's core: compassion, self-esteem, self-efficacy, balance, empathy, and joy. Examining and possibly unlearning socialization is not simple; it involves deep reflection, emotional management, relationship changes, frustration, shock, and brave vulnerability. Keep in mind these underlying, systemic influences as you endeavor to make a difference.

Experts Beyond the Text

INSIGHTFUL LEADERS KNOW ABOUT . . . LEADERSHIP AND IDENTITY

Who? How Identity Informs Leadership

By Nyasha M. Guramatunhu Cooper

Many books on leadership focus on the question, "What do leaders do?" This question is intended to help readers and learners identify the characteristics and behaviors of leaders within different contexts. However, this question offers only a partial understanding. Before one can fully understand the characteristics and behaviors of leadership, there is an accompanying and equally important question, "Who is the leader?" This question focuses on the experiences and identities that shape how leaders move about the world and their understanding of self and others.[18]

From childhood to adulthood, each leader (and follower) has had particular experiences shaping what and how they think about leadership and, ultimately, how they practice it. These mental models[19] or worldviews are shaped by one's cultural and social contexts where values, rituals, beliefs, symbols, notions of time and space, and relationships influence perspectives on leaders and leadership. An excellent way to visualize this influence is to think of a jar of room temperature water and a bowl of boiling water. If one were to put the jar of room temperature water into the bowl of boiling water, the temperature of the water in the jar would change and become warmer. This demonstrates how leaders are shaped by internal and external forces in their lives. One's identity (the question of who?) is informed by their positionality[20]—the influence of people, places, things, and events. Additionally, experiences related to race, religion, gender, sexual orientation, class, ethnicity, citizenship, language, and global location influence how leaders think and act.

Paying attention to the identities of leaders pushes leadership learners and practitioners to think deeply about how the world shapes leaders and how they shape the world.[21] There are opportunities and challenges in unveiling one's identity as a leader and unveiling the *who* can lead to creating deep connections with others based on shared lived experiences. In this case, a leader's identity can help create a leadership relationship based on establishing a sense of community. In other instances, unveiling the *who* to an unwelcoming organization, community, or institution can create tension when a leader is not seen as a "good fit" because of their identity. In this case, prejudices, resistance to diversity, and lack of social power demonstrate how the world can shape a leader's lived experience.

It is crucial to understand the relationship between who leaders are (identity) and what they do (behaviors and competencies). An insightful leader will commit to deep reflection of their own identity, be aware of how others are influenced by their own identities, and pay close attention to how they are shared. Different lived experiences influence the context in which the leadership relationship is enacted.[22] The activity that follows can help you begin that reflective journey. Without understanding the *who*, leaders risk missing incredible insights from others' experiences and enhancing their leadership practice.

Positionality and Identity Activity[23]

1. First, consider each identity element for yourself. How do you describe yourself within that category?
2. Then, think about how others view that identity, especially those who do not share that identity, and how the society in which you live and work views that identity?

Finally, consider what aspects of your identity strengthen or complicate your ability to connect with others. Choose at least three (3) identity elements that you feel are most impactful for your ability to connect. Note more details about these three elements, including what this might imply for effective leadership.

Identity Element	How I See Me	How Others See This Identity	How It Strengthens My Ability to Connect With Others	How It Complicates My Ability to Connect With Others
Gender				
Ethnicity				
Nationality/Citizenship				
Religion				
Class				
Sexual orientation				
Physical ability				
Age				
Education				
Race				
Geographic location				

Keep the notes from this activity, as they will be an essential input into articulating your leadership purpose statement. The following few segments will take you through the steps toward articulating your unique statement.

130   Module 1 ● Design Leadership Self

YOUR PURPOSE: CHARISMS AND FLOW

LEARNING OBJECTIVE
4.3   Recognize the important aspects of your charisms and flow.

Individuals spend considerable time striving to achieve their goals and ambitions, focused on the challenges at hand and the next rung on the ladder of success. But identifying your why and what requires a purposeful pause to examine and recognize your attributes. How do those seemingly natural gifts play a significant role in defining a powerful feeling of being "on purpose." If you can identify what you are truly good at and what you love to do, you can align these gifts with your goals and ambitions in a meaningful way.

Your best fit as a leader comprises the most favorable alignment of personal attributes with contextual variables to achieve the best outcome. Depending on the context or particular challenge, it may be an ideal location, level, area, or combination of factors. What are some of the best-fit activities right now in your life? Where do you feel like you are doing your best work? Where the work feels natural, easy, and fulfilling? When you reflect on these best fits (and the not-so-best fits) in life, you can get some important clues about your most fundamental gifts and how those are critical ingredients in defining your purpose in the truest sense. The following two sections highlight the following prompting questions. Take an initial look at them now:

1. What strengths, skills, or activities do you feel naturally good at and enjoy doing?

2. What could you spend hours doing and still feel energized?

3. What are the rewards (to you) for applying those strengths and/or engaging in those activities?

4. How might you bring more of your natural attributes into your daily work or learning activities?

Identify Your Charisms

Consider the following two scenarios:

1. Have you ever gone to work, worked hard all day, and came home tired but energized?

What were you doing on those days?

2. By contrast, have you ever gone to work, worked hard all day, and come home exhausted and depleted? What were you doing on those days?

One explanation for your different feelings is that on the days you got home energized, it was because, accidentally or deliberately, what you were doing all day was squarely in the zone of your most profound, most natural gifts and strengths. John J. Scherer calls these your "**charisms**."[24] Rooted in the word charisma, your charisms are those skills or activities you love to do that feel like natural abilities. As Scherer points out, when your charisms are in play, you get to exercise your fundamental strengths and gifts every day, and you are being paid for that; you no longer feel like you have a "job," you have found your "purpose."[25]

Chapter 4 ● Your Why and What for Leading   131

When you actively use your strengths and gifts, you feel like you are in the "zone." Your efforts come from what feels like your most natural areas of competence and simultaneously contribute to serving others and a larger mission in life. As for the days you went home exhausted, you were likely not nurturing your passions and gifts during the day and/or not contributing to others and/or not aligning with the mission/organizational needs.

What are your unique "charisms"? Think about your natural abilities—skills you enjoy using and things you enjoy doing; you feel good, love doing it, you can't get enough of it. Something that must be expressed—otherwise, you feel incomplete, unhappy, bored, or you feel the tension. Take a few notes and then invite a friend or someone that knows you very well and share your reflections. Do they recognize the gifts you have noted? Perhaps you've left out a few because they seemed too obvious? What else can you add to your list?

Finding Your Flow

Can you recall periods of hours or even days when time went by quickly in a flow that brought you joy and tapped into your strengths and talents? For example, when you have gotten involved in a hobby or sport or some activity where all sense of time seemed to fade away. When you are engaged in such a pursuit, you are *fully* engaged. This is a state of mind that has been called flow. Psychologist Mihaly Csikszentmihalyi introduced the idea of flow as an experience and state of total engagement.[26] Across various domains and activities, especially in creative work,[27] the flow state has been associated with numerous benefits.[28]

Some exciting things happen when you find your best fit. You have found your flow. Flow emerges from the alignment of your interests or passions (how much you value the activity), your natural charisms (your skills), and the work to be done (the task demands).[29] Sometimes, the connection is obvious, such as the person who has always loved solving mechanical problems and ends up as a mechanic or an electrical engineer. It may be less obvious, but there can also be a clear link between the person who has always loved solving various puzzles and her career as a successful molecular geneticist. When that same person realizes how much she loves bringing together teams to work on complex puzzles or problems in that branch of science and leads multiple teams, all working on complex issues, leadership happens. Take a few minutes to return to the questions posed earlier and add your thoughts to Table 4.1.

TABLE 4.1 ■ Charisms and Flow Questions	
Charisms and Flow Questions	**Your Answer**
1. What are the strengths, skills, or activities you feel naturally good at and you enjoy doing?	
2. What could you spend hours doing and still feel energized?	
3. What are the rewards (to you) for applying those strengths and/or engaging in those activities?	
4. How might you bring more of your natural attributes into your daily work or learning activities?	

Sum it up. What feels like a key characteristic of a best fit for you?

From Being to Doing: TJ Watt

TJ Watt is a professional photographer living in the city of Victoria on Vancouver Island, British Columbia, in Canada. He is cofounder of the Ancient Forest Alliance, which works to protect old-growth forests in British Columbia by raising awareness through a variety of activities. For TJ, his charism of capturing images that communicate strong messages and inspire others to act comprises a key element for the organization. You might look at TJ's success and think that he found his purpose. Indeed, he has, but that took years of engaging his charism of photography in contexts he found deeply interesting. Born and raised in the rural town of Metchosin, TJ carries a strong passion for exploring the outdoors, the environment, and life itself. TJ combines his charisms of gifted photography, personable nature, and physical endurance with the flow he finds when exploring wild areas: "My work focuses mainly on the threats to British Columbia's endangered old-growth forests, and oftentimes, I am taking photos where less than a handful of people have been—if any at all."[30]

Photo courtesy of TJ Watt

Now 36 years old, TJ has found many ways to combine his love of nature, his passion for the environment, and his gifts as a photographer. This combination has brought him significant opportunities to demonstrate leadership in the environmental conservation movement. He notes, "At the end of the day, I need to know that I did everything I could to make a difference."[31] A key step toward articulating your leadership purpose is to notice how you feel when you are using your charisms and when you are not.

Looking at TJ Watt's story, you can see that his upbringing in a nature-focused family formed his interests and inclinations. He continued to explore the outdoors and found that he had a natural gift as a nature photographer. Then, a series of his photographs published on social media sparked excitement and passion from environmentalists worldwide. This led to the realization that he could combine his passion for nature, his charism for photography, and his deeply felt concern for environmental protection. As TJ explains: "Well, it seems to have evolved naturally in that direction over the past few years. It's basically a melding of my interest in landscape photography with my strong passion for conservation work and exploring the wilderness of BC. Instead of just taking pretty pictures, I started to see it would be much more valuable if they served a higher purpose at the same time."[32] His "purpose" coalesced into his work with the Ancient Forest Alliance.

Take another look at TJ Watt's story using the questions about charisms and flow (Table 4.2).

TABLE 4.2 ■ TJ Watt: Charisms and Flow

Charisms and Flow Questions	TJ Watt's Answer
1. What are the strengths, skills, or activities you feel naturally good at and you enjoy doing?	Outdoor exploration and photography
2. What could you spend hours doing and still feel energized?	Raising awareness of the destruction of old-growth forests through photography
3. What are the rewards (to you) for applying those strengths and/or engaging in those activities?	Worldwide recognition of old-growth forest destruction photographs. Increasing donations to advocacy for the preservation of nature and old-growth forests
4. How might you bring more of your natural attributes into your daily work or learning activities?	What do you think TJ Watt would say about how he could further develop to realize his potential?

Chapter 4 • Your Why and What for Leading   133

LEARNING FROM SHADOWS

LEARNING OBJECTIVE
4.4   Translate your shadow experiences into leadership lessons for purpose.

Although staying in the zone of your charisms and where you find flow is delightful and satisfying, the world usually throws many curveballs that challenge you to go beyond these comfortable ways of being. Those challenges are more navigable when you have experiences from which you drew important lessons for yourself. In a leadership setting, these experiences may have looked like those "crucible" moments described in Chapter 2, where the heat of the difficulty transformed you. Generally in life, difficult experiences are left behind and seen as something to move past. But these are **shadow experiences**—difficult experiences that influence how and what you perceive in the world, specifically the emotions and energies that inform your behavior in similar situations. Shadow experiences can illuminate, however, and bring new insights to your leadership.

Understanding the Shadow: Hardship and Tough Life Lessons Can Bring Clarity to Purpose

Everyone has a past. Your early life experiences have significantly influenced who you are today. Sometimes, those experiences are positive, and sometimes they are not. Parents that were too harsh might have left you with a constant feeling of not being good enough. A physical disability or mental health challenge may have caused you to struggle to keep up with what others seemed to do effortlessly. Your gender identity and your cultural or religious backgrounds can be sources of deeply felt joy, and they can be sources of painful questioning and struggle. Everyone has significant shadow experiences that shape who they are and how they see the world. These experiences sometimes hold you back and may trigger strong positive and negative reactions. You might find it hard to imagine that reflecting on your shadow experiences can uncover some hidden energy sources and positively contribute to a sense of purpose. Surprisingly, this type of exploration may be the richest inspiration of all. How might you tap into the positive energy that dwells in some of your shadow experiences?

Reconsider Professor Miller's insight described earlier in the chapter (about understanding life's purpose by examining periods of unhappiness). Sometimes experiencing challenging times helps you become more explicit about what is truly important to you. Miller speaks about a nearly fatal accident that left him with permanent disabilities. The way the health care system treated him following the accident sparked his enduring interest and more significant purpose—passionately learning about and communicating what people near death want and need.[33] His experience sparked his passion for bringing greater attention and creativity to the experience of dying. His intense shadow experience inspired him to focus his strengths and talents on this opportunity to help improve an already challenging process.

In a slightly different domain, beloved educator, author, and activist Parker J. Palmer writes and lectures on community, social change, education, leadership, and spirituality. He has also spent much time reflecting on purpose and the link to vocation. Your vocation is more than a job; instead, it is like a *calling* to a career or profession. Individuals who have found their vocation feel the work is of great importance, worthy of their dedication and talents.

In his book "Let Your Life Speak" (2000), he describes his multi-year quest to find what he wanted to do in life. Despite various successes, he did not feel like he was aligned with his greater purpose. Ultimately, he got there by reflecting on personal tendencies that created roadblocks and setbacks. The most significant shadow was his long battle with severe depression.[34] This profound shadow experience ultimately opened up his awareness of his fundamental purpose and what brings him joy.

MOMENT OF AWARENESS

In reflecting on his own "further journey," Parker Palmer writes:

[There are] moments when it is clear—if I have the eyes to see—that the life I am living is not the same as the life that wants to live in me. In those moments, I sometimes catch a glimpse of my true life, a life hidden like the river beneath the ice. And . . . I wonder: What am I meant to do? Who am I meant to be?[35]

Palmer's work affirms that everyone's vocation[36] will be different and that the goal is not to copy or compare yourself to someone else's journey. He asks: *"Is the life I am living the same as the life that wants to live in me?"*

As Parker Palmer suggests, all too often, individuals are living their lives on automatic, bringing their most significant gifts to a type of work or service that doesn't feel rewarding. It is hard to accept that a career you have worked hard to succeed at isn't serving your deeper purpose and is possibly not having the impact that the world needs from you.

Dan Millman (2015) suggests that a critical step to finding purpose is to deeply consider the lessons life has given you. Millman sees the universe as "a perfect school, and daily life is the classroom."[37] Everyone can grow through challenging life experiences. The curriculum in daily life includes subjects on self-worth, discipline, well-being, money, mind, intuition, emotions, courage, knowledge, sexuality, love, and service. This curriculum can tutor you in wisdom and meaning if you listen.

Exploring the Shadow to Find the Stretch

"When jarred by life, we might unravel the story we tell ourselves and discover the story we are in, the one that keeps telling us."

—*Mark Nepo*[38]

It takes courage to examine the shadows that have formed you and that may have caused harm to you. But opening them up to reflection can lead to some freeing insights. An excellent example of someone who discovered how his dark childhood experiences could combine with his gift of spoken word and then connect to what the world needs are the work of poet Shane Koyczan. In his 2013 TED performance of[39] *To This Day*, he powerfully articulates how his early life experiences ignited an essential element of his purpose: to use his spoken word poetry to campaign against bullying.

As part of a leadership development intensive program, Dr. Ingrid Richter recounts her childhood experiences as the child of parents who had post-traumatic stress disorder (PTSD) from their experiences in World War II. Growing up with emotionally volatile family dynamics profoundly shaped her as a person and ultimately as a leader. She spent many years working

Chapter 4 ● Your Why and What for Leading   135

in the fields of corrections and policing, only to realize that these weren't corresponding to her unique strengths and gifts. She needed to delve deeper into her shadow to discover her passion for understanding how people and organizations can work together to create positive social change.

The critical insight for developing leaders is that although there are many ways the world influences you. Certain situations, experiences, stories, or events suddenly hurt you, stop you, or consistently grab your attention. Endeavor to see them as fascinating and insightful. They ask you to uncover some deeper insights hidden underneath or beyond the pain. Taken apart gently, you can identify and value the gifts of dark times and use them to help others.

Take a second look at the story of Eliane that opened this chapter. In addition to being a leader that makes a difference, hers is also a story of discovering greater purpose through combining gifts with harsh experiences. As Eliane moved into leadership positions, the present challenges summoned her shadows. In her words:

> I needed to harness skills that had not been nurtured in my academic curriculum. I immersed myself in learning how to lead myself and others. As my career grew, I worked with a coach to understand who I was as an individual, in relationship with all the groups I interacted with, and what projections I held from society. All of this has focused my journey on befriending my own shadow to present myself with as much humility as possible to face group and societal shadows. As someone deeply committed to contributing to collective healing, I knew the journey could only start by healing my wounds, the ones that were easy to see, that were historical, but also the ones that came from microaggressions over a lifetime of being Black, female, and later on a scientist. I came to understand that how we see ourselves is linked deeply to our capacity to hold space for our shadow to teach us what fears hold us back, how failure can be perceived as shaming or curiosity as lessons on our journey of emerging into a whole, more authentic self. I deeply value these words Barack Obama shared in his eulogy for John Lewis: "What gives each new generation purpose is to take up the unfinished work of the last and carry it further than anyone might have thought possible."[40]

REFLECTION QUESTIONS

1. What are your personal shadows? What can they teach you? Watch this video by Dr. Steve Mortenson with a friend. Discuss examples of your "shadows." https://strengthshadows.wordpress.com/

2. What have my "shadow" experiences taught me? What behaviors or habits do I need to learn or "stretch into" to become more effective? Where do I need to develop further to realize my potential?

3. Is your growth driven mainly through pain (kensho) or by moments of sudden positive realizations (Satori/ah-ha!)? Read about the concepts of kensho and Satori (for example, here: https://www.khaleejtimes.com/wellness/what-are-your-kensho-and-satori-moments)

THE PROCESS OF INFLUENCING OTHERS . . . FOR WHAT?

LEARNING OBJECTIVE

4.5   Appraise the range of worlds that might need your leadership.

Why should *you* lead? No doubt you can think of many general reasons, like making a positive difference, advancing an organization, or facilitating the success of others. These are all excellent reasons, but they are not specific enough to inspire you. Your challenge is to find the purpose that best fits your interests, strengths, and motivation. There are many to choose from, and this section profiles some options to consider.

Nobel Peace Prize winner Wangari Maathai would have celebrated her 83rd birthday on April 1st, 2023. In her December 10, 2004, Nobel lecture, she said:

> *"We are faced with a challenge that calls for a shift in our thinking so that humanity stops threatening its life-support system. We are called to assist the Earth to heal her wounds and, in the process, heal our own—indeed, to embrace the whole creation in all its diversity, beauty, and wonder. This will happen if we see the need to revive our sense of belonging to a larger family of life with which we have shared our evolutionary process. In the course of history, there comes a time when humanity is called to shift to a new level of consciousness, to reach a higher moral ground. A time when we have to shed our fear and give hope to each other. That time is now." (© The Nobel Foundation 2004)*[41]

Do the activities described by Wangari Maathai appeal to you? Will your leadership serve to heal the planet, pursue diversity, better appreciate beauty, or catalyze wonder for others? Embedded within this brief quote are a dozen different ends that you might adopt as your "what"—the context and focus of your leadership activities.

In designing your leadership self, you focus on your awareness as a developing leader; what you value, how you learn, where you practice, and how to prepare for the challenges. Finding your leadership activity's target requires you to transition your thinking from internal to external, from your development to the impact you seek on others. Recall that your leadership purpose integrates your internal why with your external what and will serve to energize others and align with what they value (moving toward a shared vision).

Interest-based success underlies why people are motivated to lead, according to researchers Chan and Drasgow.[42] They describe a construct called motivation to lead (MTL) as "a decision to assume leadership training, roles, and responsibilities, and that affects his or her intensity of effort at leading and persistence as a leader."[43] Their work has been expanded by others who found that leadership as an individual construct results in a cycle of finding a context of interest (or purpose), engaging and achieving because of that deep interest, and thus succeeding. Individuals find "environments that fit their interests and thus find themselves more often in leadership roles. Having more experience in such roles will give them an advantage, enhancing their chances of success. The more successful people are in their role as leaders, the more motivated they will be to take the lead in future career steps.[44,45]

The source of your MTL may be personal, such as happiness, money, power, legitimacy, legacy, success/fame; altruistic, such as a deep desire to help or serve; or something else entirely. But your fundamental motivation and approach to leadership will require identifying a context for those general, personal (and perhaps competing) objectives.

The context of your leadership may be inspired by your vision—a picture of the world you seek to create. More likely, the focus of your leadership activities will be driven by what the world needs. In this case, the "world" is defined by you. The world may comprise a field or industry, a specific interest group or organization, a company or community, or even the literal entire world. The needs of that world (i.e., the world you define and choose) provide a focus for your leadership and measure your impact.

Chapter 4 • Your Why and What for Leading   **137**

For example, look at the United Nations Sustainability Development Goals in Table 4.3. Note how each has implications at multiple levels: individual, interpersonal, group/community, and global. Which of these worlds is of great interest to you or might be a fit for your charisms? What goals might be of interest to you? At what level? Or perhaps they do not interest you at all. If so, what would it take for you to be excited about putting your energies here?

TABLE 4.3 ■ UN Sustainability Development Goals[46]

Goal 1—No Poverty—By 2030, eradicate extreme poverty for all people everywhere.

Goal 2—Zero Hunger—End hunger, achieve food security, and improved nutrition by 2030.

Goal 3—Good Health and Well-being—Ensure healthy lives and promote well-being for all at all ages by 2030.

Goal 4—Quality Education—Ensure that all girls and boys complete free, equitable, and quality primary and secondary education by 2030.

Goal 5—Gender Equality—To achieve gender equality and empower all women and girls.

Goal 6—Clean Water and Sanitation—Ensure availability and sustainable management of water and sanitation for all by 2030.

Goal 7—Affordable and Clean Energy—Ensure access to affordable, reliable, sustainable, and modern energy for all by 2030.

Goal 8—Decent Work and Economic Growth—Promote sustained, inclusive, and sustainable economic growth.

Goal 9—Industry, Innovation, and Infrastructure—Build resilient infrastructure, promote inclusive and sustainable industrialization, and foster innovation by 2030.

Goal 10—Reduced Inequality—Reduce inequality within and among countries by 2030.

Goal 11—Sustainable Cities and Communities—Make cities and human settlements inclusive, safe, resilient, and sustainable.

Goal 12—Responsible Consumption and Production—Ensure sustainable consumption and production patterns.

Goal 13—Climate Action—Take urgent action to combat climate change and its impacts.

Goal 14—Life Below Water—Conserve and sustainably use the oceans, seas, and marine resources for sustainable development.

Goal 15—Life on Land—Protect, restore, and promote sustainable use of terrestrial ecosystems, combat desertification, and halt biodiversity loss.

Goal 16—Peace and Justice Strong Institutions—Promote peaceful and inclusive societies for sustainable development; provide access to justice for all.

Goal 17—Partnerships to achieve the Goal—Strengthen the means of implementation and revitalize the global partnership for sustainable development.

Your world might focus more on helping others in a social context or a specific social group. There are undoubtedly many individual, group, and community social challenges to draw your purpose. It may be helpful to consider some of the more foundational individual needs and identify what needs may be the root of visible challenges. This has been done across many fields using Seligman's PERMA Model of Well-Being, which identifies five significant elements that foster and enable human flourishing: positive emotions, engagement, relationships, meaning, and accomplishment (PERMA).[47] A lifetime of impactful leadership could be focused on helping school-age children form meaningful relationships. Alternatively, your world could be defined by another metric of human happiness or success. For example, in his focus on racial awareness and interactions, Robert Livingston focuses on the consequences of having or lacking basic needs. Specifically, he notes that "human beings are looking for just a handful of essential things.

- Prosperity: having sufficient or surplus resources

- Belonging: being accepted and socially integrated into family and the community

- Happiness: experiencing joy and freedom
- Fulfillment: finding meaning and purpose
- Control: limiting danger and chaos."[48]

Would enhancing one of these basic needs for a specific group inspire you to choose this as your world?

What Does the World Need? Nisha Ligon

It is difficult to figure out where to focus your leadership or what world you want to impact. Sometimes you must look at the world's needs, but how do you discover that? Nisha Ligon's story illustrates how she went through several adventures before she landed on what seems to be an excellent alignment between her gifts and what the world is looking for.

Nisha Ligon is driven by her passion to bring equity in education for marginalized communities.
https://twitter.com/ElevatePrize/status/1493780934054735880

Ubongo is Africa's leading edutainment company and takes pride in creating fun, localized, and multi-platform educational media that reach millions of families through accessible technologies. Its programs significantly improve school readiness and learning outcomes and promote social and behavioral change for kids, caregivers, and educators. Nisha Ligon is the cofounder and former CEO of Ubongo. She is a Thai-American social entrepreneur with a background in media and science and a passion for education. When asked how she ended up in this field, she discusses combining her passions, talents, and interests to serve a higher purpose.

How did this evolve? In high school, Nisha began making short films and documentaries and studied biology and media production. She went to Tanzania for part of her studies. That

Chapter 4 ● Your Why and What for Leading   139

experience triggered a desire to bring her three most vital gifts together: her love of science, film, and animation and her ambition to scale up social innovation to address the plight of young African students across the continent. In a recent interview, she explained, "When I studied at University in Dar es Salaam, I became interested in education. It became clear that even the brightest students in the country didn't have the same opportunities or access to learning that I knew. I started to see education as a multiplier: you can create generational change when you give people an education foundation."[49]

Her advice to others? "Ask yourself whether the problem you seek to solve is so important to you that you're willing to focus the next decade of your life on it. If the answer is yes, you're ready, and you've got what it takes Jump right in, and don't look back!"[50]

Like TJ Watt's story, Nisha reflects the convergence between her gifts, her interests, and her awakening to what the world seemed to want from her. Consider the charism and flow questions from earlier, but this time note how identifying a world transforms charisms and passion into purpose (Table 4.4):

TABLE 4.4 ■ Nisha Ligon: Charisms and Flow	
Charisms and Flow Questions	**Nisha's Answer**
1. What are the strengths, skills, or activities you feel naturally good at and you enjoy doing?	Telling stories, creating films
2. What could you spend hours doing and still feel energized?	Using film and technology to help kids learn, especially science, biology, and other topics they might not have access to
3. What are the rewards (to you) for applying those strengths and/or engaging in those activities?	Significant recognition from previous jobs in science journalism.
4. How might you bring more of your natural attributes into your daily work or learning activities?	Creating a media company that focuses on high-quality media-based learning programs for children to access regardless of their social or economic status

Leadership by Design

Design Principle: Performance Load

Definition: The greater the effort to accomplish a task, the less likely the task will be completed successfully.[51]

In Other Words: Tasks that take too much physical or mental effort will simply not get done.

For Example: Having to decipher messy handwriting increases the performance load of a reader (see Photo 4.4).

For Leaders: Consider the performance load of your current tasks—collectively and individually. Identifying your world and purpose means focusing on what you want to accomplish (and the required performance load). How and where could you simplify? Where would the path of least resistance lead? Leaders can help themselves (and others) by reducing unnecessary steps, energy expended, repetitive tasks, and activities unrelated to their purpose. Reducing the effort to complete a task does not necessarily make it less meaningful or impactful for purpose-focused work. Instead, it may allow for greater depth, quality, or follow-through. Tasks with a significant performance load are likely to be avoided or abandoned; divide tasks into more workable loads, so you don't miss out on critical engagement. Consider the performance load to better design your leadership success.

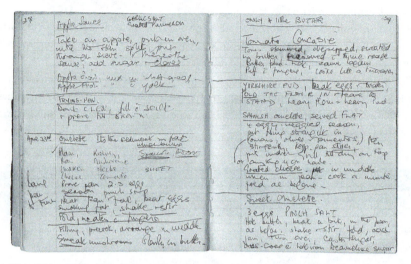

Photo 4.4 Increasing the Performance Load of the Reader
Source: ©iStock.com/whitemay

WHAT PURPOSE DESERVES YOU?

LEARNING OBJECTIVE

4.6 Distinguish what purpose deserves you through creating a Greater Purpose Statement.

What purpose deserves you? While you may be grateful to have a job or be accepted by a group, that gratitude is reciprocal—your time and talents are worth a great deal. TJ and Nisha centered their purpose on tasks at which they excelled . . . but were not necessarily great . . . at first. Every stretch comes with a learning curve, so do not judge your fit based on initial results. In his talk entitled *The Role of Deep Purpose Making in Human Flourishing*, Professor Aneel Chima[52] poses the following questions to help you identify what the world might be calling you to do:

1. What would you do if you knew you couldn't fail?

2. What contribution do you want to make to your organization/society?

3. What do you see that's exciting "out there?" (Who and what organizations are making a difference in worlds that interest you? For example, check out Young United Nations Leaders: https://www.un.org/youthenvoy/.

4. What makes you SO MAD that you would do anything to change it?

Chima labels his first question "fearless engagement." When you think about what excites or interests you, to what extent is fear holding you back? Your honest assessment of what holds you back will allow you to move forward, even in hesitant short steps.

By identifying and integrating your gifts and your world of interest, you have begun to identify key elements of your **Greater Purpose Statement or "GPS."** Like the GPS function on a phone or a vehicle, a clearly framed personal GPS helps you navigate life experiences. Sometimes your GPS enables you to stay on track amid many projects that take you in too many directions and diffuse your efforts. More critically, your GPS, in tandem with your CORE™ capacities, helps you through difficulties that might otherwise leave you deeply discouraged, burned out, confused, or feeling you have lost your way. As you craft your GPS, remember to consider your shadow experiences: tough times that left you with key lessons and your vocation—what the world is calling you to do.

Every Purpose Impacts Individuals

"It made a difference for that one."

—Loren Eiseley

Forget about this notion of leadership for a moment. You find yourself with a group of individuals in a narrow canyon quickly filled with a raging river. With the temperature dropping and daylight fading, your group needs to find a way out or a way to contact help. You try to climb the canyon wall, but it is too steep. You try to hug the wall and work your way back upriver to where you started, but the current is too strong. You could ride the river to the canyon's end, but hidden roots and rocks are a constant drowning hazard, threatening to pin you under the rapids. The situation is not good, and success is now reduced to survival.

Now bring yourself back to leadership, specifically as the leader of this canyon hike. Your group may be a team with a common vision, but it is still comprised of individuals. Who can and cannot swim? Who appears calm during this crisis, and who needs particular assistance. Who planned well for the trip, and who did not? Your purpose may be to inspire young adults through guided wilderness hikes, but that purpose and the activities that make it happen require individual consideration. Individual consideration is one of the critical elements of transformational leadership (which you will read about more fully in Chapter 10). This is the point where your why and your what meet back up with your how, within a particular world, effectively executed. What could you do to design each participant's success?

At the start of this section, the poet Loren Eiseley's quote refers to an often-told story about a boy picking up starfish off the beach and throwing them back into the ocean so they did not die in the sun.[53] A passing man told the boy that there were miles of beach and endless starfish and that the boy could not possibly make a difference. The boy picked up another starfish and threw it back into the sea, stating, "It made a difference for that one." Likewise, leaders often view their purpose as needing to impact millions, which can feel overwhelming—endless individuals and their needs and challenges. But as the story illustrates, your actions as a leader to facilitate individual success will make a difference for every person you work with. Ultimately, they will make you a more credible and effective leader.

Activate Your Purpose

Finding one's purpose is often equated to finding value in life, and individuals have been seeking their purpose for thousands of years. Finding your leadership purpose (and life purpose) is

142   Module 1 ● Design Leadership Self

a multi-faceted, dynamic process that requires considerable reflection, decision-making, commitment, and an explorative mindset that looks both internally and externally. A very common model for prompting your search for purpose is often shown as an overlapping integration of what you are good at, what you love, what the world needs, and what you can be paid for.

Take a quick moment to consider the intersection of these four answers:

1. What are you good at?

2. What do you love to do?

3. What does the world need?

4. What can you do that others value (or will pay you for)?

Then, add one additional question that will inform your initial steps toward your future: What knowledge, skills, and relationships do you need to develop further to realize your potential?

Now is the time to bring this all together. Table 4.5 intertwines the questions from this chapter with those posed in the last section. Work your way through the questions and take some quick notes. Then, consult with a close friend or family member to get additional insight. Finally, refine your thoughts and create the first draft of your Greater Purpose Statement. You can (and will) revise it over time. But if you never put a draft out there, you will have nothing to work from. As is often noted in leadership and life, do not let perfect be the enemy of good.

TABLE 4.5 ■ Putting It All Together to Create Your Greater Purpose Statement	
Greater Purpose Statement Prompts	**Your Answer**
What are you good at?	
1. What are the strengths, skills, or activities you feel naturally good at and you enjoy doing?	
What do you love to do?	
2. What could you spend hours doing and still feel energized?	
What can you provide that others value (and how so)?	
3. What are the rewards (to you) for applying those strengths and/or engaging in those activities?	
What does the world need? **What does** *your chosen* **world need?**	
4. How might you bring more of your natural attributes into your daily work or learning activities?	
Bonus: What might be hidden in your shadow experiences?	
5. What insights do you have from your shadow side and experiences? Is there something there that compels you to try and make that story different for others who might be like you?	

Greater Purpose Statement Prompts	Your Answer
Double Bonus: What is the world calling you to do?	
6. Which of these worlds is of great interest to you or might be a fit for your charisms? What goals might be of interest to you? At what level?	
Sum it up: Your Greater Purpose Statement	

CHAPTER SUMMARY

This chapter explores the importance of purpose in designing your leadership so that when you celebrate your 100th birthday, they can tell the story you want. You will spend a great deal of time learning how to lead effectively. As important is why you want to lead (the internal question) and what world you want to lead (the external question). Combined, your why, what, and how will help you design your leadership with affordance—that is, help you find your best fit. Recognizing and leveraging aspects of your identity, your charisms, and flow activities will considerably inform your purpose. So will examining the challenges from your past that form shadows in your present and provide valuable lessons regarding what is and is not essential to you.

Engaging in leadership requires a context—the process of influencing others toward . . . what? Interest-based success underlies your motivation. So finding the "world" where you seek leadership impact reinforces and energizes your purpose. There are many, many worlds upon which to focus, from the local and specific to the global and broad. Focusing on your chosen world will maximize your success and avoid performance load issues. However, your context and thus your specific purpose will undoubtedly change over time, engagement, experience, and expertise. No matter the scale, any world you choose will comprise individuals with individual needs and require individualized consideration.

After this chapter, you return to understanding how to lead and extend from designing yourself to designing relationships, success, culture, and the future. Using the prompts from the chapter, take the time to reflect and craft a Greater Purpose Statement to guide your leadership activity.

KEY TERMS

Charisms (p. 130)

Greater Purpose Statement (GPS) (p. 141)

Purpose (p. 124)

Shadow experiences (p. 133)

SKILL BUILDER ACTIVITY

Design Your Personal Leadership Brand

Your leadership brand is your trademark; it reflects your purpose and your journey of self-discovery. Your leadership brand involves identifying your assets—strengths, skills, and other desirable characteristics—and packaging them to enhance leadership efficacy and credibility. Ulrich and Smallwood, in their work, *Leadership Brand: Developing Customer-Focused Leaders to Drive Performance and Build Lasting Value*, state that your brand sets the stage for how others perceive you and thus how willing they are to engage you in collaborative working arrangements.[54]

Step #1: How Would You Like to Be Perceived by Others?

The words we use to describe ourselves are critical to becoming aware of our capacity to lead. Words like innovative, curious, and insightful reflect a personal leadership brand as transformational or creativity oriented. On the other hand, words such as task oriented, disciplined, and results oriented may reflect your leadership brand as transactional or task driven. How do others perceive you at this time? The self-analysis exercise that follows may assist in this endeavor.

Form a circle of at least five classmates, coworkers, or friends. Place your back to your classmates (facing away from others). Have the others talk about how they perceive your strengths and weaknesses. Initially, have the team focus on identifying your strengths, followed by comments about your shortcomings. Then, turn around, face your classmates, and summarize your thoughts based on what you heard.

1. **Five-word sum**—Attempt to classify the comments of others into five specific words that reflect your current brand.

2. **Dis/satisfaction**—Is the conversation about you what you wanted it to be? If so, why? If not, why not?

3. **Initial improvements**—What can you do to enhance yourself for becoming an effective leader?

Step #2: How Can You Become the Person Others Desire to Follow?

Recall that credibility is the quality of being believed. Others will follow you if you are credible. But why not be *incredible*, inspiring others to eagerly follow? That can only happen if you continue learning and finding out how *you* are most effective. Here are three things you can do to get followers to believe in you and desire to follow you.

YOU ARE WHAT YOU READ

Followers admire those who know their trade. Take the initial step to becoming educated in the discipline of leadership. What leadership topic or idea could you explore further? For example, you should explore collaborative leadership from Bernard Bass[55] or adaptive leadership from Ronald Heifetz.[56] Here is a hint: All you need to do to find out more is follow those little numbers like the one after Heifetz. Then search via your favorite browser. The more perspectives you read, the more options you have for executing leadership.

YOU ARE WHAT YOU SEE

Observing others you admire is the second way to build your leadership credibility. Identify those leaders who exemplify the behaviors and values that resonate with you and seem effective with followers. Whom do you admire for their ability to attract large numbers of followers? What about these leaders can help you form your leadership style?

YOU ARE WHAT YOU DO

The third and perhaps the most effective way to get followers to join you are by your actions—becoming a role model. This requires you to take the initiative to experiment and improve as you design relationships with others. Recall that leadership includes caring for others and making their lives successful (Rule #2: It's not about you).

Now, take a moment to complete the following table:

Read: What ONE topic are you going to search for more information to read?

See: Who are you going to observe acting in a leadership position this next week?
(See if that person will let you interview them?)

Do: Where and for whom could you act as a role model this next week? What will you purposefully try to model?

What ideas emerge from your answers to the preceding questions.

What aspects of leadership do you think are key to your success?

Step #3: State Your Leadership Brand to Others

Your leadership brand is only as valuable as applied and communicated to others. Part of that task will be finding the proper contexts for your leadership. But the other part is helping others find you, which starts with reflecting on the preceding information relating to what you would like to be known for. A personal brand also reflects your goals, beliefs, and expectations. Place your leadership brand into words that clarify who you are, and consistently communicate it to others in concise, memorable statements. For now, complete the questions that follow to begin crafting a leadership brand.

1. A follower would choose me because _____

    _____

2. I want to be known for being _____ so I can

    _____

CORE™ ATTRIBUTE BUILDERS: BUILD NOW FOR FUTURE LEADERSHIP CHALLENGES

Attribute: Engagement

Builder: Living their Purpose: *Black Panther, Hamilton,* and *Hidden Figures*

Have you seen any of the preceding three movies? Using one of these movies or another of your choice that features a strong character with a clear purpose, consider the following questions:

- How do the primary characters display purposeful leadership?

- Discuss the main character through the lens of, What are they good at? What's the world calling out for from them?

- How do the main characters live: Be, Do, Have

Module 1 ● Design Leadership Self

| CORE™ ATTRIBUTE BUILDERS: BUILD NOW FOR |
| FUTURE LEADERSHIP CHALLENGES |

Attribute: Optimism

Builder: Happiness Is a Life-long Pursuit

Read the following excerpt, then identify someone you care about. Teach them the significant points and discuss them. Do they agree, disagree, or think something different? Why would knowing this perspective help your optimism?

Part I

One of Aristotle's most influential works is the *Nicomachean Ethics*, where he presents a theory of happiness that is still relevant today, over 2,300 years later. In these lectures, the critical question Aristotle seeks to answer is:

"What is the ultimate purpose of human existence?"

What is the goal for which we should direct our energy? Everywhere we see people seeking pleasure, wealth, and a good reputation. But while each of these has some value, none of them can occupy the place of the chief good for which humanity should aim. To be an "ultimate end," an act must be self-sufficient and final, "that which is always desirable in itself and never for the sake of something else,"[57] and it must be attainable by a human.

Aristotle claims that nearly everyone would agree that happiness is the end that meets all these requirements. It is easy to see that we desire money, pleasure, and honor only because we believe these goods will make us happy. All other goods are a means toward obtaining happiness, while happiness is always an end in itself.

Part II

For Aristotle, however, happiness is an end or goal that *encompasses the totality of one's life*. It is not something that can be gained or lost in a few hours, like pleasurable sensations. It is more like the ultimate value of your life as lived up to this moment, measuring how well you have lived up to your full potential as a human being. For this reason, one cannot make any pronouncements about whether one has lived a happy life until it is over, just as we would not say of a football game that it was a "great game" at halftime (indeed, we know of many such games that turn out to be blowouts or duds). For the same reason, we cannot say that children are happy any more than we can say that an acorn is a tree, for the potential for a flourishing human life has not yet been realized. As Aristotle says, "for as it is not one swallow or one fine day that makes a spring, so it is not one day or a short time that makes a man blessed and happy."[58,59]

DESIGN LEADERSHIP RELATIONSHIPS

MODULE 2

Chapter 5	Your Values and Ethical Actions	149
Chapter 6	Decision-Making	181
Chapter 7	Influence, Power, and Motivation	209

Leadership is the process of influencing others toward a common vision. This section focuses on *others*, specifically your connection to others and how you design leadership relationships. Unless you try really hard to avoid it, most of life involves engaging with others. What advice and guidance would *you* give someone who wanted to know the most effective way to build a relationship? You would likely ask what kind of relationship—casual, professional, friendly, romantic—because each kind of relationship looks and feels different. As a leader, what kind of relationship should you have with your followers? What kind of relationship do you want? Individuals spend a great deal of time talking and thinking about relationships, much of it reactive.

Like the prior section that focused on designing your leadership self, your approach to relationships can be mindfully designed . . . or you can just see what happens and hope for the best. Perhaps a ride down the rapids would better illustrate. Imagine you are invited to kayak down a very turbulent river by a couple of friends. Both friends are experienced, but neither is an expert. One friend has taken a close look at the river, mapped out the turns and rapids, and plotted a route through each stretch of rough water. This took time, effort, and thought. The other friend is going to just *go with the flow* (pun intended), which of course required no advance work. One approach may be safer than the other, one more fun and exciting, one more interesting or more appealing. But the relative advantages and disadvantages are not the point. The important thing is the *mindful decision* about how each friend wanted to experience the kayak trip (i.e., their proposed plan, solution, or product). In other words, each friend got the experience they *designed*.

As a leader, the nature of your relationships with others will determine what and how you influence, how you and others see yourselves and the work, and a host of other variables that all add up to how it feels to be led by you. This module on designing leadership relationships comprises three chapters: Chapter 5: Your Values and Ethical Actions; Chapter 6: Decision-Making; and Chapter 7: Influence, Motivation, and Power. You can design your relationships (carefully planned or purposefully going with the flow), or you can choose not to design them and just hope everyone gets along and works well.

5

YOUR VALUES AND
ETHICAL ACTIONS

LEARNING OBJECTIVES

Upon completion of this chapter, the reader should be able to

5.1   Explain how ethics are an integral aspect of effective leadership and followership

5.2   Examine ethical issues that directly impact the student experience

5.3   Identify key foundational ideas important to ethical leadership

5.4   Recognize the roots and leadership implications of moral development

5.5   Examine the ethical challenges of leadership

5.6   Implement the cycle of liberation to advance ethical awareness and action

5.7   Design your personal approach to ethical leadership

Leadership by Design Model

Design Self
How can I design myself as a leader?

Design Relationships
AS A LEADER, HOW CAN I DESIGN MY RELATIOSHIPS WITH OTHERS?

Design Others' Success
As a leader, how can I design success for others?

Design Culture
As a leader, how can I design the culture of my organization?

Design Future
As a leader, how can I innovate?

INTRODUCTION

At the heart of effective leadership is a strong sense of self and the values that guide the leader's work. Alignment between expressed values and actions is paramount when working with others. Individuals who align values and actions not only serve as role models for others, they build trust and credibility—some of the most important ingredients for leadership. This chapter helps you better understand the importance of ethical and moral leadership, highlights values-based challenges inherent in leading others, and provides tools to help you navigate ethical dilemmas in your own life and further design your leadership.

Leadership That Makes a Difference

In 1998, a 6-year-old Canadian named Ryan Hreljac learned that there are people in the world without clean water. What started as a goal to raise $70 for a school project turned into an organization that has helped more than 1.1 million people in 17 different countries around the world.[1] Because of Ryan's efforts, these people have access to clean drinking water—what many would consider a fundamental human right. Fifteen years after its founding, Ryan's Well Foundation has dug more than 1531 wells.[2] Ryan has designed his life and professional career in alignment with the moral values of commitment to something higher than himself, with respect and caring for others. In addition, his efforts serve as a model for the virtues of charity, diligence, patience, kindness, and humility. It is important to note that no one appointed Ryan *leader*—he found a way to make a difference in the lives of others and took action. In the process, he has influenced thousands to make a difference as well.

Photo by Evan Agostini/Invision/AP

GETTING LEADERSHIP RIGHT

LEARNING OBJECTIVE

5.1 Explain how ethics are an integral aspect of effective leadership and followership.

Leadership scholar and historian James MacGregor Burns wrote, "Leadership is morally purposeful."[3] Scholar Joanne Ciulla said it like this—"leadership is about more than getting things done. The quality of leadership also depends on the ethics of the means and the ethics of the ends of a leader's actions."[4] How do you design your leadership to be ethical? Recall that leadership is "the process of influencing others toward a common vision." Ethics is an area of study that is concerned with right or wrong behavior, and every word within the aforementioned definition contains ethical implications: The decisions you make and the behaviors you take. Ethical decision-making is about how one makes decisions as well as to what end; their course of action is deemed right or wrong. When it comes to leadership, the end goal or *common vision* should leave others feeling like partners in designing a better future.

Leadership can be positional and non-positional. In other words, you can step in and out of leadership with a great deal of fluidity. As a group member, you may work to influence the group toward an ethical end without having any authority whatsoever. For instance, nobody "appointed" Greta Thunberg to the role of environmental activitist, but she certainly has influence around the globe. The key word is *influence*. You have an opportunity to engage in the process of influencing others toward a common vision multiple times every day, and the decisions you make come with the underlying decision about whether to follow your values and engage in ethical behavior . . . or not.

To *design* an ethical or moral approach to leadership (and followership), you first need to have a clear understanding of some key terminology. Once you have a baseline understanding of the core terms and ideas, it is important to ground yourself by having great clarity on your values, perspectives, and positions on important issues. Also, understanding the attributes of toxic or bad leadership helps further clarify what is and is not ethical. Each of you has faced ethical dilemmas as a student, and this will continue throughout your adult life. How will you work through those issues? In the end, each of you will have to decide your *true north*, which former Medtronic CEO Bill George describes as "the internal compass that guides you successfully through life."[5] For Beth Ford, CEO of Land O Lakes (#219 on Fortune 500), part of her true north is diversity, equity, and inclusion. She said, "I don't have that lived experience that fear for my children other than you want them to be successful happy people . . . This is going to be a long journey. What I want everybody to understand is we are committed to making sure our employees and the folks in our communities feel safe and are engaged and have the same opportunities as everybody."[6]

Ethical issues consist of many perspectives and are rarely simple, clear, or objective. The right decision often exists in the eye of the beholder. Fierce clarity about your view is critical to your leadership success. It is ultimately up to you to determine who you will be as a student, spouse, child, sibling, employee, and leader. If you are involved, engaged, and active in organizational life, your ethical decision-making will be tested on multiple occasions. You might consider these opportunities for practice and growth and having a solid base of self-awareness to work from will maximize your learning.

ETHICAL ISSUES AND THE STUDENT EXPERIENCE

LEARNING OBJECTIVE
5.2   Examine ethical issues that directly impact the student experience.

Some of you reading may not see how this topic applies to you. Moral and ethical issues seem like the stuff of classroom discussions, case studies, and corporate drama. What is fascinating is that much like corporate life, the collegiate context is filled with moral dilemmas. Just ask the fraternity members from Bowling Green State University under criminal indictment for hazing, the cadets at West Point who were caught cheating in 2021, or the former president of Penn State University who's served time in jail for his role in the child abuse case against Jerry Sundusky. In fact, when you become more in tune with what is happening around you, you will begin to see multiple situations that require your attention *every week*. Here are a few hypothetical examples of ethical scenarios you may have come across. Take a moment to consider your immediate answer to each. What should you do in each case? What would you do . . . especially if no one was looking or would find out? Then consider what other perspectives one might take on the matter. Choose one example that intrigues you. Discuss it with a friend, and note what values inform their perspective.

Rosario is a member of the hockey team. As a second-year member, this is his first time *on the other side*, part of the *in*-group of veteran players. While he joined a successful team on every conceivable metric, the team has a culture of hazing, and he is feeling pressured to participate in activities that do not feel right. In fact, they are dangerous, and he feels uncomfortable even being involved. Rather than address his concerns with the team, he finds reasons to miss *newbie* activities and feels better that he does not actively participate. He wishes he knew how to convince his teammates that what was happening violated campus policy and was illegal, and the press would have a hay day if the activities were discovered. He does not want to be associated with such behavior but does not know what to do. How should he intervene?

Jeff is a third-year undergraduate biology major. Getting into a top medical school has been a goal of his (and his parents) for as long as he can remember. But in recent months, he has been having second thoughts. The work is not exciting, and he finds himself working on anything but his coursework. He is behind and feeling desperate. He knows his grades and test scores will have a major impact on his options. Likewise, he knows if he does not bring home a 4.0 GPA, his parents will be disappointed and angry. Rather than put in the time to earn the grades, he has been focusing on how he can beat the system. In recent months, he has identified and used some unethical resources to circumvent the system (i.e., websites, technology, etc.), so he can keep up the façade. He knows what he is doing could get him kicked out of school, but he is so far behind at this point, he does not have many options. How does he unravel himself from the situation he created?

REFLECTION QUESTIONS

When was the last time you witnessed or engaged in cheating behavior? What action did you take—if any?

Latonya just witnessed one of her small group members cheat on multiple exams. Every part of her wants to bring this behavior to the attention of the professor, but she cannot bring herself to tell him. What if the cheater, Peter, finds out that it was her? Quite honestly, she does not want to deal with the potential drama of outing her classmate. However, she has become more and more agitated as he seems to move farther and farther ahead of her. People like Peter unfairly skew the curve, and the behavior has an impact on her grades. How should Latonya proceed?

Aamir is your best friend. The two of you went out to celebrate your birthday, and it has been a long night. Both of you have had more than your share of alcohol, and it is time to head home. Even though he is well above the legal limit, he is dead set on driving home. You have done all you can to persuade him not to drive, but he does not want to leave his car downtown overnight. You decide to take a hard stand and call a cab, and he has become more and more agitated. He starts calling you names and is making more and more of a scene. You know you could overpower him and take his keys, but he may become more and more physical. What do you do?

Juana is the recently elected president of the student government association (SGA) and one of your closest friends. In fact, you helped her get elected, and she was instrumental in helping

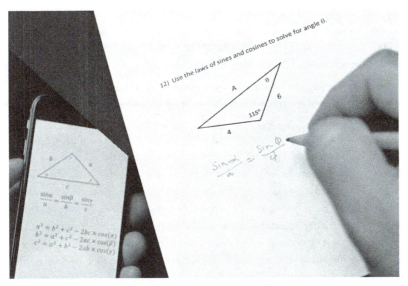

[What have you done in the past when you witnessed this behavior]
©iStockphoto.com/LarryHerfindal

you secure a senate seat. In passing, you have noticed she has been making some unilateral decisions that probably have not been discussed with others on her team. While it is likely no one will see, unilaterally allocating money to specific organizations and intentionally keeping others in the dark is becoming standard practice. In fact, she is highly skilled at not inviting key stakeholders that may stand in the way of her vision. When you bring it up, she becomes defensive and lashes out. What are your options moving forward?

If these examples are not enough to convince you that ethics should be a critical part of your leadership design, you might consider a real-world finding. When asked to choose the 15 most essential leadership competencies from a list of 74, leaders from across the world in over 30 different global organizations selected "has high ethical and moral standards" as one of the most important attributes—far more than most other competencies.[7] This finding, in conjunction with the other most important competencies listed, amounts to the importance of creating a safe and trusting environment. While morals and ethics seem to be an individual concern, the reality is that behavior shapes culture[8], which, in turn, influences both what followers expect and how they work with you.

MYTH OR REALITY?

I don't have the title, I can't make a difference.

Myth . . . and Reality. Throughout this text, leadership is described as positional *and* non-positional. Every day, people without a title or formal position (e.g., the story of Ryan Hreljac at the beginning of this chapter) influence others toward a common vision and make great change in the world. Under normal circumstances, *you do not* have to have a title to make a difference. However, to say that this is an absolute would also be false. Of course, there are situations and contexts where a title or formal power can help greatly.

154 Module 2 ● Design Leadership Relationships

ETHICS—THE KEY CONCEPTS

LEARNING OBJECTIVE
5.3 Identify key foundational ideas important to ethical leadership.

As you begin to think about how you would navigate some of the scenarios described in the previous section, understanding some key terminology is helpful. Like many other topics, ethics suffers from a lack of clarity around even the most common terms. While scholars may have clarity, most students do not; they end up using terms and concepts synonymously. As a result, the topic can be confusing and the application less effective. As you read this section, keep this basic organizing structure in mind. *Ethics* is the study of right or wrong behavior. *Laws* are rules developed by a social institution (e.g., state or nation) that govern correct behavior. *Moral principles* are behaviors deemed *correct* or *incorrect* by individuals, groups, and societies. *Virtues* are a continuum of traits, behaviors, and/or habits we can practice. *Personal values* are beliefs or ideals that guide your behavior (what you find personally important or of some worth). *Integrity* is alignment between what you say and how you behave. Your *character* is the end product—the moral qualities of *you*. Table 5.1 at the end of this section summarizes these definitions.

Ethics/Code of Ethics

Ethics is an area of study that is concerned with codifying and defending right or wrong behavior in multiple contexts. Thus, a **code of ethics** is often a document that seeks to clarify right or wrong behavior in a profession or organization. For instance, there is a nursing code of ethics, a code of ethics for social workers, and even a code of ethics for librarians.

REFLECTION QUESTIONS
Should there be a code of ethics for leaders? What would your leadership code of ethics say is right and wrong behavior?

Laws

Finally, **laws** are rules developed by a social institution (e.g., state or nation) that govern correct behavior. An act can be legal but not ethical, moral, or virtuous (e.g., cheating on your significant other). Conversely, you may break the law but still act within your values (for example, driving over the speed limit to get someone to the hospital). As a result, some values are legal, ethical, moral, and virtuous, while some are not—you can be immoral and still be following your values.

Moral Principles

Each code of ethics will highlight several behaviors that have been deemed universal—these are **moral principles.** Moral principles are *truths* about behaviors that have been widely accepted

Chapter 5 ● Your Values and Ethical Actions   155

and adopted by individuals, groups, and societies. It is important to note that moral principles held by one group of individuals may not be held in such high regard by others. For example, the Universal Declaration of Human Rights adopted by many countries in 1948 works to codify acceptable and universal norms of behavior, such as "All human beings are born free and equal in dignity and rights. They are endowed with reason and conscience and should act towards one another in a spirit of brotherhood."[9] Some countries who have not signed the document (e.g., Russia, Saudi Arabia) may not see this as a moral principle.

Another moral principle highlighted in the Code of Ethics of the American Medical Association states, "A physician shall be dedicated to providing competent medical care, with compassion and respect for human dignity and rights."[10] Other examples of moral principles may include "Do good, avoid evil; Do unto others as you would have them do unto you (The Golden Rule); The end does not justify the means; Follow what nature intends;"[11] as well as those such as committing to something greater than oneself and caring for other living things and the environment.[12] In essence, moral principles are the philosophies upon which everything else is built. For instance, if the United States is built on the moral principle that "all men are created equal," it must follow through on this expressed principle. The fact that the United States *was not* living this principle was a foundation of Martin Luther King Jr.'s *I Have a Dream* speech.

"I have a dream that one day this nation will rise up and live out the true meaning of its creed: 'We hold these truths to be self-evident: that all men are created equal.'"[13]

Personal Values

Personal values are what you find personally essential or of some *worth*. Even if you aren't aware of them or have not named them, values drive behavior. Many of your values are only visible through your behavior. For instance, in Lakota culture, seven values that guide behavior include *wacantognaka* (generosity), *wotakuye* (kinship), *wowacintanka* (fortitude), *wocekiya* (prayer), *waohola* (respect), and *woksape* (wisdom).[14] For the Inuit's values such as *Aajiiqatigiinniq* (decision-making through discussion and consensus) and *Qanuqtuurniq* (being innovative and resourceful) are central to their society.[15] You are conscious of some values, but others are not easily named or understood. Pay close attention to your behavior, and you will have a better understanding of your values—healthy and unhealthy. You could value your car, your social status, family, your wardrobe, or financial independence. Likewise, you could value "taking care of number one," but at an extreme, this may not be viewed as moral and/or virtuous. Visit https://corevalueslist.com for a list of 500 core values.

Virtues and Thoughtful Intentionality

Virtues are concerned with *living* the moral code. These are often referred to as morally good traits, behaviors, and/or habits that determine an individual's character. Virtues are practiced and are often a mean between two extremes, for example, the virtue of integrity can be seen on a scale from corruption to legalism (see Figure 5.1). Virtues are not about what is right or wrong but what a person *should* be. If the United States has a moral principle that "all men are created equal," then a virtuous person would *act* in alignment with this statement. They would potentially practice the virtues of respect and justice. It should be noted there is overlap between principles and virtues.

Thus, the real-world way of living your moral principles is by outlining and practicing your identified virtues. For some of you reading this text, you may choose to follow the thinking of others, such as Plato's four cardinal virtues—wisdom, justice, temperance, courage.[16] For others, you may choose your religion as a source. For example, in Christianity, the seven heavenly virtues are wisdom, justice, temperance, courage, faith, hope, charity (love).[17] In the Sikhism faith, Guru Nanak suggested that "Truth is the highest virtue but higher still is truthful living."[18] Some of the Canadian First Nations, Metis and Inuit peoples, use *The Seven Sacred Teachings,* which "honors the virtues necessary for a full and healthy life." These include

- To cherish knowledge is to know WISDOM
- To know LOVE is to know peace
- To honor all of the Creation is to have RESPECT
- BRAVERY is to face the foe with integrity
- HONESTY also means "righteousness," be honest first with yourself—in word and action
- HUMILITY is to know yourself as a sacred part of the Creation
- TRUTH is to know all of these things[19]

Regardless of how you choose the virtues to practice, the fact that you are intentionally working to develop your virtuous behavior is admirable.

Aristotle first developed the deficiency/excess spectrum.[20] The Virtue Continuum (Figure 5.2) communicates the concept of virtue on this spectrum (in this example through the lens of servant leadership; you will learn more about servant leadership in Chapter 13: Creating a Culture That Cares). The key point for Aristotle in highlighting this continuum is to assert that it takes practical wisdom (phronesis) to determine the *golden mean* (i.e., a desirable middle ground). For instance, sometimes selfishness can be helpful and is the right thing to do. For example, every airline instructs that in the event of cabin pressure loss, you should secure your oxygen mask first and then help others. This seems pretty selfish at first, but if you pass out because you are trying to help others first, everyone loses. The key is thoughtful intentionality. Intentionality allows the individual to *choose* the correct place on the spectrum more consciously. As you design your leadership, do you carefully consider the *golden* balance?

Practicing one's virtues helps an individual actively design their living moral principles or code. A common phrase is that "patience is a virtue." In other words, patience takes practice. For many of us, it takes intentional and deliberate work to master the virtue of patience. The American inventor and author Ben Franklin famously adopted 13 virtues[21] that he revisited on a *daily* basis. While his definitions of each virtue may not be academic sounding, they accurately describe his intentions. Following is a list of his areas of work for which, in the beginning, he struggled:.

FIGURE 5.2 ■ The Virtue Continuum: Examples of the Deficiency to Excess Spectrum

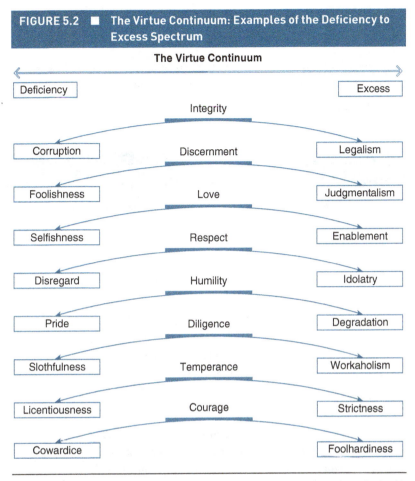

Source: Lanctot, J. D., & Irving, J. A. (2007). *Character and leadership: Situating servant leadership in a proposed virtues framework.* Retrieved from http://www.regent.edu/acad/global/publications/sl_proceedings/2007/lanctot-irving.pdf.

Franklin's 13 Virtues[22]

1. Temperance. Eat not to dullness; drink not to elevation.
2. Silence. Speak not but what may benefit others or yourself; avoid trifling conversation.
3. Order. Let all your things have their places; let each part of your business have its time.
4. Resolution. Resolve to perform what you ought; perform without fail what you resolve.
5. Frugality. Make no expense but to do good to others or yourself; i.e., waste nothing.
6. Industry. Lose no time; be always employ'd in something useful; cut off all unnecessary actions.
7. Sincerity. Use no hurtful deceit; think innocently and justly, and, if you speak, speak accordingly.
8. Justice. Wrong none by doing injuries or omitting the benefits that are your duty.
9. Moderation. Avoid extremes; forbear resenting injuries so much as you think they deserve.

10. Cleanliness. Tolerate no uncleanliness in body, clothes, or habitation.

11. Tranquility. Be not disturbed at trifles, or at accidents common or unavoidable.

12. Chastity. Rarely use venery but for health or offspring, never to dullness, weakness, or the injury of your own or another's peace or reputation.

13. Humility. Imitate Jesus and Socrates.

REFLECTION QUESTIONS

Which of Franklin's virtues do you find meaningful and important? Which are not very important? Why?

Character

In essence, all of these concepts lead to an individual's **character**, which can indicate elements such as virtues, moral principles, and values. Hazing, cheating, stealing, lying, or treating another poorly could lead to being perceived as having weak moral character. Earlier in this chapter, we mentioned the former president of Penn State University's role in the Jerry Sandusky child abuse scandal. What do his actions say about his character?

Integrity

The secondary definition of integrity describes something as having the condition of being whole, undivided, unified, and sound. When applied to a person, having **integrity** is often associated with having strong moral character and assumes alignment of one's word to deed. In the collegiate context, this may mean sticking to your word, honoring a committed relationship, following through on commitments, and when it comes to group projects . . . doing your part. These may be promises we make to ourselves or others depending on the situation. When you as a leader are whole, the values on the inside show up as behaviors on the outside.

Leadership by Design

Design Principle: Storytelling

Definition: A method of creating imagery, emotions, and understanding of events through an interaction between a storyteller and an audience. The elements of story typically consist of setting, characters, plot, theme, and mood.

In Other Words: Once upon a time . . . somewhere . . . something really interesting happened . . . and they lived happily ever after.

For Example: Consider all the fun, interesting stories that also left you with a lesson: *The Little Engine That Could, The Three Little Pigs*, and so forth. Which stories immediately come to mind for you? Or consider more personal stories, such as how your grandparents started from nothing, the day you met that best friend, or that teacher who made a difference for you. All of those stories communicate values.

For Leaders: "Tell me a little about yourself" is one of the most common yet mystifying interview questions. Incorporating storytelling into your response illustrates a strong sense

Chapter 5 • Your Values and Ethical Actions   159

of self-design. Who are you? Use elements of storytelling to help highlight and demonstrate your values. Who are you, as a character in your story? What is your setting, and how do the aforementioned elements tie into the plot? Think to yourself, how can I as a leader better design myself so I can engage in the art of storytelling when necessary? How can I help other people read my personal road map?

The key definitions and questions related to your personal ethics are summarized in Table 5.1.

TABLE 5.1 ■ Key Definitions and Questions			
	Definition	**Key Question**	**Key Question**
Moral Principles	Principles deemed correct or incorrect by individuals, groups, and societies	What moral principles underpin the major religions?	Can you identify moral principles that in hindsight were deemed immoral and/or illegal?
Personal Values	What you find *personally* important or of some *worth*	Can an individual value good looks?	Can personal values be immoral?
Virtues	A continuum of traits, behaviors, and/or habits	What are the opposite virtues associated with the seven deadly sins?	Which of Franklin's virtues intrigues you the most?
Character	The moral qualities of an individual	Are you perceived as an individual of strong character?	Which of your personal values may conflict with your objective of being known as an individual of strong character?
Integrity	Of strong moral character	Can one lack moral character and have integrity?	Can you think of an organization that lacks integrity?
Laws	Rules developed by a social institution (e.g., state or nation) that govern correct behavior	Thinking globally, can you identify a law that is immoral?	Can an act be legal but immoral?

REFLECTION QUESTIONS

- What does your online persona say about your character? Look at the list of virtues in the Skill Builder Activity and see which words do and do not align.

- What are examples of personal values you hold that could be perceived by others as immoral or lacking virtue? How could these values damage your character? Look to your behavior(s) for clues.

- What are the triggers that cause you to act in an immoral manner? Alcohol? Greed? Pride? Pressure? Ego?

- What virtues and moral principles were modeled for you in your home growing up? How about your community and school? How did your environment impact who you are today?

- Realizing that everyone is a *work in progress*, what does version "You 2.0" look and act like when it comes to this topic? Who or what will help you live a more virtuous life?

THE ROOTS OF MORAL DEVELOPMENT

LEARNING OBJECTIVE

5.4   Recognize the roots and leadership implications of moral development.

So where do your moral principles, virtues, and personal values come from? Few would deny that your parents/primary caregivers and immediate family have a significant influence on character development. Good character "consists of knowing the good, desiring the good, and doing the good."[23] In those critical early years, it is these people who model right and wrong. The literature in this realm of research is quite fascinating. As you read the following passage, reflect on your own experiences. Do they align with the research?

Parents who were responsive to children's signals and needs and had a warm, loving relationship with their children produced children of strong, multifaceted character. Families who used an open, democratic style of family discussion, decision-making, and problem-solving produced children who exhibited five characteristics (compliance, self-esteem, conscience, moral reasoning, and altruism—all but empathy, self-control, and social orientation). Parents who used *induction* (praising or disciplining with explanations that include a focus on the consequences of the child's behavior for others' feelings) produced children with relatively more mature empathy, conscience, altruism and moral reasoning. Parents who set high expectations (*demandingness*) that were attainable and supported, had children who were high in self-control, altruism, and self-esteem. Parents who *modeled* self-control and altruism had children high in self-control and altruism.[24]

Along with your parents, your early education and collegiate experience have an important impact on character development. In his article, *The Science of Character Education*, Berkowitz highlights several findings based on the character education literature—Here are a couple we found interesting: First, the quality of relationships in the child's life matters. Said relationships need to be "benevolent (nurturant, supportive), authentic (honest, open), respectful (inclusive, valuing the student's voice), and consistent (predictable, stable)."[25] Second, the child's environment is critical because they are learning about right and wrong based on what they observe. As a result, it is critical to pay attention to how people are treating one another in the child's presence. Interestingly a meta-analysis found that character education in K–12 was correlated with a higher level of educational outcomes and higher levels of expressions of "love, integrity, compassion, and self-discipline." [26]

Character development is impacted by the relationships we have with family and friends.
©iStockphoto.com/imtmphoto

The ongoing design of your character is happening even now as undergraduate or graduate students. In their research on character development and college students, Kuh and Umbach found the collegiate experience can accentuate an individual's character development.[27] Another study found that students who engage in volunteerism in high school showed the most amount of significant growth in college.[28] Opportunities to expand one's horizons in and out of the classroom correlate strongly with character development (e.g., academically, socially, culturally).[29] Opportunities for students to engage with people unlike themselves (e.g., political views, religion, ethnicity) also had a positive impact on students. In fact, roughly 60 percent of respondents reported the collegiate experience helped shape their ethical code.[30] Learning about and developing your moral and ethical self continue through life, but this happens only if you mindfully engage, recognize your value-driven behavior, and strive to be the leader you want to be.

THE ETHICAL CHALLENGES OF LEADERSHIP

LEARNING OBJECTIVE

5.5 Examine the ethical challenges of leadership.

In essence, your parents, your teachers, and your community have been training you on what is and is not moral behavior from the time you were a baby. And while you may think ethical decision-making is an academic topic relegated to political and organizational leaders, nothing could be further from the truth. In fact, as a student, each of you has more than likely encountered an ethical dilemma in the last couple of days.

Ethical Issues in Five Domains

Regardless of age, country of origin, or economic status, ethical issues for an average student occur in five primary domains (Figure 5.3).

1. The academic domain (e.g., the classroom, group projects)
2. The family domain (e.g., parents, children, siblings, extended family)
3. The work domain (e.g., jobs, internships, co-op)
4. The extracurricular domain (e.g., activities, athletics, community)
5. The friendship domain (e.g., classmates, peers)

In the classroom, the most common ethical issues involve academic dishonesty (e.g., cheating, plagiarism). In families, ethical issues often present themselves as keeping secrets, end-of-life decision-making for loved ones, or issues of fairness and equity. In the work domain, ethical problems usually have to do with individual and group decision-making around money (e.g., expense reports, spending), human resources (e.g., layoffs, hiring), and strategy (e.g., legal vs. moral, environmental impact, ensuring growth/profit). Ethical issues in the extracurricular domain are similar to others because they involve topics such as equity/fairness (e.g., who is or is not included), dishonest behavior (e.g., cheating to win), and day-to-day politics of organizational life (e.g., popularity, power, access to resources). The friendship domain can be particularly challenging to navigate because it involves close-knit social circles (e.g., groups of friends) with their norms of what is and is not appropriate behavior (e.g., drug use, drinking and driving, treatment of significant others).

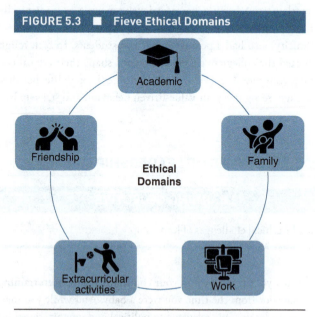

FIGURE 5.3 ■ Fieve Ethical Domains

©iStockphoto.com/musmellow, ©iStockphoto.com/LysenkoAlexander, ©iStockphoto.com/Turac Novruzova, ©iStockphoto.com/bubaone, ©iStockphoto.com/enotmaks

Chapter 5 • Your Values and Ethical Actions   **163**

You are also embedded in a broader context. Each community, state/province, and nation also faces ethical dilemmas and issues that are rarely simple. How New Zealand handed the Covid-19 pandemic was vastly different than how other countries approached the challenge—and on several metrics, they faired much better.[31] Ethical issues often involve multiple competing commitments that do not always lead to a clear resolution. For instance, between 2015 and 2017, the United States and other countries around the world struggled with the question of allowing Syrian immigrants into their country. In essence, the country's leaders were struggling with the competing commitments of inclusion and security. How leaders at the community, state, national, and global levels address issues such as terrorism, individual privacy, climate change, and trade have significant ramifications for their citizens.

REFLECTION QUESTION

Which of the five domains prove the most challenging for you to navigate ethically?

Leadership by Design

Design Principle: Propositional Density

Definition: The relationship between the aspects of a design and their meaning, specifically "a measure of how many meanings can be derived from the elements used in a design."[32] Designs that contain many elements with deeper meaning "propose" more ideas, and are "more interesting, engaging, and satisfying to look at and contemplate."[33]

In Other Words: It is better to create something simple with deep meaning rather than something with many superficial messages.

For Example: Many logos you see were designed to convey messages about organizational values, like the arrow in the Amazon logo representing speed and arched upward like a smile.

For Leaders: A leader can use the concept of propositional density to think about how they use their actions (the elements of your leadership design) to communicate their values (the deeper propositions). "Every designed object invokes multiple layers of interpretations and associations. It is not possible to produce a neutral design. In other words, there are always deep propositions involved . . . (and) will always invoke associations. (Do you) . . . leave it to chance, if the deep propositions serve or contradict the intended reading, or acknowledge their existence and use them consciously."[34] What is the relationship between what leaders do and what they *say* they will do? Successfully designing relationships means putting forth thought, energy, and effort to create the desired effect. A high propositional density makes relationships engaging and memorable. Increased engagement and meaningful values lead to stronger relationships. As a leader, how can you foster more deeply meaningful relationships that have the most impact?

Why Individuals Fail to Behave Ethically

It is a rare human being who has not fallen victim to the **decision-action gap**[35]—that space between deciding what you should do and doing it. According to the Air Force Academy's research, there are two primary reasons for this phenomenon—the individual succumbs to the challenge (e.g., pressures, fears/doubts) and/or the individual lacks the necessary character strengths (e.g., courage, self-discipline, resilience).[36] Other reasons may be that the individual simply lacks awareness that they are involved in an ethical dilemma or lacks the skills to navigate the situation successfully.[37] Interestingly, characteristics of the issue at hand may also affect an individual's willingness to follow through on an ethical decision. For instance, there may be varied levels of perceived moral intensity (the degree to which the individual sees an issue as an ethical dilemma).[38] For example, one individual may not feel drinking and driving is a significant offense, while others will perceive it as such. Another factor could be that the individual may be a victim of moral disengagement, which means they lack ownership.[39] Moral disengagement "explains why otherwise normal people can engage in unethical behavior without apparent guilt or self-censure" (e.g., hazing).[40] A lack of moral ownership will also stall action.[41] If an individual does not feel ownership for acting (e.g., curing hunger in a developing nation), it is unlikely they will engage.

So why do (student) leaders fail to act ethically? According to Schwartz,[42] the literature points to six possible reasons (of course there are others). As you read each reason in Table 5.2, reflect on when and where you have experienced each over the course of your time in school or at work.

TABLE 5.2 ■ Schwartz's Six Reasons for Unethical Behavior	
Reason for Failing to Act Ethically	**Example**
Performance pressure (us vs. them; winning at all costs)	An individual who gets so caught up in *winning* that they sidestep the rules or lose sight of their values. For instance, a college athlete takes performance-enhancing drugs to gain an advantage.
Threats to self-efficacy (pressure to be successful)	Students who feel pressure to achieve a particular score or obtain a specific grade to be successful. For instance, a student cheats on a final exam because they need an A for their graduate school application.
Decision-making autonomy (nobody will find out)	The threat of being caught is low, and the perceived *gain* is enough to take the risk. For instance, a group of resident advisors violates the hall's policy on drugs because students have not yet moved in.
Interpersonal conflicts (who cares?)	An individual fails to do what is correct or *right* out of spite toward another. For instance, a faction of members does not attend the organization's philanthropy because they dislike the coordinator—they do not want her to succeed.
Bias (friends help friends)	An individual sidesteps the routine *process* because of a relationship with the decision maker. For instance, although many qualified individuals applied, a student supervisor only interviews his friends for a position on campus.
Managing important relationships (wink-wink)	An individual in authority overlooks a rule or requirement to avoid conflict or keep a relationship intact. For instance, a professor lets a favorite student slide on the attendance policy but not others.

REFLECTION QUESTION

When was the last time you fell victim to one of the reasons listed in Table 5.2?

Toxic and Bad Leaders and Leadership

Unfortunately, not all human beings are moral and virtuous—nor do they navigate the previously mentioned challenges in an effective manner. Whether it is a boss soliciting kick-backs, an athlete accepting unapproved services and gifts, or a student leader intentionally keeping key players *out of the loop*, all are shades of what could be called toxic leadership. According to scholar Jean Lipman-Blumen, toxic leaders are "individuals who, by virtue of their destructive behaviors and their dysfunctional personal qualities or characteristics, inflict serious and enduring harm on the individuals, groups, organizations, communities and even the nations they lead."[43]

Toxic leaders result in toxic employees and a toxic environment.
©iStockphoto.com/appleuzr

People with formal power and authority have done unimaginable damage to the lives of others. Distinguishing between toxic/bad leaders and ineffective leaders is essential. We witness *ineffective* leadership each day. For instance, an athletic coach who does not achieve results on the field, an organization that does not meet its quarterly numbers, or a student leader who fails to lead their organization to success. While ineffective leadership is not desirable, it is also not surprising. Remember, leadership is a process that often requires experimentation and setbacks; hopefully, these setbacks offer new opportunities to learn and plan a new path forward. High performance and effective leadership is usually the result of many adjustments, realignments, and lessons learned as an organization grows, pivots to meet new demands, or rebuilds after a difficult challenge. Ineffective leadership is also a part of any leader's growth and development. Failure is inherent in leadership.

So what distinguishes toxic/bad leadership from ineffective leadership? Keywords and phrases, such as "dysfunctional personal qualities or characteristics" and "inflict serious and enduring harm," provide guidance. Under normal circumstances, a good individual with moderately poor results would not be deemed *toxic* by most. A team captain who is physically abusing freshmen team members or a student leader diminishing the financial health of a student organization for personal gain is another story. However, a challenge with this conversation is that one person's toxic leader may be another's heroic leader (e.g., the names Donald Trump and Joe Biden in the United States will likely yield strong reactions at the dinner table depending on your family's political persuasion).[44]

Recall again the definition of leadership—the process of influencing others toward a common vision. Embedded in the definition is the sense that followers have a *choice* and have a *voice* in what constitutes common vision. Also embedded is the distinction that leadership scholar Joanne Cuilla made in the beginning of this chapter—"The quality of leadership also depends on the ethics of the means and the ethics of the ends of a leader's actions." Choice and voice are two words that one must keep in mind when exploring the topic of toxic leadership. In the case of toxic leadership, it is often the case that one or both of these are missing and the leader and/or a small group of individuals holds power—often left unchecked. The *others* in the definition (e.g., group, organization, team members, citizens, employees) may lack voice and choice. Because of this reality, horrible atrocities are happening across the globe as you read this text.

Toxic leaders present themselves in many ways, and various types of toxic leaders have been identified (see the work of Barbara Kellerman or Jean Lipman-Blumen). While not to the extreme of some of the examples explored in this chapter, it is likely you have and/or will encounter the various shades of toxic leadership at some point in your career. Toxic leadership has a lot to do with the leader's intent. While you may disagree with the policies of former presidents of the United States, as long as they are honest and allowing voice and choice, their perspectives can be viewed as well intentioned. If they are habitually dishonest, self-centered, or ultimately focused on their own lust for power, money, or success, it may be a different story.[45] In the end, each of us may have strong feelings around topics such as gun control, voting rights, the influence of social media, social justice, individual freedoms, and vaccine mandates. These intense feelings often translate into perceiving a leader as toxic or bad. Likewise, if the leader's well-intended actions fail (e.g., had Abraham Lincoln lost the Civil War), you may perceive it as bad or toxic leadership. As a thoughtful leader and follower, you must mentally separate leadership behaviors that stifle voice or choice or have harmful intentions from those behaviors that merely differ from your values or ideas.

A starting point to determine if an individual is toxic is to view the individual and their actions through the filters of voice, choice, and intent. Some simple questions around each of these may include

- **Voice**—Did the leader actively work to minimize or eliminate the voice of the people (in particular, people who may have disagreed)? Did they do so by fear, intimidation, fostering confusion, or force? Were dissenting voices actively suppressed, dimissed, or personally attacked?

- **Choice**—Did the leader actively work to minimize access or eliminate the choice of the people? In particular, were others stuck with this individual and forced to adhere? Did the leader act with the best interest of the followers in mind?

Chapter 5 ● Your Values and Ethical Actions   **167**

- **Intent**—Did the leader have the best intentions of the people/followers in mind? Did the leader and their followers work in alignment with generally accepted moral and ethical behavior? Did the leader lie, deceive, or cheat? Were they trying to protect their personal power, authority, or wealth at the expense of the public good (e.g., economic, public health)?

Experts Beyond the Text

Insightful Leaders Know About . . . Followership

By R. Koonce and M. Hurwitz

To obsess about superiors at the expense of subordinates is to distort

the dynamic between them. And it sends a message: to underestimate, or

to undervalue, the importance of those whom Shakespeare once referred

to as underlings is to disempower. So long as we fixate on leaders at the expense of

followers, we will perpetuate the myth . . .

—Barbara Kellerman (p. xvii)[46]

The best people know when to lead and when to allow others to do the same.[47] When shared responsibility exists for accomplishing an established vision, no special emphasis should be given to a leader or a follower; they equally cocreate.[48] Leaders and followers need to work as a partnership. Hollander writes, "Though the success of a team depends upon so-called 'teamwork,' it pivots around leader-follower relations."[49] Despite the perceived importance of the partnership between a leader and a follower, the partnership is still too often portrayed as a relationship between a parent and a child,[50] as a boss and an associate, or a superior and a subordinate.[51] If a partnership is to ever exist between a leader and a follower, a follower must have a leader's interests at heart, as the leader correspondingly allows the follower to question or constructively challenge the leader's behavior or their policies.

In a paper presented in April and November 1927 conferences of the U.S. Bureau of Personnel Administration, management scholar Mary Parker Follett defined leadership as a problem of relating and the best leader as one who sought to arouse not "attitudes of obedience" but "attitudes of co-operation."[52] Her belief was that a leader who strived to organize the experience of a group in such a way that the specialized knowledge of its members could *actively* rather than passively contribute to the effectiveness of the group would inspire the group to work toward a common purpose.

Follett first used the term *followship*, pointing to the joint responsibility inherently described by the term leadership. She went on to suggest that if a follower should be expected to follow the common purpose of an organization (also referred to as the *invisible leader* in Follett's writings), so must the leader. While leadership for Follett represented a true partnership between leader and those being led, various historical accounts, such as Thersites in Homer's Iliad, rōnin in feudal Japan, and SS members in Nazi Germany, also clearly demonstrate that "not all followers 'follow' in the same way."[53]

The next time you think about leadership, consider the role and influence of the follower.

Courageous Followers and Dissent

In the face of the challenges and difficulties mentioned in the previous section, followers are often on the receiving end of toxic leadership. Sometimes designing your leadership means first designing yourself as an active follower and having to confront or address the bad behavior. Everyone is a follower at one time or another. Effective followership is every bit as important to your development and success as a leader. When considering followership, Chaleff notes a few key ideas:

- Follower is a role assumed at various times when working collaboratively.

- A follower shares responsibility for a common purpose with a leader, wants the activity to succeed, and works toward this end.

- In hierarchies, followers usually accept direction from formal leaders while influencing them to make choices that serve the common purpose better.

- Followers can dissent or can withdraw support from leadership actions they feel are not serving the common purpose well.[54]

Followers construct their role in different ways. Carsten, Uhl-Bien, West, Patera, and McGregor found these roles often comprised three general categories: passive, active, and proactive. At one end of the followership schema, *passive* followers were more likely to do what the leader wanted, displaying deference to the leader. *Active* followers sought to play a larger part in decision-making but only when leaders included them. At the other end of the followership schema, *proactive* followers wanted ownership in the endeavor: "Active and proactive followers emphasized the importance of constructively challenging their leaders and voicing ideas or concerns. Moreover, proactive followers identified blind obedience as a behavior that was associated with ineffective followership."[55] Likewise, followers who romanticize the leader and view their role as subservient are more likely to follow through on unethical requests.[56]

Pioneering scholars on the topic Robert Kelley[57] and Ira Challeff[58] have identified several follower styles that can help you better understand the choice you have when determining which role you would like to play as a follower. Take careful note that *each* of these has a time and a place; however, you need to intentionally *choose* the style most suited for the situation. Summarizing the work of Kelley and Challeff, followers often take on the following styles: partner, individualist, implementer, and resource/sheep.

The ideal style of followers for achieving a shared vision is that of *partner*. An expressed goal of every leader should be to develop a team of engaged followers who feel like partners in the process of moving toward the common vision.[59] Recall from Chapter 1 that engagement is the degree of individual involvement, investment, and enthusiasm. Creating an environment where people feel and act like partners is challenging work. The leader must give away some of their authority and open themselves up to the thoughts and perspectives of others. By doing so, followers will *feel* engaged, mobilized, and work above and beyond what they may typically give.

People who do not feel they are engaged as partners but rather are outsiders with a slightly different vision or perspective than the leader play the role of *individualist*. Individualists are often openly opposed to the direction of the leader/group, but at times, they may be silent about their opposition. Individualists can play an essential role on teams—they can keep the group in check and help the team avoid groupthink. By playing a *devil's advocate* role, the individualist helps a group explore multiple interpretations of an issue before a decision is made. However, taken to an extreme, an individual playing this role may damage group dynamics or marginalize themselves if they cannot separate their opinion from the desires of the group. Likewise, individualists must be conscious of *how* they are communicating. Is their tone negative and disagreeable or respectful and measured? Delivery can make a big difference.

A third style followers play is that of an *implementer*. Implementers consistently *fall in line* with the leader and support them in their endeavors—they are conformists or *"yes"* people. As with the other styles, context matters as to when this approach is or is not appropriate. In one sense, everyone needs to fall into this approach from time to time. If the stakes are low and you authentically agree with the direction, you can comfortably fall in line to support the leader. However, blindly following a leader in all instances can be dangerous and destructive. History's toxic leaders (e.g., Joseph Stalin, Jim Jones, William Aramony) enlisted implementers to enact their tragic visions.

A fourth follower style is *resource/sheep*. These individuals function as a *pair of hands* and will likely do whatever they are told. In many ways, they are indifferent. They are not partners, will not speak up, and will rarely take the initiative or implement anything. They merely follow instructions and do as they are told. At times, it may seem contextually appropriate for you to serve as a resource; however, the best followers are those who are mindful of *how* they are engaging and *why*. Table 5.3 summarizes followership.

TABLE 5.3 ■ Style of Followers	
Style	**Actions/Example**
Partner	"A follower operating from the first quadrant gives vigorous support to a leader but is also willing to question the leader's behavior or policies."
Implementer	"This is the quadrant from which most leaders love to have their followers operate. Leaders can count heavily on followers who operate from this profile to do what is needed to get the job done and not require much oversight or explanation."
Individualist	"Surrounding every leader are one or two individuals whose deference is quite low and who do not hesitate to tell the leader or anyone else in the group, exactly what they think of their actions or policies."
Resource	"Any group has a certain number of people who do an honest day's work for a day's pay but don't go beyond the minimum expected of them."[60]

In summary, as Ira Chaleff and Sharna Fabiano assert in the foreword of this book, followership is an emerging and *necessary* area of research. In fact, according to scholar Barbara Kellerman, the future of followership is an area ripe for investigation and consideration.[61] Leadership does not exist without followers. In her book *Lead & Follow*, Sharna Fabiano encapsulates this sentiment in the following passage:

My life as a social dancer showed me that superior work—not to mention the most satisfying work—comes *not* from everyone leading all the time, but from leaders and followers working together. Even if dancers change roles throughout the evening, or within a single dance, the roles themselves must remain intact because they each represent distinct and complimentary functions. Leading, no matter how skillful, does not remove the need for following, and neither does extraordinary following remove the need for leading.[62]

In the end, we assert that people must be prepared to engage in both roles. We are all followers *some* of the time—if you are skilled at both roles, you will be positioned well to lead and follow with intentionality and skill.

REFLECTION QUESTION

What is the followership role that you most often assume?

DEI BY DESIGN

LEARNING OBJECTIVE

5.6   Implement the cycle of liberation to advance ethical awareness and action.

Designing your leadership must include the mindful, purposeful consideration of ethics at multiple levels. As a positional leader or a follower–leader, you will likely enter an established group that operates within some explicit or implicit norms. That group's culture will be informed by that of the organization, community, and society at large. What will you use your influence for? How will you extend voice, choice, and intent? How will you readjust systems to ensure they are just and fair in how they distribute benefits and burdens (equity) and how those systems consider and welcome individual differences (inclusion)? In order to even consider these questions, you and followers must be free to see and act, and that often takes courageous followership and dissent.

The system you enter was built and reinforced over time (recall the cycle of socialization from Chapter 4), and that system can likewise be influenced and changed. Your presence can be the critical incident—the experience for others that brings awareness of and prompts action toward addressing those issues getting in the way of organizational and individual success: ethical shortcomings, inequities, or exclusivity. The cycle of liberation from the last chapter offers some specific tools that can help.[63] After experiencing a critical incident, which creates the internal strain necessary to reexamine perceptions, individuals undergo a period of *getting ready* to change. This initial phase is characterized by introspection, gaining inspiration from others, and discarding thinking, acting, and relationship-building patterns that no longer serve well. You as leader (or follower) can prompt these behaviors, seeking greater congruence between how followers see the world and the ways in which they choose to operate in it.

The work of liberation cannot be done alone, however. The *reaching out* phase of liberation involves obtaining feedback on how emerging perspectives are received by others. You and others may face pressures to go back to the way things used to be, but working with others and building those relationships helps strengthen this phase and endure to the next step.

Learning to work with others who are like you (caucuses) and those who are different from you (coalitions) is how community builds. *Building communities* with caucuses offers the support

Chapter 5 • Your Values and Ethical Actions **171**

needed to design success, while coalition-building keeps individuals accountable to the commitments made. *Both are needed to design liberatory successes.* However, working within similarities and across differences is not easy and requires continuous mindfulness about how you wield power, privilege, influence, and motivation.

Building community can lead to rich dialogue and meaningful collaboration toward changing assumptions, structures, policies, practices, and systems. Deploying time, energy, and resources toward deconstructing inequitable systems happens in the *coalescing* phase. Here, you build influence and power by sharing those same things with others in the group, which then generates proof that working together can create deep, positive, and sustainable changes.

As evidence of success grows, individuals are motivated to maintain efforts and potentially expand influence into new areas of the organization and new levels of culture. Maintaining past successes in liberation includes spreading hope for the future, modeling authenticity for others, and accepting new forms of accountability. Since the work of liberation is never done, every trip through the cycle of liberation leaves you and the group more proficient for the next time and sets the foundation for ethical awareness and action.

DESIGNING YOUR ETHICAL LEADERSHIP

LEARNING OBJECTIVE
5.7   Design your personal approach to ethical leadership.

Are you ethically fit? Athletes, musicians, and other performers put in a great deal of training and practice before the big event. How often do you consider the ethical dimensions of decisions you make, much less practice? As noted, your family, faith, school, and culture have shaped who you are and the values you hold. Have you considered the different dimensions of those values and their importance? How often do you recognize that your behavior has been influenced by one of those values? What can you do to develop and maintain your ethical fitness?[64]

Ethical Decision-Making

For leaders and followers alike, ethics is more than analyzing all the sides of a situation. Leaders make decisions (even the decision to *not make a decision* is a decision). Hence, the term ethical decision-making involves acting on what you believe to be right or wrong in a situation—do I take part in hazing? Cheat on the exam? Cheat on my partner? Drive drunk? Buy alcohol for underage friends? Misreport the expense report? Withhold critical information from my supervisor? In fact, the examples just provided are relatively straightforward examples of what students on college campuses face. And it is reasonably clear what the right or correct course of action would be in each instance. However, even though you know turning in a peer for cheating would be the right course of action, it can be challenging to act—this is the decision-action gap introduced earlier. Clarity about your values and vision of self is tantamount to ethical decision-making. According to world-renowned scholar, Dr. Mary Gentile, this work takes practice,[65] and ideally, it occurs before finding yourself in an awkward position.[66]

The decision-action gap in ethical decision-making is often substantial. Stop reading here and revisit the vignettes shared at the beginning of this chapter. Would you have acted or stood by? Would you have had the uncomfortable conversation? Would you have taken a stand or just acquiesced? Ethical decision-making involves logic *and* emotion. You may know what is right, but you feel afraid to *do* what is right. And that is why emotional intelligence is so valuable in the design of you as a leader and your leadership.

As you consider your ethical fitness, you may find you have a great deal of knowledge about ethical decision-making models, ethical perspectives, toxic leadership, and courageous follower-ship but lack the *skill* to navigate a complex moral dilemma.[67] First, it takes a great deal of intentional practice to become skilled at influencing others to behave in a way that may not serve them well in the short run (e.g., not cheating, ending the hazing). Second, consider the wisdom of leadership scholar Sean Hannah who suggests that "ethics is a team sport."[68] Arm yourself with a cadre of trusted advisors and mentors who can help you think through your approach to navigating difficult decisions. The following section is designed to provide a simple yet robust process to help develop an ethical and moral approach to leading others. The purpose was to integrate the thinking of many scholars into a framework for leading self and others.

The BASE Model

The BASE model provides a framework for building the skills of ethical leadership. As shown in Figure 5.4, BASE comprises four activities—each a fundamental ingredient to create a thoughtful starting point: (1) begin with you; (2) assess; (3) seek options; (4) elect and evaluate.

FIGURE 5.4 ■ Framework of the BASE Model

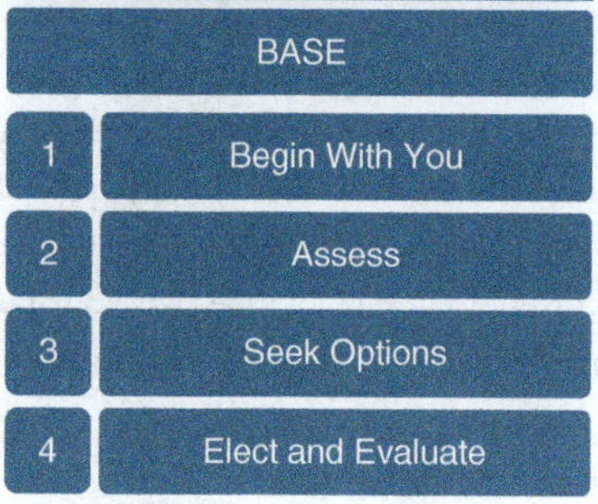

BASE
1 — Begin With You
2 — Assess
3 — Seek Options
4 — Elect and Evaluate

Begin With You

The first step in designing a moral approach to leading others is ensuring you have done the appropriate inner work. For example, you know about the topic of moral leadership—you have clarity around your moral principles, virtues, and blind spots and a vision for who you want to be (your character). What is your ethical code? Use that code as a guide, as there may be instances when it is appropriate not to follow your code. Can you think of an example?

By designing your ethical code and the virtues for practice, you are actively and intentionally entering into a state of growth and development. This becomes your *true north* to help guide your thoughts and actions during difficult times. An English proverb asserts that "a smooth sea never made a skillful sailor." In the beginning, a sailor must practice and prepare for what they will inevitably encounter; the more you engage in these turbulent waters, the more skilled you will become. The metaphor holds true for leadership—you will be tested in large and small ways. Are you ready with a basic framework (or have you developed your own), and are you practicing each day so you are prepared when you leave the harbor for the open sea?

Key questions in this phase

- What are the moral principles driving my behavior as a leader?

- What are the virtues I need to practice to help me better model a life of integrity?

- When do I have the most difficulty living a life of integrity? What are the triggers?

- What would people say about my character?

- What values do I hold that may prevent me from being who I want to be?

Assess

The second step is to assess. Although it may sound odd, many people fail to recognize when they are facing a moral dilemma. This can occur because of sheer ignorance, a lack of experience, an educational gap, an inability to scenario plan, a lack of empathy, or wrongly justifying/rationalizing behavior that is unethical. Awareness is paramount.[69] For instance, recall the brief vignette at the beginning of the chapter about Rosario, a relatively new member of the hockey team. Unless he is indeed in touch with his commitment to the moral principle of "do unto others" and his deliberate practice of the virtue of kindness, he may not consciously process that he is involved in a moral dilemma. Also, note that paying attention to your emotional reaction to a situation can be a biological indicator you are facing an ethical dilemma. Being attuned to your responses to a situation is valuable data that may trigger the next phase.

In the Assess phase, you better define the ethical dilemma and perhaps better understand the problem. This may require research or further dialogue with peers, parents, or trusted advisors and mentors who can provide guidance and counsel. By exploring your ideas with others, you can gain a better understanding of your thoughts, perspectives, and fears. Another option would be for you to benchmark the situation with your ethical code. By doing so, you may gain additional clarity on your potential courses of action and identify blind spots or cognitive biases that hinder your ability to think through the problem clearly.

Key questions in this phase

- What emotions am I experiencing because of the situation?

- What worries me about this situation? What is at stake?

- What is the ethical dilemma I am facing, and what are the competing values at play?

- What is an appropriate use of my power and access to resources in this situation?

- What loyalties are at risk?

- What authority do I have to act? Am I a leader with formal authority? If not, how should I influence those with authority? What followership style is most appropriate?

Seek Options

Scenario planning and empathizing with others are critical skills during this phase. For instance, can you identify ten options for how Latonya could respond in her vignette on cheating? At one extreme, she could do nothing; at the other, she could turn the student in for his behavior. However, there are multiple options in between the two options previously mentioned, each of which has a set of positive and negative consequences for her and the cheating student. What options provide her with a win–win? Your goal should be to identify at least five options for moving forward. Move past the obvious choices and explore more complex options to resolve the dilemma.

In his book *The Ethical Challenges of Leadership*,[70] author Craig Johnson highlights five **ethical perspectives** that can help an individual view an ethical challenge through multiple lenses. By intentionally exploring numerous perspectives and options, you will be better prepared to land on a decision with a higher level of intentionality. Be advised that perspectives overlap, and each has strengths and weaknesses depending on the context.

The first of the five ethical perspectives is **utilitarianism**, which means one should do the highest good for the most significant number of people. This approach requires the decision maker(s) explore the cost/benefits of their decision and the consequences of their actions—which can be difficult to predict.

The second approach is **Kant's Categorical Imperative**, which posits that an individual must do what is right at all costs. While this is noble and indeed a plan that has its place, it can be difficult to employ this perspective in all situations. At the extreme, the costs may be your life or the lives of others. On the other hand, this approach can be a good reminder that doing what is right at all costs helps you to take a close look at what those costs could entail in all situations.

Justice as fairness asserts that individuals in a free and democratic society should have equal access and opportunity to benefit from specific rights. This perspective contends that as a leader, you should consistently work toward the idea that all citizens should have access to fundamental rights—not just a few in power. Of course, this aligns with the founding tenets of the United States. For instance, to quote the *Pledge of Allegiance*: "I pledge allegiance to the flag of the United States of America, and to the republic for which it stands, one nation under God, indivisible, with liberty and justice for all."

Altruism means you should "love thy neighbor" and make decisions from a place of benefiting others. Highlighted in several religious texts, the principle of altruism requires you work from a place of concern for the well-being of others. Like the other perspectives, altruism is an ideal outcome of any moral dilemma. In other words, you work to keep the needs, wants, desires, and views of others in mind as you decide a course of action.

Pragmatism may engage any of the other ethical perspectives. Its strength draws from the notion that no one perspective can be correct all of the time. Back to the vignettes, it will likely benefit you always to follow the principle of not drinking and driving or getting in a car with someone who has been drinking. In this instance, having a clear line of what is and is not acceptable and beneficial will protect you and your loved ones. However, Kant's Categorical Imperative combined with altruism may cause you to help find a solution that creates a win–win (getting your friend's car home and not drinking and driving).

A hallmark of the Seek Options phase is asking questions of yourself and others (depending on the challenge). Several scholars have outlined critical questions that may help you determine a course of action (e.g., Dr. Laura Nash's brilliant 12 Questions from her article "Ethics Without Sermon"[71]). Some of these may also help you better understand the problem (assess) as well.

1. How will my decision impact others?

2. What is at stake if I do not act? What is at stake if I do?

3. Which ethical perspective is most appropriate for this situation?

4. Who will be negatively impacted by my decision? Am I willing to take this risk?

5. How do others perceive the problem? Can I empathize with their experience of the issue?

Chapter 5 • Your Values and Ethical Actions   **175**

6. What is my ultimate objective? What is the best-case scenario or ideal future state?

7. Whom will my decision injure (physically/psychologically)?

8. Is my potential solution a long-term solution, or will this problem remain in the long run?

9. What are the unintended consequences of each option?

Elect and Evaluate

In the end, you need to select an option and decide. Only the rarest of decisions ends up being perfect or ideal or addresses every nuance of the issue. There will be unintended consequences, people will respond in unexpected ways, and various other contingencies will come into play. A useful way of thinking about your decision is that you are running your best-formulated experiment to see if it yields desired results. Expecting the unexpected is a useful mindset. If everything does work out, great, but that may not be the case. As new data present themselves, you may need to revisit the Assess and Seek Options phases.

Two critical points require emphasis. First, ensure you have done your best to scenario plan the good and the bad of your decision. Second, ensure you monitor and reflect upon and evaluate the results of your chosen course. Seeking the counsel of trusted advisors *after* the decision is just as critical in this phase as it is during the Assess phase.

Key questions in this phase

- What were the unexpected consequences of my decision? Are they significant enough to warrant a reexamination?

- Are the results consistent with my future desired state, or are adjustments needed?

- How do vital players feel about the decision? What are they seeing and thinking?

Your values and ethical actions strongly impact your credibility as a leader. The previous chapter posed the questions: How would you like to be perceived by others? And how can you become the person others desire to follow? Designing yourself as a leader must include developing an awareness of your values, attention to the decision-action gap, and deliberate efforts to enhance your ethical fitness. Failing to attend to these aspects of your leadership and then subsequently failing your followers and organization, constitutes a moral failure in and of itself:

> The failure (or refusal) of a leader to foresee may be viewed as an ethical failure; because a serious ethical compromise today (when the usual judgment on ethical inadequacy is made) is sometimes the result of a failure to make an effort at an earlier date to foresee today's events and take the right actions when there was freedom for initiative to act.[72]

CHAPTER SUMMARY

This chapter examined ethical issues that directly impact the student experience and highlighted some key terminology and ideas. These concepts included foundational ideas around ethics and your ethical code, moral principles, virtues, and finding balance, integrity, values, and laws. Your moral development is the result of many influences, mainly family and education. Your growth continues even today.

All aspects of the leadership process comprise decisions, and as such, they are filled with ethical challenges. Those challenges, in leadership and life, can be categorized into five domains: academic, family, work, extracurricular, and friendship.

Perhaps most important, this chapter helps you design several dimensions of your approach to ethical leadership. Ethical leadership may feel like a set of extremes. On one end, there is an ideal state for people—including qualities such as altruism, justice, and caring. At the other extreme, there are examples of toxic and bad leaders who have engaged in horrific acts that have done significant damage. While you may not experience this extreme, it takes a great deal of moral courage to lead *and* follow.[73]

You can become a more skilled ethical decision maker by working on your ethical fitness. This starts with finding clarity about yourself and your values. Assuming your goal is to be an individual of sound character, you must determine your *true north*—who you are and what you stand for. The BASE model provides a strategy for you to practice ethical decision-making actively, so you are prepared when you face a significant ethical dilemma.

With deliberate practice, you can spend the early years of your career preparing for the next level—shaping an ethical organizational culture. As ethics scholar Craig Johnson suggests, "It's not enough just to have good character. Particularly in a large organization, people don't know you personally. So you have to be active in terms of shaping the organizational culture."[74]

KEY TERMS

Altruism (p. 174)

Character (p. 158)

Code of ethics (p. 154)

Decision-action gap (p. 163)

Ethical perspectives (p. 174)

Ethics (p. 154)

Integrity (p. 158)

Justice as fairness (p. 174)

Kant's Categorical Imperative (p. 174)

Laws (p. 154)

Moral principles (p. 154)

Personal values (p. 155)

Pragmatism (p. 174)

Utilitarianism (p. 174)

Virtues (p. 155)

CORE™ ATTRIBUTE BUILDERS: BUILD NOW FOR FUTURE LEADERSHIP CHALLENGES

Attribute: Confidence

Builder: *The Good Place, FYRE: The Greatest Party That Never Happened*, and WeWork: Or the Making and Breaking of a $47 Billion Unicorn

We know you have internalized information at a deeper level when you begin to see the concepts mentioned in this chapter in some of the television shows you binge on your favorite network. The three shows/films mentioned above are examples of programming where the main characters struggle to live a virtuous life. As you watch these and other shows, can you see some of the concepts discussed in this chapter as they occur on the screen? If so, you are

Chapter 5 ● Your Values and Ethical Actions   **177**

beginning to internalize the content. Questions to explore while watching may include the following:

- How does the primary character display attributes of toxic leadership?

- Discuss the character of the main character. What personal values guide their way?

- How do the main characters benefit from their followers?

SKILL BUILDER ACTIVITY

Moral Principles, Virtues, and Ethical Decision-Making

Part 1: Exploring the moral principles that guide your approach to leadership is a critical activity for any leader. Recall that moral principles are *truths* about behaviors that have been widely accepted and adopted by individuals, groups, and/or societies. Following, you will notice a list of widely accepted moral principles that can serve as a foundation for your approach to leadership. Use your favorite search engine to explore the meaning of the examples provided (and others as you see fit). Next, place a check mark (✔) next to your core four. The check mark indicates that you have explored its meaning, you could explain it to a friend, and it is of high value to you. The core four will serve as the foundation for your approach to leadership.

- Do good; avoid evil

- The Golden Rule

- Justice

- Rule of rescue

- Love thy neighbor

- Respect for persons

- Self-love

- Wisdom

- The end does not justify the means

- Follow what nature intends

- All people are created equal

- Do the greatest good for the greatest number of people

- Commitment to something greater than oneself

- Respect and caring for others

- Caring for other living things and the environment

- Faithfulness

- Mercy

- Love

- Sanctity of life

178   Module 2 ● Design Leadership Relationships

- First, do no harm

- Always do what is right, no matter the cost

- Equal consideration of interests

Part 2: Next, review the list of virtues provided and place a check mark (✔) next to your core four virtues you believe, with practice, will help you best model your moral principles. The check mark indicates you have explored its meaning, you could explain it to a friend, and it is of high value to you. Recall that virtues are concerned with living your moral principles. Virtues are widely accepted, morally good traits, behaviors, or habits that determine an individual's character. Virtues are practiced and are often a mean between two extremes. Virtues are not about what is right or wrong, but they are about what a person *should* be. Use your favorite search engine to explore the meaning of those we have included (and others as you see fit). Your core four will serve as opportunities for practice. Remember that Ben Franklin started his list because he *did not* have mastery of them. You *practice* the virtues. Regardless of how you choose the virtues to practice, the fact that you are intentionally working to develop them is a worthwhile endeavor. You may tell a friend you are "practicing the virtue of . . ."

- Charity

- Chastity

- Cleanliness

- Compassion

- Courage

- Diligence

- Frugality

- Generosity

- Hospitality

- Humility

- Independence

- Industry

- Justice

- Kindness

- Moderation

- Openness

- Order

- Patience

- Prudence

- Resilience

- Resolution

- Respect

- Self-control

- Self-efficacy

- Silence

- Sincerity

- Temperance

- Thoughtfulness

- Tolerance

- Tranquility

- Truthfulness

- Wisdom

Part 3: While a general framework for ethical decision-making (BASE) is explored in this chapter, it is helpful to have *your process*—a process you can recall with ease. A simple acronym can help you remember your process. It is important to remember your core four identified in previous sections can help inform your decision-making process. While not every decision will align with the core four you have chosen, it is important to acknowledge them as you move through the decision-making process.

What is *your* four- to five-step process or a visual model for making an ethical decision? Using the space following this box, draw a diagram of your process or model. After doing so, benchmark it with the mini case studies shared at the beginning of the chapter to see if your process is realistic.

6

DECISION-MAKING

LEARNING OBJECTIVES

Upon completion of this chapter, the reader should be able to

6.1 Interpret the role of decision-making in leadership

6.2 Define two types of decisions

6.3 Distinguish between a technical problem and an adaptive challenge

6.4 Describe decision-making at the group/team level

6.5 Apply the SOLVE model of decision-making

6.6 Assess several barriers to effective decision-making

6.7 Evaluate your decision-making in light of confirmation bias, stereotyping, and the availability heuristic

Leadership by Design Model

Design Self
How can I design myself as a leader?

Design Relationships
AS A LEADER, HOW CAN I DESIGN MY RELATIONSHIPS WITH OTHERS?

Design Others' Success
As a leader, how can I design success for others?

Design Culture
As a leader, how can I design the culture of my organization?

Design Future
As a leader, how can I innovate?

INTRODUCTION

Decision-making and problem-solving are at the core of a leader's work. Navigating challenges in a creative and ethical manner helps a leader stand out and best serves the organizations they work to advance. This chapter helps readers better understand the role of decision-making in leadership, acquire one very useful decision-making model, and think more intentionally about some of the inherent barriers that individuals and groups face when making decisions. The chapter

181

also highlights decision-making styles and other tips for helping leaders navigate the process of reaching the best course of action.

Let's begin by taking a look at some decisions made by business leaders today:

- Rosalind Brewer, the current chief executive officer of Walgreen's decided to confront racism head-on while serving as chief operating officer of Starbucks. In 2018, two Black men were racially profiled and arrested in a Philadelphia Starbucks (they were waiting for their business partner). Following the incident, she met personally with the men and kicked off several initiatives including a temporary closure of all stores to conduct racial-bias training.[1]

- Under the leadership of chief executive officers Ginni Rometty and Arvind Krishna, IBM has continued to move away from the hardware/laptop business and placed its bet on artificial intelligence, cloud computing, blockchain, and quantum computing.[2,3]

- In 2016, then president and chief executive officer Rose Marcario of Patagonia announced the company's intention to donate 100% of its $10 million in sales from Black Friday to charities that support planet Earth.[4] And Patagonia's current director of Philosophy shared that the company decided to change its mission to "Save our home planet."[5]

Leaders make decisions—decisions about what to do, how to do it, when, why, with whom, for how long, assuming what, and resulting in what end. Decisions can be mindful and purposeful, or they can be random, avoided, uninformed, and misguided. For anyone interested in leading, decision-making is a core activity of leadership.[6] Sometimes, your decisions result in positive outcomes, and sometimes not. Decisions are made alone, at times with others, but always relative to others. Followers, too, make decisions, which at times makes them the leader. Regardless of one's actions, a decision is always made, even if the decision is not to decide. The best leaders make decisions based on priorities aligned with their values and accept and work within the consequences of those decisions.

Leadership That Makes a Difference

Students across the globe are making a difference and tackling some real-world challenges that even the best scientists have yet to solve. Based on their expertise, they are making decisions about new and innovative ways to address our most difficult challenges. The following are three unique examples of how students, such as yourself, are using the techniques discussed in this chapter to change the world.

- At Rutgers, biomedical engineering student Katherine Lau led a team that created a prosthetic hand for a young girl. Through the use of a 3D printer, Lau and her team fashioned a device to improve the life of another. In fact, Lau said of the experience, "Getting that opportunity was a great experience. . . . The reason I want to be a biomedical engineer is to improve the lives of others. This summer, I got to see what my work can do for people."[7] Her decision to use 3-D printing as a tool to tackle this issue is unique, innovative, and potentially ground-breaking.

- In 2020, then high school student, Avi Schiffmann built a website (https://ncov2019. live/data) to help alleviate the spread of misinformation about the COVID19 virus. The home page offers easily found facts and was designed to scrape official sites and sources for the most recent data. Some reports suggested his site was receiving 300 million visitors each day, and he apparently had offers of up to $8 million to sell the site. He decided to use his skills for good and helped millions in the process by providing accurate and reliable data.[8]

Website built by Avi Schiffmann
https://ncov2019.live/data

- The iGEM Foundation is "dedicated to education and competition, advancement of synthetic biology, and the development of open community and collaboration."[9] Students from around the world were challenged to answer the following question—"How do you kill cancer cells without killing healthy ones at the same time?"[10] Teams decided upon a number of creative and innovative approaches to help scientists detect, treat, and prevent cancer. In fact, a team from Israel worked on ways to pinpoint cancer cells. "Using an innovative combination of molecular biology and engineering, the team devised a system they called 'Boomerang,' which detects cancer cells by identifying two cancer-specific promoters in cells and only targeting those cells for treatment. The team's work earned them five awards at the competition, including First Runner Up and Best Health and Medicine Project."[11]

DECISIONS, DECISIONS, DECISIONS IN LEADERSHIP

LEARNING OBJECTIVE

6.1   Interpret the role of decision-making in leadership.

If decision-making is so critical to leadership, what do you need to know about decision-making? The answer is a lot. Over the years, scholars, consulting firms, and leaders have each developed simple and complex models of decision-making to help leaders more skillfully navigate the many complex challenges they face. Consider the definition of leadership—the process of influencing others toward a common vision. Baked into the definition are many decisions, perhaps the most important being the need to determine a course of action—to decide on an idea to pursue. Consider the efforts of New Zealand's prime minister Jacinda Ardern to contain COVID-19 in her country. Widely regarded as one of if not the best responses to containing the spread of the COVID-19 virus, Ardern and her government moved swiftly and communicated consistently with her constituents. Following the containment of the virus, Ardern and her team turned to the economic challenges that, according to CNBC as of May 2021, were at pre-pandemic levels.[12] While not perfect, Ardern and her team carefully implemented policies that contained the spread of COVID-19 *and* supported struggling businesses through the process. At the core of any prime minster's work is making decisions that advance the nation from its current state to a better future state. In essence, decision-makers are often running their best experiment. While this language may sound odd, it is true, and this chapter will explore the notion of experimentation and decision-making further.

New Zealand prime minister Jacinda Ardern had to make swift, complex decisions that set a course for action.
Photo by Hagen Hopkins/Getty Images

Many of the problems collegiate leaders face are complex and challenging as well. For instance, many fraternity presidents and captains of athletic teams have worked diligently to stop hazing in their organizations. Other complex challenges on college campuses include freedom of association, decreased admissions, alcohol/drug abuse, Title IX, sexual violence/assault, student cheating and misconduct, and issues of diversity, equity, and inclusion. For instance, the president of the University of British Columbia, Dr. Santa Ono, suggested, "escalating anti-Asian racism is something that's very real in Canada very real in British Columbia and Vancouver especially" and decided to host a national forum to help raise awareness.[13] Again, there are many possible decision routes for each of these issues. No authority figure or expert can fix these problems, but leaders *can* make a difference by learning more about how to make the best decisions possible.

If those of you reading this textbook who have *entered the fray* and worked to reduce or eliminate the challenges mentioned, you know leadership is challenging work. Factions emerge. Ideologies clash. Conflict ensues. And you and perhaps a group of colleagues find yourself at the center of a proverbial storm. Leading others is not all tulips, warm-fuzzies, and chocolate bars. At times, the work of leadership is messy, high risk, difficult, challenging, and scary.

Decision-making is a core activity of leaders as they move groups from Point A to Point B. Even individuals who have chosen not to take on specific issues have decided to stay safe and maintain harmony. Sometimes a nondecision is the correct intervention—other times, this choice is damaging and dangerous.

As you move through this chapter and consider how to make more effective decisions, you may want to revisit Chapter 5 on ethics. In the final analysis, many of your decisions (and non-decisions) will either align or misalign with your "true north." Being intentional and deliberate in how your decisions align with your values is critical—it determines your character and ulti-mately impacts your relationship with others.

DEFINING DECISION-MAKING

LEARNING OBJECTIVE
6.2   Define two types of decisions.

Decision-making generally feels very difficult. People believe they prefer many options. But in reality, more choices can feel overwhelming and actually stifle making a decision. The word **decide** is defined as the process of making a choice or determining a course of action. However, the origin of the word decide comes from the Latin *de+caedere*, meaning *to cut off*. When you make a decision, you essentially cut off other options in order to pursue the decided option. No one wants to cut off options—they *might* work out. You *may* have missed an opportunity. This choice *may* never happen again. Yes, all those maybe outcomes will disappear—that is why decision-making is so difficult. But unless you make a decision and follow one option, you essen-tially follow none, and that is a problem in both leadership and life.

Decision-making is a specific process of choosing the best option, and it is often part of a more extensive process of problem-solving (see Chapter 8). The more you know about decision-making, the more comfortable you will be cutting off options, making decisions, and facilitating the decision-making of others.

There must also be a clear understanding of **decision criteria** (also known as decision rules[14]), which are factors deemed essential to consider in the process of choosing a course of action. For instance, when selecting a major, a student may use the following decision criteria for making the decision: prospects for getting a job, time, amount of passion for the topic, rigor/time com-mitment, quality of professors, and so forth. Some models suggest that weight is assigned to each criterion as well. For instance, an individual may place a higher weight on the passion for the topic than the time of day the class meets.

Levels of Decision-Making

Decision-making occurs at multiple levels. The first is the individual level. **Individual-level decision-making** consists of those decisions you make by yourself, most of which are rarely con-scious (e.g., what to wear, when to eat, your route to work, the pace of your walk, the amount of time you keep shampoo in your hair). While there is no concrete number of how many decisions an individual makes in a day, some research suggests that humans make more than 200 decisions a day about food alone.[15]

Group/Team-level decision-making is a more complicated process. A **group** is made up of individuals who are coordinating their work for some reason or another (e.g., shared gym time, where to eat, a place to study). However, there may not be a mutually shared end goal the individuals are collectively working toward. A **team** is a group of individuals with a collective target (e.g., win the championship). In a general sense, group decision-making has less emotional energy than team decision-making. For this chapter, the term group is used, but be aware there is an essential distinction between a group and a team. Table 6.1 summarizes the advantages and disadvantages to group decision-making.[16]

TABLE 6.1 ■ Advantages and Disadvantages to Group Decision-Making	
Advantages to Group Decision-Making	**Disadvantages of Group Decision-Making**
can accumulate more knowledge	often works more slowly than individuals
broader perspective, more ideas	may involve considerable compromise, which may lead to less-than-optimal decisions
participation increases individual satisfaction, support, involvement, and buy-in	often dominated by one individual or small clique
serves important communication functions	overreliance on group can inhibit management's ability to act quickly and decisively when necessary

At times, groups can be part of the problem (or the main problem). For instance, a decision-action gap exists when an individual or group knows what they should do but struggle to make the right or best decision for various reasons.[17] Another example is that the group may be unaware of what is not being discussed. Specific topics are taken off the table (consciously or unconsciously) by decision makers—these are called **nondecisions**, which are the covert issues about which a decision has effectively been taken, which will not be decided. They are controversial topics that go against the interests of the powerful stakeholders: They do not engender support, they do not fit with the prevailing culture, they are not considered acceptable for discussion, so they are quietly sidestepped or surpassed or dropped. A knowledge of what these issues are is likely to be as revealing or more so as knowledge of what is overtly being discussed. They are what is really going on, not just on the surface but underneath it. The decisions that are being discussed in the board room, in meetings, and by executives and management represent the tip of iceberg.[18]

Types of Decision-Making

When individuals and groups do make a decision, it can be rational or intuitive.[19] In a general sense, **rational decision-making** models follow a set process, such as the PrOACT model explained later in this chapter.[20] Rational decision-making models follow an established process, and potential strengths include that it provides a standardized/predictable method and compares multiple options based on similar criteria. A downside can be the speed of decision-making, and the approach may not work when working through adaptive challenges.[21] Likewise, the method does not take into consideration the role of relationships in the decision-making process. Decision-making at the group level involves others, and how the leader manages the social dimension is of critical importance. It is rare that humans are purely rational, as economists and social psychologists have discussed.[22] In fact, while it would seem logical that decision makers would work to determine the ideal solution (maximizing), they often satisfice (put up with a good enough answer).[23]

Intuitive decision-making relies more heavily on an individual's gut feeling, a hunch, or intuitions, which are "affectively charged judgments that arise through rapid, nonconscious, and holistic associations."[24] When asked if they should conduct focus groups to see what the consumer wanted, former CEO of Apple, Steve Jobs, suggested, "A lot of times, people don't know what they want until you show it to them."[25] He was famous for asserting that Apple designers and engineers just built products for themselves. Strengths of the intuitive decision-making approach may include speed, and it gives the decision maker an opportunity to experiment and better define the problem—specifically in environments called VUCA, which stands for volatility, uncertainty, complexity, and ambiguity.[26] VUCA environments lack information and predictability, so doing first will help the leader better understand the problem.[27] Downsides may include that the decision maker may be subject to any number of cognitive biases, and the approach may be wrought with difficulties, if for example, the decision maker lacks expertise, emotional intelligence, self-awareness, and clarity of values (which all humans do at one time or another). At an extreme, this approach to decision-making can feel haphazard, random, and unpredictable. Thus, the importance of the leader's relationships is critical. A leader with healthy, long-term relationships will more intuitively read their team when making a decision.

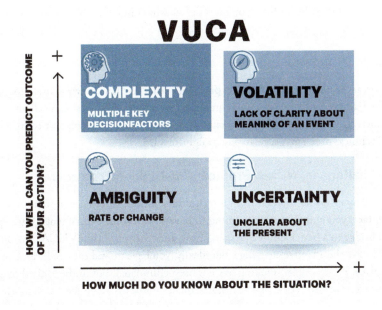

VUCA environments need decisions to take action that will bring more information.
©iStockphoto.com/300_librarians

Regardless of approach, leaders need to be skilled in both approaches to decision-making. There will be situations with a definite end state and need for a logical process, and there will be complex adaptive challenges that may not warrant a rational decision-making process. This requires intentionality in approach. The leader and group must first understand the type of problem and then intentionally choose a rational or intuitive approach.

REFLECTION QUESTION

- When was the last time you experienced the decision-action gap in a significant way? You knew what *should* be done, but you (or the group) failed to act for one reason or another.

- Which style of decision-making do you often default to—rational or intuitive? When has this default hurt you? When has it served you well?

TECHNICAL OR ADAPTIVE? TYPES OF PROBLEMS LEADERS FACE

LEARNING OBJECTIVE

6.3   Distinguish between a technical problem and an adaptive challenge.

Often, leaders and groups are deciding because they are working toward a better future state—an ideal end that will leave others in a better place. Having a clear understanding of the type of problem you are working is critical if you hope to make progress. Sometimes, a decision is relatively simple and straightforward; you could ask, "What would you tell your best friend to do?"[28] However, sometimes the decisions are much more complicated. Many terms are used, and they can mean similar things. Regardless, you must define what kind of problem you are working to solve.

Technical or Tame Problems

You know you are working with a **technical problem** when there is a known solution to the issue. For instance, fixing a flat tire or cleaning out an individual's arteries. You can call an authority figure or expert, go to your favorite search engine, or even take a course on how to fix technical problems. Technical problems are relatively straightforward.

Adaptive Challenges/Wicked Problems/Ill-Defined Problems

Adaptive challenges do not benefit from a technical solution. In essence, a solution does not yet exist. In fact, you and the team are going to have to run some experiments, learn quickly, and build a bridge to a better future.[29] Arising from and existing within VUCA environments, you may not solve the adaptive challenge, but ideally, you have moved the needle and now exist in a better place. For example, smoking has not been eliminated, but in the United States, the number of smokers has decreased drastically. Another example would be obesity. While fast food has mostly dropped in popularity, fast-casual chains (e.g., Chipotle, Panera Bread) are growing at a more rapid rate than some of the traditional fast-food chains.[30] However, the fact remains that obesity is a significant challenge in the United States. There is no expert or authority figure one can call with the answer to the solution for the problem of the obesity epidemic. Challenges such as gun control, racism/sexism, poverty, cyber-security, racial injustice, mitigating a global pandemic, combatting misinformation online, are all adaptive challenges throughout the world. It takes experimentation and engaging in continuous learning to best understand how to tackle adaptive challenges—the students involved in some of the issues mentioned at the beginning of this chapter (e.g., hazing) are working on adaptive challenges.

Chapter 6 ● Decision-Making   **189**

Experts Beyond the Text

Insightful Leaders Know About . . . Paradoxical Leadership: Adopting Both/And Thinking

By Wendy K. Smith

Our world is a complex knot of thorny interwoven tensions. Leaders face a tug of war between focusing on today or innovating for tomorrow. They struggle to ensure the financial success of their institution while seeking to address a broader set of social and environmental demands. They grapple with how to connect to the global economy while targeting the unique needs of their local communities.

Faced with such competing demands, leaders often make a choice between alternative options. We once celebrated leaders that could be so clearly decisive. Yet increasingly we know that this kind of either/or thinking can be limited at best, and detrimental at worst. In the words of Mary Parker Follett, "We should never allow ourselves to be bullied by an either-or. There is often the possibility of something better than either of these two alternatives."[31] Choosing one option diminishes possibilities. Moreover, doing so may create warring factions and trigger polarized thinking. Instead, great leaders adopt **both/and thinking**. They move away from binary opposites to adopting a more holistic approach. They engage competing demands simultaneously while seeking their deeper interrelatedness. That is, they engage paradox.[32]

Paradoxes are persistent interdependent contradictions.[33] These competing demands are interwoven such that making a decision to focus on one element ultimately triggers its opposite. For example, leaders face the ongoing tug-of-war between addressing today's needs and planning for tomorrow's possibilities. The leaders that focus too much on today will find that tomorrow becomes today sooner than they think. But leaders that are too focused on tomorrow will find they can never realize the value of their innovations in the present. The challenge is for leaders to engage the demands of both today and tomorrow *simultaneously*.

Research finds that leaders more effectively navigate competing demands by adopting a **paradox mindset**. These leaders embrace tensions as opportunities for growth, change and creativity. Rather than ask, "Should I focus on A or B?," leaders with a paradox mindset ask, "How can I accommodate A and B simultaneously?"[34] Then these leaders build organizational structures and culture to ensure they are constantly honoring the unique needs of each demand while simultaneously seeking synergies and connections.[35]

Former American President Barack Obama once noted, "It is both possible and necessary to see the paradoxes, the ambiguities, the grey areas, the absurdities of life, but not be paralyzed by them." He stressed the tensions emerging as president. "My job is to look out for the safety of American citizens as the American president, on the other hand, ensure there is a universal interest in peace and fairness and justice outside our borders. How do I reconcile those things, but then still be able to act as Commander in Chief and still be able to make a decision? Or a matter of dealing with the economic crisis, being able to reconcile the fact that our free market system creates enormous efficiencies and wealth, and that is not a system that we should want to tear down on a whim because a lot of people are relying on us making good decisions about the economy, and on the other hand there are parts of the economy that don't work and are unjust and get people frustrated and angry . . . and both things are true and you still have to make a decision."[36] Similarly, his own campaign opponent, Senator John McCain once urged us all to move beyond the "tribal rivalries that have sown resentment and hatred and violence in all the corners of the globe." Instead, he called for unity and a chance to find a both/and that connects us. "We weaken [our greatness] when we hide behind walls, rather than tear them down, when we doubt the power of our ideals, rather than trust them to be the great force for change they have always been."[37]

Great leadership follows the path of political opponents Obama and McCain. In our complex world, these leaders urge us to move beyond our binary thinking that leads to increased polarization and instead explore the complex, paradoxical and holistic solutions to our greatest challenges.

REFLECTION QUESTION

Do you tend to be an either/or thinker or a both/and thinker? Can you think of a situation in which both/and thinking can enable you to develop more creative and sustainable solutions?

Explore your own paradox mindset. See paradox.lerner.udel.edu for free access to the Paradox Mindset Inventory.

IN LEADERSHIP, DECISION-MAKING IS A TEAM SPORT (MUCH OF THE TIME)

LEARNING OBJECTIVE

6.4   Describe decision-making at the group/team level.

As soon as you take on a formal or informal leadership role, you will be making decisions in groups. Discussing the role of the team in the process and how to establish an environment that will yield success is a critical task. You will need to focus on (at least) two dimensions—process/task and relationship. The first is the process of decision-making or how the group arrives at the best way forward. The second dimension is your relationship with others in the group. Designing how you approach the relationships in the group is critical and cannot be underestimated.

Leadership by Design

Design Principle: Hick's Law

Definition: The time it takes to make a decision increases as the number and complexity of alternatives increases.[38]

In Other Words: One choice = quick decision; two choices = sort-of-quick decision; hundreds of choices = long and slow decision.

For Example: Drawing on their expertise, Secret Service agents can scan a crowd in seconds to recognize risk and take action. They combat Hick's Law by knowing what and who to disregard, knowing what they are specifically looking for, and training their eyes to limit options.

For Leaders: Leaders can enhance follower decision-making by applying Hick's Law in both directions. When and in what context are quick decisions necessary? On the other hand, when would you want to *slow down* decision-making? One thing to keep in mind: Hick's Law is not applicable as the complexity of the decision increases. In other words, a complicated decision will (and should) take some time.

Align Your Decision-Making Style

Once you have decided how to design the work of the team, how you approach the decision-making process is a meaningful discussion and intentionality is critical. As the leader, you must be intentional in your approach and how it will impact the relationships in the group. Theorist Victor Vroom and his colleagues developed five basic options a leader has (a basic summary is shown in Table 6.2).

The theorists assert that a leader must ask seven questions to help determine the appropriate path forward. The questions are designed to help the leader determine dyanmics, such as level of importance, type of problem, the need for buy-in, and potential conflict. The answers to these questions will help determine which leadership style is best depending on the situation.[39]

1. Is there a quality requirement such that one solution is likely to be more rational than another?

2. Do I have sufficient information to make a high-quality decision?

3. Is the problem structured?

4. Is acceptance of a decision by subordinates critical to effective implementation?

5. If I were to make the decision by myself, is it reasonably certain that it would be accepted by my subordinates?

6. Do subordinates share the organizational goals to be attained in solving this problem?

7. Is conflict among subordinates likely in preferred solutions?

TABLE 6.2 ■ Five Basic Options for Leaders	
Decide alone	The leader makes the decision themself and does not consult others.
Consult individually	The leader speaks with one or two individuals to gain their perspective on the issues and then decides.
Consult group	The leader speaks with the group or team to discuss the issue, solicit feedback, and then makes a decision.
Facilitate	The leader facilitates the decision-making process but does not share and/or promote their perspective.
Delegate	The leader delegates the decision to another individual or the group.

REFLECTION QUESTION

Can you think of instances where peers have used the wrong style for the situation? How did this impact their ability to lead the decision-making process?

Design Your Decision-Making Style

There are several models of decision-making with varied levels of complexity.[40] Some models outline a series of steps to take in a process-oriented manner, such as the three highlighted following.

- PrOACT: work on the right decision **Pr**oblem, specify your **O**bjectives, create imaginative **A**lternatives, understand the **C**onsequences, and grapple with **T**radeoffs.[41]

- GOFER: focus on **G**oal clarification, **O**ption generation, **F**act finding, consideration of **E**ffects, and **R**eview & implement.[42]

- DECIDE: **D**efine the problem, **E**stablish the criteria, **C**onsider all alternatives, **I**dentify the best alternative, **D**evelop and implement a plan of action, **E**valuate and monitor the solution and feedback when necessary.[43]

Other decision-making models, such as Multi-attribute Utility Theory (MAUT)[44] and Analytic Hierarchy Process (AHP),[45] involve a more complicated mathematical approach to help individuals, teams, and organizations make the best decision. In fact, there are sophisticated multiple-criteria software that support some methods and approaches.

Table 6.3 compares four decision-making models across general decision-making activities. Where do you see advantages to each of the models? What is missing (and why do you think that model does not include it)?

TABLE 6.3 ■ Decision-Making Models				
Decision-Making Activity	**SOLVE**	**PrOACT**	**GOFER**	**DECIDE**
Preparing the decision makers	**S**et roles			
Understanding	**O**utline problem and decision criteria	Work on the right decision **Pr**oblem Specify your **O**bjectives	Focus on **G**oal clarification	**D**efine the problem, **E**stablish the criteria
Strategizing—what is the best approach?	**L**ist multiple strategies			
Imagining and option/idea-generating		Create imaginative **A**lternatives	**O**ption generation	**C**onsider all the alternatives
Making a decision	**V**eer toward consensus	Understand the **C**onsequences Grapple with **T**radeoffs	**F**act finding Consideration of **E**ffects	**I**dentify the best alternative
Implementing			**R**eview & implement	**D**evelop and implement a plan of action
Evaluating	**E**valuate decision and process			**E**valuate and monitor the solution and feedback

Chapter 6 ● Decision-Making   193

DESIGNING YOUR APPROACH TO DECISION-MAKING: THE SOLVE MODEL OF DECISION-MAKING

LEARNING OBJECTIVE
6.5   Apply the SOLVE model of decision-making.

This chapter highlights the SOLVE model because it focuses on group decision-making and the role of leadership. What the SOLVE model leaves out—idea-generating and implementing—other chapters in this text cover more extensively. Of course, as the issues become more complex, so does a leader's approach to problem-solving. For most issues you will be working through in your organization, the SOLVE model will be a good starting place. However, while the model is presented as a process, steps can be skipped and/or prioritized out of order depending on the problem. For instance, if your group has an expert with *the* answer, it may be that you just begin by veering toward consensus versus taking the time to go through each step. You may have the impression the SOLVE model needs to take a lot of time. However, when you step back and think about it, athletes move through this process in seconds. Coaches do the same from the sidelines. So while in a general sense, it is important to go through all steps, it does not necessarily need to take a *long* time. For each phase of SOLVE, a brief description is provided along with common pitfalls. If you are genuinely tuned in to what is happening in the meetings you attend, you will notice many of these pitfalls. Recognizing them in real time will not only help you keep the group on track, but it will also help your team progress through the decision-making process.

Set Roles

On any athletic team, players must have clear roles. When a player moves away from their position and takes over another player's role, it can cause confusion, frustration, and chaos. Team-based decision-making is no different. People need to know their role, and they need to be clear from the onset. Who is the timekeeper? Who is the note taker, or who is recording action items? Who is leading the discussion/process? Who is building the agenda? Who is following up to ensure completion of tasks? Who is leading the meeting? At times these roles are understood by the group, other times not. *Just be sure there is clarity.*

Common Pitfalls at This Stage

- *People forget their role.* The leader forgets they are leading a process, gets immersed in the conversation, and forgets they are responsible for meeting management. This can result in wandering conversations, a couple of people taking over, and rushed decisions.

- *People take on the role of others.* A team member begins leading the meeting, and the leader no longer has control of the tone, pace, and topics being covered.

- *Roles are not defined.* This is the most common pitfall when working with young adults. Roles are not assigned, and the group wanders. At times, a couple of roles may be appointed, but others—such as timekeeper or note taker—are not.

- *One individual takes on multiple roles.* At times, the leader may take on numerous roles. The leader is so busy trying to take notes, keep time, stay on task, and facilitate the conversation that it becomes unmanageable.

Outline the Problem and Decision Criteria

Challenges, problems, and opportunities come in many different forms (e.g., technical and adaptive). While the players in the National Football League (NFL) are changing, at least the rules and other variables remain relatively constant. With leadership, the context is shifting—media, political forces, cultural norms, technology, and so forth. Taking the time to outline the problem and your decision criteria are perhaps the most critical steps in the entire process. Until the group has a clear understanding of the parameters and an ideal end state, little can be accomplished. While this first phase may seem simple, you have to go a couple of levels down to get to the heart of the matter. For instance, think of a university band that hazes. A simple problem statement such as "we want to eliminate hazing" has many other problems bundled underneath the statement that need to be defined, discussed, and considered. For instance, with the example of the band's hazing, *problems underneath the problem* may include the following:

- Student leaders avoid conflict and do not want to make a faction mad.

- A faction of band members views hazing as fun and energizing.

- A faction of band members sees hazing as an integral way of bonding people.

- The group is unsure of what could replace the hazing activities.

- Some of the student leaders enjoy the hazing themselves and do not want to change. The risk of getting caught is worth the enjoyment.

- A faction of members enjoys the tradition of hazing. The experience is a rite of passage.

- Authority figures who know about the hazing do not want to spend the political capital on this issue.

To adequately address the issue, the leader will need to examine their appetite for disruption, identify the problems underneath the problem, clarify decision criteria (items to be compared to help determine the best option), define an ideal end state, and begin working with the broader membership to address the issues, especially if an external authority figure (e.g., the university, the band director) does not impose a decision on the group. What seemed like a simple problem actually has multiple components that need to be addressed, clarified, and understood.

Common Pitfalls at This Stage

- *The problem is not accurately/completely defined.* While it is difficult to be sure you have identified all components of an adaptive challenge, give the time needed to ensure the group has a good sense of the problem or opportunity.

- *Inaccurate assumptions are made about the problem.* While defining the problem, pay close attention to statements that may limit or truncate understanding of the issues. Words such as never, cannot, always, and every are indicators that you and the group may be making false assumptions.

- *Not enough time is given to this phase.* The group blows past outlining the problem and moves straight to brainstorming. A hallmark of this phase is the number of clarifying questions asked as the group works to define the ideal end state and identify the problems beneath the problem.

Chapter 6 • Decision-Making   195

- *There is a lack of clarity around decision criteria.* The group has differing levels of agreement and/or understanding of the rules upon which they will be evaluating different options.

- *The leader does not notice some people are trying to outline the problem/decision criteria and others are brainstorming.* The leader will need to keep the group in the space of problem definition until the problem statement, decision criteria, and the ideal end state are articulated. Until these elements are clarified, it will be premature to move on to brainstorming. The leader has to skillfully keep those members who instinctually move ahead in the correct phase.

- *The problem statement is oversimplified.* In the example of the band, merely stopping at "we want to eliminate hazing" is an oversimplification of what the group is working to solve. This statement is like saying the U.S. government wants to "eliminate the deficit." The reality of what is underneath that statement has stalled lawmakers for years.

List Multiple Strategies

Once the group has consensus around the problem statement and decision criteria, it will want to move forward with brainstorming. The group will want to divide up the problems beneath the problem and address them one at a time or in small groups. Regardless, the group intends to brainstorm as many options as possible. Each of the preceding issues may have 10 to 15 ideas—do not worry about how silly or far-fetched the ideas are. Ideally, a group member is recording the thoughts in a place where everyone can see, and as discussed in previous sections, viewing the decision-making process as intentionally running a series of experiments is a useful way of thinking about how to move forward. While unlikely that the group will identify the perfect solution to please all parties, perhaps it will identify the best experiments to run. Asking the group, "What are the best experiments we should run?" will keep the group in a place of thinking in possibilities.

Common Pitfalls at This Stage

- *Perfect becomes the enemy of good.* The group searches for the one best answer and spends a great deal of time on one or two potential solutions. As a result, the group does not have many ideas to build upon and must rely on only a few options.

- *The group moves too slowly through the process.* A variation of the pitfall mentioned above, the group and its leader forget that the purpose of this phase is identifying as many potential solutions as possible.

- *Once an approach has been decided, the group stops thinking about other options.* Once the group is engaged in implementing a chosen solution, it can identify better solutions. However, the leader and members need to continue brainstorming, even in the midst of implementing a solution.

- *The group spends time discussing the merits of each idea while brainstorming.* The group stops to consider the value of each idea versus merely identifying as many options as possible. As a result, the group stalls on only one or two ideas or goes deep into one or two possibilities.

- *The group stays in a place of only seeing the barriers.* The group spends a large percentage of the time stewing on the obstacles ahead of them versus naming the barriers and then moving to brainstorming.

- *The leader is too democratic and loses control of the group.* The leader loses control of the process and is so concerned with everyone's voice being heard they ineffectively manage the process.

Veer Toward Consensus

Once the group has identified a good number of ideas, the leader wants to help the group veer toward an agreement. While consensus is ideal, it may come down to a vote as well—so be prepared. The group works to identify its best guess about the correct experiment(s) to run—rarely will one individual have the answer. So keeping the group in a mindset of experimentation will be important. With an eye on the time, the leader may want to ask individuals to clarify ideas, seek out viable combinations, or even seek new ideas based on what has been identified thus far. However, the goal is to veer toward consensus, and one way to do so is to say the following—"I am hearing a general preference for XYZ approach. Does anyone have a major problem with us trying this first?"

Common Pitfalls at This Stage

- *The leader becomes overly concerned with finding the "right" answer.* There needs to be a balance. The goal is to outline the best guess but ensure the group has given enough attention to the issue to be certain it has a good number of ideas.

- *The leader is afraid to put the decision to a vote.* The leader becomes so fixated on gaining consensus that the process stalls or critical time is lost.

- *The leader does not spend enough time hearing the opinions of others.* Balance is key. Leaders who force their ideas through with little attention for general buy-in will struggle to gain widespread support. Conversely, leaders who are easily pulled in multiple directions may lose perspective on how to move forward.

- *The leader forgets to tap the quiet members of the group.* Just because individuals or factions are silent does not mean they have given consent or support. As a leader, you may want to quickly acknowledge individuals who have not spoken up to better understand the level of support.

Leadership by Design

Design Principle: Cost-benefit

   Definition: Decisions and behaviors will only be taken if the benefits are equal to or greater than the costs.

   In Other Words: People are constantly assessing the return on investment for every action. "Whenever people decide whether the advantages of a particular action are likely to outweigh its drawbacks, they engage in a form of benefit-cost analysis[46]

   For Example: Have you ever grabbed a snack at the cafeteria and gotten in a long line and suddenly realized—you are not really *that* hungry? What is more likely happening is that you have mentally assigned the act of waiting in line a certain cost and subconsciously deemed the benefit of the food not worth it. The value you have placed on the time spent waiting is greater than the expected value incurred.

   For Leaders: Cost-benefit is a common decision-making technique that comes in a range of sophistication.[47] But as a design principle, the costs and benefits are designed as an

Chapter 6 • Decision-Making   197

informal and *perceived* factor. In other words, much of what drives decisions lies in what you *think* the costs and benefits are, versus some concrete measure. As you design your relationships with followers, consider these questions: What do followers see as the costs and benefits to working with you? How might you verify follower perceptions of costs and benefits?

Identify your costs and benefits. Then highlight what you need to for followers (while remaining authentic, transparent, and true). There are many forms of value beyond financial. Benefits might include a purposeful mission, a difference-making project, personal creativity, great autonomy, being part of something big, a fun and engaging culture, and great colleagues. Also consider benefits that might be indirect or deferred.

Evaluate Decision and Process

The group needs to circle back and evaluate its process. In the military, this phase is called an after-action review. This is a time to circle back, make sense of what occurred, and plan for next time. Groups that do not take time to evaluate may miss essential learning and could subject themselves to similar mistakes in the future. Similar to other phases, this does not need to take a great deal of time—just be intentional with the time being used.

Common Pitfalls at This Stage

- *The group does not complete this phase of the process.* The group is so caught up in the results (good or bad), they forget or do not prioritize this phase of the process.

- *The group blames or externalizes others for results versus looking within.* While external forces may have hindered the group's ability to succeed, failing to recognize what the group could have done better may be a missed opportunity for learning. The group fails to own its part in the failure.

- *The group avoids the awkward conversation.* As a result, the group fails to discuss the real issues. Or the group works around the shortcoming of individuals or factions.

- *The group and/or the leader does not keep the discussion in a constructive space.* Tempers flare, frustrations boil over, and the group struggles to keep the dialogue constructive and civilized.

MYTH OR REALITY?

The SOLVE Model Takes a Long Time

Myth. A leader can move the group through this process at a pretty good pace, and the model is merely a framework. A leader (and the group) may intentionally decide that one or two steps are not needed depending on the problem being solved. The key is intentionality. A leader who unknowingly skips or forgets steps is limited in their ability to work any problem. The leader must balance the speed of work with the quality of work, which is, at once, an exciting and challenging prospect.

SOLVE in Action: Designing (and Deciding) How the Team Will Work

There are some critical ingredients to any competent team. First, there has to be a clear mission, problem statement, opportunity, or objective. Absolute clarity in this domain will help everyone better understand the ideal end state.

Second, develop a structure that will effectively capture and facilitate the work getting accomplished. Create a shared document and let the document drive all the work. Write down each individual's name, their role, and their specific/measurable/time-bound deliverables, and develop a set of group norms—the behaviors each team member commits to (e.g., submitting work on time, attending all meetings). On this document, include everyone's contact information, the team norms, and the agenda for each meeting. Be sure to take the time in your first meeting to establish a regular meeting time and include these dates/times on the shared document as well. Note, though, that at times, perfect can be the enemy of good. You may not get everyone to every meeting—you still need to meet. See if the missing person can call in, video conference in, or at the very least, update their section of the shared document, so everyone knows where they are.

Third, each meeting should begin with a discussion of the team norms, and then each member should report on their deliverables. As the leader, you may want to send out a reminder in advance of the meeting to remind people to update the shared document with their latest information. Be ready for one or two people to not follow through and/or complete their work. Plan for these conversations in advance, and as a group, identify a consequence for those who are not prepared. By setting up the team correctly (structurally and socially), you have a better chance at creating an environment where you can capitalize on the unique talents and perspectives of your team members. This is not common practice.

Fourth, once some tasks are identified, it will be essential to delegate said tasks in an effective manner. You will want to ensure absolute clarity of mission with the individual you are entrusting. Ensure they are clear on the task, the deliverable, and the timetable, and be sure to answer any questions before they move forward. It will be necessary to check in (e.g., "How can I help?" or "Any unforeseen issues?") with each at a midway point. By doing so, you are reminding the individual, acting in a supportive manner, and providing them with an opportunity to check in. Maybe send another note to the group a couple of days before the next meeting and remind them to update the shared document, which will serve as the agenda for the next meeting.

REFLECTION QUESTION

Which phase of SOLVE do you need to focus on the most as you develop and practice?

HOW DID WE GET HERE? THIS WAS NOT THE PLAN: BARRIERS TO DECISION-MAKING

LEARNING OBJECTIVE

6.6 Assess several barriers to effective decision-making.

Just as there are a great many tools and techniques for making accurate or quick or strategic decisions, so too are there many barriers that impede those efforts. This section may be one of the most important toolkits you acquire as so much of your leadership work relies on

Chapter 6 • Decision-Making   199

decision-making. Understanding decision-making influences and barriers will help you identify (and address) those mental and behavioral habits that can confuse and misdirect your decisions. And perhaps more importantly, awareness of decision-making barriers will make you more adept at designing leadership relationships and others' success. As you read this section, take careful note of how the behaviors are unintentional and unconsciously applied. Then, see if you can spot these in your own decisions and those with whom you engage.

Cognitive Biases That Hinder Decision-Making

All humans (individually and collectively) battle cognitive biases that hinder their ability to make good decisions.[48,49] An understanding and an awareness of these biases will help you and the group be more mindful when working through the SOLVE process. In this section, some of the more common cognitive biases are highlighted. As you read, pay close attention to where you see each on campus, in your family, online/in the media, and in the workplace.

Confirmation Bias

Humans tend to pay closer attention to data that confirm their bias.[50] Their interest is peaked when a stimulus aligns with their perspective or worldview. For instance, in the United States, Republicans flock toward one television network, and Democrats tend to view another in more significant numbers. While fine, if the individual is unaware of the bias or sees no bias, then it can be difficult for the individual to understand both sides of an issue, and as a result, they may be heavily rooted in one side with little space for dialogue. Social media has exacerbated this cognitive bias.[51,52]

One-Right-Answer Thinking

Many of the challenges (e.g., hazing) discussed earlier in the chapter are adaptive challenges. In other words, no authority figure can fix the issue with their expertise. As a result, individuals who suffer from one-right-answer thinking are sure they have found the silver bullet that will alleviate the issue at hand. While possible in theory, it is important to explore several options rather than just sticking with the one right answer[53] or the first correct answer. Research on problem-solving suggests that the first solution is rarely the most effective or efficient path forward.

Groupthink

Groupthink has three classic symptoms, which are "the belief in the correctness of one's own group, negative stereotypes of the out-group, and rationalizations concerning the issues."[54] Other precursors of groupthink may include crisis, external threat, group insulation, a culture of compliance, and recent group failure.[55] This is why the promotion of diversity of thought, culture, ethnicity, personality, and so forth is critical to effective decision-making. Without said diversity (and a culture that values essential debate), a group of human beings can come to some pretty poor decisions. For instance, choosing not to comply with public health recommendations of professionals during the COVID-19 Pandemic.[56]

Framing Effect

The framing effect is characterized by coming to different conclusions based on how an issue or topic is framed. A simple example of this cognitive bias is an individual's mindset—"Is the glass half empty or half full?" Another example, in the United States, is that a Republican-leaning television network and a Democrat-leaning television network will frame a single issue such as gun control or immigration in a different way.[57] Without awareness and understanding of how an issue is framed, people are susceptible to decisions that do not take into account other perspectives and points of view. For instance, conspiracy theories were ever-present in the framing of the origins of COVID-19.[58] The *Leadership by Design* feature in this chapter highlights this type of cognitive bias.

Overconfidence Effect

This occurs when people place an unusually high value on the conclusion the individual or group has achieved.[59] Because of this cognitive bias, individuals and groups can lose sight of the limitations of their approach or strategy. Casual investors and CEOs alike can suffer from this quite easily.[60,61] While the formula may have worked last year, the addition of new players, changes in other teams, and other contextual factors will likely impact the team in ways that make the formula obsolete in the coming year.

Law of Triviality

Individuals spend a significant amount of time avoiding tough, adaptive challenges and spend the majority of their time on less important, easily solved issues[62]—for example, in the United States, Congress investigating steroids in baseball[63] versus fixing Social Security, immigration, education, or ensuring safety from cyber attacks. Student groups can suffer from this as well. More time is spent discussing T-shirt colors and food options than major issues facing the group or association. Is the group addressing the real, tough, critical problems, or is it focused on other, more trivial content?

Illusion of Control

This cognitive bias is defined as "an expectancy of a personal success probability inappropriately higher than the objective probability would warrant."[64] In essence, illusion of control is an overestimation of influence an individual has on an outcome or result. For example, an individual may view a successful sales call as a result of their skill versus luck or chance.[65] Some research suggests that cognitive diversity in teams can help mitigate this cognitive bias.[66]

Leadership by Design

Design Principle: Framing[67]

Definition: A technique that influences decision-making, risk tolerance, and judgment by manipulating the way information is presented or described.

In Other Words: What is emphasized is what you see *and* what you think.

For Example: Are you pro-bicycle or anti-car? The frame focuses your attention and influences your behaviors. How often are you lured to articles with click-bait titles: *You won't believe what happened next*!

For Leaders: Most people fail to bring the full or correct information into their conscious awareness at the right time. That is not a fault, it is a reality. Learning to expand the limits of your awareness before you make an important decision helps you avoid basing decisions solely on how the information is presented. How would you react to this photo if it were titled *Relaxing sunset yoga*? How would you react if the title were *Migrants plead for protection*? Framing is a powerful design principle that you as leader must be wary of and utilize for good. Positive frames tend to influence toward proactive and risk-taking behavior, while negative frames bring out reactive and risk-averse actions. In what ways can you frame your organization or mission? How can you frame yourself to better design your relationships with followers?

Relaxing sunset yoga, or migrants plead for protection?
©iStock.com/ipopba

> **REFLECTION QUESTION**
>
> Which cognitive biases can be seen in conservative or liberal media outlets? Why is it more difficult to see them when viewing the outlet that *you* align with politically?

Ways *You* Could Be the Barrier to Effective Decision-Making

As you become more and more deliberate in your leadership of the team, you will begin to notice themes and patterns of behaviors in yourself and others. It can be easy to identify the dysfunctional behaviors of others, but seeing them in yourself is another level of sophistication and requires cirtical reflection.[68] As you become more and more experienced in facilitating the decision-making process, you will gain confidence, and ultimately, you will drive toward successful outcomes more intentionally and thoughtfully. However, along the way, you will make some common mistakes that may stall progress. The following behaviors may diminish the quality of team decisions and your relationship (e.g., trust, credibility) with the group or team. When have you fallen victim to one or more of these behaviors?

- *Forgetful*: You forget you are leading the meeting. You get sucked into the conversation, lose focus, and wander along with the group. You may even lose track of the purpose of the meeting. This may lead to additional meetings or rushed/poor solutions that are made at the last minute.

- *Unprepared*: You set the meeting but do not prepare an agenda, outline a clear purpose for the meeting, or determine how the group will spend its time. As a result, the group wanders in multiple directions with little aim or direction and is experienced as a waste of time by others.

- *My way*: You take over and/or talk over and then wonder why others have not *bought in* and are not excited and energetic about the course of action.

- *Impatience*: You move to brainstorming before a clear problem statement has been identified. Group members have different levels of understanding about the end state and begin brainstorming before they fully understand the problem/opportunity.

- *Low energy*: You are negative or struggle to keep the energy of the group in a curious and positive place. You fail to set a positive emotional tone or actively decrease energy levels.

- *Wet fish:* You cannot keep the meeting on track when other, more dominant group members take over. And you watch and allow it to happen.

- *Overly emotional*: You get really worked up and yell, cry, and/or make others feel uncomfortable. Your lack of emotional intelligence impedes your ability to connect with the group.

- *Poor delegation*: You ensured that people were delegated tasks but did not write anything down, failed to follow the tenets of effective delegation, and ultimately did not check in until the next meeting.

- *Non-leadership*: You occupy a title, but no one really knows what you do beyond that. You are too busy, distracted, and/or overextended. You are leading nothing.

As previously mentioned, all humans fall victim to some of these dysfunctional behaviors at one time or another. Be mindful and reflective and have trusted advisors who will provide you with unfiltered and honest feedback. Leading the process of decision-making is challenging work. In a general sense, you know you have arrived at a better place if you begin to see some of the following indicators of high-functioning teams:

- There is a general sense of enthusiasm for the decision.

- Within reason, people are laughing and joking during meetings.

- Individuals volunteer without you having to beg them to do so.

- Work is consistently done early or on time.

- There is a high level of trust among team members.

- Team members know their role and enjoy their position.

- The team is securing results and collecting small wins.

- The team has a deep bench of talent.

- People feel they can voice their concerns, thoughts, and observations. There is trust that their voice will be heard.

- It is understood that not everyone will get their way all of the time.

REFLECTION QUESTION

When was the last time you fell victim to one or more of the behaviors mentioned in this section? How did it impact the group and your objectives?

Chapter 6 • Decision-Making **203**

Ways *Others* Could Be the Barrier to Effective Decision-Making

Decision-making is an emotional activity.[69] Depending on the issue, an individual or group will be asked to give something up or alter their behavior in some form or fashion. Decision-making involves change—an emotional process because "habits, values, and attitudes, even dysfunctional ones, are part of one's identity. To change the way people see and do things is to challenge how they define themselves."[70] Because decision-making often occurs in a team (especially in the collegiate context), the role of emotional intelligence is critical. At its most basic level, emotional intelligence is about awareness and regulation of emotions in self and others.[71] Throughout the decision-making process, the leader can be triggered in any number of ways, and maintaining emotional intelligence takes skill. Emotions run high around issues such as politics, religion, immigration, gender equality, gun control, the war on terror, free trade, quality, and so forth.

Leading a group of peers when you do not have formal power to hire or fire takes skill. Leading without authority is all about influence, and you may recall the proposed definition of leadership, which is "a process of influencing others toward a common vision." To do so takes a great deal of patience, wisdom, expertise, and awareness. And many leaders suffer from a cognitive bias called an empathy gap, which means they tend to underestimate "how much emotional situations influence their attitudes, preferences, and behaviors."[72] After all, some of your team members can be pretty entertaining characters. Some will be responsible and levelheaded and display a strong work ethic. However, you will come across some other characters as well. The authors asked former students to make up some fictitious characters that represent real people they have worked with during group projects (we added a couple ourselves). The results were insightful, and as you read through them, you will notice some familiar characters.

- *Distracted Dhruv*: Dhruv is famous for not paying attention to the group at all. He is elsewhere—mentally and physically.

- *Noncontributing Neema*: The only thing Neema contributed was the text every week asking you what the homework was and if you could save her . . . again.

- *Finish Line Fred*: Fred's nowhere to be found for the whole project, but he shows up right at the end—just in time to get the big win when you turn in your *A*-level work.

- *Micromanaging Min-jun*: Min-jun obsessively insists on being the group leader, and she's micromanaging to ensure you do the work her way.

- *Reliable Ryota*: Ryota is dependable, level-headed, and consistent in getting her work done. She can always be counted on as the backbone of any group project.

- *Distant Dante*: Dante is always on his phone or texting during class or in group meetings.

- *Bossy Bento*: Bento can be very close-minded about other people's thoughts and prefers to tell people what they should do. Bento believes their way is the best way, which creates little space for the thoughts and ideas of others.

- *Ghosting Giotto*: Giotto disappears for days and weeks at a time. He will reappear but may disappear just as quickly again.

- *Silent Sofia*: Sofia says three to four words throughout the entire group project. Those words often occur during the final presentation.

- *Off-Task Olivia*: Olivia is more interested in spending the group's time talking about last night's party than focusing on the task at hand. She has excessive side conversations as well.

- *Forgetful Francesca*: Whether it was intentional or not, no one knows. What we do know is that Fran did not complete her work, the project is stalled, and the meeting is a waste of time.

- *Donald the Downer*: Donald's mood is frequently negative, and he works hard to help others see the downside of the group, the project, the class, the professor, and so forth.

- *Talkative Tiana*: Tiana takes up a lot of airtime, so much so that others in the group are visibly frustrated and put off by her lack of awareness.

What behaviors have you experienced working with others in a group? What character would you add to the list? Which group members do you act like sometimes? Maintaining emotional self-control when working with any number of these individuals can feel like a Herculean effort. You will encounter these same behaviors for the rest of your life. In the end, you need to walk into any group project understanding how these behaviors might trigger you emotionally and result in you not being your best self. It will happen. Giotto will ghost, Olivia will get off task, and Bento will boss. How you navigate these realities will make all the difference. In fact, now that you know what you are looking for, you may view this as an opportunity to practice working with individuals who display unique and different behavioral tendencies, achievement orientations, capabilities, and desires to succeed.

Other Factors That Impede Effective Decision-Making

Throughout history, poor decisions have been made—and at a significant cost in some instances. It may seem like the pitfalls to decision-making are endless, which is why skilled decision-making requires practice, awareness of all of the dangers, awareness of your habits as a decision maker, and then even more practice. Some problems are more common than others, particularly for developing leaders and groups. You can read about them in Table 6.4. Which impediments have you observed in recent weeks? Consider choosing one to work on for 30 days and then choose another. Mindful engagement in decision-making will further develop your CORE™.

TABLE 6.4 ■ Potential Decision-Making Impediments	
Time	The leader/group does not spend the time needed to successfully define and solve the problem they are working.
Emotions	The leader/group is emotionally tied to how things are, one course of action, and has unconsciously or consciously taken some options off the table.
Analysis paralysis	The group is caught up in the process of analyzing all of the possible options and gets bogged down in the details and specifics.
Lack of clarity	There is a low level of clarity around the ideal end state or even the problem being solved.
Conceptual blocks	The leader/group has created fictitious rules or boundaries that hinder the ability to accurately define and/or solve the problem.
Politics	The leader/group lets internal and external politics hinder its ability to identify the *best* solution.[73]

Apathy	The leader/group does not have the energy and/or desire to work the problem.
Groupthink	The leader/group becomes *of one mind* and alternative ideas, perspectives, and opinions are pushed to the side.
Fear	The leader/group is afraid to fail or afraid to take an unpopular stance on an issue. As a result, viable options are taken off the table (consciously or unconsciously).
Power	Power dynamics in the group hinder the group's ability to have honest dialogue about the issues. As a result, individuals and groups do not bring their voice to the table.
Knowledge	At times a leader/group may not have enough knowledge to adequately solve the problem.

DEI BY DESIGN

LEARNING OBJECTIVE
6.7 Evaluate your decision-making in light of confirmation bias, stereotyping, and the availability heuristic.

The process of decision-making is never neutral. Every decision-making activity brings with it the prior experiences, knowledge, attitudes, beliefs, values, and expectations of the individual making the decision. You leverage these intellectual and emotional resources to make the best decisions at the time—however, each piece of evidence is often not weighted equally. As you just read, there are numerous cognitive biases that influence decision-making. For example, individuals tend to over-value information that aligns with our preconceived notions while simultaneously under-valuing or in some cases completely discrediting any otherwise valid data that contradicts what we already believe to be true. Hopefully, you remember this is called confirmation bias, and it is often responsible when good people make bad decisions.[74]

Confirmation bias has been understood for a long time—all the way back to the work of English philosopher and statesman Frances Bacon in the 1600s; and its effects can be seen in modern studies of political attitudes,[75] forensic science,[76] and metacognition,[77] among others. You are likely also familiar with **stereotyping**, defined as incorrectly attributing to an entire group the characteristics of one or just a few of its members. Stereotyping and confirmation biases reinforce one another, which further exacerbates faulty decision-making. Consider the stereotype: "All college professors wear plaid." While this statement is false—all professors do not wear plaid (and even when they do, they don't all wear plaid at the same time), if you were to walk around your campus with this stereotype, you would be more likely to pay attention to the clothing of your professors that do wear plaid and pay less attention to the attire of professors not in plaid. Furthermore, you would be more likely to misidentify plaid-wearers as professors (when they are not) and incorrectly identify non-plaid-wearers as not-professors, even when they are!

Unfortunately, the confirmation bias influence pushes into your mental processes, like recall. The ease with which you can bring to mind specific examples is known as our **availability heuristic**,[78] and it further influences your judgment about people, places, events, and ideas. Put plainly, it is easier to remember (or imagine) examples from your own experiences *that reflect what we already believe to be true*. It is much harder to come up with instances that contradict your beliefs, especially if you remain unaware of those beliefs. Purposefully and mindfully considering the full range of your experiences, especially those that offset the availability heuristic (i.e., those that contradict your mental model) enhances decision-making. Remember, your brain is a lean, mean pattern-making machine that loves its mental models. Your decisions impact people. Who you hear, who you see, and who you recall are influenced by your cognitive biases.

CHAPTER SUMMARY

Leaders make decisions—decisions about what to do, how to do it, when, why, with whom, for how long, assuming what, and resulting in what end. Effective leaders make mindful and purposeful decisions as they design different aspects of leadership. Many can see the problems facing an organization, but very few are skilled at helping the organization make and execute the decisions to address and move *past* problems.

Deciding means cutting off options and making a choice that determines a course of action. Decision-making can address problems that are technical or adaptive, can involve processes that are individual- or group/team-oriented, and can be intuitive or rational. All of these conditions require careful consideration of the situation, context, and persons.

Your decision-making can be greatly enhanced by determining your style and by learning a model of decision-making similar to SOLVE: Set roles, Outline the problem and criteria, List multiple strategies, Veer toward consensus, and Evaluate the decision and process. Recognizing and eliminating barriers such as cognitive biases and ineffective personal habits can also enhance your decision-making.

Decision-making is critical to designing relationships. Much of the decision-making work on teams and within organizations impacts and is influenced by how you relate to others and build relationships (e.g., consensus, coalition-building). Leaders balance two competing priorities—task and relationships. As you gain experience and wisdom in this work, you will become more and more valuable to any organization. Organizations need people who do both well.

KEY TERMS

Adaptive challenges (p. 188)

Availability heuristic (p. 205)

Both/And thinking (p. 189)

Decide (p. 185)

Decision criteria (p. 185)

Decision-making (p. 185)

Group (p. 186)

Group/Team-level decision-making (p. 186)

Individual-level decision-making (p. 185)

Intuitive decision-making (p. 187)

Nondecisions (p. 186)

Paradox mindset (p. 189)

Rational decision-making (p. 186)

stereotyping (p. 205)

Team (p. 186)

Technical problems (p. 188)

CORE™ ATTRIBUTE BUILDERS

Attribute: Engagement

Builder: The iPhone 20

At the time of this book's printing, the Apple iPhone may be in its 14th or 15th iteration. A fun question to ask a group of friends is the following: "Can you imagine the hardware and software features of the iPhone 20?" This would be a device introduced around 2028. As you

Chapter 6 • Decision-Making   207

listen to the answers, pay close attention to what happens next. Some participants will forget that you asked about hardware and software. Their minds will only focus on one or the other, and they will immediately move to brainstorming one or the other. Rarely will they remember both, and many conceptual blocks will hinder their ability to think creatively. For instance, some will continue to think of the device in its current form—a phone as it looks today. Because of this, their ability to creatively brainstorm future iterations will be limited to a device as it seems today. Finally, pay close attention to the quality of their ideas. Are they limited to ideas that are just outside of current reach (e.g., longer battery life, waterproof), or are they genuinely transformational?

Additional questions to explore while watching may include the following:

- Could you see how your friends were limited in their abilities to understand your question and brainstorm truly innovative options?

- Do you think you could intervene skillfully and engage them in identifying creative opportunities that are more in line with a device on the cutting edge of technology in 2028?

- What conceptual blocks hinder your ability to help the work of the group move forward?

SKILL BUILDER ACTIVITY

That Was the Best Group Project Ever

Group projects (as an undergrad and beyond) are rarely incredible experiences. The authors hear from students (and professionals) that group projects are a consistent source of frustration. Do you have the skills to lead a group project and at the end have people say to you—"That was the best group project I have ever worked on!" If you do, then you are a powerful individual. This is a challenging task, but you can do it. The key is to intentionally practice much of what has been discussed in this chapter.

Following are 10 key questions to consider as you think through how you will arrive at an amazing outcome *and* a positive group experience.

1. How could your personality, mindset, outlook, and style hinder progress? Do you tend to micromanage or take over? Do you struggle to remain organized and on task?

2. How will you help the group clarify the desired end state? Note this is more than just *securing an A*. In part, the task is about this being the best group project. What will that take? What are the expectations and norms of group members?

3. How will you organize your work? Would you use a platform like Google Drive?

4. What leadership style will best suit the group? A combination of democratic, affiliative, and coaching? Some other combination?

5. How will you divide the roles of group members and hold one another accountable?

6. How might Hick's Law apply to the work of the group?

7. What questions will you need to ask your professor as you outline the problem? Identify at least 10.

8. How will you hold one another accountable?

9. How will you celebrate some of the small wins and milestones along the way?

10. How will you make the experience enjoyable and fun?

While each of the questions is relatively simplistic, think through how you will navigate the project. Moreover, it will be important to revisit your answers to the questions so the group can gauge progress. When the project is complete, close the loop by going to lunch and discussing how the group did as a whole. Did you achieve your dual objective? Was it the best group project ever?

<h1>7 INFLUENCE, POWER, AND MOTIVATION</h1>

LEARNING OBJECTIVES

Upon completion of this chapter, the reader should be able to

7.1 Explain the characteristics of followers that inform leadership influence

7.2 Connect follower path-goal to your leadership style and influence

7.3 Describe the difference between influence, manipulation, and authority in one's role as a leader

7.4 Identify various forms of bias and recognize their influence

7.5 Identify 11 key approaches to influencing others

7.6 Analyze the 10 sources of power and how people use them

7.7 Analyze the difference between intrinsic and extrinsic motivation

7.8 Apply Kouzes and Posner's 5 Practices of Exemplary Leadership to your relationship design

Leadership by Design Model

Design Self
How can I design myself as a leader?

Design Relationships
As a leader, how can i design my relationships with others?

Design Others' Success
As a leader, how can I design success for others?

Design Culture
As a leader, how can I design the culture of my organization?

Design Future
As a leader, how can I innovate?

INTRODUCTION

Influencing others to be involved and engaged is a necessary skill for any leader.[1] Understanding *how* you best influence others can make all the difference for the success of the followers, organization, and leader. This chapter explores the role of influence in leadership and how an

210   Module 2 • Design Leadership Relationships

individual's sources of power can impact their ability to lead others. The chapter concludes with a discussion on how to build a culture that motivates and empowers others.

This is the last chapter in the Design Relationships module, and intentionally considering how you will relate to and influence others is critical to leadership. Your actions impact relationships, and in many ways, determine your ability to succeed or falter. As you read this chapter, try to connect with the concepts on a relational level. In other words, consider what influence, power, and motivation look like *between* you and others and how these affect your ability and others' abilities to succeed in the classroom, on the athletic field, or on the job. Whether you are inspiring a group of people to change behavior (Chapter 10), building a healthy organizational culture (Chapter 11), or encouraging others to behave in an ethical manner (Chapter 5), influence is at the heart of your work as a leader.

Leadership That Makes a Difference

A challenge that has plagued college campuses for decades is hazing. For instance, in a study of more than 325,000 NCAA athletes, more than 80% reported having been exposed to "questionable to unacceptable activities."[2] Another study found that 55% of respondents experienced hazing in clubs, on teams, or in organizations. And in more than half of the instances, a picture is posted on social media.[3] Hazing most often occurs in Greek societies, athletic teams, and the band. While one would like to think the problem has gotten better, there have been a number of high-profile cases in recent years that have brought shame and disgrace to individuals and their institutions.

The roots of hazing likely stem back to the military and other *rites-of-passage* ceremonies that new or younger members have endured. From a power and influence perspective, it is a fascinating topic because on a college campus, the desire for inclusion can be overwhelming and seemingly *good* people engage in activities that are dangerous, abusive, and demeaning. It would seem the individuals engaged in the hazing have a great deal of influence and power over the individuals being hazed. According to Chaney, the practice of hazing continues in many organizations on college campuses, even though illegal in 44 states and highly discouraged by college administrations.[4]

Unfortunately, the leadership that makes a difference in this instance is the *toxic* leadership. While not all bands, teams, or Greek organizations haze, in this instance, the *common vision* is warped, lacks morality, and is illegal in many places. Perhaps even more disturbing is the number of bystanders who may not actively engage but do not have the fortitude and courage to stand up to the ringleaders. Why? What influence tactics are used? How is power being used or abused? What motivates someone to haze or be hazed?

In 2007, Tracy Maxwell founded www.hazingprevention.org, a nonprofit whose goal is to "educate people about the dangers of hazing, advocate for change, and engage the community in strategies to prevent hazing." Maxwell saw a need in middle schools, high schools, and higher education and decided to act.[5] She and her volunteer board of directors compile resources, and research and provide educational programming. At the heart of effective leadership is a strong sense of self and the values that guide the leader's work. Alignment between expressed values and actions is paramount when working with others. Individuals who align values and activities not only serve as role models for others, they build trust—a key ingredient for leadership and relationships.

Timothy Piazza fell during an incident of hazing and drinking at a fraternity in Pennsylvania; between 1969 and 2019, at least one student died in a hazing incident in the United States.[6]

Abby Drey/Centre Daily Times via AP, File

INFLUENCE IS (MOSTLY) NOT ABOUT YOU

LEARNING OBJECTIVE

7.1 Explain the characteristics of followers that inform leadership influence.

Most definitions of leadership include some mention of leadership being a process of influence. Embedded in the work of leadership, influence feels like figuring out how to get followers to do something—how to get employees to work hard, get students to study, get constituents to vote. Note the language in those statements. Getting someone to do something is all about you and your motives, which means you are overlooking your most powerful tool as a leader, namely, the motivation of your followers. Why are your followers—each one of them, individually—doing what they do? What are their goals? What are their motives? If you do not know, you should ask. If *they* do not know, ask them to think about it. And then talk about it relative to the goals of whatever organization or entity you are leading. Assuming the individual motives of others or outright ignoring them and presuming that your goals as a leader will take precedence will only result in frustration for everyone.

Similarly, the design framework of this textbook may lead you to think that purposefully designing the different aspects of your leadership is a solitary endeavor, similar to a "craftsman in a shed with lumber and nails, hammers and a saw, and a blueprint for a chair."[7] There will certainly be times when you will need to work alone, but the model of successful design is participative, collaborative, and a mutually influential codesign. Fortunately, many of the concepts and tools in this textbook, such as empathy and design thinking, will reinforce the codesign notion.

Before you dig into the *how* of influence, power, and motivation, every leader must frame that influence in the context of their values and intentions. Why and to what end are you trying to influence others? Is that influence just and equitable? Are you fully considering the inequalities built into your context and community—even the ones you cannot readily see? How does the system perpetuate who does and who does not have power? Embedded within all influence are issues of privilege, class, protection of unjust systems, inequality, bias, and the potential to wield that influence in ways that can harm others and/or perpetuate unjust beliefs and systems. Only those who are vigilant about the dynamics of power and powerlessness—either leader or follower—will truly foster effective leadership.

As you read about the influence tactics and sources of power described in this chapter, reflect on the range of their application—when they have been used to achieve good and when they have been abused and caused great destruction. Many individuals see the word influence (and design in some cases) as manipulation. In reality, you influence others all the time, and in turn, others influence you. The keys are to (a) be aware of that influence, (b) be aware of how that influence fosters justice and equity within the larger context, and (c) mindfully and justly decide what and how you will influence others. If you want to be the leader who makes a just, equitable, and sustainable difference, then you must continue to develop your awareness of the full range of influence: visible and invisible; leader to follower; across and within genders, ethnic distinctions, and socioeconomic differences; and from the individual level through the cultures and systems that influence assumptions. You can further explore this topic across the different DEI by Design sections within each chapter and within the broader leadership field in John Dugan's book *Leadership Theory: Cultivating Critical Perspectives*.[8]

THE PATH TO THE GOAL AND YOUR STYLE

LEARNING OBJECTIVE
7.2   Connect follower path-goal to your leadership style and influence.

Leadership is the process of influencing others toward a common vision. Let's pretend for a moment that the goal is not so common or, more likely, that the purpose (for the organization) is broad enough such that many other goals fit within it. Excellent organizational missions and visions are specific enough to guide the organization yet broad enough to allow many individuals to find the piece that motivates them. Each follower has unique, individualized goals for themselves relative to the organization. This reality is even more prevalent in creative and professional fields where great autonomy, innovation, and self-direction are necessary.

What happens on their path to that goal is where you, the leader, have significant influence. Path-goal leadership theory[9,10] highlights the variables that affect a follower's motivation to travel the path from the present to their goal. In simple terms, here is what you can do as leader:

1. Help define the goal(s)

2. Help clarify the most effective path

3. Remove obstacles (even if that obstacle is you)

4. Provide support in a variety of ways (that do not unintentionally become obstacles)

Chapter 7 • Influence, Power, and Motivation   213

The key to maximizing follower motivation lies in how the leader goes about addressing these four elements, often called a **leadership style**. What does each of these elements look like from your perspective as a leader? How would you go about accomplishing these for each follower?

A leader's *style* represents the beginning of you understanding your tendencies but only as a springboard from which to shift and alter your behaviors to maximize follower and organizational success. Many leaders will justify their ineffective behavior by saying (and thinking), "Well, that is my leadership style; my followers will just have to get used to it." Maybe . . . or maybe they (your followers) will disengage, sabotage the mission, or just find another organization.

The great news is with work, you can change your default leadership style, and doing so is as easy as refocusing on what each follower needs, their goals, the path to those goals, and what the task/s requires. The fit between these variables, as shown by leadership scholar Peter Northouse,[11] is shown in Table 7.1.

TABLE 7.1 ■ Fitting Leadership Behavior With Follower and Task		
Leadership Behavior (aka, your style)	**Follower Characteristics**	**Task Characteristics**
Directive Provides guidance and psychological structure	Dogmatic, authoritarian	Ambiguous, unclear rules, complex
Supportive Provides nurturance	Unsatisfied, need affiliation, need human touch	Repetitive, unchallenging, mundane
Participative Provides involvement	Autonomous, need for control, need for clarity	Ambiguous, unclear, unstructured
Achievement oriented Provides challenge	High expectations, need to excel	Ambiguous, challenging, complex

Effective leaders discern what style will work best given the situation, to what degree, at what point, and with whom.[12,13] If you are working with high-achieving individuals who are very self-directed, using a directive style will not only be ineffective but will be perceived as condescending and an obstacle in the path. We will explore this notion in greater detail later in the chapter.

There are many leadership styles—including more to this particular theory. However, the essential message remains: *To be effective, leaders need to facilitate followers by providing those things that will help their progress and by removing obstacles from that progress.*

FORMS OF INFLUENCE

LEARNING OBJECTIVE
7.3 Describe the difference between influence, manipulation, and authority in one's role as a leader.

Just like many other topics, there is an entire literature base on the topic of influence.[14,15] It is a complex subject and requires self-awareness, awareness and empathy for others, and a sound grounding in your values. **Influence** is the process of moving individuals or groups to the desired mindset, position, behavior, or place. Leaders need to consider an even more fundamental idea of influence—namely, that while they are influencing others, they too are subject to being influenced. Once this reality is understood, leaders can more fully understand their motivations. The leader can consider five dichotomous elements. For instance, what would be more effective, direct influence, like an appeal to why this task is important, or an indirect influence, like appealing to a follower's colleagues who then influence the follower? Should the influence be overt such that they know you are trying to influence them in a specific manner or covert such that the influence is masked?

There are also physical, psychological, and contextual dimensions to influence, as shown in Table 7.2. For instance, are you using some kind of psychological/cognitive means of influence (e.g., appeal to relationship, guilt inducement, etc.); a physical means (i.e., something more tangible like bonus pay); or contextual, where you alter the environment as part of influencing (e.g., play soothing music, take away the chairs so folks have to stand and talk)?

TABLE 7.2 ■ Forms of Influence

Direct: Leader focuses influence efforts on the specific subject of influence.	Indirect: Leader seeks to influence the subject by way of other individuals.
Overt: Leader's efforts to influence are clearly seen.	Covert: Leader's efforts to influence are hidden.
Conscious: Leader wants subjects to be aware of efforts to influence.	Unconscious: Leader wants subject to be unaware they are being influenced.
Active: Leader is currently purposefully trying to influence others.	Passive: Leader is influencing others even without purposefully trying.
Individual: Influence is focused on a single person.	Group: Influence is focused on a group and utilizes group dynamics.

Leadership by Design

Design Principle: Signal-to-Noise Ratio

   Definition: The ratio of relevant to irrelevant information.

   In Other Words: How much junk is in the way of important stuff?

   For Example: How does a mascot clearly express themselves or tell a story without using any words? They have a strong signal-to-noise ratio since their actions are not muddled by speech. Likewise, PowerPoint presentations with too much information on each slide are filled with noise that distracts from key points.

   For Leaders: What is your signal-to-noise ratio when it comes to your followers? How much of what you communicate is relevant (to them) versus not relevant? Leaders influence others through the many ways they communicate, but those messages need to be clear, focused, and relevant. Be mindful of the signal-to-noise ratio that you put forth in all the ways you and your organization communicate. Confirm shared meaning. Edward Tufte said, "Clutter and confusion are failures of design, not attributes of information."[16] What *noise* is getting in the way of your designing leadership relationships?

> **REFLECTION QUESTION**
>
> Which of the forms of influence listed in Table 7.2 have you used in the last couple of days with your peers, at your job, or in your student organization?

The Difference Between Influence and Authority

In addition to forms of influence, leaders should understand the difference between influence and authority or what is called legitimate or formal power. An **authority figure** is an individual whose role provides them with formal power to determine the fate of individuals or groups. **Formal power** is legitimate power bestowed upon an individual who holds a position or role (e.g., judge, police officer). For instance, a police officer has the formal power to give you a ticket, a judge can put you in jail, and your professor has the authority to issue you a grade. And while you may not agree with their decisions, they have the authority afforded to them by a larger body because of their role. Leadership scholar Ron Heifetz has a unique and interesting perspective on this concept.

> Our language fails us, too, when we discuss, analyze, and practice leadership. We commonly talk about "leaders" in organizations or politics when we actually mean people in positions of managerial or political authority. Although we have confounded leadership with authority in nearly every journalistic and scholarly article written on "leadership" during the last one hundred years, we know intuitively that these two phenomena are distinct when we complain all too frequently in politics and business that "the leadership isn't exercising any leadership," by which we actually mean to say that "people in authority aren't exercising any leadership."[17]

While some leaders influence through the use of formal power and authority, leadership is more often about using **informal power**, which is derived from an individual characteristic, such as charisma, expertise, experience, wisdom, and so forth. Leadership is about influencing others toward a shared vision. They are partners in the process and want to engage and commit to a better future.

Leadership is more often about informal power rooted in expertise, charisma, experience, or relationships.
©iStockphoto.com/JohnnyGreigs

The Difference Between Influence and Manipulation

There is also a very important difference between influencing someone and manipulation. **Manipulation** is similar to influence but often with more of a hidden or inauthentic intent. Manipulation usually involves an ulterior or hidden motive.[18] There is a level of deceit in manipulation. A general objective would be that leaders are transparent and upfront about their motives as they work to move individuals or groups to a desired mindset, position, behavior, or place.

DEI BY DESIGN

LEARNING OBJECTIVE
7.4   Identify various forms of bias and recognize their influence.

Much of this chapter focuses on influence as mindful, purposeful action in the practice of leadership—the tools leaders use to influence followers. Equally important is an awareness of who or what is influencing you, the individual in the leader position. The actions of followers will certainly influence you, but the key factor informing that influence is . . . you. In Chapter 9, you will read more about your brain's ability to construct meaning (recall: your brain is a lean, mean, pattern-making machine from Chapter 2). These constructed meanings influence how you see the world and how you judge the world and those in it. **Biases** are your associations in favor of or against a person or group in society.[19] In some cases, you are aware of such associations, which make them **explicit biases** that impact your behaviors and judgments.

However, because your construction of the world appears (to you) to be how the world really is, your biases sometimes go unrecognized by you. These take the form of automatic assumptions about others that you see as "true" when they are really your perspective. This is called **implicit bias**. These biases form patterns of judgment that reinforce prejudices, which can in turn lead to discriminatory behaviors. For example, you may have experienced some wealthy children who were ill behaved, from which you have developed a negative bias. Consequently, when you find out that a child comes from a wealthy family, you judge their actions as entitled, have little patience for their personal challenges, and are unlikely to hire them. Your constructed idea is influencing your judgment and behavior.

It is important to consider and enhance self-awareness of your implicit and explicit biases, especially when they oppose your stated beliefs and values. Leaders especially need to be aware of how biases impact the ability to craft and maintain relationships, the ways bias can corrode credibility and trustworthiness, and how you as a leader might be influencing biased processes, practices, and structures.

Perhaps you are biased to disbelieve what you read in textbooks. In that case, check out one or more of the implicit association tests by visiting the following website: https://implicit. harvard.edu/implicit/takeatest.html. Harvard University's *Project Implicit* "is a non-profit organization and international collaboration between researchers who are interested in implicit social cognition—thoughts and feelings outside of conscious awareness and control".[20] Their goal is to educate members of society about implicit biases and to collect data about bias and disparity. The results from these assessments help you see your own biases more clearly while contributing to the overall understanding of how biases impact society.

Chapter 7 • Influence, Power, and Motivation   217

Self-awareness of your biases will help design leadership relationships. However, as you expand into designing success for others and designing culture, it becomes your responsibility to navigate the biases of others. *The Kirwan Institute for the Study of Race and Ethnicity* at The Ohio State University helpfully provides some strategies for interrupting bias and repairing its effects.[21] Collectively referred to as becoming an **active bystander**, the steps include: (a) recognizing when an instance of bias occurs, (b) choosing to confront those situations, (c) taking action (including educating others and inviting them to try different approaches in the future), and (d) creating positive future patterns of thinking and acting. Additionally, using humor, being literal about assumptions, asking questions to generate conversation, stating your own discomfort, and using direct communication are strategies to speak out against bias when it occurs.

DESIGNING YOUR INFLUENCE WITH INDIVIDUALS AND TEAM

LEARNING OBJECTIVE
7.5   Identify 11 key approaches to influencing others.

You influence others—up, down, and across. The process of influencing others is multidirectional, and you have been influencing others your entire life. Whether interacting with your peers when making plans on a Friday evening or that time you talked your parents into letting you stay out just a little later in high school—you were practicing influence. Organizational life is very similar. Throughout your career, you will be influencing your peers, your followers, and even your supervisor. An adage goes that "we all answer to someone." If you view your current organizations, internships, or job as practice fields, you will be ahead of the game. Likewise, if you pay close attention to how others in the organization are successfully influencing up, across, and down, you will glean important data as you progress through the organization.

People skilled at influencing others have power, but not everyone in a position of authority has influence. As discussed, influence is a central activity when leading others, and as a result, it is an important skill whether you have formal authority or not. In other words, even when you are not *in charge*, you still have an opportunity to influence others. A number of the concepts discussed in this chapter are relevant regardless of your title or formal role.

People with real or perceived power can wield a great deal of influence.[22] An individual who brings a great deal of experience or expertise to a situation will often have influence over the group. People will place trust and confidence in their opinion. But this quality of being believed (i.e., credibility) is a powerful force that must be used with care. Individuals can overestimate their abilities, or they may underestimate the complexity of the context, which can mean proposed solutions are really not as straightforward and simple as suggested.[23] Likewise, group members need to think critically about the suggestions from people who have a great deal of expertise or experience. Blindly trusting can be a recipe for disaster.

REFLECTION QUESTIONS

Can you think of a time when you blindly placed too much trust in an individual who had a great deal of experience or expertise? What was the context? What were the positive or negative results on you or the group?

Influence Tactics for Leaders

The following section comprises a list of influence tactics that is by no means exhaustive but provides a strong foundation for anyone hoping to lead others. **Influence tactics** are actions designed to move others to a desired mindset. Three words need to be top of mind as you influence others—*experimentation, authenticity*, and *intentionality*. First, no single resource will tell you exactly how to influence—not your mom, the team, your peers, or your supervisor—but they all will provide clues. In essence, you are running a well-planned *experiment*. Similar to the sciences, some experiments work, and others do not. The second word, *authenticity*, means you are open and honest about your intentions. People do not want to feel manipulated or duped because of your ulterior motives. Likewise, tactics such as manipulation and deceit diminish trust—the foundation of stable relationships. The third word is *intentionality*. Purposefully plan and prepare for how you will influence others. An *off-the-cuff* influence attempt likely will not yield the results that a planned intervention will. As a result, you need to be intentional about how you intervene. It is not merely a default reaction or a last-minute, knee-jerk response.

Involve Others/Consulting

By involving others, you are providing them with a voice to help set the course and determine their role in the group's or organization's success.[24] Jacinda Ardern used this approach as New Zealand fought the COVID-19 pandemic and relied heavily on her experts.[25] Also, you are helping them acclimate to the new direction, provide input, and gain enthusiasm based on the energy of the group. By involving others, there is a shared sense of mission and shared vision that can unleash the energy needed to accomplish great things.[26] Where have you seen this approach work in the last week?

Leadership by Design

Design Principle: Horror Vacui

   Definition: A fear of emptiness that results in a tendency to favor filling that emptiness with objects, sound, or meaning.[27]

   In Other Words: People fear empty space and are compelled to fill it.

   For Example: Essay questions on exams should be answered concisely, but if there is still room left over to write more, students may feel compelled to fill in the blank space with redundant information. Likewise, if you post a question with a blank space, people will be compelled to _____.

   For Leaders: Leaders who can overcome the *horror* of empty space add considerably to their influence toolkit. When you leave open space for your followers, they will fill it—with activity, with meaning, with innovative ideas—all of which communicate that you value and trust their contributions. The simplicity of unfilled spaces can more clearly highlight and focus on what is in the space—like the mission or a particular project. Try sitting in silence with someone—they are inevitably compelled to speak—to fill the space with words. When you are comfortable with the empty space of silence, it communicates confidence, gives you time to think, and provides an opportunity for others. What empty spaces are you compelled to fill? When you purposefully leave an empty space, others will be compelled to fill it, often with their own meaning. Be cautious with *horror vacui* though. Who or what are you silencing when you choose to fill an empty space versus encouraging others to do so? Taylor Swift even sings about *horror vacui*—she has a blank space, so she wants to write your name.[28]

Chapter 7 ● Influence, Power, and Motivation   219

Facts/Logic/Rational Persuasion

While it is well established that humans do not always make decisions based on what makes logical sense,[29] helping others understand the logic behind your thinking is important because it will resonate with a faction of the individuals you are working to influence.[30] The key is to align your logic with the values and needs of the group you are working to influence. For instance, if you are influencing a group of sales managers, you would want to provide concrete information on how your solution could improve sales and increase their return on investment. When have you used this with a professor?

Relationships

Relationships and influence are closely interconnected.[31] As a result, it is vital that you do your best to build strong, lasting relationships when possible. While this is easy in concept, building relationships takes time and energy, which at times, individuals do not feel they have. However, strong relationships are an investment and a critical influence strategy. More often than not, people are influenced by others they trust and like. Do you have a relationship with the last person you asked to write you a letter of recommendation?

Lead a Coalition

The adage of *strength in numbers* is an important concept when it comes to the topic of influence.[32] A lone voice has much less power than a group of individuals with a shared mission or vision for a better future. An example is the Beyond the Bag Initiative, a coalition of companies working to eliminate single-use plastic bags in retail settings.[33] However, just because you have a coalition of motivated individuals does not mean everything is set. It will be wise to weave in elements such as logic, relationships, win-win, and empathy as well. When was the last time you were part of a collation of friends who wanted to get your way?

Emphasize win-win

When influencing others, it is important to emphasize the win-win. In other words, you are helping others see how they will benefit from the approach or strategy you are suggesting.[34] For instance, proponents of COVD-19 vaccinations used this approach by offering lotteries or college education for those who participated.[35] Framing an option as a win-win allows all parties to benefit from the proposed solution. This approach requires empathy, which means you can place yourself *in the shoes* of the other individual. You can see the issue from their perspective and identify approaches that will help them accomplish their goals. When have you used this influence tactic on your parents?

Create Positive Energy

If you have enthusiasm and energy for your proposed solution, it is likely others will too.[36] Create positive and authentic energy around your recommended course of action. While not a silver bullet, positive energy is a necessary ingredient. When combined with other influence tactics in this section, positivity and optimism have enormous power to influence. One caveat—it is vital that your optimism and enthusiasm are authentic, measured, and appropriate. Who among your peers does this best?

Inspirational Appeal

Similar to creating positive energy, inspirational appeal is more focused on aligning your proposed direction with the values, mission, and vision of the group or organization.[37] You are appealing to the core of what the group was intended to be. An example of this would be Amanda Gorman's poem "The Hill We Climb," in which she aligned her words and hopes for creating a more perfect union in the United States when she said, "So let us leave behind a country better than the one we were left with."[38] With an inspirational appeal, it is all about bringing your argument back to the mission and living into the purpose of the organization or institution. Can you think of the last cause you gave to? How did the concept of inspirational appeal influence your decision?

Amanda Gorman sharing her inspirational poem *"The Hill We Climb"* at the inauguration of U.S. president Jospeh Biden
Photo by Patrick Semansky-Pool/Getty Images

Negotiation/Bargaining/Exchange

Humans have been influencing one another via bargaining and exchange since the beginning of their existence. Also known as *reciprocity*, it means an exchange of *this* for *that*.[39] It is likely you have been using this influence strategy your entire life with peers, parents, siblings, and supervisors. It is an important tool because if both parties can feel like they are gaining something, it is more likely that an agreement can be made. The key is empathy. What do they need, and how will your exchange help them achieve *their* goals? How is this similar to but different from win/win?

Personal Appeal

A personal appeal relies heavily on the relationship between two individuals.[40] In a sense, it is using the connection as a primary reason for compliance. While it is true that relationships are critical to the influence process, it is important to observe when you are being asked to make decisions that go against what is ethically appropriate, fair, or at an extreme, illegal. Personal appeal is a powerful force. Most people want to see their friends and inner circle succeed and progress. Have you used personal appeal in the last couple of days?

Chapter 7 ● Influence, Power, and Motivation   221

Pressure/Coercion

An individual using this influence strategy is often using their formal power or authority to dictate behavior.[41] There are many shades of this influence strategy, from offhand comments, such as "you better start studying because you cannot afford to fail this exam," to outright threats and violence. While pressure and coercion can seem extreme, they are valuable tools that most people in leadership have to use at one time or another. For instance, a manager may need to reprimand her chronically underperforming employee, or an individual working outside of the rules and expectations may need to be pressured to act in line with organizational expectations and norms. When was the last time you witnessed this approach being used?

Ingratiation

An individual using this influence tactic is concerned with increasing the level of positive feelings among the key decision makers.[42] Making oneself more likable to followers in order to influence them can be direct or through association. A statement such as, "Under Xiaoting's leadership we have come so far, and this strategy is a way for us to continue his legacy," purposefully appeals to the positive feelings Xiaoting elicited as a leader. A leader using this appeal wants to influence followers to adopt the proposed strategy in the statement because followers liked Xiaoting and his actions. Similar to many other influence strategies (see Table 7.3), this approach combined with logic, win-win, inspirational appeal, and so forth can be a powerful combination. Can you think of a time you could have used this tactic?

TABLE 7.3 ■ Influence Tactics for Leaders	
Influence Tactic	**Definition**
Involve others/consulting	Involving others in the decision-making process
Facts/logic/rational persuasion	Sharing facts and using logic to persuade others
Relationships	Using personal relationships to sway opinions
Lead a coalition	Convening a group of like-minded people to convince decision makers
Emphasize win-win	Helping others see how they will benefit from your idea or solution
Create positive energy	Building enthusiasm and energy for your proposed solution
Inspirational appeal	Aligning your proposed direction with the values, mission, and vision of the group or organization
Negotiation/bargaining/exchange	Exchanging *this* for *that* or engaging in dialogue to establish a path forward
Personal appeal	Appealing to personal relationships as a way to sway opinions
Pressure/coercion	Using formal power or authority to dictate behavior
Ingratiation	Increasing the level of positive feelings among the key decision makers

GAINING POWER IN GROUPS AND ORGANIZATIONS

LEARNING OBJECTIVE
7.6　Analyze the 10 sources of power and how people use them.

In the context of relationships, the word *power* can be perceived as negative. In truth, power is neither good nor bad. Humans make it so. In other words, what people do with their power will make all the difference. As we explored in Chapter 5, some have used their power for destructive purposes or show up as "bosses from hell," as scholar Ron Riggio[43] suggests. These individuals are using personalized power, which is about using power for personal gain.[44] Another type of power is called socialized power, which is used to benefit the masses. For instance, for years, UNICEF has existed to "provide a better future for every child." Its results over the years are quite staggering. For instance, in one year (by the end of 2020), UNICEF reached

- **106 million people** with critical water, sanitation and hygiene services and supplies
- **3 billion people** with information on risks and safety precautions
- **2.5+ million health workers** with personal protective equipment (PPE)
- **4 million health workers** with training on infection prevention and control[45]

This story is an example of an organization using its power and ability to mobilize hundreds of thousands of men and women toward one cause and make a difference in the world. Leaders should consistently reflect upon how they are using their power. Likewise, a strong ethical foundation (see Chapter 5) and awareness can help leaders ensure they are clear on what they stand for and that they are living their values.

Sources of Power: Personal and Positional Power

How does an individual gain power in an organization? What is the source of that influence? **Sources of power** comprise the specific origin of your capacity to influence others. After all, many of you reading this text hope to take on positions of leadership in your organization, in your community, and perhaps across the globe. As you read this section, note that you have already achieved power and authority in multiple domains throughout childhood. For instance, as you review the sources of power in the following section, think about your peer groups, athletic teams, internships, organizations, and so forth. It is likely you have three or more sources of power in many of these domains. The key to gaining power in an organizational context is intentionality. Are you purposefully working toward multiple sources of power? Are you consistently working to develop your knowledge, skills, and abilities in various domains? If so, you are likely on the right path.

Reward Power

Often associated with a formal position of power, reward power means you can formally reward an individual for their efforts.[46] This recognition could be a monetary reward or some other perk you have the authority to grant (e.g., vacation time, free meal). It could also mean you can reward an individual with a promotion or opportunity to advance their career in some form or fashion. In many respects, your parents had this form of power and could reward you with benefits, such as special privileges (e.g., staying out later), money, or gifts (e.g., a car). Here are some questions to help you determine your level of reward power:

- Do you hold a position on campus or in the community that allows you to reward others with special perks or money?

- Do you have the ability to reward an individual in your organization with something they would value in appreciation for their hard work or effort with something they would value?

Personal Charisma/Referent Power

Some people have that *it* factor others find attractive. Perhaps it is their optimism or enthusiasm[47] or perhaps their charisma that you read about back in Chapter 2. Not necessarily in a physical sense, but their humor, their zest for adventure, perspective on life, positive energy, view of a better future, endearing quirks, and ability to *connect* set them apart from the rest. Think of the person in your circle of friends who attracts others to be a part of their club, organization, or festivities. Those with referent power have strong interpersonal skills. Here are some questions to help you determine your level of charisma/**referent power**.

- Are you an individual who is a *hub* for the action? Do you have a wide variety of friends in many contexts? Are you a connector?

- Do your energy and enthusiasm attract others?

- Do people tell you that you are charismatic and an *attractor* when it comes to people?

Outmatched Effort

This source of power is exemplified by individuals who consistently display superior effort. The term *outmatched effort* is contextual.[48] For instance, in an accounting firm during the busy season, it is not uncommon to work 12- to 14-hour days. In a similar vein, it is not uncommon for young medical residents to work very long hours—it is a part of the culture. In other contexts, an individual who worked these hours is an individual who puts in an extraordinary amount of time and energy. Here are some questions to help you determine your level of effort.

- Do your professors know you and your work? Would they say it is above and beyond the work of others or middle of the pack?

- Would your internship supervisor advocate for you? Did they see you work above and beyond the other interns, or are you in the bottom 50% when it comes to effort?

- Are you a *go-to* person because people in your organization know you will get the task done?

Wealth/Resource

At first blush, you may be thinking about wealth as money, which of course is a source of power. However, wealth can be thought of as a *span of control*. Obviously, the president of a sorority has more wealth or span of control than a new member in the organization—the president is in charge of a $500,000 budget, the actions of 100+ women, and so forth. In corporate life, an individual running a multimillion-dollar division has more wealth than a director with a team of six (unless it is an exceptional group of six). Here are some questions to help you determine your wealth:

- Do you have a significant level of responsibility in your organization? Are you the captain of the team? President of the club? Senior resident hall advisor? Student body president?

- In the position(s) you hold, do you have control over how money is spent and allocated? Do you set the budget? Distribute the funds? Collect the dues?

- Do people see you as critical to the success of the organization?

Expertise

Individuals who display this source of power have a superior command of domain-specific knowledge. They have continually pushed well past the threshold of competence and are focused on developing their knowledge.[49] However, like other domains, expertise is relative. For instance, a senior resident advisor naturally has more expertise than junior advisors; however, one senior advisor likely knows policy much better than others. In a similar vein, some football players have spent more time studying the playbook than others—they have a strong command of the content. In organizational life (e.g., corporate, nonprofit), the individual with the most expertise has a great deal of power. Here are some questions to help you determine your level of expertise.

- Do colleagues or peers comment on your knowledge or command of the content?

- Have your peers, professors, or faculty advisors commented on your expertise?

- Do you enjoy the process of learning and building expertise in and out of the classroom?

Relevance

Relevance as a source of power means you have responsibility for mission-critical work in your organization.[50] In health care, nurses and physicians are highly relevant to the task. At a college or university, the president is relevant to advancing the mission and vision of the institution. Individuals with highly relevant roles have power and authority. For instance, a job applicant with a dual major in data science and accounting will find their skills in high demand based on the needs of today's market. Here are some questions to help you determine your level of relevance.

- Are you a hub for activity? Do people need to work through you to complete their work?

- Is success in your role mission critical to the success of the organization?

- Is your role highly regarded as an honor?

Visibility

Visibility means key decision makers or influential figures see you in action.[51] They see your skills or expertise in action, and this can open doors—quickly. Think of a coach watching a new

Chapter 7 • Influence, Power, and Motivation   225

player on the field display her talent—that visibility is a source of power because the individual moves forward from the pack in the eyes of the decision maker. Of course, this applies in the workplace as well, so how are you aligning yourself with committees, philanthropic endeavors, or projects that are critical to organizational success? If you don't, you may reside in the *cube farm* for longer than you would like. Here are some questions to help you determine your level of visibility:

- Your CEO, division leader, or department head knows your name and has seen your work, and they were impressed.

- On campus, you have an extensive network in and outside of your various organizations. Because of your involvement in the community, influential people in the community have seen your work and were impressed by your efforts.

- Strangers know who you are—and for good reasons.

Network

An individual's network is another source of power. The saying "it is not what you know, but who you know" can ring true. Individuals with a broad and vast network merely have access to resources that others may not.[52] So it is wise to invest in your network on campus, in your organization, and in the community. Investing in your network can pay off in many ways. First, your network can open doors that would otherwise be difficult to enter. Also, your network can provide guidance and mentoring in times of transition or change. Third, your network can serve as a peer group and social outlet. Investing in your network is a long-term process. It is a way of being. Here are some questions to help you think about your network:

- Do people make comments about the number of people you know on and off campus?

- Do you have coffee, lunch, or a drink with at least one or two people outside of your immediate peer group each week?

- Do you think of your family (e.g., aunts and uncles), family friends, and your friends' parents as part of your network? Have you connected with people in these realms to learn more about their paths?

Legitimacy

Legitimacy means you align with the written and unwritten norms, values, and goals of the group.[53] On an athletic team, an individual with this source of power may be a team player, behave well off the field, excel in competition, know the sport well, practice with great determination, embody the values of the team, and so forth. If the list previously mentioned: is what the team values, we could likely judge each team member on those dimensions and determine the person who most closely aligns with the list. Likewise, there would be some individuals with two or three but who are missing one or two important attributes (behave well off the field and practice with great determination). It is important to note that every group and organization has unwritten rules as well. It is important to observe these at play and understand how you do and do not align with them. For instance, it could be an unwritten rule that your boss promotes the people who work the longest hours. It is never said, per se, but her value for long hours is something you need to pick up on to be successful in that context. Here are some questions to help you think about your legitimacy

- Do people say, "If we just had more of you, we would be in a better position"?
- What did legitimacy mean at your last internship or job? What were the written and unwritten rules for success?
- What does a student with legitimacy look like in the classroom? Think of your courses and explore this concept.

Investing in your personal and professional network is a critical consideration for every young professional.
©iStockphoto.com/jeffbergen

Legitimate Power

Different from *legitimacy*, **legitimate power** means you have actual authority over an individual or group.[54] For instance, a professor may have legitimate power over you as a student—they hold your grade in their hands. Or you may have the authority to hire or fire an individual at your job. These are forms of legitimate power—a power granted to you by function of your role. Before using legitimate power to change behavior (e.g., putting someone on a 90-day plan or firing them), you should use influence to encourage a change in behavior. Here are some questions to help you think about legitimate power:

- Have you served in a role where you had specific authority over others? Examples may be approving expenditures, setting someone's schedule, approval of requests, the power to hire someone, and so forth.
- When have you witnessed someone (coach, boss) using legitimate power to ensure compliance of a group? How did their use of this source of power impact the group's motivation or morale?
- Do your parents have legitimate power? If yes, how so? If no, why?

Chapter 7 ● Influence, Power, and Motivation **227**

One final note on power. Reflect upon what happens if an individual lacks specific sources of power. In other words, you could have five to six of the sources of power listed in Table 7.4 but lack *expertise*, and you will be limited in your ability to connect at the highest levels. Likewise, it is likely you have a few of these sources of power in one domain (e.g., your athletic team) but not in others (e.g., the club you just joined). Depending on the context, it can take years to gain a position of formal authority or prestige. For instance, in your internship, it is unlikely you gainfully obtain many of the sources of power listed in Table 7.4 in three to six months. All of this takes time, perseverance, resilience, patience, and a little luck.

TABLE 7.4 ■ Sources of Power	
Source of Power	**Definition**
Reward power	You can formally reward an individual for their efforts.
Personal charisma/ referent power	You attract others through your enthusiasm, energy, humor, and optimism.
Outmatched effort	You consistently display superior effort.
Wealth/resource	You have financial wealth or, in an organizational context, a wide *span of control* under your purview.
Expertise	You have a superior command of domain-specific knowledge.
Relevance	You have responsibility for mission-critical work in your organization.
Visibility	Key decision makers or influential figures see you in action.
Network	You have a wide and vast network.
Legitimacy	You align with the written and unwritten norms, values, and goals of the group.
Legitimate power	You have actual authority over an individual or group.

MOTIVATION

LEARNING OBJECTIVE

7.7   Analyze the difference between intrinsic and extrinsic motivation.

Motivation is the internal desire for a person to act. Everyone—believe it or not—is motivated. The trouble lies in *what* they are motivated to do and, in some cases, *how* they are motivated. According to scholars, "To be motivated means to be moved to do something. A person who feels no impetus or inspiration to act is thus characterized as unmotivated, whereas someone who is energized or activated toward an end is considered motivated."[55] In this section, you will explore ways to create a culture that is energizing by capitalizing on intrinsic motivation and other sources of motivation that activate others toward a desired (by both the individual and the leader) goal or vision.

Intrinsic and Extrinsic Motivation

In 1971, Deci asserted that some activities have inherent benefits and do not need external rewards. These came to be known as intrinsic motivators.[56] **Intrinsic motivation** is about engaging in an activity for the inherent joy of the task, while **extrinsic motivation** is about partic-ipating in an activity because of external rewards for doing so. Interestingly, many scholars found that intrinsic motivation diminished with the presence of external rewards.[57] Other scholars have found that both intrinsic and extrinsic motivators jointly predict performance.[58]

> ### Leadership by Design
>
> *Design Principle:* Entry Point
>
> *Definition:* A place where one enters, physically or in their attention focus, into a deeper space of your place, product, context, or concept.
>
> *In Other Words:* Where and how do you enter or begin?
>
> *For Example:* Common entry points you know: Judging a book by its cover; a class by its course title; a person by their look or handshake; or a store by its front space and door. An airport is an important entry point to a city that can influence the rest of the trip.
>
> *For Leaders:* A first impression is the entry point of a person; it influences perceptions and attitudes that affect future interactions. Physical entry points have progressive lures to attract and pull people into the space, such as footsteps painted on the floor entering the door or sidewalk tent signs. How do you progressively lure followers to enter your organiza-tion, the mission, or the team? Good entry points also have minimal barriers and clear paths. What might be or appear too complicated or difficult for followers that keeps them from entering a project or the culture of your organization? Consider the entry point as a highly influential aspect of any design, including the design of your leadership relationships.

Sources of Intrinsic and Extrinsic Motivation

Sources of power represent your capacity to influence. **Sources of motivation** comprise the con-ditions you design to alter someone's internal desire to act. The following section is a list of strate-gies that leaders and managers must have in mind when exploring the concept of motivation. By doing so, you can create a system that fits the needs and desires of your team members and your organization. And like other concepts explored in this text, you need to experiment. It is likely your first attempt will not yield perfect results. Also, pay close to attention to your employees. Are they behaving in a way that a motivated team member would? What are they motivated to do, and what is the source fueling that motivation?(see table 7.5)

Financial Compensation

Financial compensation is a motivating factor for some but not all.[59] Is your organization below the average income in your industry? At the top? Somewhere in the middle? What is your strat-egy? Starbucks has a history of compensating (pay and benefits) its employees in a very different manner from the industry standard.[60] In fact, it was an essential element of their strategy to make Starbucks your *third place* (first being home, second being work). By compensating their employees fairly, they bet on the fact that they would retain good people who had relationships with their customer base. Is money everything? No, but it is an important consideration.

Alignment With Values

Research has found that an individual will feel more motivated to perform when the mission and values of the organization align with their value system.[61] For instance, an individual who values service to their community will resonate with an organization that prioritizes *giving back* to the community as a core priority. Does your organization promote and live its values? Do your team members make connections between their values and the organization's?

Meaning

People who find significant meaning in their work are more motivated to perform at the highest levels.[62] For instance, an individual who sees purpose by helping people in the writing center will be more energized to produce *above and beyond* in their role. Of course, the key is to find work that is intrinsically meaningful to you. This takes exploration and a great deal of self-awareness. When you become a supervisor, it is important to coach and mentor others through this process as well.

Showing Appreciation

It sounds so simple; but think about all the people in your life who struggle to show appreciation[63] with a simple *thank you*. In addition to verbal appreciation, managers can praise via text, email, or handwritten note. Develop a habit of mind when it comes to appreciating others. Do you notice and acknowledge the *good* that your parents, peers, teachers, coaches, supervisors, and mentors do? People are motivated to work above and beyond when they feel appreciated for their efforts. If someone has given you their time, they deserve your appreciation.

Reward and Recognize

A more formal and sometimes more public way of showing appreciation, reward, and recognition are other sources of motivation.[64] Often, reward and recognition involve structured systems of recognition (e.g., an employee of the month or employee of the year) or a bonus structure for meeting goals and objectives. While not a silver bullet, a reward and recognition program is an excellent addition to many of the other motivational techniques explored in this section.

Recognition for the hard work of team members is a critical task for leaders.
©iStockphoto.com/Wavebreakmedia

Empowerment

The term **empowerment** has multiple meanings. In general, empowerment means that individuals feel a sense of ownership/control and competence in their work or projects.[65] From a situational leadership perspective, it may take some time until the leader can genuinely *turn over the reins* to a team member or employee. However, the most competent and committed followers are those individuals who are autonomous and who can be trusted to produce high-quality work with little or no direction. **Autonomy** and self-determination are significant sources of motivation. But in most cases, it is unrealistic to think that someone can achieve this level of trust and autonomy from the beginning. The road to empowerment is complicated and is a process that involves organizational analysis, coaching, and experience.[66]

MYTH OR REALITY?

About 50% of US employees are actively looking or watching for opportunities

Reality. Here is an excerpt from the article:

> A new Gallup analysis finds that 48% of America's working population is actively job searching or watching for opportunities. Businesses are facing a staggeringly high quit rate—3.6 million Americans resigned in May 2021 alone—*and* a record-high number of unfilled positions. And Gallup discovered that workers in all job categories, from customer-facing service roles to highly professional positions, are actively or passively job hunting at roughly the same rate.[67]

Belonging

Feeling a sense of belonging and comradery with the group is another source of motivation that is founded in relationships.[68] As a result, it is important to focus on creating a sense of team so all members understand their role and contribution to the team. In part, leaders have an opportunity to ensure they have worked to create a sense of belonging.[69] And while it is unrealistic to think every team member will always mesh or fit in with the larger group, it is an important task and goal for anyone leading a team. Given the statistic shared at the beginning of this section (see Myth or Reality), this topic is especially critical as companies transition to differing versions of in-person, hybrid, and remote work.

Achievement/Success/Competence

When people feel like they are successful in their endeavors, it is a source of motivation.[70] So a feeling of competence and achievement can drive motivation. As a leader, you have an opportunity to ensure that team members are provided with the correct coaching and feedback to develop as members of your team. The challenge can be to not overwhelm and to provide adequate tasks and activities that fit the individual's ability level.

Fairness

A lack of perceived fairness can diminish trust, which, in turn, can reduce an individual's motivation.[71] So as a leader, ensure (a) you are fair in your interactions with people and (b) you do everything possible to ensure fairness is a norm in the organizational environment—especially in a hybrid or remote work environment.[72] At times, *in-group*[73] members (people with close relationships to decision makers) can be given (consciously or unconsciously) preferential treatment, which can lead to lawsuits, mistrust, decreased levels of motivation, and lower productivity.

Autonomy

People with a sense of independence feel ownership in the decision-making process.[74] **Autonomy** is a significant source of motivation for individuals who appreciate and enjoy the freedom to decide how their work is completed. However, like the other sources of motivation, this is not a panacea. Too much autonomy too soon can be disastrous for both the individual and the organization.

Feedback/Coaching

Feedback and coaching help the development and growth of team members.[75] As a formal or informal leader in your organization, coaching from one's immediate supervisor is vital. Without effective coaching and feedback, team members will struggle to work to their full potential and may struggle to meet expectations. At times, supervisors can feel uncomfortable when taking on a coaching role because it may involve conflict and accountability. When a supervisor avoids these opportunities, teaching moments are missed.

Flexibility/Freedom

Some individuals are motivated by flexible working hours, flextime, and remote working options.[76] In fact, McKinsey found that nearly three-quarters of the roughly 5,000 employees surveyed preferred a hybrid option of working from home at least two days a week. More than half wanted to work from home three days each week.[77] Perhaps they can work from a home office or in a city removed from the home office. Another form of flexibility/freedom is that the role has clear benchmarks for success but does not require a set number of hours in one specific location. In other words, "we do not care when or where you work, we just care that you produce results."

The days of everyone going to an office are over—it's a blend of remote, hybrid, and in-person.
©iStockphoto.com/nensuria

Career pathing

Team members want clarity about how their career will progress in the organization.[78] Providing team members with clear objectives, goals, and deliverables will help them better understand what they need to do to progress in the organization. **Career pathing** can be a challenge for some organizations that may not have this information clearly outlined or described. Again, the key is clear baseline expectations with consistent follow-through for reward once expectations are met.

Psychological Safety

Trust is a fundamental ingredient for any human relationship. People want to have trust in the organization, their supervisor, and their peers. When trust is missing, it is difficult for employees and team members to bring their *full selves* to the work.[79] In addition, when trust is lacking, individuals begin to focus more and more energy on their safety or well-being versus the task at hand. Note that as a leader, there will be times when you are actively holding people accountable or having difficult conversations with people. They may have reason to mistrust you, or they may feel unsafe . . . because they are. They are not living up to expectations. So you need to think about trust and safety in a general sense—do your high-performing, well-adjusted, functioning employees feel like you have their best interest at heart? Do they trust that you want them to succeed? Do they know that if they meet baseline expectations, they will be *safe* and know where they stand?

TABLE 7.5 ■ Sources of Motivation	
Source of Motivation	**Definition**
Financial compensation	You are fairly compensated for your work.
Alignment with values	The mission and values of the organization are aligned with your value system.
Meaning	You experience great meaning in your work.
Showing appreciation	Your superiors and peers show appreciation for your efforts.
Reward and recognition	You are formally rewarded and recognized for your results.
Empowerment	You feel a sense of ownership/control and competence in your work.
Belonging	You feel a sense of belonging and comradery with your team or group.
Achievement/success/competence	You feel competent in your work and enjoy a sense of achievement.
Fairness	You feel your supervisor is fair and consistent.
Autonomy	You feel ownership in how tasks are accomplished.
Feedback/coaching	You receive consistent feedback and coaching on your performance.
Flexibility/freedom	You have flexible working hours, flextime, and/or remote working options.
Career pathing	You have a clear sense of how you can progress and move forward in the organization.
Psychological safety	You have trust in the organization, your supervisor, and your peers.

Chapter 7 • Influence, Power, and Motivation   233

There is no *silver bullet* for guiding the motivation of human beings and no guaranteed way to influence others. However, some concepts have emerged that, as a leader, you need to know. Your awareness of each of these concepts will allow you to more intentionally build a culture where both intrinsic and extrinsic motivators work in concert to influence individuals and the group to the desired end. Likewise, you will be in a better position to diagnose or understand why some individuals are not motivated to engage the task at hand or working to their full potential. For instance, *person/job fit* is an umbrella term for many of the elements explored in this section. In a general sense, when individual motivation and the job are aligned, it appears as a good fit.

THE LEADERSHIP CHALLENGE: DESIGNING LEADERSHIP RELATIONSHIPS

LEARNING OBJECTIVE
7.8   Apply Kouzes and Posner's 5 Practices of Exemplary Leadership to your relationship design.

People are complicated. That seemingly trite statement truly captures the greatest challenge you will face as a leader. Designing yourself takes time and effort; designing others' success requires insight and engagement, and designing culture means seeing the bigger picture. But *designing relationships* requires approaching all of the preceding along with extraordinary patience, forgiveness, and emotional intelligence. Continuing to build your CORE™ (confidence, optimism, resilience, and engagement) will also help you design relationships.

Another key set of tools comes from the research of Jim Kouzes and Barry Posner, who interviewed thousands of individuals about their best leadership.[80] Kouzes and Posner captured these answers in five broad *Practices of Exemplary Leadership*: (a) model the way, (b) inspire a shared vision, (c) challenge the process, (d) enable others to act, and (e) encourage the heart. The seminal book in which they elaborate on these five practices and offer many practical applied tips is aptly named *The Leadership Challenge*. Take a second look at the five practices. Can you identify the common factor that ties them all together? Yes, they all focus on designing and developing relationships with others. Kouzes and Posner provide an invaluable how-to/what-to-do list of leadership practices that will come in handy long into your future career. The exemplary practices also supply a framework by which you can begin to address the greatest leadership challenge—designing relationships (see Table 7.6).

TABLE 7.6 ■ Designing Relationships With Kouzes and Posner's Practices of Exemplary Leadership	
When you . . .	**You design relationships by . . .**
Model the way	Providing a vision and route to achievement; building credibility and establishing parameters of the relationship and acceptable behavior
Inspire a shared vision	Sharing power and responsibility, which develops mutual respect
Challenge the process	Guiding others to their best while reinforcing the importance of making mistakes and improving; building resilience
Enable others to act	Building motivation and trust through autonomy, confidence through self-efficacy, and optimism through achievement
Encourage the heart	Understanding and connecting with emotions, which in turn becomes the greatest source of influence and inspiration

MYTH OR REALITY?

Leaders cannot and should not be friends with their followers.

Myth . . . and Reality. You already know this is a misconception from reading Chapter 2. But why is it both myth and reality? Consider a time when you were working on a group project or with a team and a new member joined the group. If the new member was someone you knew well and considered a friend, your interactions with them would be considerably different than if they were a stranger. You would place greater trust in them, have more meaningful conversations, discuss actions and decisions, and feel a mutual respect and equality even if you were the leader of the group. The rest of the group would likewise see this new person as part of the team based on your relationship with them. But now consider what it feels like to be the new person joining the group when you do not know the leader or the others in the group. You likely are welcomed, perhaps even with enthusiasm, but the leader does not know you nor do you know the leader. So; you assume the role of follower, listener, and learner; you are more cautious about taking action or making decisions; you follow the rules and your conversations with the leader are more professional. You might even feel like an outsider for a time.

These situations highlight the importance of the dyadic (two-person) relationship between the follower and the leader. Researchers who focus on this dyadic relationship have developed a theory called leader-member exchange theory or LMX.[81] They have found many positive individual and organizational outcomes when there is a high-quality relationship between a leader and follower. For example, you may have witnessed a boss, teacher, or coach taking the time to talk with and get to know each individual follower. Sometimes those conversations are about the task at hand, soliciting ideas about the work, or guiding individual development. But all of the time, those individualized conversations are moments where the leader indirectly communicates how much they value the individual. Those individual moments can add up to a relationship of mutual understanding, credibility, and trust.

Focusing on each individual relationship and building these relationships from stranger to acquaintance to partner, as leader-member exchange theory explains, leaders are able to design a higher quality of interaction and performance from each member and the team as a whole.[82] In addition, once individual followers feel good about their relationship with their leader, they are freed up psychologically and emotionally to take the focus off of themselves and shift it to focus on the greater success of the group.

When should a leader not befriend a follower? Leader-member exchange theory also focuses on what happens as these relationships form and what happens when some relationships with the leader are close and others are not. When a new person joins a group, all the other individuals in the group have been building a relationship with the leader—they are considered the *in-group* while the new person feels like they are in the *out-group*. The leader is not trying to form in- and out-groups, they just naturally occur because the dyadic relationships vary. This perceived unfairness can be detrimental.[83] The best thing you can do as a leader is work hard to build relationships with new individuals, be aware of the perception of in-out groups and the appearance of possible favoritism, and find unique ways to connect new and veteran followers.

CHAPTER SUMMARY

Designing relationships involves the mindful application of influence, power, and motivation. These three constructs comprise a reality of leadership activity that requires careful consideration to ensure just, equitable, sustainable, and ethical application. At a minimum, leaders can capitalize

Chapter 7 • Influence, Power, and Motivation   **235**

on the natural motivation of followers by defining the goal, clarifying an effective path, removing obstacles, and providing support. Awareness of the appropriate behavioral style is also key.

Influence can come in many forms, and there are key differences between influence, authority, and manipulation. There are also many influence tactics leaders can use to design relationships and effectively mobilize others to action. The roles and sources of power can drive influence tactics and often dictate the initial form of a relationship. Effective and ethical leaders should recognize these sources and their appropriate use.

Finally, leaders can design a culture that fosters motivation through a number of conditions and behaviors. Some of those characteristics enhance intrinsic motivation, while others rely on extrinsic motivators. This chapter provides many tools of influence, all of which can be employed to design relationships and ultimately influence others toward a common goal.

KEY TERMS

Achievement oriented (p. 213)

Active bystander (p. 217)

Authority figure (p. 215)

Autonomy (p. 231)

Bias (p. 216)

Career pathing (p. 232)

Directive (p. 213)

Empowerment (p. 230)

Explicit bias (p. 216)

Extrinsic motivation (p. 228)

Formal power (p. 215)

Implicit bias (p. 216)

Influence (p. 214)

Influence tactics (p. 218)

Informal power (p. 215)

Ingratiation (p. 221)

Inspirational appeal (p. 221)

Intrinsic motivation (p. 227)

Lead a coalition (p. 221)

Leadership style (p. 213)

Legitimate power (p. 226)

Manipulation (p. 216)

Motivation (p. 227)

Outmatched effort (p. 227)

Participative (p. 213)

Psychological safety (p. 402)

Rational persuasion (p. 221)

Referent power (p. 223)

Sources of motivation (p. 228)

Sources of power (p. 222)

Supportive (p. 213)

Win–win (p. 221)

CORE™ ATTRIBUTE BUILDERS: BUILD NOW FOR FUTURE LEADERSHIP CHALLENGES

Attribute: Engagement

Builder: Influencing others

It is likely you see opportunities for improvement in your workplace, internship, family, student organization (fraternity, residence hall), or athletic team. For instance, recall the hazing statistics shared at the beginning of this chapter. Can you influence others to act upon the opportunity you see? Can you build a coalition of like minds in an effort to help the organization better live its values, achieve results, improve culture, and so forth? First, determine the opportunity and get clear on your thinking. How will your solution help? Next, read the influence strategies listed in this chapter and circle four or five you think could work—perhaps it is inspirational appeal, building a coalition, and emphasizing win-win. As you plan, think through *how* others will respond and be clear about the factions that will and will not support you. You could even run your thoughts by a few peers or a mentor as well to get some preliminary feedback. Finally, determine how you would like to communicate your plan and see who you can engage and *win over* to your perspective or thoughts. Be sure to focus on listening, and be aware that you may need to compromise or collaborate with others. It is unlikely—especially if the issue has some heat around it—that your plan will move forward without some adjustments and tweaks.

After the meeting or discussion, some critical questions may include the following:

- What happened that was unexpected? How did this impact results?

- In hindsight, what other influence techniques may have helped you make your case?

- Did you change the minds of individuals from other factions or subgroups? If not, why?

- How did your mindset and delivery help or hinder your ability to sell your ideas?

SKILL BUILDER ACTIVITY

Motivating Leadership Presentation (Part I)—Conditions for Intrinsic Motivation

Your (large) group has been invited to present an introduction to leadership theory and practice to a group of high school students. Your presentation must be informative, accurate, entertaining, engaging, and memorable.

Your presentation must last between five and eight minutes.

Every person in the group must be involved in a visible manner.

Your (small) leadership team has four weeks to prepare for this event (and all those events following):

How would you, as the leader, motivate your group—individually and as a group?

1. To what extent could you, the leader, incorporate the following conditions:
    a. Autonomy? How so?
    b. Individual achievement/success/competence? How so?
    c. Responsibility and/or sense of meaning? How so?

Motivating Leadership Presentation (Part II)—Influence, Power, and Motivation

Your (large) group has been invited to present an introduction to influence, power, and motivation to a group of high school students. Your presentation must be informative, accurate, entertaining, engaging, and memorable.

Your presentation must last between five and eight minutes.

Every person in the group must be involved in a visible manner.

Your (small) leadership team has four weeks to prepare for this event (and all those events following):

How would you, as the leader, motivate your group—individually and as a group?

2. How could you more effectively . . .
    a. define the goals of the task?
    b. clarify the path to achieve the goals?
    c. identify and remove obstacles to achievement?
    d. seek out needs and provide support?

MODULE

3

DESIGN OTHERS' SUCCESS

Chapter 8	Creativity, Problem-Solving, and Idea-Generating	239
Chapter 9	Effective Practices for Leading Others to Success	273
Chapter 10	Utilizing Change Processes Effectively	307

What can you do as a leader to design others' success? This section flips the typical organizational chart upside down, putting those individuals who interface directly with the product or customer or service as most important and placing those with lead titles in the support position—creating conditions for others to succeed—designing others' success. When a problem occurs in the typical organizational hierarchy, everyone looks down from the top to place blame—because, after all, that is where the problem happened. But when you are a leader who designs others' success, *blame-finding* transforms into problem-solving. And the first question for you as a leader is, Did I create the conditions for this problem to occur, or did I create conditions for success? Did the problem occur because the person was not the right fit for the position or task? Was the person properly trained? Did they have the necessary resources to succeed?

Throughout this text, your approach to facilitating others has been framed as a choice: You can mindfully design, or you can just *see what happens* and hope for the best. This next module on designing others' success provides a wealth of tools that you will need to serve others on their journey. Three chapters comprise this module: Chapter 8—Creativity, Problem-Solving, and Idea-Generating; Chapter 9—Effective Practices for Leading Others to Success; and Chapter 10—Utilizing Change Processes Effectively. The first of these chapters introduces the value and role of creativity in leadership. Leaders solve problems—big and little, proactively and reactively, all day, every day, even in their sleep (more on that later in this chapter). The range of problems leaders face requires both creative problem-solving processes and a big toolbox full of idea-generating techniques to prompt innovation.

8 CREATIVITY, PROBLEM-SOLVING, AND IDEA-GENERATING

LEARNING OBJECTIVES

Upon completion of this chapter, the reader should be able to

8.1 Explain the myths and reality of creativity

8.2 State the impact of fragility and vulnerability in building creative confidence

8.3 Distinguish between different types of problems

8.4 Differentiate between the four Ps that define creativity

8.5 Construct your creative problem-solving toolbox with a variety of idea-generating techniques

8.6 Demonstrate explorative activities that will continuously fill your creative problem-solving idea stockpile

8.7 Compose a plan to continuously build your creative activity and confidence

Leadership by Design Model

Design Self
How can I design myself as a leader?

Design Relationships
As a leader, how can I design my relationships with others?

Design Others' Success
AS A LEADER, HOW CAN I DESIGN SUCCESS FOR OTHERS?

Design Culture
As a leader, how can I design the culture of my organization?

Design Future
As a leader, how can I innovate?

INTRODUCTION

Creativity. The concept is shrouded in mystery—filled with the awe of amazing innovations and special individuals whose gifts are both enviable and unexplainable. Creativity stands as a prized and highly sought-after attribute, generally credited for the success of innovative organizations and on the grand scale, hope for the future (i.e., if only we could find an innovative solution to [your problem inserted here]).

Creativity is perhaps the most valuable yet misunderstood attribute to personal and organizational success as well as the most talked about yet least purposefully developed. Organizations, schools, policymakers, and leaders generally proclaim their affinity for creativity and how dedicated they are to the pursuit of innovation. Every leader wants to be innovative, and they value and seek creativity in their followers. Creativity, originality, initiative, analytical thinking, and innovation sit in the top five skills perceived as growing in demand by 2025.[1] **Innovation** can be defined as new things or methods that deliver value, and it is the *new things* part of innovation where creativity lives. Both innovation and creativity conjure images of magic, genius, and solutions that make all your dreams come true. And then . . . they wait and hope for a flash of inspiration and that breakthrough idea.

There is indeed great promise in creativity, and endorsing the concept can begin and sustain creative activity. Unfortunately, if you inquire as to how a leader is going to bring their love for creativity into practical reality, you will find considerable hesitation, misinformation, generalizations, and wishful thinking. After you read this chapter, you will not be that leader.

Leadership That Makes a Difference

Leaders and experts in every field struggle to concisely explain the complexity of their world, especially to those outside that world. How could one effectively popularize complex topics in a simple and fascinating manner? Have you seen a TED talk recently?

One of the most important things a leader can do to have an impact on both knowledge and practice is to alter and expand the way others see the world and its possibilities. Innovation is about opportunity—seeing potential challenges. Richard Saul Wurman—author, architect, urban and graphic designer, cartographer, teacher, and most notably the creator of TED, the entity that has brought innovative ideas from a broad variety of fields to millions—has been helping others see differently since his first books were published in 1962. As noted on his bio, "The acknowledged father of Information Architecture, Wurman has written, designed and published 83 books on a range of topics, while creating conferences and new mapping projects. All contribute to a greater understanding of complex information. They spring from his particular brand of innovation: *doing the opposite of what is rote or expected*."[2]

The now-ubiquitous intellectual events themed TED were born in 1984 out of Richard Saul Wurman's observation of a powerful convergence among three fields: technology, entertainment, and design. The first TED included a demo of the compact disc, the e-book, and cutting-edge 3-D graphics from Lucasfilm. Designer Stefan Sagmeister states about Wurman, "He created and chaired TED Conferences, which might have become the single most important communication platform for our own field and many others, and thereby connecting design effectively to science, technology, education, politics and entertainment."[3]

As the TED history notes, "The roster of presenters broadened to include scientists, philosophers, musicians, business and religious leaders, philanthropists and many others. For many attendees, TED became one of the intellectual and emotional highlights of the year."[4] While others have grown TED into a multifaceted success, it was Wurman's initiative that provided the foundation. By 2012, TED Talks had celebrated its one billionth video view.[5] As of 2018, there have been over 11 billion views with about 3.2 billion views a year.[6]

Amusingly, Richard Saul Wurman's latest book "chronicles the adventures and musings of the eccentric main character, the Commissioner of Curiosity and Imagination."[7] If every organization, community, and culture had such a position, everyone would have the chance to see the world differently and further inspire creativity.

Richard Saul Wurman, the innovator behind TED.
Getty Images/Jerod Harris / Stringer

YES, YOU REALLY ARE CREATIVE

LEARNING OBJECTIVE
8.1 Explain the myths and reality of creativity.

Creativity. The bolt of lightning from the gods that makes the light bulb appear above the head of the lone genius—eureka! Here is the real flash of genius for you: Yes, *you* can develop creativity. When students are asked if they are creative, most will initially say they are not. But asking why generally elicits answers like, "I am not artistic," or "I do not wear crazy clothes or do wacky things." The myths and misconceptions surrounding creativity rival those of leadership. Many of these false ideas stifle any chance for individuals or organizations to develop and utilize creativity. As a leader, you will need to know, confront, and debunk these myths in order to design others' success. Take some time to talk with others about their concept of creativity. The Creativity Myth Bingo card (Table 8.1) can help guide your conversations.

The answers from those who identify as creative generally reveal more accurate answers about creativity. Why are you creative? "Because I think of lots of options and ideas before I make a decision." And "I consider many perspectives and try to see things in different ways." Those answers make creativity sound like it is more about *how* you think than something you produce. **Creativity** is defined as the personal capacities and process of generating a unique product that has value. The next section examines a more comprehensive definition of creativity, highlighting the components in this concise definition: person, process, product (and more).

242 Module 3 ● Design Others' Success

TABLE 8.1 ■ Creativity Myth Bingo!			
Eureka Myth New ideas are a flash of insight! But . . . research shows that such insights are actually the culminating result of prior hard work on a problem.	**Breed Myth** Creative ability is a trait inherent in one's heritage or genes. But . . . evidence supports just the opposite. People who have confidence and work the hardest are the ones most likely to come up with a creative solution.	**Originality Myth** New ideas are thought up by one person. But . . . history and research show more that new ideas are actually combinations of older ideas and that sharing those helps generate more innovation.	**Expert Myth** Only an expert or group of experts can generate creative ideas. But . . . research suggests that particularly tough problems often require the perspective of an outsider.
Incentive Myth Bigger incentives, monetary or otherwise, will increase motivation and hence increase innovation. But . . . incentives often do more harm than good, as people learn to game the system.	**Free Space!** Yes . . . just like in real Bingo, you get a free space—it is true!	**Most Common Myth** What have you heard the most that seems like it probably is not true?	**Cohesive Myth** If everyone gets along and plays, there will be creativity. But . . . creative companies are not *zany*, instead they find ways to structure dissent and conflict into their process to better push creative limits.
Constraints Myth Constraints hinder creativity, and the most innovative results come from people who have *unlimited* resources. But . . . research shows that creativity loves constraints, as it helps prompt creative potential.	**Lone Creator Myth** One person's hard work is how creativity happens. But . . . creative work requires supportive work, collaborative preliminary efforts, and a great team.	**Brainstorming Myth** Throwing ideas around, no matter how far out, will yield creative insights. But . . . without a focused problem, identifiable goal, and managed idea-generating techniques, there is no evidence that just *throwing ideas around* consistently produces innovative breakthroughs.	**Mousetrap Myth** Once you have the creative idea, the work is done. But . . . great ideas are only valuable if we communicate them, market them, and find the right customers. We all know of at least one *better mousetrap* that is still hidden.

Source: Based on Burkus, D. (2014). *The myths of creativity: The truth about how innovative companies and people generate great ideas.* San Francisco, CA: Jossey-Bass.

Even with an accurate understanding, individuals tend to limit or even avoid creativity. How can you design others' success when those others do not want to engage? The answer lies back in the introduction to this module on what facilitates engagement. Engaging in creativity is like any other task. Followers must feel competent, included, appreciated, and that their creative work is meaningful. Translating the engagement questions into facilitating creativity results in a leader asking questions such as

- How can I provide opportunities to create and co-create with others?

- How can I recognize creative behavior and production?

- How can I encourage and/or facilitate the personal creative development of each individual in my organization?

- How might I create a culture that encourages creative activity?

Try this thought exercise. Starting right now, you have five minutes to come up with a creative idea for any context you like, addressing any problem—as long as it is really unique and will work. Even with encouragement, this exercise is pretty stressful—not because of the time or expectations but because of the uncertainty[8]: Will I get a good idea? Will it be unique? Will others like it? Will it work? Everyone asks these questions *while they are thinking* about possible ideas, in effect scaring themselves and simultaneously stifling their creativity.[9] Self-editing or self-censoring kills creative ideas—what Matthew May calls *ideacide*.[10] Unique ideas are exactly that—unique. They are different—which makes you different. Recall that your brain is a lean, mean, pattern-making machine, and it loves the concept of the world you have constructed. Creative ideas, by definition, challenge the usual perspectives and are met with suspicion, skepticism, and sometimes even envious rejection.[11] Creativity requires courage; facilitating the creative capacity of yourself and your followers requires purposeful design.

Leadership by Design

Design Principle: Desire Line

Definition: Indications of common and frequent use that indicate preferred methods of interaction and activity.

In Other Words: You can see how people like to use things by looking at how that object or environment wears out.

For Example: A pumpkin patch may have premade rows that afford easy walking, but that is not where you will find the pumpkins. New paths are worn where people desire to walk.

Desire line

©iStock.com/jeffbergen

For Leaders: Have you ever been in a creative session where ideas seem to have dried up, yet you just know there are many more ideas locked inside the group? When problem-solving, it is typical to follow the methods of thinking that have previously been laid out in front of you. Treat pumpkins in a pumpkin patch as solutions to your problem—you will not find the perfect one by taking the same path everyone else did. Thinking within the constraints of a certain situation is a barrier to creative problem-solving. You will only find that new idea if, as leader, you foster group brainstorming sessions in a way that encourages *mental off-roading*, which forces people to venture off the beaten track. When you allow desire lines to form, you get a more candid perspective that challenges what has already been done before and highlights its inefficiencies. Be attentive to desire lines to gain an unbiased understanding of how people interact with something.

Your concept of creativity has been shaped by many years of education and social norms. Those rules dictate that creativity is acceptable once in a while and only if there is a good idea attached. Beyond that, creativity as a focus or pursuit is fruitless, distracting, uncertain, and probably downright frivolous. And by the way, you are not that creative. Ouch. That thinking is not helpful, nor even accurate. In fact, that perspective is so bad you can almost smell it—hold your nose and exclaim, "That idea is thinky!" Even if puns are not your thing, how many different ways could you modify the word *think* to create new meanings? You would likely surprise yourself. In *Creative Thinkering*, expert Michael Michalko highlights a number of important realities about creativity that nicely frame the mindset you will need moving forward—12 ideas[12]:

1. You are creative.

2. Creative thinking is work.

3. You must go through the motions of being creative.

4. Your brain is not a computer (and that is a good thing).

5. There is no one right answer.

6. Never stop with your first good idea.

7. Expect the experts to be negative.

8. Trust your instincts.

9. There is no such thing as failure.

10. You do not see things as they are; you see them as you are.

11. Always approach a problem on its own terms.

12. Learn to think unconventionally.

Creativity takes work, and our brains do not like to work if they do not have to. Early research on brain activity shows it takes less cognitive effort to choose a sure gain than a risky gain, and engaging in creativity is a risk (in many ways) with the potential gain of innovation.[13]

DEI BY DESIGN

> **LEARNING OBJECTIVE**
>
> 8.2   State the impact of fragility and vulnerability in building creative confidence.

Being the person who puts their ideas forward as solutions to technical and adaptive problems can be scary. The fear associated with expressing creativity, attempting to solve a problem, or innovating new initiatives may stem from the discomfort of being vulnerable. This **fragility** comes from the perception of threat and is triggered by uneasiness or anxiety.[14] Sometimes it can turn into anger, fear, silence, or withdrawal from stress-causing conditions. Creative and innovative leadership requires enduring these uncomfortable feelings in order to arrive at novel solutions. Understanding how feelings of fragility impacts your approach to leadership can help dismantle your own fear and open new pathways to creative leading.

Prominent vulnerability scholars describe **vulnerability** as, "uncertainty, risk, and emotional exposure."[15] Most of us, under normal conditions, would try to avoid these conditions, yet you will need to risk discomfort in order to lead authentically, intentionally, and by design. If you can inhabit the mental and physical spaces characterized by vulnerability, creativity and innovation can flourish. As a leader, however, you should also be aware that some individuals risk more social losses than others. Given the unequal distribution of power, access, and resources at both the organizational and societal levels, it may be unfair to challenge the least protected among us to embrace vulnerability in leading unless those individuals and groups have what is necessary to thrive.

As you strive to move away from fragility and toward vulnerability, you may seek both safe and brave spaces; for ourselves and others. Safe spaces are those environments where all can candidly express, "ideas and feelings, particularly around challenging areas such as diversity, cultural

Design others' creative success by building safe spaces that encourage creative confidence.
©iStockphoto.com/undefined undefined

246 Module 3 ● Design Others' Success

competence, and oppression."[16] These physical environments are co-constructed by everyone in them to offer protection from psychological harm, especially among individuals who have multiple targeted social identities. The goal in creating such safe spaces is to confront uncomfortable issues in a productive way, which in turn can further clarify who you are, what you believe, and how you lead. For the creative leader, these spaces will also foster creative thinking and ultimately creative confidence.

However, for some, no place is safe enough to meet the definition of safety. Those situations require significant bravery to lead by design in an unequal and inequitable world. By acknowledging the uneven risk among diverse leaders, you begin to craft brave spaces—arenas where you explicitly understand leading and offering creative ideas is risky and admit that it is more risky for individuals with fewer social protections.[17] Operating within brave spaces allows you to understand and own differences in privilege and power; embrace fragility, discover vulnerability, and lead with courage. Together, all of these factors improve our creative problem-solving, innovative idea-generating, and DEI-designed leadership.

MOVING FROM REACTIVE PROBLEMS TO PROACTIVE OPPORTUNITIES

LEARNING OBJECTIVE
8.3   Distinguish between different types of problems.

Do you have problems? Oh yes, you do. And if you do not have problems, that is, oddly, a problem. **Problem** can be defined as a challenge or difficult matter of uncertain outcome, and your ability to spot problems is key to effective leadership. After all, you cannot address much less solve a problem you do not even realize exists. Most often problems are considered troublesome and troubling—something that pops up and gets in the way—a dissatisfaction with the current state. Addressing problems of this kind in this manner happens all the time in both leadership and life. This is the *reactive* problem-solving noted in the module introduction. By contrast, **proactive** problem-solving involves anticipating and addressing problems before they occur. The ability to see potential problems is even more powerful. What if you created problems (i.e., saw opportunities) by visualizing a more ideal outcome than the present? In other words, what if you visualize making something better? Researchers have found some interesting benefits to motivational imagery including higher levels of motivation, anticipated pleasure, and anticipated reward for the planned activities, as compared to control groups.[18]

Proactively exploring problems is key to innovative leadership. Right now, it probably seems a bit strange to go looking for problems. But when organizations (and individuals) redefine problems as *opportunities*, finding new problems can lead to great success. Try addressing some of these questions as a way to seek out problems:

- Over the course of one day, what annoys me? Make a list. What annoyance, if solved, could be a great new product, process, or service?

- By contrast, what is working really well in my life that I use a lot? How could it be just a bit better?

- Who could I talk to in order to discover new problems? What could I find if all my friends and family kept track of what annoys them over a week?

Once you see the problem—reactively, proactively, or idealized—leaders set about solving the problem by engaging in a process. Your default, constructed process may or may not be effective for all problems, and it may or may not fully utilize the three general phases of problem-solving explained in Chapter 1: Understand, Imagine, and Implement.

Understanding the problem includes much more than simply knowing it annoys you. Consider the many questions that could prompt your understanding of the problem. What are the costs and consequences—current and long term? What has been done to solve the problem in the past, and what worked and did not work, and why? Who are the key stakeholders, and how are they affected? What are the different variables within the problem, and how are they connected? What is the history and context around this problem? What are the little problems within the larger problem? What would the ideal solution look like, and what consequences might that solution produce?

Unless you understand the problem, you may be working to solve the wrong thing. Experienced leaders appear to solve problems much more quickly than the time needed to answer all those questions because their experience has answered those questions already. The good news, as you may recall, about your pattern-making machine of a brain is that your experiences help make problem-solving more efficient. However, experienced leaders also know to take a slightly different approach to the Understand phase, namely, making sure they understand their own assumptions, biases, and limitations to how they see the problem. Knowing what might be influencing your perspective or at least that your perspective is only one of many possible perspectives, positions you well for learning from experience.

Algorithm, Heuristic, and the Important Thing

Expert problem solvers recognize the different forms of problem and then apply the most effective tools and approach for that specific problem. **Algorithmic problems** are those with a well-defined set of rules or instructions for solving, such as a mathematical equation. There are not very many algorithmic problems in leadership. Most leadership problems are open-ended, which means they have many parts that are often ill-defined and changing. These kinds of problems are referred to as heuristic. A **heuristic problem** is an open-ended problem with no specific formula for solution and thus needs a general set of guidelines to address. A heuristic approach is flexible enough to allow for variations in persons, situations, and context. For example, there are some general steps to things like building a team, strategic planning, crafting a vision, and conflict resolution. You can imagine how very different these heuristics look with differing players and situations. And that does not even include the other great variable—*you*. If you had to explain to someone how you generally solved problems, you would likely discover that you have already created a habitual pattern—your informal problem-solving heuristic. Effective leaders design their problem-solving with a clear awareness of their tendencies and have a range of heuristics to draw upon.

Problems are complicated, and every problem is comprised of many pieces—variables that lead to the problem, others that influence the problem, and still others that may be part of the problem some of the time. Heuristic problems include wicked problems (that were introduced in Chapter 3)—those generally social problems that are difficult to solve due to their incomplete, interconnected, and dynamic variables. How can you address such confusing and complex problems as a leader? You might start with *the important thing*. The children's book author Margaret Wise Brown (who also wrote *Goodnight Moon*) wrote *The Important Book,* in which she illustrates a very important point about life (and leadership and problems):

The important thing about a shoe is that you put your foot in it. You walk in it, and you take it off at night. And it's warm when you take it off. But the important thing about a shoe is that you put your foot in it.[19]

There are many characteristics about a given thing, but out of all those there is a fundamental characteristic—the important thing. The same is true of problems. Understanding the problem space helps you identify the important thing, which in turn focuses and specifies your problem. Trying to solve a problem that is too general leads to frustration and wasted effort because the solution is likely not targeted at the important thing. As management guru Peter Drucker notes, "There is nothing quite so useless as doing with great efficiency something that should not be done at all."[20]

When there is so much to understand about a given problem and limited time to learn and explore, how does a leader make a decision and move forward? Decision-making research tells you that when faced with seemingly endless variables and an unclear path to the goal, the best thing to do is utilize the information you have, make a decision, and move forward. At first thought this approach is frightening. "What did I miss?" is the usual worry. Fear not. Effective problem-solving is *iterative*, which is to say, if you missed something important, you will notice it as you go through the process. Iteration happens automatically when you have developed the design-thinking capacity of iterative thinking—the mindset of always seeing solutions in process—assessing and improving (you should revisit this from Chapter 3). As you read on into the Imagine phase of idea-generating, keep in mind that you may start to see the problem differently simply by generating possible solutions, which may then lead you to reframe the problem. That is not wasted time, it is effective problem-solving.

YES, CREATIVITY WILL HELP (A LOT)

LEARNING OBJECTIVE
8.4   Differentiate between the 4Ps that define creativity.

Leaders solve problems—big and small, near and far, individual and organizational, algorithmic and heuristic, reactively and proactively, and in some cases, creatively. Moving from a good problem-solving leader to a creative one consists of understanding the broad range of what facilitates and inhibits creativity, both in yourself and others. One effective way of organizing this understanding is around the classic 4Ps that are often used to define creativity: Product, Person, Press, and Process. **Product** defines the qualities and criteria that distinguish a solution as creative—namely, that it is unique and of value. **Person** is characteristic of knowledge, skills, and dispositions that support individual creative activity. **Press** describes the contextual variables that foster or inhibit creative thinking and behavior. **Process** outlines the steps of thinking and doing that maximize creative possibilities. Each of these Ps can prompt activities that will encourage creativity.

Product: Unique and Valuable

Often, when you come upon something that is very unique, you consider it creative. Indeed, uniqueness is one of the key criteria for a creative product. Note that the term product implies all forms of solution, which might be a design, a service, a strategy, or any other solution. What if you were to draw a messy scribble on a piece of paper right now and offer to sell it to your classmate? Would they buy it? You can claim it is unique—no others like it in the world. Try it and see what happens. From the conversation with your colleague, it quickly becomes clear that the quality of unique is both relative (ranging from unique to you, all the way through unique to the world) and varied (ranging from pretty much anyone can produce this, all the way through very few to perhaps only one person can produce this).

Did your classmate like your scribble? What if you clarified that this was done by someone famous or that it was done at the top of Mount Everest? In addition to *unique*, a creative product must have value. The notion of value, however, may differ greatly in terms of both persons and forms of value. Usually, the creative product is valued based on the degree to which it *solves* a problem. Your scribble may also be valued for its uniqueness and therefore translate into monetary value. But it may have sentimental value, spiritual value, referential value, and a host of other forms of value as defined by individuals assessing it.

Both uniqueness and value are relative criteria for a creative product. That does not mean that anything you deem creative is so. In fact, what *you think*w is creative is probably not. What matters more are numerous other measures, including how well the product solves the problem, how different the product is relative to a broad audience, and how and in what ways users value the product. Thnsider both target population and value throughout the process.

Creative products must be unique and of value.
©iStockphoto.com/Vicky_bennett

Person: Divergent Thinking, Open-Mindedness, and Creative Confidence

Defining creativity as a product (i.e., this solution is creative... or not) helps leaders understand the nature of the solution, but it does not speak to the route to that end (process) or the tools to get there (person, press). The creative person comprises the knowledge, skills, and dispositions that support creativity. You are unique and of value, and you are the tool of creative production. Utilizing, emphasizing, and developing some key characteristics will best encourage creative outcomes (Table 8.2).

TABLE 8.2 ■ Characteristics of Creative Individuals or Effective Leaders?

Adventurous	Expressive	Open	Self-confident
Aggressive	Flexible	Open-minded	Self-sufficient
Ambitious	Humorous	Original	Sensation seeking
Assertive	Imaginative	Perceptive	Sensitive/perceptive
Autonomous	Impulsive	Persevering	Thorough
Complex	Independent	Playful	Tolerant of ambiguity
Courageous	Individualistic	Prefer complexity	Tolerant of disorder
Curious	Industrious	Questioning	Tolerant of incongruity
Dissatisfied	Inner-directed	Radical	Unconcerned with
Dominant	Internally controlled	Recognition seeking	impressing others
Emotional	Introspective	Reflective	Unconventional
Energetic	Intuitive	Resourceful	Uninhibited
Excitable	Liberal	Risk taking	Varied interests
Experimenting	Non-conforming	Self-aware	Versatile

Research into the creative person started much like effective leader research—identify individuals producing creative things, observe, and label their characteristics.[21] Over time, the list of characteristics became so long it described lots of individuals, and it became too unfocused to identify what one should develop for greater creativity. Interestingly, many of these characteristics would be of great value to effective leaders. Look at Table 8.2. Can you tell if it is describing creative individuals or effective leaders?

REFLECTION QUESTION

How many of the above characteristics can you recognize in yourself? Put a check by those that describe you. Circle the five you think are most valuable to your effectiveness as a *leader*. Now ask a friend to look at your choices and see if they agree that these are your most effective characteristics for *creativity*.

Many characteristics that you now possess can be leveraged to facilitate creativity. Three personal characteristics that are both skills and dispositions (mental habits) can be further developed to bring out your most creative self: divergent thinking, open-mindedness, and creative confidence. These three characteristics work together to enable you to see differently and generate new ideas from those new perspectives. Divergent thinking, introduced earlier as one of the key dispositions in design thinking, is defined as the mindset of generating many, many ideas for a single problem. This capacity underpins idea generation, and it pushes your thinking *outside the box* where unique solutions can be found.

Back in Chapter 3, you were challenged to come up with 100 different uses for a pencil—to think divergently. In a typical group of 50, with each person generating 100 ideas, you would be surprised to learn that out of that pile of 5,000 ideas there might be 10 that are original to *just that group*. You are more alike than you think, which is why it takes extra effort to be unique. Researchers have expanded the notion of divergent thinking to better assess creativity. The total number of ideas you are able to generate to a specific problem is called **fluency**, while the total number of unique ideas is termed **originality**. Guilford's alternate uses test[22] measures how many different uses you can generate for a common object—such as a pencil or a lollipop—and it measures how many different categories those uses comprise. This is called **flexibility**. Generating ideas that cut across many categories indicates that you are not stuck in one perspective. For example, a lollipop might be used for a variety of things in the category of *golf course* (e.g., a tee, a way

Chapter 8 • Creativity, Problem-Solving, and Idea-Generating   251

to mark your ball on the green, a way to clean off your golf cleats), the category of *hospital* (e.g., a mini splint, test your reflexes hammer, cover one eye for an eye test), or the category of *landscape* (decorate your yard, aerate the lawn, create a squirrel lure). Finally, very few answers show **elaboration**, another measure of creativity based on the degree of detail in the answer. Saying you can use a pencil as a coffee stirrer is less elaborate than a temperature-sensitive coffee stirrer only found at literary cafes upon which famous phrases emerge with different temperatures to prompt writers.

MYTH OR REALITY?

The phrase *thinking outside the box* just means to think creatively.

Myth . . . and Reality. The phrase *outside the box* originally refers to a psychology experiment by Karl Dunker in 1945 where he asked individuals to solve a problem where they had to affix a candle to the wall using only a few items, one of which was a box of tacks. The key to the solution was to overcome what he called *functional fixedness*, which is your lean, mean, pattern-making machine at work. Individuals were stuck seeing the box as a holder for the tacks rather than seeing it as an item available for use in solving the problem. When you take the tacks out of the box, you can tack the box to the wall to hold the candle. Thus, thinking (with the tacks) outside the box.

The phrase was popularized by management consultants in the 1960s and 1970s in reference to a classic puzzle from 1914[23] where you are challenged to connect nine dots (three rows of three . . . . . forming a box) with four lines.[24] The solution is to extend the lines out of the box formed by the dots. Try the puzzle and really *think out of the box*.

The metaphorical box you must now escape from is your own perspective and way of thinking. So, in reality, it does refer to thinking creatively.

Open-minded can be defined as the mindset of being receptive to new ideas and perspectives. You cannot see new perspectives and possibilities if you are not receptive to doing so. Many individuals will claim they are open-minded, but their behavior says otherwise. Open-mindedness requires both an awareness and a level of humility. In Chapter 3 (and earlier), you learned that your brain constructs information. When you encounter new ideas, your brain struggles to fit them into the way you see the world. And if you cannot, those perspectives are rejected. However, when you know your perspective is only one of an endless parade, you open yourself up to looking more closely at new ideas. Admitting you have much to learn becomes more difficult as you become more experienced and expert, which is why open-mindedness requires humility. Can you admit the fallibility of your beliefs and perspective, or can you at least put them aside long enough to really consider something different?

Supporting your open-mindedness and divergent thinking is a concept more recently popularized by David Kelley and his brother Tom from IDEO called creative confidence.[25] If the root of confidence is trust in yourself, **creative confidence** is trust in yourself as a creative individual or as Kelley describes it (individuals), a "natural ability to come up with new ideas and the courage to try them out."[26] A strong creative confidence, like a strong CORE™, opens the door to many related creativity attributes such as comfort with ambiguity, the willingness to play and try things, and the willingness to take risks and to see failure as a learning opportunity.[27] The Kelleys note a number of things you can do to build your creative confidence, all of which entail your active creative engagement and exploring new perspectives. Here are some specific suggestions:

- Choose creativity—at some point you need to simply make the decision that you are going to be creative and then go practice and engage.

Module 3 ● Design Others' Success

- Build a creative support network—it is hard to be creative when everyone around you wants to stay in the box . . . ... and keep you in as well.

- Think like a traveler—seeing the world, even the one you live in every day, with wonder (as in, "I wonder why . . ....") helps you practice seeing differently.

Press: Context and Culture

The creative press comprises those things in the environment that press on your creativity, either inhibiting or encouraging. Consider two scenarios as a practical way to understand press. In both situations, your team has been tasked with putting together some new, creative ideas for holiday gifts for your clients. In one scenario, the team meets in a windowless room, seated in rows facing the leader, given only a notepad and pen, and they are frequently reminded that the deadline is looming. In the other scenario, the team is sent off to visit other stores to explore and observe. They return to a wide-open, sunny space filled with arts and crafts materials and walls to write upon. They are encouraged to share their explorations and ideas, and they are told that even though there is a deadline, they should set the project aside for a few days and revisit it later.

Both scenarios really happen. Which one sounds more appealing? Which one would you choose if you had to focus on studying for a big test? And which one would more likely foster creativity? There is a great deal of research on what fosters and inhibits creativity in the immediate context and environment, in the local and larger culture, in the design of the space, timing of the activities, and style of interactions between individuals. Leaders can develop the creative capacity of their followers, and they can strategically engage elements of the creative press to influence creative behavior. Chapter 14 focuses exclusively on how to create a culture of innovation and will greatly inform how you design your leadership future.

Process: Understand, Imagine, Implement, and Iterate Revisited

Problem-solving is a process, and many models and approaches have been tried, recorded, and developed. Humans have been solving problems for a long time and learn processes from one another through experience and modeling. Everyone, including you, has a default problem-solving process that you learned through experience. Effective leaders have a range of processes they can draw from depending on the needs of the problem and situation. By now, you should be familiar with the three phases of problem-solving: Understand, Imagine, and Implement. This general framework can be used to help you sort and organize other models you come across, taking the important steps and stages from each as you find useful.

Two of the earliest models of creative problem-solving were laid out by Graham Wallas (an economist) in 1926 and by James Webb Young (an advertising executive) in 1939. Wallas asserts four stages of the creative process: Preparation, Incubation, Illumination, and Verification.[28] Preparation clearly relates to understanding the problem, illumination is that mythical *aha* of imagine, and verification seems to fit implementation. But what is incubation? **Incubation** is a purposeful stepping away from consciously focusing on the problem to allow unconscious processing and connections. Wallas called it *mental relaxation*, and its importance to creativity has become increasingly recognized. Similarly, Young terms his model a technique, and it includes five steps:

1. Gathering raw material

2. Digesting the material

3. Unconscious processing

Chapter 8 ● Creativity, Problem-Solving, and Idea-Generating   **253**

4. The aha moment

5. Idea meets reality

Again, it is easy to see which steps comprise understanding the problem, imagining, and implementing. Many of the myths that have since been debunked are also evident because these models were based on experience and observations rather than research. When you look at Wallas's and Young's models, how do you think their professions influenced them?

Perhaps the most famous and highly used process model has been the Osborn-Parnes Creative Problem Solving Model. Another advertising executive, Alex Osborn, took a reflective approach to his work, partnering with Professor Syd Parnes to develop tools and techniques to enhance creativity.[30] The original model outlined seven steps in the creative problem-solving process,[31] but the power of this model has been its flexibility. Over the years, it has undergone many revisions, each striving to be a more useful tool. One of the recent iterations of this model identifies six steps within three stages (not surprisingly, they mirror Understand, Imagine, and Implement) (Table 8.3).

TABLE 8.3 ■ Osborn-Parnes Creative Problem Solving Model—Stages and Activities

Stage	Activities
Explore the challenge	Objective finding Fact finding Problem finding
Generate ideas	Idea finding
Prepare for action	Solution finding Acceptance finding

While not evident in Table 8.3, this model emphasizes two dynamic elements of the creative problem-solving process. First, the process is cyclical and iterative. In other words, reaching the end of the process is seen as additional insight to start again seeking further innovation. This dynamic mirrors the notion of continuous improvement and proactively seeking opportunities of effective leadership. The second dynamic is the complementary relationship between divergent and convergent thinking *at each stage* of the process. Divergent thinking is often characterized as the idea-generating mental habit, but in reality, you will need to think of many, many ideas throughout the creative problem-solving process. For example, during Fact Finding, you may have to generate many ideas for what to research and where to get that information, and then you have to converge those ideas into the best information and sources. Or for Acceptance Finding you could generate a list of the many individuals you may need to influence to bring an idea to practice, and again you need to converge on the most impactful individuals with whom you will work.

All of these models and processes can be a bit confusing. One very different and insightful approach is offered by creativity guru Roger von Oech, highlighted in his books *A Whack on the Side of the Head* and *A Kick in the Seat of the Pants* (sounds promising already).[32] Von Oech asserts that rather than go step by step, stage by stage, you should instead assume four different roles as you progress through the process: Explorer, Artist, Judge, and Warrior. An explorer seeks out new things but also talks with people, takes careful notes, and does considerable background work so they know where to look in the first place. Explorers probably feel excited, focused, eager, curious, and perhaps a little anxious. The explorer must be thoughtful, strategic, observant, courageous, and engaged. Take a moment to consider what each of these roles does, what they feel like, and what kind of personal characteristics are needed (Table 8.3).

TABLE 8.3 ■ Four Roles in the Creative Process

Role	What Do They Do?	What Does It Feel Like?	What Should They Be Like?
Explorer			
Artist			
Judge			
Warrior			

Von Oech notes, "When you're searching for new information, be an Explorer. When you're turning your resources into new ideas, be an Artist. When you're evaluating the merits of an idea, be a Judge. When you're carrying your idea into action, be a Warrior."[33] These roles can be translated into action by considering what divergent and convergent activities comprise each role. Figure 8.1 outlines these activities by role.

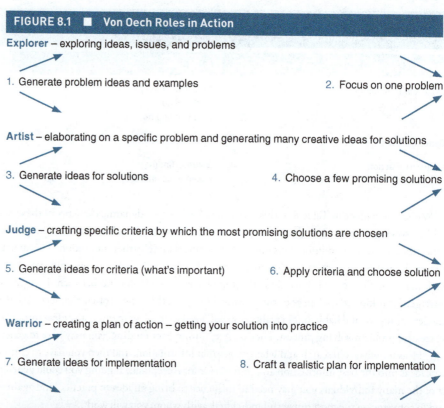

FIGURE 8.1 ■ Von Oech Roles in Action

Explorer – exploring ideas, issues, and problems

1. Generate problem ideas and examples
2. Focus on one problem

Artist – elaborating on a specific problem and generating many creative ideas for solutions

3. Generate ideas for solutions
4. Choose a few promising solutions

Judge – crafting specific criteria by which the most promising solutions are chosen

5. Generate ideas for criteria (what's important)
6. Apply criteria and choose solution

Warrior – creating a plan of action – getting your solution into practice

7. Generate ideas for implementation
8. Craft a realistic plan for implementation

Chapter 8 • Creativity, Problem-Solving, and Idea-Generating   255

Creative problem-solving processes are easy to find and easy to follow, but they are challenging to fit to the appropriate problem and context. Your best approach as a leader is to know the general Understand—Imagine—Implement model and then continue to explore and add specific steps from other models to your problem-solving toolbox. The next section shifts exclusively to the Imagine phase, specifically looking at the many techniques for generating ideas. Get ready to put your divergent thinking to work.

YES, YOU CAN GENERATE MANY, MANY IDEAS

LEARNING OBJECTIVE
8.5   Construct your creative problem-solving toolbox with a variety of idea-generating techniques.

Ideas. Solutions. Innovative answers. At the heart of creative problem-solving is finding a unique idea of value. But using the word *finding* takes leaders down the path of innovation as a treasure hunt without a map, playing into the Eureka myth. Great innovations are the result of many other ideas building off one another, crossing disciplinary silos, being tested and improved, and evolving over time and context.[34] This process was evident in the most recent great innovation – the Covid-19 vaccine.[35] "We like to think our breakthrough ideas . . . are state-of-the-art technology, but more often than not, they're cobbled together from whatever parts happen to be around nearby," notes Steven Johnson, who researches where ideas come from.[36] That systemic and often random process, however, does not help individual leaders and organizations address immediate, real-world problems. Ideas are not *found*, they are produced or generated. This section introduces a number of idea-generating techniques useful in creative problem-solving.

If you went about making cookies the same way individuals typically make ideas, you would sit around looking at the empty cookie sheet for a while and wait for cookies to appear. Then you might put the sheet in the oven, again hoping cookies would form on the sheet. The more analytical or ambitious might buy a cookie and break it into small pieces, examining it carefully to see how it came to be. Others may grab handfuls of random ingredients, possibly mix them, and then shape them into what could look like a cookie. Fortunately, that is not the cookie-making process, nor should that be the idea-making process.

Cookie-making by an experienced baker serves as an excellent metaphor for idea generation. As a novice, you follow a recipe with ingredients and instructions on how to put them together and end with how to transform them. The process is almost algorithmic—follow the formula, get the cookies. As you become more experienced, the recipe becomes more of a general guide for your experimentation and improvisation. You might add a bit more flour, substitute M&Ms for chocolate chips, or bake them at a higher temperature for less time. Finally, as an expert, you know and understand the ingredients and process at a more intuitive level (recall the characteristics of an expert from Chapter 1). This expertise allows for greater flexibility in your approach and process. Asking someone to find an idea is like asking a baker to find a cookie—both inaccurate and improbable.

Generating ideas may start as formulaic, using the algorithm of the techniques found in this chapter and beyond. However, idea-generating techniques are really heuristic because they prompt and guide your thinking in different directions. At the heart of all idea-generating techniques is a push to *see differently*. Think about all the ways that you could see something differently. You could look at the details or zoom out to see the larger

256 Module 3 ● Design Others' Success

context, you could see the opposite or reverse, or you could see through someone else's eyes. As you explore each of the idea-generating techniques, consider how each prompts you to see differently.

Divergent Thinking Techniques

Some problems are best solved by generating many, many ideas and then finding the best ones and developing them into something great. Divergent thinking, introduced in Chapter 5 as one of the dispositions of design thinking, consists of the mindset of generating many, many ideas from a single problem. While all the idea-generating techniques utilize divergent thinking, there are some for which that activity is central.

How often have you been asked to *brainstorm* for ideas? Generally, individuals use the term brainstorming when they really mean "let's just talk and shoot out some ideas." But brainstorming is a specific technique developed by advertising executive Alex Osborn back in the 1940s. Brainstorming has rules that facilitate the generation of many ideas[37]:

1. Go for quantity.

2. Withhold criticism and judgment—negative and positive.

3. Encourage wild ideas.

4. Combine and improve ideas by building off each other's ideas.

It may seem strange to apply rules to enhance creativity. Rules, however, provide guidance and context that foster idea generation. For example, each of the brainstorming rules prompts very specific thinking behaviors that would otherwise not emerge. This reasoning is noted in Table 8.4.

TABLE 8.4 ■ Brainstorming Tips	
Brainstorming Rule	**Why It Is Important**
Go for quantity	When solving problems, people tend to satisfice—settling on the first idea that will satisfy our needs—rather than generating more to find the best.
Withhold criticism and judgment—negative and positive	Asserting an idea is a bit of a risk and takes courage. The judgment of others is a very powerful influence. Individuals will withhold ideas to avoid negative judgments. On the other hand, positive judgments set a standard for idea quality that, if not met in your mind, will also stifle idea generation.
Encourage wild ideas	Individuals need encouragement and permission to escape their own self-editing and self-judgment. You can often see others dismissing their own ideas in their head for fear the idea is not feasible, viable, desirable, or unique enough. But without those *wild* ideas as seeds, there are no ideas to develop and build upon.
Combine and improve ideas by building off each other's ideas	The great power of brainstorming lies in the interactions between individual ideas. Without the constraints of judgment and quantity, the room fills with many spare parts that comprise an inventory of new possibilities.

Brainstorming has many variations that suit different problems and contexts. Try this example: Take out a blank piece of paper and draw a line down the middle of the page from top to

Chapter 8 ● Creativity, Problem-Solving, and Idea-Generating   **257**

bottom. Writing only on the left side, generate as many ideas as you can for how to create the worst classroom space ever. Follow the brainstorming rules—go for quantity, go wild, with no judgment, and have some fun with others. Once you have filled up the left side, reverse your answers and build upon the reversals. Because the problem is really, How can we create the best classroom space ever? *Reverse brainstorming* allows you to see aspects of the problem and ideas that you would not have considered had you simply addressed the problem directly. For example, you might have said the worst classroom would have a really bad odor. Reverse that—a good space would not have the bad odor—and build off it. What if we added some pleasant scent to the classroom or perhaps a series of fun and pleasant scents? Take a few more minutes to work down your list and develop some ideas.

Sometimes as a leader you need to address a sensitive problem, one that others are hesitant to discuss. Likewise, you may have followers who are more quiet or private and simply not ready for the wild, no-judgment discussion in brainstorming. A technique called *Pass the Note* is an effective technique for generating ideas when discussion is limited. Write the specific problem on the top of the page and explain that you are looking for any and all ideas. Then, pass the note from person to person—either at a meeting or around an organization—allowing each person to write down their ideas after reading those that were written before (this allows some building off other ideas). The note can be sent around as many times as you like, but eventually, you end up with a big list of ideas for further development.

Problem Analysis Techniques

Another category of useful idea-generating techniques involves seeing the problem differently by analyzing it in different ways. Imagine you work for a local restaurant and the manager asked you to come up with a new sandwich for every day . . . for the next five years. That would be 1,826 different sandwiches (assuming one leap year). That is a lot of ideas to generate. You try brainstorming with a few groups but seem to stall out around 50 new sandwiches. So instead, you take a closer look at what generally makes up a sandwich: some kind of protein, some kind of garnishment like a cheese or vegetable, and then some way to hold it all together (i.e., the bread). Now instead of thinking divergently about the whole sandwich, you generate a list of different kinds of proteins (ham, tofu, turkey, etc.), different additions (Swiss cheese, cheddar, sweet peppers, etc.), and different wraps (wheat bread, lettuce wrap, pita, etc.). If you generate a mere 13 ideas for each of these three and then cross them in a 13 × 13 × 13 matrix, you will end up with 2,197 sandwich combinations—more than you needed. If you add another category such as sauces (ketchup, mayo, jelly), a list of 13 sauces would then bring the total combinations to 28,561. That is an incredible number of ideas, and it would take you nearly eight hours to list out if you could write one every second. This technique is called *morphological synthesis*, and the multiple effect of categories is made possible by the act of seeing the problem in parts rather than the whole.

Thinking about the *parts* as *attributes* helps to better identify the essential features of a problem. For example, the attributes of a sandwich include the generalized ingredients but also might include things such as (a) holdability—you can hold it in one hand and do other stuff; (b) preservation—you can pack it in your bag without cooling, and it will not spoil by lunch; (c) nutritional completeness—it includes all the necessary nutrients; (d) 10-bite timing—it does not take long to eat—about 10 bites. Of course, these terms are made up, but the idea behind them is not. Remember *The Important Book* noted earlier in the chapter? *You* need to determine the important attributes of the problem. And once you do so, those attributes can be modified.

258   Module 3 • Design Others' Success

The *SCAMPER* technique further prompts how you might modify attributes to generate new ideas. SCAMPER stands for Substitute, Combine, Adapt, Modify, Put to another use, Eliminate, and/or Reverse each attribute.[38] Each of these prompts represents numerous questions that could elicit new ideas. For example, for Substitute you might ask, Can we substitute one part for another? Could we change the name? The shape? The color? Can we use this in a different place or for a different purpose? Could we substitute different materials, processes, individuals involved, rules, and/or terms used? Attribute modification offers a seemingly endless supply of new ideas, each of which could be the seeds to your next great innovation.

At this point, you are probably thinking, yes, this is all good and perhaps fun, but how do techniques like this apply to something abstract like leadership? Many leadership problems can be reversed and brainstormed or broken into attributes that can be modified (again, problems include proactive opportunities, not just reactions when things go wrong). Quite often followers lose track of the vision, and leaders need to somehow help others remember and align their work with the mission. At the next meeting, you might ask, What are all the ways in which we can stray from our mission? You will be surprised at the number of creative answers. Following that question to the group, of course, reverse the answers to see the unique possibilities.

Relatedly, what attributes comprise the *work* of individuals? For each of these attributes, note all the ways you might make the mission more evident or connected? Perhaps your organization is trying to come up with ideas for how to increase membership. You could come up with attributes of membership recruitment activities, such as forums, themes, activities, and follow-up.[39] Brainstorming a short list for each attribute, you could then apply morphological synthesis (remember the sandwich types example) to come up with a variety of events for recruitment. Try it out by adding to Table 8.5 (the columns need not be even). From the examples that follows, you have $5 \times 5 \times 5 \times 4 = 500$ event ideas. Who could resist a "Take a Selfie With an Ice-Skating Monkey Party," especially when the following week you get a singing email reminder for the next meeting?

TABLE 8.5 ■ Brainstorming by Attributes Example			
Forums (the when and where)	**Themes**	**Activities**	**Follow-Up**
Classroom	Circus	Playing board games	Hand-written card
Local park	Cheese	Taking stuff apart	Picture of person
Main street	Monkeys	Eating	Singing email
Swimming pool	Presidents	Taking pictures	Singing telegram
Ice rink	80s music	Balancing on things	

Visualization Techniques

Everyone is familiar with automobiles and their safety features. Many of those features were designed in response to an accident. But many were designed by visualizing what *could* go wrong. Your capacity to play out scenarios in your mind—even, if not especially, fictitious ones—represents a fundamental building block of creativity. The term ideation is often used to describe the entire creative process; however, it really means to form ideas in your mind. This capacity can be directed and used to generate new ideas.

The *Worst Case* technique asks you to visualize all the things that could go wrong and then address each of these *worst cases* by generating solutions, which may end up being new ideas.

Chapter 8 ● Creativity, Problem-Solving, and Idea-Generating   259

Worst cases need not actually be the worst, but rather they are all the things that might or could happen contrary to intent, use, or success. Try using this technique regarding your next organization meeting:

- What worst-case uses, interactions, or interpretations have you observed in the past?

- What could be misused or abused?

- What might your biggest critic say?

- What might wear out?

- How might I minimize the consequences if one of these bad things happens?

Visualization techniques more often focus on the ideal and fantastical. A common set of techniques (e.g., What would happen if . . .. magic wand, wish list) essentially entails asking the group to imagine ideal outcomes without the constraints of rules, budgets, personalities, procedures, or any of the other pesky implementation barriers. While the ideas generated are not practical, they do provide a different way of seeing the problem and possible solutions. What if we could fly like a bird? What if all that power in a river could be captured? What would happen if we had light during all hours of the night? If you had a magic wand, what would your organization be doing right now? If you were granted three wishes for your followers, what would you wish for them? Each of these questions prompts new ways of seeing and ultimately new ideas.

The way that problems are framed and the level at which you view a problem can also change the way you see. *Framing* cars as a way to get from point to point is quite different from seeing cars as a status symbol or a sports implement. The designs would be (and are) significantly different depending on the frame. Likewise, designing a car from different perspectives results in very different innovations. Try the activity in Table 8.6. How would you innovate a car from each perspective? For example, at the microlevel, you might consider new materials that would wick water off the windshield glass or conform the seat to your body, or perhaps you might infuse a pleasant scent to the exhaust. Those ideas are very different from those at the parking lot planning level, where the innovation might be wheels that turn to a full right angle to allow you to slide into a parking spot or a retractable bumper that makes the car two feet shorter.

TABLE 8.6 ■ Framing, Perspectives, and Ideas	
Perspective	**Your Ideas for Car Redesign?**
1	Car from a distance—in action	
2	In the showroom	
3	Interior from driver's perspective	
4	Interior from passenger's perspective	
5	Engine level	
6	Microlevel	
7	Urban setting—street level	
8	Parking lot planning level	
9	Urban core and evacuation route level	

Play and Build Techniques

Idea-generating in the Imagine phase is all about seeing differently . . . and playing. Many of the examples given are simply wacky and would not work for many reasons. But you are not judging those ideas at this point, only generating them. And again, quite often the bits of crazy ideas end up inspiring insights that lead to viable, feasible, and desirable innovation. Play and build techniques emphasize this iterative and cumulative notion in idea generation. Leaders need an open mind and trusting culture to engage their followers in play, which is discussed further at the end of this chapter (and a major focus of Chapter 14 on Creating a Culture of Innovation).

Many organizations promote the notion of play in their culture, but play in idea-generating is the specific, focused application of play to purposefully see differently. Of the many types of play, some specifically facilitate idea-generation, such as exploratory play, which expands your storehouse of ideas from which new ideas can be built.[40] Other types of play, such as role play and building play, provide rich mediums for iteration and for alternative perspectives.[41] For example, Ismail al-Jazari was a highly successful 12th Century Turkish engineer whose mechanical toy designs are considered some of the first programmable robots and ideas from which created valuable civic innovations.[42]

No doubt, you have dressed up for Halloween at some point, and perhaps you have even taken on the role of your character to some extent. Likely, some of you have also performed in plays or other dramatic productions in which you had to take on a role. What was it like to see through that role? Everything looks like a chew toy to a baby; serious athletes structure their days and months around preparing for peak performance. Experienced professionals see the world in a manner that highlights their expertise. So too, as you learn more about leadership, you will begin to see more and more examples of good and bad leadership in your day-to-day life.

One of the origins of the word creativity is from the Latin *creare*, which means *to make*. For as long as humans have built things, they have used their hands as a tool to think and to generate ideas. Sometimes *making* ideas means you have to actually make stuff outside your mind so you can see different dimensions of the problem and solution. Every design field incorporates sketching and prototyping into their process—not because they are *artsy* but because each sketch is a step toward a more refined solution. Each prototype is a tool to help the designer see and try a solution.

In an introductory leadership course focused on creativity, students are challenged to create an innovation that makes dorm life easier and to build a cardboard prototype of their idea. Inevitably the cardboard models look terrible, but that helps emphasize the point. Making the model is not about how pretty it looks but about how well it illustrates and communicates the solution. Even more important, the process of making the model highlights alterations, improvements, and impossibilities that the students were unable to see without the physical model.

Senses and Emotions

Problems and solutions spend lots of time in your head. The power of play and build techniques brings that activity into the concrete world where there is more room to process. Have you ever worked on a paper or project where you had to spread different resources all over a table or an entire room? Why? Because you could not juggle all of those different elements in your head. Similarly, there are facets of problems that are often overlooked because they live in your brain. Applying role play, you are trying to conceptualize the world through someone else's mind. That effort can be significantly enhanced by adding two elements: senses and emotions.

Go on a sensory scavenger hunt, and focus on *all* of your senses. Most of our attention relies on the visual, but inputs to the other senses can make a huge difference. Think about how sound

Chapter 8 ● Creativity, Problem-Solving, and Idea-Generating   261

(a soothing voice versus a screech), touch (the firm handshake versus the limp), or smell (well . . . you can imagine this one yourself . . ....) impacts the relationship you design with your followers. In her book *The Senses: Design Beyond Vision*, designer and writer Ellen Lupton summarizes many advantages to integrating different senses relative to health and well-being, diversity, inclusivity, richness of story and experience, and influence.[43] Considering a sensory component adds to your idea-generating as well. Attuning yourself to multiple senses promotes attending to this valuable perspective. Try this sensory hunt.

SENSORY SCAVENGER HUNT

Sight: Find a defined space that is not the classroom.

Where is your immediate focus? What is in the background? What is on the floor? What is over your head?

Sound: Close your eyes and listen carefully for a period of time. Note nine things you hear. Now plug your ears—what/how do you hear (besides your own breathing/chewing)?

Smell: Find 10 different smells . . . describe them . . . rate them.

Item	Description of Smell	1 (Hated) to 5 (Loved) the Smell
1		
2		
3		
4		
5		
6		
7		
8		
9		
10		

Taste: Find five items to taste—pick some usual and some unusual. Close your eyes; take your time. Try small bites and big. Move the food around in your mouth and focus on the primary flavor and then the more subtle flavors.

Item	Description of Flavors	1 (Hated) to 5 (Loved) the Taste
1		
2		
3		
4		
5		

Touch: Find five items to touch—again, pick some usual and some unusual. Close your eyes; take your time. Use your whole hand and then your fingers; touch without moving your fingers, then moving. Then try feeling touch with your body as a whole—close your eyes and feel the weather, wind, clothes on your body.

Item	Description of Touch
1	
2	
3	
4	
5	

Taking time to consider the emotional aspects of a problem can also contribute to idea generation. *Solving* a problem looks different when the outcome is to induce a specific emotion. For example, hotels gather extensive user-centered data to give people what they need and want. But what kind of room would you have if the hotel were designed to make you *feel* a certain way—like calm or nostalgic or energized? As you recall from the section on emotional intelligence, expanding your emotional vocabulary helps you better discern and work with your and others' emotions. In the most applied sense, consider what it feels like to be led by you. How do you want it to feel? Design your relationships with emotions in mind.

Incubation Techniques

The Eureka myth seems most applicable when you are least engaged with the problem. Although you may feel this as a flash of inspiration, that *moment* is really a culmination of many pieces of information swirling around over time. As that early Wallas model asserted, incubation in idea generation consists of any number of activities where you intentionally shift your attention away from the problem, with the intention of revisiting it later.

Suggestions such as "Why don't you sleep on it?" or "You should set it aside for a while" are suggestive of your brain's continuous processing. Attention and focus narrow your thinking and may further add stress, neither of which allow for new and random connections. Engaging in routine activities frees up one's cognitive load to process, even if unconsciously. In a world of increasing efficiency, multitasking, and on-demand instant expectations, incubation is looked at with skepticism if not contempt. A boss might ask, "Why should I pay you to sit around and process?" Nevertheless, shower notepads were invented for a reason—to capture that brilliant idea that only seems to hit you when you do not have a pen. Contrary to the importance of engagement and the great value of engaging the problem, its components, other perspectives, and play, when generating ideas you sometimes need to engage in disengagement. Meditate, take a walk, play a game, or simply set a project aside for a few days. You will be pleasantly surprised by the creative results.

Alternative Perspective Techniques

Perhaps the most straightforward way to see differently is to see with someone else's eyes. Alternative perspective techniques take your idea-generating efforts outside the problem space, asking you to explore the problem from the outside in, through the eyes of another. Deep empathy becomes a vehicle to see differently and generate ideas. Two design-thinking capacities contribute to generating ideas in this manner: user-centeredness and multidisciplinary. Utilizing user-centered data collection methods (again, recall Chapter 3) directs your attention to see through the user's eyes and feel what they feel. And multidisciplinary thinking encourages you to invite other fields of practice and experience to the process. Together, these design-thinking practices assist you in working as the T-shaped person described in Chapter 3, where working in the margins of your discipline helps you see ideas in the spaces where disciplines meet and overlap.

Alternative perspectives extend beyond other individuals and their disciplines. How else might you parse and pursue differences? Maybe a child would see the problem differently, or a veteran, or a small business owner, or a coin collector, or someone who has lived through a hurricane. There are endless ways to identify difference, each holding a unique and valuable perspective for contributing ideas. Yet another way of altering perspective lies in how people think: conservative, liberal, progressive; optimistic, pessimistic, nihilistic; and so forth, to include any number of values and beliefs that would contribute a unique perspective.

Chapter 8 ● Creativity, Problem-Solving, and Idea-Generating   263

REFLECTION QUESTIONS

Consider a problem on which you are currently working. Who would see this problem differently? Who has nothing to do with this problem or even the context? Whose opinion could you ask?

YES, YOU CAN *FIND* MANY, MANY IDEAS

LEARNING OBJECTIVE

8.6   Demonstrate explorative activities that will continuously fill your creative problem-solving idea stockpile.

Hopefully, it is now clear that ideas are generated, not found. What is found, however, is inspiration—ideas from sources outside the problem. Ideas build on other ideas and contexts, and the more you explore and experience the world, the greater your storehouse of concepts that can be applied, combined, and adapted into a new context and a new idea. If, as Steven Johnson noted earlier in this chapter, ideas are usually cobbled together from spare parts that happen to be around, where do you find the parts? You could work on your explorative design-thinking capacity and be more of an explorer of the world (review Chapter 3). But seriously, how much stuff can you have, and how many experiences can you keep track of before you are overwhelmed?

Inspiration and Exploration Techniques

Many individuals who work in a stereotypical creative field (remember, all fields should be creative) often surround themselves with a literal museum of interesting objects and images and regularly explore for new sources of inspiration. This approach can be fun and effective, but it is not always possible. Rather than random exploration, look to contexts that may parallel the problem you are addressing. For example, the natural world provides a wide array of time-tested solutions. Janine Benyus, co-founder of the Biomimicry Institute, has championed a wide array of applications where experts in a specific field look to nature to identify a problem-solution similar to their focus. The concept of biomimicry purposefully seeks out solutions from nature that can be mimicked.[44] For example, no one likes to go to the doctor and get a shot. It hurts. How could scientists develop a pain-free needle? Turns out that there is an expert in the natural world at pricking others without getting caught or squished—the mosquito.

> Materials researchers and engineers at Kansai University in Japan saw amazing potential in the structure of the mosquito's mouth. They used sophisticated engineering techniques that can carve out structures on the nanometer scale. The result of this blend of materials science and biology was a needle that penetrates like a mosquito, using pressure to stabilize and painlessly glide into skin.[45]

What could leaders learn from how nature influences others or how to best work as a team?

Leadership by Design

Design Principle: Mimicry

Definition: The act of copying or imitating properties of something familiar. In design, looking to other objects, organisms, or environments for ideas and solutions.

In Other Words: Observe, copy, and paste.

For Example: Examples of mimicry are all around you. The famous Spanish architect Antonio Guadi mimicked patterns in nature for many of his very unique building features, such as the roof in this photo.

Mimicry
©iStock.com/sneska

For Leaders: Creativity does not always suggest that an idea is brand new. Many great innovations take concepts and inner workings already found elsewhere and simply apply them to a new framework. Mimicry is actually one of the oldest and most efficient methods for achieving major advances in designs. Leaders should use mimicry to further develop effective systems that have been previously designed—in their field and in others. Benchmarking identifies the goals of mimicry and helps quickly discern what ideas or practices would work in your organization without having to reinvent the wheel. Even from a self-design standpoint, leaders can develop desirable skills the fastest by mimicking role models. Who is already doing a great job? Who can you mimic? When should an idea be entirely your own? How can you also use mimicry to model desired relationships after already established connections? A new idea can be created from two old ones.

If looking to nature to mimic how problems are solved is a good idea, why not look all over the place and find comparable ideas? *Metaphorical thinking* is an idea-generating technique wherein you compare two different things that share similar characteristics and then draw ideas for your context from the new context. For example, say your group has been challenged to find ways to improve the new student orientation at your college. Using metaphorical

Chapter 8 • Creativity, Problem-Solving, and Idea-Generating 265

thinking, you would take a moment to generate ideas about what being a new college student is like—not the real experience, everyone has thought of that already. Instead, you think about metaphors.

Being a new student at college is like . . . stepping onto a school bus full of strangers . . . tasting a new food . . . visiting a country where no one speaks your language . . . walking through a haunted house where people jump out at you. You can probably already see the connections, but the next step is to make them explicit and then translate them back into your context as ideas. Table 8.7 provides an example. Note, the ideas generated are not necessarily good ideas . . . yet. But they are the result of seeing differently, and they may lead to innovation.

TABLE 8.7 ■ Metaphorical Thinking			
Being a New Student in College Is Like . . .	Because . . .	Which Means . . .	So, Here Are Some Possible Ideas . . .
Entering a strange forest at dusk	You cannot see very far down the path.	It would be helpful to be able to see what is next and where the path leads.	Create a visual journey through the major, showing what comes next. Connect students across grades to discuss their experiences.
	Every little sound is new, strange, and distracting.	Keeping new information and distractions limited to only those necessary for success.	Put together an easily accessible quick directory rather than separate flyers. Limit involvement in certain things to more experienced students.
	It feels fully immersive, like there is no way out.	Understanding where there are breaks (exits) and that there are guides in and out of the forest.	Have each new student return to their high school and share their experience. Build *take a break* days into the semester where students share things about their home.

Many creativity experts assert that great ideas come from connecting with other ideas and making connections that others have not seen. *Forced connections* comprise a wide variety of techniques that direct you to examine and play with how one idea might fit with, enhance, combine with, or otherwise alter another idea to create something unique. Say, for example, that you loved pizza and really wanted to create an innovation in pizza. This could include a unique new product, delivery system, restaurant, product packaging—any facet of the total pizza realm. The fun part is to find rich sources of inspiration with which to connect. See if you can force connections using the sources in Table 8.8 (a few examples are noted—you should add to them).

TABLE 8.8 ■ Sources of Inspiration

Draw From This Source . . .	. . . to Create These Ideas for Pizza Innovation!
Random objects on your person (yes, make a list of them)	Rolled Pizza—like you would roll up your sleeves Pizza Passport—get stamped for each type of pizza until you have traveled the pizza world
Small businesses on Main Street (any Main St.—again, make a list)	Pizza Train—like the sushi train where you sit and the conveyor belt goes by with different, small pieces of pizza, and you take what you want Pizza ATM—put in your card, get a slice out of the machine
Toys and board games	Pin the Pepperoni on the Pizza—a fun game for families at the restaurant
Random words—open a book at random, point to a word	
Tools and other things you would find in a hardware store	
A walk through the park	

Sources for ideas and inspiration are everywhere. Techniques like metaphorical thinking and forced connections are advanced techniques that involve some of the other idea-generating techniques (such as role play, attention to senses and emotions, attribute modification, visualization, play, and of course divergent thinking); however, the success of these techniques depends on your effort and ability to explore. Remember Roger von Oech's roles for guiding you through the creative problem-solving process (Explorer, Artist, Judge, and Warrior)? The Explorer role, while meant for finding and understanding the problem, offers considerable guidance for finding rich idea-generating sources.

Retype these, blow them up, and post them in front of your desk:

1. Ask questions and be curious.

2. Start your explorations with a goal in mind.

3. Be present and see what is around and in front of you.

Retype these, cut them into strips, put them in a hat, and pick one to do each time:

1. Look at other disciplines, fields, practices, and industries.

2. Allow yourself to wander and be led astray

3. Break up your routine.

4. Look at different levels—up close to big picture.

5. Visit places very different from your usual.

And tattoo this one on your hand:

1. Remember to take notes.

Chapter 8 ● Creativity, Problem-Solving, and Idea-Generating **267**

MOMENT OF AWARENESS

Sources of inspiration are everywhere.

There are always new ways to take your ideas to the next level. Never again can I say, "I don't have any ideas." There are idea-generation techniques where you can just take a random image and start brainstorming ideas from there. There is no longer any barrier to entry to having an idea and no excuse for being unable to create something new! We drew inspiration from cartoons, skateboarders and our environment. We made connections between random words to form wild ideas. The number one problem I hear from people who say that they're "not creative" is that they don't have any ideas. After learning and experiencing all the techniques from this class, I'm confident that I could help people believe in their own creativity.

—Zachary Jones, Undergraduate

All the idea-generating techniques introduced in this chapter bring you to the heart of creativity—the ability to see differently. Table 8.9 summarizes the different categories of idea-generating techniques with numerous examples. As you solve problems as a leader, know that there are many tools to help you and your organization imagine, generate innovative ideas, and develop your creativity.

TABLE 8.9 ■ Categories and Techniques for Generating Ideas

When You Want to:	Use These Idea-Generating Techniques
Maximize ideas: Techniques that maximize quantity	Divergent thinking techniques: Brainstorming Reverse brainstorming Pass the note
Examine problem and modify parts: Techniques that analyze and deconstruct the problem and then alter some part or attribute of the problem	Problem analysis techniques: SCAMPER Morphological synthesis
Visualize outcomes: Techniques that involve mental simulation of various outcomes or scenarios	Visualization techniques: What would happen if . . . . Worst case Reframing problem Wish list Magic wand
Play and build: Techniques that emphasize idea emergence through random and/or playful manipulation of the problem and related facets	Play and build techniques: Prototyping Role play Sketching
Sense and feel: Techniques that bring attention to the human facets of the problem, such as emotions and multiple senses	Sense and emotion techniques: Emotional prompts Sensory focusing

(Continued)

TABLE 8.9 ■ Categories and Techniques for Generating Ideas (*Continued*)	
When You Want to:	**Use These Idea-Generating Techniques**
Incubate: Techniques that purposefully relax and disengage the mind away from the problem	Incubation techniques: Meditation Exercise
See through other eyes: Techniques that apply a framework that is outside the problem	Alternative perspective techniques: Cross-disciplinary Empathy
Get ideas from elsewhere and purposefully explore: Techniques that acquire ideas from sources and contexts outside the problem	Exploration techniques: Metaphor Biomimicry Forced connections Be an explorer

NO, YOU ARE NOT "DONE": ITERATION, CONVERGENCE, AND ASSURANCE

LEARNING OBJECTIVE
8.7   Compose a plan to continuously build your creative activity and confidence.

Generating ideas consists of many iterative reassessments and refinements. In classic brainstorming, the rule is to build off each other's ideas. In problem analysis, different attributes spark new modifications. In play and prototyping, there is a rapid cycle of try, assess, alter, try again. No matter how hard you try to withhold judgment (another brainstorming rule), you cannot help but make micro-judgments about each idea, which in turn spurs on more ideas. This iteration is crucial to idea-generating, and it can be purposefully built into the process.

As a leader trying to facilitate this process, you need two important actions: convergence and assurance. Convergent thinking as a complement to divergent thinking was explained earlier as happening at every stage of the problem-solving process—generate lots of ideas (divergent), then pick the best one (convergent). The convergent–divergent complementary process is a very important activity that is generally overlooked, primarily because in practice, divergent thinking is relegated to the Imagine phase. Convergent thinking drives those little micro-judgments during idea generation. This is the Judge role presented by von Oech. You can put the Judge to work before the final solution decision. In reality, judges only render a decision after they spend a lot of time weighing arguments and evidence. In other words, the Judge helps refine the problem, which in turn generates more ideas. Here are some prompting questions by the Judge role that ultimately help generate ideas:

- What is the idea trying to do?

- What assumptions are you making, are they still valid, and are there assumptions you are not even aware of (ask someone)?

Chapter 8 ● Creativity, Problem-Solving, and Idea-Generating   269

- What's interesting and worth building on?

- What are the idea's drawbacks?

- Have I made things overly complicated?

- Are we playing by rules? What if we did not?

Like idea-generating techniques, there are many convergent thinking tools that facilitate your analysis and decision-making as you converge on the best ideas from the divergently generated list. You will learn some of these techniques in Chapter 14: Creating a Culture of Innovation.

Leadership by Design

Design Principle: Iteration

Definition: A process of incrementally developing and refining a design based on feedback until a specific result is achieved.[46]

In Other Words: Go back to the drawing board. Again. On purpose.

For Example: Your educational curriculum is likely different now than it was when the program was first created; fields of study are often iterated to keep up with new knowledge and an increasingly complex, competitive society.

For Leaders: Iteration is arguably the most important component to a successful solution. It allows intricate ideas to build naturally on simpler ones, which brings order to complexity. Often leaders shy away from iteration because they fear failure; however, a failing design provides just as much, if not more, valuable information as a successful idea. People have an unlimited capacity for creativity—there is no reason to halt the process after the first idea. How can a leader involve as many constituents as possible to test concepts and solicit feedback? Why is that important? When should the iteration of a design actually stop, if at all?

Creativity takes practice. Creativity is (sometimes) hard work. These two assertions by Michael Michalko from the start of this chapter sum up the only thing between you and innovation. You have set aside your fears and recognize the myths of creativity. You understand creative problem-solving processes and idea-generating techniques. How, then, do you further develop your creative capacity? Frequent, purposeful engagement in creative challenges, along with the following suggestions, will help you maximize your creative potential.

1. Develop your CORE™—creative activity involves risk. Taking creative risks is easier when you are confident, optimistic, and resilient.

2. Believe in yourself as a creative individual—this belief will grow as you engage.

3. Recognize and eliminate blocks—creativity **blocks** are the many things that stifle your creative thinking. When someone says, "That is a terrible idea!"—that is a creative block. Blocks can also be psychological (fear), cultural (norms), social (others' judgment), conceptual (how you see things), and literal (deadlines, distractions, environment).

4. Play and have fun—positive emotions and humor enhance creativity and motivation to engage.[47]

5. Give yourself a kick—the idea doctor said, "It's a picture of the shoe I used to give you a kick in the seat of the pants. When you look at it, I want it to trigger these questions in your mind: Am I getting lazy? Am I too busy? Am I becoming arrogant? Am I getting timid?"[48] Developing your creativity takes work, time, humility, and courage. Some of these are internal and some external, but all are in your control.

CHAPTER SUMMARY

Yes, you really are creative, and the first step toward developing your leadership is to understand the many myths that surround the concept. Perhaps the greatest obstacle to your creativity is you—your fear of being different, your self-editing and self-censoring, and the mental habits formed over the years.

But as a leader, you will have problems. Even if you do not have problems, you want to proactively seek out problems because those kinds of problems are heuristic opportunities to innovate. Creative leaders see more possibilities.

Creativity can be defined with the 4Ps. Creative products are unique and of value, and that uniqueness and value need to be clearly defined. Creative persons think divergently and are able to generate many, many ideas from a single problem. They are also open-minded and have creative confidence. The creative press are the things in the environment that impact creativity. And there are many creative processes, all of which offer some interesting divergent–convergent steps and stages, all of which fall into the general organization of Understand—Imagine—Implement with iteration. But the important thing (remember to identify the important thing) is to follow a process.

Yes, you can generate many ideas. Wow, can you generate ideas. So many idea-generating techniques to add to your creative problem-solving toolbox. Fortunately, your toolbox is organized by category of technique: divergent-thinking techniques, problem-analysis techniques, visualization techniques, play-and-build techniques, human-centered techniques, incubation techniques, alternative-perspective techniques, and inspiration and exploration techniques.

KEY TERMS

Algorithmic problem (p. 247)

Blocks (p. 270)

Creative confidence (p. 251)

Creativity (p. 241)

Elaboration (p. 251)

Flexibility (p. 250)

Fluency (p. 250)

Fragility (p. 245)

4Ps (p. 248)

Heuristic problem (p. 247)

Incubation (p. 252)

Innovation (p. 240)

Open-minded (p. 251)

Originality (p. 250)

Person (p. 248)

Press (p. 248)

Proactive (p. 246)

Problem (p. 246)

Process (p. 248)

Product (p. 248)

Vulnerability (p. 245)

Chapter 8 ● Creativity, Problem-Solving, and Idea-Generating   **271**

CORE™ ATTRIBUTE BUILDERS: BUILD NOW FOR FUTURE LEADERSHIP CHALLENGES

Attribute: Confidence (Creative)

Builder: Creating creativity workshop

Teach some idea-generating techniques to your friends. Better still, work with friends to put together a brief workshop (15 minutes) that engages your organization in divergent thinking activities or idea-generating techniques. Take the techniques and challenges right from this chapter or make up your own. The important thing is to continue to practice and involve yourself in creative activities.

SKILL BUILDER ACTIVITY

Imagine Imagine Imagine what if . . .

Invite three friends out to coffee and discuss the questions that follow. Any time an interesting idea comes up, one you think is really fun and has potential, write it down. Really push yourself and the group to have fun and be wacky.

- What would happen if animals became self-conscious?
- What would happen if men had babies?
- What would happen if college courses were only taught after 10 p.m.?
- What would happen if students wore uniforms?
- What would happen if all students used a wheelchair?
- What would happen if there was a 3 to 6 p.m. siesta?

SKILL BUILDER ACTIVITY

Practice the creative process: Mission Positive Idea Challenge

Yay for happy!

Your challenge: Design an inexpensive, reproducible, product and/or experience that induces positive emotions in others. The broader the appeal (that is, the more people you impact), the better. If your idea can create positive emotions in the same person over and over again . . . well, that is really cool.

- Remember to *understand* the problem, context, solutions, and so forth.
- Remember to think *divergently* and generate many, many, many, many, many, many, many, many ideas . . .
- Remember to *iterate* and test and improve and test and improve and test and improve . . .
- And keep those other design-thinking habits of mind in mind: Explorative, User-Centered, Multidisciplinary, and Integrative.

SKILL BUILDER ACTIVITY

Activate multiple senses to generate ideas

Here are three challenges that ask you to activate as many of the senses as possible:

1. With a partner—Design a *date* focusing on each of the five senses (taste, touch, smell, sight, sound) and a sixth sense—a feeling of beauty, expectations exceeded, deep comfort, or an alternative you choose relative to positive emotion.

2. Create a campus map that is based on something other than geography (e.g., smells, mood, colors, etc.). Incorporate as many of the senses into the map itself or what it represents.

3. Design a greeting card for someone who needs a thank you. Again, think about a card that includes and activates as many of the senses as possible.

9 EFFECTIVE PRACTICES FOR LEADING OTHERS TO SUCCESS

LEARNING OBJECTIVES

Upon completion of this chapter, the reader should be able to

9.1   Identify important broad influences that may impact effective leadership practices

9.2   Translate important information about the brain into designing leadership relationships and others' success

9.3   Describe the context behind adopting a new set of leadership practices

9.4   Explain how leadership and management functions are different but complementary

9.5   Engage in leadership practices to inspire those around you

9.6   Apply managerial practices to implement a strategic plan

9.7   Use a situational leadership approach to design others' success

Leadership by Design Model

Design Self
How can I design myself as a leader?

Design Relationships
As a leader, how can I design my relationships with others?

Design Others' Success
AS A LEADER, HOW CAN I DESIGN SUCCESS FOR OTHERS?

Design Culture
As a leader, how can I design the culture of my organization?

Design Future
As a leader, how can I innovate?

INTRODUCTION

Leadership is ultimately about influencing others. But influencing someone to do something is not nearly as effective as influencing them to do that something better. Designing others' success means creating the conditions for maximizing potential and multiplying value—well beyond immediate work toward the common goal. Much like building your leadership CORE and other capacities, a process-oriented perspective and growth mindset *applied to followers* prepares your organization for unknown challenges and unique opportunities. For example, the resounding theme across stories of organizational success during the pandemic was that of a willingness and ability to creatively adapt and a focus on present resources.[1] Leadership practices that helped facilitate success in that crisis provide a valuable roadmap for capacity-building.[2]

In a leadership role, you have the opportunity to design many things, including and perhaps especially the capacity of your followers. This chapter begins by exploring the foundational elements of what followers need and the practices you can use as a leader to meet those needs—first in the most fundamental way that everyone's brain works (or does not) and then in terms of their role and experience operating in your organization. The next section outlines key practices that will help you IGNITE success as a leader and DELIVER success as a manager, capturing these two very important aspects of leadership. The chapter concludes with an overview of how situational leadership theory can assist you in designing the right approach for facilitating others' success.

Leadership That Makes a Difference

Life is about confronting those special moments we all experience and stepping up our game to grow and change. In this regard, it is not what is thrust upon us during these moments that is important but how we respond to these occurrences. Imagine yourself growing up in a public housing project where crime is all around you. Imagine yourself living in a chaotic family situation where your parents eventually divorce. Imagine yourself having little chance of escaping poverty and accomplishing something special in your life. Growing up, Cynthia did not see many Black women in leadership roles. Nonetheless, she studied exceptionally hard while in school and became the first African American student body president at her high school. After receiving a scholarship to attend the University of California, Berkley, and graduating with a business administration degree, she took a job working at AT&T. During her next 30+ years, she worked her way up the ladder of success to become a senior vice president. Her mantra was building an organization that prioritizes diversity, inclusion, and equity. She applied aspects of the IGNITE practices you will read about in this chapter to rally others to change their ways of interacting with their colleagues. For example, she practiced the (I) in IGNITE by *instilling* a culture that despised complacency while motivating those around her to go beyond the expectations at that time. Similarly, she applied the (T) by *thinking differently* about how to treat people and demonstrating she cared about them and their future. She (E) *ensured* a clear vision that diversity, inclusion, and equity were achievable and added value to AT&T by building extraordinary customer relations. Her legacy reflects an intriguing philosophy that promotes the leadership principle that people generally do not care about how intelligent their leaders are or how much knowledge they possess. They are concerned about how their leaders care about them. Her leadership style reflects achievement and excellence by listening to others, learning from others, and loving to help others achieve success. Breaking down barriers to women of color was her vision. Today, Cynthia Marshall is the CEO of the Dallas Mavericks professional basketball team and the first Black woman to serve as the business leader for an NBA team. During her time with the Mavericks, Marshall has transformed a previously toxic culture into an inclusive environment where everyone can speak up and have a voice. Throughout her life, she not only transformed herself but changed both organizations and the people within them by promoting total acceptance of one another as valuable and contributing members of a team. By the way, she insists on being called Cynt instead of Cynthia.

Cynt Marshall has been a transformative leader for the Dallas Mavericks.
Associated Press/Rebecca Blackwell

DEI BY DESIGN

LEARNING OBJECTIVE
9.1   Identify important broad influences that may impact effective leadership practices.

A **practice** is an activity used typically to maintain or improve one's performance. At the broader level, five leadership practices have been identified by James Kouzes and Barry Posner,[3] as discussed in the last section of Chapter 7: (a) model the way, (b) inspire a shared vision, (c) challenge the process, (d) enable others to act, and (e) encourage the heart. These practices are strongly correlated with successfully changing the behavior of those around us. Kouzes and Posner suggest that assessing your own capacity to put these practices into operation is an excellent way to begin your journey, learning how to grow into an effective leader.

Effective practices, like everything about leadership, involve relating to and working with others in constructive, equitable, and inclusive ways as well as facilitating the same amongst the group. Every member (leaders and followers alike) is empowered to bring the best of their knowledge, skills, and abilities forward in order to help the community advance.[4] Information sharing can take the forms of perspective-making and perspective-taking. **Perspective-making** occurs within a group when members share their individualized knowledge with one another, thereby raising collective knowing. **Perspective-taking** happens when any community member attempts to see the world from someone else's point of view, which may or may not change their opinions on what they know or expect is true. Both perspective-making and perspective–taking are impacted by our social identities, identity intersectionality, and our unique blend of social advantages and disadvantages (i.e., our social location). Organizations that are intentionally inclusive make space for a variety of perspectives and the meaning behind those perspectives, as they meet their goals.

When leading others to success, effective leaders consider the relative proportion of social identities among the membership to avoid tokenism. **Tokenism** occurs when followers with underrepresented social identities are viewed by leaders (or other members) as the representative for all people who share that underrepresented identity and are subsequently treated as though their experiences are reflective of everyone who shares that identity.[5] This tokenizing is harmful to the focal person because it places unfair responsibility on them to act as the proxy for everyone else with a similar social identity, even though they may not experience salience around that identity. In other words, just because you happen to be from Texas does not mean you speak for all Texans, nor do you necessarily act as all other Texans.

Tokenism also limits the effectiveness of the organization because false conclusions can be drawn from the experiences of a limited number of individuals. Socially just groups and teams seek perspectives from a wide array of people to inform their progress and prevent tokenizing members, and recent research indicates that organizational culture plays a key role in limiting and even eliminating tokenism.[6]

One additional social dynamic impacting leadership practices is **essentialism**, which occurs when robust and intersectional social identities are flattened down to one or just a few characteristics. Chimamanda Adichie refers to this as the danger of a single story.[7] By reducing complex individuals to one (often pejorative) narrative, you limit their ability to flourish alongside other members of the community.

PRACTICES FOR YOUR FOLLOWER'S BRAIN

LEARNING OBJECTIVE
9.2   Translate important information about the brain into designing leadership relationships and others' success

Individual behavior comes from individual brains. If you know how the brain works, you can influence behavior. How you see and act regarding yourself, others, the world, and its influences all happens between your ears—in your brain. And yet, despite how much is known about the brain and thinking, leaders apply very little of this knowledge to designing and practicing leadership. How, for example, would you lead differently if you knew that the brain—everyone's brain—could only focus on work after a short rest and being flooded with oxygen? Perhaps you would incorporate more breaks into meetings or install a treadmill desk. Or maybe you would invest in an oxygen bar for the break room and a set of bunk beds in the spare office. This *physiological* dimension of the brain is one of six that form a handy framework to help you apply these brainy lessons.

Your brain constructs how you see the world based on how you have experienced the world (remember the model from Chapter 2 that illustrated your choice between having a narrow, rigid view versus a broad, open view). Another thing you know about your brain is that it likes to form habits. What you construct can become habits in how you think—habits that are referred to as dispositions. Some thinking habits are helpful, and some are not. As you should recall from the introductory chapter, the mental habits comprising design thinking consist of a very useful set of dispositions, which you can apply to a wide variety of challenges.

Brain Leading in Six Dimensions[8]

Take another look at the title of this section. Can you imagine what the title means or what this section will talk about? Does it sound like a science fiction movie? Is the title so odd that you simply breezed over it and moved on? Whatever your interpretation and reaction, your brain was the star of the show. Think about all the things your brain was able to do with this simple request: focus and refocus attention, interpret symbols into letters into words into a sentence, dig into memory for definitions and examples, compare and contrast memories with new ideas, judge the amount of time worth spending, assess the accuracy of your answer, and imagine new possibilities. And you did all this without anyone else, and you did it quite quickly. That is amazing.

Consider for a moment what you know about the brain. Better still, consult with a friend and consider what you know about your friend's brain.[9] You will probably start your list with some of the physical properties you know or have heard. But think hard about what your friend's brain can really *do*. For immediate example, your friend's brain can speculate about you and your brain—like they are doing right now.

There is a lot to know about the brain. One important thing everyone knows about the brain, especially students, is that long, random lists of unrelated facts are very difficult to remember, much less use. Luckily your brain is a lean, mean, pattern-making machine, and it loves to categorize and organize information. Michael Dickmann and Nancy Stanford-Blair provide a framework you can use to keep all this brain information organized so you can apply it to your leadership—the six dimensions: physiological, emotional, social, constructive, dispositional, and reflective.

The six **dimensions of the brain** imply significant applications for leaders (Figure 9.1). As you learn more about the brain beyond this class, you can utilize this framework to translate that knowledge into leadership action. The key question is: *If I know x about the brain, then to be effective as a leader, I should do y*. What will you do differently because you now know something about the brain?

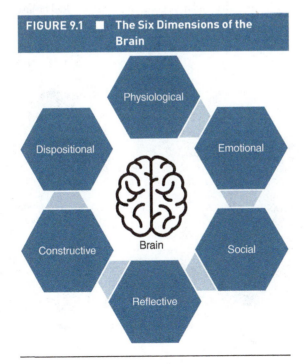

FIGURE 9.1 ■ The Six Dimensions of the Brain

Image of brain—©iStockphoto.com/Pavlo Stavnichuk

The sections that follow include the story of Ralph, a typical employee who wants to be successful. The only thing getting in Ralph's way is his own brain. Read on to find out how you as Ralph's leader can use each of the six dimensions of his brain to design your relationship and his success. You may want to read through these sections now and take a few notes. Then, reread the sections and discuss the reflection questions with a peer. Finally, read through the sections one more time (yes, a third time) and note what *you could do* to positively use each dimension.

> ### REFLECTION QUESTIONS
>
> How did you initially feel about being asked to read something three times? How and why is it useful to look at (or read) something multiple times focusing on different things? After you have read (and reread) these sections, what dimensions of the brain explain the benefits of rereading?

Physiological, Emotional, and Social Dimensions

Ralph arrives at work with a huge yawn, still sleepy from the night before when he decided to stay up for that movie marathon. Because he was in a rush, he did not get a chance to grab his usual morning coffee or even eat any breakfast. Now, Ralph sits at the staff meeting, tummy grumbling, eyes falling shut, and unprepared. Up for discussion is an item that involves Ralph having to shift projects. He considered the shift when the meeting agenda came out and thought through the advantages to both himself and the company. But right now, he is too tired to remember those reasons. When the item is brought up, Ralph finds himself feeling very angry, and he reacts with sarcastic comments and then stone silence. His colleagues, generally very collaborative and fun to work with, react to Ralph's behavior by cutting him out of the conversation and disregarding his perspective. Poor Ralph—and to think this all could have gone a different way had he just eaten a donut.

What physiological, social, or emotional factors are limiting your engagement and performance?
©iStockphoto.com/Blue Planet Studio

This example highlights the three dimensions of the brain discussed in this section: physiological, emotional, and social. More importantly, the preceding scene illustrates the real-world nature of the brain in action. *The six dimensions work together, complementing and contradicting each other, and they cannot be separated in practice.* Thus, the six-dimension framework is simply an organizational and strategic tool for applying brain knowledge to leadership activity, also known as brain leading. One way to think about this interconnectivity is with the old-school puzzle called the Rubik's cube. The Rubik's cube consisted of a 3 × 3 × 3 cube with each of the nine blocks on each side of the cube a single color. Each of the nine blocks could be moved by physically spinning rows and columns, with the goal to get the cube back to having each side a single color. If you consider each side one of the six dimensions of the brain, it becomes quite clear that the dimensions blend into one another pretty much all the time, and the single configuration of each dimension being clearly alone is a remote probability.[10]

So back to poor Ralph—physiologically, he is a mess. Physiological refers to the functions and activities of your body. The **physiological dimension** of the brain recognizes there is a fundamental connection between your brain and your body. This is not a surprise, but it does seem to be constantly overlooked in leadership. Ken Robinson, in his wildly popular TED talk, asserts that university professors "look upon their body as a form of transport for their heads. It's a way of getting their head to meetings."[11] Although slightly in jest, his assertion accurately sums the approach most leaders have to designing relationships with their followers: I, as leader, will interact with your head, overlooking the fact that your brain is comprised of water, chemicals, and electricity, all of which are connected to larger systems in your body. When we want optimal performance from a car, we do not limit our tinkering to the software that controls the systems and overlook the need for oil and other physical parts.

In addition to the very basic physical needs, the physiological dimension also recognizes the brain is made of physical structures that grow (and recede) based on activity. The neural connections throughout your brain that make thinking happen continue to change, physically, as you engage the world—experiencing and learning. Experiences can be positive or detrimental, like the stress of some jobs or work cultures. If manageable, that stress can stimulate neural growth; if never-ending or traumatic, stress can damage the brain.[12]

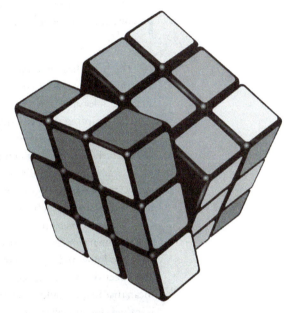

Rubik's Cube

Source: Image by Booyabazooka via Creative Commons BY-SA 3.0 https://creativecommons.org/licenses/by-sa/3.0/deed.en

REFLECTION QUESTIONS

What physical conditions might be contributing to Ralph's situation? What role is stress playing in this culture and context? What other friendly or unfriendly brain conditions can you identify?

Leadership by Design

Design Principle: Biophilia Effect[13]

   Definition: Environments rich in nature, real or in views and imagery, result in mental and physical health benefits such as reduced stress and enhanced focus and concentration.[14,15]

   In Other Words: Go outside and get some fresh air or at least look at a picture of nature!

   For Example: Hospitals incorporate large murals of natural settings for their restorative effects. Pushing your desk up against the window can help you emotionally, cognitively, and physically do better in school.

   For Leaders: As a leader, think about what conditions have impact on you and your team. Incorporating nature or natural images into daily work will prove beneficial to your team in a variety of ways.[16] No matter how trivial they may seem at first, every element of engagement can provide a greater return on invested time or effort. What areas and/or activities in your organization require a context of healing, creative thinking, stress reduction, greater concentration, or enhanced learning? Apply nature.

The brain has an **emotional dimension** that influences how individuals see and react to situations and others based on feelings. Emotion is formally defined as a brief experience of pleasure or displeasure; however, that definition highlights one of the shortcomings most individuals have regarding their emotions—their very limited emotional vocabulary. Remember Ralph and his not-so-good morning at work? How would you describe the emotions he is feeling? You would likely use the most common emotions—angry, happy, sad—rather than more complex yet accurate descriptors like anxious, disaffected, or lethargic. How aware of his own emotions do you think Ralph is at this meeting, and how are those emotions influencing his thinking and behavior? Knowing the answers to these questions is partly a matter of emotional intelligence.

You can be smart in many different ways. As you read in Chapter 1, one very important way of being smart for leaders regards emotion. Emotional intelligence (EI) was defined as a person's ability to know and regulate their own feelings, perceive and understand the feelings of others, and effectively work between their own and others' feelings. Being smart with feelings would mean that Ralph would also be able to read the emotions of others, understand how his behavior is influencing his colleagues, and manage his emotions more effectively, even if he is hungry and tired. The interrelated nature of the dimensions becomes even more apparent when you look at the central role of emotion. What physiological and social conditions elicit emotions? What emotions result in social and physical outcomes?

A great deal of work on EI urges leaders and followers to better understand and manage their emotions for better health, performance, and success.[17] Although research in EI is relatively recent, the notion of understanding and managing emotions dates back to early philosophers. The implications and applications to leadership are apparent in this quote by Aristotle: "Anyone can become angry—that is easy, but to be angry with the right person at the right time, and for the right purpose and in the right way—that is not within everyone's power and that is not easy."[18]

As a leader, what can you do to attend to the emotional dimension of the brain? As Ralph sits through the meeting described, he is feeling defensive, unsupported, and generally uncomfortable. In any context, when you are more concerned with feeling accepted, safe, and comfortable, you are not going to be able to concentrate or focus on the higher-level thinking tasks. For example, if you are worried about the judgment of your colleagues, if you are sitting across the table from an angry ex-boyfriend, if someone in the meeting threatened you before the

Chapter 9 ● Effective Practices for Leading Others to Success   **281**

meeting—those emotions will overwhelm the agenda, making you far less effective for the task at hand. Effective leaders are aware of and proactive in designing the emotional climate and consequently influencing followers.

REFLECTION QUESTIONS

What emotions does Ralph's situation elicit? What are the levels of emotional intelligence of the individuals involved?

The **social dimension** of the brain focuses on the critical and inextricable role that others play in how you see and react to the world. Much of your mental model was (and continues to be) constructed from interactions you have with others, even instances where you only interact with others by observing their behavior. Effective leaders utilize the social dimension of the brain, realizing the power that others have on the individual in problem-solving, seeing other perspectives, generating ideas, engaging complementary strengths, observing the environment, and modeling and upholding norms and culture. Surprisingly, many leaders overlook the power of the social dimension, instead falling back on outdated notions of individualism and fears of losing control. The education world is a prime example of this shortsightedness, where only recently have some educators moved away from the rows of individual note-taking students listening passively to a lecture. One of the authors of this text begins each course with the assertion, "Just because I am not talking does not mean you are not learning." In other words, creating opportunities for individuals to learn from one another—directly, as models, or even as a process of working toward understanding—makes for a far richer emotional experience and learning outcome.

Kouzes and Posner's practices of exemplary leadership introduced earlier lie at the heart of the social dimension, primarily because each of those practices focuses on designing relationships and others' success. When you think about who in your life has made the greatest difference, the list is not filled with celebrities but rather with family or friends—those who have connected with you emotionally. When leaders model the way, inspire a shared vision, challenge the process, enable others to act, and encourage the heart, they tap into the social dimension of the brain.

REFLECTION QUESTIONS

How would Ralph's situation differ if he was alone versus in a meeting with peers? Looking again at Kouzes and Posner's effective leadership practices, what would you do as a leader in the context of Ralph and the other staff? What have you experienced as benefits to sharing, discussing, or working with others?

Reflective, Constructive, and Dispositional

Ralph arrives at work with a huge yawn, still sleepy from the night before when he decided to stay up for that movie marathon. Here we go again, except this time we know the physiological, emotional, and social implications Ralph is facing. These challenges impact the three higher-level dimensions of the brain: reflective, constructive, and dispositional. Ralph thinks about his situation throughout the meeting—tired, hungry, frustrated, defensive—and knows this is a temporary state. His prior interactions with his colleagues and the leader have established his credibility, and he knows them well enough to know they have good intentions. Even though this has been a less than productive or positive interaction, Ralph is optimistic and a creative problem solver who persists at projects and learns from mistakes.

Purposeful reflection can (re)construct your view of a situation, and your performance.
©iStockphoto.com/Blue Planet Studio

This example again highlights three dimensions of the brain, in this case, the reflective, constructive, and dispositional. And again, note the six dimensions continue to operate together, reiterating that the six-dimension framework is only a tool for brain leading. In the preceding example, it seems there is less to worry about with Ralph. He has a good deal of self-awareness, a positive mental model that goes beyond this instance, and some productive dispositions.

The brain has a **reflective dimension**, which is the capacity to consider and modify information and understanding. Your reflective capacity allows you to engage a variety of critical thinking capacities, such as the ability to critically question both a situation and your understanding or mental model. Reflection enables you to predict outcomes, envision futures, prioritize information, and revise both real outcomes and conceptual models. The reflective dimension also allows you to translate information into implications and action.

The power of the reflective dimension, however, is only as effective as you allow or a leader facilitates. In other words, leaders must provide time, space, and in some cases, guidance for reflection. Unfortunately for Ralph, he will have to find that time himself after the meeting.

REFLECTION QUESTIONS

What opportunities do others have to reflect on the situation? What prompts are guiding and framing their reflection... and yours? How can you integrate project/work-focused reflection into team meetings?

The object and outcome of the brain's reflection is the mental model you construct. The notion of a mental model was introduced in Chapter 2—your mental representation of things in the world—not just the picture in your head but how you understand things and even how you process information. Mental models are key to the **constructive dimension** of the brain. The constructive dimension emphasizes your process of conceptualizing the world based on what you interact with in the world. This includes how you later reflect on that construction, feel about those constructions, test those constructions in interactions with others, and continue to modify your constructions.

As noted many times in this text, your brain is a lean, mean, pattern-making machine. As a leader, you can use the constructive dimension to help followers understand and apply information by providing organizational frameworks (like the six dimensions of the brain as a way to organize what you know and how to use it). What knowledge matters most for your followers, and how do you need them to understand and prioritize that information? What mental models might be holding followers back from thinking more creatively or seeing alternative perspectives? As the famous economist John Kenneth Galbraith noted, "Faced with the choice between changing one's mind and proving that there is no need to do so, almost everyone gets busy on the proof."[19] The constructive dimension is a powerful tool for designers of leadership. A strong first impression or concept will withstand many contrary examples.

A leader who understands that the brain has a constructive dimension will address these questions. What is the follower's mental model of this situation? What is your mental model? What other constructions of the world (and the context) may be influencing others and your leadership?

The best news for Ralph and his situation is that he has strongly constructed some positive ways of thinking, so strongly that they have become habits. These habits of mind, as you might recall from Chapter 1, are called dispositions—habits of mind often seen as tendencies or characteristics. The **dispositional dimension** of the brain asserts that everyone has formed habitual ways of processing information and these mental habits influence what individuals perceive and how they conceive information. For Ralph, seeing the positive and the possible will carry him through this tough day, and ultimately, it will bring him success. His leader wishes all of Ralph's colleagues were as optimistic and persistent.

Dispositions are often thought of as personal characteristics because they appear to be so constant, but that is the nature of habits. Leaders who understand the dispositional dimension of the brain will seek to understand the different dispositions of their followers, as well as purposefully develop dispositions that will lead to success. Research has identified a number of dispositions related to effective thinking.[20] These include a disposition (a) to be broad and adventurous, (b) toward learning, problem-finding, and investigation, (c) to build explanations, (d) to make plans and be strategic, (e) to be intellectually careful, (f) to seek and evaluate reasons, and (g) to be metacognitive.[21] **Metacognition** means thinking about your own thinking. In other words, if you have developed the mental habit of reflecting on how you thought about something—the approach or strategy you used, what you know and do not know, what you did well and did not do well in how you thought it through—then you have a metacognitive disposition, and that is part of good thinking.

Understanding different dispositions allows leaders to more effectively communicate and structure tasks to suit different strengths, which in turn help highlights the assets of what might appear otherwise. For example, what might appear as rebellious might be the perfect disposition for a team that tends to the status quo. Table 9.1 is a list of troublesome characteristics, some of which could be dispositions, and how they might be alternatively seen as strengths. As a leader, how could you build a disposition that sees the strengths in others?

284 Module 3 ● Design Others' Success

TABLE 9.1 ■ Develop a Strength-Seeing Disposition		
What Might Be Seen As	**Could Be This Strength**	**What Do You Need to Do . . .** **1. To see the strength?** **2. To bring out the strength?**
Scattered	Creative	
Schedule-driven	Prompt	
Rigid	Organized	
Pushy	Assertive	
Loud	Outgoing	
Meek and deferential	Thoughtful and respectful	
Shy	Reflective or observant	
Very sensitive	Empathetic	
Unrealistic	Optimistic	
Pessimistic	Cautious and prepared	
Uncooperative and rebellious	Independent	

Effective Leadership: Creating Conditions Using Dimensions of the Brain

You are organizing a workshop for your regional managers. The regional managers are having a hard time with the site managers under their supervision, specifically, the regional managers are not happy with the leadership efficacy they expect from their site managers. The regional and site managers know all sorts of information and practices of effective leadership; however, what they do not know is *how to create the conditions for effective leadership and success utilizing the dimensions of the brain*. What specific ideas and insight can your group offer the managers for how they might achieve the latter? Use the grid In Table 9.2 to help guide crafting your recommendations.

TABLE 9.2 ■ Practices for Leaders From Connecting Leadership to the Brain[22]		
Dimensions of the Brain	**Key Questions for Leadership**	**Practices for Your Follower's Brain**
Physiological	What physical conditions might be contributing to the situation? What role is stress playing in this culture and context? What other friendly or unfriendly brain conditions can you identify?	— attend to physiological needs — stimulate neural growth — protect against stress
Social	To what extent do individuals work and/or communicate with others? How do they do so advantageously and otherwise?	— create social opportunities — cultivate shared vision — invite diversity

Dimensions of the Brain	Key Questions for Leadership	Practices for Your Follower's Brain
Emotional	What emotions does this situation elicit? What are the levels of emotional intelligence of the individuals involved?	— cultivate climate of trust and support — cultivate climate of challenge and passion — cultivate climate of emotional intelligence
Constructive	What are individuals' mental model of this situation? What is your mental model? What other constructions of the world (and the context) may be influencing others and your leadership?	— provide sites and structures for knowledge construction — construct knowledge that matters — challenge constructions of knowledge
Reflective	What opportunities do others have to reflect on the situation? What prompts are guiding and framing their reflection . . . and yours?	— supply time, space, and structure for thinking — provoke thinking otherwise
Dispositional	What dispositions (i.e., thinking habits) have individuals brought to this situation? What mental habits, in followers and yourself, would facilitate success?	— proactively exercise multiple dimensions of intelligence — target productive thinking dispositions

Get to know *your* brain. The more clearly you understand how *you* are influenced by your own brain, the more effectively you will be able to maximize your success and apply those lessons to leading others. The CORE™ Builder activity at the end of this chapter explains 11 different activities you could have some fun with as you consider what dimensions are at work and how they are influencing you and others.

PRACTICES FOR FOLLOWERS' NEEDS AND MOTIVATION

LEARNING OBJECTIVE
9.3   Describe the context behind adopting a new set of leadership practices.

Designing success for others begins with how you *see* others. You are likely someone who wants to make an impact—an individual who wants to be seen by colleagues as a valuable contributor who makes a difference. Leaders need to see the same in their followers. Everyone wants to feel like they matter, whether the organizational objective is maximizing shareholder value in a for-profit corporation, better meeting an important social need through a nonprofit, or building sustainability, citizenship, or perhaps spiritual well-being through a public or religious organization. Leading others to success is actually pretty easy—it is already where they want to go. Facilitating that journey to success and designing the conditions and actions to do so is the tricky part for you as a leader. That facilitation begins with understanding what followers need and changing your mindset from *what can you (follower) do for me* to *how can I (leader) bring out your best*.

Know What Followers Need to Succeed

Your greatest achievements at work will ultimately be related to helping others around you succeed at their jobs. Organizations function as complex, interconnected systems where the actions of some impact the success (or not) of others. Knowing what those around you need to become successful requires constant vigilance and consistent planning. As you create conditions for others to succeed, their growing confidence will perpetuate those conditions for others.

Followers Need the Freedom to Raise Issues

You cannot help someone develop into a productive, confident employee if you do not know what concerns them. People generally know when you are truly interested in them. Asking thoughtful questions and providing serious consideration of answers to problems results in creating an atmosphere where success becomes a team effort. This is the objective of appreciative inquiry theory, whereby you build unity among subordinates by focusing on what they are talking about, such as their achievements, stories, and dreams.[23] You will learn more about appreciative inquiry in Chapter 11. Applying this approach creates an open dialogue by permitting and encouraging those around you to ask questions unconditionally. This will likely result in a working environment where innovation and dream-making become a reality.

Followers Need to Be Believed In

People generally want others to believe in them regardless of how successful they might be. By showing support in the form of encouragement, it may be possible to get an individual to believe in themselves for accomplishing great things.[24] Recognizing the contributions of others on a daily basis shows respect and interest in their accomplishments. Giving credit to others for their successes will result in generating more confidence since the energy and enthusiasm at work become commonplace. When others see themselves as being respected and trusted, they are less likely to become negative and critical of others.

Followers Need to Possess Cutting-Edge Job Skills

Having the latest technology available, as well as up-to-date policies for using that technology, will help coworkers more readily gain access to information, connect with and network with others, and remain on the cutting edge of their work. While building relationships with coworkers requires a high degree of face-to-face interaction on your part, networking digitally around the world is also part of bonding with a wider audience. Competence in the use of various forms of social media, cloud computing, and connectivity enables coworkers to become more efficient in getting tasks done and more effective in designing their relationships. Network-enabled devices being *cloudy, social,* and *mobile* also allows individuals to complete many job routines remotely but in real time.[25]

Followers Need Time to Think Creatively

The ultimate confidence builder is coming up with a new idea that becomes a reality for an organization. Accordingly, you as a future leader must promote a framework that provides coworkers sufficient time to get away from job routines to think about innovative ways for getting things done. Setting time aside on a consistent basis, perhaps one day a month, allows individuals to think, plan, and organize their thoughts to advance the best interests of the organization. With organizations needing to stay on the cutting edge, having many employees at all levels of an organization spending time thinking outside the box and comfort zone increases the likelihood that new ideas will come forth.

What cutting-edge technology will give you the edge?
©iStockphoto.com/nespix

Followers Need to Capitalize on Their Strengths

The Strengths-based approach introduced in Chapter 3 suggested you build on what you are good at instead of focusing on rectifying weaknesses. As a leader, you should take the same approach with followers—identify their unique strengths and abilities, and then help them use those skills to excel in their own way. Matching employees with a partner who has complementary skills can form a bond where individuals can focus on what they are good at in the workplace. During this match-up, reconfiguring work neutralizes weaknesses among coworkers and can lead to unconventional work designs that help individuals overcome obstacles. Offering incentives such as time off for planning creative approaches for getting things done can result in bringing out employee ingenuity.

> **Experts Beyond the Text**
>
> ### Insightful Leaders Know About . . . Women and Leadership
>
> ### Women and Leadership: Why It Matters
>
> *By Sherylle J. Tan and Lisa DeFrank-Cole*
>
> Women make up half the population in the United States. Since the late 1980s, more women than men have earned baccalaureate and master's degrees, and since 2006 more doctorate degrees.[26] This pattern is consistent among all racial and ethnic groups. Women participate in the workforce holding more than half of all management, professional, and related occupations.[27] Though women possess all the qualities required for impactful leadership in the 21st century, men continue to outnumber women in senior leadership positions in nearly every sector.[28]
>
> This underrepresentation of women in senior leadership does not appear to be an issue of qualification or ability to lead. Women are capable of being effective leaders and exhibit the expertise and skills necessary to advance contemporary organizations and society.[29] While

researchers have found few differences between women's and men's leadership, there are some variations. For example, women tend to use more democratic and/or transformational forms of leadership that take followers into consideration.[30]

Despite research that shows women are equally effective leaders as their male counterparts,[31] women face what is known as *second-generation gender bias.* These subtle biases are the cultural, structural, and attitudinal beliefs and behaviors that exist to maintain the status quo and hold women back from ascending into leadership positions.[32] People have preconceived ideas of what a leader should look like, typically a White cisgender male, and these conceptions often reinforce pervasive gender norms. These ideas result in less favorable perceptions, attitudes, and evaluations of women leaders.[33] The bias persists, creating obstacles for women to become leaders and achieve success.[34] As a result, women must work harder to prove their worth as leaders.

In addition to factors in the workplace and in society, women face additional responsibilities with home and family. Though men have become more involved in doing domestic chores, women continue to hold the majority of those responsibilities even when they work outside the home.[35] This gap in *domestic labor* contributes to the leadership gap in all segments of the workforce.[36]

Why does it matter? One significant reason to advocate for women in leadership is that women are more likely to be committed to the public good, to equality, and to social change.[37] Acknowledging that one role of a leader is to solve problems, when women are at the table they influence and make decisions on how resources are allocated and invest in issues related to social good such as children, education, and health care. Diverse perspectives in senior leadership teams allow for more beneficial and innovative outcomes.

If women continue to be underrepresented in decision-making, then the expertise and skills of a significant part of the workforce are being underutilized. Though great strides have been made and many "glass ceilings" shattered, there continue to be challenges and barriers to women's advancement in leadership. For equity in leadership to be realized, we need to see shifts in accepted gender roles and stereotypes. This needs to take place in the home with true equality in the division of labor as well as in all areas of work and society.

Strategies to support women's leadership and move toward gender equity include:

- *Shifting gender roles and norms:* Re-evaluate and expand the gender norms for men. Change stereotypical roles for both women and men. For example, encourage boys and men to pursue female-dominated professions while encouraging girls and women to pursue male-dominated professions.

- *Move toward a collective organizational culture:* Masculine organizational cultures, ones that promote competition among teams, aggressiveness, and domination, can be inhospitable for women by reinforcing second-generation gender bias. Organizations that promote an environment that focuses on cooperation, rather than competition, and values the needs of the collective over the individual can support women and enhance employee satisfaction. Organizational policies and initiatives that focus on diversity and inclusion help promote collective organizational climates.

- *Encourage men to be advocates and allies:* Men often carry authority; they can use their power to mentor, sponsor, and advance women in their careers. Women need access to a wide range of networks to increase their social capital that includes people from all genders.

Chapter 9 • Effective Practices for Leading Others to Success   289

- *Establish positive belief systems:* Positive belief systems, such as leader self-efficacy and growth mindset, can buffer the negative effects of stereotype threat and have positive impacts on women's motivation to lead and their leader identity development.

What other strategies could support gender equity in leadership? How can society (including women, men, and nonbinary individuals) advance women to leadership positions, and thus provide more diverse and inclusive environments? What can you do?

Followers Want to Have Impact

Like you, followers want to make a difference. Highly engaged employees are driven by purpose among other variables.[38] And, highly engaged employees who contribute more of themselves at work are more likely to produce innovations that change the world.[39] In this regard, how employees organize and collaborate does matter. You can generate a highly engaged work ethic among your followers by applying Kanter's three Ms theory, which consists of three components: mastery, membership, and meaning. Read the brief description of this strategy and compare your own capacity for designing others' success with each of the following factors.

Mastery of Problem-Solving Skills

When individuals are competent in identifying and resolving especially difficult problems themselves, they possess the fundamentals for getting things done in a smarter way. Therefore, when coworkers possess the feeling they can literally shape the future by being an active player at work, the pace of accomplishment increases.

Membership Through Community Solidarity

Working in teams effectively is a strategy for developing community solidarity and a contributor to high performance.[40] **Community solidarity** is defined as unity (as in a group), which produces collegial interests, objectives, and points of view. It refers to the ties in a society that bind people together as one. By encouraging coworkers to network with others across an organization, you will enhance overall engagement and the opportunity for new ideas to be generated. Thinking laterally across organizational functions (marketing, human resources, accounting, research, design, etc.) results in an awareness of how the existing organizational system works. To build community solidarity among employees, clearly communicate unity whereby ideas, points of view, and feelings may be shared without fear of recrimination.

Meaning by Focusing Upon the Big Picture

Having a view of the big picture takes a mental shift from the mundane to that of curiosity. Rather than continuously focusing on job routines and getting specific tasks done as part of an operational system, sitting back and looking at the overall purpose and impact of the work expands your perception of personal importance and that of others. Clarity about how organizational products or services improve the lives of others also results in guideposts for making future decisions. Changing the daily conversation about how to create new products energizes others to think beyond the typical.

290 Module 3 ● Design Others' Success

REFLECTION QUESTIONS

When you have worked with others in the past, did you trust them enough to open your mind to their ideas? How did you help them feel comfortable enough to share concerns or new ideas? Do you think they felt like you believed in their capabilities? If you had to convince someone right now that you thought they could be successful, what would you say or do?

As a leader, you work to build your CORE™. To design success for others, the bottom line is that you need to help others gain confidence, see optimistically, build up their resilience, and inspire them to more fully engage. Another way to accomplish this is to consistently and authentically let others know they are doing something important for the organization. People want others to believe in them. By showing support in the form of encouragement, you help others succeed at becoming innovative by tending to their needs rather than focusing solely on your own.

Leadership by Design

Design Principle: Garbage In—Garbage Out

Definition: The quality of system output is dependent on the quality of system input.

In Other Words: Bad inputs result in bad outputs. You may also have heard this as *you get out what you put in*, or *you reap what you sow*.

For Example: The time and effort you put into studying for an exam is usually directly proportional to the grade you receive. Here is another example: If you make an apple pie with rotten apples, you will get a lousy pie. If you make a pie with good apples but add salt instead of sugar, again you get a lousy pie. The fault does not lie with the apples. Ponder, and read on.

For Leaders: This design principle captures the essence of designing for others' success. When follower performance fails, leaders often focus on that individual. But the real answer to why things went wrong lies long before the problem actually occurred. Assume for a moment that the source of the *garbage* is not the person—where could the garbage have been added? Did you advertise for the wrong positional skills? Was your hiring process flawed? Was the orientation lacking? Were the necessary resources not provided? Did the individual get any prior feedback or training?

Investing time and resources into the input processes (screening, interviewing, orienting, training, etc.) will ensure that you minimize the amount of garbage in so you can maximize the quality of output. Can you trace the process of recurring issues back to the inputs and redesign it for follower success?

REFLECTION QUESTIONS

Think of a time when you worked with an individual of a different culture from yours. How did you build a relationship with that individual? What did you learn from that experience that may assist you in getting things done efficiently in the future?

Chapter 9 • Effective Practices for Leading Others to Success   291

PRACTICE LEADERSHIP AND MANAGEMENT: WHEN MULTITASKING REALLY MATTERS

LEARNING OBJECTIVE
9.4   Explain how leadership and management functions are different but complementary.

There has been some dissension over decades as to how leading and managing relate.[41,42] The idea that leading and managing are both important is not new, and both bring a large repertoire of practices for leaders. Revisit the definitions: Leadership is the process of influencing others toward a common vision. Management is the process of organizing, controlling, and coordinating resources to achieve organizational value. The function of leadership is to mobilize individuals—human resources—in an effort to move toward accomplishing something significant. The function of management is to coordinate the efforts of people to get those tasks done that achieve specific objectives.

Lead and manage, mobilize and organize. As noted in Chapter 2, these two functions require different but complementary skill sets. A leader in a relatively small organization generally takes on both functions simultaneously since limited resources invite a leader to be multifunctional. However, as organizations get larger and the complexity of operations becomes apparent, the need for considering both functions becomes less apparent. In large organizations with many levels of responsibilities involving possibly thousands of individuals, it is practically impossible for those in leadership roles to manage coworkers on a daily basis.

Effective leaders are fully aware of leadership and management systems and activities as both impact success at many levels. Visualize yourself down at the beach observing the ocean current. As you enter the ocean, you make waves. Similarly, in an organization, there are existing currents—the flow of activity emanating from others, systems, and the overall culture. What waves do you introduce into the overall current, and how might your waves be most influential? How can you use the currents that already exist to your advantage? Creating waves requires the initiative of leadership. Directing your waves and those that already exist requires management. Only by designing others' success can you maximize the combined impact of both. Visualize how leadership and management are complementary functions (Table 9.3).

TABLE 9.3 ■ Management Linking Leadership		
Management	**Linking**	**Leadership**
Riding waves	Functions	Making waves
Ask how to do it?	**Planning**	Ask why it is being done?
Match talent to task	**Organizing**	Hire the right people
Delegate tasks	**Implementing**	Volunteer to engage
Micro-manage/monitor activities	**Controlling**	Empower others to act
Use top-down benchmarks	**Assessing**	Emphasize accountability

As implied in the illustration, management has the responsibility of maintaining order and discipline by ensuring the right people are in place to perform required tasks. On the other hand, leadership is about obtaining and mobilizing resources to enable others to take on challenges to get things done. In the next segment, you will look at several critical practices individuals in leadership roles may undertake in order to make things happen in their organizations. But for now, reflect on your own past experience in regard to working with or for a leader and what you learned from that process.

> ### REFLECTIVE QUESTIONS
>
> Consider a project you led in the past whereby you were working with a highly diverse team consisting of members from different corners of the world. How did things actually get done? What practices of leadership and management did you exhibit to get things done? Why (do you think) you were successful or not? How could you have maximized the success of others to enhance the project outcome?

IGNITE AS A LEADER

LEARNING OBJECTIVE	
9.5	Engage in leadership practices to inspire those around you.

In the leadership role, you act as a facilitator who brings people together in a united effort to accomplish something special. The practices you bring to that task need to include both leadership and management. To get followers to think for themselves, engage others, and overcome obstacles, you need to IGNITE their passion that will lead to action on their part. Here are six leadership practices that will enhance your capacity to IGNITE as a leader: I = Instill, G = Grow, N = Notice, I = Invest, T = Target, and E = Ensure.

Instill a Culture That Despises Complacency

As a human being, you have a tendency to become complacent. You often settle for doing things that are comfortable and routine. Complacency does not require much effort. To counter an organizational culture where complacency becomes the norm, your leadership should reflect an open work climate where all ideas for change are welcome. Organizations need to grow and change faster than the competition. You as a leader spur that change by designing new ways to address that reality. In other words, change what you are doing before you are forced to actually have to change due to competitive forces. We have witnessed a number of companies that at one time were among the top in their industries in 2010 but then failed to change and lost their prominence a few years later, such as Kodak, Toys R Us, Lands End, Radio Shack, and Payless Shoes. To counteract failure, creating a work culture where *there is no place for complacency* reflects a new reality.

Grow Engagement and Innovation With Compassion

Your engagement and willingness to innovate increases with a growth mindset. Shifting from a fixed to a growth mindset, as explained in Chapter 3, frees you to take the risks you need to try

Chapter 9 • Effective Practices for Leading Others to Success   293

new things and keep learning. With a growth mindset, you approach your capacity and challenges as a process of continuous growth versus unchangeable and limited. These advantages extend to your leadership practice. Believing that followers have an endless capacity to learn and acquire new abilities dictates that you emphasize that learning and empowers followers to more fully engage. When you are the leader who says, "I know you can learn to do this," you model the very CORE capacities that will facilitate their success.

Compassionate practices, including self-compassion, can greatly add to the practice of modeling and encouraging a growth mindset. Compassion can be defined as being attentive to the needs of others and further moved to alleviate another's suffering. Compassion is most evidently needed if followers are working through personal or professional difficulties or if the nature of your organization regularly deals with crisis situations. Many stories that emerged from the terrible challenges of the pandemic highlighted the importance of compassionate leadership to follower and organizational success.[43] However, research on compassion shows considerable advantages in everyday operations, including coping with stress, work engagement, less burnout, and greater connection to the organization (organizational citizenship).[44,45] Growing compassion starts with recognizing and practicing self-compassion, which is essentially being mindful, kind, and patient toward your own shortcomings and mistakes. As you consider the increasingly dynamic nature of leadership, compassion toward yourself and your followers sets the stage for resilience and may be the key to enhancing your other leadership practices.[46,47]

REFLECTION QUESTIONS

What comes to mind when you hear the word compassion? How much do you know about compassion? Find a compassion measure online, or try this one: http://www.goodmedi-cine.org.uk/files/other-compassion%20scale,%20tahoma.pdf Then think carefully about someone you know who is going through a difficult time. What do they most need to succeed right now? How do those needs relate to what a compassionate friend or leader would provide?[48]

Note and Study Your Competitors and Collaborators

Staying alert as to what competitors are doing enables you to remain on the cutting edge of your profession. Striving for great in any endeavor is your priority, especially your career. And, being focused on winning is a way to make certain that competitors do not suddenly overtake your product line or service.[49] Winning may mean different things to different organizations, but focusing on continuously improving and innovating is often driven by the competition for markets, grant dollars, reputation, or rankings. In both the public and private sector, leaders scan the marketplace and competitors to get new ideas and strive to provide high-quality services and an infrastructure to better achieve the organizational vision. Knowing what competitors and other public service agencies are doing is an opportunity to reinforce what is currently being done or a source for new ideas. Consider one of your favorite products: If you were starting a similar company, how would you out-compete that product? If you think about this carefully, you will quickly realize there are many ways you can compete beyond the product itself, like better customer service, faster delivery, or a better warranty. Incorporate this winning spirit and competitor-scanning behavior to ignite your followers.

Invest in Real-Time, Data-Driven Decision-Making

Leadership is about more than making the right decision at the right time, it is about making decisions in the right way. Chapter 6 explained the many facets of smart decision-making, including the distinction between intuitive and rational decisions. Working in an environment of ambiguity, uncertainty, and change adds urgency for useful, timely data. Highly effective organizations create systems to collect real-time information, which provides a framework for making decisions. Pulling together the latest technology along with an effective data analytics team produces the information required to become an informed decision maker.[50] In addition, distributing decision-making among coworkers by connecting data to people results in more effective outcomes. Your ability to diagnose issues, identify alternative solutions, and make decisions propels your credibility and your effectiveness as a leader.

Tackle Candid Conversations

In order to generate a working environment where individuals are inspired to produce big ideas, followers require a feeling of support and appreciation. However, when critical or conflicting issues arise that are not addressed by an organization's leadership, obstacles to getting things done quickly arise. For example, if followers perceive their working environment as being unfair or lacking in inclusiveness, holding candid conversations allows for a quick recognition and solutions that demonstrate that leaders care about them.

Thus, resolving important issues between leaders and followers enables a workforce to focus on thinking of big ideas rather than dwelling on distractions. For example, a company called Intuit values the human aspect by permitting their employees to spend 10 percent of their work time generating big ideas for new products.[51] This now common practice emerged through frank discussions relating to a perceived unfair lack of time for employees to actually think about creating new products due to pressures to get job routines completed each day. Tackling inequities in the workplace may need to start by having these crucial and candid conversations.[52]

REFLECTION QUESTIONS

Can you think of a time when you should have initiated a candid conversation? What kept you from doing so? How would you like to be approached by someone wanting to talk about a difficult subject or disagreement?

Ensure a Clear Vision to Make It Happen

Effective leaders communicate their vision using clear, vivid messages that both motivate and provide direction. This involves identifying key constituencies that need to support your initiatives, enrolling them, and getting into place the support system that would give your efforts staying power.[53] Your vision as a leader promotes your leadership brand. It establishes the expectations behind the work culture in that organization. In this regard, Simon Sinek's Golden Circle for Communication[54] depicts an intriguing strategy for connecting your vision to a successful effort. For example, leaders traditionally communicate their vision to coworkers by first focusing on *what* product or service is being produced, then explaining *how* to produce the end result efficiently, and finally emphasizing *why* the product will generate a profit. To Sinek, successful organizations take a different approach. You inspire others to buy into your vision by first convincing followers on *why* there is a need for the product or service, then stipulating *how* to build the product or service creatively, and finally identifying *what* lifestyle need of consumers you are serving.

These IGNITE leadership practices should become part of your repertoire when helping others succeed, especially in a workspace where personal preference for getting things done becomes more prevalent. IGNITE those surrounding you by adopting these practices for becoming an exemplary leader (Figure 9.2).

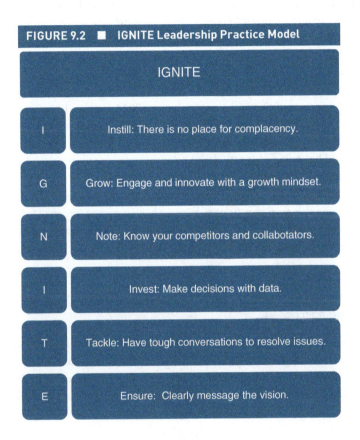

FIGURE 9.2 ■ IGNITE Leadership Practice Model

IGNITE

I — Instill: There is no place for complacency.

G — Grow: Engage and innovate with a growth mindset.

N — Note: Know your competitors and collabotators.

I — Invest: Make decisions with data.

T — Tackle: Have tough conversations to resolve issues.

E — Ensure: Clearly message the vision.

REFLECTION QUESTIONS

Can you recall at least three leadership practices depicted in Figure 9.2 that will likely help you influence others to follow your lead? List them below in order of preference. Circle the one you perceive yourself as being particularly adept in implementing right now. Put a square around the one you need more confidence to use. What have you learned to ignite in yourself as a result of this reflection?

1. _____
2. _____
3. _____

296 Module 3 ● Design Others' Success

DELIVER AS A MANAGER

LEARNING OBJECTIVE
9.6   Apply managerial practices to implement a strategic plan.

A leader's vision is only as good as the delivery of resources toward that vision. In other words, things need to actually get done. In a leadership role, you also need knowledge of management practices that will result in moving followers and the organization along a path of success. The collaborative nature of work today reinforces the notion that gaining knowledge is not a solitary act but a community affair.[55] An intriguing challenge for you as a leader is dealing with a growing number of **freelance workers**, defined as individuals who desire to work for more than one employer on a part-time basis rather than full-time for only one organization. Researchers predicted that 50 percent of the workforce in the year 2020 may not be receiving a paycheck from just one employer.[56] The pandemic brought forth more uncertainty but also a degree of organization and new platforms for engaging freelance workers.[57] With this new mobile worker emerging, you will be testing your capacity to prioritize tasks, motivate others for getting tasks accomplished, and hold individuals accountable for their results.

The acronym DELIVER reflects a set of practices that can focus you on managing to get things done. Placing this term in your own memory bank is a great way to expand your leadership presence because DELIVER should help remind you how to make your vision become reality: D = Designate, E = Empower, L = List, I = Initiate, V = Verify, E = Encourage, and R = Redesign.

Designate One Individual Who Will Have Responsibility Over the Implementation Process

Selecting the right person for this responsibility is crucial. For credibility, this individual must have the capacity for communicating widely across all levels and functions (marketing, accounting, research/design, etc.) of an organization. Holding one person accountable allows for a quick assessment of the change process being undertaken. Getting continuous feedback as to how things are proceeding increases the pace of change.

Empower Followers to Make Thoughtful Decisions by Delineating Clear Lines for the Scope of Their Authority

As a leader, establish the framework for letting subordinates know what kind of decisions they are able to make without seeking approval from another. This practice provides clarity for determining when those surrounding you must seek permission before acting. Without such clarity, there will be a tendency for chaos or confusion. Pushing decision-making to lower levels in an organization enables followers to gain confidence. Giving individuals authority to perform is part of developing a learning organization whereby the work culture reflects an expectation to perform responsibly.[58]

List What Is Unique About Each Person, Then Capitalize on It

Turn talent into performance by challenging each employee to excel in their own way. Setting goals based on uniqueness is part of this process. Involve people in setting their own implementation goals, instead of dictating them. In a leadership role, you desire an individual's commitment, not just compliance. When people believe they can influence and shape their own goals, they are more likely to be motivated to achieve them. Implement work practices that encourage the views and suggestions from individuals from diverse backgrounds. Being a part of an operation where individual uniqueness is perceived as a strength generates not only a feeling of equity but a correspondingly healthful and respectful relationship for inspiring collaborative effort.

Initiate a Risk Response Team to Assist Those Being Subjected to Significant Obstacles and Possible Failure

Having a tolerance for failure is important. During the implementation process, mistakes will likely occur. If followers are encouraged to learn from their mistakes, implementation efforts will proceed with less chaos and frustration. During this process, releasing resources to support risk-taking efforts (some of which fail) reassures followers they are not left alone when difficult times occur. And making mistakes may also become a learning opportunity for followers, especially if they are encouraged to get together and discuss what is working and what is not. Creating a risk response team reduces the fear and frustration associated with setbacks.

Leadership by Design

Design Principle: Factor of Safety

Definition: The use of more elements than is thought necessary to offset the effects of unknown variables and prevent system failure.

In Other Words: Anticipating and addressing possible issues and trouble in your design.

For Example: Being asked a security question in order to verify your identity when logging into an online bank account. That verification step is designed to save you and the bank from fraudulent activity.

For Leaders: Think about all the many ways your followers might be *unsuccessful* at a given task. What can you add now to their knowledge, attitude, mindset, context, and so forth that can insure against possible future failure? One possible way to design around failure is to embrace small failures by encouraging controlled risk taking, using mistakes as an integral part of follower development. Consider how you can better design others' success by using factors of safety.

A note about designing your leadership self: Do you remember the most catastrophic error in leadership? Tarnishing your reputation and losing your credibility. What factors of safety can you design into your leadership to avoid this error?

Verify Progress by Establishing Checkpoints for Accomplishments

Convening coworkers on a periodic basis to evaluate work progress keeps everyone on track. Meeting, talking, and thinking together often brings the best out from each coworker. Creating momentum leads to systematic progress. Often, momentum itself will take on a life of its own for creating a winning climate. By having verification meetings, you learn about what actually works as you move forward—and you don't have to wait until the end to find out what worked and what did not. As individuals experience success, they will get better at implementation. They learn how to manage their own expectations, make better decisions, allocate scarce resources appropriately, and understand what actually works.

Encourage and Exhibit Calm When Under Fire

Dealing with ambiguity, uncertainty, turbulence, and chaos that arise suddenly requires a steady hand and the ability to rally those around you to stay on track. An example of exhibiting calm came during an attack using aircraft by terrorists on September 11, 2001, when a large number of employees at different levels of operational responsibilities assumed leadership roles at the World Trade Center in New York City. In this instance, self-appointed leaders assessed that something was wrong and acted quickly to save lives. They reacted rationally during this tragedy by remaining calm when diagnosing the severity of the situation, then making decisions as to how to proceed, and finally executing those decisions quickly and effectively.

Redesign Work Patterns and Assignments so They Are Cross-Functional

Getting things done by yourself is very difficult. It generally takes a variety of individuals with complementary skills to get things done effectively. For example, by redesigning work assignments across functions, those in marketing can learn about product design by engaging in joint projects with those associated with manufacturing. Using the diversity of a workforce to your advantage leads to very impressive results. By redesigning work patterns, you energize workers to accomplish more than they think they can. Creating a learning organization propels managers to a vital role since they are the coaches in an organization.

REFLECTION QUESTIONS

Who have you met that is great at energizing workers to accomplish more than what those employees think they are capable of? What managerial practices did this leader implement to get followers to critically think about achieving important organizational goals? During your own previous work on a project where you were designated as the leader, what management practices did you adopt for generating results? What checkpoints did you put into place to ensure your teammates were working efficiently? What did you learn from this experience that will help you as a future leader?

The acronym DELIVER should be helpful in remembering that management practices complement leadership practices (Figure 9.3). Managers are the organizers and the doers; they get things done. Adopting practices that inspire others into action reflects the goal of leadership. However, change and innovation can also bring chaos and turbulence. Those in leadership positions must be capable of leading and managing others during times when things are going well and when things get chaotic and unpredictable. Bringing out the best in followers is the goal of leadership but requires management practices as well.

REFLECTION QUESTION

Form a small group of at least three individuals. Put together a list of at least five managerial practices a leader should be knowledgeable of for getting others to complete those tasks necessary for implementing a vision. List them below in order of preference. Place a circle around that one practice in which you feel you already excel. Put a square around that practice in which you need some work in order to be confident in performing. What did you learn about yourself as a result of this reflection?

1. _____
2. _____
3. _____
4. _____
5. _____

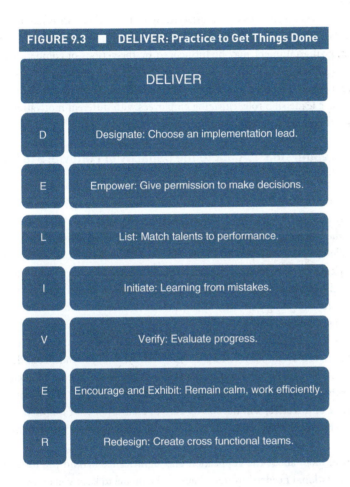

FIGURE 9.3 ■ DELIVER: Practice to Get Things Done

DELIVER

D — Designate: Choose an implementation lead.
E — Empower: Give permission to make decisions.
L — List: Match talents to performance.
I — Initiate: Learning from mistakes.
V — Verify: Evaluate progress.
E — Encourage and Exhibit: Remain calm, work efficiently.
R — Redesign: Create cross functional teams.

DESIGN OTHERS' SUCCESS WITH A SITUATIONAL LEADERSHIP APPROACH

LEARNING OBJECTIVE

9.7 Use a situational leadership strategy to design others' success.

Applying both leadership and management practices will help enhance your effectiveness as a leader. How these practices are implemented depends on the situation in which you find yourself. New generations growing up with new technology will think and work in new and different

300 Module 3 ● Design Others' Success

ways. The present generation has high expectations in regard to balancing work responsibilities with personal lifestyle choices. They desire to grow on the job, share their strengths with others, and be part of an organization that produces goods and services that make a positive difference in people's lives. Working with different generations within different fields and across different levels of experience and expertise all comprise aspects of the *situation* within which you as leader must operate. For example, a study by Deloitte revealed that two thirds of new entrants into the workplace now believe it is the leader's job to provide them with accelerated career development opportunities.[59]

In reality, leadership effectiveness is affected by situational factors often not under control of the leader. For example, in companies such as Google, Time Warner, and Samsung, in the private sector, goal attainment may be influenced by the actions of competitors, new legislation, and new technologies. Thus, situations shape how leaders must behave. Correspondingly, the kinds of followers you engage will likely vary in both readiness and willingness to perform. When assuming a leadership role, engaging employees with different motivations, goals, ambitions, and skills demands your attention.

Situational Leadership®: Adapt to the Capacity of Followers to Perform

Designed in the 1960s by Paul Hersey and Ken Blanchard, the Situational Leadership° Model promotes the idea that leaders generally must deal with a wide range of readiness levels of followers, namely their competence and commitment for a specific task.[60] **Situational Leadership°** is defined as the behaviors used by leaders of an organization adjusting to fit the development level of the followers they are trying to influence.[61] With Situational Leadership°, you as a leader adapt your style based on specific parameters of your followers. There is no single best behavior to utilize at all times. Situational Leadership° Theory is arguably one of the most ubiquitous tools used by leaders for designing a strategy to engage others—however, research on the model only supports the importance of a more directive style for new employees.[62]

The process for applying the Situational Leadership° Model starts with your initial identification of the most important tasks to be accomplished. Second, you must consider the readiness and willingness of each follower, from which you will determine whether that employee needs: direction, coaching, support, or delegation. The leadership strategy you adopt, whether it be more supportive or directive, will depend on careful analysis of your followers' readiness level. The four universal leadership behaviors in the model should prepare you for any situation you may find yourself in no matter the size or purpose of the organization.

As you read more about the application and significance behind the different leadership behaviors in Situational Leadership°, refer back to the model to keep you on track. Try applying this model to a current task you are working with others on. Do those individuals need your direction, coaching, support, or delegation?

- *Directing:* Directing others in exactly what to do is an appropriate leadership behavior when your followers cannot actually do the job or may be afraid to try. In such a situation, such behaviors as prescribing actual tasks to be performed and then directly supervising followers closely are in order. With less confident followers, you as a leader must recognize that being totally in charge of the work process is necessary, if actions of followers are to be meaningful.

- *Coaching:* Coach employees by explaining decisions and providing opportunities for clarification is most appropriate when your followers are very willing to work but lack the skills necessary to perform effectively. Coaching may involve working on a one-on-one basis—listening, advising, and helping your followers to gain necessary skills in order to do the task without assistance the next time. The outcome of coaching is convincing others that they can do the task with your guidance.

- *Supporting:* Supporting others is the most appropriate leadership behavior when your followers can do the job, but they also may show a lack of commitment or just refuse to perform to expected organizational standards. The key practice is you identifying incentives for both motivating followers and building their confidence. Behaviors such as getting others to participate in open dialogue by asking for input, listening to their comments, and empowering others to act are directed at changing the perspectives of those followers who are currently refusing to commit.

- *Delegating:* Entrusting others to perform on their own is an appropriate leadership practice when followers are very skillful and also have a great willingness to get things done. You should rely on delegating when your followers can do the job and are also motivated to succeed. You as a leader must become involved in the decision-making process, but the execution of those decisions is in the hands of the followers. The strategy of putting the follower in control of work processes enables a greater degree of creativity on their part. You as their leader are less involved in daily planning, organizing, and controlling of actual work.

Match your leadership style to follower competence and commitment.
©iStockphoto.com/fizkes

Leadership by Design

Design Principle: Control

Definition: The level of control provided by a system should be related to the proficiency and experience levels of the people using the system.

In Other Words: Provide instructions and tasks that match understanding and capability.

For Example: Rock walls are designed to provide multiple courses to get to the top that vary based on a climber's ability.

For Leaders: As a leader, you should know the capabilities of your followers so you can provide an appropriate range of delegation. Are they beginners who need structure—or experts who need autonomy? Control as a design principle could mean a limit to follower authority when the task is above their experience. Accommodate varying abilities by offering multiple ways to perform a task. Can you identify tasks that are not so easy that they bore followers but not so difficult that they frustrate and overwhelm? What can be built into the system to allow your followers to succeed at each level of their development?

The Situational Leadership® Model is about demonstrating flexible leadership by adapting both leadership and management practices that address specific situations associated with followers. Situational Leadership® provides the flexibility to match a multiplicity of practices with appropriate behaviors to motivate others to perform above their own perceived expectations. Having a common purpose means you and your coworkers are in this together. By respecting and dealing with differences, you as a leader have an added obligation to enhance the success of others by building quality relationships based on trust. Your behavior (whether directing, coaching, supporting, or delegating) is the ingredient that forms the foundation for putting your leadership practices into play. The innovation process requires utilizing and motivating individuals with the capacity to move a project forward at a reasonable pace. Getting workers with different levels of readiness for participating in a team effort is a challenge you will likely address as you assume a leadership role in the future.

REFLECTION QUESTIONS

Think of a time when you found yourself in a situation where individuals were not being treated fairly or with respect. Using the Situational Leadership® Model explained, what would you have done differently to meet the challenges of the situation you were in at that time? Give at least three examples.

1. _____
2. _____
3. _____

Understand the (New) Rules of Engagement

The leadership and management practices explained in this chapter reflect a new era whereby a different set of behaviors is required for getting others to buy in to your vision. They also reflect the emergence of a different kind of engaged workforce that relies on advanced technology to perform. Today, new recruits do almost everything on a smartphone or tablet, with new apps and platforms emerging regularly. Apps on cell phones are the primary means of accessing information and expertise on the Internet.[63] And with the rise of Zoom and other web-based meeting platforms, it is easy to forget that organizations are comprised of people who form an organizational culture that impacts job performance, positivity, and possibilities.[64] Accordingly, 95 percent of job candidates currently believe a culture of engagement—the kind of engagement described in the introduction to Module 3—at work is more important than compensation.[65] Achieving a common purpose requires an expanded outlook as to how people connect, interact, and support one another in an environment where face-to-face communication may be less of a reality.

CHAPTER SUMMARY

Leaders need a new set of practices to inspire a different kind of follower—one who now desires to succeed but also somewhat on their own terms.

Relating to others and influencing them requires understanding how people think and how their brain operates. There are many brain features and processes all individuals share. If a leader understands these processes, they can more effectively relate to and lead others. While the brain consists of many, many detailed elements, your lean, mean, pattern-making machine brain loves when things are simplified and organized. Thus, one helpful way to understand the brain is by using six dimensions: physiological, emotional, social, constructive, reflective, and dispositional. The six dimensions can be examined separately for their impacts and influences on overall performance, even though the dimensions all overlap and influence one another.

IGNITE as a leader; DELIVER as a manager. IGNITE followers by instilling a culture that despises complacency, growing engagement and innovation with compassion, noticing what competitors and collaborators are doing, investing in real-time data-driving decision-making, tackling tough issues with direct conversations, and ensuring a clear vision. DELIVER results by designating responsibility, empowering followers to make thoughtful decisions, listing employee strengths, initiating risk response, verifying progress, encouraging and exhibiting calm while under fire, and redesigning work patterns. Your practices as a leader matter. Having command of both leadership and managerial practices enables you to set the direction for an organization and design a working environment that produces results.

Design others' success by flexibly altering your supportive versus task-oriented behavior based on what followers need. Situational leadership considers followers' competence and commitment as a basis for the kind of leadership practices that will best facilitate follower success. By adding this thoughtful, purposeful flexibility, you effectively manage while empowering those who have demonstrated greater self-direction and capability.

KEY TERMS

Community solidarity (p. 289)

Constructive dimension (p. 283)

Dimensions of the brain (p. 277)

Dispositional dimension (p. 283)

Emotional dimension (p. 280)

Essentialism (p. 276)

Freelance workers (p. 296)

Metacognition (p. 283)

Perspective-making (p. 275)

Perspective-taking (p. 275)

Physiological dimension (p. 279)

Practice (p. 275)

Reflective dimension (p. 282)

Second-generation gender bias (p. 288)

Situational leadership (p. 300)

Social dimension (p. 281)

Tokenism (p. 276)

CORE™ ATTRIBUTE BUILDERS: BUILD NOW FOR FUTURE LEADERSHIP CHALLENGES

Attribute: Confidence, Optimism, Resilience, and Engagement

Builder: Getting to Know Your Brain activities.

Engage in the following described activity, then think carefully about how leaders are influenced (and how they influence others) and what this means about what leaders know, do, or are like. As you do so, you will find many opportunities to build your confidence, practice your optimism, test your resilience, and engage. Be sure to note your insights for later reference.

Assignment #1: Eye Contact

Monitor your eye contact with others. For at least one day, try looking directly into the eyes of others. What are your thoughts and reactions? What reactions do you notice in others? Do you notice a reaction from others in days after?

Assignment #2: Dominant Hand

Consider things you do with your dominant hand—eating, brushing your teeth, steering your car, turning the pages of a book, and so forth. Choose two to three of these activities and complete them with your nondominant hand for a couple of days. Reflect on the experience.

Assignment #3: Emotional Quotient x3

Choose three individuals you interact with every day. Assess their emotional intelligence by observing their reactions to situations. Choose a day in which you are purposely contrary with these individuals and another in which you are consistently agreeable. Add this to your assessment.

Assignment #4: Big Smile

For the last five minutes of your commute to work or school, smile continuously—five minutes for a couple of consecutive days. Assess your mood and emotions each day and at the end of the week.

Assignment #5: Emotional Quotient Machine

Identify a machine that is used frequently (you decide the context). Inconspicuously place an "Out of Order" sign on the machine and observe the comments and emotions you observe for one hour. Note how many individuals try the machine despite the sign. For added fun, step up and use the machine as dejected parties step away. Caution: Make sure you choose a machine that is not life or career threatening—to you or others.

Assignment #6: Routines

Consider a routine you have. It might be a morning routine before you start your day, when you first arrive at work, or a routine before going to sleep at night. Choose one routine and alter it so you do something different or in a different order every day for a few days. At the end of that time, consider how the experience felt and what you thought.

Assignment #7: Decision-Making Perspectives

Consider a decision you are about to make. On what are you basing your decision? Find three individuals very different from yourself: one of a different gender, one of a different generation/age, and one of a different ethnicity/culture. Find out their perspective on the decision (the one you are about to make). What would they decide, and on what would their decision be based? Write a letter to a friend explaining the decision, what you decided, how you decided and why, and what you learned from consulting with those different than yourself.

Chapter 9 ● Effective Practices for Leading Others to Success   **305**

Assignment #8: Reflection

Choose a time during your day to sit alone in a quiet space for 15 minutes and listen to your own breathing— no television or phone, no colleagues, no Internet, no reading material, no lunch— nothing. Do this every day for a few days. After spending the time doing this, reflect on any changes in your reactions and interactions with others, as well as the overall experience.

Assignment #9: Something New

Resolve to find and experience something completely new (really, really new) to you every day for a few days. It may be eating a new food, listening to music you are unfamiliar with, going into a store you have never been in, visiting a town you have never been to, or talking to someone you do not know. At the end of this time, consider how you felt and what you thought during and after the experience. Did this change your view of things you were familiar with and the idea of exploring new things?

Assignment #10: Worn Out

Wear something out of character for you—not something ridiculous so others assume you are being silly but rather something that clearly gets attention, has others questioning, but would not necessarily be considered a joke. Note how others react and interact with you. If you are really feeling daring, try wearing something that crosses gender or other cultural assumptions a bit, like wearing a sparkly decorative pin or pulling a little red wagon—if that is out of character for you, of course.

SKILL BUILDER ACTIVITY—GO DO SOME LEADERSHIP!

IGNITE as a leader, DELIVER as a manager—put your practices into practice and see what works for you.

Go do some leadership! What exactly does that mean? What would it look like? What should it look like?

Try using the components of the definition:

1. Choose a goal. (goal/vision)

2. Consider what other individuals can help meet that goal. (others)

3. Assess the extent to which those others buy into the goal and then help them better understand the goal and why they should make it their goal too. (common)

4. Craft a strategy (with others) to meet that goal. (process)

5. Craft and execute a plan for persuading others to further adopt and work toward the goal. (influence)

6. Assess your progress toward the goal and then improve your plan. (toward)

Your challenge is to go out and do some leadership. Follow the steps, record both your actions and reflections, reflect, discuss with a colleague, and summarize what you did and learned.

10

UTILIZING CHANGE PROCESSES EFFECTIVELY

LEARNING OBJECTIVES

Upon completion of this chapter, the reader should be able to

10.1   Compare three levels of change typically initiated by those in leadership roles

10.2   Describe how individuals experience change

10.3   Examine key aspects of change that impact your leadership

10.4   Differentiate between transactional and transformational leadership approaches to leading change

10.5   Identify common barriers to change

10.6   Design a change strategy for implementation

10.7   Identify activism and advocacy as essential leadership skills

Leadership by Design Model

Design Self
How can I design myself as a leader?

Design Relationships
As a leader, how can I design my relationships with others?

Design Others' Success
AS A LEADER, HOW CAN I DESIGN SUCCESS FOR OTHERS?

Design Culture
As a leader, how can I design the culture of my organization?

Design Future
As a leader, how can I innovate?

INTRODUCTION

The idea of change filters through nearly everything. People are changing. Times are changing. You should make this change. Be open to change. At each level of leadership design within this textbook, change plays a significant role. Designing leadership self, relationships, others' success, culture, and especially designing the future—all talk about some facet of making things different (and hopefully better). Even embedded within the definition of leadership—the process of influencing others *toward* a common vision—speaks of movement from one state to another. Generally, people are not so good at change, and they dislike it. The current way of doing things is easy and efficient, and you really do not even need to think much about it. The new way, the changed way, requires learning and practice. Sometimes, you feel frustrated and uncomfortable, and even if you know the change is for the better, you resist.

Change happens because the world and all those within it are dynamic. Even time changes. Every interaction you have with your world reinforces or changes your view of the world (remember your lean, mean, pattern-making machine brain?). Some of those changes are subtle, such as when you do not notice the paint fading on the fence in your backyard or how your sibling grows up a little every day. Those changes are easy to deal with—little changes require little change. But many changes, particularly in leadership, are a bit more significant and sometimes sudden. Those kinds of changes can overwhelm you since what you believed in the past may no longer be true.

This chapter helps you understand and lead change. In keeping with the general approach of this textbook, the important premise is that you proactively design how changes will be addressed rather than simply react to changes. And by facilitating change for yourself, others, and your organization, you help design others' success.

Change is intriguing in that it happens because someone cares to do something different and hopefully useful. People are making changes all the time. If you fail to pay attention or wait too long, especially in your job, organization, or industry, it may be difficult to maintain relevance. Designing others' success includes helping others change before they actually have to in order to remain a key player in adding value to the organization. What kinds of opportunities will you have to do something truly different from the past? Following is an example of an individual holding a PhD from Stanford University who decides to build a nonprofit organization to assist children suffering from diseases that are likely to end in death if untreated. As you read this story, note how one individual changes the process for delivering health care to families around the world who cannot get treatment due to its high cost, and consider how that one change resulted in myriad changes for many others.

Leadership That Makes a Difference

Krista Donaldson was not certain early in her career as to how one uses design to serve the public good. In the past, design seemed more about art or products rather than people. However, she pondered "Why do I exist on this planet?" and her answer was to serve people. She found herself in a career choice that focuses on solving problems while generating a product or service that enhances the quality of life for others. Krista concluded that the field of design results in outcomes that have significant social impact. She continued to be curious about the connection of products and the people who use them. Since she desired to help people, she decided to seek a position in government. After finding employment with the U. S. Department of State, she learned how difficult it is as a leader to align public policy with the understanding of what people actually need. It was during this time that she noticed there were thousands of children dying from jaundice and other childhood diseases. Being frustrated with the ineffectiveness of government to deliver products and services to those in need around the world, she created a nonprofit organization that brings medical devices to families that earn generally less than $4 per day. The aim was to design first-rate medical equipment targeting children's health needs in developing countries. She desired to change the way organizations can partner to produce and distribute products to those who cannot afford to purchase health care at all. Her leadership style promoted collaborative strategies between those employed in the nonprofit and private sectors for designing world-class products that perform better than the best product currently on the market. She became obsessed with a user-centric leadership framework in that the end users of medical devices, the patients, are key contributors in the design of their medical devices. She realized that to build a better world, you need to *adopt leadership change practices* that include building new relationships between the consumer and the designer for generating medical devices that deliver quality health care to those in desperate need.[1]

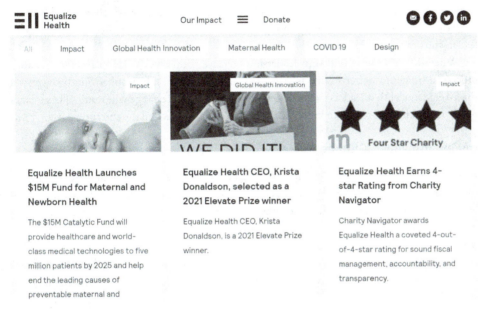

You too can be a leader that makes a difference in changing the world much as Krista Davidson of Equalize Health is doing.

This is a real person and real story. In 2009, Krista Donaldson created a nonprofit organization known as Equalize Health (formerly known as D-Rev (short for Design Revolution). Since then, she has led the design and scaling in emerging markets of Brilliance, an affordable treatment for babies with jaundice, and the ReMotion prosthetic knee, which is worn by over 5,500 amputees. She has been recognized by *Fast Company* as one of the 50 designers shaping the future and by the World Economic Forum as a Technology Pioneer. The bottom line is that this could be you. Changing the way things have been done in the past provides opportunity to innovate and ultimately enhance the quality of life of others. You have the ability to innovate, but it takes action on your part to take an idea and make it happen.

IDENTIFY LEVELS OF CHANGE

LEARNING OBJECTIVE

10.1 Compare three levels of change typically initiated by those in leadership roles.

Change is the process of becoming different yourself or fostering difference in other persons or things, which is exactly the order for facilitating change. To successfully innovate within an organization, you need to be willing to change yourself first. If you cannot change yourself, it is difficult to inspire others around you to change. As a change agent, you are both a role model and a change manager. People look to you for setting the tone in the organization and, in the case of this chapter, how you deal with change. Do you model openness to change or resistance? Do your actions communicate a purposeful, goal-oriented focus, or one that is disorganized, hesitant, and lacking a vision? Back in Chapter 3, you considered your strengths and skills and made a commitment to further develop yourself and put those attributes into action. Both of those activities comprise change, and both should be purposefully, mindfully designed, led, and managed. One helpful model for leading change comprises three levels of change action.[2] As you read about each of the three levels, think about those things you would like to change and perhaps some that need to change. Ultimately, it is you who will change—into an effective change agent leader who designs others' success.

When others surrounding your leadership perceive themselves as key players in a change process, a bridge to better results is generated. In this regard, Christopher Smith suggests a three-stage model that leaders can utilize to ensure sustainable change will result. These stages reflect the change process at an individual level, the project level, and the enterprise level.

Initiate Individual Change (Level 1)

How do *you* deal with change? What can you do differently to enhance your capacity to drive that change? **Refining personal change capacity** refers to making modest changes in your own behavior that people notice and, at the same time, convince them to follow your lead. As a role model, even minor things help refine your capacity to lead. Setting an example by getting to work a little earlier each day, engaging subordinates in opportunities to innovate, or becoming more complimentary by recognizing innovative efforts among coworkers are all symbolic of convincing others that you are the real thing. Can you identify at least three changes you made in yourself over the past 6 months that have enhanced your capacity to drive change? Consider one thing you could do over the next month and do it.

Smith notes that everyone has a natural resistance to change. However, when people are open to new ideas and support change, they can become very resilient. He suggests that to champion change, you must understand your feelings and emotions about undertaking new methods, as well as help others make a transition from the old to the new. In other words, ask yourself: What messages do I need to tell myself personally as well as what others need to hear from me to inspire a collective effort?

Support Change at the Project Level (Level 2)

Leading a project team requires extra effort in order to build effective working relationships for gaining the confidence of those with whom your future success depends. The importance of designing relationships with others was highlighted in the previous module. Trusting relationships with your followers makes you more influential, and that influence will be necessary to persuade others that a specific change is worth the effort. Incremental changes provide others the opportunity to test change and assure a supportive relationship. What changes can you introduce to prepare followers for greater change? How can you highlight the importance and value of these changes? For example, having special recognition days in which individuals are acknowledged for their innovative efforts creates an appreciation of change. Setting aside

Chapter 10 • Utilizing Change Processes Effectively   **311**

time for individuals to reflect upon their past change accomplishments elevates the value of the change to coworkers. Can you identify at least three things you could do to encourage supportive relationships?

When leading during project work, the challenge is to enlist the support of others by getting them to buy-in. According to Smith, this process begins by identifying those stakeholders who need to change and boosting their awareness as to why that movement is needed. Involving stakeholders in every step of the change process is critical if they will eventually embrace your ultimate goal. At the core of inspiring others to change is the capacity to build quality relationships along the way.

Generating a Change Culture at the Enterprise Level (Level 3)

For change to be sustainable, it needs to be embedded in an organization's core values. When change becomes part of each individual's culture while also matching an organization's values, all those supporting your leadership will know exactly what they need to do to excel in their overall performance. This involves collectively embracing strategic initiatives, adopting new technologies, and improving the capacity to continually change as a competitive advantage.

Leading innovative efforts throughout an organization and putting together a network of new thinking throughout an organization comprises a large-scale change. **Large-scale change** is a more complex process that requires integrating a strategic vision into change initiatives that redirect attention to entirely new processes, systems, or structures. Large-scale change requires a more extensive level of innovation than those indicated in the preceding two levels. For example, reducing the levels of hierarchy in an organization, designing an entirely new product line, or initiating a work-sharing practice reflects innovative processes at Level 3. What large-scale change would you recommend that benefits an organization with which you work? If you had a magic wand, what would that change process look like?

Effecting change relies on leadership to make it happen. It has been often said that what gets done in an organization is what leaders attend to. If you can design a framework where innovation occurs systematically, your credibility will become apparent to others. As opportunities emerge, you must be vigilant to change yourself routinely, then at the next level to lead innovative efforts by building productive relationships, and finally at the highest level to redesign operational systems to streamline functions. The key role leaders play in the change process is what this chapter is all about. The next section will focus on how change not only impacts you but also how it affects people around you.

CHANGE YOURSELF BEFORE YOU CAN CHANGE OTHERS

LEARNING OBJECTIVE
10.2   Describe how individuals experience change.

How you view change influences how you communicate, make decisions, and solve problems. Ultimately, your view of change determines how quickly you will adjust to it. Change often comes suddenly, and it can be overwhelming if you are not prepared. Fortunately, there are many things you can do to anticipate change. If you view change as an opportunity to move on in a different role, then seeking alternatives becomes part of your plan. Entering into a dialogue about the change with others is also important as this is an opportunity for you to see new directions for yourself. However, if you view change with anxiety, frustration, and fear, you will likely struggle in attempting to find meaning as to what has happened to you.

Individual Change in Stages

Change affects how people interact with you and each other as innovative practices, policies, and expectations come into existence. For example, such innovations as Amazon.com with online retailing, Costco with membership consumption, and Walmart with warehouse direct shopping have resulted in structural changes in daily operations. Such innovations have led to employees being retrained to acquire new skills, transferred to another facility, and promoted with new responsibilities. These changes may also feel like loss, resulting in followers going through the classic stages of grief: shock, anger, depression, and possibly leaving the organization. You as a leader need to be sensitive to the five stages that you personally, as well as colleagues and followers, will likely go through as you attempt to move from denial to acceptance of change (see Figure 10.1).[3]

FIGURE 10.1 ■ Recognizing the Personal Change Process

Shock/Denial → Anger → Depression → Dialogue → Acceptance

The first stage of *shock* or *denial* reflects an individual who is extremely confused and may blame others for what is happening. Following shock and denial is *anger*, whereby the individual has great anxiety, frustration, and embarrassment. The next stage is *depression*, which is characterized by being overwhelmed and helpless. This is where leadership is most needed and most influential. Moving from depression to dialogue, an individual begins to become more open to alternatives. As they continue *dialogue* with friends, cohorts, and others, the individual is ready to move on by *accepting* the need to explore options and place a new game plan into action.[4] As a leader, you may have witnessed those with whom you work not necessarily liking the change being undertaken. Individuals affected by radical change, such as losing a job, are likely to require your assistance for developing a new game plan.

The CORE™ attributes you are building are of great value to you in facing and working through change. Likewise, facilitating others to draw upon their confidence, optimism, resilience, and engagement will help them work through change. You may want to revisit some of the ways you can build these capacities (back in Chapter 1). One way to enhance resilience through a change is to commit to the change and craft a plan. Recall that the four CORE™ elements interact with and reinforce one another. Resilience can be strengthened by striving to remain optimistic, reinforcing your confidence, and fully engaging in the activities leading up to and through the change. You will need to be positive, focused, organized, and proactive rather than fight or run away from the change.

Understanding that change unfolds, and it results in somewhat predictable changes in individuals, empowers you to anticipate and prepare. How ready you are to convert these stages into personal action depends on how willing you are to change aspects of yourself by initiating a significant change in your own behavior. An intriguing and proactive model of personal behavior change is Prochaska's model for change.[5] This model, based on research in changing health behaviors, provides a practical guide for what individuals think and feel through the change

Chapter 10 ● Utilizing Change Processes Effectively   **313**

process. Note that the actual change—the action—is only one of the five stages of the model, and three stages come *before*p any changing activity. The first stage, re-contemplation, is often overlooked in leadership. Individuals do not want to change because they do not even recognize that a change is merited, needed, or even possible. Thus, the earliest activities of a leader facilitating change should include pointing out all the possibilities for change—helping followers see differently (recall Chapter 8 on creativity)—what could be better, refined, reconsidered, or even simply noted.

The other stage of Prochaska's change process that is often overlooked is the final stage: maintenance. People try to eat better, and then they do not; they try to quit smoking and pick it up again; they strive for work-life balance and slip back into working weekends. Change is challenging, and changing habits is even harder. But once the change has been made (especially after contemplation and preparation), individuals need a strategy, plan, and context to reinforce that change on a regular basis. When a change is dependent on individual willpower alone, it likely will not last. Leaders need to fully design change from before the need for change is even noticed to long after the change has occurred.

The prompting worksheet in the following exercise uses Prochaska's model to prompt you through a change, as well as assess where you are in the change process and consider your capacity to change. Think about a behavior you would like to change about yourself—such as stereotyping people into categories, isolating yourself from different cultures, or engaging in an unhealthy behavior such as arguing too much or being too negative—and follow the change process shown. See how things work out and what insights you find about changing yourself.

Exercise:

Prompting Change With Prochaska's Model

Note a change that you would like to make in your life: _____

Follow a Path to Personal Change

Pre-contemplation (Not Ready for Change): Generally, the first aspect that you are likely to feel is that of not being ready to change your behavior. This is what Prochaska depicts as "I won't" or "I can't." This is the time you need someone who can work with you closely to understand your feelings. During this phase, you need to reflect on your own feelings without fear.

Ask Self: Who has spoken to you about changing your behavior?

List: Who can motivate me to change?

Act: Talk to someone you trust about possibly changing your behavior.

Contemplation (Thinking About Change): This is the "I may" change, but I am not sure. At this stage, you are beginning to think about changing an unhealthy behavior. You need to gather some information to gain an understanding of the dimensions to such a change.

Ask Self: What does my behavior look like to others?

List: What are my reasons for wanting to change?

Act: Talk to someone who has struggled and succeeded in making a change similar to one you are considering.

Preparation (Preparing for Action): This is the "I will" change. At this point, you begin to experiment with possible solutions. You realize you need a plan.

Ask Self: What steps do I need to follow to change my behavior?

List: Who will help keep me going when things get difficult?

Act: Write out your plan and share it with a friend.

Action (Make Change Happen): This is the "I am" committed to implementing a change. You know what you have to do, so you begin to monitor your progress.

Ask Self: What do I not have to give up when changing my behavior?

List: What are those things that make me give up?

Act: Avoid those things that make you want to give up.

Maintenance (Maintaining Your Changed Behavior): This is "I still am" committed to change. This phase begins when the new behavior change has become a habit and is done automatically. You are now confident that you can maintain the new behavior. In this stage, your own self-efficacy is both high and self-reinforcing.

Ask Self: How can I continue with this behavior with ease?

List: What are those things that will help keep me on track?

Act: Ask someone you trust to keep track of your changed behavior.

Prochaska's model of change emphasizes your capacity for accessing information about the effects of a proposed change, being moved emotionally to act, and reflecting how others are going to perceive you in the future. Therefore, making a commitment, being sensitive to cues around you to guide you in the right direction, and recruiting trusted friends to help you are all part of changing yourself. The storyline here is that you need to be able to first change yourself before you are likely to convince others to change aspects of themselves. Using your own example, were you successful in changing aspects of your own behavior as a result of applying Prochaska's change model to your own situation?

CHANGE DIRECTLY AFFECTS YOUR CAPACITY TO LEAD EFFECTIVELY

LEARNING OBJECTIVE

10.3   Examine key aspects of change that impact your leadership.

During a change process, you will learn a lot about yourself. Take a brief look at some situations where you may find yourself as change is implemented in the workplace. How would you personally react to each of these kinds of changes described in the following section?

Be Reactive or Proactive

Remember how you felt and the stress upon you when you personally moved to a new school or neighborhood. As you just read, during the early stages of experiencing radical change, people generally feel fear, anxiety, and loss of control. A changing environment is like a problem to be solved. As you read in Chapter 8, problems can be approached in many ways, including reactive and proactive. A reactive approach, where you let an issue emerge before you act, frames change as a loss or threat. The opposite approach is being proactive whereby you plan for change before

Chapter 10 ● Utilizing Change Processes Effectively 315

it occurs. A proactive approach frames change as a problem to be solved or even an opportunity to strategize a successful outcome. When you were subjected to a significant change in your life, how did you react? Were you a reactive victim of change or a proactive strategic leader of change?

Experts Beyond the Text

Insightful Leaders Know About . . . Crisis Leadership
By Ralph A. Gigliotti

Of the many competencies required for effective leadership, perhaps none are as timely and relevant as **crisis leadership**. Crisis leadership can be defined as the ability to demonstrate courage and care during times of collective disruption. The convergence of challenges facing leaders during this historic period—a global pandemic, growing economic concerns, sweeping racial unrest, heightened partisan polarization, and the ongoing impact of climate change, among others—pose tremendous challenges for leaders across organizations and sectors. A growing body of research supports the fact that crises are growing in magnitude, frequency, and complexity.[6] You will likely face these challenges. What do you need to know? What can you learn from the current crises of the moment to adequately prepare for those moments of discord that inevitably lie ahead?

Although there is some degree of subjectivity involved in describing an event or situation as a crisis, many of the existing definitions and perspectives characterize a crisis as an event or series of events that create uncertainty, threaten lives and/or organizational operations, and require an immediate response from those engaged in leadership.[7] As Matthew Seeger and Robert Ulmer acknowledge, crises are high-impact events that often strip an entity to its core values.[8] This means that during these periods of great turbulence, the purpose and foundational values of the organization provide a shared foundation for all members of the community. In the spotlight of crisis, leadership decisions, actions, and words need to focus on that core purpose. However, crisis also presents opportunity for leaders to reinforce and showcase the espoused values of the group, team, or organization.

The three Ps are foundational for effective crisis leadership: *preparation, perception, and principles* (Figure 10.2). Beginning with preparation, it is important for leaders at all levels to take the time to prepare for these unexpected yet inevitable periods of disruption. Although you may not be able to predict the type and timing of a specific crisis, adequate preparation and prevention can prove advantageous for an organization and its leaders when crises strike. Moving on to perception, leaders must take the perspectives of others seriously and recognize that the *perception* of crisis implies the existence of a crisis requiring the attention of leaders. Time and time again, situations snowball into widespread and overwhelming crises because leaders neglected to understand that perception can bring forth reality, and they failed to hear those early concerns. Finally, aligned with the approach of this textbook, the design of your leadership requires attention to the principles and values that guide leadership practice in your organization. Do you know what you and your organization stand for, believe in, and define as your core purpose? When faced with a crisis, these principles will influence both the immediate and long-term response, setting the stage for success or further disruption.

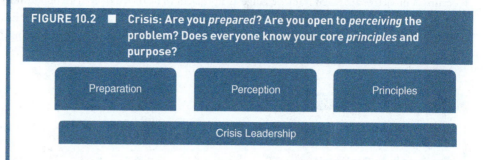

FIGURE 10.2 ■ Crisis: Are you *prepared*? Are you open to *perceiving* the problem? Does everyone know your core *principles* and purpose?

Crises often cause disruption, danger, and destruction for individuals impacted by the event(s); yet within crisis lies an opportunity for healing, growth, reinvention, and renewal. Take a moment to reflect on the types of crises you might encounter in your current or future leadership role. What skills or capacities (like CORE) will you need to be an effective crisis leader? As Nancy Koehn writes, effective crisis leaders engage in the following behaviors: (a) acknowledge people's fears, then encourage resolve, (b) give people a role and purpose, (c) emphasize experimentation and learning, and (d) tend to energy and emotion—yours and theirs.[9] Relatedly, there are numerous leadership approaches and strategies one might engage in to leverage and advance individual and organizational change when faced with a crisis.[10] As you continue your leadership journey, the most certain future is one of uncertainty and possible crisis. Prepare now so you can turn crisis into opportunity and engage in the following:

1. Monitoring the internal and external environment for potential crises that might impact your group, team, or organization
2. Modeling care and courage when responding to a crisis
3. Triaging immediate needs and encouraging the group, team, or organization to explore the longer-term implications of any given crisis

Suggested Readings

Gigliotti, R. A. (2020). The perception of crisis, the existence of crisis: Navigating the social construction of crisis. *Journal of Applied Communication Research, 48*(5), 558–576.

Koehn, N. (2020). Real leaders are forged in crisis. *Harvard Business Review.* https://hbr.org/2020/04/real-leaders-are-forged-in-crisis

Stern, E. K. (2009). Crisis navigation: Lessons from history for the crisis manager in chief. *Governance: An International Journal of Policy, Administration, and Institutions, 22*(2), 189–202.

Gain or Lose Control Over Work Life

Change can evoke some intriguing reactions for those who appear to be losing control over their work life. One reaction is to continue to do those tasks the way they have always been done and to undercut the change process. This individual will likely resist change and make coworkers uncomfortable about accepting any change. Others, however, may desire to accelerate change by setting new goals and work routines to adjust to new conditions in the workplace. The challenge with change is that job routines remain to be done as a new system is designed and put into place. With two systems operating simultaneously, confusion and despair can become game changers.

Discarding old ways of doing things is stressful. As a future leader, you need to be observant to the degree that coworkers deal with change. Here are four typical reactions by you and perhaps your coworkers as changes in how tasks are done are made:

- You embrace change in doing tasks to become better.

- You accept the need to do tasks differently although reluctantly.

- You resist changing at all and need some time to adjust.

- You are skeptical about doing tasks differently and undermine the change process.[11]

Adjust or Reject a Set of New Organizational Core Values

Changes in an organization's core values, such as those arising from a merger or acquisition, will directly impact upon your willingness to change. Depending on the size and impact of the innovation being proposed, employee engagement often declines initially when a change is actually proposed. However, as the process proceeds, employee engagement is likely to improve somewhat as the inevitable becomes apparent. In this regard, you—in a leadership role—are among the top drivers of employee engagement. In terms of organizational culture, the impact that you as a leader have on an organization's culture can be immense. This is the moment that the CORE™ attribute of *engagement* comes into play as individuals having conflicting personal and organizational values may need some interaction with their leaders. When designing others' success, the leader needs to be assured that coworkers are united in purpose for attaining the goals of the organization.

Transform How Careers Evolve

Typically, in the past, you entered an organization with the expectation of competing against your counterparts who are also attempting to move up the ladder of success. Particularly in a hierarchy, the path to success has been to work your way up the different levels of leadership (e.g. from supervisor to manager to director to senior leadership). As the career path emerges, the individual adjusts the career plan as new job openings become available. However, a change in the structure of an organization motivated by a merger, acquisition, or downsizing puts you at the mercy of external factors over which you have no control. As indicated earlier in the text, there appears to be some interest among new job entrants to stay in control of their careers by becoming freelance workers. In this regard, careers being multimodal, you will likely find yourself in a leadership role where employees may choose to work for more than one employer and thus receive more than one paycheck. The prevalence of a fluid workforce will challenge you when mobilizing resources for undertaking an innovative effort.

REFLECTION QUESTIONS

1. Think about some examples of how you have responded to change. Were you proactive or reactive? What could you have done differently to improve the process?

2. How do you feel about working in an organization where your core values are inconsistent with that of proposed changes in the way you operate? Can you give an example of when this has happened to you? How did you react and why?

3. How do you feel about becoming a freelance employee who works for more than one employer? How do you feel that will impact your capacity to assume a leadership role?

TRANSFORMATIONAL VERSUS TRANSACTIONAL LEADERSHIP

LEARNING OBJECTIVE

10.4 Differentiate between transactional and transformational leadership approaches to leading change.

Your approach to your followers and the way you fundamentally view your role in their life represents one of the most consequential and influential aspects of leadership. Some leaders view their interaction with followers as a transaction: You (follower) work for me, and I (leader) pay you—a simple transaction that does not include anything beyond the terms of the agreement. In contrast, some leaders strive to maximize the success of followers—not just their success at work or for the organization, but their overall success as an individual—their personal fulfillment.

Transactional leadership is defined as a process whereby those in leadership roles directly supervise change by the setting of clear objectives for their followers as well as the use of either punishments or rewards in order to encourage compliance with these goals.[12] In this regard, transactional change leaders also prefer to utilize rewards and punishment in traditional ways according to organizational expectations. Transactional leaders appeal to the self-interest of employees who seek out rewards for themselves, in contrast to transformational leaders, who appeal to group interests and notions of organizational success.

Transformational leaders strive to "*engage* with others in such a way that leaders and followers raise one another to higher levels of motivation and morality." According to James MacGregor Burns (you read about him way back in Chapter 1), **transformational leadership** is defined as a change process in which leaders and followers help each other advance to a higher level of morale and motivation.[13] The transformational approach creates significant change in the perceptions, values, expectations, and aspirations of employees. These include connecting the followers' sense of identity and self to the mission and the collective identity of the organization.

Transformational leaders focus on the higher-order motivational needs of followers (i.e., helping followers and the organization reach full potential).[14] At the individual relationship level, transformational leaders appeal to followers' intrinsic motivation through what Bass and Avolio identified as four specific leadership actions[15]:

- *Individualized consideration:* The leader respects each employee and pays attention to their individual needs. How would you as leader make every individual feel special, noticed, and/or relevant?

- *Intellectual stimulation:* The leader provides tasks of considerable but possible challenge, encourages addressing problems in new ways, inspires critical thinking, and shares new ideas. How would you as leader keep every individual interested, intrigued, and positively challenged?

- *Inspirational motivation:* The leader articulates an energizing vision that connects with each follower and provides a meaning for tasks at hand. How would you as leader infuse each individual with energy for the task, position, and organization?

- *Idealized influence and charisma:* The leader acts as a role model for the employees, communicates and demonstrates a clear set of values, and builds trust and credibility. How are you as leader explicitly modeling the energy, engagement, and behavior you want in your followers or employees?

Chapter 10 • Utilizing Change Processes Effectively   **319**

In practice, an effective leader influences others by modeling excellence, motivates others by emotionally connecting with them and steering their attention to the higher purpose, provides them with challenging and interesting work that is within their reach, and communicates the message that each individual is important, noticed, and considered by the leader. If what intrinsically motivates individuals is feeling competent (mastery) and feeling like they are doing something important (purpose), then having a transformational leader should significantly enhance the engagement of followers.

Designing others' success relies on you to create a proactive work culture that instills pride, promotes involvement, and generates new ideas for change that become ingrained in an organization. The design process is a collaborative effort that results in mutual support and respect, meaningful work, and continual learning through timely feedback. In this regard, you will need to design a process that matches organizational and individual needs, moves innovative ideas forward by asking the right questions, and executes outcomes so all participants can see their contributions as part of a new reality.

Based on the premise that those leaders who act more as facilitators are generally more successful at change, four more keys to enhancing your effectiveness are also offered by Higgs and Rowland.[16] First, effective leaders are very self-aware of the importance of their physical presence to the change process. A second key is for you to learn everything there is to know about your organization, which involves mastering the politics of the workforce and in particular identifying those who will likely distort your ideas, such as agitators, distractors, or combatants. Third, those effective at innovation are able to work in the moment, staying attentive to what is happening around them. A change that dramatically increases organizational discomfort is doomed. Plan ahead by involving employees in planning changes. This will ameliorate some of the effects of change before you proceed. Fourth, effective change agents remain in tune with the bigger picture to ensure the change process remains clearly connected to the wider audience. Resistance to change is likely at some point, but the preceding keys and a transformational approach should help tremendously.[17]

REFLECTION QUESTIONS

Having an insight that helps you grow in a leadership role can provide you with confidence that will help you endure through the bad times. Anybody can lead during good times. However, when things go bad, this is where your knowledge about effective leadership becomes critical. How can you distinguish yourself as a leader prepared for anything?

1. Identify at least three other companies or organizations that were well-known and are no longer in existence. Why did they fail? What can you learn from each that will help you in the future to not fail?

2. What is the most important thing that a leader has to know about confronting resistance during the change process? Can you identify a time when you had considerable resistance to your change idea? How did you react?

BARRIERS TO CHANGE

LEARNING OBJECTIVE

10.5   Identify common barriers to change.

Organizations do not change unless the individuals within them change. Resistance to change at both the individual and organizational level is a normal response, so you need to plan for it, expect it, and accept it as part of the change process. People only change when they are Aware of the need for change and the alternatives, Desire the change, Know how to go about changing, are Able to implement the change on a day-to-day basis, and Reinforce the change so it stays in place. This is called the **ADKAR model of change**, and many of the activities for successful individual and organizational change essentially follow these criteria.[18]

MYTH OR REALITY?

Implementing change is based on using analytical tools and algorithms to justify moving in a new direction.

Myth. Matthew Lieberman, a founding father of the field of social neuroscience, says this is a myth. In his book *Social: Why Our Brains Are Wired to Connect*, he points out that another driver of equal importance, if not greater, is the need to be socially involved in the change process by connecting to the values and expectations of others. A leader who knows their staff really cares about will be able to succeed at change more effectively than one who is simply focused on the elements of a project.[19]

Thinking Rationally About Change May Not Work

Changing from one thing to another is effectively a decision, and decisions are best if rationally calculated . . . right? As you may recall from Chapter 6 on decision-making, rational calculation is just one aspect of how decisions are made. Interestingly, it is not a lack of analytical skills but rather a lack of social skills among organizational leaders behind some of the biggest failures in organizations. If you are not good at understanding the needs of followers and their confidence levels, you are likely to develop a change strategy in a vacuum and thus fail. In fact, just 30 percent of change initiatives succeed, according to 15 years of data from McKinsey & Co.[20] Limiting your thinking to a rational analysis rather than social (or emotional) inhibits getting buy-in from followers who need to perceive how they fit into proposed changes.

If you adopt a mindset that discounts social cues, you are going to miss a lot of important information around you. A notable example of organizational failure is video game giant Atari, an early entrant in the video gaming industry in 1975. Rationally, the leaders in this company had the best technology at the time and thus gave little attention to social cues from both employees and customers by ignoring the increasing popularity of home computers for accessing such games. Other examples of notable failures are Blockbuster video, Kodak cameras, and Borders bookstores. Their leaders had rational plans for dominating their markets but again ignored the social aspects of their operations (employee input and customer feedback). Correspondingly, they failed to recognize that changing consumer preferences for online convenient access to video and reading materials would lead to their demise.

Not All Opportunities for Change Are Worth Taking

Change is about taking risks. The moment you stop looking for new opportunities, your organization is likely to become complacent. However, taking risks without thinking about consequences may be foolhardy. On the other hand, not taking risks may also be foolish since leadership is all about weighing the pros and cons of change for achieving something different. Therefore, a

Chapter 10 • Utilizing Change Processes Effectively   321

calculated risk is in order. **Calculated risk-taking** is making a decision that involves careful consideration of the possible outcomes. A calculated risk-taker has the following qualities[21]:

- Decisive, having good judgment as to whether information that is incomplete is sufficient for action

- Analytical, being insightful when comparing the costs and benefits to a proposal

- Predictive, using information to calculate the probability that actions will be successful

Are you someone who can assess opportunities for change with a critical eye? Are you primarily driven by emotion, fear, or frustration? Or do you have confidence when taking on a challenge? Having a network of advisors in place to provide you with some objectivity is quite helpful. Realize that it is not feasible to pursue all proposals for change as you will likely be presented with numerous ideas for new approaches on how to operate. Moreover, once you initiate a change process, you may have to adjust your strategy, as you may lose key personnel or the market may change. For example, it may be in your best interest to stop a current change proposal due to the emergence of a new technology that revolutionizes your industry.

Someone Will Resist the Change

As a change agent, you can expect to run into resistance from unexpected sources. For example, individuals who initially support your innovative idea may become active resistors over time. In addition, most significant change involves dealing with the power structure within an organization or within a culture. Some people will gain influence while others will lose some. In addition, there is no guarantee that the change process you follow will work. Change is not only chaotic at times, it is quite unpredictable; all the planning in the world may not prevent failure from occurring. Therefore, the side effects to change are difficult to predict, maneuver, and manage. For example, change fatigue may set in over time. **Change fatigue** is a general state of disengagement from the change process due to natural cognitive, emotional, and social demands. When coworkers refrain from sharing or commenting on data generated during the change process or when progress reviews are not well attended, change agents should be on notice that an issue has arisen.[22] In this regard, you must be prepared to react to resistance, chaos, change fatigue, and other surprises that arise at times spontaneously. What could you do as a leader to work through these barriers and facilitate successful change?

LEADING CHANGE

LEARNING OBJECTIVE
10.6 Design a change strategy for implementation.

You can unlock the keys to effective change. One fundamental key lies in rethinking the way in which you as a leader see yourself relative to your followers—focusing efforts on doing change *with* people rather than doing change to them. Based on interviews of leaders from 33 organizations, findings indicated that leader-centric behaviors, those shaping and controlling the actions of others, have an adverse impact on change implementation. In contrast, the behavior of leaders who are more facilitating and engaging is positively related to change success. The negative impact on change success of leader-centric behaviors (such as conflict, confusion, and resentment) was noted from data derived from their interviews, whereas more enabling behaviors (engaging and facilitating others) appear to promote a greater degree of successful change implementation.[23]

Preparing to Execute Change

Change models used by those in leadership roles are important in that they set the stage for how individuals will go about achieving something new and different. Change by definition requires a new system and then institutionalizing the new approaches for getting things done.[24] While effective change depends on your mindset and approach as a leader, there are numerous models and strategies from which you can select to help you plan change execution.

As you prepare to implement any level of change whether personal, interpersonal, or organizational, you need (1) to operate within the work climate already in existence, (2) to adapt to the capacity or skill levels of your workforce, and (3) to identify the kind of support you will require for change to occur. One very helpful model is the Initiation, Implementation, Institutionalization (I3) model noted in Table 10.1 with prompting questions. This model can be used in advance to plan out the important elements and variables, or it can be revisited during a change process to reconsider the approach and improve the process.

TABLE 10.1 ■ The I3 Change Process With Prompting Questions [25]
Initiation
What is the need?
What is the vision of the end state?
What is the vision or model of how the process will unfold?
Who are your advocates?
What steps need to be prepared?
Implementation
Who communicates what to whom, when, and how?
Who should/could be part of the decision-making (i.e., *control*)?
Who/What will be supportive? And who/what opposed?
What technical assistance will be needed?
What intrinsic and/or extrinsic rewards could be engaged?
Institutionalization
How can the association between need and change be reinforced?
What assessment methods can inform further development?
How can the change be widened to include others/other areas?
What competing priorities/activities exist?
What policies need to be changed to make the change part of *doing business*?
Who are strong advocates that can offer continuing assistance/reinforcement?

When people are truly invested in change, it is 30 percent more likely they will be successful.[26] Leaders today need to make decisions quickly in a fast-paced environment where having a competitive advantage comes to those who can set new priorities and implement change more quickly than their rivals. Perceiving yourself as being prepared at the start will bring along followers who are dedicated, strong, decisive, and organized.

Leadership by Design

Design Principle: Stickiness

Definition: The degree to which an idea, expression, product, or service is dramatically recognized, recalled, and/or shared with others.[27]

In Other Words: Designs that stick are remembered.

For Example: How can you make sure people remember your store? Try using an address that looks like someone dove into the wall and got stuck! Closer to home, college admissions tour guides work hard to ensure your campus experience *sticks*. They use attention-grabbing elements of surprise, emotion, and storytelling to create a memorable experience.

Stickiness and success

For Leaders: Leaders designing success for others, particularly through a change process, need new ideas to stick. Anything that can be seen, heard, or touched can have an element of stickiness. To increase the memorability of a change, keep messaging succinct, yet thoughtful.

Consider what exactly you need to stick. Use the elements of SUCCESS: Simplicity, Unexpectedness, Concreteness, Credibility, Emotions, Stories, and Sincerity to increase the stickiness.[28] You may know what you want your audience to recall, but it is equally as important to think about what you *do not* want them to remember and make sure those items are not sticky.

Executing Change for Others' Success

Executing your plan is, of course, always more complex than you have envisioned. Your credibility, presence, and relationships with individual followers will have significant impact upon how change is actually implemented and accepted. Adopting an empathetic (or user-centered mindset from design thinking in Chapter 3), you will be more likely to effectively lead change. Perhaps the most effective way to frame your thinking before acting is to consider how *you* would want to experience a change. Table 10.2 highlights nine common mistakes leaders make in how and what they communicate (or fail to communicate) throughout the change process.

TABLE 10.2 ■ Mistakes During Change
1. Failing to be specific about the change
2. Failing to show why a change is important or necessary
3. Failing to allow those affected by the change to contribute to the planning
4. Using only personal appeal to gain acceptance of change
5. Disregarding a work group's habit patterns
6. Failing to keep stakeholders informed about change
7. Failing to allay stakeholders' worries about possible failure
8. Creating excessive pressure/stress during change
9. Failing to deal with emotions and anxiety over individual issues during a change

Like any good design process, a good change process is iterative. In other words, as you execute the change you are constantly assessing, improving, and altering activities. A great change process strives to ensure others' success as much as achieving the change since practically they are one and the same. Suppose you have been at a university for four years and have never met any administrator over that period. You could not recognize the president, provost, or even the dean of the college in which your major exists. You would like to create an innovative mechanism that would enable students to connect directly with such administrators face-to-face throughout a semester. You recognize this as a Level 3 change effort in which you are attempting to modify organizational culture in the way students and administrators connect. You could execute that change using an excellent model, such as John Kotter's foundational eight-step change model.[29] Detailed explanations of Kotter's model provide a very powerful tool for executing change. Adding a design frame enhances that process by focusing on the success of others through that change process (see Figure 10.3).

Justify an Opportunity to Act by Creating an Urgency for Change

The initial step in any change process is to justify that an opportunity exists. This involves gathering data from as many sources as possible to conceptually understand the need for change. As a design thinker, this is the opportunity to accurately define the challenge you are taking on by making sense of all the information you have gathered. In order to craft a clear definition of the issue at hand, you require data. Alternatives for gathering data digitally are conducting online interviews with current administrators, generating a Facebook discussion group, or placing a survey online for students, administrators, and faculty to participate, among others. You decide

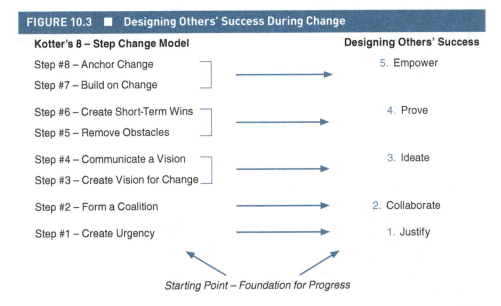

FIGURE 10.3 ■ Designing Others' Success During Change

to create an online forum where you can interact with administrators and students directly for getting ideas about how to proceed.

Collaborate With Those Affected by Forming a Coalition

Now you realize you need to identify individuals who are likely to be affected by your innovative strategy. You must convince them that change is necessary on your campus. These individuals also will be those to whom you send out survey forms and connect with digitally, and so forth, as indicated in the first step. You decide to put together a leadership coalition of key administrators, faculty members, and students for designing actual questions for gathering data. You realize you need to understand the people with whom you will be working as well as those who will be impacted once the change is implemented. Having a change project leadership team in place will enable you to identify pockets of resistance as well as those who will support you.

Ideate and Communicate Possibilities Through a Clear Vision for Change

Using the divergent-thinking process, individuals working in teams build on each other's ideas for arriving at an innovative change idea. This step is about using your imagination to generate a wide range of ideas for solving an issue—and not simply determine the one most apparent. Based on the data obtained from your digital forums, online surveys, and interviews, three alternative solutions are proposed by your leadership team. One is to have a daily administrator-on-call online (similar to a physician's office). A second alternative is to schedule online meetings with a variety of students each month. Finally, a third possibility is to have special ask-the-administrator online chat sessions on the university website. This part of the change process encourages lateral thinking, defined here as having individuals step beyond the obvious solutions.[30] Getting back to the change project, in addition to the alternatives indicated, another atypical solution could be using email or posting notes to a Facebook discussion group for enhancing communication. Having the capacity for students to directly connect to administrators more frequently on their own time schedule is reflective of extending the conversation beyond the obvious.

326   Module 3 • Design Others' Success

> ### REFLECTION QUESTIONS
>
> The capabilities of new technologies allow leaders and followers to communicate more quickly, more broadly, and more personally. In what ways might you utilize technology to provide just-in-time feedback? Build empathy, community, and shared purpose? Demonstrate progress?[31] Enhance any of the specific steps of the change process?

Prove the Change Is Acceptable

Ensuring the changes proposed are realistic and compatible with existing organizational values, norms, and goals is critical if they are going to be ingrained into a new work culture. Pretesting the effects of alternatives allows for flexibility for possibly changing direction without committing excessive time, energy, and resources. Eliciting feedback from colleagues is a great way to get everyone involved. This is also an excellent time to gain an understanding of people you are designing the change for. This is similar to pilot testing the solution with a small group of individuals for gaining insight as to whether you are on the right track or not. After analyzing all of your findings, after collecting data by means of your surveys and interviews, you decide to experiment with the innovative idea of having a *provost-on-call* for an online discussion for one hour per week per month.

Empower Others to Implement and Build

After pilot testing a solution, you and your leadership group decide that having an online administrator forum once a month at the provost's level is feasible. However, you know nothing will happen unless the necessary work is done to implement the proposed change. You put together a project management team to get the innovative strategy to actually happen. **Project management** is defined as the application of knowledge, skills, tools, and techniques to a broad range of activities in order to meet the requirements of a particular project.[32] Managing a project includes (a) putting together a team charter outlining the tasks to be completed, the budget required, and the deadlines for delivering important outcomes, and delegating authority to make decisions; (b) launching the implementation plan by identifying expectations of everyone in the change process and alerting stakeholders as to what is coming; (c) verifying that deadlines are being met according to actual implementation plans adopted; and (d) assessing the effects of the change process completed and the outcomes achieved. You also anchor the new practice of engaging an administrator by assigning a staff member to monitor the practice each day.[33]

While each step is critical, the task of getting others as advocates for the change process will make or break your effort. A large aspect of design thinking focuses on the human factor—that is, getting others engaged in the process of thinking about change. Therefore, Step #2 relating to understanding the needs and desires of those around you forms the backdrop for effective action. Without the support of your subordinates or coworkers, change at best will only be temporary.

> ### Leadership by Design
>
> *Design Principle:* Progressive Disclosure
>
>   *Definition:* A strategy for managing information complexity in which only necessary, requested, or user-understandable information is displayed at any given time.[34]
>
>   *In Other Words:* People get overwhelmed when they see too much information at once.

For Example: Having multiple small quizzes leading up to a final exam is not a form of punishment from your professor; it is a way to introduce students to the concepts a little bit at a time. Progressively disclosing prevents information overload.

For Leaders: When it comes to eliciting change, leaders and followers undergo many different phases: awareness of the need to change, desire to participate and support change, knowledge of how to change, what that change looks like, implementing the change, and then reinforcing it to keep the change in place. To facilitate this complex series of steps, use progressive disclosure with your followers to ensure only the necessary information is provided at any given stage. This does not mean keep secrets. Share the big picture and be transparent; but do not expect deep, focused understanding of everything at once.

Progressive disclosure
©iStock.com/diane555

Break tasks and information into small, understandable, and achievable chunks. How can you, for example, teach unskilled people how to accomplish something as big as building a house? Hide options that are not essential at the moment and teach people as they go. Progressively disclosing big changes will help leaders design others' success.

Sustain Momentum and Resilience After Change Is Implemented

Perhaps the most challenging and frustrating aspect of change is how quickly and easily things can change back. How does one sustain the change? Maintaining a change once implemented also requires planning, persistence, and collaboration. Establishing an inclusive, positive working environment to involve as many individuals as possible for designing others' success is important to ensure a strong finish and an institutionalization of the change.[35] Most change plans fail to adequately anticipate internal resistance and other unforeseen factors that cause change to derail over time. Most resistance to change remains underground as managers and employees decide whether to support change, wait it out, or undermine it through inaction and sarcasm. Passive resistance is not lethal in small doses, but over time, it leads to a crippling of the change results. As a change agent, you need to create an organizational culture that reflects a rhythm for change, similar to how lyrics and a musical score, when put together properly, endure endlessly. Initially, having a work culture that performs in a rhythmic pattern sets the stage for accepting change.

Having change as an everyday expectation makes it easier to sustain it. Second, identifying and nourishing those individuals who both accept and initiate change themselves provides inspiration for others to follow along the same path. Creating an organizational culture that embraces change and nurturing change agents go hand in hand. To sustain change in an organization requires establishing an organizational DNA whereby change becomes a constant in the everyday flow of activities. You can reinforce sustaining change by holding a series of post-change meetings to keep on top of how things are progressing. In this regard, you must make certain that the infrastructure (e.g., performance management and reward systems) supports the continuation of the change and makes returning to the previous state less attractive. Having special recognition for those who excel in demonstrating the positive effects of the changes implemented will model an appreciation for follow-through and outstanding productivity. Finally, you can celebrate successes along the way, not just final outcomes. People who see the connection between behaviors and outcomes are much more willing to embrace the desired change and sustain it over time. This keeps the focus on the achievement of the desired behavior in the short term as well as in the long term.[36]

Implementing Positive Organizational Scholarship as a Basis for Performing

Having a positive working environment when promoting change enables those in leadership roles to engage with others through a collective discourse, creating a culture that nourishes individuals through the change process. In this regard, Cameron and Quinn suggest that leaders exhibiting a form of positive energy enhance the chances for achieving greatness.[37] For example, positive energy is demonstrated by leaders using language that is *reflective*, using words like excellence, thriving, flourishing, abundance, and resilience Focusing on positive human attributes results in change leaders who act in an unselfish and altruistic manner. This strategy is an attempt to address those leaders who are obsessed by greed, selfishness, manipulation, and secrecy when focusing primarily on wealth creation. Leading individuals by promoting distrust, anxiety, fear, and abuse results in the emergence of a culture of disrespect that becomes a mainstay as social relationships are developed.

If leaders engage change as problem solvers, managers of uncertainty, and conflict resolvers, then they are able to create an environment that embraces compassion, honesty, and respect, resulting in a workplace that is more inviting where change can occur. Too often those in leadership roles tend to focus on efficiency, profitability, and reduction of costs as critical measures of successful change. Cameron and Quinn's framework of positive organizational scholarship brings forth change agents perceived as positive and respectful motivators. Through their design of administrative practices, leaders are able to mobilize a more diverse and inclusive workforce that attends to human needs for attention, inclusiveness, and dignity.

Chapter 10 • Utilizing Change Processes Effectively 329

DEI BY DESIGN

LEARNING OBJECTIVE
10.7 Identify activism and advocacy as essential leadership skills.

Leadership embodies change, by definition. Often the impetus and aim of that change involve solving a problem; addressing market changes, organizational growth and changing systems; or sparking innovation. In those cases, leading and managing change is critical to success. In some cases, however, you want to be a change-maker—initiating numerous actions and advocating around a larger goal or cause. **Activism** comprises executing numerous direct, vigorous activities to bring about a change, generally social or political. **Advocacy** is the process of recommending or supporting that change. Both are naturally connected to leadership when considering our ability to use change processes effectively for the betterment of our families, communities, organizations, and society. You may have seen these kinds of change efforts in action with student activism—that is, "students work to interrupt the status quo of their campuses with the goal of (in this example) shifting toward being socially just."[38] Activism includes but is not limited to implicit and explicit resistance, challenging harmful policies and practices, interrogating problematic organizational features, and the creation of safe and brave spaces (detailed in an earlier chapter). Efforts toward folding diversity, equity, inclusion, and justice into the culture of your organization may require that your leadership encompass activism, knowingly and authentically engaging change processes toward full and equal participation, access to opportunities, and physical and psychological safety and security.

Becoming a leader activist includes consideration of two specific elements: activism psychology and activism behavior.[39] Activism psychology includes your internal thoughts and feelings about external environments. These thoughts and feelings include your expectations, aspirations, the demands you perceive being placed on some by others, your sense-making tendencies and cognitive structures, your biases, sense of control, and your personality traits, among other factors. Your natural dispositions can impact your activism psychology, and you may need to nurture new patterns of thinking and feeling to aid your psychological development toward activism.

Activism behavior consists of the actions you take (or choose not to take) in response to your psychological processing. These actions can be measured in frequency (how often do you act as an activist), duration (how long are you engaged in activism), and quality (the relative worth or value of your activism efforts). Your ability and willingness to engage in activism behaviors hinges significantly on your personalities, identities, and social locations. Designing your leadership includes creating congruence between your thoughts, feelings, and actions regarding activism in daily life.

Leader advocacy is another related way to use change processes effectively. For advancing DEI, leader advocacy goes beyond what you model and build into organizational systems and is rather a direct, explicit support of others as they take action to ensure fair treatment, access, or opportunity. Long- and short-term advocacy improves the chances that others are successful in their attempts to implement a culture of DEI and overcome the resistances that hinder progress for everyone. Through leader advocacy, you help others become leader activists themselves and, in turn, sustain progress.

Leadership planning, advocacy, and activism result in sustainable change that benefits future change-makers.
©iStock.com/Steve Debenport

CHAPTER SUMMARY

Designing others' success is rooted in change because your charge as a leader involves facilitating others and the organization to become something better than before. Change is fundamentally a people process. Organizations do not change unless the individuals within them change. To achieve and sustain change, those in leadership roles need to look for new approaches for inspiring others to follow their lead. Change can be considered at three levels: personal, project, and large scale.

Individual change happens in stages, which includes how people think about things (cognitive), how they feel (emotional), and how they interact with the leader and one another (social). Most people are uncomfortable with change and can initially react in very negative ways. The Prochaska model can help prompt individual change from initial awareness of a need for change all the way through maintaining a successful change.

Resistance to change at the individual level translates to challenges implementing change at the organizational level. The general ADKAR model can help remind leaders where followers are in their change process. Change fatigue, overreliance on rationality, and failure to fully consider the risks are just some of the many barriers to effecting change.

Transformational leaders are contrasted with transactional leaders by their focus on advancing each follower to be their best self versus simple compliance and organizational goal attainment.

Chapter 10 • Utilizing Change Processes Effectively   **331**

Adopting a transformational leadership approach, along with other interpersonal factors, comprises an initial step in executing change. The I3 and Kotter models of change execution provide concrete steps for planning, executing, and maintaining organizational change efforts. Adding a design framework further highlights the transformational human aspect of the change process.

It takes a special person to lead change efforts, and in many cases, you will want to be an advocate or activist. Suggesting change is rather easy. Designing, initiating, and leading change is challenging. You will need to continue to develop your CORE™ to persevere through to successful change and design others' success.

KEY TERMS

Activism (p. 329)

ADKAR model of change (p. 320)

Advocacy (p. 329)

Calculated risk-taking making (p. 321)

Change fatigue (p. 321)

Change (p. 310)

Crisis leadership (p. 315)

Large-scale change (p. 311)

Lateral thinking (p. 325)

Project management (p. 326)

Refining personal change capacity (p. 310)

Transactional leadership (p. 318)

Transformational leadership (p. 318)

CORE™ ATTRIBUTE BUILDERS: BUILD NOW FOR FUTURE LEADERSHIP CHALLENGES

Attribute: Confidence

Builder: Align your strengths—take on a change challenge

Test your capacity to take on changing something of interest to you. First, align your change mindset, whether transformational, transactional, or a hybrid. Generate alternatives for solving either a person, interpersonal, or organizational issue confronting you today. Using the five-step design-thinking framework along with the Kotter model that you learned in this chapter, select something you would like to change on campus, at work, or in a community organization where a team of individuals is involved. Here is your guide:

1. Step #1—Justify the Challenge—(Level 1) (Level 2) (Level 3)—Give specifics

2. Step #2—Form a Coalition—Gather data from numerous sources

3. Step #3—Ideate Possible Solutions—Think laterally about alternatives

4. Step #4—Prototype for Credibility—Pretest alternatives for practicality

5. Step #5—Empower Others to Implement—Take a transformational or transactional role—Get your final alternative to work

Be prepared to discuss with others what worked and what did not work. As a result of this experience, how do you see yourself leading change?

332   Module 3 ● Design Others' Success

SKILL BUILDER ACTIVITY

Reflect upon a significant change you personally experienced while at work, at home, or at school. What was the change process? Was the leader transactional or transformational when acting as a change agent? How did you feel about the change process followed? What would you have done differently in bringing about that change if you were the leader at that time?

SKILL BUILDER ACTIVITY

Leading Change I: How did leaders facilitate significant organizational change?

Learn from others how they addressed a change in their organization. Following are five organizations that have changed significantly in terms of moving from their original mission to a new product line. Select any one of the following and put together a profile of the process the leader used to change the behavior of those surrounding them. Was it a transformational change style or transactional—or perhaps a hybrid model? Put together a report no more than three pages long analyzing the process used and what you learned from this investigation.

Possible Alternatives to Select One for Study and Analysis

Netflix—starting as a DVD in the mail service to streaming of video/TV shows

Google—moving from a search engine to telephone access to cloud storage services

National Geographic—moving from a magazine to producing TV shows on Discovery and other channels

Nokia—transforming itself from a rubber-producing company to cell phone distributor

ELEVEN—complementing a fantastic career as a superb athlete by designing an intriguing new clothing line

BONUS: You identify an organization from a world that interests you. Dig a little deeper into the history of that organization.

SKILL BUILDER ACTIVITY

Leading Change II: How did leaders navigate significant personal change within their field?

Take a moment and study the leadership change style of specific individuals who have inspired others to stay on the cutting edge of their field. They challenged the status quo and generated solutions that others never thought of in their field. Select one of the following and determine how they were so different in their approach to being successful:

Anna Maria Chavez—CEO of Girl Scouts of America: How did she revamp an organization with a great history into the 21st century with a new direction?

Mark Cuban (Shark Tank TV)—CEO of Dallas Mavericks basketball team: Each basketball game is sold out. How did he change team marketing efforts to make millions of dollars?

Bill James—Sports Analyst: An analyst who discovered new approaches for helping sports teams, specifically in baseball, utilize data to produce winning seasons. How did he use design thinking to put together a strategy to convince others that he has the winning formula to be successful in baseball?

Marissa Mayer—Yahoo CEO: How did she change Yahoo from basically an email service to a major advertiser of business services?

Ayesha Curry—Entrepreneur: How did she use design thinking for creating a new kind of cookware?

Keith Dorsey—Entrepreneur: How did he reshape the field of entertainment by challenging the status quo?

BONUS: You identify a leader from a world that interests you. How did they change the field? What aspects of the change process did they utilize to make that happen?

MODULE 4

DESIGN CULTURE AND COMMUNITY

Chapter 11	Culture	337
Chapter 12	Leading a Team	369
Chapter 13	Designing a Culture That Cares	399

Over the past 10 chapters, you have focused on designing yourself, your followers, and your relationship with them. The chapters in Module 4 expand your leadership lens beyond the individuals to focus on the organization as a whole. Individuals make up an organization, but the organization also makes up the individuals. Here is a simple example: Holiday dinner with the family.

No matter who you are and how you act as an individual, when you return home for a holiday dinner with your family, there is a general feeling that influences everyone to act a certain way, to be a certain person. This applies regardless of where or what you call home, what your family looks like, and whatever holiday/special occasion you gather to celebrate. You feel the vibe, the relationships run deep, and the culture supersedes individual behavior. Simply put, culture is the way we do things. All groups have a culture—teams, organizations, communities . . . and families—a set of rules that defines the group. Culture happens, but a good leader *designs the culture* to influence others toward a common vision. The chapters in this section will guide your understanding and design of culture (Chapter 11), with a special emphasis on leading effective teams (Chapter 12) and creating a culture that cares (Chapter 13).

11 CULTURE

LEARNING OBJECTIVES

Upon completion of this chapter, the reader should be able to

11.1 Recognize the extensive and influential nature of culture

11.2 Distinguish the characteristics of culture

11.3 Interpret how the characteristics of culture at the societal level influence organizational culture

11.4 Identify how personal values reciprocally inform organizational values within a culture

11.5 Describe characteristics and examples of how organizations design their culture

11.6 Use the eight scales of culture to map perceptions and expectations

11.7 Apply various tools to design organizational culture

Leadership by Design Model

Design Self
How can I design myself as a leader?

Design Relationships
As a leader, how can I design my relationships with others?

Design Others' Success
As a leader, how can I design success for others?

Design Culture
AS A LEADER, HOW CAN I DESIGN THE CULTURE OF MY ORGANIZATION?

Design Future
As a leader, how can I innovate?

INTRODUCTION

If you were asked to explore another culture, you would likely start thinking about where you were going to travel. The popular notion of culture brings forth images of foreign lands and native peoples with extremely different foods, clothing, language, housing, and other obvious visible characteristics. As you will learn in this chapter, the latter image is only a small example of culture, in terms of both where culture lies and what it entails. Here is another example that illustrates the depth and breadth of culture. Have you ever moved to a new neighborhood, joined a new group or club, switched schools, or started a new job with an established organization? If you have, you undoubtedly felt confused and a bit uncomfortable at first. You felt this way because you stepped into another culture.

Culture is a set of shared assumptions that guide the behavior of members of an organization of any size, from a small group of friends to a workplace to the larger society. Culture is the way things are done around here. Many of those things are invisible and unspoken. No one wrote them down; no one explained them to you. You are just expected to behave in accordance with the established culture. And until you do so, you are going to feel a bit out of place, uncertain, and uncomfortable.

In this chapter, you will learn how culture permeates every group, organization, and society; come to understand why it is important to you now and in the future; and learn how you can design and change culture. It is also important to learn how your personal and organizational values inform culture, how cultures originate, and most importantly, how you can design and change your group or organization's culture in the future.

Leadership That Makes a Difference

Imagine being a first grader walking an hour home from school to a remote village in the jungles of Bangladesh, crying the whole way because the teacher smacked your hands with a cane because you would not speak up when asked a question. But you could not speak up because you did not understand the teachers—your native language was Marma, and the teachers were speaking Bengali. It seems pointless for you to attend school since you do not understand the teacher, nor can you read the textbooks, so you beg your mother not to send you back to school. She finally agrees; however, you have to continue studying at home. You studied at your mother's side learning the Bengali language and went back to school four years later.

This is the story of Maung Nyeu, now a doctoral graduate from Harvard University. Maung Nyeu was a first-grade dropout.

Decades-long internal strife in Bangladesh led to the resettlement of a significant number of the indigenous people of Chittagong Hill (where Maung grew up)—primarily to India. In fact, one night, when he was six years old, Maung and his family heard gunshots and were warned by the village headmaster to run, and into the jungle they escaped. The next day, they saw both their village and the Buddhist temple nearby burned to the ground. Tens of thousands of indigenous people fled to escape the civil war and social marginalization. When the children who had settled in refugee camps in India returned to their native Chittagong Hill, it was apparent that they had not been in school. Moreover, with Bengali now the official language, they lost most of what they knew of their native language. So too had Maung Nyeu.

Today, the schoolchildren continue to struggle with language issues. Less than 28% of individuals in Maung's village are literate, with 60% of students dropping out of primary school and even more dropping out in the higher grades. Maung was one of the lucky ones who won a scholarship to a residential school far from his home, and he was ultimately able to get into Harvard University and obtain his master's degree and complete his doctoral degree. Still, he does not know how to write in his own language, like many of the children of his village.

So he wanted to give back. In 2009, along with other community members, he opened a school, and 12 students attended. Six years later, as a residential school on the grounds of a Buddhist Temple, the school serves 650 students, and Marma and other native languages are taught along with Bengali.

One issue that always bothered him was the absence of native stories from the Marma culture and for the children's lives to be validated (textbooks in Bengali barely referenced indigenous people like him). He decided to do something about it. Tim Brookes, a faculty member at Champlain College and fiction writer, is passionate about saving vanishing languages through his project Endangered Alphabets.[1] He was excited to meet Maung and collaborate with him on a cultural preservation project. Endangered Alphabets is about preserving cultural identity: "In countries all over the world, members of indigenous cultures have their own spoken and written languages—languages they have developed to express their own beliefs, their own experiences, and their understanding of the world."[2]

When the children attending Maung's school go home for vacation, they listen to the stories that their grandparents tell, practice the stories, and then tell them again when they return to school. Each story is captured on film, and when Maung returns to Harvard with them, they are transcribed into Marma, illustrated, and a book is returned to the school. Because they have been so marginalized, it is important for the students to see that they have a voice and that their stories are as important as everyone else's. Now they are important; now they have a voice. Through his leadership, one man is changing lives, one culture, one story at a time.

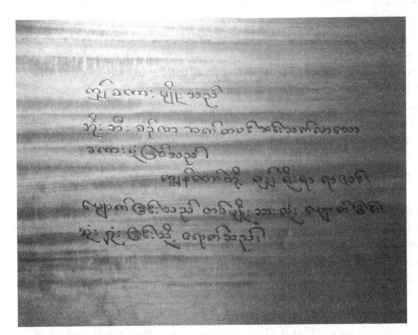

Marma language in Myanmar script
Photo courtesy of Tim Brookes

Marma language in Myanmar script. Poem and carving by Tim Brookes. The poem reads, "All human beings are born free and equal in dignity and rights. They are endowed with reason and conscience and should act towards one another in a spirit of brotherhood."

THE WAY WE DO THINGS AROUND HERE: UNDERSTANDING CULTURE

LEARNING OBJECTIVE
11.1   Recognize the extensive and influential nature of culture.

Culture surrounds you every day, in every group to which you belong—your family, school, work, community, and the larger society. Maybe you only think about it when you see or meet someone from a *very* different culture from your own—someone who does not look or behave in the same way as you. In college, you may meet quite a few of those individuals, or you may experience cultural differences in the ways in which groups do things differently than you are used to. Maybe you selected a particular college because of its culture or the values that it articulates. Did you pick the local school, the religious institution, or maybe a field-specific university? However you selected your school, there was a cultural component that was in some way attractive to you.

Culture is a very complex phenomenon.[3] Authors have tried to simplify the concept by defining it as how things are done around the organization[4] or how people behave when no one is looking.[5] But culture is much more complicated than those simple definitions would have you believe.[6] Consider the differences in what you might see and feel when visiting a friend's home for the weekend. They may eat different foods than you, they may go to bed earlier or later than you, or they may behave in a manner that is more formal or more relaxed. There are differences you may also notice while traveling to different cities, such as the slow pace of life in some parts of the United States versus the frenetic activities in an urban center like New York City.

Traveling abroad often provides the most obvious cultural distinctions. For example, there may be an expectation to bargain for goods in a street market that is unlike the way that others accept prices as fixed when shopping at a market in the United States. All these differences can be attributed to the various cultures within different types of groups or organizations, families, locals, and countries or societies. One notices different rules, different behaviors, and different values for the activities that take place. These experiences are differences in the observed behaviors that manifest from differences in cultural values. Despite how it may feel to you, those values and activities are not *weird*, they are just different . . . to you. For those who are part of that culture, it is simply the way things are done around here.

As individuals seek positions and enter the workforce, an engaging organizational culture with similar values is important to them. Each year *Forbes* and *Fortune* report the top companies to work for, taking into account organizational culture in their assessments, and *Comparable* reports the top 100 large and medium/small companies for culture.[7,8] With the high cost of hiring, organizations that are transparent in their cultural values can ensure a good fit. Think about when you started applying to college or to your first job. The *good fit* that you felt (or did not) was culture.

Effective leaders design culture intentionally, establishing the values, norms, and beliefs that guide group members' daily behavior within the organization, as well as their interactions with those outside the organization. Culture within an organization can be established as members of the organization share learning experiences that provide meaning to both themselves and the organization. As a leader, you will endeavor to establish a good fit between your values and the values and beliefs embraced by the members of the organization. These shared values inform and will become embedded in the culture of the organization and manifest through the norms and what you see, hear, and feel when you interact with members of that organization.[9]

MYTH OR REALITY?

The best way to understand an organization's culture is to read examples of exit interviews with employees who leave the company.

Myth. People do not leave companies just because they do not like them; the reasons are many and varied. But often people are reluctant to give the *real* reason at an exit interview because they fear they will not get a good job reference when they need one next. To get the best pulse of your company, walk the floors of the organization and talk with people.

Leaders are critical in crafting the organization's culture through providing the organization's vision and purpose.[10] Additionally, it is important for the leader to "determine what the most effective culture is for their organization and, when necessary, how to change the organizational culture effectively."

UNDERSTANDING ORGANIZATIONAL CULTURE

LEARNING OBJECTIVE

11.2 Distinguish the characteristics of culture.

Take a moment to think back to what your home was like when you were young. Do you remember what the inside of the house looked like? What did you do after school? What was mealtime like? What kind of traditions did you have when you celebrated a holiday? Did you have any special routines, such as reading every night before bed?

Your first experiences with culture may have come from family or close friends. These people implicitly teach us about common values, beliefs, norms, and rules. They may share experiences in which they learned how to behave at home, in the groups in which they are a part (such as church, social groups, athletics), and in the greater society. The members of those groups reinforce the values and behaviors as well. Encountering people who did things differently may have felt a little strange. Culture is a powerful influence on how people see the world, and experiences with different groups and settings create expectations for the *way things are done around here*.

Your foundational knowledge of culture, similar to that just described, is not unlike the culture in everyday organizations that you experience now or will in the future (e.g., like where you will work). As you grew up, you had the opportunity to experience different cultures in a variety of settings. For example, you may have attended a public school, where the focus was on making sure the students successfully passed standardized tests; or you may have attended a college prep school, where academics were rigorous and 100% of the student body got into good colleges. Now perhaps you attend a private liberal arts college that has as its foundation many long-standing traditions, such as an outstanding football team. Maybe you have experience at a community college where many of the students are working to put themselves through college, for whom extracurricular activities are not in the plan. Some of you may be working full time and because of responsibilities at home, need to take online classes. In any event, these kinds of experiences help shape who you are, the values you have, your philosophies about life, and your understanding of organizational differences—differences in organizational culture.

Culture has been researched and observed from a variety of different perspectives. With its roots in sociology and anthropology, researchers from management, leadership, organizational behavior, and organizational development have studied culture, each from a slightly different perspective. *How* you experience culture is very different for each organization you encounter. That is, you experience culture specific to an organization through events and activities that you can see, such as symbols (the American flag), rituals (the honor society initiation ceremony), group norms (the dorm—the quiet study area), and heroes (Nelson Mandela). These function as the outward signs (behaviors) of the inward culture (values) that result from integrating these various aspects of the organizational culture with your own values and background.

Every organization has a culture that has been crafted and created, purposefully or otherwise, by founding members—family, partners, owners, or leaders.[11] Culture has been compared to an individual's personality—what you see on the outside (behavior) is the result of the personality (values) that you cannot see. Similarly, culture guides the behavior of individuals within the organization, which has a set of core values that you often do not see. These are the values and beliefs the founders thought were important to the organization—the shared basic assumptions of the group.

There are three levels of culture within organizations:

1. **Artifacts** *and symbols*—physical objects that represent organizational values (i.e., those things that you can see). These might include organizational logos, rituals (staff celebrations), language, and manner of dress
2. *Beliefs and values*—such as aspirations, goals, and ideals
3. *Underlying assumptions*—unconscious beliefs and values that determine behavior but are unseen and often difficult to ascertain without significant time spent within the group[12]

Google has a culture very unique from traditional organizations.
Photo by Brooks Kraft LLC/Corbis via Getty Images

What does all this mean for you? You need to be aware that there are important underlying values and beliefs in groups, organizations, and societies that answer why and how its members behave in certain ways. You learn how to behave in different organizational cultures by interacting within various experiences where you learn the meaning of that particular world.[13] Much of this happens below the surface—out of your awareness, and thus, your understanding. "Every organization develops its own distinctive culture. . . . One can often tell within a few minutes of visiting a company, college, or even a restaurant whether employees enjoy their work, whether they take pride or some form of partial 'ownership' in their organization."[14] You will need to look more closely to understand the culture. Anyone not part of that culture is likely to make assumptions using their lean, mean, pattern-making machine brain, resulting in the usual partial and flawed mental model of that culture.

Now that you have had a chance to learn about organizational culture, a more micro view, take a step back and look at culture from the macro perspective—the societal level.

REFLECTION QUESTIONS

Think about an organization to which you belong and reflect on the following questions:

- Are you aware of the founding members' values and beliefs for the organization? Can you articulate them?
- What are the underlying assumptions that guide the organization?
- What are the beliefs and values, aspirations, goals, and ideas that organizational members espouse? Are they congruent with founding values?
- What kinds of artifacts represent the beliefs and values of the organization?
- What messages and values are taught to new members of the organization? How are those cultural values communicated?

CULTURE AT THE SOCIETAL LEVEL

LEARNING OBJECTIVE

11.3   Interpret how the characteristics of culture at the societal level influence organizational culture.

Two primary views of societal culture have been put forth by those studying this concept. These groups of authors examine the differences in the behaviors, beliefs, and values of individuals based on their country of origin. One group defines culture as a social phenomenon that is "the collective programming of the mind that distinguishes the members of one group or category of people from others."[15] The other group believes the concept of culture should refer to societies (nations, ethnic, or regional groups within or across nations). The first definition centers more on the individual and how they come to identify with the values of the group, while the second definition focuses more on specific societies as collectives. This text will use the second view, defining the term **societal cultures** as differences across nations, regions, or ethnicities.

Both organizational and societal cultures have visible elements, which include stories, heroes, and rituals.

- **Stories** are the words, gestures, pictures, and objects that carry often complex meanings recognized as such only by those who share the culture.

- **Heroes** are persons, alive or dead, real or imaginary, who possess characteristics that are highly prized in a culture and thus serve as models for behavior.
- **Rituals** are collective activities that are technically unnecessary to the achievement of desired ends but that within a culture are considered socially essential, keeping the individual bound within the norms of the collectivity.

These visible elements are known as *practices*. Although you (the outside observer) can see them, their meanings are not visible—those are only known to members of that culture. Many cultures around the world have different practices that are not immediately understood by others.

Understanding the Iceberg

The concept of the cultural iceberg may shed some light on understanding the various levels of culture. Whether organizational or societal, there is much about culture that you see and experience; however, there is a significant amount that remains unseen. The concept of the cultural iceberg has been attributed to Edward Hall, a cultural anthropologist. He explored the differences between and among the American cultural systems and the many other cultures in which he lived, studied, and visited—Navajo, Hopi, France, Germany, and Japan, among others. Hall inferred that there is only a small part of culture that is visible, and much of what drives you in your day-to-day life is below the surface, not visible to others, similar to an iceberg (see Figure 11.1). In some respects, culture primarily operates at the unconscious level.[16] While the iceberg gives us a physical representation of the elements of culture (those that are visible and tangible; and those that are less visible or not visible at all), the concept of culture is anything but visible. The iceberg is a metaphor that allows us to visually connect with and understand elements of culture that we experience in day-to-day life, both personally and organizationally.

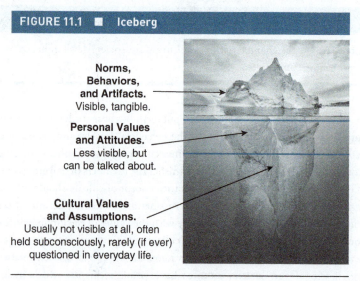

FIGURE 11.1 ■ Iceberg

Norms, Behaviors, and Artifacts. Visible, tangible.

Personal Values and Attitudes. Less visible, but can be talked about.

Cultural Values and Assumptions. Usually not visible at all, often held subconsciously, rarely (if ever) questioned in everyday life.

Source: ©iStockphoto.com/posteriori.

One very important cultural dimension is context, which is what we pay attention to (or not) when we are experiencing events. Contexts provide individuals with *part* of the meaning of an event. Whether a context is high or low is determined by your culture and by what you have to pay attention to in order to gain meaning from the event. There are five categories of events that must be perceived to fully interpret an event: the activity, the present situation, your position/role within the social system, past experience, and culture.[17]

To fully understand the meaning of a culture, you need to understand the context in which culture occurs and on *what* members focus their attention. An interesting example of cultural context is how you perceive personal space, which is based on how you grew up, where you live, and how you adapt to new contexts. You may have had a communication class in which you learned about norms for personal space—those are intimate space (typically one and a half feet), personal space (approximately four feet), social space (12 feet), and public space (25 feet). These distances can vary greatly from country to country, and you may find yourself quite annoyed and uneasy the first time you visit a country where the norm for space is significantly different from what you are used to experiencing. For example, in large cities in some Middle Eastern countries where there are large populations of individuals, personal space feels nonexistent due to overcrowding—individuals have gotten used to very little personal space, and those individuals experience daily what Americans would consider intimate space.

Time is also a function of culture and is identified as either monochronic (M-time) or polychronic (P-time). Cultures that adhere to a monochronic time schedule, such as Americans and Northern Europeans, adhere to a strict time schedule where days are scheduled and appointments are made and kept on time. In cultures that are polychronic, however, people juggle multiple tasks at one time, and their focus is on people, not on the task. That is to say, it is more important to pay attention to the needs of the individual rather than adhere to a strict schedule.

The GLOBE Study

This classic study has become even more relevant today. Not only leaders but employees alike must understand the nuances of "doing business" globally to assist in developing high-quality relationships. The differences in these culturally based values and practices become critical for organizations that maintain an international presence or have individuals with international backgrounds working in their organizations. In fact, researchers have "identified more than 160 competencies that are relevant for global leadership effectiveness."[18]

Several researchers over the years have collected data on cultural differences around the world. One of the largest studies collected data from more than 17,000 middle managers in 62 societies in what is called the GLOBE (Global Leadership and Organizational Behavior Effectiveness) study.[19] Similar to the definition provided earlier, this group defined culture as "shared motives, values, beliefs, identities, and interpretations or meanings of significant events that result from common experiences of members of collectives that are transmitted across generations." Looking at cultural practices and values in world cultures, their model incorporated numerous leadership-related theories resulting in 15 propositions that drove their research. For example, "Societal cultural norms of shared values and practices affect leaders' behavior" and "Societal cultural values and practices also affect organizational culture and practices."[20] If you were looking at leadership in another country, what would you focus on? The GLOBE research group used the following constructs to examine leadership practices and values:

1. *Power distance*: The degree to which members of a collective expect power to be distributed equally

2. *Uncertainty avoidance*: The extent to which a society, organization, or group relies on social norms, rules, and procedures to alleviate unpredictability of future events

3. *Humane orientation*: The degree to which a collective encourages and rewards individuals for being fair, altruistic, generous, caring, and kind to others

4. *Collectivism I (institutional collectivism)*: The degree to which organizational and societal institutional practices encourage and reward collective distribution of resources and collective action

5. *Collectivism II (on-croup collectivism)*: The degree to which individuals express pride, loyalty, and cohesiveness in their organizations or families

6. *Assertiveness*: The degree to which individuals are assertive, confrontational, and aggressive in their relationships with others

7. *Gender egalitarianism*: The degree to which a collective minimizes gender inequality

8. *Future orientation*: The extent to which individuals engage in future-oriented behaviors, such as delaying gratification, planning, and investing in the future

9. *Performance orientation*: The degree to which a collective encourages and rewards group members for performance improvement and excellence

The GLOBE study resulted in some surprising outcomes. Despite all the differences across cultures, 22 of the leadership attributes were desirable across *all* societies. And eight attributes were universally undesirable. The study also found that, based on leader characteristics, there were three universally accepted theories of leadership that contributed to effective leadership across cultures: charismatic/value-based leadership, team-oriented leadership, and participative leadership. Lastly, researchers were able to place societies into culture clusters based on how they scored on the nine cultural dimensions. How might this fascinating work connecting leadership to world cultures inform your leadership design work?

Numerous companies in the United States are adept at focusing on the importance of cultural differences around the world. The Colgate-Palmolive Corporation is one among them that has implemented global standards and criteria for excellence around the world, which are critical to the core strategy of the company. They focus on customers in over 200 countries and understand the preferences of each in order to create products that match local needs and preferences. For example, they understand that people in Latin America like stronger fragrances and flavors than North Americans and that individuals in rural Asia can't afford to buy larger-size products, so they market smaller sizes there.

In order to understand these cultural preferences around the world, Colgate-Palmolive has an extensive infrastructure that gives them a competitive advantage. Not only do they hire local individuals from around the world who know and understand local culture, they also "borrow from each other's cultures" and become "homogeneously global." High-potential individuals who work for Colgate-Palmolive are sent around the world to become immersed in local cultures—each must work in both a developing and a developed country and focus on different departments within the company. These assignments are vital to the success of the company by providing international perspectives, which permeates the company and allows them to gain the best solutions worldwide.[21]

Chapter 11 ● Culture **347**

Experts Beyond the Text

INSIGHTFUL LEADERS KNOW ABOUT . . . LEADERSHIP IN OTHER CULTURES

Features of Leadership in Japan

By Ryosuke (Reo) Watanabe

Japanese leadership has been characterized by collectivism with a strong focus on collaboration, teamwork, low conflict, and shared decision-making that paradoxically functions in a hierarchy with deference and loyalty to positional leaders.[22] The collective leadership in Japan offers a remarkable case study of a different leadership style than in the West, particularly because of recent shifts in theory and practice of leadership away from individualistic approaches to more collective beliefs and processes in the West.[23]

Visitors to Japan often experience a juxtaposition of tradition and technological innovation, as Japan is one of the most technologically advanced economies in the world.[24] However, a 2,000-year history of tradition and seniority represented through extensive honorific language still permeates the culture. Japan has a collectivist culture with strong group emotions and loyalty to authority. Its collectivism is not egalitarian, but highly hierarchical.[25] Thus, the most acceptable practices and qualities of leadership in Japan are based on *hierarchical collectivism*, which puts importance on authority and self-sacrifice for the good of the group.[26]

This conceptualization of leadership values harmony and avoids direct conflict. It also places high importance on respecting authority figures, which corresponds to a high level of obedience.[27] At the same time, leaders are expected to care for group members and maintain equality. Group harmony is usually considered more important than making profits or overall productivity. A Japanese proverb, "The nail which sticks out gets pounded down," demonstrates how individuals are not singled out in Japan for praises or criticisms, because such feedback is supposed to be directed at the group, emphasizing collective responsibility.

Japanese collective leadership enabled the "economic miracle" in the post-war period, when government policies led by a strong bureaucracy supported the growth of leading companies in strategic industries. The policies also incentivized companies to adopt lifetime employment, thereby offering workers job security. Furthermore, employees were rewarded for working long hours, doing precisely as directed, and not causing disruption. The outcome was the world's role model of lean manufacturing and quality excellence in the twentieth century.[28]

The collective leadership approach in Japan, however, is not effective in adapting to the unparalleled challenges caused by dynamic changes such as a globalizing economy, technological innovation, and declining/aging population. In other words, Japan's consensus-based collective approach slows down the decision-making process that requires agility and innovation as a response to the new challenges. In the last three decades, the Japanese economy has experienced the "lost decades"—persistent slow growth and low inflation.[29] Additionally, Japanese collective leadership has faced severe ethical problems in recent years. These include scandals at corporate giants such as Toshiba, Nissan, and Mitsubishi with issues ranging from accountancy to quality control and certificate falsification.[30] These negative outcomes are examples of an authoritative leader's arrogance and the malfunction of collective responsibility. Another Japanese proverb warns, "The boughs that bear most hang lowest." Japan's collective leadership presupposes top authorities to act modestly and avoid egoism. After all, significant problems occur if leaders fail to behave accordingly.

Japanese collective leadership has both advantages and disadvantages because it not only contributed to the "economic miracle" in the post-war period, but also caused the "lost decades" afterward. This collectivism provides a useful contrast to the individualistic leadership in the West and offers helpful insights regarding the effective leadership required to thrive in the future.

Reflection Questions

Ask someone from another country or culture the following:

1. Describe a typical day [in your country or culture].
2. What are the types of foods that you eat? What is your favorite dish?
3. Tell me about the educational system.
4. How do individuals engage in business transactions? Do they quickly get to the point? Do they converse over a long, leisurely dinner?

THE LEADER'S ROLE AND ORGANIZATIONAL CULTURE

LEARNING OBJECTIVE
11.4 Identify how personal values reciprocally inform organizational values within a culture.

Inculcating values throughout an organization starts with the leader, who sets standards of behavior for everyone in the organization. Someday, that could be you. Leaders work hard every day to gain alignment with the company's values, reinforcing positive actions, and swiftly taking action with employees who do not emulate these values.[31] Leadership author and scholar Warren Bennis[32] wrote about the importance of understanding your own personal values, understanding the **organization's values**, and knowing any difference between the two. You will be happiest in your organization when there is congruence between your personal values and the values of your organization. Each person brings a personal set of values to the organization, and together those collective sets of values are what create the organization's culture.[33] For that reason, it is important for leaders to know and understand the values and beliefs of followers.

Personal Values—Forming and Informing Organizational Culture

One of the most important elements of culture is values—both personal values and those reinforced at the organizational level. Based on the family in which you grew up, your social structures (e.g., religious, schools, groups), and your national and regional identity (e.g., American from the west coast), your values define who you are, what you believe, and how you interact with others. As you read in Chapter 5 on values, designing your leadership self requires a full understanding of the values by which you live, simply because when you join an organization you want to make sure it is representative of those values.

One model for helping you see how your values align with those of an organization is the Competing Values Framework.[34] Two cultural dimensions comprise organizations in this model: an internal to external focus dimension and a flexibility to stability dimension. Within these emerge four generalized values-based cultures: clan, adhocracy, hierarchy, and market. The clan is described as like a family, valuing nurturing, teamwork, loyalty, and concern for people. The adhocracy is entrepreneurial, valuing risk, innovation, freedom, and challenges. These two cultures tend toward flexibility, while the next two—hierarchy and market—tend toward stability and control. The hierarchy is described as controlled and structured, valuing organization, efficiency, security, and stability. The market is competitive, valuing achievement in reaching goals and outdoing competition.

Each of the cultural types holds forth values important to the success of an organization, particularly in certain circumstances. For example, in times of disruption or uncertainty, organizations with more flexible cultures will more easily adapt. Each type also aligns with a set of leadership behaviors and follower expectations—the way things are done around here. How would you describe your current organizational culture? Would you call it a clan, where everyone is very involved similar to a big family and the leader focuses on mentoring and nurturing followers? More important for you as a leader, which of the four cultures described best aligns with your approach to leadership?

Do Your Values Align With the Organization's Values? Ensuring Fit

Just as important as the organizational culture is to the success of the organization, your success is driven by a match between personal and organizational values. The average cost to hire a new employee is roughly 20% to 50% of an individual's annual salary. That is a lot of money to any organization. So losing employees because of poor values or cultural fit can be extraordinarily costly to the bottom line in both time and money (no matter what type of organization—public, private, governmental, or nonprofit). Organizational leaders hire individuals to get the best fit between new employees and the organizational culture—an important consideration regarding whether or not employees will stay the course. Moreover, prospective employees need to engage in self-reflection regarding their own values to determine whether the organizational values and culture are congruent with their own personal values.

The notion of aligned values for organizational success is a consistent theme for effective leadership. In the book *Leadership Matters*, the authors reported "that getting the culture right is a top priority" and "every organization has to create its own culture and encourage one that serves its particular mission."[35] While they acknowledged there is no one *right* culture, there are certain characteristics that most organizations desire in their members. Use the Cultural Values Assessment exercise at the end of the chapter to do an assessment of one culture to which you belong.

Leadership by Design

Design Principle: Figure-Ground Relationship

Definition: Elements are perceived as either figures (objects of focus) or ground (the rest of the perceptual field).

In Other Words: Looking at anything, you will focus on some things while all the rest sits in the background.

Another exciting day of class
©iStockphoto.com/PeopleImage

For Example: Take a look at the picture, entitled *Another Exciting Day of Class*. What is the first thing you notice? The sleeping student is the figure, all the rest is the ground. But what important things does the *ground* contain? Every picture, like every context, tells a story and raises questions. What class is this? What are they studying? What put him to sleep? Is he sleeping or playing a game? The figure is key, but the ground can be important too.

For Leaders: Leaders must be aware of both figures and ground. When followers interact with you and the culture of your organization, what do you want them to notice and remember? If they cannot distinguish the figure from the ground, then they may not put their effort into the important things. Have you ever seen the optical illusion where a white vase sits on a black background, until suddenly that background appears to you as two profiles facing one another? This perceptual instability happens because it is unclear what is figure versus ground. For followers, this uncertainty diffuses their focus and results in frustration. Leaders should also consider what followers might be missing that may be getting lost in the background. What are the key elements that reinforce your culture?

Vision, Mission, and Values in Organizational Culture

From lofty aspirations to day-to-day details, an organization's vision, mission, and values provide declarations to the world about who they are and for what they stand. A vision is a forward-thinking and aspirational image that sets the direction for the organization that others might follow. Unlike Alice in Wonderland, who did not know which way she ought to go, leaders must set a compelling vision that moves followers *somewhere*... and that somewhere is different for each organization. Excellent leaders listen to the wants and needs, the hopes and dreams of followers, and craft their vision of the organization around those so that followers will feel a part of that vision. Crafting the vision is one of the first and most important tasks of the leader.[36]

The organizational **mission** describes an organization's reason for existence—articulating the business they are in. Mission statements guide organizational members in their day-to-day work and serve as a reminder of the reason the organization exists and that each and every activity in which they engage meets that end.

Finally, an organization's values inform the organizational culture. From the founders, there is reciprocity between organizational members and organizational leaders, and together they have a mutual understanding of what they stand for and in which direction they need to move the organization forward.

CONTEMPORARY APPROACHES TO ORGANIZATIONAL CULTURE

LEARNING OBJECTIVE
11.5   Describe characteristics and examples of how organizations design their culture.

The face of organizational cultural identity is changing. You need only look as far as Warby Parker or Google to see the contemporary approach to organizational culture. Numerous organizations have broken the mold, and gone are the days of the *white shirt and dark suit* that drove organizational culture in years past. Outlined in their Impact Report 2021, Warby Parker outlines that they were "founded with a mission: to inspire and impact the world with vision, purpose, and style." Their culture is driven by their core values:

- Inject fun and quirkiness into everything we do
    - Take our work and our impact seriously (but not ourselves)
    - Help others have fun

- Treat others as they want to be treated
    - Design with empathy
    - Have a positive attitude

- Pursue new and creative ideas
    - Embrace change and uncertainty
    - Continually challenge ourselves

- Do good
    - Impact the world in a meaningful way
    - Value our customers, our peers, the community, and the environment

- Take action
    - Set ambitious goals and measure results
    - Take the first step

- Presume positive intent
    - Trust but verify

- Lead with integrity
    - Be honest
    - Give and take direct feedback
Learn. Grow. Repeat[37]

Warby Parker is at the forefront of transforming the way that organizations treat and engage with customers, employees, the community, the environment, and partners. In addition, they have a 10-point racial equity strategy that seeks to make their organization more diverse, equitable, and inclusive.

Similar to Warby Parker, Starbucks, Apple, and many other contemporary organizations, Google's culture focuses on its people who "share common goals and visions for the company. . . and reflect the global audience that we serve." Moreover, their corporate culture encourages interactions that focus on both work and play. Rather than a vision and/or mission, Google focuses on the "Ten things we know to be true":

1. Focus on the user and all else will follow.

2. It's best to do one thing really, really well.

3. Fast is better than slow.

4. Democracy on the web works.

5. You don't need to be at your desk to need an answer.

6. You can make money without doing evil.

7. There's always more information out there.

8. The need for information crosses all borders.

9. You can be serious without a suit.

10. Great just isn't good enough.[38]

Sounds like a great environment that focuses on both work and play. How does each set of values differ from the other? What would you need to value to succeed (or to lead) in each culture?

The Great Pandemic

No one could have predicted the far-reaching effects of the 2020 Covid pandemic. Schools, restaurants, airlines, and thousands of businesses shut down while trying to figure out how to manage and do business while individuals sheltered at home. Importantly, the world had to pivot. Some individuals were able to work remotely, while others could not. Those who could go out, found their world quite different. Streets were quiet, and people who ventured out were masked. People slowly started working from home.

Many organizations had previously, intentionally not allowed work-from-home but immediately found that this was the only alternative to keeping businesses up and running. How would not seeing and interacting with colleagues on a regular basis affect organizational culture? Not surprisingly, individuals reacted and were affected *differently*. Some individuals adapted more easily than others; some organizations were able to design culture from a distance better than others. Although in-person interaction may be considered the best way to create "rapport and trust," leaders now need to shift methods for gaining that through empowerment and other strategies.[39] Helping to maintain an adaptive culture will be assisted by three ideas: (1) Hire and promote people who are resilient, adaptable, and exhibit grace under fire; (2) curate and communicate examples of how the organization is adhering to its cultural values through new practices; and (3) model transcendent values.[40] Having weathered a challenge as significant as

Chapter 11 • Culture   353

the 2020 Covid pandemic, your organization will be ready to face the next pivot with grace and understanding.

REFLECTION QUESTION

Think of a societal culture with which you are somewhat familiar (one such as Japan) and a story, hero, or ritual (such as bowing) exhibited within that culture that you find different. There is obviously some cultural meaning behind that practice that only insiders understand. Find a member of that culture or someone who has lived in that culture for an extended time. Ask them about the practice, and try to understand the meaning behind the behavior.

DEI BY DESIGN

LEARNING OBJECTIVE

11.6   Use the eight scales of culture to map perceptions and expectations.

The interplay of social culture with organizational norms impacts expectations, actions, and interactions. Erin Meyer's 2014 book, *The Culture Map* provides leaders and managers eight scales to understand culture and see leadership environments more clearly.[41] The eight scales described help decode how individuals from different cultures interact as well as offer some insights on designing culture for your areas of influence. As you are introduced to each, consider where on the scale your current organization might fall.

1. *Low-context to high-context* cultures. In low-context cultures, communication is direct, explicit, and meant to be understood literally. In high-context cultures, messages often contain implied information and typically draw on common references or shared prior knowledge to be effective.

2. *Direct to indirect.* In direct cultures, negative feedback is provided bluntly, without additional positive remarks, and can be shared publicly without shame. Conversely, in indirect cultures, positive feedback is used to soften negative feedback, absolute terms (totally, completely, always, etc.) are not frequently used, and criticisms are almost always provided in private.

3. *Principles (why-first) to applications (how-first).* In a why-first culture, persuasion begins with an underlying theory, concept, or model before presenting an opinion, perspective, or solution. In how-first cultures, facts, statements, or positions are presented first, and theoretical orientations, conceptual frameworks, or practical models are supplied after—and only if necessary.

4. *Egalitarian to hierarchical* approaches to leadership. In cultures that favor egalitarianism, the power difference between leaders and members is small, organizational structures are flat, and communication patterns radiate throughout organizations. Cultures with hierarchical preferences tend to favor a large power difference between leaders and members, organizational structures that are

multilayered, and communication pathways that mirror the organization's chain of command.

5. *Consensual to top-down.* Decisions are made by leaders and members through unanimous agreement in consensus-favoring cultures. Inversely, decisions are made by one or a small group of bosses, leaders, or managers in top-down cultures.

6. *Cognitive to affective* cultural trust. In cognitive (task-based) cultures, trust is built on practicality, consistency, and reliability. In affective (relationship-based) cultures, trust is forged through experience-sharing, quality time spent together, and shared values orientations.

7. *Confrontational to avoidant* disagreement. In confrontational cultures, disagreement is valued as positive, open confrontation is welcomed, and relationships are (generally) not harmed by debate. However, in avoidant cultures, disagreement is regarded negatively, direct challenges are considered inappropriate, and harmony in relationships is disturbed by dissension.

8. *Linear to flexible* norms about scheduling. In linear-time cultures, scheduling is focused on benchmarks, deadlines, and sticking to a pre-determined timeline, with an emphasis on promptness and reliable organization of tasks. In flexible-time cultures, project steps are approached in an emergent fashion, with priorities that shift as teams work together, with a clear focus on adaptability.

These scales can help you plot your culture and develop a map to compare your expectations with those of others. Noting the areas of overlap and difference between you and those you lead can help uncover the mismatches that may be limiting success. Building this type of cultural awareness also helps bridge cultural divides and teaches the cultural flexibility needed for intentionally designed success.

DESIGNING CULTURE

LEARNING OBJECTIVE

11.7 Apply various tools to design organizational culture.

Designing culture may be the most difficult, long-term design challenge. Culture is built from the ground up, by those who were there in the beginning, no matter the type of group or organization. It can take years to craft and years to change. Organizational change has been defined as "planned alterations of organizational components to improve the effectiveness of the organization." These components include the "mission, vision, values, culture, strategy, goals, structure, processes or systems, technology, and people in an organization. When organizations enhance their effectiveness, they increase their ability to generate value for those they serve."[42]

As discussed in Chapter 10, leaders are often challenged to manage organizational change in response to changes such as fluctuations in the market, new leadership, fast-paced technological change, a changing workforce, a multigenerational and diverse workforce, increased scrutiny by stakeholders, more government oversight, and an ever-increasing global presence. Traditionally, organizational change occurs from the top down where executive leaders, in response to these internal and/or external pressures such as those noted, respond each in their own way but often in a manner that imposes new requirements by others on the organization. In contrast, today organizational members want to be informed, involved, and engaged decision makers in the organizational processes that affect their work. Recall from the previous chapter the work of John Kotter and his eight-step change model. That model was introduced as a way to facilitate organizational change. Here are the steps again:

1. Establishing a sense of urgency

2. Creating the guiding coalition

3. Developing a vision and strategy

4. Communicating the change vision

5. Empowering broad-based action

6. Generating short-term wins

7. Consolidating gains and producing more change

8. Anchoring new approaches in the culture[43]

Note the last step—anchoring new approaches in the culture. Changing organizational culture can take quite some time, which can lead to frustration on the part of organizational members; enthusiasm can drop, and changes that were made early on can be lost in the process. In fact, the point is that cultural changes need to be secured and built into the social norms and shared values if you hope to make organizational changes *stick*. Unfortunately, too many leaders fail to be attentive to the organization's culture during the process of implementing change. You cannot make changes to design success for others unless you also design the culture that will support and sustain that success.

Kotter's eight-step process for organizational change has stood the test of time. While the steps are numbered sequentially, Kotter noted that most organizations are engaged in various steps simultaneously, with some steps completed to various degrees while others are being started. The majority of change efforts that fail are a result of leaders jumping ahead and trying to complete only Steps 5, 6, and 7. The *failure* to address the critical components of assisting members in understanding the importance of the change effort (urgency), getting key individuals on board (a guiding coalition), and creating and communicating a compelling vision can undermine all the subsequent steps to get the change implemented successfully. And as noted, the last step— the culture step—is critical to making the changes more permanent. Kotter reminds leaders that when they have been indoctrinated into and steeped in the culture of the organization's norms of behavior and shared values, change comes slowly; and although it can come, it must be anchored for change to be effective. Designing and facilitating organizational and cultural change is not easy, particularly at large corporations or organizations steeped in years of history, but it is nonetheless necessary for sustained organizational and individual success.

Tools to Facilitate Culture Change

Does the culture of the organization get in the way of change or does it foster or even encourage change? Leadership guru Warren Bennis wrote about the importance of change to organizational leaders: "All of the leaders I talked with believe in change—in both people and organizations. They equate it with growth—tangible and intangible—and progress."[44] Growth and progress are extraordinarily relevant today given the rapid pace of change that continues to accelerate. In order to move *any* organization forward, leaders need to be cognizant of the types of pressures for change that affect their organizations—no matter what the organization type: for-profit, non-profit, governmental, or educational. Environmental factors, most of which are beyond a leader's control (i.e., changing demographics, technology, globalization), affect all organizations. So the question is not how do leaders react to external pressures but rather how do leaders proactively engage their organization to be responsive to the changes they know are inevitable?

Organizational change or any type of personal or professional change can be difficult and stressful. Effective leaders recognize those intrapersonal demands and take measures to ensure a smooth transition for the individuals and the team. Make sure that you have put into place and communicate an action plan that makes the change process transparent to everyone in the organization. The leader needs to be attentive to the following issues and decisions during the change:

- What are the strategies for dealing with the politics that will be involved in the change?

- What are the conditions for a successful change, and how will you know when you have achieved them?

- How will you communicate both the change plan and the results organization-wide?

- What strategies/resources will you use to generate new information to inform the plan?

- How will you support the staff through their emotional reactions to the change?

- How will you measure the success of the change effort (the new state) and the change process itself?

- What rewards will you implement to support the change process and the outcomes?

Again, while the change process will likely carry some stress for most individuals, being as transparent as possible will minimize that stress and keep the rumors to a minimum.

Appreciative Inquiry

Another method for facilitating organizational change is appreciative inquiry (AI).[45] **Appreciative inquiry** is defined as the cooperative, coevolutionary search for the best in people, their organizations, and the world around them. This positive approach focuses on changing organizational cultures by examining what is *right* with the organization. It involves systematic discovery of what gives life to an organization or a community when it is most effective and most capable in economic, ecological terms. Conceived in the late 1980s, AI has gained momentum and is now considered one of the foremost methods for organizational change. Different from traditional change methods, AI focuses on organizational strengths and stories of success rather than on problems and what has gone wrong—a glass-half-full approach that is transformational for the organization.

AI's focus on what is right in the organization is uplifting and transforming for members who are used to always examining what is wrong. AI has been defined as "the study of what gives life to human systems when they function at their best."[46] AI uses process mapping to map the positive core of the organization. **Process mapping** is an activity where leaders and followers visually represent what an organization does, noting the flow of activities, decision points, roles, and any other variables involved in getting things done. AI engages the organization's entire

Chapter 11 • Culture   357

community (or as many as possible), as well as all key stakeholders—board members, customers, suppliers, and so forth—in the process of inquiring into "extraordinary moments of high engagement, commitment, and passionate achievement."

Rather than focus on problem-solving, AI utilizes a structured *appreciative interview* process involving all stakeholders to glean out the best from the organization. Originally a four-step process called the 4-D Cycle, one author has added a fifth step. The five phases are as follows:

- *Discovery*: Mobilizing the whole system by engaging all stakeholders in the articulation of strengths and best practices. Identifying "The best of what has been and what is."

- *Dream*: Creating a clear, results-oriented vision in relation to discovered potential and in relation to questions of higher purpose, such as, "What is the world calling us to become?"

- *Design*: Creating possibility propositions of the ideal organization, articulating an organization design that people feel is capable of drawing upon and magnifying the positive core to realize the newly expressed dream.

- *Destiny*: Strengthening the affirmative capability of the whole system, enabling it to build hope and sustain momentum for ongoing positive change and high performance.

- *Define:* Emphasizing the importance of a clear and compelling theme for the inquiry.

Table 11.1 displays sample AI interview questions for visioning for both individuals and groups. Notice the positive focus of the inquiry.

TABLE 11.1 ■ Sample Appreciative Inquiry Questions for Visioning

Individuals

1. Describe a time when you felt the team/group performed really well. What were the circumstances during that time?

2. Describe a time when you were proud to be a member of the team or group. Why were you proud?

3. What do you value most about being a member of this team/group? Why?

4. Tell about a time you were most excited about your contributions to this group.

5. What are you most excited about with respect to future contributions?

Groups

1. Discuss examples of the best practices that people have seen within the organization.

2. Determine what circumstances made the best practices possible (describe in detail).

3. Take the stories and envision what might be. Write an affirmative statement (a provocative proposition) that describes the idealized future as if it were already happening.

When an AI effort is successful, an organization's culture change sticks. The power of focusing on the positive provides hope for organizational members. Moreover, the process is generative in that it focuses on coming to a collective understanding of what members want for the organization versus only solving problems.

358 Module 4 ● Design Culture and Community

Strategic Planning Toward Culture Change

Imagine if you were part of a soccer team where

Only 4 of the 11 players on the field would know which goal is theirs

Only 2 of the 11 would care

Only 2 of the 11 would know what position they play and know exactly what they are supposed to do

All but 2 players would, in some way, be competing against their own team members rather than the opponent[47]

Hardly a culture of success. Yet Stephen Covey, in his book *The 8th Habit*, describes a poll of 23,000 employees drawn from a number of companies and industries. He reports the poll's findings:

Only 37 percent said they have a *clear understanding* of what their organization is trying to achieve and why.

Only one in five was *enthusiastic* about their team's and their organization's goals.

Only one in five said they had a *clear line of sight* between their tasks and their team's and organization's goals.

Only 15 percent felt that their organization *fully enables* them to execute key goals.

Only 20 percent *fully trusted* the organization they work for.[48]

These numbers are the same as those of the dysfunctional soccer team and are clearly a problem for any leader.

Take a look at those elements again (in italics), paraphrased here:

1. Clear understanding of purpose

2. Enthusiasm for goals

3. Clear connection between actions and goals

4. Fully enables to act

5. Trust one another

Effective leaders can address each of these elements separately because they are each critical to individual and organizational success. But what if there were a larger process that conceptualized these elements as parts of a bigger whole? Fortunately, there is such a process—it is called strategic planning (among other names). **Strategic planning** is the process by which an organization (a) clarifies (identify, develop, refine) values and vision, (b) translates those into goals, and then (c) creates action plans or strategies to achieve those goals. Action plans generally include an analysis of the external and internal context and resources, activities tied to a specific goal or subgoal, a description of what success will look like, who is responsible, the timeline of activities, the resources needed, and how goal achievement will be assessed. Figure 11.2 helps illustrate.

FIGURE 11.2 ■ Strategic Planning

At first, strategic planning may appear to be a very logical, straightforward process. As explained, the process is quite simple. However, in practice, strategic planning requires a good deal of time, focus, and thought. Consider how long it would take you to generate *your* core values and vision for your future and then to translate them into concrete action steps. Now, multiply that by the number of individuals who comprise an organization—because together you are seeking a shared vision. The time and effort, though, is well worth it; strategic planning results in a clearer understanding of purpose and a clear connection between actions and goals (Items 1 and 3 preceding) and clarifies culture. The discussions, thinking, and decision-making done throughout the process bring individuals together in a shared understanding of both how they see the organization as well as how well they know and trust one another. In other words, strategic planning builds culture; and a well-designed and well-executed strategic planning process comprises a very powerful way leaders can design culture.

Strategic planning is like the creative problem-solving process introduced throughout this text. First, you must *understand* your organization, then you must *imagine* how to best achieve the goals and vision, and finally, you craft a plan for *implementing* those activities. The process can be applied to designing culture and the path forward for organizations of any size, even groups of strangers seeking to build community and a shared vision. For example, a Collective Action Toolkit can be used to facilitate community leaders in a range of problem-solving and strategic planning activities.[49] As you can see from Figure 11.3, understanding, imagining, and implementing are all part of the process that centers around the shared goal.

As you continue developing your effective leader toolkit, strategic planning introduces a whole new set of tools that can be used to more effectively execute each phase of the process. Some of these tools have already been introduced, such as the creativity and idea-generating techniques to facilitate the imagine phase that you learned about in Chapter 8. Strategic planning begins with understanding—first the organization and then the organization relative to the internal and external context. Organizational management legend Peter Drucker developed a self-assessment tool that poses five *most important* questions (with many related prompts) from which organizational members can begin understanding themselves.[50] How many of these questions can you readily answer about an organization with which you work?

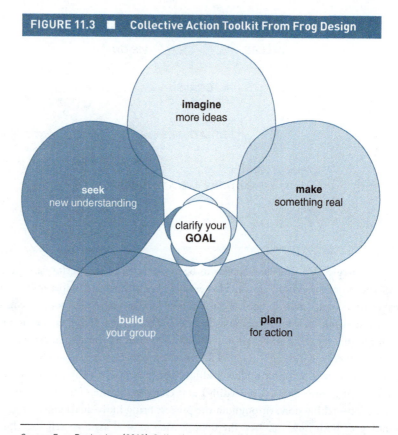

FIGURE 11.3 ■ Collective Action Toolkit From Frog Design

Source: Frog Design Inc. (2012). Collective action toolkit: Groups make change (p. 4).

The Five Drucker Questions

Question 1: What is our mission?

    What are we trying to achieve?

    What specific results are we seeking?

    What are our major strengths?

    What are our major weaknesses?

    Does our mission need to be revisited?

Question 2: Who is our customer?

    Who are our primary customers?

    Who are our supporting customers?

    Have our customers changed?

    Should we add or delete some customers?

Question 3: What does the customer consider value?

    What do our primary customers consider value?

    What do our supporting customers consider value?

How well are we providing what our customers consider value?

How can we use what our customers consider value to become more effective?

What additional information do we need?

Question 4: What have been our results?

How do we define results for our organization?

To what extent have we achieved these results?

How well are we using our resources?

Question 5: What is our plan?

What have we learned and what do we recommend?

Where should we focus our efforts?

What, if anything, should we do differently?

What is my plan to achieve results for my group/responsibility area?

What is our plan to achieve results for the organization?

REFLECTION QUESTIONS

Relook at the five important questions posed by Drucker. How would you answer each of those if you were examining your own leadership?

What is *your* mission? Who is *your* customer? What does the customer consider value? What have been *your* results? What is *your* plan?

Understanding your organization and culture starts with introspective and aspirational questions like those posed by Drucker. The next step in understanding entails carefully examining the real and present internal and external attributes of the organization. A **SWOT analysis** is a strategic planning and decision-making tool used to evaluate the current strengths, weaknesses, opportunities, and threats relevant to an organization or specific situation that requires understanding. The typical SWOT matrix looks like Figure 11.4, illustrating the four categories for which you would analyze the organization. The SWOT analysis tool is simple to understand but very complex and powerful. A thorough SWOT analysis of your organization will yield both an assessment of current capacity as well as a glimpse of what might be possible.

FIGURE 11.4 ■ SWOT Analysis Matrix		
	Positive\Helful	Negative\Harmful
Internal: Attributes of the organzation	Strengths	Weaknesses
External: Attributes of the environment outside the organization	Opportunities	Threats

REFLECTION QUESTIONS

Again, reinterpret an organizational tool like SWOT into a tool for better understanding your-self. You have likely already assessed your (internal) strengths and weaknesses. What are your external opportunities? Your external threats?

Identifying opportunities and mapping out how to pursue and attain those opportunities are the primary and most straightforward aims of strategic planning. Quite often, leaders plan reactively based on immediate problems and challenges rather than starting with values and vision to clarify what actions make the most sense. As Peter Drucker famously stated, "Doing the right thing is more important than doing the thing right."[51] The Drucker questions and the SWOT analysis are just two of many tools that can help identify the values, vision, mission, and specific goals your organization seeks. From this point, the challenge is to craft a plan for meeting those goals. Typically, this step is called action planning, which involves working through the questions in Table 11.2 for each goal.

TABLE 11.2 ■ Action Planning					
Goal	Actions	Owner	Timeline	Resources Needed	Assessment Criteria
What is the specific goal?	What activities need to happen to reach the goal?	Who is responsible for leading, coordinating, and monitoring this activity?	What are the specific time goals for each activity and final goal?	What time, personnel, funds, or other resources are needed?	What does success look like, and how will progress be assessed?

Action plans can include many other categories to clarify the process. These might include a breakdown of long- and short-term goals, broad and subgoals, rationale for each goal, stakeholders involved or impacted by the activities, necessary partners or collaborations, and next steps or future actions after the goal is attained. Because strategic planning significantly catalyzes organizational progress, countless templates and technology-based tools have been developed to facilitate the process. However, there is no substitute for the actual time spent thinking and discussing among organization members.

One very useful tool that will help prompt action planning is the POWER Up method (see Figure 11.5). POWER is an acronym that stands for *positives, objections, what else, enhancements,* and *remedies.*[52] As you talk through possible actions to reach a goal, some of those ideas may be difficult to put into practice. The POWER Up method asks you to list all of the positive outcomes of that idea, then all the possible objections that others might raise. Then, similar to effective creative problem-solving, the method asks you to set your idea aside for a moment and generate more ideas (What else?). Returning to the original idea (or another if you found a better one), you then revisit the list of positives to discuss what enhancements you could make to the idea. Finally, addressing the list of objections, what remedies would help address those objections?

FIGURE 11.5 ■ POWER Up Method to Prompt Action Planning

The idea/solution: _____

Positives	Objections	What else?	Enhancements	Remedies
Positive outcomes of that idea:	Possible objections to that idea:	Additional ideas\solutions:	Ways to enhance those outcomes:	Ways to address those objections:

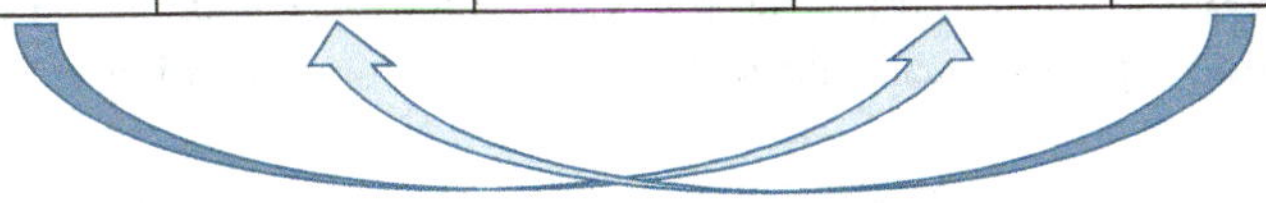

Strategic planning can be as fun as it is useful. And building in elements of culture (How do we all *want* to do things around here?) addresses the complete picture of what drives organizational success: the plans and the people. Highlighting what is amazing in your organization, what lofty and fantastic things you might achieve, and clarifying the ideal can add extraordinary energy to a strategic planning process. As a leader, it is about what you do and how you do it (recall Rule #1), all while making it about the organization's success and positive culture (Rule #2: It's not about you.). You will find that this balance continues to require your attention as you make your way through Chapter 12 on Leading a Team and Chapter 13 on Designing a Culture That Cares.

Leadership by Design

Design Principle: Immersion

Definition: A state of mental focus so intense that awareness of the *real* world is lost, generally resulting in a feeling of joy and satisfaction.

In Other Words: When you are so intensely engaged with something, time seems to fly by, and you really enjoy the activity.

For Example: Have you ever been so engrossed in a great movie that when it ends, you had to take a moment to remember where you were or what day it was? You may have had the same experience with a captivating book or a challenging role-playing video game or even while engaged in a sport. Everything else disappears, and you are solely focused on the task at hand.

For Leaders: Immersion often occurs when you have found the zone between too much and too little cognitive and perceptual challenge. In other words, your context and task are neither overwhelming nor boring; they are just right—capturing your focus and energy to the exclusion of all else. Consider experiences you have had with immersion—in a job, at a party, at a museum, on an amusement park ride. What elements contributed to your immersion?

Leaders can apply the principle of immersion to increase satisfaction and enjoyment, enhance focus and engagement, deepen learning, and guide motivation. Creating a culture with clear and appropriate goals, limited distractions, and immediate feedback with tasks in that possible-but-not-easy challenge zone will help achieve that immersive experience. Leaders should monitor, assess, and adjust elements of context and culture to find and fully utilize immersion as they design culture. You may need to remind followers to eat and go home—immersion is a powerful state.

CHAPTER SUMMARY

In this chapter, you have learned about the importance of culture from how individuals contribute to both organizational and societal culture. Organizational culture was defined, and the elements that make up the visible and invisible parts of culture were outlined. Additionally, you learned about differences between individuals based on societal culture. Individual and organizational values as they define culture and the organization's vision and mission were described. Finally, changing organizational culture and new tools for facilitating cultural design were outlined.

Culture surrounds you every day in many ways. Personally and professionally, you navigate between worlds with values that may or may not be in concert with your own. No two cultures are the same. Groups have different values; organizations differ in their visions, missions, and values; and most importantly, the people who belong to those groups and organizations differ in the backgrounds, skills, talents, and values they bring. Culture is something individuals rarely think about, even though it is everywhere and its roots run deep.[53] You are affected not only by the culture in the organizations to which you belong, but you acquire cultural roots from your family and groups, as well as society. Your own cultural roots run deep, are difficult to change, and are definitely influenced by where and how you spend your time.

Although organizational cultures are crafted by the beliefs and values of founding members, over time, they are influenced by the beliefs and values of organizational members. Much of organizational culture is the visible norms, behaviors, and artifacts, which are significantly influenced by the less visible personal values and the usually not visible at all cultural values and assumptions. All culture is influenced by context, which influences the differences between and among societal cultures. These differences are vitally important to understand when interacting in either a personal or business setting with individuals from around the world.

Everyone wants to feel comfortable within their groups. The emotional aspects of culture fit or misfit result from ensuring that your own values align with the organization's values. When you become a leader in your own organization, it is important to take the time to listen to your followers. Make sure you fully understand their values and beliefs and treat that culture with the same respect you would hope for your own.

Finally, you can design your culture, beginning with efforts to fully understand that includes mapping perceptions and expectations across eight scales. There are a variety of tools that offer very specific steps and activities. In some cases, these tools help design culture as part of addressing organizational change. In all cases, engaging the tools of mindful, purposeful strategic planning will help guide you and your followers from the *why, what, and how we do things* to impact *the way we do things around here*.

KEY TERMS

Appreciative Inquiry (p. 356)

Artifacts (p. 342)

Heroes (p. 344)

Mission (p. 351)

Organizational values (p. 348)

Process mapping (p. 356)

Rituals (p. 344)

Societal cultures (p. 343)

Stories (p. 343)

Strategic planning (p. 358)

SWOT analysis (p. 361)

> ## CORE™ ATTRIBUTE BUILDERS: BUILD NOW FOR
> ## FUTURE LEADERSHIP CHALLENGES

Attribute: Resilience and Engagement

Builder: Engage global events and persons

Many communities offer lots of opportunities for you to get involved with individuals from other countries, and through these opportunities, you can expand your cultural understanding. Many larger communities offer international cultural exchange programs for community members to visit other countries. Some communities have international festivals where local residents showcase their cultural background through food, costumes, music and dance, and exhibits—take the time to visit and learn about your community members from other countries. Additionally, assimilating into a new country can be difficult for individuals—take the time to volunteer to help teach English as a second language to a new international member in your community or assist in helping them navigate through your city. However you engage with members from other countries, make sure to listen and absorb all you can about their culture— you never know when understanding differences might work in your favor.

> ## CORE™ ATTRIBUTE BUILDERS: BUILD NOW FOR
> ## FUTURE LEADERSHIP CHALLENGES

Attribute: Confidence (cultural)

Builder: Create a cultural guidebook

Developing your awareness of your own and other cultures will enhance your ability and comfort when encountering new cultures. With that increased confidence, you are more likely to explore and engage other cultures, which will broaden your sources for perspectives, approaches, solutions, and ideas for innovation.

Part I—Start building your cultural competence by exploring a group or organization

Individually or with a small group of peers, identify a group—the more different from you, the better. Interact with and explore all you can about that group. Visit places they visit, eat what they eat, listen to what they talk about and how, interview a few individuals in that culture— immerse yourself in any way possible. As you do this, take notes. What are the written rules of behavior and the unwritten and unspoken norms? Compare your observations and insights to your own culture. You are building what is called *cultural competence*, which includes cultural knowledge, awareness, sensitivity, and ultimately the ability to effectively navigate and work with individuals in that culture.

Part II—Create a cultural guidebook

Organize your insights into a *guidebook* that you could hand to someone entering the culture you explored so they would be able to read it and understand what to do and not do in order to be successful. Show your guidebook to some of the individuals in that culture to get their feedback on its accuracy. Consider what you got right . . . and what you missed.

Take a moment to reflect on what in *your* culture others need to know in order to succeed. How can you best communicate your culture to others?

366   Module 4 • Design Culture and Community

SKILL BUILDER ACTIVITY

My Cultural Perception

First, examine your world: Look around your classroom right now. What artifacts—those things that you can see—do you see that represent the culture in this specific room? How is the room set up? What does that tell you about the culture in the room? What beliefs and values are represented by the individuals around you? Ask the instructor too. And what underlying assumptions—unconscious beliefs and values—exist? Ask those around you.

Second, examine someone else's world: Find an organization or a local business where you can visit and observe. A local coffee shop or other place where you can linger without disruption is ideal. As you engage as a customer, observe the work culture of those employed (or members of an organization). Can you describe *the way things are done around here*? How do individuals interact and work with (or against) one another? How does the culture of the employees differ from the culture the customer or visitor experiences?

Cultural Values Assessment

Take the following assessment of the values within a culture to which you belong (e.g., your workplace, your church, your team). Provide a brief answer to each question.

Do you take pride in the mission of your organization? How do you express that?

_____

Do you have a sense of urgency about the work to be done? How?

_____

Do you have a passion for your work? Describe in what way.

_____

Do you understand the way in which you are contributing to both your organization's success and society? Describe.

_____

Do you recognize that, although it is okay to make mistakes, you have to quickly learn from them? In what way do you learn from your mistakes?

_____

Do you promote teamwork, collaboration, and trust? Identify how you accomplish that.

_____

Do you understand the importance of stopping to fix broken processes?

_____

Do you understand the critical importance of honesty, integrity, and ethical considerations?

_____

Do you have a skill set that matches the tasks at hand? Describe.

Do you understand customer needs, the competitive market, and the need to capitalize on comparative advantages? How would you accomplish those?

Do you understand the importance of using good judgment in all situations?

Do you understand the importance of eliminating waste and inefficiencies?

Do you understand that high quality and continual innovation are everyone's responsibility? How do you engage in those?

Do you celebrate breakthroughs at all levels of the organization and encourage the joy and fun of solving problems, serving customers, and doing good?

Do you recognize the crucial importance of both personal renewal and organizational renewal strategies, all aimed at fostering agile, nimble, and adaptive flexibility?

Do you fight unnecessary bureaucracy and standard operating procedures that create bloat and kill spark?

Take a second look at the questions you just answered. Each of these items represents a design challenge for you as leader. Many represent multiple levels of leadership activity. For example, having a passion for your work can be designed in yourself, into your relationships with followers, and for others—all of which culminates in influencing culture. Identify the items that represent important challenges you would like to see addressed. Note how you might utilize the past 10 chapters of this book to address these different culture design challenges you face as a leader.

12 LEADING A TEAM

LEARNING OBJECTIVES

Upon completion of this chapter, the reader should be able to

12.1 Describe the difference between teams and groups

12.2 Compare various types of organizational team models

12.3 Formulate the essential elements needed for a great team

12.4 Apply intergroup dialogue techniques to team leadership

12.5 Interpret Tuckman's stages of group development

12.6 Describe the key activities of team leadership

12.7 Interpret the various roles that comprise an effective team

12.8 Contrast the differences between organizational, team, and individual issues that can arise in teams

---

Leadership by Design Model

Design Self
How can I design myself as a leader?

Design Relationships
As a leader, how can I design my relationships with others?

Design Others' Success
As a leader, how can I design success for others?

Design Culture
As a leader, how can i design the culture of my organization?

Design Future
As a leader, how can I innovate?

INTRODUCTION

It seems as if everywhere you look today, organizations are engaging in teamwork to accomplish organizational goals. At this point in your life, you have likely been a member of many different teams. Think back to a time when you were part of a team. Were you and the others focused on a common problem or goal? Did you have a choice as to who was part of the group? How did everyone relate and get along? What did the leader do that made the team more or less effective? As you recall, some teams seemed to work and some did not; some teams were fun and energizing, while others felt like a burden. What made the difference between those experiences? Would you have been better off working alone?

Even when there are no organized teams, groups will form in any organization or anywhere, for that matter. However, it is up to leaders to purposefully design those groups to create the most effective and best performing group—in other words, design and lead a *team*. A team is defined as two or more individuals aligned in a common purpose. Effective selection of team members for long- or short-term assignments provides the opportunity to bring the collective strengths of a group to organizational teams while simultaneously creating motivated performance and continuous improvement toward achieving organizational objectives.

Just as organizations have a culture, so do teams. This chapter highlights the distinctions and advantages of designing and leading a team. The chapter begins by distinguishing between a group and a team, and then it describes various types of teams, the stages of team development, and the very important roles that members play in the effective functioning of a team. Finally, the notion of team leadership is introduced, examining several models of team leadership, your and others' role on the team, and how to take corrective actions when things go awry.

Leadership That Makes a Difference

Danny Iny and Mirasee

Successful entrepreneur Danny Iny, founder and CEO of Mirasee, successfully navigated an Internet marketing company from nothing to over $5 million in just 5 years.[1] Mirasee focuses on business training programs, calling their customers *students* and training programs *education* and *courses*. Mirasee is driven by six core values: empowerment through learning and growth; enthusiasm and positivity; innovation and adaptability; support, appreciation, and humility; openness and transparency; and partnership and ownership. The company is committed to seeing that the companies it serves focus first on *their* audience, on making a difference second, and finally, on profits. Mirasee is a contemporary company, whose team conducts day-to-day business operations from around the globe—on four continents, in six countries, and in five different time zones. In those 5 years, Iny has mastered the art of successfully engaging and keeping connected with the members of his virtual team, all prior to the necessity of virtual teams during the pandemic!

In an article on navigating successful remote teams, Iny answered the questions many of us would ask regarding how to keep connected in a virtual organization.[2] He offered ten suggestions to keep the members of his team connected with one another—they communicate daily, weekly, and monthly and actually convene in person on a periodic basis—noting these frequent connections as key to their team's success. Each week begins with Danny's Monday morning email, which highlights examples from team members who have exemplified one of the company's core values. Each day begins with team members checking in on their messaging app to see what was accomplished the previous day, see what is upcoming for the current day, and make requests for their work needs from team members. Additionally, individuals instant message each other throughout the day to ask and answer questions, share information, or simply to share a joke.

Additionally, the Mirasee team has weekly all-team meetings via web conferencing. At the beginning of the meeting, each team member gets an opportunity to share, and each meeting concludes with an open session to ask questions of Danny. Periodically, extracurricular team meetings happen where members *get together* via web conferencing to chat over lunch or discuss topics of interest to members who choose to join in.

Each month, the chief financial officer provides a financial report to the team, which provides an incentive for all team members to work toward the company's success. Additionally, the team is committed to learning, so one day per month, they focus on the entire team learning a skill. Finally, once every eight months or so, they gather all team members from around the world to connect in person in order to "get away from distractions to brainstorm, deliberate ideas, and devise strategies."[3] As leader, Danny Iny has created a successful organization in the world of virtual teams. There is a lot to be learned from his ability to keep his staff members connected, engaged, and working together effectively as a team.

mirasee.com

JUST WHAT *IS* A TEAM?

LEARNING OBJECTIVE

12.1 Describe the difference between teams and groups.

Growing up, your experience with groups and teams might have included being on a sports or academic team or maybe you worked on some group projects in classes or were part of a club. Some of those groups were bigger than others, more formal than others, and felt more connected than others. In any case, you got an introduction to what the future might hold for you in working with teams, where individuals come together with specific knowledge, talents, or gifts and work hard to achieve for the team. In college and work, you are likely to experience working in teams—from coming together for a short time, such as one class period, or a much longer time frame, such as a months-long project. When groups are formed in classes, your professor is providing you with the opportunity to experience the benefits of and learn the skills necessary for teamwork that you will need when you start your career upon graduation.

As far back as the late 1990s, leadership guru Warren Bennis commented that "the problems we face are too complex to be solved by any one person or any one discipline. Our only chance is to bring people together from a variety of backgrounds and disciplines who can refract a problem through the prism of complementary minds allied in common purpose."[4] The complexity of the world today has only magnified, needing solutions with broader viewpoints from multiple individuals. Bennis noted that "the more I look at the history of business, government, the arts, and the sciences the clearer it is that few great accomplishments are ever the work of a single individual."[5] Teams serve organizations much more effectively than a mere collection of individuals. This is a very important leadership lesson.

Teams have the distinct advantage of bringing synergy to a task, which would otherwise not occur. **Synergy** is defined as a group's energy, where the output of the entire group is greater than the combined output of each individual. That is to say, the output of a team far exceeds the sum of what each individual on the team can provide. When team members work collaboratively toward a shared vision and have developed into a team, each individual produces more in the team environment and the total outcome is greater still. Why does this happen? Team members provide mutual support for one another and contribute to continuous improvement and innovation.

Team synergy gives all members the opportunity to provide input.
©iStockphoto.com/Wavebreakmedia

The definition of leadership combined with the process of problem-solving comprises a process made more effective with a team. Leadership is the process of influencing others toward a common vision. Leaders intentionally design teams to effectively and efficiently meet the needs of the organization. An effective team often leads itself, with members influencing each other and reinforcing the common vision. Teams also solve problems more effectively. They mutually *understand* the vision of the organization, they utilize multiple brains and perspectives to *imagine* solutions to the problem at hand, and they complement one another to *implement* a solution to an issue or problem.

Today's organizational leaders need to be on top of or ahead of the rapid pace of change, and they need individuals who have the flexibility to move in and out of teams as necessary to accomplish the work of the organization. In fact, employers purposefully look for individuals who have teamwork skills. Many of these skills you have learned about in this textbook, such as decision-making, problem-solving, and creativity. Many more skills are critical to working with an effective team, such as clear and direct communication; critical thinking; collaboration; and trust, support, and respect for one another.[6] Employers want graduates who are prepared for the challenges they will face as new employees, and being an effective team member is top among them.

Teams Versus Groups

A group is defined as a collection of individuals who are coordinating their work for some reason or another. As contrasted with a team, groups of individuals have no mutual accountability, and they may likely work for personal gain over group gain and each member has their own definition of *winning*. There are no shared consequences and no shared accountability.[7] While some groups may have a common end, group members work either individually or with each other; however, the ultimate focus is on "what's in it for me," without regard for the group as a whole. In fact, individual members often simply share information only so that each person's individual performance can be enhanced.

Team was defined earlier as a group of individuals with a common purpose, aligned with collective goals for the good of the entire team. Teams are "aligned toward a common purpose. They are guided by shared leadership and share a mutual understanding—and therefore accountability—of team roles, responsibilities, the scope of work to be accomplished and the purpose for which the team exists."[8] Think about the groups of individuals with whom you work in various settings—at work, in school, at home, or elsewhere. Are they a group or a team?

One difference between groups and teams is that groups designate a leader, who holds authority and power, while teams often have **shared leadership**[9] where individuals share authority and power and one may take a leadership role for a specific time and then another steps up to lead; or an individual may take a leadership role depending, on the task at hand and on their areas of expertise, so that leadership is dependent on a specific task at any different moment. Importantly, shared leadership increases team performance.[10] Maybe you have experienced shared leadership in a team for a specific task in class—the team comes together and designates one individual to take the lead for a specific part of the project because of their expertise in that area while, at another time, someone else takes the lead because of their knowledge. You have engaged in shared leadership in the team. Shared leadership is different from team roles. **Team roles** comprise the functions that each individual plays in the team (e.g, technical, interpersonal). Team roles are often discussed and agreed upon in advance, whereas shared leadership is more dynamic and emergent based on the current needs of the group.

Members of a group have individual accountability for completing group tasks, while team members have **shared accountability** for setting and meeting outcomes for the team.[11] In fact, for groups, the reasons for the specific work of the group reflect the purposes of the organization wherein they operate within the boundaries of the organization. However, members of teams often develop their own specific vision and/or purpose and are not constrained by organizational boundaries. Teams have a shared sense of mission and collective responsibility for carrying out that mission. After team members set the overall mission for the project and take shared responsibility for the outcome, members outline the specific tasks, assign *leads* for different parts of the project, and meet regularly to share progress. All team members are constantly cognizant of the big picture of the task at hand.

The appropriate size for a team seems to be a challenging question. What is the right number of members? Many authors suggest that between 3 to 10 but no more than 12 is a good and manageable size for a team. Larger than that, and it becomes difficult to find time to bring all members together. Moreover, members start to form subgroups, which can have a detrimental effect on the work of the team. Here is an amusing rule of thumb from Amazon's Jeff Bezos: "If I see more than two pizzas for lunch, the team is too big."[12]

It is very important that the team leader carefully select team members for the skills and talents they bring to the table. Designing your team means selecting team members intentionally and strategically so all members understand their role on the team. Members need to trust one another and feel safe enough to open up to all members of the team. If individuals have been included as a *favor* to the boss, people may not feel they can open up and trust the entire team.

The 2020–2021 pandemic created some real strains on teams. In discussing what strategies helped successful teams during the pandemic, Lindsey Pollak found that keeping an open dialogue between leaders and team members through an "Ask me anything" session helped ally fears. Additionally, she suggested that team members be allowed to share feelings and concerns regarding the new normal work environment.[13]

REFLECTION QUESTIONS

Besides taking this class, what are you doing to expand your team experience and develop your teamwork skills? Are you involved in clubs and organizations at school or in your community?

TYPES OF TEAMS

LEARNING OBJECTIVE

12.2 Compare various types of organizational team models.

Having experienced a team or two may lead you to believe that there exists only a couple of types of teams. However, in the workplace, there are a number of different types of teams that you may encounter. Primary among those are functional; cross-functional; self-directed or self-managed; permanent and temporary; and contemporary teams, such as virtual and high performing. Each type of team has and serves a specific purpose. Moreover, different types may be more appropriate at different times or in different environments, depending on the situation and tasks to be performed.

Functional teams generally include department leaders and their subordinates. These types of teams typically operate within traditional organizational hierarchies and are structured along departmental lines. Leadership styles within these groups vary according to organizational and team needs.

Cross-functional teams are comprised of members from different departments who may be selected as a representative of that particular department or due to their areas of expertise. This type of team structure allows organizations to assemble teams that are quickly able to respond to problems or issues within the organization. Moreover, with such diverse organizational representation, members get a broader view of problems and their potential solutions.

Self-directed or self-managed teams are similar to cross-functional teams and are comprised of members from across department types within the organization. The primary difference is that self-directed team members take responsibility for the quality of the work process and the sharing of management and leadership functions, and they are involved in the training, hiring, and disciplining of group members. Self-management is related to high levels of productivity and engagement.[14]

Permanent teams are those that work together continuously on various projects either simultaneously or consecutively. These teams can be composed of members with similar areas of expertise or with various complementary backgrounds for the projects to which they are assigned.

Temporary teams are comprised of members who come together for the specific purpose of completing a task or project and then disband when the work is complete, returning to their regular positions within the organization. They, too, can have similar or varied areas of skills and expertise, depending on the task at hand.

Virtual teams that are geographically dispersed have emerged as a result of today's mobile, global, and technological society. Virtual teams pose significant challenges for organizations. Many of the challenges that are present in traditional teams may be even more pronounced in virtual settings. Virtual organizations and virtual teams are the results of efforts to look for novel ways to manage rapid change and global reach, with the advantage of hiring the best talent from anywhere in the world. Specific to internationally dispersed teams, issues surrounding cultural differences (see Chapter 11) need to be top of mind for leaders, and attention must be paid to educating team members on both understanding and capitalizing on these cultural differences.[15]

As a result of the 2020–2021 pandemic, the necessity and use of virtual teams expanded dramatically. Researchers find that communication and trust were the most important factors for virtual team performance, arising from leaders who create conditions for empowerment and team cohesion.[16,17]

High-performing teams are those teams that display extraordinary effort, productivity, and consistently meet their goals. As the name implies, the results-focused teams perform well beyond that of an average team. Researchers[18] have found these important characteristics of high-performing teams: purpose and values; empowerment; defined relationships; flexibility; optimal productivity; recognition and appreciation; and morale. Moreover, trust, clear communication, defined roles and responsibilities, engaged leadership, and collective goals are all important to a high-performing team.[19] Additionally, "high performance teams don't just happen—they are developed and nurtured . . . [they] take the combined efforts of a visionary leader, willing and competent team members, and a facilitator with expertise in team building."[20]

REFLECTION QUESTIONS

Of the types of teams that have been outlined, which are used most frequently in your college or work setting. Are they working well? Would another team structure work better?

ENVISIONING A GREAT TEAM

LEARNING OBJECTIVE

12.3 Formulate the essential elements needed for a great team.

Teams come together in a variety of ways. The organization may need to solve a specific problem, develop a new product, solve a complex task, or work with a specific client. Each of these needs requires that a leader craft a team based on skills needed or temperaments necessary for a specific project. Effective teams need to be comprised of members with complementary skills in the following three categories: technical or functional expertise; problem-solving and decision-making skills; and interpersonal skills—in short, task, procedural, and social-emotional roles.[21] While attempting to maintain an ideal team size of between 3 and 12, team members normally will be selected who are adept at *several* different skills (e.g., problem-solving and interpersonal; technical and decision-making).

How Do Teams Come Together, and What Makes Them Excellent?

Many individuals can describe their experience with an excellent team. The difficulty with that description is that it is from their perspective, which is likely to highlight those characteristics most meaningful and relevant to that team member. You will find many lists profiling the characteristics of an excellent team. Four well-established profiles are listed in Table 12.1. Several foundational elements are generally agreed upon by researchers and practitioners: a meaningful mission that is shared and understood by all members; a climate of respect and trust; clear, agreed-upon roles and processes; external organizational support; and attentive leadership that designs success.

TABLE 12.1 ■ Table 12.1 Profiling Characteristics

Hackman (2010)	Larson and LaFasto (1989)
• Teams must be real. Everyone needs to know who is in and who is out. • Teams need a compelling direction. • Teams need enabling structures. • Teams need a supportive organization. • Teams need expert coaching. Too often organizations only focus on individual coaching.[22]	• A clear, elevating goal • A results-driven structure • Competent members • Unified commitment • A collaborative climate • Standards of excellence • External support and recognition • Principled leadership.[23]

Silva (2016)	Crawford (2016)
• Common purpose • Clear roles • Trust • Solid relationships • Competent leadership • Effective processes • Excellent communication[24]	• Embrace excellence • Accountable to each other • Excellent listening • Collaborative delegating • Flexible, adaptable • Ok with making mistakes • Sense of humor[25]

> ### MYTH OR REALITY
>
> #### A talented leader and talented team members will result in a great team.
>
> Myth and Myth. Effective teams are carefully, thoughtfully designed. Leaders create conditions for success by encouraging collaboration, listening, setting a clear vision and goals, admitting one's flaws, building relationships, developing others, and complimenting the team often.[26] No amount of leader talent can make up for failing to design appropriate conditions for success.

There is indeed an *I* in team—it is called *individuals*. While the common sentiment of emphasizing the *we* aspect of shared vision, common purpose, and collaborative effort is important, you cannot overlook the individuals who comprise the team, both during the advance design of the team as well as during the team's work. Individuals have different perspectives, needs, strengths, ways of communicating, levels of investment, means of influence, and personal goals outside of work. Maximizing the engagement and enthusiasm of each individual enhances the team outcome.

The other *I* in team might be called *irritating innovation*. Although teams have a specific purpose or problem, typically a more innovative solution is preferred. Innovation, however, is not fostered by consensus, common perspectives, or compromising collaboration. Rather, as you recall from Chapter 8 on creativity, innovative ideas emerge when individuals are forced to see differently. Teams comprised of purposefully differing perspectives are likely to conflict, and from that conflict springs innovation. Controlled conflict to catalyze innovation happens when leaders design the team, focusing on the roles, rules, and elevated common goals within which team members operate.

When creating a team, whether it is for a project for school or work, it is important to make sure to clearly define each of the following elements for your team members. The more closely aligned members are to understanding and embracing them, the better performance your team will have on its tasks, purpose, or outcomes.

Key elements for teams include

- *A meaningful mission that is shared and understood by all members.* Teams need a common purpose, specifically one that is clear and compelling. Team members must have a clear understanding of the reasons why their task is being given to a team (rather than just an individual)—teams are the means to an end, not the end in and of itself. This must be clearly articulated to the team by organizational leaders or crafted by members of the team themselves. It is critical not to begin the work of the team before the purpose is clearly articulated and understood by all members.[27]

- *A climate of respect and trust.* Trust forms one of the most important foundations of teams. As such, "being trustworthy means keeping confidences; carrying out assignments and following through on promises and commitments; supporting others when they need support; giving both honest, positive feedback and helpful constructive feedback; being present at team meetings; and being available to help other team members,"[28] in effect, being predictable and consistent. Trusting relationships in teams allows members to openly communicate and not feel threatened by other members.

This openness of communication is what allows teams to become highly competent and successful. It is not necessary that team members be friends but simply that they have respectful, trusting relationships where they know that all members of the team have the best interest of the team at heart and they can trust one another to do the right thing.

- *Clear, agreed-upon roles and processes.* Critical to the effective functioning of the team is an understanding on the part of each member as to why they have been selected to be a member of the team (i.e., what unique skills and abilities they bring to the table). Each person needs an understanding of the role that every other team member plays and their skills and abilities. Leveraging the strengths of each team member together will increase the likelihood of a successful outcome for the project. Additionally, highly effective teams function because they have established effective processes. Consider any athletic team sport. The team works many hours in advance of the game to craft each of its plays with precise processes and then practices their moves over and over again. Organizational team processes include decision-making, problem-solving, innovation, project management, and many more.

- *Attentive leadership that designs success.* Teams need attentive, effective leadership to design the team experience and launch. Attentive leadership then continuously ensures that the group is working within their agreed-upon roles and rules, has the resources they need, and is heading on the right path toward the mission.

Leaders must particularly attend to the team communication process. Excellent communication facilitates the work of the team. The more efficient the communication process, the more expeditiously the team can accomplish its work. Team members get straight to the point and say what they mean—members of the team do not waste time with beating around the bush or lack of straight talk, which can lead to miscommunication or misunderstandings. They work hard at making communication effective and efficient and *meta-communicate*. That is, they talk about the process of communication to ensure that all members are on the same page.

Experts Beyond the Text

INSIGHTFUL LEADERS KNOW ABOUT . . . HUMAN CAPITAL MANAGEMENT (HCM)

Human Capital Management and Leadership: Investing in Your Human Resources

By Lauren Miltenberger, Villanova University, and Ralph A. Gigliotti, Rutgers University

Have you ever thought about the term "human resources"? Many organizations have an individual or an entire department called Human Resources (or HR), but consider the literal words: human beings—people—as a resource. HR functions typically administer all the organizational aspects of employees: Workforce planning and job analysis; employee recruitment and selection; compensation, benefits, and employee engagement; assessing and managing employee performance; and employee training and development. But what if HR retooled activities toward their literal aim—to maximize the value of the individuals in whom the organization invests? How would you treat followers if you were always reminded of their great value—not just as persons but as a present and potential profit generator?

Chapter 12 • Leading a Team   **379**

Human capital management (HCM) is an employee-centered approach for assessing individual performance, predicting organizational results, and guiding the investments made in the area of human resources.[29] In the HCM model, leaders strive to engage employees in meaningful work experiences, support their employees in achieving specific goals, and encourage their learning and development. Cultivating positive relationships with employees is rewarding for the leader and highly advantageous for the organization at large. Research suggests that companies with an HCM approach to employee relations produce higher financial returns and value to their shareholders.[30]

Great HCM leaders understand the needs of their employees, emphasize the importance of skill development, and seek to create a positive work environment that both engages the employee and contributes to their ultimate success. Leaders can cultivate a human capital environment by doing the following:

- Focus on the strengths and strive to understand how to balance the skills and needs of the employee with the competencies and skills needed for the job.
- Recognize both extrinsic and intrinsic rewards: recognize and celebrate individual achievements, promote continual learning, draw connections to mission, encourage democratic decision-making, and build positive relationships grounded in trust and respect.
- Devote time and attention to the development of workplace plans, hiring strategies, and recruitment and selection techniques—all of which are aligned with the mission of the unit, department, and organization.
- Recognize the value of performance management. Instead of using evaluations as once-a-year opportunities to discuss employee performance, use them as real-time benchmarks to connect each employee to the larger purpose of the organization, as well as to co-create goals that clarify expectations and outcomes.
- Above all, demonstrate empathy and work with each employee to help develop strengths and achieve excellence.

As you learn more about building a great team and the mindful design of organizational culture, consider the extraordinary HCM impact of making the shift from seeing employees as something to manage versus resources that can exponentially grown and produce returns on investment.

Shared Vision, Values, and Culture—Key to Team Success

Teams need to establish their vision, values, and culture for the team. These provide both a shared purpose and reason for existence, as well as assist in keeping team members aligned with the same values and moving in the same direction toward the same goal. You have learned about the overall organizational vision, values, and culture elsewhere in this book. As you may recall, those terms were defined like this:

- Vision: An aspirational image that provides short- and long-term direction for an organization and its members
- Values: Beliefs or ideals that guide a person's behavior
- Culture: Shared values and assumptions by organizational (or group) members; the way we do things around here

Notice that all three have something very important in common—all of them are highly influential in motivating and guiding individual behavior. If team members do not embrace a common purpose and performance goals, they revert to subpar performance. Additionally, common values are especially important in virtual teams when individuals are not engaging in day-to-day activities with one another and can easily lose sight of the common goal.

> **Leadership by Design**
>
> *Design Principle:* Accessibility
>
> *Definition:* Objects and environments should be designed to be usable without modification by as many people as possible.
>
> *In Other Words:* Can everyone perceive, understand, and operate within the context, organization, and culture?
>
> *For Example:* Online portals allow everyone to receive the same information efficiently and participate fully, no matter what their physical capabilities or geographic location.
>
> *For Leaders:* Accessibility is generally associated with wheelchair ramps and other physical characteristics, but the principle really comprises a much broader range in what it means to have access. Accessibility is a very powerful design principle that also applies to designing the culture and community of your team. When those on your team are able to perceive the culture, understand and operate with it, and make a few mistakes without getting too off-track, then you as leader have designed an accessible culture. As the team grows larger, how can you ensure you remain accessible to a diverse group of people? What must you consider when designing a community where information and social interaction flow unimpeded throughout the organization?
>
>
>
> ©iStock.com/goalkeeper

Teams also have a culture. If you have ever joined a well-established team, you felt that culture right away as you tried to figure out those invisible rules of behavior. While some team

Chapter 12 ● Leading a Team   **381**

cultures mirror the culture of the larger organization, others create and live their own culture. In fact, Schumpeter observed that "teams work best if their members have a strong common culture."[31] Moreover, in virtual teams, where members represent cultures from around the world, expectations and understandings can differ, requiring extra time and attention to make sure that all members understand and are clear on issues and goals facing the team. Refer back to Chapter 11 to refresh on the importance of culture in the organization.

Team Charter: Agreeing on the Basics

Your team will function with greater efficiency and success if the specifics of the team's purpose, individual roles and responsibilities, and other "rules" are discussed and outlined in writing. The team charter is done in advance of the team getting to work. Crafting a team charter ensures that all team members have an opportunity to consider, contribute, and ultimately agree to the specifics regarding how the group operates. Members will know why the team exists (its mission and objectives) and each member's responsibilities toward that end. Importantly, a team charter should always be crafted specifically for that team's explicit purpose.

Every team is unique and will differ based on the individuals, nature of the assignments, and depth and breadth of responsibilities. Nonetheless, there are some common elements that can guide the discussion and development of your team charter:

Inputs
1. Identify team's mission, purpose, expected outcomes/results, and scope of project (specifically what is included/excluded)

Process
1. Develop goals/milestones/timeline and identify what success will look like
2. Identify key stakeholders
3. Identify team member roles
4. Create member accountabilities—the 3 Ws (<u>Who</u> is responsible for <u>What</u> by <u>When</u>)
5. Craft team norms
6. Outline decision-making/problem-solving methods
7. Define meeting management (see Running an Efficient and Effective Meeting)
8. Create a communication plan (both internally among team members and externally within and outside the organization) to include project tracking and updates on progress
9. Build working relationships
10. Periodically give and receive feedback
11. Work to create effective working relationships with team leader(s)
12. Understand and assess the external environment

Outputs
1. Prepare final deliverable and execute
2. Team process assessment

Signature and approval page for all members and supervisors to sign.

Upon completion of the team's project, be sure to evaluate both the team's process effectiveness as well as the outcome of the project itself.

382 Module 4 ● Design Culture and Community

DEI BY DESIGN

LEARNING OBJECTIVE
12.4   Apply intergroup dialogue techniques to team leadership.

Designing a great team is a dynamic process that is highly dependent on the interactions between members and between leader and members. Consider again the key elements for teams: meaningful and shared mission, climate of respect and trust, agreed-upon roles and processes, and attentive leadership. Leaders can create conditions where all group members feel included and equitably treated, helping the key elements of a great team more easily emerge and grow.

Intergroup dialogue (IGD) is a technique team leaders use to manage within-team and across-team interactions. Defined broadly, IGD is an intentional group interaction designed to promote safe expressions of anger, fear, and resentment (among other feelings) about the unfairness, inequality, and inequity that surrounds us all.[32] The goal of IGD-based interactions is to communicate more effectively across social differences, develop new and better listening skills, and develop shared meaning around leadership and followership in an inherently imbalanced world. When applied to team leadership, IGD has the potential to transform people and their communities as well as resolve long-standing conflicts between groups in society and create new pathways toward cooperation and collaboration for the common good.

Producing healthy and productive IGD involves four stages: setting an environment for dialogue; developing a common base; exploring questions, issues, and conflicts; and moving from dialogue to action.[33] *Setting the dialogue environment* involves establishing the purpose, mission, and structure of conversations. Through this process, leaders (or IGD facilitators) start to build the trust and safety needed to have these difficult but necessary discussions. In this part of the process, leaders also develop the guidelines for dialogue as well as introduce, describe, and clarify ground rules and norms. To model brave vulnerability, IGD leaders can also disclose their personal beliefs about the topics at hand and share experiences that inform their opinions.

Setting the dialogue environment is an ongoing process that naturally tends toward *developing a common base.* In this second stage of IGD, all participants regardless of role explore their own beliefs, assumptions, and expectations around the dialogue topic, with special attention to the commonalities and differences among those present. Dialogue members are also encouraged to listen without judgment to build understanding across differences. Through this open sharing and active listening, members can negotiate meaning to develop a common language to guide the rest of the dialogue. Discussion leaders actively question participants about their perceptions around the problem, issue, or topic at hand to start naming and mapping relationships and obstacles. Everyone contributes to this common base by offering their perspectives, owning their biases, and revising their perceptions based on feedback from others.

Developing a common base for IGD is messy work and necessitates an *exploration of questions, issues, or conflicts.* Much like in the previous stage, this enhanced exploration calls for even greater bravery, vulnerability, and trust. The intergroup conversation continues to identify sources of conflict, in- and out-group tensions, and systemic barriers to inequality. This is also when members can begin expressing hope toward a fairer and more just future. The map that has been built continues to be refined and framed by identifying the policies, procedures, and practices that allow problematic circumstances to persist. What if-style scenarios can be generated to begin reconsidering relationships and communication patterns necessary for social change to occur and for social justice to thrive.

Chapter 12 • Leading a Team   **383**

Finally, IGD involves *moving from dialogue to action*. Here, the dialogue formally shifts focus from how things are to how they can be. Conversations center on transferring what was learned together into new and different daily behaviors. Alliances toward change are crafted, and action plans are developed. Each participant bears some responsibility to enact agreed-upon changes with appropriate individual and collective accountability. Although IGD is a complex process, filled with the potential for discomfort, stress, and pain, effective team leaders practice and refine the skills necessary to manage circumstances in order to design conditions where they, and others, can thrive.

FROM GROUP TO TEAM: STAGES OF DEVELOPMENT

LEARNING OBJECTIVE
12.5   Interpret Tuckman's stages of group development.

As individuals work together as a group, they inevitably move through various stages of development (much like you did when you were growing up). Leaders and team members who understand these developmental stages and what to expect can design ways to navigate those challenges more effectively and move the team to its next level more quickly. Sometimes the team can get stuck in one stage, sometimes it moves forward and then back again, and sometimes it works through the stages sequentially. The best team development is when everyone recognizes that there *are* developmental stages, *what* they are, and *how* to move through each one and on to the crucial stage of getting the work of the team completed. Finally, when the project is over, team members move on, either back to their regular positions or on to the next task.

Tuckman's Stages of Group Development

Tuckman's stages of group development stand as one of the most used and useful models describing how groups commonly move from strangers to team.[34] Originally conceived as four stages (forming, storming, norming, and performing), in a follow-up analysis, Tuckman and Jensen added a final stage (adjourning).[35]

In the first stage, **forming,** group members come together and behave in a very tentative way while trying to understand the task, the interpersonal dynamics, and each other. He referred to this as the stage of *testing and dependency*. The next stage, **storming,** is where individuals are in *conflict* as they attempt to find their place in the team and gain an understanding of the task, rules, and roles at hand. The third stage, **norming,** is where *cohesion and consensus* come together and teams establish their mission, goals, responsibilities, and culture. The fourth stage is the **performing** stage, which Tuckman indicated included *functional role relatedness,* where members attend to their work and their interpersonal skills and celebrate accomplishments.

Adjourning, the final stage, occurs when the work of the group is completed and the group as presently composed disperses. During this stage, members may mourn having to disband.[36]

As individuals and the group move through each stage of development, a number of needs must be addressed. Because individuals will behave in a manner that meets their own needs, a group will muddle through each stage. However, as stated at the outset, leaders can facilitate a group's progress (and thus their performance) by understanding those needs and taking action to address them. Table 12.2 lists the needs at each stage of development. What specific activities could you do to address any of the needs either before or during each stage?

384 Module 4 ● Design Culture and Community

TABLE 12.2 ■ Table 12.2 Needs at Different Stages of Development			
		As Leader, How Could You Facilitate?	
Stage	Individual Need	Before the Stage	During the Stage
Forming	Understand the mission and vision Channel excitement of new project Allay fears of uncertainty Get to know others Understand culture and norms Understand their role and how I fit		
Storming	Assurance that my contributions are noticed, appreciated, and important Understand and address individual differences Allay the uncertainty of others Revisit mission and remember that progress takes time Refocus goals Acknowledge frustration and establish trust		
Norming	Elaborate on true feelings and ideas Capitalize on differences Deepen trust and engagement with others Utilize critique for individual progress Benchmark team progress		
Performing	Enhance team performance Enhance engagement with others Expand individual role and enrich others' work Acknowledge and celebrate success Reestablish goals and next steps Assess and address internal and external changes		
Adjourning	Acknowledge relationships and connections with others Celebrate and archive accomplishments Allay impending fear of loss and feelings of sadness Understand my next steps		

REFLECTION QUESTIONS

Think about the last time you were in a group . . . maybe it was in class, maybe it was the start of the new school year, or maybe it was a new job; do you remember moving through Tuckman's various stages of group development? If your team ended—did you mourn the loss?

LEADING AND BEING A TEAM

> **LEARNING OBJECTIVE**
>
> 12.6 Describe the key activities of team leadership.

It is important to understand the difference between being a leader and leading a team. Where a leader generally oversees and directs the work of others, the team leader is an integral part of the team, participating in the work of the team—in many cases, this makes the team leader a leader among equals. Team leaders are principled leaders who show respect for team members and support an action-oriented, decision-making environment where team members are valued and encouraged.[37]

Models of Team Leadership

Leaders of great groups share four traits: They "provide direction and meaning; generate and sustain trust; display a bias toward action, risk taking, and curiosity; [and] are purveyors of hope."[38] Note how each of the four could facilitate a group working through the stages of development outlined in the previous section. For example, when leaders provide direction and meaning to followers in a variety of ways and often, individuals maintain the direction of

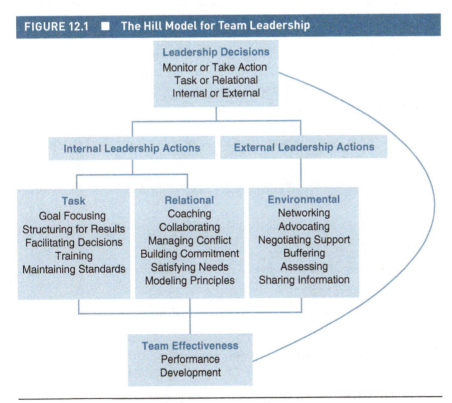

FIGURE 12.1 ■ The Hill Model for Team Leadership

Source: Hill, S. E. K. (2016). Team leadership. In P. G. Northouse (Ed.), *Leadership: Theory and practice* (7th ed., p. 367). Thousand Oaks, CA: SAGE.

their work, the vision as shared is reinforced, minor relationships and communication issues are put in perspective, and followers feel that the leader is attentive and invested. A number of leadership theories, models, or styles work well for team leadership, including transformational (Chapter 10), servant (Chapter 13), and authentic (Chapter 16), which all focus on working closely with others.

One model specifically focused on leading a team is the Hill Model for Team Leadership (see Figure 12.1). This model frames the actions necessary for ensuring team effectiveness. Hill's model specifically delineates the decisions or actions necessary at the leadership level for the team to effectively problem solve at each decision level. As a team's agenda unfolds, the leader faces many issues and challenges. Hill's model directs the leader to ask three initial questions:

1. Should I simply monitor the situation or take action?

2. If taking action is necessary, does the most useful action address an internal or external aspect?

3. If the action should be internal, would the most useful action focus on tasks or relationships?

As you can see in the model, the answers to those three questions lead to a short menu of areas that might be the solution to the present issue. Hill's model is particularly useful in that it guides a leader to more accurately assess an issue before acting and highlights the idea that taking no action and simply monitoring can also sometimes be an effective answer.

Another model for effective team leadership provides seven drivers of success for teams. Leaders and team members need to focus on the following key drivers and fundamental questions that inform successful teams and team leadership:

Driver Fundamental Question

1. Capability: Do we have the right people with the right mix of knowledge, skills, and other attributes?

2. Cooperation: Do team members possess the right beliefs and attitudes about their team?

3. Coordination: Are team members exhibiting the necessary teamwork behaviors for team success?

4. Communication: Do team members communicate effectively with each other and with people outside the team?

5. Cognition: Do team members possess a shared understanding about key factors, such as priorities, roles, and vision?

6. Coaching: Does the leader and/or team members demonstrate the necessary leadership behaviors?

7. Conditions: Is the context in which the team operates favorable for performing effectively (e.g., ample resources, supportive culture).[39]

YOUR AND OTHERS' ROLE ON THE TEAM: WHAT MAKES A GOOD TEAM MEMBER?

LEARNING OBJECTIVE
12.7 Interpret the various roles that comprise an effective team.

Over the course of this chapter, you have been asked numerous times to think back on your experience with teams. Similar to much of leadership, leading teams is about how you can influence others, and that is most effectively accomplished (or thwarted) by how someone feels. If you felt lousy about a team experience, reflecting on why and what made it feel that way invariably advances your understanding and practice of leadership. Thinking again about your experience with teams, would you say you were a good team member? Why or why not? Who on those teams would you characterize as a good team member or who not? You might have said a good team member is someone who gets along with everyone, builds bridges, contributes great effort, or has some skill that makes a difference. Take a moment to reflect, discuss, and write a quick list of good and not-so-good team member characteristics.

The assets you think you bring to a team can often be different from what the team thinks you bring. As you consider your strengths and what you *could* bring to the team, you realize that individual attributes are more complicated than a short list of characteristics. The attributes of a good team member are dependent on what the team needs and who else is on the team and what they bring. In other words, what you might recall as your strength on a team may likely be your strength *in that particular role on that particular team.* That is why designing your team is such a critical activity for the leader.

One way of categorizing attributes is to separate the task from the people and process. LaFasto and Larson found that team members' abilities and behaviors matter in two areas:

1. Working knowledge factors
   - Experience (practical knowledge)
   - Problem-solving ability (clarifying, bringing them into focus, getting them understood, developing strategies for overcoming)

2. Teamwork factors
   - Openness: The basic ingredient for team success (willing to deal with problems, surface issues that need to be discussed, help create an environment where people are free to say what's on their minds, and promote open exchange of ideas—these folks are effective communicators)
   - Supportiveness
   - Action orientation
   - Personal style[40]

As noted earlier, team member selection can be based on a variety of factors, but it is critical that you have a good mix of content, process, and people members. In other words, individuals who know and are skilled at the task to be accomplished, those who understand and can facilitate the process, and those who are skilled in emotional and social intelligence—working well with, among, and between others. Many team members will likely have some of each, but leaders should strive to identify and design a complementary mix. A number of instruments provide insight into individual strengths, including the Myers-Briggs Type Indicator® (MBTI®), Multiple Intelligences, StrengthsFinder, DISC®, and the Big Five, to name a few.[41]

What Strengths Do I Bring to This Group?

This is a great time for you to revisit your strengths, in this case, what attributes you might bring to a team. You may want to take one or more of the assessments listed in the preceding paragraph and find out more about yourself and your own preferences for interacting with others. Having a richer picture of yourself is also very helpful for understanding the dynamics that occur in teams. For example, one assessment instrument that has been popular for quite some time, the MBTI®, assesses 16 different personality preferences along four dimensions: extraversion/introversion, sensing/intuition, thinking/feeling, and judging/perceiving. Knowing how you and your teammates see and interact with the world allows you to more accurately find the best fitting roles for each person, as well as explain and problem-solve when the team seems not to be working.

Likewise, the Gallup StrengthsFinder (SF) explained in Chapter 3 can bring a more specific analysis of who is bringing what strength to your team.[42] The 34 strengths identified by SF will fall into one of four leadership-focused categories: executing, influencing, relationship building, and strategic thinking. Will the *ideal* team have individuals who have strengths in each of those categories? Maybe. Like leadership, the development of a team is a dynamic process that evolves over time, context, situation, and specific challenge. Designing other's success as a team requires purposeful, mindful assessment and (re) assignment on a regular basis.

WHEN TEAMS GO WRONG

LEARNING OBJECTIVE
12.8 Contrast the differences between organizational, team, and individual issues that can arise in teams.

At this point, you might be thinking, "Great, so if I just use all these tools, my team will run just fine." Not exactly. While the strategies you have learned so far will clearly help your team move along smoothly, teams are still made up of people with different personalities, different motives, and different agendas they bring to the team. Moreover, while some individuals may have great technical skills they bring to the team, they may lack effective communication or people skills to be successful team members or vice versa. This section examines how teams can fail and what you can do as a leader to avoid failure or minimize the consequences.

Reasons Teams Fail

Things can go wrong on teams from an organizational perspective, within the group itself, or with individual team members. Here are eight reasons researchers have found that teams fail:

1. Lack of clear purpose and goals

2. Unsure of what requires a team effort

3. Lack of accountability

4. Lack of effective or shared leadership

5. Lack of trust among team members

6. Inability to deal with conflict

7. Ineffective problem-solving skills

8. Lack of focus on creativity and excellence[43]

An awareness of these potential pitfalls allows teams to proactively take measures to ensure they are addressed (i.e., design for success). Clearly, there are numerous issues or problems that can arise for teams—from within or outside the team and before or during team activity. Three additional, well-researched team pitfalls are explained in the next sections: Abilene paradox, groupthink, and the Five Dysfunctions of a team. As you read about how teams can go wrong, note which challenges are the responsibility of the team members, the leader, the organization, or a bit of each.

Abilene Paradox

Have you ever gone along with the group because you thought everyone wanted to do something, so you agreed to follow that particular plan? Well, the Abilene paradox is just that—it is a story about a family that ends up on a car trip to Abilene, Texas, from their home in Coleman because each individual thought all the others wanted to go since that is what each person articulated to the group. It was not until their return home that everyone confessed to the group that they had not really wanted to go but would have preferred to stay in Coleman. There was plenty of blame to go around, as each blamed the other for not speaking up in opposition to going on the trip.

Professor Jerry Harvey, who conceived the Abilene paradox, indicated that it is the *failure to manage agreement*, which means in reality, even though individuals disagree with a particular decision, no one comes forward to indicate their disagreement.[44] As a result, the organization, team, or group ends up moving in a specific direction that no one wants to go. People do not speak up for fear of being ostracized by or left out of the group, no matter the negative consequences or outcome that might happen as a result of moving forward with the plan.

So what does the team do to overcome this dilemma? First, determine whether the organization is facing a *conflict-management* or an *agreement-management* problem. If it is the latter, all members of the team meet together and one person expresses their real position on the decision or problem at hand. Results can be confronted on either a *technical* or *existential* level. The technical level addresses the ability or inability of the team to solve the problem or issue with the resources at hand. Conversely, the existential level exposes to the team true interpersonal conflict within the group. In either case, it opens the possibility for either satisfaction having come from confronting the problem or dissatisfaction with opening up to critical dialogue toward the problem-solving. Finally, the individual may simply have to face living with the consequences.

Groupthink

Groupthink is a theory of social conformity in groups that was developed by Irving Janis[45] after reviewing the group dynamics involved in several key historical blunders. He found that as group cohesion increases, so too does the incidence of groupthink. Groupthink occurs when members of a cohesive group fail to raise objections in group discussions for fear of being too harsh on colleagues, bow to group pressure to go along with the group, or desire not to create conflict and provide social support among group members. Janis summarizes eight symptoms of groupthink. As you read each, can you identify a time when you experienced this on a team?

1. An illusion of invulnerability, shared by most or all of the members, which creates excessive optimism and encourages taking extreme risks;

2. Collective efforts to rationalize in order to discount warnings which might lead the members to reconsider their assumptions before they recommit themselves to their past policy decisions;

3. An unquestioned belief in the group's inherent morality, inclining the members to ignore the ethical or moral consequences of their decisions

4. Stereotyped views of rivals and enemies as too evil to warrant genuine attempts to negotiate, or as too weak and stupid to counter whatever risky attempts are made to defeat their purposes;

5. Direct pressure on any member who expresses strong arguments against any of the group's stereotypes, illusions, or commitments, making clear that this type of dissent is contrary to what is expected of all loyal members;

6. Self-censorship of deviations from the apparent group consensus, reflecting each member's inclination to minimize to themselves the importance of doubts and counterarguments;

7. A shared illusion of unanimity concerning judgments conforming to the majority view (partly resulting from self-censorship of deviations, augmented by the false assumption that silence means consent);

8. The emergence of self-appointed mind guards—members who protect the group from adverse information that might shatter their shared complacency about the effectiveness and morality of their decisions.[46]

Dysfunctional Teams

The Five Dysfunctions of a Team describes a fable about a new CEO who took over a previously successful company and taught them about the five dysfunctions that can derail a team.[47] Table 12.3 notes each of these dysfunctions, along with some possible ways to overcome each.

TABLE 12.3 ■ Five Dysfunctions of a Team			
Dysfunction	Described as ...	Could Be Overcome With	What Else Could You Do as Leader?
First: Absence of trust	Team members are not open to one another about *mistakes and weaknesses* that are foundational to effective teamwork	Personal histories, team effectiveness, and personality profiles	

Dysfunction	Described as . . .	Could Be Overcome With	What Else Could You Do as Leader?
Second: Fear of conflict	Lack of open communication and debate of ideas	Acknowledging that conflict can be constructive and giving themselves permission to raise issues and deal with them openly	
Third: Lack of commitment	lack of commitment to decisions	Imposing a clear deadline or engaging in a worst-case scenario analysis	
Fourth: Avoidance of accountability	Evidenced when team members "hesitate to call their peers on actions and behaviors that seem counterproductive to the good of the team"[48]	Clarifying group goals and standards, regular progress reviews, and team (not individual) rewards	
Fifth: Inattention to results	Where individual or other needs are put ahead of the needs of the team	Publicly declaring the specifics of intended results and tying results to team-based rewards	

Finally, team problems can also arise from personal issues with individuals who are on the team. One primary concern is a lack of motivation to contribute to the goals of the team. Additionally, individuals may have ineffective communication skills that lead to problems between and among members. There may be difficulties getting an individual to adequately coordinate with team members, and individuals may have personal or professional conflicts with other team members. Some individuals may simply withdraw from participation in the team. *Forbes Coaches Council* offered 14 warning signs when a team is near dysfunction:

1. A communication breakdown

2. Absense of trust

3. Unresolved conflict

4. A mass exodus of talent

5. Withdrawal

6. Becoming too comfortable

7. Lack of decision-making

8. Tattling

9. Blame and lack of responsibility

392   Module 4 • Design Culture and Community

10. Silos

11. Avoidance of vulnerability

12. Workload imbalance

13. Scapgoating and subgroups

14. Fixating on past and current problems[49]

How to Fix It When Things Go Wrong?

Leadership is a process. Sometimes things go great, sometimes not. Leaders with strong CORE™ capacities are well-positioned to persistently and positively work through the challenges of teamwork. If you were steering a boat that drifted off course, you would guide it back, but it would not happen immediately. If you had a leak in the boat that slowed you down and threatened to sink your boat, you would fix the leak, but you would also need to bail out the water and recalculate your progress. Of course, if the boat falls apart, you abandon it and build a new boat. So the notion of *fixing* a team is perhaps better stated as facilitating the process.

Too often the challenges of teamwork appear so daunting that organizations and individuals either avoid them or avoid teams altogether. However, many of those challenges are actually benefits in disguise, and (as per Hill's model) it only requires the patient monitoring of the leader to take effect. If you have ever thought to yourself, "If the leader would have just stayed out of this, it would be fine," then you know the power of purposeful nonaction. These challenge–benefit opportunities are nicely summed by Edmondson in the *Harvard Business Review*.[50] For example, the challenge of navigating individual differences yields the benefit of multiple perspectives finding innovation, expanding individual skill sets, and providing a broader, more cohesive view of the organization.

The teams of the future are moving toward a more dynamic, situational model, and thus, they are more challenging to lead. Edmondson distinguishes between traditional teamwork and the more agile yet chaotic notion of teaming. **Teaming** represents a temporary group put together to solve a problem, often with a diverse group of experts. This is quite different from the more stable team that has worked their way through the developmental stages. In some ways, the classroom teams of which you have been a part were more teaming than traditional team. Leading teaming still requires advanced planning of process and structure; however, the social and emotional aspects take on more importance and take greater skill to facilitate.

> ### Leadership by Design
>
> Design Principle: Priming
>
> *Definition:* The activation of specific concepts in memory for the purposes of influencing subsequent behaviors.
>
> *In Other Words:* Exposure to certain things now will influence a later response.
>
> *For Example:* Highlighting a preconceived stereotype before a task could influence performance. For example, there is a common misconception that females are poor at math. Indicating gender prior to taking the test primes the student to think a certain way and may influence performance.

For Leaders: Priming occurs outside of conscious awareness. Concepts in memory are automatically activated via the five senses, so as a leader, you can capitalize on this natural phenomenon to reinforce culture and better lead your team. Set your team up for success by creating the desired environment within your followers' subconscious. What images, sounds, or interactions have been associated with organizational success? Priming that goes unnoticed is the most effective. What other behaviors might a leader require from followers that could be primed for later influence?

Just as leaders need to remember to reward individuals for their work accomplishments, teams also should be rewarded. When teams accomplish a major milestone, members should be rewarded *as a team*, not as individuals. While most companies claim they value teamwork, few really know what great teamwork looks like. If teaming were clear, then there would be more team-based rewards rather than corporate incentives that promote individualism.[51] Rewarding members as a team assists in keeping team cohesion and unity. Rewards can take the form of personal thank you notes, public praise, time off with pay, special celebrations, and special awards among many others. Bob Nelson has written a comprehensive book titled *1,001 Ways to Reward Employees* that outlines rewards that are just as appropriate for teams as they are for individual successes.[52]

REFLECTION QUESTIONS

While there is no foolproof way to avoid the problems outlined, what do you need to look for when composing a team that might minimize the occurrence of issues? Take a look back through this entire chapter at the many aspects of effective teams and team leadership. What steps can you take to minimize teamwork issues?

CHAPTER SUMMARY

More and more organizations are moving to the use of teams, recognizing the power and value in bringing different perspectives to a project. A group of individuals has the potential to bring more than the sum of individual contributions. This is known as synergy and can be accomplished by ensuring that the group has a shared purpose, vision, and accountability to one another. This is what makes a team different (and more than) a group.

Teams also have shared leadership. Although one person may have the leadership position, the strength of the team lies in the roles each person agrees to take. As different situations and needs arise, those roles may best serve the team by assuming the lead. Teams are carefully selected to include the right mix of content, process, and people skills and strengths.

There are many different kinds of teams, each suited for a different challenge or purpose. Effective teams are characterized by a meaningful mission that is shared and understood by all members; a climate of respect and trust; clear, agreed-upon roles and processes; external (to the team) support; and attentive leadership that designs success. A sense of humor helps, too.

Individuals remain an important element of the team, as each person brings their unique motivations, attributes, and perspective. Bringing out the best in each individual team member requires considerable attention and ability by the leader but, inevitably, doing so provides great return in productivity and innovation. Being a good team member depends on one's fit for the specific role. However, understanding your attributes and what you are capable of contributing to the team helps clarify.

In addition to their shared vision and values, teams share a culture. The culture of a given team goes through specific stages of development: forming, storming, norming, performing, and adjourning. Understanding what each stage entails and feels like for team members informs a leader as they facilitate the group's formation into a team. Numerous models help further inform leader activity, including Hill's model that begins with asking whether action is even necessary (versus monitoring).

Teams can fail for many reasons. Preparation in designing the team and its launch is perhaps the most important preventative measure. Team leadership is a process comprised of people, and the attentive, mindful leader will choose from their many tools to facilitate the team to success.

KEY TERMS

Adjourning (p. 383)

Forming (p. 383)

Human capital management (HCM) (p. 379)

Intergroup dialogue (IGD) (p. 382)

Norming (p. 383)

Performing (p. 383)

Shared accountability (p. 373)

Shared leadership (p. 373)

Storming (p. 383)

Synergy (p. 372)

Team roles (p. 373)

Teaming (p. 392)

Tuckman's stages of group development (p. 383)

CORE™ ATTRIBUTE BUILDERS: BUILD NOW FOR FUTURE LEADERSHIP CHALLENGES

Attribute: Optimism

Builder: Tuckman team development (on) stage

When you understand and can anticipate what is coming, it is much easier to be optimistic. Build your optimism for working with and leading a team by role-playing each stage of Tuckman's model. With a small group of peers, create a two- to three-minute skit based on one of the stages:forming, storming, norming, performing, or adjourning. Strive to illustrate both what happens and what it feels like at that stage. Following each performance, have a conversation about what you were trying to portray and what others would add to your performance.

Once you have gone through the performances, have your group change their focus, this time to create a new two- to three-minute skit illustrating how a leader could effectively facilitate a group through that specific stage.[53]

Chapter 12 • Leading a Team   **395**

CORE™ ATTRIBUTE BUILDERS: BUILD NOW FOR FUTURE LEADERSHIP CHALLENGES

Attribute: Resilience

Builder: Learn to do (something new to you)

Nothing requires resilience quite like learning to do something new, and doing so as a group can build your resilience as you see others acquiring the skill faster than you. Here is your group's task:

1. Your team must learn *to do* something new. All members must learn to do it proficiently. Only *one* member of the group may have tried it, and *no* member may be an expert in it.

2. What you choose to learn must be more interesting, creative, valuable, and challenging *than all the other groups*. This means no beer pong, t-shirt folding, simple recipe-making, flip cup, or other skills a small child could easily learn. *Be interesting, distinctive, and excellent.*

3. You must learn how to do it from a credible *source*.

4. Be prepared to *demonstrate* what you learned to do for the full group.

5. As a group, discuss:
   a. How did it feel to have to learn something new . . . at the start, as you learned, after you learned?
   b. What did you bring to the group?
   c. What did you need from the group?
   d. What traits and/or skills were most helpful for this task?

For an added challenge, have each group *assign* what another group needs to learn.

SKILL BUILDER

Run an Efficient and Effective Meeting

"Too many meetings!" How often have you heard that complaint? Building a great team takes time, often meeting time. But poorly planned and executed meetings can quickly wreck a team. Use this document to outline the key points to run your efficient and effective meeting.

1. Most important, determine whether a meeting is required. There is nothing more annoying than showing up to a meeting and quickly determining that the information communicated could have easily been distributed by memo or email and that your presence did not make any difference in any decisions, which leads you to believe that you don't have any skin in the game on decisions that were made.

   Why is this meeting being called? What is the anticipated outcome?

   _____
   _____
   _____
   _____

2. Send the agenda with the meeting invitation. Identify the purpose and goals of the meeting.

This provides attendees the opportunity to plan appropriately and determine what documents and other items need to be available at the meeting itself.

Does the agenda identify the purpose of the meeting and include any items/documents that should be brought to the meeting? What are those documents?

_____

_____

_____

_____

_____

3. Review the list of attendees. Limit the number to 8 to 10 members.

Most of us would like fewer meetings. Ensure that among the attendees are decision makers and those who have information pertinent to the decisions that will be made.

Who should be invited to this meeting? What information should they be requested to bring?

_____

_____

_____

_____

_____

4. Start and end the meeting on time. Enough said!

5. Indicate how decisions will be made at the beginning of the meeting. Will the ultimate decisions be made by the leader? Will the decision be made collaboratively by team members?

Who will be involved in the decision-making?

_____

_____

_____

_____

_____

6. Take notes during the meeting. Identify someone who can be attentive to the task of notetaking to leave the leader to focus on content and process.

Who will be the note taker, and when should those notes be expected to be delivered to the meeting convener for distribution?

_____

_____

_____

_____

_____

7. Make time for participants to ask questions. If any questions are unable to be answered, be sure to write them down and follow up with all members who were at the meeting so no one feels left out and everyone is fully informed.

Who will follow up on questions posed and left unanswered at the meeting? What are those questions?

Chapter 12 • Leading a Team 397

_____

8. Identify action items and members who are responsible for each.
   Who will catalog the action items and follow up with responsible individuals?

   _____

9. Evaluate the effectiveness of the meeting. Do a formal evaluation with each attendee.
   Who will craft the evaluation, disperse evaluations, and receive and collate responses?

   _____

10. Follow up with a list of action items with detailed actions for each meeting attendee.
    Who will craft the list of action items and disperse to attendees?

   _____

SKILL BUILDER

Teamwork Is Like a Jigsaw Puzzle

List all the ways you can think of in which a jigsaw puzzle is similar to the composition and operation of a team.

Some Possibilities

1. There are boundaries (the straight-edged pieces).

2. Each piece plays a specific role in the solution.

3. Pieces are highly interconnected when teamwork occurs.

4. Each piece is unique in its nature (similar to the individual differences among people).

5. The solution is a fragile one (easily broken).

6. The whole is more (better) than the sum of its parts.

7. Some pieces are central; some are peripheral.

8. There are natural groupings (e.g., by color or design).

9. Pieces need someone to move them.

10. Rapid solution is aided by someone with an overall vision.

Discussion Questions

1. Are you surprised by the number of similarities?

2. What are the ways in which you can use this metaphor?

3. What action guidelines does this point toward?

13

DESIGNING A CULTURE THAT CARES

LEARNING OBJECTIVES

Upon completion of this chapter, the reader should be able to

13.1   Describe the important characteristics that shape a caring culture

13.2   Explain the concept of service and the application of servant leadership

13.3   Practice radical empathy in leadership to build cultures of care

13.4   Apply the Social Change Model to translate a culture that cares into real-world leadership activities

13.5   Recognize the breadth of opportunities to make a difference through leadership

Leadership by Design Model

Design Self
How can I design myself as a leader?

Design Relationships
As a leader, how can I design my relationships with others?

Design Others' Success
As a leader, how can I design success for others??

Design Culture
As a leader, how can i design the culture of my organization?

Design Future
As a leader, how can I innovate?

INTRODUCTION

In what kind of place would you like to work—a place where colleagues do what they need to do for themselves to be successful or one where colleagues sincerely care for one another? It is likely you have a pretty good vision for what kind of workplace or organization you are striving to build. However, set aside the notion of success and achievement for a moment and consider the idea of *care*. What might a culture of care look like? How do people communicate, make decisions, and work through challenges and change?

At this point in the textbook, you have focused on the success of others—designing their success, designing your relationship with them, and designing the team and culture within which you and your followers will work. While you are always designing yourself as a leader, many of the last chapters move beyond that and focus on Rule #2 (It's not about you.). This chapter takes Rule #2 and your design of culture to the next level—where your values and intentions find organizational success through a lens of care and service. Every chapter of this textbook starts with *Leadership that Makes a Difference*. This chapter positions you to be that difference.

Leadership That Makes a Difference

Tawanda Jones and the Camden Sophisticated Sisters

In a world filled with poverty, violence, and despair, there shines a bright, caring light in Camden, New Jersey. Not long ago, Camden had been known for being one of the most violent cities in America. As a young teen, Tawanda Jones saw her friends having kids, dropping out of school, and struggling with poverty, a life that she did not want for herself. At age 13, Tawanda knew she needed to do something to change the course of her life and the lives of those around her.

Tawanda loved dance and drill team, so she went to the local community center to get involved with the drill team—the director saw something in her and asked if she would help with the younger kids, and so she did. However, within a couple of years, the city program lost funding and it closed. At age 15, her grandfather challenged her to make a difference in her community; however, she was not sure she could. Her grandfather showed faith in her and told her he knew she would make it work. In 1986, he bought her 80 uniforms and one drum, and thus began the Camden Sophisticated Sisters (CSS). Tawanda set out to serve the youth in Camden and make a positive change in her community.

Students who enter the program come from very difficult circumstances where murder, drugs, single-parent homes, and families working multiple jobs to make a living wage are common. Students must have and maintain a C grade point average, audition, and complete an essay on *How Can I Improve Where I Live*. In addition, each student is required to participate in 200 hours of community service annually, instilling in them the importance of caring and giving back to their community. Tawanda exposes high school students to colleges, and out of over 5,000 students, 100 percent have graduated high school, and 90 percent of those have gone on to some form of post-secondary education—in a city where the high school graduation rate is only 66 percent, well below the state average of 90 percent.

Within the last few years, she has been recognized many times for the wonderful work and service she has provided to the children of Camden. Tawanda Jones is changing lives one kid at a time in Camden, New Jersey. "Under her unwavering leadership through many challenges, trials and tribulations, CSS has impacted lives, prepared young people for a successful life, and proved that, despite appearances, there is genuine goodness in Camden, New Jersey." Tawanda Jones exemplifies caring and service to others, and she credits her grandfather as the one who taught her to give back.[1]

The Camden Sophisticated Sisters Drill team Inc.
March 13 · Instagram

THANK YOU @usatoday FOR ACKNOWLEDGING ME FOR WOMAN OF THE YEAR. I CANT WAIT TO SEE MY NEWBIES!! THANK GOD FOR CONTINUOUSLY BEING IN THE MIDST 😊🙏🖤

164 39 Comments 4 Shares

👍 Like   💬 Comment   ➤ Share

http://camdensophisticatedsisters.org/

A CULTURE THAT CARES

LEARNING OBJECTIVE
13.1 Describe the important characteristics that shape a caring culture.

As a leader, how can you design the culture of your organization? Perhaps the more important question is, What *kind* of culture do you want to design? A *culture that cares* impacts employee morale, engagement, retention, and productivity; and consequently, has a significant impact on achieving an organization's vision. As a leader, you can design a culture that cares, strengthening your organization, even its bottom line.[2] Caring in any organization begins with the top leaders and permeates throughout the entire organization. A culture that cares should be evident from a person's very first interaction with an organization.[3] Organizations that embrace caring in the workplace comprise leaders and coworkers who provide support and empathy for one another and foster connections and conversations among employees. A caring workplace utilizes mistakes as teachable moments and focuses on individual and team strengths.

Individuals who **care** act in a manner that provides for and shows concern regarding another's needs and well-being. In Chapter 7, you learned about the style approach to leadership where, based on the current needs of the organization, leaders shift their emphasis and focus between task and relationship. Designing a culture of care goes well beyond what a leader emphasizes at a given moment in order for the group to be successful. A culture of care means the unwritten rules emphasize concern for the health, wellness, and protection of the individuals—it is the way things are done around here.

Values and Intention

Individual values and intentions guide those actions that distinguish how a caring culture will feel and act. Culture is ultimately a product of the individual actions that model the rules of behavior for others. While you and your followers may hold values and intentions that truly care about others, those values need to be both aligned with actions and reinforced by the culture. For a leader, the alignment of values and actions communicates credibility. More importantly, showing others that you care (in any situation) helps model the cultural expectations, helps followers feel good about themselves, and ultimately prompts them, in turn, to care for others. The cycle of caring can permeate throughout the organization, emphasizing values that many individuals hold deeply but did not believe were part of their work or organizational culture.

The notion of *care* for leaders represents a broad set of activities and intentions that incorporate elements from other leadership approaches. For example, in Chapter 10, you learned that transformational leadership was defined as a change process in which leaders and followers help each other advance to a higher level of morale and motivation.[4] Sounds very much like caring. Individual consideration, one of the four used to describe transformational leader behavior, emphasizes the importance of communicating that you as a leader care about each and every individual within the organization. When you give others individualized consideration, you strongly communicate that you care—about who they are, what they are doing, what they need, and even why they are part of your team.[5]

Authentic Leadership is another approach that centers on an ethic and culture of care. (You will learn more about Authentic Leadership in Chapter 16) Authentic leaders are working from a place where their central motivation is to help the movement, group, organization, or team.[6] They authentically care in a way that is both transparent and sincere. They do not take on a leadership role or engage in leadership activities for status, honor, or other personal rewards.

Chapter 13 ● Designing a Culture That Cares **403**

> **REFLECTION QUESTIONS**
>
> Revisit your values—the ones you explored in Chapter 4. Which of your values could contribute to a culture that cares? What important values do you hold that you hesitate to display because the culture does not support them? In what other ways does the culture of your group, organization, or society influence how much you behave in a way that cares?

Care, Empathy, and Compassion

In Chapter 5, you learned about virtues, values, and altruism—that you should love thy neighbor and benefit others. In a culture that cares, these become very important and manifest through caring, empathy, and compassion. Although these concepts may seem similar (and are sometimes used interchangeably), there is a difference in their meaning that separates one from another in important ways.

Self-compassion helps you connect with the organization and helps you to be kind to yourself and learn to be resilient. It is also critical to learn care, empathy, and compassion for *others* in the workplace as well. Showing care for others lets them know that you have a concern or interest in what is going on in their lives that might affect their lives in the workplace. Heather Younger, who hosts the podcast, *Leadership With Heart,* notes that "the caring leader makes sure to set time with their people one-on-one and listens intently to what their employees need from them to do their best work." She says that the caring leader focuses on the "whole" person and makes them feel like "they matter." Caring leaders act with empathy and kindness for the benefit and well-being of others.[7]

Empathy and compassion take care to the next levels. Empathy, one of the skills of both servant leadership and emotional intelligence, involves the ability to listen to others, recognize, understand, and share their thoughts and feelings. Empathy is crucial to establishing relationships and being compassionate. Empathy has been noted to be the most important leadership skill, particularly in this day and age with multiple stressors, such as mental health issues, increased stress, increased anxiety, emotional exhaustion, compromised sleep, and workplace incivility. Empathy can have positive effects—when employees reported that their leaders were empathetic, they were more innovative, more engaged, had higher retention rates, and more life-work balance.[8]

Compassion is distinguished from empathy through the feeling that one has when one sees someone else struggling and wants to take action to relieve that suffering. It is the desire to act that is the differentiator between compassion and empathy. Similar to empathy, individuals who work for compassionate leaders are 25 percent more engaged, 20 percent more committed to the organization, and 11 percent less likely to burn out.[9]

Vulnerability

Prior to Brene Brown's extraordinarily popular 2010 Tedx Houston presentation titled *The Power of Vulnerability* (which has over 17.6 million views to date), the idea of vulnerability received scant attention in the leadership literature.[10] Since that time, both academic and popular leadership literature have seen an expansion in the growing importance for leaders to be authentic and show vulnerability in the workplace. To many individuals, expressing vulnerability was thought of as a sign of weakness, but actually, the opposite is true. It takes great courage and strength to open yourself up and be vulnerable. In fact, "If we only share our best moments . . . we don't convey an authentic version of ourselves or empower others with the confidence to discuss challenges in their own lives."[11] Through being transparent and showing vulnerabilities, leaders create a "culture where people feel trusted, safe and secure."[12]

Importantly, being open and transparent does not mean revealing your deepest, darkest secrets; it does mean admitting you don't have all the answers and being open and honest about yourself and the current state of affairs within the organization. Leaders who express vulnerability do "not feel compelled to be the first to answer or come up with an idea."[13] This allows others the opportunity to spread their wings and be creative, involved, and invested in idea creation and innovation within the organization. By empowering your employees, you create in them the will to give their best effort for the organization.

Among others, here are several benefits of practicing vulnerability in organizations:

1. **Improved productivity.** Working in a positive environment leads to individuals working harder for those who value them.

2. **Excellent teamwork.** Vulnerability in the workplace leads to an openness to share great ideas and work together collaboratively.

3. **Reduced turnover rates.** By treating employees with respect and care, they will stick with the organization, even during the tough times.

4. **Increased sales.** Happy employees often have happy customers who are willing to purchase more products![14]

Make sure that you are leading with authenticity and integrity. Sincerely apologize when you are wrong. Share new or different ideas to keep others out of a rut (change is important for growth). Discuss sensitive matters honestly and respectfully. Make sure to set your own, and respect others' boundaries. Don't expect everything to be perfect—individuals make mistakes. Help them to use mistakes as learning opportunities. Get to know your employees. Knowing about them and being able to ask about their family, big events, and so forth, shows that you care. Call out inappropriate behavior. Don't look the other way—address issues honestly, respectfully, and directly. Standing up for what is right requires vulnerability (and models the culture you are designing).[15]

Remember that being vulnerable is authentic, and authenticity builds trust. While it is important for everyone, it is especially important for the CEO and senior leaders.[16] Practice now by opening up to people a little at a time. By the time you are the CEO or president of an organization, you will have had lots of practice in being vulnerable and authentic!

Motivation and Maslow's Hierarchy of Needs

Have you ever been really hungry in the middle of class? All you can think about is ending the class and getting some food. Even if the class would normally be very interesting or engaging, your grumbling tummy has taken over your attention. Or imagine that you have an abusive classmate who glares at you in a threatening manner all through the class. You would likely put all your mental energy into wondering what you did, why they are targeting you, and what will happen to you after class rather than exploring and learning the course content. What if these situations (hungry or threatened) were a constant part of the classroom culture? This would definitely not be a culture that cares. But sometimes leaders rely on their values and intentions and overlook some of the other forces that drive behavior and culture—forces that may distract from the vision.

The preceding scenarios describe one of the most well-known models for what drives individual behavior—Abraham Maslow's Hierarchy of Motivational Needs. **Maslow's Hierarchy of Needs** illustrates progressive categories of needs that drive human behavior.[17] There are four lower-order needs, which Maslow called *deficiency needs*, that must be satisfied (typically thought to be sequentially but not always) before moving up to the higher-level needs. As individuals grow and fulfill needs, they are motivated by the gratification of these lower-level needs. Then higher-level needs emerge and are pursued to satisfaction. This progression fosters continual growth in the person.[18] One way that you come to know and appreciate yourself is through an understanding of your own motivation and needs.

The lower-level needs include the following:

- Physiological—basic air, water, food, and shelter; required for survival
- Safety—safety from harm, health, and economic security
- Belonging and love—family, friendships, social, community and religious groups, and intimate relationships
- Esteem—self-esteem and self-respect, respect and appreciation from others, and feelings of accomplishment[19]

Maslow's Hierarchy was originally developed with only one highest-level need, called *self-actualization*. He later reexamined that top level and added three more, reordering the higher levels into the following: cognitive needs, aesthetic needs, then self-actualization, followed by transcendence, in which individuals move outside themselves to help others (see Figure 13.1).[20]

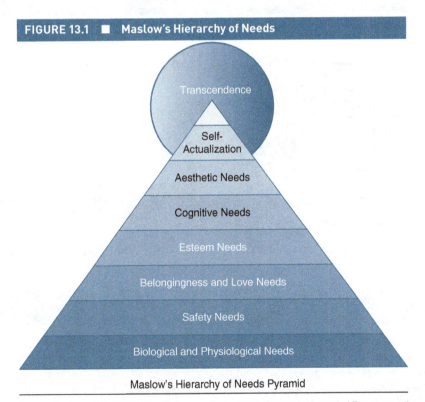

FIGURE 13.1 ■ Maslow's Hierarchy of Needs

Maslow's Hierarchy of Needs Pyramid

Source: Maslow, A. H. (1969). The farther reaches of human nature. *Journal of Transpersonal Psychology, 1*(1), 1–9.

- Cognitive needs—gaining knowledge
- Aesthetic needs—understanding and appreciating beauty and the arts
- Self-actualization—realizing one's personal potential and being able to provide service to self
- Transcendence—helping others by being altruistic[21]

Maslow's Hierarchy illustrates an important point: Everyone has needs that drive them, and some of those basic needs must be satisfied before one can move on to other needs. Further, needs get satisfied in whichever order is important to life circumstances. Designing a culture that cares means you must also be aware of the individuals within that culture . . . and their needs.

As you design yourself as a leader, note what needs are driving *you*. Most of you have acquired your basic needs, such as food and shelter from harm. But perhaps you are still working on a desire to feel a part of something bigger than yourself—friends, family, and community. At some point, everyone wants to be self-actualized and live a life that is happy and fulfilled. The ultimate outcome in the leadership quest is to attain transcendence—to give of yourself. Through transcendence, you are able to focus on caring for and serving others. Maslow reminds you that you must design your leadership self before you can (or are willing to) focus on designing a culture that cares. Use Figure 13.2 to assess your needs using Maslow's Model.

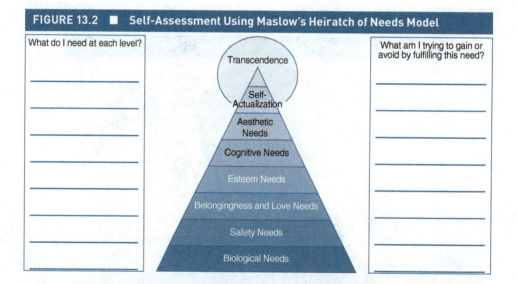

FIGURE 13.2 ■ Self-Assessment Using Maslow's Heiratch of Needs Model

REFLECTION QUESTION

Where are you in the hierarchy? Are all your lower-order needs met? Are you currently pursuing your cognitive needs by taking a college class or program? What do you think it means to become self-actualized? What more information do you need or what intrapersonal issues do you need to resolve to achieve self-actualization? Are you ready to help others?

Chapter 13 • Designing a Culture That Cares

LEADING WITH SERVICE

LEARNING OBJECTIVE
13.2 Explain the concept of service and the application of servant leadership.

Designing a culture that cares includes your values and intentions, aligning your actions with those values, and meeting the individual needs of your followers. When you shift your focus from your needs and well-being to those of others, you are leading with service. **Service** can be defined as action that is done for others—putting others' needs ahead of your own. The concept of service to others as an aspect of leadership goes back thousands of years. Nearly every religion in both ancient and contemporary history describes (and promotes) some form of service to others as a part of its foundational principles. Recent leadership authors also note the importance of service. For example, Peter Northouse identifies *serving others* as one of five key components of what ethical leaders do.[22] And in Kouzes and Posner's *The Leadership Challenge* (see the intro to Module 2), the first practice, "Model the Way," speaks to the importance of understanding and following your own guiding principles and values.[23] All around the world, many organizations exist specifically to serve others. Many schools, businesses, and organizations have embraced the idea of providing service to others to benefit the organization and its members, local communities, and society in general.

Leading with service means changing the way you fundamentally see your goal—elevating achieving a culture of care to an equal place as part of the vision of the organization. Former AT&T executive Robert Greenleaf is credited with the modern leadership notion of placing oneself in the service of others as a core component of leading. Organizations with cultures that espouse a leadership model of service not only have employees with high loyalty but also high engagement, high performance, and high productivity. This section examines the nature of service to others and of leadership *with* others for positive good.

The idea of service with others is critical to the definition of leadership: the process of influencing others toward a common vision. Organizations today are moving toward designing organizations that give back to the community and to the world as well. But even more than giving back, organizations want to be positive contributing citizens. The idea of sustainability as an organizational goal includes the common notion of environmental sustainability, yet it also includes financial sustainability (so you do not go out of business) and the idea of social sustainability—creating a culture within your organization such that individuals thrive and want to stay. This description of sustainability is referred to as the triple bottom line (environment, finance, social), and it will be explored more extensively as you design your future in the final chapter of this book.

In a growing number of organizations, individuals are given time off from work to volunteer in the community. Teams of individuals travel the world to effect change in countries less fortunate than ours. The challenge as you move into a leadership role is to determine how and when your organization can give back and how the culture encourages sustainable behavior. The vision of making the world a better place is important to engaging today's employees in the workplace because it provides a sense of purpose and a feeling that you are working toward something bigger than yourself. Look to very involved contemporary organizations for the new model of how this is working. In the most recent list of the Best Places to Work, there is also a list of Best Workplaces for Giving Back, where you will find such places as Nationwide Insurance, Cisco, PricewaterhouseCoopers, Etsy, and American Express.[24]

Servant Leadership and the Servant Leader

The concept of **servant leadership** has been around since 1970, when Robert Greenleaf wrote an essay titled *Servant as Leader* and subsequently expanded the concept.[25] His concept of servant as leader came after reading Hermann Hesse's novel entitled *Journey to the East*. In the story, a character named Leo acts as a servant to a group of travelers. He does chores, but he also keeps up the spirits of a group of travelers, which keeps them together. One day he disappears, and then the travelers fall apart—they cannot make it without him. Years later, Leo is found, and it is discovered that he is a "great and noble leader" (who first served).

Greenleaf asked the question, "Who is the Servant-Leader?" In the most often quoted passage, he noted,

> The servant-leader *is* servant first—as Leo was portrayed. It begins with the natural feeling that one wants to serve, to serve *first*. Then conscious choice brings one to aspire to lead. That person is sharply different from one who is *leader* first. . . . The difference manifests itself in the care taken by the servant-first to make sure that other people's highest priority needs are being served. The best test and difficult to administer, is, Do those served grow as persons? Do they, *while being served*, become healthier, wiser, freer, more autonomous, more likely themselves to become servants? *And* what is the effect on the least privileged in society; will they benefit or at least not be further deprived?[26]

Thus, servant leadership is defined as a leadership approach that focuses first on others' needs, aspirations, and success. Over the years since Greenleaf's first writing about servant leadership, numerous authors have tried to capture and articulate the concept of servant leadership and define it in a way that is easily communicated. Authors have examined traits, behaviors, and characteristics of servant leaders; various concepts related to servant leadership; and personal values of servant leaders. Larry Spears, who led the Greenleaf Center for Servant Leadership for 17 years, had the opportunity to dive deeply into Greenleaf's writings and found that "servant leadership seeks to involve others in decision-making, is strongly based in ethical and caring behavior, and enhances the growth of workers while improving the caring and quality of organizational life."[27] He identified the following 10 characteristics, which he views as being critical to the development of servant leaders:

1. *Listening*—listening intently to others for both what is said and what is unsaid, clarifying the will of the group after a period of reflection

2. *Empathy*—striving to both understand and empathize with others; accepting and recognizing others for who they are

3. *Healing*—taking the opportunity to heal oneself and others and "help make whole those with whom they come in contact"[28]

4. *Awareness*—self-awareness, especially regarding ethics, power, and values

5. *Persuasion*—the ability to convince others, especially through effective consensus building within the group

6. *Conceptualization*—the ability to dream and conceptualize beyond the day-to-day with a delicate balance between conceptual and operational thinking

7. *Foresight*—the ability to learn from the past and apply lessons to future decisions

8. *Stewardship*—the ability to hold the organization and its people (staff and trustees alike) for the greater good of society with the commitment to serving others

Chapter 13 • Designing a Culture That Cares **409**

9. *Commitment to the growth of people*—individual members of the organization have intrinsic value and the servant leader commits to providing resources that will add to the personal and professional growth of each one

10. *Building community*—moving toward a focus on building community for those individuals within an organization

Leadership is a process; the leader is the person. Beyond these 10 characteristics of servant leadership, there are several scholars who looked for the most important characteristics of servant leadership. From the over 100 they found in the literature, they found the following 12 characteristics most important for servant leaders: valuing people, humility, listening, trust, caring, integrity, service, empowering, serving others' needs before their own, collaboration, unconditional love, and learning.[29]

Take a look at two of the characteristics of servant leadership and see how they play out in organizations: empathy and community building.

Empathy

Empathy has been defined as a leader characteristic that "extends listening when leaders are able to put themselves in the circumstances of others" and "operationalized as the ability to appreciate the circumstances that others face."[30] Within a social system, empathy "creates [a] level of belonging, safety, trust and coherence."[31] Empathy can not only enhance members' feelings of belonging, it can add to the bottom line as well.

One consulting firm in the United Kingdom (Lady Geek) has discovered that companies that act with empathy are more profitable. In fact, the top 10 companies in their 2015 Global Empathy Index "increased in value more than twice as much as the bottom 10 and generated 50% more earnings." The topmost empathetic companies for 2016 included (in rank order) Facebook, Alphabet (Google), LinkedIn, Netflix, and Unilever.[32] It pays to engage in organizational empathy.

Community building

In his article, *The Servant as Leader*, Nicko Batsios, describes leaders who engage in community building as those who "encourage and foster the building of communities among those who work together within a certain organization, people that have shared interests and a need for unity and relatedness. Servant leaders provide a place where people can feel safe to express their own views while being connected with others."[33] Community building is relationship oriented and focuses on shared power, the common good, and long-term relationships.[34]

One example of an organization that has practiced servant leadership and, more specifically, focused on the people aspect of community building, is TDIndustries, an employee-owned company that has been listed in the Fortune Best Companies to Work For since the inception of the honor in 1998. TDIndustries has inverted the pyramid at their organization that puts their employees at the top—serving their needs first through holding their managers accountable for employee growth and development. They facilitate listening forums and employee surveys and are known for their servant leadership training and generous tuition reimbursement program.

Organizational Benefits of Servant Leadership

An article in the *Harvard Business Review* suggests that a new style of leadership is needed for individuals in today's workforce, who often work in a team environment (see Chapter 12) and want organizational leaders to be honest, open, transparent, and trustworthy. Employees feel engaged, respected, perform at high levels, and feel trust in their leader.[35] Servant leadership fits the bill for today's workers. In order to gain the influence that most leaders desire, the servant leader removes the attention from themself and focuses on the achievements of the organization, the success of team members, and their contribution to the organization. The leader becomes the facilitator between the employee and the success of the organization.

The servant leader will "ask more questions, listen more carefully, and actively value others' needs and contributions. The result is more thoughtful, balanced decisions." Moreover, "an employee who believes her boss understands her strengths, values her input, and encourages her growth is likely to stick around for the long-term."[36] The benefits of servant leadership include increased worker morale and greater organizational commitment by employees, thus leading to lower employee attrition.

Why is it important for a leader to understand and apply servant leadership? Organizations that are led by servant leaders are extraordinarily successful from both a financial and personnel point of view. For example, one study compared the 10-year average performance of the S&P 500 with Jim Collins' Good to Great Companies[37] and servant-led companies. The S&P 500 averaged a 10.8 percent gain, Collins' companies averaged a 17.3 percent gain, and the servant-led companies averaged a 24.2 percent gain.[38] That is a massive financial and productivity difference.

Servant leaders lead a significant number of top-performing organizations. In fact, during the pandemic, there was a distinction between self-serving organizations and servant-led organizations. Self-serving organizations looked out for their own self-interests, to the detriment of their employees, while servant-led organizations created innovative ways to serve their employees and the communities they serve.[39] Large organizations that have embraced servant leadership have included (among others) Chick-fil-A, Home Depot, the U.S. Marine Corps, Ritz-Carlton, Whole Foods, Starbucks, and Southwest Airlines. Ritz-Carlton, which has consistently been among the top servant-led organizations on numerous lists, stands out not only for being an exemplar in service but for having a corporate training arm that focuses specifically on teaching servant leadership principles, both in-house and to others who want to emulate their extraordinary service philosophy.

Servant leadership blogger Ben Lichtenwalner found an absence of a comprehensive list of organizations that embraced servant leadership principles and set about to create his own list. To date, his list contains 114 companies that value servant leadership.[40] Additionally, each year more and more companies that espouse servant leadership principles are popping up on lists of best companies to work for. He noted that five of the top 10 *Fortune* magazine's Best Companies to Work For had servant leaders who run the organizations.

Experts Beyond the Text

INSIGHTFUL LEADERS KNOW ABOUT . . . LEADERSHIP AND SPIRITUAL CAPITAL

Leadership Success as Redefined Through Spiritual Capital

By Alain Noghiu

Being a leader is a popular aspiration and a coveted organizational and societal status. Yet there is something both inspiring and troubling about the notion of leadership, both leading back to the same source: human nature. Leadership authors, of course, distinguish between less ("authoritarian") and more desirable ("transformative" or "servant") forms of leadership, but the field of study as a whole tends to abstain from judgments, instead focusing on presenting nearly all forms of leadership as valid in particular contexts. Hence, individuals must grapple with questions of right and wrong—the why and to what end—to pursue leadership and ponder how they need to address prevailing leader-follower dynamics.

Judging by the course of history, it may seem pointless to challenge power-based leader-follower paradigms, since it appears that most societies have structured themselves along these lines. One might conclude that such a dynamic represents a "natural societal order." The 21st century, however, is not "business as usual." Our globe and societies are transforming at an incredible pace, characterizing this time as one of complexity and interconnectedness. These come with evident social benefits, such as technological progress and global communication, as well as considerable costs, like environmental degradation. Might this new reality require a rethink of how leadership acts and what it wants?

The concept of **spiritual capital** addresses complexity and interconnectedness and takes a stance about society and the future. Spiritual capital is a form of value but unlike other forms (like money, time, social connections, etc.). Samuel Rima, perhaps the most thoughtful author on the topic, defines the notion as

> a metaphysical impulse that animates and leverages other forms of capital to build capacity for advancing the common good. As such, spiritual capital exists to bring life, vitality and empowerment to people and the societies in which they live, rather than for the material or economic satisfaction and advancement of one individual, social group or corporate entity.[41]

Spiritual capital speaks to the fact that if leaders seek positive impact, they need to connect with something deeper, something transcendent. Within themselves, aspiring leaders need to seek sources of motivation more noble, principled, and moral. Toward others, leaders must "disappear" so their peers may also gather "life, vitality and empowerment." Spiritual capital as a form of leadership value looks like

> individual dispositions that manifest as a sense of meaningfulness through: (a) belief in something larger than self, (b) a sense of interconnectedness, (c) ethical and moral salience, (d) a call or drive to serve, and (e) the capability to transfer the latter conceptualizations into individual and organizational behaviors, and ultimately added value.[42]

Spiritual capital challenges leadership to rise above itself, transcending organizational structures to inspire human progress. As such, it fully represents the exciting paradoxical reality of our times.

Leadership by Design

Design Principle: Veblen Effect

Definition: A willingness and at times tendency to find a product desirable and pay a higher price simply because the product has a high price.[43]

In Other Words: It must be good because it costs more . . . so I want it.

For Example: Brand-name clothing, brand-name shoes, brand-name foods, pretty much brand-name everything.

For Leaders: The perception of high value influences others. Valuable things are sought after, elicit great effort, and are cherished and kept nice. In reality, price does not always equate to quality or efficacy. But price does often compel individuals to perceive and desire one thing over another. As a leader designs a culture of service, the Veblen Effect (and research on engagement and motivation) suggests that followers will more likely want to be a part of an organization that has explicitly high value. Individuals want to be a part of something valuable—they desire the feeling of status, which in turn provides a feeling of belonging. While excellent service can translate into profits, it more often arises from efforts to better the human condition. How can you as a leader recast the common good as uniquely great? Where and when might you need to unveil the misperception of overvalued, unproductive goals?

REFLECTION QUESTIONS

Have you ever worked for an organization that cares? How did you see that play out? What can you do in the future to ensure that your organization engages in caring?

DEI BY DESIGN

LEARNING OBJECTIVE

13.3 Practice radical empathy in leadership to build cultures of care.

As you strive to lead and serve, you express empathy—effectively feeling another person's reality as though it were your own. As noted earlier in the chapter, empathy is a natural part of leadership because leading always involves other people and people cannot be separated from their emotions; all people have emotions and are influenced by their and others' emotions (see expert feature on emotional intelligence in Chapter 1). Leading and following involve continual emotional management—within self, between you and other people, and among others. Understanding empathy in leading helps move toward organizational and communal lives dedicated to care and concern.

The traditional focus on empathy in leadership describes leaders who communicate a fairly basic level of concern about member well-being. This is generally appropriate since leaders do bear some responsibility for followers' health (and subsequent success). However, when you strive to cultivate caring cultures, empathy must take on a significance beyond simply acknowledging others' feelings. For empathy to have enough impact to create change, members need to feel as though their leaders have been moved to think and act differently by the realities those followers face. The **radical empathy** that fosters caring organizations goes beyond daily niceties and becomes a "vehicle for deep learning and acknowledgment of the power relationships where both [types of] people experience growth."[44] Leaders express radical empathy when they tell members how they have been changed through their stories, questions, and ideas, which in turn, sparks followers' sense of partnership in leading processes.

Radical empathy in leadership is sometimes called *mattering* (in higher education research).[45] Regardless of the term used, radical empathy or mattering is made up of five parts: attention,

Chapter 13 • Designing a Culture That Cares   413

importance, ego-extension, dependence, and appreciation. *Attention* is the awareness that someone else notices you, your actions, and the impact of those actions. *Importance* takes attention one step further to include positive assessments of what you think, how you act, and what you are capable of in the future. *Ego-extension* is the sense that others will be proud of your successes but also share the sadness of failures. Your feelings of being needed, as well as needing others, comprise *dependence*. Finally, *appreciation* is a form of gratitude associated with the effort, energy, and time you dedicate to helping and being helped by others. Radically empathic leaders seek to maximize each of these elements as they create cultures of care and concern.

However, carrying the expectation of maintaining radical empathy with every member or in every interaction is a surefire path to emotional burnout. As you engage in the social construction of leadership, you are likely to experience some emotional triggers of your own. Learning to move through them instead of disconnecting improves your capacity for radically empathic leadership. When you feel overwhelmed by others' emotions, you can try to stay present through that feeling and seek trusted others to process your potential feelings of anger, anxiety, fear, shame, or doubt (among others). Reflecting on your own emotional connection (and disconnection) patterns can also provide some clarity on how to proactively prevent empathic exhaustion as well as how to recover when it happens. Finally, practicing self-empathy in the forms of self-care, intentional disconnection from the responsibilities of leading, and self-patience actually serve to increase your self-awareness, re-energize you, and role-model well-being for members and followers.

Designing cultures of care calls you to participate in radically empathic leadership. Although the vulnerability required for this type of leading seems to contradict many leadership lesson you may have been taught, formally and informally, it is only through these forms of attention and intention that you can move toward an organization and community defined by their ethic of concern. Building a sense of mattering among members can be taxing work, but not engaging these forms of empathy risks losing the progress needed to make a fairer and more just world.

MAKE A DIFFERENCE: DESIGNING A CULTURE THAT CARES

LEARNING OBJECTIVE

13.4   Apply the Social Change Model to translate a culture that cares into real-world leadership activities.

In what kind of a place would you like to work? That was the question posed at the start of this chapter. Some say if you want a workplace that employees love, you need to create a high-energy workplace where work is fun, employees have space to dream, and everyone shares the success so employees feel like owners and have a real incentive to contribute to the organization's success.[46] Sounds like a great culture. But what if within that high-energy culture no one *authentically* cares about each other? Although everyone has their own set of values and goals, everyone—every single person—wants to feel like they matter. Adopting a servant leadership approach and incorporating those specific behaviors into your culture will make a great difference.

Designing a culture where each individual matters means fully engaging The Leadership Challenge exemplary practice entitled "Encourage the Heart."[47] In their workbook by the same title, Kouzes and Posner outline seven essential activities. Take a moment to look over each of these seven practices listed in Table 13.1 and try to complete the table: What are you doing now that helps meet that essential for encouraging the heart? What could you be doing?

TABLE 13.1 ■ Seven Essentials for Encouraging the Heart[48]		
	What Are You Doing Now?	**What Could You Be Doing?**
Tell the story		
Set clear standards		
Expect the best		
Pay attention		
Personalize recognition		
Celebrate together		
Set the example		

Source: Kouzes, J. M., & Posner, B. Z. (2011). *Encouraging the heart workbook.* San Francisco, CA: Jossey-Bass.

Tell the story of your organization. What makes you excellent? Who are the main characters, and what role do they play? What challenges do you overcome, and how do you do it? When you tell the story of your organization, you are setting the example and clear standards. Your story is about expecting the best, working together with everyone's strengths, and celebrating your accomplishments. Telling this story again and again, in word and deed, models and reinforces a culture that cares. The story, through the culture, becomes a self-fulfilling prophecy—if much is expected from an individual, they will rise to the occasion and achieve higher goals. You may want to revisit the Leadership by Design featuring "Storytelling" in both Chapter 4 and ahead in Chapter 16.

When you feel like you matter, people notice when you do a good job and then provide recognition for that job well done. Recognition that is personal. Personalized recognition singles out a person and specifically notes what they did, why it mattered, and how that person contributes to the greater mission and overall good. Appreciation for a great job goes a long way to make a person feel they are an important part of the organization. Sometimes, a simple *thank you* can go a long way to making an individual feel valued as well. If you currently work on a team, with a group, or in an organization, who could use a personal thank you or note of accomplishment? In what ways could you make individual recognition a regular activity such that it becomes the way things are done around here (as culture is simply defined)?

Leadership by Design

Design Principle: Personas

Definition: A technique to build data-based archetypes of fictitious users/clients/customers to profile their needs, wants, and expectations in order to guide decision-making regarding features, interactions, and aesthetics.

In Other Words: Who are the *typical* users, and what do they tend to be like?

For Example: Visitors can log into a university website from a number of different perspectives—a student, an alumnus, a parent, a faculty/staff member, and so forth. The subsequent information each person sees is tailored specifically to that subpopulation.

For Leaders: A leader's role is often ambiguous. There are no guidelines for every specific situation, context, time, and individual follower that demonstrate how to lead. Crafting

Chapter 13 • Designing a Culture That Cares   **415**

personas comprising different roles in the organization and different stakeholders helps a leader anticipate and better design culture and community. In the same way that a persona helps make the intended user more real to a designer, a leader can use personas to more effectively find the *common* vision across many individuals. Personas provide a framework around which a leader can test decisions, understand situations, and further develop. Personas ensure that different needs are being met while also creating empathy and expanding perspectives.

Social Change Model of Leadership Development

One model that many universities have adopted to help students develop their capacity to design a culture that cares and makes a difference is the Social Change Model of Leadership Development (SCM) (shown in Table 13.2).[49] The Social Change Model of Leadership is based on the assumptions that leadership is concerned with effecting change on behalf of others and society; that leadership is collaborative; that leadership is a process rather than a position; that leadership should be value based; that all students are potential leaders; and that service is a powerful vehicle for developing student's leadership skills.[50]

TABLE 13.2 ■ The Seven Cs of the Social Change Model of Leadership Development	
	Start Making a Difference by Doing the Following:
Consciousness of self	Find what motivates you to take action.
Congruence	Find what values your actions communicate, then find the right actions that align.
Commitment	Find the social issue or challenge that inspires your investment of time and energy.
Collaboration	Find others who share your commitment, and find ways to work with them.
Common purpose	Find the shared values, visions, and aspirations of those sharing your commitment.
Controversy with civility	Find where others disagree, and then find resolution (even if it is, agree to disagree).
Citizenship	Find how your values and your issues connect with others and the community, and find your responsibility to those others.
Change	Find out more about change management and how your service can effect positive social change.

Often used as a foundation for co-curricular programs, the SCM asserts that the hub of leadership development is the pursuit of positive social change (the relationship among the seven Cs is reflected in Figure 13.3). The model focuses on three different perspectives: the individual, the group, and society/community. Each perspective has values that drive the model: individual values of *consciousness of self, congruence,* and *commitment*; group process values of *collaboration, common purpose,* and *controversy with civility*; and *community/societal values of citizenship,* all centered on a hub of *CHANGE,* which gives meaning and purpose to the seven Cs. "Change, in other words is the ultimate goal of the creative process of leadership—to make a better world and a better society for self and others."[51]

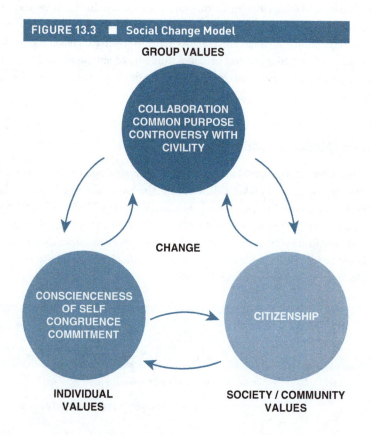

FIGURE 13.3 ■ Social Change Model

Individual Values

- *Consciousness of self* means to be self-aware and be a person who can function collaboratively with others and participate in shaping the common purpose of the group. A good citizen who can help to resolve conflicts and problem solve.
- *Congruence* is the ability to be authentic and honest in interactions with others. Someone whose actions are consistent in upholding their values and beliefs.
- *Commitment* is investing time in the development of the leadership process. Effectively working with others in the group to strategize and find a common purpose and implementation of actions to achieve that purpose.

Group Values

- *Collaboration* is about working with and relating to people. It empowers the group to work toward a common purpose.
- *Common purpose* is a shared set of goals and values. Groups can achieve a shared vision and mission by developing trust with group members to work toward achieving common goals.

Chapter 13 ● Designing a Culture That Cares **417**

- *Controversy with civility* speaks to the notion that challenges within groups will arise, there will be differences in opinion and viewpoints. These differences should be acknowledged and discussed with engagement toward finding resolutions that work for the benefit of the whole. Discussions should be open, honest, and cooperative.

Community Values

- *Citizenship* means engagement with the group in an effort to serve a socially or civic-minded purpose. The forefront of citizenship is the ability to keep responsible values and beliefs in mind that connect the group to larger communities and the greater need or good.

Each of the Seven Cs within the model provides a prescriptive goal around which many college programs have built leadership programs to develop social responsibility and drive positive social change. Look at the statements after each of the Seven Cs in Table 13.2. How might you translate each of the values into a practicable action in your university community or the greater community in which you live?

MAKING A DIFFERENCE NOW AND LATER: OPPORTUNITIES AND ACTIONS

LEARNING OBJECTIVE
13.5   Recognize the breadth of opportunities to make a difference through leadership.

Reflect back on several of the "Leadership That Makes a Difference" stories you have read throughout this book. What you were reading were actual stories of caring and service to others. Remember in Chapter 5, Ryan Hreljac at age 6 was determined to solve the issue of access to clean drinking water? He was serving others, doing something greater than just for himself. And in Chapter 11, Maung Nyeu sought to save his native language for future generations of his hometown. And in this chapter, you learned about Tawanda Jones, who cared about and served her community by saving children from the devastating effects of murder and drugs in the streets of Camden, New Jersey. These three examples of caring and service to others reflect ordinary people doing extraordinary things and touching the lives of many individuals. These leaders made a difference by serving others, and they acted from the heart to serve as leaders for their communities and their causes.

MYTH OR REALITY?

Participating in a service project is a great way to get experience for a job upon graduation.

Reality. Not only does gaining service experience look great on a resume, it provides you with an opportunity to gain skills that are important and useful in today's work environment, especially if you have worked in a team environment.

Perhaps the best training for designing a culture that cares is through practicing service yourself. The more mindful, reflective service engagement you experience, the more you will notice what is and is not effective. Service to others is embedded in many families, communities, organizations, and national cultures. Service plays out in many different ways, through many different organizations. **Nonprofit organizations** focus on achieving a type of value different from financial. As an organization, they strive to achieve a cause or mission, funneling any financial profit back into serving the organization's efforts (versus paying investors or stockholders). Many nonprofit organizations are service oriented, with missions to tackle difficult social challenges. Working with or for a nonprofit organization can be extraordinarily rewarding because serving others and a culture that cares are often built into the mission. For-profit companies can also serve or make a difference. But their underlying responsibility is to maximize profit and/or shareholder value.

It is quite likely you have already participated in service. Every major religion engages in service to others in numerous ways—this call to service, to serve others, is reflected in each of the holy books. Maybe when you were growing up, your church, synagogue, mosque, or other religious institution engaged in feeding the poor or building or cleaning up homes for those less fortunate. Possibly you were involved with a nonprofit organization such as the local animal shelter and helped walk dogs or clean cages. Perhaps you had a bake sale to donate the proceeds to a specific charity or visited with senior citizens at a community center. Each of these provided you an opportunity to feel good about making a difference in your community. Moreover, it provided an opportunity to improve your community, meet new people, and gain work and leadership experiences. But most important, these activities shape and reinforce the culture people seek to encourage. Consider the many ways you can continue and extend your involvement—this time as a leadership learning opportunity.

Service to Others in College

Although some students come to college already having engaged in service learning or volunteerism in high school, their workplace, or simply from a desire to give back, often students have their first experience with service learning in college.[52] **Service learning** refers to campus-based volunteer opportunities that combine academic learning with principles of service to community. **Volunteerism** comprises individual or group engagement with others and/or an organization for no compensation. In fact, many colleges and universities have created service learning opportunities both inside and outside the classroom. Most sororities and fraternities have had some type of socially responsible service opportunities since early in their inception; and now, more college clubs and organizations outside of fraternities have taken on service projects. Colleges and universities are most interested in assisting the local community, being good community partners, and being stewards of the neighborhoods in which they reside. Many universities offer lots of opportunities for students to become involved.

Besides the simple benefit of feeling like you are doing something to help the greater good of the community, research has consistently found many educational and developmental benefits, including increased social and interpersonal skills, cultural competence, communication skills, and enhanced moral reasoning to name a few.[1] And, these benefits cut across disciplines, including global experiences.

---

[1] Salam, M., Awang Iskandar, D. N., Ibrahim, D. H. A., & Farooq, M. S. (2019). Service learning in higher education: A systematic literature review. Asia Pacific Education Review, 20(4), 573-593.

Chapter 13 • Designing a Culture That Cares   **419**

Types of College Service

The types of student engagement in service or volunteerism that are offered are quite varied and are foundational for a lifetime of volunteering:

- *Service learning*—typically engages students in combining learning goals with service in the community, usually making a difference for some local nonprofit organization. This type of activity enhances student growth and the common good.

- Community engagement—focuses on community action goals, combined with learning. Beneficial outcomes occur for learning, personal, and social outcomes, and career development.

- *Volunteerism*—often not as structured as service learning or community engagement but can provide just as valuable a service to external (or internal) organizations.

In addition to on-campus resources for service learning (e.g., your professor, the service learning office), there are numerous off-campus groups that coordinate service experiences. Among some are the Corporation for National and Community Service; Campus Compact; BreakAway (alternative breaks); and Idealist. Several colleges stand out as exemplars in service learning—or creating service for others. Brandeis University has consistently provided global volunteering and service-learning programs as well as being actively engaged in research on service learning. You only need to do a web search for "best colleges for community service" to come up with a list of the top 10 colleges most involved with community service. For colleges that are interested in participating in education for civic and social responsibility, Campus Compact has been a leader in coordinating activities for college since the 1980s. It offers "research, online tools, and other initiatives to help campuses create effective service-learning programs that meet academic and service goals."[54]

Service Outside College

For some of you, college represents a time and context where the full responsibilities of adult life have been put off. This time ideally helps you focus on developing yourself (like your CORE™), so you can be even more impactful when you graduate. Service activities in college are excellent practice for leading the design of a culture that cares across many contexts. These opportunities to practice and make a difference continue after college. And in fact, your participation is critical to the success of others and community—it is the citizenship value in the Social Change Model. You will find some of these opportunities within your career field or organization, and there are also many venues to make a difference outside your organization.

One context that will always appreciate your attention is your community. Every individual exists in a community of one type or another. Some people are very involved, while others prefer to simply act as good citizens. Either way, communities usually have individual and societal needs—needs that can be addressed through community service. In her blog for *PrepScholar*, Christine Sarikas defines community service as "work done by a person or group that benefits others." She poses four questions that can guide your thinking about your involvement in community service:

1. Who would you like to help?

2. Do you want a community service activity that is reoccurring or a one-time event?

3. What kind of impact do you want to have?

4. What skills would you like to gain?[55]

420   Module 4 ● Design Culture and Community

The list of opportunity ideas in this article seems endless, and indeed there are many, many creative and interesting ways you can contribute. Once you have thought about and discussed those questions with others, consider what *you* are interested in, have specific strengths and skills in, and would find fun and fulfilling. Then, realistically consider how much time you can devote to community service. As with leadership, the more you know about yourself, the more likely you will identify your preferred avenue for serving . . . and creating a culture that cares.

REFLECTION QUESTIONS

What worlds, hobbies, activities, or ideas do you find important or interesting? Then, research groups or organizations in your community that align with those interests. Who could you contact to find out how you could get involved? Remember, service is not about fixing, it is about engaging.

Service Within the Organization

In today's turbulent times, many organizations are encouraging employees to spend time in service to others in both the local community and beyond, sometimes even internationally. Often called names such as volunteerism, community service, or corporate volunteering, many allow these opportunities during the work hours.

Volunteering is alive and well in America. The most recent statistics on volunteering from the Corporation for National and Community Service found that "1 in 4 Americans volunteered through an organization," and that adults volunteered 7.8 billion hours, time that is valued at $184 billion. Additionally, they found that volunteers are "twice as likely to donate to charity as non-volunteers." In their study, Gen X had the highest volunteer rate (28.9%), followed by Baby Boomers (25.7%), and 21.9% of Millennials volunteered. Individuals attending college volunteered at twice the rate of non-college peers (25.7% vs. 13.6%), and working mothers have the highest rate of volunteerism (36%).[56] The latest research by the Higher Education Research Institute (2017) on Gen Z indicated that 79 percent of college seniors volunteered or provided community service either occasionally or frequently.[57]

Many individuals are eyeing potential employers that have a focus on purpose and making an impact on society. "Younger workers increasingly want to work at companies that pursue equity, diversity and community."[58] It is good for business to involve employees in volunteering. In fact, the Macquarie Graduate School of Management found that 93 percent of employees are happier and 54 percent are proud of their company and engaged at work.[59]

Volunteerism provides numerous benefits to the organization. It can assist with attracting employees who are motivated to work in an organization that gives back to the community, it can improve a corporate image, it can enhance employees' skills, and it can build stronger local communities in which the organization resides. The best kind of volunteer program is one that is employee driven, which leads to more organizational engagement by employees.

Service Outside the Organization

In the United States, the federal government offers numerous opportunities for service. Public service and volunteer opportunities are available at https://www.usa.gov/volunteer, which includes a repository for information on Peace Corps, Citizen Corps, and Volunteer.gov and a link to the Corporation for National & Community Service, where one can find information on AmeriCorps and Senior Corps. Information is also available on disaster services, education, vets and military families, and environmental stewardship. Gaining experience in one of these meaningful types of service organizations can position college students or recent graduates for significant leadership experiences upon return and will be looked upon favorably by employers when seeking a permanent position.

The United States also has numerous **service clubs** made up of people whose purpose in belonging to those organizations—in addition to fellowship—is to serve others. Three highly regarded international organizations that were founded in the United States are Rotary International,[60] Kiwanis International,[61] and Lions Clubs International.[62] The mottos for each of these organizations are "Service Above Self" (Rotary), "Serving the Children of the World" (Kiwanis), and "We Serve" (Lions). In turn, each of the service organizations has social issues that its members undertake to solve and give back—whether those are for local, state, or international communities (sometimes for all three). For example, Rotary strives to foster intercultural peace; fight diseases such as polio and malaria; provide clean water, sanitation, and hygiene; save mothers and children; support education; and grow local economies, and they engage in these activities both here and abroad. No matter the type of service organization, all have similar desires for the outcomes of their service—to make the world a better place than they found it, to solve a need that affects large numbers of individuals.

The concept of organizational caring may seem like the latest *buzzword* in the lexicon of leadership and management. But an organizational culture that provides a culture of care is a setting that employees (and others) would love to spend their time in every day. The website FastCompany.com wrote an article titled "How to Create a Workplace People Love Coming To" in which they found the five traits in organizations that made them "Employers of Choice" in the annual list of Best Places to Work.[63] Those traits are people matter; employees feel heard; people are empowered to grow; leaders are strong; and employees are appreciated. In other words, these organizations and their leaders *care* about their employees.

So now it is up to you. What steps will you take to design a culture that cares?

Take the Service Learning Preference Inventory (SLPI) at the end of this chapter to learn which type of service learning activity fits best with *your* personality type. Are you a *direct* type, where you like to be involved in direct contact with people in need of service? Maybe you are *indirect*, where you prefer to work on resources to solve problems that affect individuals in need. Alternatively, you might be into *advocacy*, where your skills fit the opportunity to solve specific problems. Finally, you might be more interested in participating in a *research-based*, task-oriented service-learning project by researching the underlying causes for specific community problems. Whatever fits your specific style of involvement, there is always a place for you in serving others.

REFLECTION QUESTIONS

If you were to engage in service learning in your class today, what type of organization would you engage with and why? Based on your skills and expertise, what type of contribution can you make to a service project?

CHAPTER SUMMARY

In what kind of a place would you like to work? Designing a culture of care significantly impacts both individual and organizational performance. Organizations that embrace caring in the workplace involve leaders and coworkers who provide support and empathy for one another; foster connections and conversations among employees; avoid blame, forgive mistakes, and use them as teachable moments; have a positive workplace; and focus on individual and team strengths. The concept of care is rooted in the values, intentions, and motivations of leaders and followers. Care, compassion, vulnerability, and radical empathy comprise some of the practices that contribute to a culture that cares.

Leading with service and the approach of servant leadership, comprises one of the most impactful approaches to designing a culture that cares. While people have been serving others for millennia, leading with service is more complex than helping or fixing. Robert Greenleaf, who created the idea of servant leadership, found servant leaders in business who were making a difference in their organizations. Numerous attributes characterize the servant leader, including listening, empathy, healing, awareness, foresight, stewardship, building community, and a commitment to the growth of others. Valuing people and caring are at the heart of the servant leader.

Designing a culture that cares is really about making a positive social difference, whether in your organization, your community, or the larger world. Many strategies, approaches, and venues exist for maximizing your impact, such as those related to *Encouraging the Heart* of others or the seven C values that comprise the Social Change Model of Leadership Development.

Many of today's organizations are engaged with local, national, and international community projects where giving back and assisting others is a primary end goal. This chapter includes suggestions for numerous types of opportunities for service to community as well as a number of organizations that provide those opportunities.

KEY TERMS

Care (p. 402)

Community engagement (p. 419)

Maslow's Hierarchy of Needs (p. 405)

Nonprofit organization (p. 418)

Radical empathy (p. 412)

Servant leadership (p. 408)

Service (p. 407)

Service clubs (p. 421)

Service learning (p. 418)

Spiritual capital (p. 411)

Volunteerism (p. 418)

CORE™ ATTRIBUTE BUILDERS: BUILD NOW FOR FUTURE LEADERSHIP CHALLENGES

Attribute: Confidence and Engagement

Builder: Engaging servant leadership

Complete each of the following activities by yourself or with a small group of others. Explain how you accomplished each item, and consider which characteristics of servant leadership are most applicable for each activity:

Chapter 13 ● Designing a Culture That Cares   **423**

Help someone.

Do something exceptionally courteous.

Interact with positive people.

Praise someone.

Make someone else feel good.

Work on something with a positive person.

Tell someone that you care about them.

Meet someone new (more than just *hello*).

Recognize someone for something.

Listen to someone talk through their goals and ambitions.

Make an unhappy person laugh.

Recognize someone for doing something excellent.

Send someone a thank you note.

(Adapted from http://gx.gallup.com/dipper.gx)

CORE™ ATTRIBUTE BUILDERS: BUILD NOW FOR FUTURE LEADERSHIP CHALLENGES

Attribute: Resilience and Engagement

Builder: First-year student servant leader care package

First, review the 10 characteristics of a servant leader:

1. Listening

2. Empathy

3. Healing

4. Awareness

5. Persuasion for empowerment

6. Conceptualizing a positive vision

7. Foreseeing possibilities

8. Stewardship and sustainable behavior

9. Commitment to the growth of people

10. Building community

Second, remember when you were a first-year student in college? What aspects of servant leadership would have facilitated your success?

424 Module 4 • Design Culture and Community

Third, design and put together a care package for a first-year student at your school incorporating as many of the servant leadership characteristics as possible. Explain which characteristics you used, why you chose them, and how you incorporated them into your care package.

Finally, deliver your care package to a deserving first-year student.

SKILL BUILDER ACTIVITY

Service Learning Preference Inventory (SLPI)

STEP 1: Conduct Inventory

Each row contains descriptions of two service activity options. Circle the number closest to the service activity you would *most likely* prefer of the two options given in each numbered row. Look at the sample, then begin when you are ready.

Wash cars to raise money	1 2 3 4	Research social issues and create a report

_____

_____

_____

Begin Inventory Here

1. Visit elderly in long-term care facility	1 2 3 4	Organize a letter-writing campaign
2. Deliver food to needy families	1 2 3 4	Collect/analyze data to solve organizational problem
3. Assist a group with cleaning a local park	1 2 3 4	Conduct a nonpartisan voter registration effort
4. Create marketing materials (flyers, brochures)	1 2 3 4	Analyze survey data for a school district
5. Help people register for recreation classes	1 2 3 4	Assist a political office with a social issue
6. Mentor teens on basic living skills or career preparation	1 2 3 4	Evaluate effectiveness of a new program
7. Design a website or use social media to market an agency	1 2 3 4	Design and deliver presentations on a social issue (e.g., poverty, obesity)
8. Assist with raising funds to build a local playground	1 2 3 4	Conduct energy audits in public buildings

Horizontal score = _____
Add your circled responses and place the sum on the line above
This is your Horizontal score

Continue With Inventory . . .

9. Pack boxes to send shoes to third-world countries	1 2 3 4	Create community awareness for Alzheimer's
10. Conduct an analysis to determine impact of agency on its community	1 2 3 4	Give series of presentations regarding resources for diabetics

11. Serve behind the scenes	1 2 3 4	Work directly with people
12. Analyze data—look for trends	1 2 3 4	Work one-on-one with people
13. Arrange baskets of food for local pantry	1 2 3 4	Give small group presentations in the community
14. Conduct a needs analysis on an organization	1 2 3 4	Create community awareness for a social issue
15. Serve while working among a group, following their lead	1 2 3 4	Serve by working independently, taking your own initiative
16. Service focused on a project (tasks)	1 2 3 4	Service focused on people (relationships)

Vertical score = _____
Add your circled responses and place the sum on the line above
This is your *Vertical* score

Estimate (plot) your horizontal and vertical scores on the graph's horizontal and vertical lines. Draw a line to connect your two scores to create an intersecting mark in one of the quadrants. For example, scores of 30 (horizontal) and 14 (vertical) would display as shown in Figure 13.4 to indicate *research-based* as the preferred type of service.

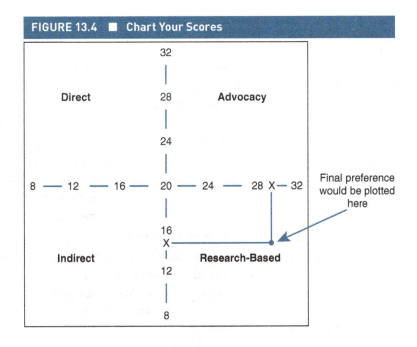

FIGURE 13.4 ■ Chart Your Scores

STEP 2: Chart Your Scores

On the graph in Figure 13.5, plot your horizontal and vertical scores; then connect the two to view your preferred type of service.

FIGURE 13.5

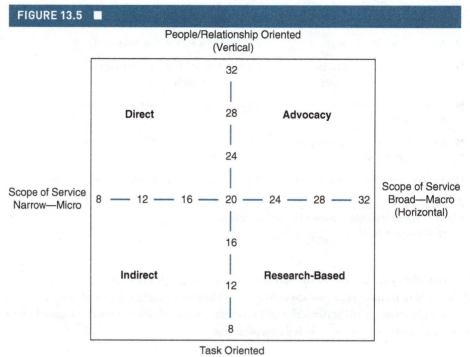

Service Learning Preferences

Direct (people oriented; narrow scope of service)—Activities that require personal contact with people in need. This type of service is generally the most rewarding since you often receive immediate positive feedback during the process of helping others. Examples of direct service activities include working with senior citizens, providing direct services to the homeless, or being the front receptionist at a women's center.

Indirect (task oriented; narrow scope of service)—Activities that are centered on channeling resources to the problem rather than working directly with an individual who may need the service. Often you do not come in contact with the people being served. Examples of indirect service include collecting food or toys for disadvantaged families, participating in landscaping a community park, or transferring hard-copy policies to an online format.

Advocacy (people oriented; broad scope of service)—Requires you to lend your skills and talents to the effort of eliminating the causes of a specific problem and/or to make the public aware of the problem. Activities may include making presentations to the community about particular social issues, distributing literature about the issues throughout the neighborhood, or making phone calls to help raise funds for a notable cause.

Research-based (task oriented; broad scope of service)—can be defined as a partnership of students, faculty, and community who collaboratively engage in research with the purpose of solving a pressing problem or initiative for change. Typical research projects include creating survey tools for an agency in order to assess a specific community need/problem, conducting a needs analysis to implement a new initiative, or evaluating a current process or organizational need. Once data are analyzed, recommendations are typically developed to address the needed change.

Source: © Dan Noel. (2015). Direct, indirect, and advocacy types of service learning were originally suggested by Dunlap, Drew, and Gibson (1994). All four types of service are mentioned and supported by Kaye (2004) as well as used by other institutions of higher education (i.e., Colorado State University-tilt program).

Dunlap, N. C., Drew, S. F., & Gibson, K. (1994). *Serving to learn: High school manual.* Columbia: South Carolina Department of Education.

Kaye, C. B. (2004). *The complete guide to service learning: Proven, practical ways to engage students in civic responsibility, academic curriculum, & social action.* Minneapolis, MN: Free Spirit Publishing.

DESIGN THE FUTURE

MODULE 5

Chapter 14	Creating a Culture of Innovation	431
Chapter 15	Entrepreneurial Leadership	461
Chapter 16	Systems and Sustainability	489

There has been a lot of talk over the decades about the future in space. After successful use of satellites, trips to the moon, shuttles, space stations, and now seeing to the edge of the Universe, the next big thing seems to be getting people to Mars. A personal trip to Mars requires a lot of planning and inventing a few things that do not yet exist. The more scientists, engineers, policymakers, and all of those involved learn about what such a trip might entail, the more clearly the challenges can be anticipated and prepared for. Designing a successful trip to Mars means knowing what you will need to have, know, be able to do, and be like—all so you can expect the unexpected and survive if the worst possibilities happen. Everyone, using all that they know, strives to build accurate scenarios that can then be analyzed for best and worst cases. The best-case/worst-case scenario analysis is a tool used in many fields to predict risk and guide decisions.

You have a much more difficult challenge on your hands than designing a trip to Mars. You have to design *you* . . . to make a successful trip into the future. No one has been to the future, nor have any probes been sent to gather information. Despite the best efforts of many very smart people through time, none have consistently predicted what the future will bring—what challenges, new ideas, or even accurate best-/worst-case scenarios. Many have imagined the future, and in some cases, those imaginations helped guide those designing the future. The hard reality is that no one knows what to expect, how it will feel, what needs to be known, and so forth. That reality is one of the essential tenets of this textbook: How do you prepare for that unknown future?

All the way back in the introduction to this textbook, design was defined as the process of originating and developing a plan, solution, or product. Initially, the plan was all about you, the leader—designing a plan for your success by becoming more aware of your conceptions, values, and capacity. Then it was a plan to enhance leadership relationships by understanding design-thinking dispositions, dimensions of the brain, decision-making, and motivation and influence. The focus shifted to the follower, designing a plan to facilitate others' success through creativity, management practices, and change processes. You shifted your focus from yourself, to you and others, to others, and finally, in the previous set of chapters, to the larger culture—the "we"—where the focus was on team, group norms, and the collective action of a culture of service. This final module moves into the future—"Design the Future"—first by building a culture of innovation (Chapter 14), then by learning more about how to forge your own way as an entrepreneurial leader (Chapter 15), and finally understanding the broad notion of sustainability and how to develop systems that will perpetuate your success (Chapter 16).

14 CREATING A CULTURE OF INNOVATION

Jules Bruck, PhD

LEARNING OBJECTIVES

Upon completion of this chapter, the reader should be able to

14.1   Recognize innovation's role in advancing the marketplace of the future

14.2   Interpret innovation as a collaborative process that extends creativity

14.3   Demonstrate convergent thinking techniques for innovation

14.4   Apply design-thinking dispositions to build an innovation culture

14.5   Practice cultivating and harvesting diversity to foster innovative teams

14.6   Apply the dimensions of the brain to enhance innovation for individuals and teams

---

Leadership by Design Model

Design Self
How can I design myself as a leader?

Design Relationships
As a leader, how can I design my relationships with others?

Design Others' Success
As a leader, how can I design success for others?

Design Culture
As a leader, how can I design the culture of my organization?

Design Future
As a leader, how can i innovate?

INTRODUCTION

Innovation is perhaps one of the most overused and misunderstood terms in leadership. Take a minute to search online for a *process of innovation*. You may be surprised to find about 2.1 billion results in less than one second (thank you, Google). It would take a lifetime to sort through all the results. Even if you review the first three screens of results, you find many resources with vastly different advice, definitions, tips, and ideas. Some of the information online can be confusing. Recall the definition from Chapter 8: Innovation is new things or methods that deliver value (as a noun); and the collaborative process of translating creative ideas into something of value (as a verb). Innovation is more than a new invention. Innovators may work to bring a product to the

431

marketplace, but they also deliver new processes, services, and experiences to consumers. And for the most part, innovation is built upon prior advances in a field of study.

Dr. Mae Jemison, the first Black woman in space, leads a project called 100 Year Starship, "which is about making sure the capabilities for human travel beyond our solar system exist within the next hundred years. And so, notice I say make sure the capabilities exist. I didn't say that it's about having the Starship Enterprise ready to go and warp out. But why do we want the capabilities to exist? Because it pushes us very radically to come up with new ideas."[1] As the project notes: "We believe pursuing an extraordinary tomorrow will build a better world today."[2]

This chapter focuses on you as the designer of the future, specifically, how you can effectively foster a culture of innovation. Throughout this textbook, you have been challenged to design leadership. Designing for innovation means addressing all levels of leadership—building your own innovative capacity, developing creativity and innovation in other individuals and teams, and designing a culture that encourages and sustains innovative thinking. In this chapter, you will discover processes, perspectives, and possibilities that will enhance idea generation and the translation of those ideas into value.

Leadership That Makes a Difference

All successful innovative organizations involve collaboration, but it is often the case that certain charismatic individuals become the face of the organization's success. Individuals possessing creative confidence (see Chapter 8) trust in themselves as creative individuals, and they are courageous enough to pursue their unique ideas. When you hear the word innovation, you likely think about those highly creative tech geniuses. Their genius, however, lies not in the idea attributed to them but more to their leadership and ability to foster a culture of innovation relative to the problem they address. These leaders have the creative confidence to innovate: Marissa Mayer, Julie Zhuo, and Jane Marie Chen. How were they able to come up with new ideas, and what gave them the courage to try them out?

New ideas define the career of Marissa Mayer, the former president and CEO of Yahoo! In her prior role at Google and subsequently for Yahoo!, she embraces ideas that come from all levels of the organization. Mayer says, "Ideas come from everywhere." In a video filmed for Stanford's eCorner, she explains there are "myriad of different places that ideas come from," and the goal is to set up a system where people feel they can contribute those ideas. "The best ideas will rise to the top in sort of a Darwinistic way by proof of concept of the powerful prototype, by demonstrating that it's going to fill a really important user need."[3] She continuously built platforms for people throughout the organization to share their ideas, leading to a culture of innovation. She also believes creativity comes from constraint. At Google, she evaluated the vision, which was to have Google run on 90 percent of computers, and concretely set down the constraints created by the vision. For Google to run on so many machines, it had to have a small memory footprint, and it could only consume a certain amount of disk space. Ruling out features based on size constraints led to very exciting levels of product innovation. According to Mayer, "That's when you see a lot of really interesting innovation happen, is when you actually pen in the constraints."[4] You can read more about constraint as a design principle later in this chapter.

Facebook's vice president of product design, Julie Zhuo, refers to the generation of new ideas in concrete terms of problem-solving and asks if the problem is worth solving. She asks, "Is this one the one we should pick out of thousands or millions of problems that are out there?"[5] Confidence comes from knowing that the problem is not being solved because of organizational self-interest, rather it is decidedly a problem faced by their audience. To determine the right problem at Facebook, Zhuo relies on talking to a lot of people and looking at a lot of data. Courage to try out new ideas comes from knowing the implementation of the idea will solve a real problem.

Embrace Innovations CEO and cofounder, Jane Marie Chen, gets her courage from optimism. Embrace Innovations aims to help over 20 million premature and low-birth-weight babies born into vulnerable populations by providing low-cost infant warmers. After years of working within corrupt and broken systems and witnessing a lot of pain and suffering, she began to feel negative and pessimistic. Her conscious choice to see the beauty around her motivated her to continue generating ideas to bring the vision to reality. She meets amazing, selfless doctors, nurses, parents, and community workers who provide her hope.[6]

Innovation is bigger than individual personality traits and more intricate than the end product. The individuals described are the face of their organization's success because they generate creative ideas and lead their organization guided by a strong vision of the future.

Facebook's Julie Zhuo uses her leadership to manage innovation.
San Francisco Chronicle/Hearst Newspapers via Getty Images

WHY INNOVATE? DESIGNING THE FUTURE

LEARNING OBJECTIVE
14.1 Recognize innovation's role in advancing the marketplace of the future.

What do *you* think of when you hear the word innovation? Often technology comes to mind because major technological advances and discoveries are significant drivers of large periods of innovation. **Technology** is the practical, material, and human application of scientific knowledge. This means technology includes everything from the most complicated machines to the most simple, everyday devices—such as a pencil. As you learn more about innovation in this chapter, know that the ideas, objects, and processes familiar to you were once the cutting-edge technology. Those now-common ideas sprung from prior ideas, and in turn, they will prompt the next set of ideas, in a chain of inspiration that will continue on into the future.

Technological innovation generally brings to mind things like the Internet and perhaps some of the big Internet companies, such as Google. Everyone is familiar with Google, the company and search engine, and individuals even use the word Google as a verb, meaning to search for answers or information online. What was Google's innovation? Larry Page and Sergey Brin, who founded Google, actually designed a PageRank algorithm to rank web pages, making the search engine faster and more accurate for users. They did not invent the idea of search engines—they creatively improved the process. From there, creativity in advertising-based financial innovations drove their business, allowing them to expand and innovate in new directions.

You live in an amazing time, where search engines give you answers to most of the questions you can dream up—in fact, it is more challenging to think up the questions than acquire the answers. Access to knowledge is easier than it has ever been. So, what might differentiate you, your team, or your organization from others who have the same access to information? You possess an un-Googleable talent—creativity. Innovation is powered by creativity, so to distinguish yourself from others, it is imperative that you maximize and capitalize on your creativity and learn to lead an organization that collects and fosters individual and team creativity.

Through time, individuals have contributed personal creativity to the development of exciting new technologies that transformed access to new markets and ideas. Yet the practical reality is that innovation remains collaborative. As a collaborative process, innovation benefits from today's connectivity, which allows for efficient sharing of information. Not surprisingly, innovation occurs more rapidly now than in any other point in history. If two parties are working on ideas to solve the same problem on opposite sides of the globe, they can connect and collaborate to expedite new discoveries. This was not always the case.

One of the most important innovations of all time, the magnetic compass, became readily available for European explorers in the 15th century, but it was originally invented in China over 1000 years earlier. In today's world, we navigate easily with the help of satellites within the Global Positioning System (GPS). Without innovation, there would be no GPS, nor all the jobs along the way as humans moved from star navigation to magnetic compasses to the present technology.

"Cutting-edge" innovation builds off prior ideas. What might the next innovation in this chain look like?
©iStockphoto.com/HadelProductions, ©iStockphoto.com/DNY59, ©iStockphoto.com/pagadesign

Likewise, organizations that failed to innovate and chose instead to propagate the then-current technology inevitably became as obsolete as the technology they embraced. Effective leaders (and designers) accurately read the current marketplace. Innovative leaders read the *future* marketplace, continually questioning the market and the process and iterating existing ideas or selecting new creative ideas to translate into value.

Chapter 14 • Creating a Culture of Innovation   435

Drivers of Innovation

The development of navigation story highlights several facets of the innovation definition. Again, innovation is the collaborative process of translating creative ideas into something of value. In the upcoming sections, you will learn more about two key concepts within this definition: collaboration and translating ideas into value. For now, notice how creativity is embedded in the definition of innovation. Creativity was defined in Chapter 8 as the personal capacities and process of generating a unique product that has value (remember the 4 Ps: *person, process, product,* and *press*). Innovation and creativity processes are indeed similar. However, there are additional features that differentiate innovation from creativity, including a number of unique tools to help in the thoughtful selection of bringing an idea to reality.

From the beginning of time, humans have innovated to survive and thrive in their environment. The creation of basic tools over thousands of years represents many examples of how humans innovate to create items of value. Through time, innovation in tools used to hunt, carry and store food, build secure shelters, and move easily from place to place have meant everything from basic survival to increased quality of life and additional leisure time. Several factors continually drive innovation throughout time, including *necessity, desire,* and *advances.*

Innovation From Needs

Necessity is perhaps the most fundamental reason for innovation.[7] Look around the room and notice all the things you see around you. What do you categorize as items you need? Certainly, you need the shelter of the room, as well as food and drink. What about electricity? The need for electricity is debatable—but it is unfathomable to exist without it in most parts of the world today. As you explore the drivers of innovation, you could focus on the evolution of absolutely anything you see, but a quick study of something all humans need allows for an easy exploration. Stop for a moment to think about how building techniques for shelters, vessels to hold and conveniently carry water, or even the clothes on your back have evolved over time.

Innovation driven by necessity extends beyond basic needs to higher-order needs. Recall Maslow's Hierarchy of Needs from the previous chapter. In Maslow's model of what motivates human behavior, each of those levels (physical, safety, belonging, esteem, cognitive, aesthetic, self-actualization, and up to transcendence) contributes a set of needs and thus provides the potential for future innovation. What innovations are possible in each of these various need categories?

Innovation From Desires

When considering what items were in the room that you *need*—you likely differentiated between two types of items. The ones you need and the ones you want. There are many items that are not necessary to own but are desirable. *Desire* is a second driver of innovation. The desire for entertainment and fun has driven creativity and innovation in many industries. Most notably, Disney has capitalized on the desire for both a safe escape from everyday life as well as high-quality entertainment. Fitness is another industry capitalizing on desire. The promise of improved physical health based on new programs or equipment is desirable over the alternative, not to mention the many desirable conveniences of modern health clubs.

Innovation From Advances

The third driver of innovation is advances. *Advances* in materials, machines, manufacturing, and processing (i.e., technology—applications of scientific knowledge) change the look, durability, use, and cost of our everyday products and services. Drive through an old neighborhood and you will find houses made of stone and brick. Advances in composite materials and plastics have transformed many industries resulting in many new product introductions. You can tell the age of a newer housing development by the use of composites for siding, railings, fences, shutters, decks, and patios. Creative people and organizations continually dream up new uses for new materials and machines, and innovators translate those uses into value.

The three drivers of innovation—needs, desires, and advances—provide you with an accessible framework to begin imagining a new and different future. This useful framework provides prompts for innovative thinking and demonstrates that creativity and innovation do not necessarily come from a place of creative genius but rather from an ability to reframe existing information.

Need will always be a primary driver of innovation, so as you consider how to design the future of an organization, think about the problems you want to solve. What will people need in the future? What material advance might provide a strong barrier against increasing UV exposure? How might nanotechnology be used to improve health at the molecular scale? Could microbes be used to create self-healing fabrics or structures? What materials and equipment would be required to monitor the health of or provide safe shelters for refugees?

In your daily life, you have seen how innovation is driven by needs and desires as well as advances in materials, machines, manufacturing, and technology. Right now, inventors, scientists, and entrepreneurs are working on ideas for new products and processes to introduce to the marketplace of the future. The future holds the promise of many wondrous innovations that you will interact with over time. The ability to combine advances with a need or desire in a way that creatively solves a problem will lead you to innovation and provide countless opportunities to generate creative ideas. The ideas and activities of innovation are just as applicable to your work as an effective leader as you design the future.

REFLECTION QUESTIONS

Innovation will change the marketplace of the future.

How do you imagine the needs and desires of the future?

What current trends can you find in technology and material innovations?

Can you connect knowledge about recent breakthroughs with human needs and desires? How might sustainability factor into the future marketplace? Will society continue to have a tolerance for products that consume natural resources and are quickly obsolete, or will consumers demand innovation shifts that consider a healthier environment?

UNDERSTANDING INNOVATION

LEARNING OBJECTIVE

14.2 Interpret innovation as a collaborative process that extends creativity.

"Innovating requires identifying the problems that matter and moving through them systematically to deliver elegant solutions."

—*Larry Keeley*[8]

Chapter 14 • Creating a Culture of Innovation   **437**

This section highlights key components of the definition of innovation: the collaborative process of translating creative ideas into something of value. Each of these elements prompts you to start thinking about ways to clearly identify and articulate problems as a means to communicate a clear organizational goal. Importantly, innovation requires both individual and collective creativity, and it takes place within an environment that supports creativity. Those additional aspects of innovation related to creativity, culture, and climate are discussed in the sections that follow.

Collaborative Process

In *Ten Types of Innovation*, Keeley states, "Innovation is a team sport. In fact, an organization that depends on individual innovators alone is destined to fail."[9] **Collaboration** is two or more people working together to create or achieve greater success than can be achieved individually. Naturally, collaboration involves both teamwork and partnerships, and therefore, it has importance as an *internal* organizational tool (recall Chapter 12 on Leading a Team) and as a means to communicate with experts and stakeholders outside the organization (*external* partnerships). The most valuable collaborators are those who are open to new ways of looking at existing information and who engage in multidisciplinary exploration. Leaders who wish to foster a collaborative organization should expertly define problems so all members of the organization have a strong sense of purpose and clarity of vision.

Defining a Problem

Albert Einstein is reported to have said that if he only had an hour to solve a problem, he would spend 55 minutes thinking about the problem and 5 minutes solving it. Whether proper attribution belongs to Einstein or someone else, the point is an emphasis on problem definition over solution. A poorly defined problem results in an ineffective solution, or worse, it results in a solution that does not even address the problem. Effective collaboration requires leaders who are able to clearly define the problems they are seeking to solve. Leaders want to solve real problems that will make a big difference over time, so it is important to get into the habit of actively defining problems as long-range challenges that you can tackle within your organization.

If you are going to design the future, you must think proactively—anticipating and preparing for a possible outcome. Proactively exploring problems is the key to innovative leadership. As discussed in Chapter 8, looking for problems may seem a bit odd, but practicing this mental habit now allows you to think more critically in the future. Once you see problems, you will automatically want to generate ideas to solve them. At that point, stop your innovation process and take the time to fully define the problem. Only by clearly defining a problem are you able to identify areas for further exploration, select measures for how to successfully solve the problem, and articulate a clear vision of the problem to share with others.

Have you ever used Mad-Libs™? Filling in blanks to complete a sentence is a fun game that is likely to lead to hilarious answers. The Buck Institute for Education (BIE)[10] created a helpful problem-defining tool called a TUBRIC™. The tool functions similarly to Mad-Libs™ and provides an easy structure to fill in blanks to generate a clear problem statement. There are four blanks you must fill in to complete the problem statement: Frame, Person/Entity, Action/Challenge, and Audience/Purpose.

In the first blank, called the Frame, select a word or phrase to frame the statement as a question, such as how might, could, what if, and so forth. The partially completed chart in Table 14.1 provides examples for each of the blanks. For the second blank, Person/Entity, write down the group who is taking action. This could be you (I), your organization (We), a school

438 Module 5 ● Design the Future

TABLE 14.1 ■ TUBRIC Tool for Problem-Finding and Defining			
Frame	**Person/Entity**	**Action/Challenge**	**Audience/Purpose**
How might	Universities	Design a campus facility	To engage students in creativity?
How can	Supermarket managers	Create networks	To provide food to hungry individuals?
How might	Health providers in low-income communities	Engage parents to ensure	Children thrive in their first five years?
Could	We	Improve delivery strategies	To cut back on fuel costs?

or community, or a group, such as all high school seniors or moms. The third blank is for the Action/Challenge. It requires a strong and concise verb, such as create, design, plan, solve, propose, or decide, followed by a challenge. For example, *design a network* or *organize a better process*. The last blank identifies the Audience/Purpose. The more specific your answers, the better your problem definition. Try filling in each blank for a problem relevant to you. Here is an example: "Could (frame) universities (entity) consolidate the application process (action/challenge) to save applicants time and money (audience/purpose)?"

A strongly defined problem often reads as a challenge. Formulating the challenge takes time and may be one of the hardest parts of the creative process. But a well-defined problem is well on its way to being solved. The problem gives you clues as to where to seek ideas, who to engage, and where to start to look for a better understanding of the problem, including what has been done before to solve the problem.

As highlighted in this chapter's "Leadership That Makes a Difference" feature, the future requires you to define challenges that solve real problems. Practice defining problems using the preceding method. Keep track of problems you have defined, so you can see how your ideas evolve over time. Once you have identified a clear problem—practice communicating your idea to someone to see if it is clear and concise before embarking on the next steps of the design process, which are highlighted subsequently.

REFLECTION QUESTIONS

What are some ways you could mindfully build your collaboration network? How does clearly defining a problem lead you to seek out additional collaborators?

Translating Ideas

Creativity comprises the personal capacities and process of generating a unique product that has value. Innovation is the collaborative process of *translating* creative ideas into something of value. At first glance, these two definitions seem pretty similar. As you analyze both terms, you will begin to see the differences.

Creativity requires divergent thinking. As you learned in Chapter 8, there are many techniques you can use to think divergently and generate many, many ideas. Individuals and teams able and willing to generate many ideas will develop more creative solutions to a defined problem.

Innovation also requires generating ideas that solve a well-defined problem but includes selecting one idea and moving it toward the marketplace or other measure of value.

Imagine you were hired to work at the Idea Factory. Your job description states your compensation is based on the quantity of ideas generated for a given problem. This would require creativity fluency, the ability to generate many ideas. If you were successful at your job, you would generate many ideas each day and become well-compensated. What if your pay was reduced each time your colleague thought of the same idea as you? You would have to ramp up your originality to keep up your earnings. Originality in idea-generating refers to a unique idea. Think of each unique idea as an individual marble, and then imagine all the marbles together in a canvas bag. It took a lot of creativity to generate all those ideas, and you are holding a large bag of marbles. You are a divergent-thinking success.

Now it is time to choose an idea. Which one do you select? How do you pick one idea from a big bag of unique ideas? It requires a different skill set called convergent thinking. **Convergent thinking** is the mental process of finding a single best solution to a problem.

Imagine *innovation* is represented by arrows pointing in all directions (Figure 14.2). The arrows suggest movement toward the implementation of a given idea—movement toward greater value. Select an idea and put it in the center of the arrows as a way of visualizing innovation. Is it possible to have creativity without innovation? Absolutely. Creativity gets you a bag of marbles. Can you have innovation without creativity? No, because you have nothing unique to *move* to the next phases of the process, which is implementation. You need to select a creative idea (or combination of ideas) to move forward for innovation. If the selected idea is prototyped and tested, it may be put into the marketplace. Some of those arrows lead to very valuable implementations, and some do not. The next part of the innovation definition highlights how the idea is translated into *something of value*, and later in the chapter, you will learn about several convergence methods for how to select one idea from many.

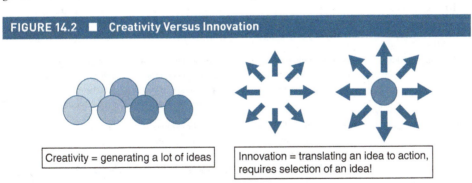

FIGURE 14.2 ■ Creativity Versus Innovation

Creativity = generating a lot of ideas

Innovation = translating an idea to action, requires selection of an idea!

Translating Ideas Into Something of Value

There are many ways to return value to the organization. Economic viability requires that an innovation generate enough revenue to sustain the organization. The innovation may be in the form of a product, system, process, or service. Innovation within an organization frequently includes other forms of value, such as social or environmental strategies, which may also be good for an organization's bottom line. Note there are many forms of value beyond economic.

Identifying the full range of possible innovation-value connections can be driven by the value you seek or by the idea and its possibilities. As you design for the future, what are the values you and your organization seek to enhance? Likewise, consider the many ways innovation in different areas of your organization can return value to you and others. A number of models have

440 Module 5 ● Design the Future

been developed that explicate many of the different types of innovation, each offering a different form of value. One concise model based on the work of Keeley organizes the innovation into 10 types across four major categories. Table 14.2 illustrates these innovation types along with a key descriptor and prompting question.

TABLE 14.2 ■ Ten Types of Innovation			
Innovation Type[11]	Description	Ask Yourself	Example—Not-for-Profit Summer Camps
Finance—business model	How you make money	How might I generate extra capital?	Create new for-profit division to support your not-for-profit work
Finance—networks and alliances	How you join forces with other companies for mutual benefit	How might I partner to eliminate local or regional duplication of services?	Offer advanced lessons (tennis, golf, swimming) through local partners
Process—enabling	How you support the company's core processes and workers	How might I enhance compensation or benefits for my employees?	Provide an educational development pipeline for staff wanting to become school teachers
Process—core	How you create and add value to your offerings	How might I create a new system that will optimize resources?	Design a new bus scheduling system reducing bus rental costs
Offerings—product performance	How you design your core offerings to improve performance	In what ways might I improve my product's performance?	Offer campers high-tech training on useful design programs
Offerings—product system	How you link and/or provide a platform for multiple products	How might I link programs, products, and processes to enhance offerings?	Turn school-year activities into clubs, and transition clubs to camp themes
Offerings—service	How you provide value to customers and consumers beyond and around your products	How might I enhance services or special offerings to my customers?	Add before and after camp care, parents' nights, and advanced booking
Delivery—channel	How you get your offerings to market	What are the key channels through which my audience finds products, services, and so forth?	Partner with students' home school for location
Delivery—brand	How you communicate your offerings	What unique message will capture the attention of my audience?	Focus marketing campaign on student achievement
Delivery—customer experience	How your customers feel when they interact with your company and its offerings		Provide team t-shirts and hold a youth expo to highlight projects

Chapter 14 • Creating a Culture of Innovation   **441**

DIVERGE FOR CREATIVITY, CONVERGE FOR INNOVATION

LEARNING OBJECTIVE
14.3 Demonstrate convergent thinking techniques for innovation.

Generating many ideas is a hallmark of creativity. Remember, the more ideas you generate, the more likely you are to find that unique and valuable idea. Divergent thinking—a mindset of generating many, many ideas for a single problem—and divergent techniques are critical to creativity. But the opposite—convergence—is key to the process of innovation and the selection of one idea to move into action.

Convergent thinking was defined as the mental process of finding a single best solution to a problem. Sometimes it is described as the ability to give the *correct* answer, but this is misleading. Unlike a standardized exam question, there is hardly ever one right answer, especially in design or leadership. It is best to think of convergence as a process. Convergence as a process gives room for a level of creativity in choosing an idea—whether combining two or more ideas or allowing for iteration on an original idea. You use convergence every day when you work to support an argument in writing or conversation. For example, you may know many facts and figures about gun safety, but when you are responding during a discussion, you have to evaluate the particular facts that best support the idea you are sharing.

In contrast to divergent thinking, a process pursuing wildly outward directions, convergence is focused. Both are critical for innovation, and both are generally associated with the imagination phase. Before you can implement, you must evaluate each of the best ideas to select one to put into action.

Convergent thinking is a disposition (habit of thinking) that you have been well trained in over a lifetime of schooling. Unfortunately, your convergent habit is usually put to use in cutting off the idea-generating process and choosing an answer. Effective innovators (and those that lead them) learn to manage both divergent and convergent thinking within the process. Convergent thinking is also a skill set with many techniques that are used to select and prepare an idea for action. Deciding which technique to use is often based on the situation. Using convergent techniques is a good way to choose an idea without biasing the process, which is very useful when groups are involved in decision-making. For example, you may find your team has a bias toward solving problems with ideas that are easy to implement or seem familiar. If that is the case, they may be seriously limiting innovation. Convergence strategies help you to evaluate ideas free from bias and make decisions free of judgment.

Benchmarking

One method to converge on an idea is a process called benchmarking. **Benchmarking** is evaluating ideas by comparison with a standard. Consider a team of engineers asked to design something new, such as an innovative floating wetland. A floating wetland is a manufactured floating island designed to provide filtration and treatment services to waterways to improve water quality. The engineers will compare their idea, as well as several others, including solutions already on the market (standard), against criteria developed during the definition of the problem. Perhaps they were asked to design a floating wetland treatment that reliably floats, supports plants, eliminates nesting waterfowl, and is safe for the environment. After creating the matrix, each person on the project team independently scores each product, ranking each idea using a numerical

442   Module 5 ● Design the Future

system (for example, 1 to 4) against the criteria. The addition of each product's score will yield a number that represents a quantitative result. Benchmarking allows ideas to be numerically ranked to determine the best idea of several.

As seen in Table 14.3, the high score based on the four criteria seems to indicate a clear best choice. However, using the tool to see where other products/ideas scored higher than the overall winner in different categories is useful too. In this example, it may lead the team to consider changes to *Our Innovative Idea* based on *Market Product B*'s score on Criterion 4, and *Another Idea We Had*'s score on Criterion 3. Use the scoring to guide team discussion. Work to understand differences in individual values.

TABLE 14.3 ■ Benchmarking

Product	Criterion 1—Reliably Floats, No Sinking	Criterion 2—Supports Plants	Criterion 3—Does Not Allow for Nesting	Criterion 4—Safe for the Environment	Score
Our Innovative Idea	4	3	2	3	12
Market Product A	4	2	1	1	8
Market Product B	3	1	2	4	10
Another Idea We Had!	1	1	4	3	9

How? Now, Wow![12]

Another useful tool to select ideas while making sure no potentially viable ideas are lost is a technique called *How? Now, Wow!* This convergence tool is also a matrix that has two selection criteria—*originality* and *ease of implementation*. To use the tool, draw four boxes—two stacked on top of two (see Figure 14.3).

The top two boxes represent ideas *impossible* to implement, and the bottom two are for *easy* ideas to implement. Looking at the four boxes—the two on the left are for *normal ideas* and the two on the right are for *original ideas*. This tool allows a team to quickly sort through the many ideas they generated during the imagination phase to converge on the most suitable idea to develop. The value of this matrix is that it also enables the group to look at all ideas simultaneously. A team using this tool then has an opportunity to look beyond practical project selection criteria (How much weight does it hold? How stable is it? How durable is it?) that solve the problem to actively deciding to pursue a more innovative idea. As a team, ideas are reviewed and each one placed into a box. *HOW* ideas are original but impossible to implement. These are ideas for the future—dreams and challenges that inspire awe and wonder—think human colony on Mars. *NOW* ideas are the ones that are easy to implement and low risk. They are pre-accepted—maybe because they are slightly different versions of an older idea. The *WOW* ideas are easy and original breakthrough ideas that are exciting because they are feasible and ready for action.

Chapter 14 ● Creating a Culture of Innovation   443

FIGURE 14.3 ■ **How? Now, Wow!**	
Impossible to implement/ Normal ideas	Impossible to implement/ Original ideas HOW?
Easy to implement/ Normal ideas NOW!	Easy to implement/ Original ideas WOW!

As a leader, you help determine which type of idea is most feasible for the organization. Do you have the time, resources, and talent to go for a HOW idea? Is this the direction you want to move into as an organization? What may be needed to help you achieve those original, impossible ideas? Perhaps it requires you to focus on a product or process in the NOW category that becomes the ongoing revenue generator for the development of a HOW idea. WOW ideas are those that will be easy but position the organization as unique or innovative.

Force Field Analysis

Another useful convergence technique is Force Field Analysis. You can use Force Field Analysis when you want to explore the forces for and against several ideas once you have narrowed down your possibilities. To use this technique, at the top of a blank page write down the idea under consideration. Draw a line down the middle of the page. On one side of the line begin to list all the forces *for* the idea. In other words, list out all the things that might promote the idea or change. This could be specific individuals, connections, assets, trends, policies, partnerships, funds—absolutely anything. On the other side of the line, list the forces *against* the idea. Similar to making a pro/con list, use logic to determine different forces that have the potential to act on a solution if those are understood. For example, if a team generated an idea to create a *shared food pantry* for a community to combat food waste while feeding people in need, there would be forces for the pantry and forces against. The forces for a shared food pantry may be a new policy that limits food waste in household garbage, centrally available space near a homeless shelter, and an existing transportation network of deliveries from a single distribution to neighborhood grocery stores. Forces against the idea may be health concerns, high transportation costs, and high rent.

Once you have the forces defined and written into the diagram, you can lead a team in determining how to neutralize or otherwise address the forces against the idea, as well as capitalize on and/or increase the forces in the for category. Figure 14.4 illustrates the Force Field Analysis using another example. After looking it over, choose an example of your own and briefly outline the forces for and against your desired goal. The act of purposefully thinking about these two seemingly obvious sides of a change leads to insights that ultimately inform and facilitate implementation.[13]

The $100 Test

Benchmarking is a method used to determine the quantifiable ranking of an idea. Economists see the world differently. Through the lens of an economist, the way to gauge the acceptability of a product or policy is to equate it to something valuable that everyone can relate to—dollars. Would you put your money on an idea?

FIGURE 14.4 ■ Force Field Analysis

Force Field and Change Analysis Template

Describe the current situation or problem (what is happening now, or what the status quo is). Outing Club is exclusively for registered university students. Only registered students can attend outings.			
Describe the contemplated change (desired goal) that needs analysis. Proposed change to allow alumni of the outing club to attend trips.			
List the driving forces that are promoting change.	Weight (1–5)	List the restraining forces or obstacles that are opposing change.	Weight (1–5)
Alums have experience they can share with the club members	4	University liability will not cover alums	4
Alums have friends in the club post-graduationand want to participate	2	May limit younger students from emerging as leaders	5
Alums may provide additional financial support for larger trips	3	Alums may take the place of undergraduates on trips with limited space	3
Are there some common themes?		Why are these forces occurring? Are there some common themes?	
Totals	9		12

People make very different decisions about how to allocate dollars versus points on a chart. Another convergence technique is *The $100 Test*. Assume each team member has $100 to spend on developing several ideas. After presenting a range of suitable ideas, each team member distributes their money across the ideas under consideration. This works best if team members have money (real or play) to allocate. Direct the team to think of each allocation as a real investment and allow members to divide their $100 between different ideas. After everyone invests, add up the total dollar amounts for each of the ideas to determine how the team values each idea. This can lead to a deeper conversation about how distributions were made among team members.

Convergence is part of the ideation phase of the innovation process. It leads to the selection of an idea to move forward into implementation phases of the process. As a leader, you now have selected an idea—so what is your next move? You should consider ways of testing the idea. During the implementation phase, you must practice an iterative mindset—constantly assessing and improving on ideas. Circle back to revisit old ideas and be open to new ideas along the way. As you can see, there is a balance between multiple variables, ideas, and design constraints. The innovation process is about creatively resolving the tensions between multiple factors. As a leader, you should continuously ask, "What if . . .?" regardless of how satisfied you are with your solution and be willing to make design decisions conditionally with the awareness that they may or may not work out as you continue toward a final solution.

CREATING A CULTURE OF INNOVATION WITH DESIGN THINKING

LEARNING OBJECTIVE

14.4 Apply design-thinking dispositions to build an innovation culture.

What would an organizational culture look like if it were designed to support creativity and innovation? One way of approaching this question is to think about ways creative individuals are *taught* from their earliest encounter with a culture outside their family—in school. Educators, similar to all professionals, must strike a balance between competing constraints. The culture of a school is likely to prioritize many values above creativity, in part because of time constraints. If achievement is high on the list of priorities, resources dedicated to the development of individual skills related to creativity may be lacking.

Have you ever wondered why leaders, especially political and business leaders, always seem so concerned about education? They are interested in education because what students are taught now will influence who they become and how they think about business and politics as adults. If you want to design the future, you start where the future lies—within the developing minds of children. The same is true of developing the minds of adults and those you lead. As you think about creating a culture of innovation, consider what you might do now that will affect your organization 10 or 20 years from now. Read about what creativity expert Ronald Beghetto highlights about creativity in the classroom and note those things you can do now in the teaching aspects of your leadership.

Experts Beyond the Text

INSIGHTFUL LEADERS KNOW ABOUT . . . CREATIVITY IN THE CLASSROOM

Creativity in the Classroom: Quick Insights for Leaders

By Ronald A. Beghetto, University of Connecticut

What do leaders need to know about creativity in the classroom? In what follows, I provide a brief overview of what creativity is and what it means in the context of the classroom. I then highlight a few important things to know about creativity. Specifically, I highlight a few problematic beliefs that can undermine classroom creativity and offer alternative perspectives from the creativity studies literature. I close by briefly discussing why it is important for leaders to know about this topic.

What Is Creativity?

Creativity researchers generally agree that creativity is some combination of originality and meeting task constraints as defined within a particular context.[14]

One way to think about creativity in the classroom is striking a balance between helping students share their own ideas, interests, perspectives, and ways of doing things (originality) while at the same time helping them learn how to meet academic criteria, standards, and expectations (task constraints) during particular learning activities and assignments (context).

Here's an example that may help. Imagine a student who is asked to provide an illustration of the life cycle of a plant on a science test. The student draws a picture of a plant turning into a zombie. Although such a drawing is an *original* response, it would not be considered creative in the *context* of the science test (because it did not meet the *task constraints* of representing the features of the plant life cycle). Similarly, a student who copies a picture found on Google Images would not be considered creative because it lacks originality, even though it meets the task constraints (i.e., has all the required features of the life cycle). A creative response, in the context of the science test, would require students to come up with their own, unique way of illustrating the required features of the plant life cycle.

Important Things to Know About Classroom Creativity

Here are a few problematic beliefs about creativity in classrooms and some new ways of thinking about them based on the creativity studies literature:

- **Problematic belief:** Only certain people can be creative
- **Response from the literature:** There are different levels of creative experiences and actions. Learning something new and meaningful (even if it is only new and meaningful to you) can still be considered a creative act. This is called mini-c creativity and is a sign of creative potential.[15] Mini-c creativity can grow into larger C creativity through (among other things) honest and supportive feedback, hard work, deliberate practice, sensible risk-taking, persistence, the development of expertise, and time.[16] There are no shortcuts or magical strategies for developing creative potential into creative achievements.
- **Problematic belief:** Creativity is only about the arts
- **Response from the literature:** Creative thought and action are possible in any subject area.[17] Just because someone is creative in one subject area (science), however, doesn't mean they will be creative in another (language arts). Creative accomplishment requires developing domain-specific knowledge and skills.
- **Problematic belief:** Creativity is about thinking outside the box
- **Response from the literature:** In the context of classrooms, it's often more about thinking and acting creatively inside the box rather than outside of it. Of course, there are times when it is necessary to imagine and build a new box. In most cases, however, it's about being creative within curricular constraints.[18]
- **Problematic belief:** Creativity is always good
- **Response from the literature:** There is a time and a place for creativity. Creative thought and action always involve risk, which sometimes involves negative, unintended consequences. Taking creative risks makes sense when old ways of thinking and acting don't work or when we are trying to make improvements.
- **Problematic belief:** Schools kill creativity
- **Response from the literature:** The possibility for creative thought and action is always and already present in schools and classrooms. Schools can't give creativity to students, take it away, or kill it, but schools can establish situations that suppress or support it.[19]

Why Is It Important for Leaders to Know About This Topic?

A common goal of education is to prepare young people for the future. This is a challenge because the future is uncertain. Creativity is a capacity that enables people to successfully navigate the uncertainty they face, solve complex and ill-defined problems, and make necessary changes in thought and action. Moreover, if we want students to engage in possibility thinking and take the risks necessary for creative thought and action, then we need to lead the way by doing so ourselves.

Chapter 14 ● Creating a Culture of Innovation   **447**

Another way of approaching the question of how to foster creativity is to think about ways creative individuals *habitually think* as they approach each stage of the creative process—in other words, design thinking. As you learned in Chapter 1, design thinking is a set of dispositions defined as habits of mind that are often seen as a tendency or characteristics. Leaders who provide the cultural conditions to support the characteristic dispositions of creative individuals as they progress through each stage of their process will set the organization on a path to innovation.

In Chapter 10, culture refers to "a set of shared assumptions that guide the behavior of members of an organization of any size from a small group of friends to a workplace to the larger society." Social norms can enhance individual creativity, which in turn positively influences leadership.[20] Effective leaders design culture *intentionally*, which means actively designing the shared set of beliefs and values that drive behaviors as well as all aspects of organizational conduct. You want meaningful organizational values to be the driver of culture rather than empty words. In other words, stating "At this organization we value excellence, service, and innovation" does not mean a whole lot because the words have little clarity. Instead consider, "At this organization, we value innovation and believe in adopting a user-centered approach to problem-solving." The second statement clearly shares how the value is related to the belief and is influential in shaping the organization's behavior.

Design-thinking dispositions can guide your efforts as a leader to create a culture of innovation. Look at the design-thinking dispositions in Table 14.4. The specific dispositions include user-centered, *explorative, divergent, multidisciplinary, iterative, collaborative,* and *integrative*. As you review the column titled "We make it so by . . ." consider ways a statement in each category could be expressed as part of the organizational values and beliefs. On the left are the dispositions by phase of the design process, and on the right are the ways leaders can *make it so* by engaging in the specific tasks.

TABLE 14.4 ■ Creating a Culture of Innovation With Design Thinking	
Design-Thinking Disposition	**Creating a Culture of Innovation—Our Vision**
Design thinking is a cognitive approach to engaging problems that embodies a specific mindset that is	We make it so by . . . We encourage/foster the notion of . . .
Understand the Problem, Person, Process, Context	
User-centered—mindset that focuses on the user and how they experience and feel	Adopting a user-centered approach Engaging in user research to acquire a deeper understanding of the user Looking toward users to define problems rather than those who successfully solved the problem before
Explorative—mindset that assumes purposeful ambiguity and curiosity	Allowing time and space for preflection and reflection on the problem, person, process, and context Proactively seeing opportunities to improve by unearthing new problems Embarking on the unknown with optimism

(Continued)

TABLE 14.4 ■ Creating a Culture of Innovation With Design Thinking *(Continued)*	
***Imagine* the Possibilities and Impossibilities**	
Divergent—mindset of generating many, many ideas for a single problem	Modeling and pushing beyond preconceived limits of generating ideas
	Incentivizing the generation of new ideas
	Encouraging people to speak up with new ideas
Multidisciplinary—mindset that engages many minds and pursues multiple areas of expertise	Imagining and/or engaging using multiple disciplines and perspectives
	Purposefully displacing people out of routine thinking
	Engaging a diverse group of colleagues
Iterative—mindset of always seeing solutions in process—assessing and improving	Incorporating revisions and multiple iterations
	Testing new ideas
	Prototyping
	Providing constant feedback
***Implement*, Assess, Iterate**	
Collaborative—mindset that working with others is always far more effective	Inviting collaboration and co-design
	Engaging across functional boundaries
Integrative—mindset of attending to and balancing multiple criteria, particularly viability, feasibility, and desirability	Assessing competing goals of the solution and revising

Culture is complex and multifaceted. Organizational leaders strive to influence members of their organization and guide them toward a common vision. The most effective visions are deeply embedded in the culture through the expression of values and norms. Most importantly, the expression of values and norms influences how people within the organization act (i.e., "the way we do things around here"). The *ways we make it so* in Table 14.4 demonstrate several possibilities to guide the development of clear organizational values that are supportive of creativity and innovation.

REFLECTION QUESTIONS

Evaluate which statements in Table 14.4 you believe are most important, necessary, and true to support a culture of creativity and innovation. Imagine an organization you are familiar with while evaluating the design-thinking dispositions and the innovation culture statements. Does the organization you are thinking about support one or more aspects of creativity? Which ones do they value and where could they become more supportive?

DEI BY DESIGN

LEARNING OBJECTIVE

14.5 Practice cultivating and harvesting diversity to foster innovative teams.

Chapter 14 • Creating a Culture of Innovation 449

Solving organizational problems requires team innovation.[21] Each individual on the team brings their unique perspectives, experiences, and resources to the group. The more diverse the team, the more divergent the content coming together to generate ideas . . . if those individuals feel comfortable enough to share that diversity with the group. In inclusive and creative leadership environments, members feel they can authentically express themselves, especially with regard to their unique problem-solving perspectives. DEI-minded leaders harvest the benefits of diversity by inviting all organizational or community members to fully engage in and uniquely contribute to leadership processes.[22] Additionally, inclusive leaders cultivate value-in-diversity beliefs by actively promoting positive perspectives on diversity to drive members' engagement across differences. These leader behaviors promote team-authentic inclusion and grow team creativity.

Harvesting diversity includes actively inviting members to offer their unique knowledge, skills, and abilities, as well as supporting the voicing of opinions and critical perspectives. By inviting a wide array of identities, attitudes, and experiences across multiple lines of difference, leaders create members' perceptions of being a valuable contributor to the team.[23] However, simply harvesting the benefits of diversity will not necessarily improve feelings of inclusion among members. "Increasing the volume of diverse perspectives, without creating an environment that enables team members to cope with and value such differences, highlights to individuals how they are different from others, making them feel less rather than more included."[24] Hence, the positive influence of diversity depends on leaders also **cultivating value-in-diversity** beliefs among members.

For team-authentic inclusion to bloom, leaders also need to unambiguously promote the collective belief that differences among members represent an advantage for the team as a whole. Team leaders do this by framing social differences as natural and positive team features as well as encouraging beliefs that interpersonal differences are assets for the group. When leaders embolden and reward unique attitudes and beliefs, while instilling a shared faith in the team that differences are desirable, members feel more integrated into their teams. Teams characterized by a well-developed sense of inclusion are more inclined to discuss, reconfigure, and integrate innovative ideas and perspectives. Empowering members to share their unique views (harvesting), while building an environment that appreciates differences (cultivating) aids in creating a culture of innovation.

CREATING A CLIMATE OF INNOVATION WITH THE DIMENSIONS OF THE BRAIN

LEARNING OBJECTIVE
14.6 Apply the dimensions of the brain to enhance innovation for individuals and teams.

The design of an organization's culture based upon the design-thinking mindsets ensures the values of an organization will support creativity. The culture sets the overall tone for a group, but it does not address individual needs within the context of the workplace. Therefore, it is important to consider how people within an organization function at a fundamental and perceptual level and how they relate to one another to further design a workplace climate conducive to creativity.

The organizational climate differs from the culture. An organization's culture is a stable articulation of beliefs, values, and norms. The **organizational climate** is the recurring, often dynamic, patterns of behaviors, attitudes, and feelings that characterize what it is like to work within an organization. The difference can be thought of as what the team *values* versus what the team members experience. It is well-documented that a supportive, creative climate increases levels of innovation, well-being, and even profitability.[25]

In Chapter 9, you explored how understanding six dimensions of the brain could inform your leadership. These six dimensions were physiological, emotional, social, constructive, dispositional, and reflective. In this section, three of the dimensions are revisited to provide a valuable framework for leaders interested in designing an innovative organizational climate supportive of and enhancing individual and team creativity. While all six dimensions are contributing factors to a creative climate, the social, constructive, and reflective dimensions are particularly useful when designing the future.

Like today, organizations of the future will compete for talented individuals. When designing for either climate or culture, it is important to start with an understanding of the many different people who share the work environment. Because each individual has a unique set of motivators, attitudes, and personal preferences, there is no one-size-fits-all approach to creating a perfect climate for all. The most impactful leaders maintain open and honest communication with teams about the positive and negative aspects of the working environment. Leaders familiar with applying the dimensions of the brain have a great head start in conceiving of a workplace environment in tune with a variety of individual needs and styles.

Social Dimension: Collaboration and Community

At this organization, we foster interaction and the notion that there is a collaborative spirit where individuals are able to take risks while advancing a shared vision.

Collaboration is key to innovation. As discussed earlier in this chapter, innovation does not happen individually in a vacuum. Rather, it requires the engagement and creativity of many people with unique skill sets coming together to focus on the collective vision of the solution to a problem. How does collaboration fit within the overall context of a society that values individual achievement and success? What do high schools do to foster collaboration among students in the classroom? On the playing field? In the band? And as students prepare college applications? Collaboration may be hard to imagine since some level of competitive structures are in play in almost every one of those examples and individuals are not taught *how* to collaborate.

Collaboration embodies the social dimension. The leader plays a key role in designing a climate of innovation, starting with modeling creative activity and confidence.[26] In a collaborative environment, people must enjoy working on teams, accepting critical feedback, and putting into place systems for selecting valuable ideas. Leaders communicate that they and the group must be willing to leave good ideas behind in the pursuit of great ideas. For these reasons, it is perhaps asking a lot of an organization to expect individuals to have the ability to collaborate effectively and efficiently. Instead, assume people are not accustomed to collaboration nor comfortable putting their ideas out there and critiquing others' ideas. You, the leader, need to design and foster a climate of psychological safety to encourage innovation.[27] It is also critical to articulate the goals of the group clearly. Investing in a shared vision is the best way to overcome any obstacles to collaboration. Table 14.5 summarizes some key activities from the social dimension that a leader could do to foster a climate of innovation.

Chapter 14 ● Creating a Culture of Innovation   **451**

TABLE 14.5 ■ Creative Climate Using the Social Dimension	
Actively Support the Social Dimension of Creativity and Innovation by Providing:	**In My Organization, I Could . . .**
Opportunities for collaboration with and within diverse individuals and groups from inside and outside the organization	Join a team and become a co-collaborator Provide collaboration training Hire/Populate teams with diversity in mind
Freedom to make mistakes and room to fail	Build and encourage a climate of psychological safety
Clear problems to solve, criteria for success, and a project plan to recognize successful solutions	Use a methodology to clearly define problems and help teams craft a vision for successful solutions
A strong sense of community	
Rewards to teams that take appropriate risks	Nominate groups for awards based on their process rather than their end result
Modeled behaviors by myself and other leaders showing creative confidence	

Constructive Dimension: Seeking and Seeing Different

At this organization, we believe in other ways of seeing the problem, and we seek to challenge the existing constructions of knowledge.

Your brain is a lean, mean, pattern-making machine (remember that phrase?). To challenge a construction of knowledge requires one to determine how individual mental models influence your way of seeing a problem. Mental models were defined way back in Chapter 2 as your mental representation of things in the world, including how you understand things and how you process information. On the positive side, the constructive dimension helps you and your team establish a clear and shared vision of what you are trying to achieve. On the troubling side, differences in mental models can affect how two people arrive at different conclusions when provided the same information. Generally speaking, it is common for people to pay attention to some but not all data presented to them, while others may pay attention to different aspects of the data. The way both individuals impose their interpretation of the data and draw conclusions has a profound effect on the conclusion. It is easy to lose sight of your personal thinking process and obtain conclusions that seem obvious. When conclusions seem obvious but are different from others, it can lead to disagreements. It is often difficult to resolve a conflict that arises from your constructed reality for a given situation.

Mental models frame how one sees a problem, which consequently limits how one sees a problem and the possibilities for solution.[28] By definition, it inhibits new ways of seeing and limits innovation. In a culture of innovation, there needs to be a conscious effort to recognize the constructions that are dictating how you are seeing problems and solutions and look beyond mental models to frame a problem in a unique way. Are you open to different ways of seeing the world?

What are some ways to challenge your mental model? First, *understand* the nature of your mental model and how it works to frame information. *Reflect* on your mental model—how are you defining things, describing situations, assuming—what are the ways you see the world that may influence how you make decisions and process information? *Inquire* about others' mental models; specifically, learn to ask questions that shed light on what data people are paying attention to and how they interpret the data. *Advocate* for your way of thinking and the conclusions you draw by clearly expressing your thought and reasoning process.

According to Confucius, "True wisdom is knowing what you don't know." Being aware of mental models and actively expanding your knowledge base are useful ways of thinking about your own constructions of the world. If you were asked to make a list of what you do not know, it should be very, very long. If it is not, you are not even aware of what you do not know, which means raising that awareness is your first step. Find out more about the world, explore different perspectives. It is helpful to explore cultures different from your own, to travel, and to be open to new ways of seeing the world.

Mental models structure what individuals see, how they respond, and the conclusions they draw. Mental models describe how information is organized in your mind and what you draw on when faced with complex yet seemingly familiar situations. They also describe how an individual may adapt to a new situation or see a new problem or frame the future. As you design a culture of innovation, what ways of seeing the world do you bring to the table? How similar are the constructed mental models of those in your organization? What perspectives are you missing that could spark innovation? Table 14.6 summarizes some key activities from the constructive dimension that a leader could do to foster a climate of innovation.

TABLE 14.6 ■ Creative Climate Using the Constructive Dimension	
Actively Support the Constructive Dimension of Creativity and Innovation by Providing:	**In My Organization, I Could . . .**
Opportunity to travel	Send groups to new places to gather information
	Hold a meeting in a new location—somewhere unexpected
Time to explore and understand before being asked to draw conclusions	Give my team excused time off of email to allow time for focused problem solving
	Work with my team to create a labyrinth—encourage people to use it and lead the way
Opportunity to get involved with a culture different from your own	Host cultural events that allow individuals to share foods and customs
Explore societal mental models when implementing ideas	Provide the team prompts to ensure societal mental models are considered

Leadership by Design

Design Principle: Constraint

> *Definition:* A method of limiting the actions that can be performed on a system.
> *In Other Words:* Challenge your creativity with limits—advance your innovation
> *For Example:* A spending limit on your credit card constrains how much shopping and acquisition of debt you can do.
> *For Leaders:* Constraints may seem like the last thing a leader should be imposing on a creative project, but constraints can prove beneficial when implemented correctly. When

Chapter 14 • Creating a Culture of Innovation   **453**

the sky is the limit, many people become paralyzed by the infinite opportunities. As a leader, helping to take away some of the choices can provide a more focused path to begin exploring. Constraints are put in place as a means to simplify systems and minimize errors. Constraints also help with the convergence process, helping to identify the best ideas from the long list of divergently generated ideas.

When would a leader want to limit the actions of their followers? How might counter-intuitive approaches make a culture more creative? It is important to use constraints wisely and only when appropriate. Wouldn't innovation come to a halt without the occasional dissent?

Reflective Dimension: Time, Space, and Structure

At this organization, we believe in supplying time, space, and structure for other ways of seeing the problem.

Every Sunday night Julie looks at her calendar to see what she has on the schedule for the week ahead. Recently, she had a week that was jam-packed with meetings. Back-to-back meetings. Each meeting required some preparation on the front end, and of course, each required follow-up afterward. But with each meeting stacked one on top of the next, there was no time to *reflect* on the purpose or conclusion of any meeting. What was decided? Was it a good decision? Does it require additional follow-up? Where is the best source of follow-up information? What does the outcome of the meeting mean for the project?

In a work climate that requires a lot of meetings, who is allowing for and protecting the important non-meeting time where individuals have a chance to think and be thoughtful? This thoughtful thinking time is called reflection. It may come naturally directly following the meeting if you are fortunate enough to have a decent walk (15–20 minutes) outside of a building between meetings or if you schedule time between meetings for reflection, exercise, meditation, or naps.[29] These mental breaks after intense collaborative or individual work often lead to the greatest ideas, and they can foster creativity as well as reduce stress.

When working in groups, reflective time may seem more like the alternative definition of reflective—as in images or sounds *bouncing back* at you. Your brain needs individual reflection time, and teams need their people engaging in both individual and group reflection to fully foster their creativity (recall the idea-generating technique called incubation from Chapter 8). What opportunities are provided for your organization to reflect on current decisions, processes, ideas, or products? How have you and your team structured time and space to actually think about decisions already made?

Reflection is an essential dimension of the brain, and it is a key component of all work; but it is an inseparable part of creative work. Further, metacognition (reflecting about your own thinking) may facilitate different aspects of the creative process.[30] When during the work day are you provided time to reflect? Is time to reflect valued in the organization? Promoted? Understood? Do you understand it? Think about it. Now read this section again, and then put the book down. Go for a 20-minute walk. You may prefer to reflect quietly—or to the sound of nature or music—but try both. When you walk, you think about things differently.[31] In fact, the authors of this textbook did just that—took a break and walked a bit to think about how to organize and write up the idea of reflection for this section. Table 14.7 summarizes some key activities from the reflective dimension that a leader could do to foster a climate of innovation.

TABLE 14.7 ■ Creative Climate Using the Reflective Dimension

Actively Support the Reflective Dimension of Creativity and Innovation by Providing	In My Organization, I Could . . .
Time for people to reflect	Structure my meeting blocks to keep the most productive part of the day open for creative work and reflection
Space for people to reflect	Seek out places and encourage team members to exercise after long meetings
	Seek out places for team members to work on hobby projects or engage in mindful meditation; encourage people to take a break and work on alternative hobby projects
Opportunities for people to relax during the work	Encourage people to enjoy time in a café
	Take a walk together
Education about the value of reflection	End the meeting 15 minutes early; prompt your team to stop and write down their thoughts before they leave
	Take time to share success stories

Leadership by Design

Design Principle: Von Restorff Effect

Definition: A phenomenon of memory in which noticeably different things are more likely to be recalled than common things.

In Other Words: Leverage the element of surprise to increase memory. Do something a little bit different.

For Example: The Macy's Thanksgiving Day Parade uses the von Restorff Effect every year to deliver a memorable experience to its millions of viewers. Nowhere else would you see Smurfs and a giant ice cream cone floating through the streets of New York City. Macy's capitalizes on these unique sights and experiences to engrain themselves in people's memory.

©iStock.com/RightFramePhotoVideo

Chapter 14 • Creating a Culture of Innovation   455

For Leaders: Leaders can create a culture of innovation by applying the von Restorff Effect. Apply von Restorff to raise awareness of the mental models that may be restraining the team, emphasize important points, and generally spark individuals thinking in new ways. What do you really need followers, clients, or stakeholders to notice or remember? How can you introduce that message in a manner that is very, very different than they might expect? Note that this technique in leadership should be used sparingly—if everything is highlighted, then nothing will stand out.

While the dimensions of the brain applied to innovation for individuals and teams provides a broad framework to design a creativity-supporting climate, there are several other dispositions a leader should consider when designing a future innovative workplace. Recall the concept of *press* introduced in Chapter 8. Press refers to those things in the environment that press on your creativity, either inhibiting or encouraging. Beyond what was discussed with the dimensions of the brain, what other ways could you strategically engage elements of the creative press to influence creative behavior?

Finally, recall that the CORE™ capacities discussed throughout this textbook are fundamental to your overall leadership success. They are also key to you and your team's innovation capacity. When designing the workplace of your future, note what might inhibit those CORE™ capacities and what you might do to design a culture that is encouraging of each one. Think critically about what would inhibit or undermine *confidence* in a workplace environment. Perhaps it would be inhibited by fear stemming from lack of information or an impending change that was not well explained. Undermining *optimism* may be an overall pessimism that pervades the culture. What is the source of pessimistic viewpoints? Are there misunderstandings around deadlines or availability of resources? How might *resilience* be undermined? Perhaps there are significant challenges that are not addressed in a timely manner. This may lead to discouragement and the overall feeling that there are insurmountable deterrents to organizational success. In what ways might *engagement* be inhibited? When individuals or teams are not recognized for their efforts or if the people in the organization do not understand how their work fits into the overall goals of the organization, lack of engagement ensues.

Many of these prompting questions about confidence, optimism, resilience, and engagement point to the value of clear and meaningful communication as a standard for organizational success. While it is often not explicit in the values and beliefs that comprise an organizational culture, there is no reason to discount the importance of communication in making sure the culture is not undercut by pessimism, misunderstandings, discouragement, or lack of engagement. Your job as the leader of an innovative culture is to understand all the cultural and climate variables that lead to greater innovation and to communicate to ensure the press encourages an individual's CORE™ capacities.

MYTH OR REALITY?

Transformational leadership is the best approach for encouraging followers' creativity and organizational innovation.

Myth . . . and Reality. Transformational leadership—characterized by the four I's of *individual consideration*, *intellectual stimulation*, *inspirational motivation*, and *idealized influence*—generally feels like the leadership approach that would most likely establish the conditions for individuals and organizations to innovate. And the reality is that there are numerous studies suggesting transformational leadership has significant effects on creativity at both the individual and organizational levels and across different contexts.[32] At the individual level, transformational leadership influences employees' creativity through psychological empowerment and intellectual stimulation.[33] At the organizational level, it is positively associated with organizational innovation. But . . . in some cases, the effect is mediated by promotion focus and creative process engagement,[34] by emphasizing a learning orientation,[35] or by applying leadership to a specific part of the creativity process.[36] But . . . other studies indicate limited effects of transformational leadership and even negative effects, such as increasing follower dependency that decreased creativity.[37]

This is a great example of why leadership needs to be a mindful process that you design. There are no simple recipes that say do this leadership style and it will result in that performance outcome. Leadership and innovation are simply too complicated, individual-based, context-based, and situational. Nonetheless, research on what factors promote and inhibit creativity and the variables that mediate those effects are worth exploring, understanding, and applying as appropriate.

CHAPTER SUMMARY

When you think of the future of innovation, it is likely that you think about technology. Technology and innovation are closely related because major advances in technology tend to drive the largest periods of progress throughout time. Innovation would not be possible without creativity. Innovative leaders accurately read the future marketplace, continually questioning the market to iterate upon existing ideas or select new creative ideas to translate into value.

Innovation is enhanced if you understand the drivers of innovation, which include necessity, desire, and advances (in methods, materials, etc.). Innovative leaders have an understanding of how to use these drivers of innovation as a starting point to imagining future possibilities.

Innovation is a collaborative process of translating creative ideas into something of value.

The best leaders and collaborators have a clear understanding of the problem they are trying to solve. You benefit from learning how and practicing defining problems clearly. A clearly defined problem is well on its way to being solved.

Innovation is a creative process that relies on iteration and the translation of creative ideas into something of value for an organization. Many types of innovation result in value for an organization, and you can select one or more once you choose the type of value that you and your organization seek to enhance. As you look at the many creative ideas that you generate, you also use a process to find a single best solution to a problem. Selecting the one idea, out of many, to translate to value occurs through convergence. There are many convergence techniques used to help you understand a variety of ways to go about selecting an idea to pursue.

Innovative organizations are designed to support creativity. Supporting creativity requires an understanding of how creative individuals habitually think as they approach the creative process. Using design-thinking dispositions as a guide to create a culture of innovation allows you to design a culture that is sympathetic to creative individuals' characteristics and mindsets. Culture is the values and beliefs of an organization, but climate is the patterns of behavior and attitude that characterize what it is like to work within an organization. It is equally important

Chapter 14 • Creating a Culture of Innovation 457

to design culture and climate. With no one-size-fits-all approach, using the six dimensions of the brain as a way to design the climate of an innovative workplace environment is a good place to start.

KEY TERMS

Benchmarking (p. 441)

Collaboration (p. 437)

Convergent thinking (p. 439)

Cultivating value-in-diversity (p. 449)

Harvesting diversity (p. 449)

Organizational climate (p. 450)

Technology (p. 433)

CORE™ ATTRIBUTE BUILDERS: BUILD NOW FOR FUTURE LEADERSHIP CHALLENGES

Attribute: Engagement

Builder: Read, post, or comment to OpenIDEO.com or Innocentive.com

How might mobile technology help improve access to health care? How might we better prepare all learners for the needs of tomorrow by reimagining higher education? These are two of the current open challenges offered on the online open-source innovation platform called OpenIDEO. According to their website, "A challenge is usually a three to five-month collaborative process that focuses our attention on a specific issue and creates a space for community members to contribute, refine and prototype solutions."[38] Innocentive.com offers a similar platform for you to engage your creative, problem-solving leadership.

Get involved. Read, comment, or post on the current challenge. The most valuable part of their platform is the engagement of innovators from all over the world connected and actively involved in solving pressing global issues.

CORE™ ATTRIBUTE BUILDERS: BUILD NOW FOR FUTURE LEADERSHIP CHALLENGES

Attribute: Confidence and Resilience

Builder: Space and feeling awareness

What kind of space brings out the best or most creative in you? Raising your awareness of how different spaces elicit different emotions in you empowers you to both seek out the spaces that best fit you as well as know what spaces might require an extra effort to deal with unwanted feelings. Try this activity to build your confidence and resilience through awareness of space and feeling:

1. Go to three separate locations:
   a. One space that feels really good to you—a place you really enjoy spending time and where you feel focused and energized
   b. Another space that seems very unique
   c. And another space that seems very popular or that many individuals walk through or occupy

2. What feelings does each space communicate and incite in you as you occupy the space?

3. What about the space, specifically, do you think brings on those feelings?

Here are a number of feeling words to help you describe your experience:

Feelings When *Are Not* Being Met		
Angry: enraged, furious, incensed	Annoyed: Aggravated, Dismayed	Hostile: Animosity, Appalled, Aversion
Afraid: apprehensive, dread, foreboding	Confused: ambivalent, baffled	Embarrassed: ashamed, chagrined, flustered
Sad: depressed, dejected, despair	Vulnerable: fragile, guarded helpless	Disconnected: alienated, aloof, apathetic, bored, cold, detached, distant
Upset: agitated, alarmed, discombobulated, disconcerted	Tense: anxious, bitter, cranky, distressed, distraught, edgy	Pain: agony, anguished, bereaved, devastated, grief, heartbroken
Yearning: envious, jealous, longing	Fatigue: beat, burned out, depleted	Surprised: disbelief, shocked, startled

Feelings When Needs *Are* Being Met

Joyful: amused, delighted, glad	Excited: amazed, animated, astonished	Affectionate: compassionate, friendly
Hopeful: expectant, encouraged	Inspired: amazed, awed, radiant	Exhilarated: blissful, ecstatic, elated
Grateful: appreciative, moved, thankful	Confident: empowered, open, proud, safe	Intrigued: interested, fascinated
Peaceful: calm, clear-headed, relaxed	Engaged: absorbed, alert, curious	Refreshed: enlivened, rejuvenated

Source: http://www.celebrateempathy.com/Needs-&-Feelings.pdf

SKILL BUILDER ACTIVITY

Creative Climate Interview and Memo

Choose an organization (not your own). Observe and talk to folks about the creative context and culture. Analyze the data you collect. Write a one- to two-page memo to the organization highlighting what they should start doing, stop doing, and keep doing to facilitate creativity.

Interview someone in that career about the role, process, and context of creativity. Choose five to seven questions from the following list:

- Do you believe in divergent thinking? What methods do you use?

- What do you do to inspire creativity?

- What do you do when you encounter someone who is not creative?

- How do you recover from failing?

- What is the most effective way to start your day in your organization?

Chapter 14 ● Creating a Culture of Innovation   459

- Why do you do what you do?

- What is the key factor to make you successful?

- What is the future of your industry?

- How do you generate ideas?

- What do you fear?

- What brings you joy?

- Where do you come up with your ideas?

- What is involved in your daily routine?

- Does your family influence your creativity?

- Do you intentionally surround yourself with creative people?

- How do you overcome adversity to your creative idea?

- How do you remain entrepreneurial?

- Do you feel pressured to maintain a level of creativity?

- When did you know being different was a good thing?

- How do you find new ways to stay creative?

SKILL BUILDER ACTIVITY

Build a Better Block

As a leader, individuals look to you for guidance, assurance, answers, decisions, and success. Individuals also look to you to foster a culture of innovation. This Skill Builder Activity challenges you to create a space that encourages creativity and innovation, specifically redesigning a city block in your neighborhood or town.

The Build a Better Block program is a relatively new social design endeavor that has grown exponentially. Why? Because it is critically needed, is flexible to accommodate a variety of locations, and engages individuals in a real-world effort to make a difference. You can (should) read more about it here: http://betterblock.org/.

From the website http://betterblock.org/how-to-build-a-better-block/, it is best to address the following four areas when developing a Better Block, which we will break down in greater depth:

1. **Safety (real and perceived)**—First and foremost, if an area feels unsafe, then everything breaks down. Whether it be businesses, schools, or neighborhood revitalization, the key to changing a place is addressing its perceived safety. When approaching blocks, we ask the questions: Does it feel safe to cross the street? Does it feel safe to stand on the sidewalk? Does it feel safe to linger in the area?

2. **Shared access**—The next goal we focus on is looking at ways to bring more people into the area by various modes of transportation. We ask the questions: Do pedestrians have easy and clear access to the area? Do bicycles feel welcome in the area? Is the area easily accessible from neighborhoods? Are there way-finding signs that direct people into and

out of the area? Are there amenities that allow people to linger in the space (seating, tables, etc.)?

3. **Stay power**—How can we encourage people to visit the area, have them linger, and invite their friends?

4. **8—80, dog owners**—Lastly, we look at amenities that create invitations for children, seniors, and dog owners on a block. These groups tend to be indicators of a healthy environment that feels welcoming and attracts other people.

You can attempt this challenge individually, but it is far more fun as a group or as a class project.

You will need to *understand* the problem, its history, context, efforts to solve, and so forth.

You will need to *imagine* great ideas . . . thinking divergently far beyond *the box*.

And you will need to *iterate* your ideas until you have something feasible, viable, desirable, and innovative.

15 ENTREPRENEURIAL LEADERSHIP

LEARNING OBJECTIVES

Upon completion of this chapter, the reader should be able to

15.1 Explain the broad domain of entrepreneurship

15.2 Describe the entrepreneurial mindset

15.3 Evaluate the possible benefits of a social entrepreneurial venture

15.4 Recognize the entrepreneurial process

15.5 Design your future as an entrepreneurial leader

Leadership by Design Model

Design Self
How can I design myself as a leader?

Design Relationships
As a leader, how can I design my relationships with others?

Design Others' Success
As a leader, how can I design success for others?

Design Culture
As a leader, how can I design the culture of my organization?

Design Future
AS A LEADER, HOW CAN I INNOVATE?

INTRODUCTION

Did you ever play musical chairs as a kid? Musical chairs is that game where you and a group of others walk around a bunch of chairs while music is playing. Then, when the music stops, everyone has to find a chair and sit in it. The challenge, however, is there is always one less chair than people playing, which of course means someone is left standing and that person is out of the game. The marketing guru Seth Godin shared this analogy in regard to how individuals approach their career—constantly competing and looking over your shoulder, making sure you have a chair when the music stops.[1] This is playing the game within rules that only exist in your head. The reality of today's rapidly changing technology means career path instability and organizational disruption. In other words, disappearing chairs. But what if you brought

461

462   Module 5 • Design the Future

your own chair or even built your own chair and made your own music? That is the essence of entrepreneurship.

Being a leader often requires designing and making your own path. The previous chapter introduced creating a culture of innovation, fostering yourself and others to generate unique ideas and translate them into value. This chapter introduces the broad domain of entrepreneurship and, more importantly, the elements from entrepreneurship that can make you a more effective, innovative leader—the *entrepreneurial leader*. At a fundamental level, entrepreneurship can be viewed as an exercise in leadership that involves bringing people together around a shared vision to launch something new into the marketplace and make a positive impact on others. Entrepreneurial leadership comprises a unique set of concepts, mindsets, and activities used by leaders to identify opportunities, deepen understanding, and initiate and develop innovation— in other words, leaders who spot value, translate that value, develop it, and then put the ideas into action to realize greater value for their organization and beyond.

Entrepreneurial leadership is more important and needed than ever. Although every era has enjoyed the benefits of new ideas and the individuals who translated these ideas into real-world value, the trending patterns indicate an acceleration of invention and innovation, faster adoption of new technologies, and increasing disruption to products and services resulting in shorter life spans for companies that cannot adapt.[2] The World Economic Forum estimates that 50 percent of the entire workforce will need to be reskilled by 2025.[3] These trends impact individuals and their career choices and options. Within the next decade, nearly half of all current jobs will be replaced with automation and artificial intelligence, and one third to one half of the workforce will be independent contract workers.[4] All of this adds up to a critical need for entrepreneurs and strong career advice to acquire and develop the mindsets and skills of entrepreneurial leadership. Design the future before it designs you.

Leadership That Makes a Difference

Leadership for what? The specific social challenge that drives the work of social entrepreneurial leaders can emerge from many sources. Often your personal experience with a particular issue serves as the spark that ignites the idea that you could and should do something to make a difference. Story after story of social entrepreneurs follow that trajectory: I was minding my own business, living my life, and then I experienced this . . . and I knew I had to do something. That was the case with a young prince who was an unusually talented warrior and statesman, despite his relatively low rank in the royal household. Applying those talents, he led with the same style as those around him—decisive brutality and conquest—and rose to become king. However, one experience changed his mindset, his life, and the future of social entrepreneurship: "The morning after a victory he went out to survey the state of things and encountered nothing except burnt houses and scattered corpses. Having been brought face to face with the consequences of war, for the first time he felt overwhelmed with the brutality of his actions. He vowed never to practice violence again and devoted himself completely to Buddhism."[5] This ruler's name was Ashoka, one of the most powerful kings of India, reigning from 273 to 232 B.C.

Ashoka's personal transformation resulted in his embrace of principles of nonviolence and leading with integrity. His legal reforms and administration effectively followed and implemented the ten precepts of a perfect ruler that Buddha noted. These include avoiding selfishness, maintaining high moral character, being kind and gentle, practicing patience, and respecting public opinion to promote peace and harmony, among others. Ashoka extended these into a series of edicts that he inscribed on rock and spread throughout the land to remind and encourage followers. The edicts emphasize tolerance for all sects and religions, respect and generosity, humane treatment, and openness to feedback on governance.[6] These edicts brought a shared vision and ethic to a multi-cultural, multi-caste, multi-religious land.

Fast-forward a few thousand years and a young undergraduate student named Bill Drayton creates an informal series of dinners where local leaders can share ideas. He names it the Ashoka Table. After earning his law degree and working for a decade as a management consultant, he founds an organization that gives rise to the phrase "social entrepreneur:" *Ashoka: Innovators for the Public*. Since 1980, Ashoka (which means "absence of sorrow" in Sanskrit) has educated, trained, and supported thousands of change leaders throughout the world through a wide variety of programs. The resulting social entrepreneurial ventures empower leadership across every conceivable social challenge. For example, in their latest issue of *The Social Entrepreneurs and Their Ideas*, profiled projects address civic participation, growing up, environment, full economic citizenship, health, and human rights.[7] The Ashoka Support Network continues to support these projects and more, long beyond the direct programs.

Ashoka (the ancient king) was a leader who made a difference, as is Bill Drayton (the modern social entrepreneur). Social entrepreneurship may be your preferred venue for becoming a leader who makes a difference. If so, start with the Ashoka.org.

Indian emperor Ashoka the Great redesigned his leadership and inspired social entrepreneurship.
Photo Dharma from Sadao, Thailand

ENTREPRENEURSHIP: RE-ENVISIONING LEADERSHIP

LEARNING OBJECTIVE
15.1   Explain the broad domain of entrepreneurship.

What comes to mind when you hear someone mention *entrepreneurship*? Do you think about starting and operating small businesses, taking risks, and seeking to make a profit? Do you think about famous entrepreneurs like Mark Zuckerberg (Facebook), Bill Gates (Microsoft), and Jeff Bezos (Amazon)? If so, you are certainly not alone. Many definitions of entrepreneurship focus on starting businesses, and popular culture has made celebrities out of a handful of entrepreneurs who have founded companies and become exceptionally wealthy by creating innovative goods and services used by millions of consumers. These are some of the many misconceptions individuals hold regarding entrepreneurship.[8]

Defining Entrepreneurship

Entrepreneurship originates from the French verb *entreprendre*, which means to undertake or do something, and that *something* has been to start a business venture for hundreds of years. As entrepreneurship has evolved to the present day, it has come to comprise four very important distinguishing features that were added to entrepreneurship over centuries: creating value, managing that value, assuming risk, and innovating.[9] Indeed, the notion of reaching for something new and taking action is fundamental to entrepreneurship, as the origins of the word go even deeper into history, combining the Latin words *entre* (to swim out) and *prendes* (to grasp, understand, or capture). This chapter presents a broad perspective on entrepreneurship that extends beyond startup businesses to include innovation within existing companies, social venturing, and other entrepreneurial endeavors. This broader perspective is anchored by an updated definition of **entrepreneurship** stated as the process of pursuing opportunity through the conception, validation, and launch of new ideas into the marketplace. Each element of this definition tells a story about who entrepreneurs are, how they think, and what they do as leaders to make an impact on the world.

Entrepreneurship Is a Process

Entrepreneurship involves engaging in a series of actions in an attempt to achieve a desired outcome. In *Disciplined Entrepreneurship*,[10] Bill Aulet describes the first 24 steps needed to launch a successful startup, beginning with "Step 1—market segmentation" and ending with "Step 24—develop a product plan." Although few entrepreneurial endeavors progress in the type of orderly, linear sequence implied by numbered steps (on the contrary, most are characterized by repeated false starts, pivots, iterations, and feedback loops), descriptions like Aulet's help to elucidate the many actions involved in executing the entrepreneurial process.

Entrepreneurship Involves Pursuing Opportunity

Like all processes, entrepreneurship has a defined beginning. It starts with the recognition and pursuit of opportunity. **Opportunity recognition** occurs when entrepreneurs become aware of a problem, dissatisfaction, or gap in current offerings that they find interesting and believe themselves capable of solving. Opportunity pursuit occurs when an entrepreneur decides to take action. For example, Seth Goldman, co-founder of Honest Tea, noticed a gap in the market for iced tea that was not heavily sweetened and decided to develop a new, lightly sweetened formulation to

Chapter 15 • Entrepreneurial Leadership   **465**

pursue this opportunity. Similarly, Muhammad Yunus recognized a common problem for many would-be entrepreneurs in developing countries—they were poor and lacked access to even small amounts of startup capital. Yunus pursued this opportunity through the founding of Grameen Bank, a microcredit and microfinancing organization that has helped countless people to break out of poverty, and was awarded the 2006 Nobel Peace Prize for his efforts.

REFLECTION QUESTION

"What do you believe that no one else does?" That's a question Peter Thiel, co-founder of PayPal, asks the people he interviews. Seeing a truth that others are missing may represent an opportunity to change the world.

Conception, Validation, and Launch of New Ideas

The pursuit of opportunity involves three major buckets of activities corresponding to the conception, validation, and launch of new ideas. Conception-related activities include problem exploration, creativity, idea generation, and visioning (using many of the techniques you have learned in prior chapters). Validation-related activities include identifying risky assumptions, conducting tests, and iterating based on evidence. And launch-related activities include influencing others, building a team, and establishing a sustainable business or social impact model.

As Table 15.1 shows, the conception, validation, and launch of new ideas require a broad and diverse skill set that goes far beyond small business management. It also requires a strong leadership CORE™, as entrepreneurship tends to be similar to riding a roller coaster—there are a lot of uncontrollable ups and downs that will test your confidence, optimism, resilience, and engagement.

TABLE 15.1 ■ Knowledge and Skills Relevant to the Broad Domain of Entrepreneurship				
Recognizing Opportunity	**Idea Conception**	**Validation**	**Launch**	**Growth and Management**
• Adaptability • Effectual thinking • Entrepreneurial mindset • Resourcefulness	• Creativity • Design thinking • Problem-solving • Visioning	• Evidence-based decision-making • Experimentation • Mindfulness • Prototyping and iteration	• Boundary spanning • Networking • Pitching and selling • Teamwork	• Business fundamentals • Continuous learning • Efficient execution • Goal setting
Confidence	Optimism	Resilience	Engagement	

Into the Marketplace

The final component of this updated definition of entrepreneurship—into the marketplace—implies that someone or some entity (a business, governmental organization, or nonprofit) must benefit from the entrepreneur's new idea. In other words, mere **invention**—the creation of a new method, device, or process—is not sufficient for entrepreneurship. Rather, the new creation must provide value to a customer or a beneficiary by helping them to solve a problem or address an unmet need. If so, then the new creation can be referred to as an innovation—a new method, device, or process that is useful to people—that is developed and delivered into the marketplace through the process of entrepreneurship.

The Broad Domain of Entrepreneurship

Defining entrepreneurship as involving the pursuit of opportunity through new ideas broadens its domain to include entrepreneurial activity across many contexts. These contexts might look like new ideas for policies, projects, and programs that solve important problems and create benefits for people within the entrepreneurial domain. For example, **social entrepreneurship** is the process of utilizing the marketplace to solve social problems (generally wicked social problems) in a novel manner. It encompasses new ideas for social ventures to address chronic societal problems, such as environmental degradation, poverty, and access to health care, education, and clean water. **Intrapreneurship** comprises entrepreneurial behaviors within an existing organization, such as risk-taking and generating ideas for new products and services to be developed as companies seek to remain competitive or grow revenues and profitability. The entrepreneurial leader brings a mindset and understanding of how to execute the entrepreneurial process and a skill set that is relevant and useful across the broad domain of contexts where opportunity can be turned into value.

Entrepreneurship and Leadership

Entrepreneurs need the leadership skills and dispositions that build relationships and engage others to realize the potential of their venture. Yet interestingly, entrepreneurial success stories are filled with tales of vexing problems solved by someone with a brilliant insight and then a series of heroic journeys—challenging situations; tough decisions; and a path to growth, enlightenment, and often unexpected outcomes. As you hear these stories, you may get the mistaken impression that leading an entrepreneurial venture is the act of a single great leader who initiates and drives everything—the *great man* theory that represented one of the early notions of leadership. Entrepreneurs may mistake their willingness and initial effort to *do something* with an image that they do everything. This shortsighted conception often results in considerable organizational difficulties, and it is referred to as founder's syndrome. **Founder's syndrome** is an organizational disorder characterized by overreliance on the charisma, involvement, and decisions of one or more founding members in place of mindful, collaborative, and strategic management and leadership.

The moment any endeavor begins to develop beyond an idea, other individuals become involved. At that point, you are trying to facilitate a process of influencing others toward a common vision (i.e., leadership). Researchers have found significant overlap between the characteristics of leaders and entrepreneurs.[11] The dynamic nature of a growing venture requires different knowledge, skills, attitudes, and others at every stage of the entrepreneurial journey—and consequently different types and facets of leadership.

Leading an entrepreneurial venture differs from entrepreneurial leadership.[12] Entrepreneurial leadership begs the question: What would you know, do, or be like as a leader if you were more entrepreneurial? The most basic notion of entrepreneurship by Jean-Baptiste Say in 1804 states, "The entrepreneur shifts economic resources out of an area of lower and into an area of higher productivity and greater yield."[13] In other words, the entrepreneur finds ways to make the most out of things—to bring out the greatest value—not just in economic terms but in other currency

Chapter 15 • Entrepreneurial Leadership   467

aligned with the context, such as greater employee engagement, a more accessible bike trail, less diabetes in a community, more indictments of corrupt officials, or more citizens voting. Successfully achieving these kinds of outcomes requires that leaders see and think differently—like an entrepreneur. Thus, a recent definition states, "Entrepreneurial leaders are individuals who, through an understanding of themselves and the contexts in which they work, act on and shape opportunities that create value for their organizations, their stakeholders, and the wider society."[14]

Design Revisited

Seeing leadership through the lens of entrepreneurship will once again ask you to see differently. As you try on different lenses that provide insights for your leadership, you are continuing to add to your toolbox, from which you will draw to design your leadership. This would be a good point to remind you of the three powerful design elements that will power your new tools. Design process, design principles, and design thinking were briefly explained in the introductory chapter. You should flip back and reread those sections . . . for a couple of reasons. First, this design framework is both highly unique and uniquely effective in helping you see differently, ultimately enhancing your innovation and efficacy as a leader. Second, the more times you revisit information, the more you strengthen the connections in your lean, mean, pattern-making machine brain and the better you will be at using that tool. Finally, revisiting what you previously learned will position you to more effectively learn the new stuff. Seriously, go back and reread—it will only take a few minutes. Then check out Table 15.2 and add a reminder for yourself.

TABLE 15.2 ■ Design in Brief and Why You Should Care		
Wait . . . What? . . .	**You Need It Because . . .**	**How Will *You* Remember This Concept?**
Design process—the process of originating and developing a plan, which comprises three phases: understand, imagine, and implement	*Following a process ensures you remember each important part.* Try doing something in random order that you normally have a process for doing. Get dressed in random order, brush your teeth, cook a meal—you will likely miss a few things and end up with a poor outcome.	
Design principle—the rules that designers apply to help guide their process and enhance their product	*Certain rules and reminders help enhance your outcome.* What *rules* do you normally follow that enhance your life? Say "please" and "thank you," wear sunscreen, hydrate on hot days, call your mom—these rules make things better.	
Design thinking—the habits of mind (dispositions) that designers use to help enhance and guide their process. A cognitive approach to engaging problems that embodies a specific mindset that is (a) user-centered, (b) explorative, (c) divergent, (d) multidisciplinary, (e) iterative, and (f) integrative	*Certain ways of thinking and seeing enhance your process and outcome.* Your brain is a lean, mean, pattern-making machine that forms habits. You can form habitual ways of thinking that are detrimental ("people always disappoint") or form mental habits that are helpful ("mistakes help others learn to do better next time").	

THE ENTREPRENEURIAL MINDSET

LEARNING OBJECTIVE

15.2   Describe the entrepreneurial mindset.

Entrepreneurs think differently. They notice problems and dissatisfactions that others fail to recognize. They utilize effectual thinking to develop a vision of what is possible given the means at hand. And they draw from a deep reservoir of passion and persistence to overcome the many impediments to developing novel solutions that make people's lives better. Using analysis on psychological testing from 4,000 successful entrepreneurs and 1,800 business leaders (self-describing as general managers who are not entrepreneurial), Butler found that entrepreneurs have three distinguishing characteristics: the ability to thrive in uncertainty, a passionate desire to author and own projects, and a unique skill at persuasion.[15]

Some people seem to be wired this way—naturally comfortable with ambiguity, seeing themselves as surrounded by abundant opportunity, compelled to take action, and charmingly persuasive. However, most do not possess this hardwiring, and instead, they need to develop the ability to see the world through an entrepreneurial lens. Doing so can provide incredible rewards—empowerment and the capacity to capitalize on unlimited possibilities for having a good and fulfilling life.

Consider this quote by Steve Jobs, founder of Apple and creator of iMacs, iPods, and iPhones:

When you grow up, you tend to get told that the world is the way it is and your life is just to live your life inside the world, try not to bash into the walls too much, try to have a nice family, have fun, save a little money. That's a very limited life. Life can be much broader, once you discover one simple fact, and that is that everything around you that you call life was made up by people that were no smarter than you. And you can change it, you can influence it, you can build your own things that other people can use. Once you learn that, you'll never be the same again.[16]

This quote captures the distinction between the two general approaches for how you see the world: a fixed mindset versus a growth mindset, which was introduced in Chapter 3.[17] Recall that with a fixed mindset you see your abilities and capacity as set versus a growth mindset wherein you believe you can continuously learn, grow, and acquire new abilities. The growth mindset underpins the more specific entrepreneurial mindsets discussed in this section because you see things for their potential, including your own capacity as a leader and innovator, and believe the only limit lies in your effort. Further, your role as a leader is key to establishing the context and culture for encouraging a growth mindset in others.[18]

REFLECTION QUESTION

If you had the power to change anything in the world, what would you change? What in your life right now is getting in the way of your success? What could you add to your life, real or magical, that would enhance your success?

Now, really believe the advice of Steve Jobs: You have the power to make things change. Do it.

Chapter 15 • Entrepreneurial Leadership   **469**

The next sections discuss the entrepreneurial mindset—a series of dispositions or mental habits that drive the process of pursuing opportunity through the conception, validation, and launch of new ideas into the marketplace (Table 15.3).

TABLE 15.3 ■ Entrepreneurial Mindset
See more opportunity: Mindful, observant, and open to new ideas
See different: Reframing problems as opportunities
See more answers: Ideation, effectuation, and resourcefulness
See it started: Predilection for action . . . and reflection
See it through: Remembering your purpose

See More Opportunity: Mindful, Observant, and Open to New Ideas

Have you ever wondered why school starts early in the morning and ends in the afternoon? Have you ever thought about why we frequently eat food such as eggs and cereal for breakfast but choose them less often for other meals? Have you ever sat at a red light in the middle of the night with no other cars around and wondered why you are required by law to just sit there? As Steve Jobs rightly pointed out, everything in the world—from the schools we attend to our food consumption patterns to the traffic laws we are required to follow—was made up by people and can be changed.

Training yourself to be open and observant is a lot like trying to see your surroundings through the eyes of a foreign traveler. It involves continuously questioning your understanding of the *what* and the *why* of the people, products, processes, and other things that we encounter on a daily basis. Most of the time, we take the what and the why for granted and just accept the world at face value. Seeing the world through an entrepreneurial lens involves actively looking deeper to discover the hidden cracks of opportunity that surround us. For example, you likely have heard of TOMS Shoes, the company that gives a pair of shoes to someone in need for every pair it sells. What you may not know is that the founder, Blake Mycoskie, was already a serial entrepreneur. He thought up the idea for TOMS while traveling in Argentina. There he noticed how many individuals were lacking shoes and the effect it had on their health and success. While many would simply see an interesting culture and people, Blake Mycoskie saw a problem . . . and then he saw an opportunity.

Seeing opportunities is not as easy as the stories of entrepreneurship make it seem. Yes, you may find an opportunity simply jumps out at you, particularly if you have developed the habit of looking for them. Throughout this text, you have read about many other developing leaders and their moments of awareness. As an entrepreneurial leader, *you need to seek out* and maximize those moments, raising your awareness of opportunities. Try this exercise:

Take a trip to a public place, such as a park or a mall, and watch the people around you. Try to understand what they are doing and why. Are there unspoken social norms guiding their behaviors? If so, what are they? Start a few conversations and really listen to what others are saying—are they complaining about things that could be addressed by an entrepreneurial venture? Next time you use a product, consider why you are really using it and whether it truly meets your needs. Next time you are at work, map out the steps involved in doing your job and ask yourself whether there might be a better way.

Take notes during and after each of these experiences. Then consider how you might meet a need, enhance an experience, add to a current use, make something more user-friendly, or create the next evolution in a product, service, or experience. The great news is there are many techniques you can utilize to both direct your focus as well as develop the mindset of mindfully observing. Try the specific opportunity—finding methods in this section to raise your awareness. Table 15.4 outlines six general approaches to exploring opportunities along with a few of the many user-centered data collection techniques that can guide your explorations. Purposely find some time individually or with a partner to engage in some of these activities. See what opportunities you can discover.

TABLE 15.4 ■ Opportunity-Finding Methods*	
Explore Data and Analyze It **Historical Analysis**—Compare features of an industry, organization, group, market segment, or practice through various stages of development. **Competitive Product Survey**—Collect, compare, and conduct evaluations of the product's competition.	**En/Vision the Ideal** **Predict Next Year's Headlines**—Invite clients to project their company into the future, identifying how they want to develop and sustain customer relationships.
Observe, Map, Analyze **Fly on the Wall**—Observe and record behavior within its context, without interfering with people's activities to see what people actually do within real contexts and time frames. **A Day in the Life**—Catalog the activities and contexts that users experience throughout the entire day.	**En/Vision the Worst Cases** **Error Analysis**—List all the things that can go wrong when using a product and determine the various possible causes.
Recognize and Map (Your/User) Culture & Concepts **Extreme User Interviews**—Identify individuals who are extremely familiar or completely unfamiliar with the product and ask them to evaluate their experience using it.	**Investigate Personal Preferences** **Personal Inventory**—Document the things that people identify as important to them as a way of cataloging evidence of their lifestyles.

* Methods directly quoted from IDEO Method Cards[19]

See Differently: Reframing Problems as Opportunities

Think about the last time you encountered a problem. How did you react? Did you try to avoid it, or did you embrace the problem and immediately begin to consider solutions? Back in Chapter 8 on creativity, you learned about being reactive and proactive—dealing with problems as they occur or trying to anticipate problems and address them before they become problematic. Entrepreneurs completely reframe problems and see them as opportunities—a hint that there is something of value missing that can be filled by a venture. Entrepreneurs love to encounter people who have problems because they know their complaints, frustrations, and pains represent opportunities to make a positive impact. The ability to empathize greatly enhances the entrepreneurial mindset.[20] Consider the examples of persistent problems in the following list. Try to reframe them to represent opportunities to make a positive impact on the world through the conception, validation, and launch of a new idea into the marketplace:

- People are unhappy about their weight
- People are busy and feel time-poor
- People want to find fulfilling employment
- People lack access to affordable medical care

Can you see the connection between people being unhappy about their weight and the thousands of diet and exercise solutions that have been introduced into the marketplace? How about time poverty and the invention of countless time-saving devices (many of which do not actually save time and end up failing to gain traction in the marketplace)? The point is that the world is full of problems. As a result, when you learn to view the world through an entrepreneurial lens, you will see that these problems represent opportunities and opportunities are everywhere.

Leadership by Design

Design Principle: Simplicity (a.k.a. Ockham's Razor, the law of parsimony)

Definition: "Simplicity is about subtracting the obvious and adding the meaningful."[21]

In Other Words: Keep it simple. Unnecessary elements decrease efficiency, increase the likelihood of unanticipated consequences, and discourage use.

For Example: A single-speed bicycle rarely needs a tune-up.

For Leaders: When asked to improve something, people generally add a new feature. What is better than a car that performs well? A car with cup holders . . . and seat warmers . . . and keyless entry . . . and, and, and. While these features may be desirable, they also add layers of necessary instruction and possible repair. Complexity is simple addition, but simplicity requires seeing the bigger system and designing a more fundamental solution. For example, when followers are not performing, leaders often add more instruction or more rules. The principle of simplicity, however, would suggest starting with asking why:[22]

- Why are followers doing this?
- Why are we concerned about this performance?
- Why are we adding this?
- Why are we taking this away?
- Why would users care?
- Why can they do this?
- Why will they still do this?

What can be reduced, reorganized, relocated, or relearned, rather than added? This may take time. Added time is also added complexity, and some things cannot be made simple. But simplicity frees up room for new activities and innovative directions.

See More Answers: Ideation, Effectuation, and Resourcefulness

Entrepreneurs see more opportunities, and they see more ways to take advantage of those opportunities using two mental habits: ideation and effectuation. **Ideation** is the mental process of forming ideas. Entrepreneurs envision what *could be* as they encounter opportunity. In other words, what would the ideal outcome look like? Applying divergent thinking to generate many possibilities enhances this approach. However, another kind of thinking helps entrepreneurs flexibly alter their venture as new opportunities emerge.

When researcher Saras Sarasvathy conducted a study involving 27 expert entrepreneurs, she discovered that they think differently.[23] Rather than using **causal reasoning** to set a goal and then consider the means through which the goal can be accomplished, entrepreneurs use effectuation. **Effectuation** is defined as a type of reasoning that starts with one's given resources that subsequently forge goals as the resources are applied.[24] Effectual thinkers start by considering their means: Who am I, what do I know, whom do I know? Entrepreneurs also consider the other resources at their disposal—facilities, funding, equipment, and more—to determine what they can accomplish.

The distinction between causal reasoning and effectuation is perhaps best illustrated with a cooking metaphor. If you were going to prepare dinner for yourself, which approach would you take: Do you decide what you want to eat and use a recipe to cook it? Or do you look around to see what you have on hand, and then figure out how to use the ingredients to make something you want to eat. Typical businesspersons tend to plan their actions based on the goal (i.e., the recipe). Entrepreneurs, however, often begin with their means. Activities from that starting point result in emergent goals, which in turn produce new means, in a cycle that drives their venture in unexpected but fruitful new directions.[25] To begin to think like an entrepreneur, start by considering your means and resources. What opportunities can you pursue with your ingredients?

See It Started: Predilection for Action . . . and Reflection

Entrepreneurs are doers. They do not just sit around dreaming of new ideas. Rather, they think about what they can do to pursue an opportunity, and they take action. This approach has been described as *ready-fire-aim*,[26] but it might be better to think of it as *ready-fire-reflect* because the most successful entrepreneurs thoughtfully consider the outcomes resulting from their actions. They ask themselves, "why did the action succeed or fail?" and "what might work better next time?" as they search to find solutions that will win in the marketplace. The single most valuable resource entrepreneurs possess is their time. Having a mental bias toward action and reflection enables entrepreneurs to efficiently allocate their time while executing a continuous series of dream, do, learn, and repeat loops.

MOMENT OF AWARENESS

There's no such thing as being fearless. If that's something you aspire to, you've been duped! But fear not, I was duped too. Being a Misfit Entrepreneur requires that you be fear-facing. For me, fear manifested as debilitating, getting-in-my-own-way self-doubt. It literally stopped me from doing necessary things, and for no good reason.

It's one thing to feel doubt; it's another to let it limit your potential and hold you back. My self-doubt would stop me from following up with a potential client. I would meet someone at a networking event who seemed interested in my elevator pitch. I'd get their card and think to myself, I should follow up with them and schedule a coffee meeting. But then I'd tell myself, I need to get a flyer together—it's more professional to have packages I can show. Days would go by, and I hadn't made a flyer. A week later, I still hadn't followed up. Then I would tell myself that I'd missed the magic 48-hour window to follow up, which just showed how much I was failing at business, so why should I even bother.

You must learn to listen from within and distinguish between the voice of your inner critic and the wisdom of your inner genius. Understanding yourself isn't about making excuses. It's not saying, "It's just the way I am—there's nothing I can do about it." Understanding yourself is a constant process of self-discovery.

—Ariana Friedlander, from A Misfit Entrepreneur's Guide to Building a Business
Your Way[27]

See It Through: Remembering Your Purpose

Conceiving, validating, and launching a new idea into the marketplace is a *huge* challenge. To succeed, you will need to overcome obstacles, push through points of resistance, avoid pitfalls, and quickly recover from rejection and failure. During dark times it is important to remember your purpose—the *why* behind your actions. With a strong and clear purpose—for example, providing world-class educational opportunities, creating jobs and economic well-being for others, making a strong positive impact on people's lives—you can keep yourself on track. Having such a purpose will also help you to bring people together around a shared vision and keep your team on track while you execute the entrepreneurial process.

> **Experts Beyond the Text**
>
> ### INSIGHTFUL LEADERS KNOW ABOUT . . . PANARCHY AND ADAPTIVE CYCLES
>
> #### Thinking in Adaptive Cycles
>
> By Dr. Kathleen E. Allen
>
> When we see a living system, like nature or an individual person, there are cycles that are natural to the evolution of these systems that occur at all levels of scale. One of these **adaptive cycles** is called panarchy.[28] **Panarchy** names the deep patterns that occur in the transformation cycles all human and natural systems go through. This specific cycle looks like an infinity loop and includes the following phases: exploitation, conservation, release, and reorganization (see Figure 15.1).
>
>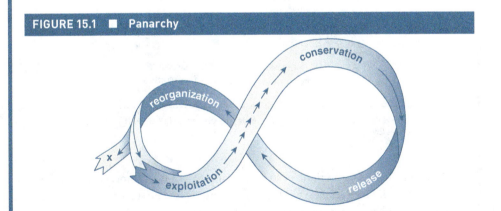
>
> **FIGURE 15.1 ■ Panarchy**
>
> The front side of this loop includes exploitation and conservation. Exploitation occurs when there is a buildup of resources that can be used to launch a new phase of business or life cycle, and this front loop continues into conservation when things become systematized and the successful forms that have achieved the function become set. The front loop is slow. At some point, the focus on conservation builds rigidity and an adherence to form. This rigidity makes the system vulnerable to a collapse, which starts the back loop of this adaptive cycle. The collapse creates a release of resources that are needed to build the next stage of evolution for an ecological system, business model, or individual transformation. This release occurs when the system is not adapting to changing conditions and creates a reset in the system. The other

part of the "back loop" is reorganization, which is in the upper left side of the loop. After the collapse of the system, an exploration phase occurs that allows for the system to adapt or reset.

When disruptive technologies occur in business, this panarchy cycle is seen. A business develops a business plan that launches a successful enterprise. They move to launch their product and solidify their market niche. One example of this was the shift from desktop computers to mobile devices, or from internal data storage to the cloud. Swiss watchmakers and their successful dominance of the analog watch design had their business model collapse when digital watchmaking emerged as a disruptive technology. This triggered a release of the traditional paradigm of watchmaking and created a lot of creative energy to explore and reorganize the assumptions behind how to tell time. New businesses and market share were created that split the analog market niche into analog and digital timepieces.

In human organizations and communities, there is a constant evolution occurring. In business, disruptive technologies are occurring all the time, even if we can't see them coming.[29] Leaders of the future will need to learn how to think in adaptive cycles. Organizations are built on structures. Systems aren't just structures, they are also movements.[30] These movements have a pattern, one of which is panarchy. The concepts of panarchy have been adapted into using an ecocycle framework for understanding movements and cycles in organizational systems and applying it to planning and leading.[31] The ecocycle in Figure 15.2 shows four main phases cycling in an infinite loop.

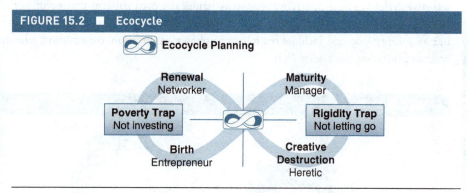

FIGURE 15.2 ■ Ecocycle

Source: http://www.liberatingstructures.com/31-ecocycle-planning via CC BY-NC 3.0 https://creativecommons.org/licenses/by-nc/3.0/legalcode

Traditionally, businesses think of strategic planning as a linear process moving the organization forward. However, in typical strategic plans, there is no space for release or creative destruction of what an organization is doing. An ecocycle invites an intentional letting go of all preconceived assumptions or structures to release energy and resources. These resources are then used to explore and launch new products or thinking. The questions that leaders need to focus on are related to the ecocycle.

- What needs to be explored?
- What needs to be launched?
- What needs to be sustained and systematized?
- What needs to be let go of or released to make room for the next innovation?

This allows for intentional releasing of energy, capital, attention, and form that no longer serves the organization's main function.

Chapter 15 • Entrepreneurial Leadership   **475**

DEI BY DESIGN

LEARNING OBJECTIVE
15.3   Evaluate the possible benefits of a social entrepreneurial venture.

Choosing to take your own path as an entrepreneur needs to include the important aspects of a thriving organization such as leadership, engagement, a culture of care, and fostering diversity, equity, and inclusion. Even when focused on a social challenge, entrepreneurial ventures may short-change internally positive conditions for the external cause.[32] Recall, social entrepreneurship is the process of utilizing the marketplace to solve social problems in a novel manner. There are now a great many social ventures comprising a wide range of organizational and impact structures, tackling an even wider range of issues.[33]

In the general sense, social entrepreneurs are driven by the acknowledgment, evaluation, and realization of opportunities to benefit the common good. They strive to meet those needs through innovative organization of members and their talents. Apart from the focus on social value, commercial and social entrepreneurship function quite similarly, and the leadership knowledge, skills, and abilities used in pursuit of profits are oriented toward improving societal conditions.[34] However, the desire for purpose in work is a strong motivator. Afdhel Aziz, co-founder of Conspiracy of Love, a global brand purpose consultancy, notes:[35] "The Cone Communications Millennial Employee Study found that 64% of Millennials won't take a job if their employee doesn't have a strong CSR policy, and 83% would be more loyal to a company that helps them contribute to social and environmental issues." Further, "Deloitte Insights *2020 Global Marketing Trends Report* found that purpose-driven companies had 40% higher levels of workforce retention than their competitors. Capitalism needs to evolve dramatically to keep up with these changes, and purpose is the key to doing so authentically and sustainably, in a way that creates a durable prosperity for the many, not the few."

Social innovators and social entrepreneurs are also agents of social change when they engage in efforts to address a social issue. These endeavors, however, are not without challenges. Since it is not primarily concerned with turning a profit, aspiring social entrepreneurs may face difficulties in amassing much-needed financial resources. Initiating new social ventures frequently requires connecting with funding sources that share an interest in creating social value and improving the common good. This scarcity of resources also applies to locating human workers. All too frequently, social ventures face challenges paying labor market rates for employees, despite the expressed desire of employees for purpose and impact in their work. As a consequence, social innovators become heavily reliant on volunteers and employees who care more about social change than building financial wealth.

Scholars envision a spectrum of organizational structures where commercial entrepreneurship and social entrepreneurship sit at the two opposing ends.[36] In this conceptualization, organizations can pursue purely commercial entrepreneurship, purely social entrepreneurship, or some hybrid of both. Not all entrepreneurship experts agree that a person or organization can pursue both bottom lines and still be considered socially entrepreneurial. Those who suggest such mutual exclusivity point to companies that engage in cause-related marketing not to produce social change per se, but rather to increase sales, profits, and shareholder wealth based on the perception that they intend on driving social value. The question of motive in social entrepreneurship is something each entrepreneur needs to decide for themselves. As it regards the

476 Module 5 ● Design the Future

organization generally, Aziz continues: "Companies who take things one step further and adopt a stakeholder-focused model (that explicitly serves employees, customers, suppliers, business partners, investors, local communities, the environment, and society) have historically shown even higher returns than standard ethical companies."[37]

LEADING THE ENTREPRENEURIAL PROCESS

LEARNING OBJECTIVE
15.4   Recognize the entrepreneurial process.

Entrepreneurs and their unique way of seeing and thinking design the future by seeing opportunities and translating them into value. Leaders adopting these entrepreneurial mindsets can apply them to any context to maximize innovation. Entrepreneurs also engage in unique processes that can further enhance leadership. The entrepreneurial process is best described as a sequence of activities that includes opportunity recognition, idea conception, validation, launch, and growth. However, in practice, it is decidedly nonlinear, often involving false starts and pivots before launching into the marketplace and continuous iteration thereafter. Until recently, best practices for executing the entrepreneurial process once an idea was conceived involved emulating the strategic planning process of large companies. Specifically, entrepreneurs would allocate their time to developing a comprehensive business plan that describes the company, its organization and management, products, marketing plan, and financial projections for the next three to five years. They would then seek to execute their plans, often resulting in failure because the plans relied on critical untested assumptions, which are inherent to bringing any truly new idea into the marketplace.

A different set of best practices has since developed for executing an *evidence-based* entrepreneurial process based on a key book: *Four Steps to the Epiphany*.[38] **Evidence-based decision-making** means that decisions are researched and made based on collected data rather than relying on your experience and expertise, personal observations, advice, hopes, or hunches. These practices build from the observation that all new ideas are associated with a variety of untested assumptions. When left untested prior to launch, each of these assumptions represents a potential cause of failure. For example, if you conceived of a new program to reduce homelessness, then the success of your idea would likely depend on untested assumptions about why the people you want to help are homeless, how the specifics of your program would benefit them, how you would reach beneficiaries to let them know about the program, the extent to which participating in the program would appeal to prospective beneficiaries, and how the program would be funded for sustainability. If any one of your assumptions ultimately proved to be invalid, then the program would be likely to fail.

The basic idea underlying evidence-based entrepreneurship is that you can systematically reduce the risk associated with bringing new ideas into the marketplace by testing assumptions, starting with the riskiest. As you do so, many of your assumptions will be invalidated by evidence. Each time this occurs, you can change an aspect of the idea based on what was learned (this is called a **pivot**) or start over with a completely new idea. Entrepreneurs employ impact modeling and lean startup methods as highly useful toolsets for executing an evidence-based entrepreneurial process.

Impact Modeling

Impact modeling is a general term for describing the decomposition of a new idea into constituent elements that are relevant to its viability. Business modeling and social impact modeling are closely related, but they are distinct varieties of impact modeling. A **business model** represents a company's rationale for how it creates value for customers, delivers its products to them, and captures value to make a profit. A category of tools called **business model canvas** are useful for illustrating the components of a business model. The first such tool to gain widespread use, which was developed by Alexander Osterwalder and Yves Pigneur,[39] is aptly named the business model canvas. The business model canvas decomposes businesses into nine components: (1) key partners, (2) key activities, (3) key resources, (4) value proposition, (5) customer relationships, (6) channels, (7) customer segments, (8) cost structure, and (9) revenue. Figure 15.3 displays the common business model canvas; however, it is important to know that other versions of this tool have been developed for different contexts, types of organizations (such as nonprofits), and different facets of entrepreneurship, such as social entrepreneurship.

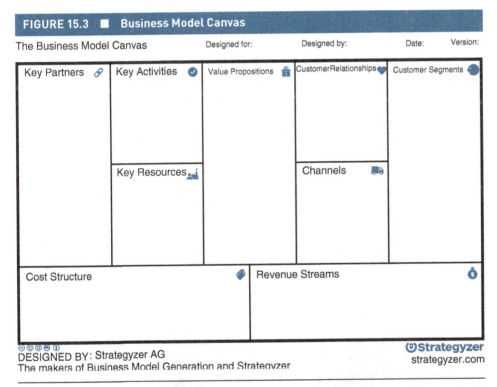

FIGURE 15.3 ■ Business Model Canvas

Source: Strategyzer, Business Model Canvas, https://strategyzer.com/canvas/business-model-canvas via CC BY-SA 3.0 https://creativecommons.org/licenses/by-sa/3.0/.

In combination, these components describe how the company creates value (through its key partners, activities, and resources), the value it offers and to whom it is offered (its value proposition and customer segments), how value is delivered (through its customer relationships and channels), and the economics of capturing value from customers (its cost structure and revenue streams).

Another form of business model canvas is the lean canvas developed by Ash Maurya[40] for startup businesses. The lean canvas decomposes new business ideas into nine components: (1) problem, (2) solution, (3) key metrics, (4) unique value proposition, (5) unfair advantage, (6) channels, (7) customer segments, (8) cost structure, and (9) revenue streams. One benefit of using the lean canvas as part of the evidence-based entrepreneurial process for startup businesses is that it emphasizes the problem (or unmet need) being addressed. The biggest risk most startups face is building a solution that no one wants. By identifying assumptions about the problem and who has it, the lean canvas can save entrepreneurs from spending a lot of time and money to develop solutions to non-problems.

A **social impact model** represents the rationale for how a policy, program, project, or social venture creates value for beneficiaries, delivers the value to beneficiaries, and sustains its impact over time. A variety of social impact canvases are available, most of which include key partners, value propositions, channels, customer segments, and other elements. The best one for decomposing your idea into constituent assumptions for testing will depend on the nature of your idea. Some components that are unique to social impact canvases include type of intervention, key points of resistance, intended societal impact, and potential unintended consequences (see Figure 15.4).

FIGURE 15.4 ■ Social Impact Canvas

Unintended Consequences		Social Impact		
Problem	Solution	Unique value proposition – Beneficiaries	Channels to beneficiaries	Beneficiaries
Key resistances	Key enablers	Unique value proposition – Payers	Channels to payers	Payers (customers)
Financial Costs		Revenue Sources		

Source: Dan Freeman, Ph.D., Horn Entrepreneurship, University of Delaware.

Lean Startup Methods

Once you have modeled your idea using an appropriate canvas, you can begin to identify and test your riskiest assumptions using lean startup methods.[41] **Lean** refers to an approach to organizational development that engages flexible, rapid methods to test and revise products and services before heavily investing. Two of these powerful methods include customer discovery interviewing and prototyping minimum viable products.

Customer Discovery Interviewing

The **customer discovery interview** involves using a structured interview script to qualify an interviewee as a member of your assumed target segment and elicit beliefs and experiences relevant to the problem you are trying to solve and the solution you are working to develop. One of many user-centered data collection techniques discussed previously, customer discovery interviewing tests and/or enriches understanding of the problem members of the customer segment

Chapter 15 ● Entrepreneurial Leadership **479**

experience and identifies core *must-have* features and benefits that your solution will need to offer to deliver compelling value. The most important guideline for customer discovery interviewing is simply to do it early and often during the entrepreneurial process.

The second most important guideline is to remember that a pitch is *not* included. Customer discovery interviews should focus on the interviewee's experiences, pains, and desires. Listen, do not talk. As Seth Godin notes, "The other person is always right. You'll need to travel to this place of 'right' before you have any chance at all of actual communication or understanding" and influence.[42] *The Mom Test* by Rob Fitzpatrick also outlines many general rules that will help spark a rich conversation, summed as, "1. Talk about their life instead of your idea. 2. Ask about specifics in the past instead of generics or opinions about the future. 3. Talk less and listen more."[43] Table 15.5 provides a few sample interview questions.[44]

TABLE 15.5 ■ Sample Customer Discovery Interview Questions (from *The Mom Test*)
Good Questions:
1. Why do you bother doing _____?
2. Talk me through the last time you did _____.
3. What else have you tried?
4. What would your dream (product/service) do?
Bad Questions:
1. Would you buy a product/service that did _____?
2. How much would you pay for _____?
3. Do you think _____ is a good idea?

Prototyping Minimum Viable Products

Once you have validated your ideas for core product features and benefits, you can prototype a minimum viable product to test its appeal. A **minimum viable product (MVP)** is the smallest, simplest thing you can build that conveys the product's value proposition to customers. Your MVP does not need to be a physical prototype, but it could be a promotional flyer or a landing page that describes the product and what it offers. Different variations of MVPs provide information from customers that allow you to iterate based on evidence before spending the time and money needed to actually develop a marketable version of your product or service.

The lean practices associated with evidence-based entrepreneurship can be successfully applied to the process of bringing any type of new idea—including ideas for programs, policies, social ventures, products, and startup businesses—into the marketplace.

THE EVOLVING ROLE OF THE ENTREPRENEURIAL LEADER

LEARNING OBJECTIVE
15.5 Design your future as an entrepreneurial leader.

Up to this point, entrepreneurial leadership has been described largely as mental habits and process activities, such as idea generation and validation. However, there are at least four distinct roles that entrepreneurial leaders can play as they execute the entrepreneurial process by conceiving, validating, and launching new ideas into the marketplace: the founder, the innovator, the team builder, and the chief executive. This section describes these roles as well as the tremendous challenges associated with any one person attempting to fill all of these roles by going from founder to CEO.

The Founder

The entrepreneurial process begins with the recognition and pursuit of opportunity by a founder (or inventor/creator). The founder's role as an entrepreneurial leader involves seeing opportunity and utilizing creativity to conceive of a new idea that has the potential to disrupt the status quo. New ideas are inherently associated with greater uncertainty and risk vis-à-vis established ideas. As uncertainty and risk are aversive, an important part of the founder's role involves developing and communicating a compelling vision for the unique value that will be provided by the new idea. This vision needs to articulate who will benefit, how they will benefit, why it matters, and why the benefits should be expected to greatly outweigh any potential risks. For founders, creativity, compulsion to disrupt the status quo, and vision are essential personal characteristics.

MYTH OR REALITY?

You cannot be an entrepreneur unless you have a disruptive idea.

Myth! There are many entrepreneurial roles—founder, innovator, team builder, and chief executive. Only one requires that you be involved in idea generation. In other words, you can still be an entrepreneur if you are involved in the validation and launch of a new idea into the marketplace or guide the growth of an entrepreneurial venture as its chief executive. Ideas emerge from engaging other ideas and perspectives. The more you are involved in entrepreneurial activities and the more you are mindful, observant, and open to new ideas, the more likely you will one day see that opportunity and find that disruptive idea. But that activity is just one small part of entrepreneurship.

The Innovator

Once a vision has been developed, the entrepreneurial leader's role transitions to that of the innovator. Recall that innovation is defined as the collaborative process of translating creative ideas into something of value. Thus, the innovator's role is to translate the vision into a series of testable impact model assumptions, prioritize and conduct tests, and iterate as needed until a viable model is identified or the project is terminated. This process, which often involves active collaboration with members of the founding team and many turns of the do–learn–repeat loop, requires the innovator to maintain flexibility and persistence in response to a roller coaster of excitement, rejection, and uncertainty. Riding the roller coaster is not for everyone. Possession of the passion and optimism needed to persist through difficult times and the capacity to continuously reprioritize and rapidly adapt based on learning are essential characteristics for innovators.

Chapter 15 ● Entrepreneurial Leadership   481

Leadership by Design

Design Principle: Fun

Definition: A feeling of enjoyment or pleasure (as a noun), a way to describe something as such (as an adjective—that was a fun game—or even a verb if you think "funning" is a word).[45]

In Other Words: A purely and often instantaneously pleasurable experience. For example, you fill in the blank: "I have fun doing _____." Fun is subjective.

For Leaders: Fun can play a key role in every facet of your leadership design. Designing fun into yourself and your time has positive effects on health and creativity. Fun in your leadership relationships increases engagement, job satisfaction, and performance while reducing anxiety and emotional exhaustion.[46] Fun increases organizational citizenship behavior and creates a culture of connectedness and innovation (see Chapter 14). Fun and funny often emanate from connecting ideas that generally do not belong together—such as when a comedian makes an unexpected or inappropriate face relative to their joke. Or why do witches fly around on broomsticks? Because vacuum cleaners do not have long enough cords. Fun can catalyze innovation and designing the future.

Because everyone defines fun in their own way, leaders must buy in, facilitate, and find ways to bring everyone in on the fun—to make it a shared experience.[47] Likewise, too often, activities and interactions imposed by managers are perceived as juvenile, condescending, and inauthentic, resulting in employee cynicism. That is no fun.

What can you do to design fun into your leadership?

The Team Builder

After the innovator succeeds in validating a novel impact model, the entrepreneurial leader's role shifts to growing the team. Leadership is the process of influencing others toward a common vision. At this point, the entrepreneurial leader's role of team builder focuses most heavily on effective leadership activities, such as recruiting new personnel and communicating a purpose that will align everyone's activities and make all team members feel as if they are part of something important and larger than themselves (i.e., a shared vision). Research on motivation shows that purpose is often more powerful than money in promoting high performance among the types of employees who are most likely to drive the growth of an entrepreneurial venture—those who are creative problem solvers and knowledge workers.[48, 49] Therefore, being growth oriented, willing to make personal sacrifices to advance a shared purpose, and capable of influencing others are essential characteristics for team builders.

The Chief Executive

Once the core team is assembled and scope and scale of the venture have expanded, often with considerable velocity, the entrepreneurial leader's role transitions to chief executive. In this capacity, the leader becomes responsible for setting strategic direction and accountable for the overall performance/impact of the business, social enterprise, project, or program. Providing strategic direction requires cognitive ambidexterity.[50] Similar to being able to use both hands equally well, cognitive ambidexterity describes the ability of someone to think creatively as well as logically. The chief executive must guide the development of rigid policies and processes to extract efficiencies from existing products. On the other hand, the chief executive must also encourage ongoing experimentation to explore and pursue new opportunities. Accountability for performance requires managerial discipline while energizing innovation requires leadership autonomy and inspiration. Thus, characteristics pertaining to mental agility, efficiency, and management are essential for chief executives.

REFLECTION QUESTION

What entrepreneurial leadership role are you best suited for—founder, innovator, team builder, or chief executive? Do you think you have the characteristics and skills needed to go from founder to chief executive?

The Leadership Challenge: From Founder to Chief Executive

The skills approach to leadership explained in Chapter 2 outlined the shifting skills required of leaders as they rose in the organization—transitioning from the technical skills of doing the job to the human skills of managing to the conceptual skills of heading the organization. These shifts also apply to the value of personal characteristics in the transition from founder to chief executive, with each level demanding new skills from entrepreneurial leaders. Two skill set-based challenges associated with making this transition are going from technician to strategist and going from star player to coach of the year.[51]

During idea generation, validation, and launch, entrepreneurial leadership is about pace setting and being actively involved in all aspects of value creation, delivery, and capture. Throughout these stages of the entrepreneurial process, leaders need to be close to customers to ascertain whether they are on the right track. Technical expertise and operational skills are valuable in this context, as they enable the leader to meet the challenge of execution, which is about doing things right.

However, as the business grows, entrepreneurial leadership transitions to being about doing the right things. Chief executives simply do not have enough time to be actively involved in the day-to-day operational aspects of a business or social venture. Rather, they need to focus on setting the strategic direction of the company and determining how to put their limited time to its highest and best use. Transitioning from working in the business to working on the business can be difficult for many entrepreneurial leaders (thus, founder's syndrome). Whereas working in the business emphasizes attending to details and constantly making decisions in real time, working on the business emphasizes big picture and making a relatively small number of strategic decisions. This requires a different skill set. Table 15.6 summarizes the shifting focus of entrepreneurial leadership.

Transitioning from a nascent startup to a growing company also involves a shift in the nature of leaders' relationships with team members. The shift from founder to chief executive is akin to going from the star player to coach of the year. During startup, entrepreneurial leaders are the stars of their teams; others look to them for direction and making the big plays that result in the company beginning to win in the marketplace. Growth forces entrepreneurial leaders to rely more on the operational capabilities of others and less on their own abilities to execute the company's business model. This means another shift in skills—away from execution and toward talent development. Just as in sports, the star player does not necessarily translate to excellent coach or scout or trainer. The entrepreneurial leader must focus on and develop new skills to become an effective coach who prepares top executives and devises a strategic game plan that puts them in the best position to succeed.

Chapter 15 • Entrepreneurial Leadership   483

TABLE 15.6 ■ Entrepreneurial Leadership Roles and Shifting Focus		
Role	**Venture Focus**	**Leadership Focus**
Founder	Find opportunity Generate idea Craft vision Initiate venture	Clarify and communicate vision Inspire and recruit partners Model CORE™ amidst risk
Innovator	Translate value Develop viable model	Manage collaborative iteration work Maintain optimism and resilience
Team builder	Maximize value Engage and manage others	Identify, screen, onboard Communicate vision and purpose Clarify direction and strategy Engage, motivate, and manage
Chief executive	Maximize, sustain, and reinvent value Set strategic direction	Foster innovation Create management systems Inspire and model the ideal

REFLECTION QUESTION

With which entrepreneurial leadership role are you least comfortable? What are your personal shortcomings and weaknesses that might affect your success as an entrepreneurial leader? The capacity to conduct an honest self-assessment and strive for personal improvement will make you a better entrepreneurial leader.

Chief Engagement Officer: Entrepreneurial Leadership at Every Level

While your focus and role as a leader will vary, one constant will apply from founder through executive: Extending your impact and influence will always require talented, engaged others. Throughout this textbook, you have learned about building *your* CORE™—confidence, optimism, resilience, and engagement. And then you learned about designing others' success by helping your followers build their CORE™ through creating conditions that build confidence and optimism, ensuring that challenges are manageable but difficult enough to build resilience, and encouraging engagement. Designing *your* future success means designing *others'* future success. At any leadership level, this means serving as a chief engagement officer.

The idea of engagement has become a popular topic as it relates to employees.[52] Chapter 1 defined engagement as the degree of individual involvement, investment, and enthusiasm within and for a specific context or situation. There are considerable individual and organizational benefits to having engaged followers, and many leaders focus on how they can increase their employee engagement in addition to their own.[53] The Gallup organization measures employee engagement and has created an assessment called the Q12—12 questions that best predict who will and will not be engaged and consequently perform and succeed. Gallup notes three categories of employees: engaged employees who work with passion and feel connected to their company; not-engaged employees who put in the time but without energy or passion; and actively disengaged employees who are both unhappy and busy undermining the organization.[54]

Gallup's extensive research highlights both the importance of engagement as well as the key role that leaders play in fostering that engagement. For example, if you have ever worked for a bad leader, it will not surprise you to learn that 50 percent of employees leave their job to get away from a manager. Further, 70 percent of the variance in employee engagement scores are tied to the manager.[55] Note that in the business setting, Gallup refers to leaders as managers and limits their definition of leader to those holding a supervisory position.

At the heart of engagement is follower satisfaction, but let's aim for enthusiasm. Satisfied, enthused individuals become cheerleaders for and long-term invested members of the organization. They also become high performers. The consulting firm Aon Hewitt calls this the Say, Stay, and Strive model.[56] How will you engage individuals such that they will say great things, stay part of the group, and strive for greatness? The simple yet challenging answer, as always, lies in the human side of leadership. As a leader, you must do more than design others' success, you must *serve* others' success. In short, supporting others, attending to social and emotional needs, and emphasizing the meaningfulness of the work bring forth the positive culture that leads to engagement.[57]

The Gallup Q12 measure illuminates what you might do to increase engagement. Following are a few questions based on the Q12 and reframed as prompts for generating ideas, specifically, ideas for ways that you might increase engagement and design future success.

In what ways might I . . .

- Identify what others and I do best? And in what ways might we provide opportunities to share and/or apply what we do best?

- Receive and show others praise and/or recognition for good work or accomplishment?

- Show or communicate to others that they are noticed and cared about?

- Encourage and/or facilitate personal development of each individual in my organization?

- Create a culture where everyone's opinion matters? How might I solicit those opinions and recognize/acknowledge them?

- Consistently achieve really high-quality work? How might I ensure every activity greatly impresses others?

- Build deeper relationships with others?

- Regularly reflect on and discuss goals, activities to reach those goals, my role in those activities, and how I am progressing?

- Create more opportunities to learn and grow both personally and professionally?

CHAPTER SUMMARY

This chapter added another perspective and set of tools to your leadership toolbox—that of the entrepreneurial leader. Entrepreneurs benefit greatly from understanding leadership, but leaders who seek to thrive in times of change must learn to innovate and take on an entrepreneurial leadership mindset. As you continue to learn more about leadership, it should become more and more apparent that leadership is about you and not about you simultaneously. Navigating that balance will allow you to harness innovation and maximize your success.

The classic children's book *Harold and the Purple Crayon* tells the story of young Harold, who decides to create his own world and adventure by drawing what he wants with his purple crayon

Chapter 15 ● Entrepreneurial Leadership **485**

and then watching it come to life. At heart, it is a story about creating your own opportunities and solving problems with your imagination and effort. Harold draws a mountain from which to see, "But as he looked down over the other side he slipped—And there wasn't any other side of the mountain. He was falling, in thin air. But, luckily, he kept his wits and his purple crayon. He made a balloon and he grabbed on to it."[58] Effective leaders must design and make their own path, seeing and pursuing opportunities for innovation. The field of entrepreneurship provides a unique set of concepts, mindsets, and activities that can help leaders spot, translate, and develop value.

Entrepreneurship is the process of pursuing opportunity through the conception, validation, and launch of new ideas into the marketplace. This activity goes beyond the field of business and can include every field including social, political, and within existing organizations. Each action within the definition requires specific knowledge and skills as well as a number of mindsets that enable entrepreneurs to see differently. This includes a growth mindset, being mindful and observant, reframing problems as opportunities, ideating and effectuating, taking reflective action, and staying focused on purpose.

Leading the entrepreneurial process using tools such as the business model canvas and lean start-up methods enable entrepreneurial leaders to minimize risk and iterate to find the most successful path forward.

As a venture grows, entrepreneurial leaders must shift their role and focus from founder to innovator to team builder to chief executive. Each role requires a differing skill set aligned to the needs of the developing venture. However, designing for future success at all levels involves creating conditions for engagement.

KEY TERMS

Adaptive cycles (p. 473)
Business model canvas (p. 477)
Business model (p. 477)
Causal reasoning (p. 471)
Customer discovery interviewing (p. 478)
Ecocycle framework (p. 474)
Effectuation (p. 471)
Entrepreneurial leadership (p. 462)
Entrepreneurship (p. 464)
Evidence-based decision-making (p. 476)
Founder's syndrome (p. 466)

Ideation (p. 471)
Impact modelling (p. 477)
Intrapreneurship (p. 466)
Invention (p. 465)
Lean (p. 478)
Minimum viable product (MVP) (p. 479)
Opportunity recognition (p. 464)
Panarchy (p. 473)
Pivot (p. 476)
Social entrepreneurship (p. 466)
Social impact model (p. 478)

CORE™ ATTRIBUTE BUILDERS: BUILD NOW FOR FUTURE LEADERSHIP CHALLENGES

Attribute: Engagement

Builder: "Eye of the Tiger," by Steve Boerner

Can you recall a movie where the hero is facing terrible obstacles and then the hit soundtrack kicks in and the hero has that moment of conviction—a moment that marks the beginning of a

486   Module 5 • Design the Future

determined journey toward conquering the impossible? In the Academy Award-winning movie *Rocky*, that song is "Eye of the Tiger" (by the band Survivor). In the movie, Rocky is faced with the impossibility of rising from the streets of South Philadelphia to become a world-champion boxer. Only when he truly commits (and fully engages) does he take on the eye of the tiger—the tenacious will to reach his goals.

Your challenge: Choose an implausible outcome you desire. Then pursue it with a new lens, a creative approach, and with heightened ambition.

Apply your eye of the tiger to accomplish a micro-success and then another and another. Perhaps you want to meet someone? Learn a skill?[59]

What do you really want but right now think is impossible? Get the eye of the tiger and take the first step!

CORE™ ATTRIBUTE BUILDERS: BUILD NOW FOR FUTURE LEADERSHIP CHALLENGES

Attribute: Confidence and Resilience

Builder: 25 things to celebrate

Entrepreneurs are on the lookout for opportunities, take risks, spearhead initiatives, and constantly try things for the purpose of assessing and improving. They are always looking for the next thing on their to-do list. And effective leaders are often no different. What both fail to do often enough is note and celebrate their success.

1. Take a moment right now to write out 25 things of which you are proud. These can be accomplishments big or small, interactions or reactions, a risk taken, a moment of emotional intelligence, or anything that *you* are proud to have done, been like, and so forth.

2. When you are done with the list, read it out loud to yourself without comment or judgment. You will be surprised how you feel.

3. Date your list and file it somewhere. Repeat this activity every so often, and soon you will have quite a record of your big and small accomplishments. Taking the time to remind yourself of these accomplishments boosts your confidence, knowing that your work is more than the list that remains undone. The list also builds resilience, reminding yourself of the many things that you have managed to achieve.

As an added dimension, do this activity with friends and/or colleagues. Remind them that during the reading, there is no judgment or comment. Of course, there will be lots of smiles and congrats afterward.

SKILL BUILDER ACTIVITY

Practice Your Pitching

Develop a 30-second description of your business (an elevator pitch) and field test it at a community networking event. Do people seem to get it? What can you learn from their reactions?

Chapter 15 ● Entrepreneurial Leadership   **487**

SKILL BUILDER ACTIVITY

Plan a Venture

Planning an entrepreneurial venture takes a good deal of time, information, collaboration, and leadership. Use the list of activities that follows to guide you and/or a team through the venture-planning process.

	Prompt/Activity	Business Model Canvas	Innovation Process Phase
1	Consider and list issues of interest to you—what do you want to know more about and make a difference regarding?	Pre-canvas	Understand
2	Write a brief history of your issue—both a professional history and your personal history with the issue.	Pre-canvas	Understand
3	Create a visual model of your issue—a mental map or a systems diagram.	Pre-canvas	Understand
4	Write the story of solutions as it regards your issue and highlight best practices (using the storytelling framework). If customers have a problem, right now they are doing something to solve it. What has been done? What is being done?	Pre-canvas	Understand
5	Engage user-centered methods to collect information about your issue, identifying the stakeholders and potential customer segments. Consider what kind of relationship you want with each customer segment.	Customer segments Customer relationships	Understand
6	Envision the ideal solutions and/or outcomes of your issue—what would/ could it look like and how?		Understand Imagine
7	Generate many, many, many ideas for *solving* your issue.		Imagine
8	Examine multiple views and perspectives on both your issue and some of your proposed solutions.		Imagine
9	Research and establish criteria by which you will judge the success of your solution; create metrics as applicable.	Key metrics	Implement
10	Engage in customer discovery interviewing and other techniques to determine solution viability and desirability.		Iteration
11	Assess unique value proposition and how to frame it.	Unique value proposition	Implement
12	Assess your unfair advantage: Why are *you* the one to take on this problem? What do *you* have that no one else has or can buy? What gives you an advantage that others can only dream of?	Unfair advantage	Implement
13	Craft a strategic implementation plan for your solution using the business model canvas or other applicable tool.	Overall canvas Sales channels Key resources Key activities	Iterate Implement
14	Add a plan to maximize value and revenue.	Revenue streams (or value types)	
15	Consider and plan possible cross-sector collaborations and further innovations in the solution and/or implementation of your solution. Who could help you advance your venture?	Key partners	Iterate Implement

(Continued)

488   Module 5 • Design the Future

	Prompt/Activity	Business Model Canvas	Innovation Process Phase
16	Consider unintended consequences, worst cases, and ethical issues arising from your solution.	Overall canvas	Iterate
17	Create and test a minimum viable product.		Iterate
18	Envision the next iteration and innovation.	Revisit problem and solution, then overall canvas	Iterate

16 SYSTEMS AND SUSTAINABILITY

LEARNING OBJECTIVES

Upon completion of this chapter, the reader should be able to

16.1 Explore how systems thinking is critical to the success of leaders

16.2 Identify systems thinking as a key part of a learning organization

16.3 Apply concepts of generativity and identity to sustain your leadership beyond your time as leader

16.4 Describe several dimensions of sustainability

16.5 Integrate mindful practices to sustain your personal growth

16.6 Personalize the concept of authentic leadership

Leadership by Design Model

Design Self
How can I design myself as a leader?

Design Relationships
As a leader, how can I design my relationships with others?

Design Others' Success
As a leader, how can I design success for others?

Design Culture
As a leader, how can I design the culture of my organization?

Design Future
AS A LEADER, HOW CAN I INNOVATE?

INTRODUCTION

Great leaders design a future of success long past their time as leader. This chapter focuses on systems thinking and sustainability in the broadest sense. How can the leader ensure long-term financial viability, environmental stewardship, socially just practices, and development of the next generation of leaders for the organization? The chapter concludes with a discussion of authentic leadership as a foundation for sustainable leadership.

Designing the future as a leader means understanding two facts: Everything is more complicated and interconnected than it appears, and actions in the present will impact the future in some way. In other words, individuals, groups, organizations, and cultures are all part of complex systems and may or may not be sustainable over time. Sustainable, effective leadership is less about having the answers and much more about a leader's ability to see wider, deeper, and into the future. Most senior leaders would agree that leadership is about identifying the right questions to help achieve the mission—questions that help unmask hidden variables and influences that drive activity and attitudes. It is a complex endeavor to determine what an organization needs to hold on to and what it needs to let go of to live in a better future (see IBM and Kodak for two interesting case studies). Consider the following poem entitled "The Blind Men and the Elephant" by American poet John Godfrey Saxe (1816–1887) based on an Indian folktale. The individuals in the poem are big on firmly held answers but lack the questions that could have changed their results.

The Blind Men and the Elephant*

It was six men of Indostan,
To learning much inclined,
Who went to see the elephant,
(Though all of them were blind),
That each by observation
Might satisfy his mind.
The first approached the elephant,
And happening to fall
Against his broad and sturdy side,
At once began to bawl:
"God bless me! But the elephant
Is very like a wall!"
The second, feeling of the tusk,
Cried: "Ho! What have we here,
So very round and smooth and sharp?
To me 'tis very clear,
This wonder of an elephant
Is very like a spear!"
The third approached the animal,
And happening to take
The squirming trunk within his hands,
Thus boldly up and spake:
"I see," quoth he, "the elephant
Is very like a snake!"
The fourth reached out an eager hand,
And felt about the knee.
"What most this wondrous beast is like
Is might plain," quoth he;
"Tis clear enough the elephant
Is very like a tree."
The fifth, who chanced to touch the ear,
Said: "E'en the blindest man
Can tell what this resembles most:
Deny the fact who can,
This marvel of an elephant
Is very like a fan."

Chapter 16 • Systems and Sustainability   491

The sixth no sooner had begun
About the beast to grope,
Than seizing on the swinging tail
That fell within his scope,
"I see," quoth he, "the elephant
Is very like a rope."
And so these men of Indostan
Disputed loud and long,
Each in his own opinion
Exceeding stiff and strong.
Though each was partly right,
All were in the wrong.
Moral:
So oft in theologic wars,
The disputants, I ween,
Rail on in utter ignorance
Of what each other mean,
And prate about an Elephant
Not one of them has seen!
*Source: Saxe, J. G. "The blind men and the elephant." Retrieved from http://www.noogen-
esis.com/pineapple/blind_men_elephant.html

"The Blind Men and the Elephant" encapsulates the focus of this final chapter. The elephant could be said to represent an organization; however, the world is full of complex, interconnected systems in which there are elephants everywhere. Even this textbook is an elephant—without reading and understanding the overall structure and how each idea fits with the others, each idea could be interpreted in a variety of ways, many of which would not be accurate without the big picture.

Looking at individual parts of a larger system can be an exercise in futility. As you read in earlier chapters, developing an ideal culture means understanding and addressing the many hidden variables at work in the more extensive system. You need to understand the system to facilitate long-term, lasting change. It is more likely that a system of interventions will lead to a sustainable organization versus a single solution. And to better understand the system and create sustainability (defined broadly), there are some characteristics and tools that you will need—things like remaining humble, surrounding yourself with an incredible team, and identifying central questions for the group to explore.

Leadership That Makes a Difference

Many of you reading this textbook may be unfamiliar with Unilever. However, you know its products—Ben & Jerry's, Dove, Axe, Vaseline, Klondike, and Lipton to name a few. The reality is that as of July 2021, Unilever's market cap was at 152.76 billion and it's the 83rd most valuable company.[1] What's interesting about Unilever is its overt commitment to being a company that is not only profitable but also sustainable. According to *Fortune*, it's the 30th most admired company in the world.[2] Unilever's vision and purpose clearly communicate its commitment to sustainability—it understands its role in the larger system. Its vision statement states, "Our vision is to grow our business while decoupling our environmental footprint from our growth and increasing our positive social impact," and under 'purpose,' the company states, "We continue to believe that business must make a positive contribution to addressing the challenges the world faces and that this is the only way a business will succeed. In 2009 we launched The Compass—our strategy for sustainable growth setting out our determination to build a sustainable business for the long term." According to Unilever's sustainability report, the company has yielded some impressive results since unveiling The Unilever Sustainable Living Plan launched in 2010. Unilever has set an ambitious goal of net zero emissions by 2039. Likewise, it has a goal of cutting the greenhouse gas impact of its products across the lifecycle in half by 2030.[3] The company values transparency, and its website highlights several topics, such as deforestation, farm animal welfare, genetically modified crops, human rights, microplastics, sugar reduction and a host of other topics.[4]

As of 2020, the company reported some significant results. For instance, 83 percent of its procurement spend was through suppliers that met mandatory requirements of the Responsible Sourcing Policy. Likewise, there was a 34 percent decrease in the waste impact of its products across the lifecycle (per consumer). The company reached more than 1.3 billion people through its programming on handwashing, sanitation, oral health, and safe drinking water. Interestingly, 168,489 women gained access to initiatives designed to create opportunities in Unilever's value chain.[5]

While not perfect, it's clear that Unilver is invested in more than just the financial bottom line. Sustainable business practices are at the core of its long-term strategy. In fact, the company was named the Dow Jones Sustainability Indices Industry Leader in 2020.[6] Ex-CEO Paul Polman sums up the company's mindset well—"At the current rate we'll get there in 2072 and we cannot really wait for that. The most burning issues at the moment are climate change and inequality. You see that being played out now every day in the news one country after another people in the streets or businesses being boycotted and all these other things. What companies can do best is integrate the SDGs into their strategies which are I think a business opportunity."[7] As industry expert Helle Bank Jorgensen suggests, "We need a plan and we need that plan right now. And we need to follow up on that plan. We need to report on that plan. We need to tell our stakeholders about our plan."[8]

Unilever has a plan. Does your favorite company? Do a quick search and find out.
©iStockphoto.com/JHVEPhoto

Chapter 16 • Systems and Sustainability   **493**

SYSTEMS AND SYSTEMS THINKING

LEARNING OBJECTIVE

16.1   Explore how systems thinking is critical to the success of leaders.

Every system is perfectly designed to get the results it gets.—W. Edwards Demming[9]

A **system** comprises a group of interconnected, interdependent parts that make up a complex whole. A bag of marbles is not a system because each marble functions independently. However, the ball in a pinball machine is part of a system—without the other parts of the game, there is no game (and no fun). The concept can sound complicated and confusing. However, you interact and work with systems every day. A primary example is the Earth. There is a system—multiple variables interacting with one another—all in place to facilitate life on planet Earth. A similar system does not exist on Pluto, Venus, or Mercury. Another example is your weight. Based on your metabolism, eating habits, workout regimen, environment, culture, microbiome, and any number of other variables, there is a system in place that yields your weight. One final example is your family—a system as well. For example, if your primary caregivers modeled a healthy relationship with strong communication, valued education, modeled moral integrity, and promoted a growth mindset, you likely come from a family system that set you up for a well-adjusted life.

Organizations have systems in place as well. Chapter 7 highlighted the importance of engagement in organizational life. Some organizational systems facilitate a culture of engagement, while others do not. As a leader, establishing a culture of engagement is no small task. You have to focus on many variables, such as how you set the vision, hire, conduct performance management, reward and recognize, assign work, develop your employees, model norms of behavior, and so on.

REFLECTION QUESTIONS

Think back to your last job or internship. Did the system facilitate engagement of employees? Why or why not?

Leaders influence others toward a common goal; they affect the relationships, context, and culture of a group or organization. Influencing such a complex system requires the ability to see and think about the systems making up the whole. **Systems thinking** is a habit of mind (disposition) used to examine and understand the connections and interactions between individual parts making up a complex whole.

Systems thinking was first introduced in organizational life as a tool for decision-making, often relative to organizational productivity as explained by management legend W. Edwards Deming.[10] Systems thinking is a way to *see* the whole of a problem or opportunity versus the individual parts (as highlighted in the poem at the beginning of the chapter). Only seeing or addressing the parts of a problem can lead to unintended consequences or failed efforts. For instance, a community experiencing low unemployment and an increase in crime could push full steam ahead on business development—attracting several new businesses to town. However, unless the community has the educated workforce, resource infrastructure (e.g., roads, water, airport), and other components (e.g., resources for families, high-quality education, strong police force) to accommodate the new demand, their efforts will fail. The issue of unemployment and high crime links to education, skills training, community resources, and so on.

As you become more and more familiar with systems, certain archetypes emerge. An archetype is a *typical example* of something. In systems thinking, archetypes allow you to see typical configurations of parts influencing one another—a whole picture that you might not readily see. For instance, one archetype of system thinking is called Fixes That Fail. This archetype models a situation where a solution to the problem is really only addressing a symptom, which then fails because it does not target the root cause. For instance, many popular diet plans provide tools or *fixes* that often do not address the actual root cause of overeating and/or low activity levels (e.g., depression, addiction, environment). As a result, they often fail to work long term—thus, resulting in the multi-billion-dollar diet industry. If these diets worked, the obesity epidemic would have been eradicated by now.

Another systems-thinking archetype is known as Limits to Growth, which occurs when resource constraints eventually limit growth, quality, and service. Imagine a college campus that is growing its international population rapidly. If the school does not have the support resources (e.g., housing over breaks, year-round meal plans, onboarding programs) to accommodate large numbers, the quality of their experience will diminish. Only so much growth will occur under the current system. For the organization to move to another level, it will need to address other dimensions of the system.[11]

Seeing Interconnections

As discussed, systems thinking means that you can see the many interconnections and relationships among the variables. Leaders can often default to looking for a single cause for low motivation among employees (e.g., "we are hiring the wrong people") or a lack of results; however, in reality, the system is yielding results for many reasons. At least, that is a real possibility. As a result, think about your organizations with a level of complexity so you can push past simplistic thinking as you work to create a better future. Peter Senge, a leader in this realm, suggests the following:

> Systems Thinking helps us challenge counterproductive assumptions about authority in a productive way. Rather than pointing fingers, it fosters compassion. We realize that systems work the way they do, not because of any one person's individual agency, but because of our collective agency.[12]

Similar to the leader/follower relationship, everyone owns a piece of what works and what does not work—that which functions and the dysfunction as well. At times, you are a bystander to dysfunctional behavior, which allows or creates a culture that will not yield desired results. In reality, everyone is shaping culture. A common misconception is that you need to have a position of authority to influence or change the system. By now, you know this is not necessarily the case. Great acts of leadership have occurred throughout history by people who did not have a formal position of authority (e.g., Steven Biko, Larry Kramer, Greta Thunberg, Jane Goodall, Malala Yousafzai).

If we were mapping a human being, the major systems to be mapped would include circulatory, respiratory, digestive, nervous, immune, skeletal, and so forth. A heart cannot function without other parts of the system, and it will be difficult to understand the system by merely exploring the heart. Thus, to understand a human being, you need to look at the whole to better understand the system. Interestingly, the universe, a rainforest, and a corporate community are systems as well. For example, when an organization embraces a community, the two become more and more interdependent.

Chapter 16 • Systems and Sustainability **495**

Experts Beyond the Text

INSIGHTFUL LEADERS KNOW ABOUT . . . CYNEFIN FRAMEWORK AND EMERGENT PRACTICE

Cynefin Framework: Decision-Making for Complex Times

By Dr. Kathleen E. Allen

The global economy, social media, the internet of things, political unrest, and the environment are connected to each other. Change in one area impacts changes in other domains. Nothing seems to "stay put" anymore. As the world becomes more interconnected and interdependent, leaders no longer lead a closed-system organization. This new reality has implications for how we think about leadership and decision-making.

Traditional decision-making frameworks held a deep background assumption that organizations and businesses were closed systems. If a problem came up, leaders sought to identify and analyze all the variables to the problem. Once the parts were understood, the solution would show up as good or best practice. In closed systems, solutions are found in the parts, not the whole.

When leading in open, complex organizations, many problems have multiple systems that impact one another. The turbulent external environment shows up inside the organization, and traditional decision-making of good or best practice doesn't fit these situations. As systems become more open, interconnected, and sophisticated, decision-making practices also need to shift.

In open complex systems, solutions are found by going up to the balcony and observing the dance floor to see the patterns of the dance. In other words, leaders need to seek out and see the bigger picture. Once the patterns are found, a strategy can be designed through emergent practice. Sometimes open systems are very dynamic and become chaotic. Chaotic challenges require novel practice instead of best practice because nothing is static or known.

The Cynefin Framework helps leaders see how open systems develop an emergent practice approach to decision-making.[13] These open systems have many different variables that impact the system. The weather system is an example of a nonlinear dynamic system where the interdependent nature of weather variables can create disturbances at a distance. The popular idea from chaos theory that the flap of a butterfly's wings in China can create a snowstorm in New York City is an example of how open and interdependent systems have unexpected events as a natural part of the system.[14] The nonlinear nature of the dynamics of an open complex system fits with emergent practice rather than best or good practice.

Figure 16.1 is a visual of four different kinds of problems and the decision-making practice that best fits the problem. A *simple* or *complicated* problem occurs in a closed system. The variables are either known or can be known, and no new variables show up. The leader seeks to analyze all the variables and then decide based on good or best practice.

Complex or *chaotic* problems can't use "best practice" because there are always new variables that emerge as the problem is being solved. The situation is dynamic and changing, so the leader must shift their decision-making process to emergent or novel practice. Emergent practice has an element of adaptation and experimentation, which is necessary for leaders seeking a culture of adaptation and innovation.

FIGURE 16.1 ■ The Cynefin Framework

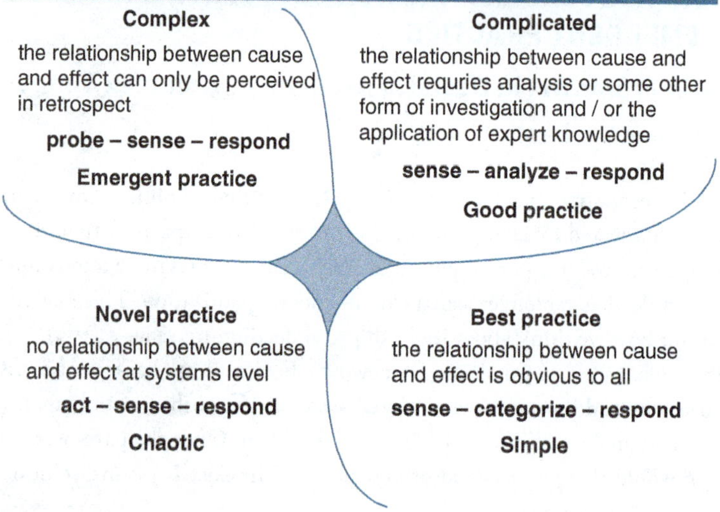

Complex

the relationship between cause and effect can only be perceived in retrospect

probe – sense – respond

Emergent practice

Complicated

the relationship between cause and effect requries analysis or some other form of investigation and / or the application of expert knowledge

sense – analyze – respond

Good practice

Novel practice

no relationship between cause and effect at systems level

act – sense – respond

Chaotic

Best practice

the relationship between cause and effect is obvious to all

sense – categorize – respond

Simple

Source: Snowden, D. J., & Boone, M. E. (2007, November). A leader's framework for decision making: Wise executives tailor their approach to fit the complexity of the circumstances they face. *Harvard Business Review, 85*(11). Retrieved from https://hbr.org/2007/11/a-leaders-framework-for-decision-making.

REFLECTION QUESTIONS

Think about your campus as a system. What are some of the major components of the system? Which components are successful and filled with energy? Which struggle and why?

Where's the Energy in the System?

Energy is an important concept to consider when discussing systems. All systems use energy. As discussed in Chapter 7, an organizational system is unleashing positive energy and engagement, or in many cases, it is quite the opposite, according to Gallup's research. Leaders need to have a keen eye for energy, and in their article "Energy Optimization and the Role of the Leader," Kathy Allen and William Mease highlight this point elegantly.

> Energy exists in all systems. When energy is used positively, it is optimized, and like the riptide, is generative instead of continually consuming resources. Positive energy naturally flows in a direction that brings the system into greater alignment with itself. We've all had the expansive experience of being "on the same wave length" with others. It is a freeing, energizing experience.[15]

Leaders have an opportunity to unleash energy in a system. This phenomenon has occurred throughout history—for good and evil. For instance, Wangari Maathai and her Green Belt Movement or Nelson Mandela focusing the energy of the South African people. In a similar vein, Adolf Hitler tapped into the fear and unrest of the German people, which led to evil and destruction. You likely experience this systemic energy on a daily basis in the classroom, at your job, on your team, or in your student organizations. In some contexts, the professor, coach, or

Chapter 16 • Systems and Sustainability **497**

supervisor does an excellent job of unleashing and focusing energy. At other times, this is not the case—and you can feel it—almost instantly.

REFLECTION QUESTIONS

Can you think of a teacher, coach, clergy member, supervisor, or relative who was skilled at unleashing the untapped energy in a group? What attributes made them have such an impact on others?

Once energy is released, what does success look like? Some would say that in a capitalistic society, profits will determine success. Others define success more broadly—in more of a systemic manner. For instance, proponents of the triple bottom line assert that long-term, sustainable success is about three fundamental factors: people, planet, and profit.[16] Does the culture engage and develop people? Does the organization sustainably use natural resources? Does the firm minimize its footprint? And does the company maximize profits for shareholders? By defining success more broadly, some would assert that there is a better likelihood of long-term, sustainable results.

THE LEARNING ORGANIZATION

LEARNING OBJECTIVE

16.2   Identify systems thinking as a key part of a learning organization.

The notion of systems, interconnections, systems thinking, and energy can be nebulous and confusing. It is likely that no one individual has a clear understanding and awareness of the whole. As a result, it is crucial that leaders establish an environment where individuals and groups can learn together. To further develop this notion, Peter Senge coined the term *learning organization*. According to Senge, learning organizations are "organizations where people continually expand their capacity to create the results they truly desire, where new and expansive patterns of thinking are nurtured, where collective aspiration is set free, and where people are continually learning to see the whole together."[17] Senge identified what he termed five disciplines or *component technologies* (in Table 16.1) for developing and fostering a learning organization.

TABLE 16.1 ■ Component Technologies for Fostering a Learning Organization	
Systems Thinking	Seeking to better understand the whole and seeking to better understand the relationships and interconnections of the parts
Personal Mastery	Living in a state of continuous learning, exploration, and sensemaking
Mental Models	Exploring (and at times challenging) the assumptions, biases, generalizations, and mental pictures that shape and inform our world
Building Shared Vision	Unleashing energy in others to work above and beyond toward a desired future
Team Learning	A habit of dialogue that fosters an environment where individuals are engaged in shared learning and collective meaning making

In essence, a learning organization maximizes the use of systems thinking to make sense of complexity. Systems thinking is rarely the work of one individual—it is a collective effort that requires a culture where individuals are invited to own and engage in the design of a better future. The creation of a learning organization is perhaps the ultimate goal of a leader. By doing so, the leader will ensure a focus on dialogue, collective energy, continuous growth, and a better understanding of the larger whole.

DEI BY DESIGN

LEARNING OBJECTIVE

16.3 Apply concepts of generativity and identity to sustain your leadership beyond your time as leader.

Someday your position as leader will end. And at some point, you may leave an organization, taking your leadership with you. What kind of organization will you leave to the next generation of leaders? How do you want to be remembered as a leader? What do you want people to say about your leadership after you are gone? What leadership practices do you hope others will strive to mimic in your absence? These are questions you will consider if you are practicing generative leadership. In perhaps the widest sense, **generativity** describes the process of guiding the next generation of individuals through purposefully crafting your own legacy. Like leadership, generativity is based on engagement with others. Generative activities might include offering guidance, pursuing positive well-being, acting in mutually beneficial ways, designing the future of others, enduring challenges and hardships, and celebrating milestones and victories.[18] Taken together, these six elements help chart a path to sustainable leadership and leadership that is rooted in developing a legacy of diversity, equity, and inclusion.

As you might imagine, culture and social identities play a significant role in personal and leader generativity. They determine what is worthy of passing on to the next cohort of leaders, as well as shape how that process of passing on occurs. Culture shapes perceptions, values, and ways of expression, acting as a filter that highlights what you believe future others will need and what is no longer necessary for their success. Although you inherit your leadership environments from your leader predecessors, acting as a link in the chain of leadership history, your effort to purposefully design your legacy enables you to choose or not choose the generative content. Nevertheless, your social identities, the values associated with them, and the priorities you implicitly and explicitly impart form key parts of the leadership systems you co-construct with others over time.

In the development of the leadership identity development model for college students, Komives and colleagues included a three-part definition of generative leadership—including, recognizing a larger purpose in leading, attending to the developmental needs of younger or newer organizational members, and cultivating a leadership pipeline to enhance the viability and sustainability of their organizations.[19] However, their model doesn't clearly describe the role of social identities in those generative processes. Your identities always impact leadership because you cannot be separated from those social identities. As you craft the plans your organizations, communities, businesses, groups, and teams might carry out after you are gone, pay attention to how your identities are showing up in those plans in order to design future systems that are inclusive and sustainable.

One important practice of generative leadership is mentoring—having someone who models, coaches, and talks to you about your leadership development. Studies find that students who mentor had stronger generative leadership, were more committed to sustainable leader actions, and demonstrated an enhanced commitment to leading than those who did not.[20] Consider how you want to be remembered as a leader, what you want people to say about your leadership, and how you hope others follow your examples. Then, note that your identities will undoubtedly play a role in your legacy as well as in the systems and relationships you leave behind.

DESIGN FOR SUSTAINABILITY

LEARNING OBJECTIVE
16.4 Describe several dimensions of sustainability

Sustainability is defined as the ability to endure, specifically the process of using the resources of the present to ensure success in the future. Another definition developed by the Brundtland Commission is that "Sustainable development is development that meets the needs of the present without compromising the ability of future generations to meet their own needs."[21] Although the term sustainability is often associated with the environment, there are many more facets to the concept and its applicability (see Figure 16.2). As a leader, you have a responsibility to co-design *sustainable* systems—those that facilitate long-term success. To this point, the concept of systems and the energy within a system have been explored. It is essential that as a leader you have both in mind—the system and energy within the system. Healthy systems will yield desired results. This text is all about designing your leadership, and the ultimate end of your design work is a team and organization that will be a successful and thriving organization for years to come.

This section explores several aspects of sustainability—many of which have been explored elsewhere in this text. However, when viewed together, you can see a system of interrelated components (ideally) working together to facilitate long-term success. The ultimate goal is to build

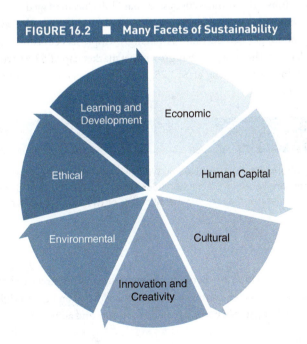

FIGURE 16.2 ■ Many Facets of Sustainability

500 Module 5 • Design the Future

a sustainable system that addresses the areas explored (and others). Given what you have learned about systems and complexity, a lack of balance in one area will impact other areas. For instance, if an organization is placing too much priority on giving back to the community and pleasing employees, it could lose sight of its economic sustainability. Likewise, if it is too focused on only benefiting shareholders, it may lose good employees and have a poor reputation in the community. The keys are clarity of values and a long-term, balanced approach.

The Sustainable Culture

Determine what behaviors and beliefs you value as a company and have everyone live true to them. These behaviors and beliefs should be so essential to your core that you don't even think of it as a culture.

—Brittany Forsyth, CTO Shopify[22]

Culture was defined as the shared values and assumptions by organizational (or group) members (from Chapter 11). Creating a sustainable culture means maintaining what is good and healthy about organizational culture. Likewise, there will always be areas for improvement as contextual shifts occur (e.g., changing employee demographics, economic forces). The thing to remember is that culture is like a plant—metaphorically speaking, it needs sunlight and water to thrive. While some plants are sturdy and can withstand many environmental shifts, others are much more delicate and susceptible to the elements. The key is that as a leader, you have a consistent eye on culture. Is the system yielding the results you would like? Are your team members engaged, energized, and excited?

After the death of Apple's long-time co-founder and chief executive officer, Steve Jobs, the role was turned over to former chief operations officer Tim Cook. A primary concern among investors, long-time Apple enthusiasts, and employees was how the organization would shift under new leadership. And while this story is still being told, it is interesting to explore how Jobs attempted to solidify norms for the culture of Apple—even before his death. Cook has reported that the single most significant piece of advice from Jobs was to "never ask what he would do" and to just "be himself."[23] In fact, in their article, "Why Apple Doesn't Need Steve Jobs," the authors suggested that "Jobs has managed to perform the ultimate feat of leadership—he's embedded himself so deeply within the cultural fabric of Apple that the company no longer needs him."[24] Amazingly, Apple has continued to prosper, and under Cook's leadership, the company has grown to a market cap of $2.41 trillion. In today's terms, stock under Jobs was trading at $12.75, and as of December 2021, it was trading at about $160 per share.[25]

REFLECTION QUESTIONS

Think of an organization to which you belong. What aspects of the culture have endured, and which components are based on the personalities of key individuals involved? What could be done to solidify the features that are dependent on one or two key personalities?

Environmental Sustainability

In a few decades, the relationship between the environment, resources and conflict may seem almost as obvious as the connection we see today between human rights, democracy and peace. —Wangari Maathai, Nobel Prize winner and activist[26]

Environmental sustainability is defined as the degree to which organizations can minimize their impact on the environment. For example, the *Leadership That Makes a Difference* segment at the beginning of the chapter highlights the efforts of Unilever to minimize its footprint, utilize renewable energy, invest in its people, and so forth. While environmental sustainability is an important topic, organizations take three distinct approaches—compliance, commitment, and core. Organizations that are simply compliant with external regulations such as state and federal laws often see the topic of environmental sustainability as a necessary evil versus a core value of the organization. At times, the term *greenwashing* is used to describe organizations that publicize their efforts as more of a promotional or marketing tactic than a sincere commitment to renewing resources that have been harvested or depleted.

Organizations that are authentically committed to environmental sustainability have found ways to prioritize and perhaps monetize their efforts. Unilever has identified a way to help the environment *and* add revenue for doing so. This win–win approach facilitates commitment on the part of the organization and its stakeholders. Other organizations have environmental sustainability at the core of their existence. For instance, in 2016, Patagonia donated 100% of its profits from Black Friday to charity.[27] Perhaps their business strategy rests upon products that promote renewable energy, such as wind and solar power. Or maybe the business exists to encourage a more efficient use of water in faucets, showerheads, or toilets. Or maybe Patagonia has a deep commitment to more than just the bottom line, as exemplified in its mission statement: "Build the best product, cause no unnecessary harm, use business to inspire and implement solutions to the environmental crisis."[28]

MYTH OR REALITY?

Sustainability initiatives are just another cost to the organization.

Myth and Reality. It is potentially true if the sustainability initiatives lack alignment with the organization's core strategy or mission. For instance, an organization that allows employees to give time to the community but has no substantial purpose or reason for doing so may be missing an opportunity to achieve the mission and do good for the community. The statement becomes a myth if the organization can achieve the win–win. For example, Walmart has identified a way to profit from their goal of targeting zero waste. In fact, not only does it divert waste from landfills, across the many stores, the organization adds hundreds of millions of dollars in revenue each year selling its recycled goods to companies that use the materials in any number of ways (e.g., cardboard, plastic, fryer grease).[29]

Sustaining Creativity and Innovation

There is no innovation and creativity without failure. Period.

—*Dr. Brene Brown, author/scholar*[30]

In Chapter 14, you learned how to foster a culture of innovation, much of which you can use as a leader to ensure that innovative behavior continues into the future. By definition, innovation is an experimental activity—generating lots and lots of ideas, choosing the best, testing and assessing, iterating, and then putting those solutions to work as quickly as possible. Various tools for divergent thinking (Chapter 8) and convergent thinking (Chapter 14) contribute to establishing and perpetuating this culture. Innovative teams "know that integrative decision-making often involves more than simply and mechanically combining ideas. Rather, it requires a willingness to play with ideas and experiments until they *click*."[31]

In the article "The Capabilities Your Organization Needs to Sustain Innovation," the authors suggest three capabilities: creative abrasion, creative agility, and creative resolution.[32] Creative abrasion means creating a culture where people with different values, viewpoints, knowledge, and life experiences can search for solutions, discuss ideas, and passionately explore new directions. As discussed, this requires a culture with strong norms that encourage multiple perspectives and a willingness to openly share, dialogue, and search for the best idea. These groups can maintain their focus on the problem at hand and drop their egos in search of the best outcome.

Ethical Sustainability

My parents were both born and raised in the Depression. They instilled great values about integrity and the importance of hard work and I've taken that with me to every job.

— *Mary Barra, CEO of General Motors*[33]

The foundation of a sustainable career is a solid grounding in who you are and what you stand for. Given the topic of this chapter (sustainability), it is essential to think about ethical sustainability at a few different levels. The first is the individual level, which was the focus of Chapter 5: Your Values and Ethical Actions. Two others are the group and organization levels.

Ethical sustainability at the group level means you have developed shared norms that the team is committed to living. As a leader, you must engage your team in this conversation to ensure the team members have a clear understanding of what is and is not acceptable. If you think about organizations on campus or in your community, you can understand why this is critical. For instance, it is likely you can identify incidents on your campus where the actions of a few individuals have reflected poorly on the entire organization or campus community. Not only do leaders need to have their own shop in order, they need to ensure the group-level norms are established and followed as well.

At the organizational level, cultural norms are even more critical. While the point seems obvious, a leader must have a keen eye for many organizational dimensions that could lead to (or even encourage) unethical behavior. An example is the incident at Wells Fargo that began in 2016 and resonated in the news for years. More than 5,300 employees created false accounts. According to one news source, "The phony accounts earned the bank unwarranted fees and allowed Wells Fargo employees to boost their sales figures and make more money."[34] The organizational culture of meeting numbers was creating an environment where thousands of employees acted unethically. By some estimates, employees opened more than 1.5 million unauthorized accounts. This is just one example of many that could be considered. Thus, unethical behavior at the individual, team, and organizational level is not sustainable. As a leader, you must have an eye on how the system influences behavior. A culture with strong behavioral norms and accountability for not meeting said norms is vital. One final point—it is easy to feel like this topic is foreign and far away. In reality, it exists all over campus. Just look at an organization that you belong to. Does the culture promote ethical behavior, look the other way, or worse, actively enable unethical behavior?

Chapter 16 • Systems and Sustainability **503**

Economic Sustainability

If climate change issues are not adequately addressed—if we keep running those nice energy subsidies if the price on carbon is not adequately set if policymakers don't have it on their radar screens—then financial stability in the medium and long-term is clearly at stake.

—Christine Lagarde, president of the European Central Bank[35]

In a general sense, sustainability is about a sensible use of resources. From an economic standpoint, the primary resources are money, capital resources, intellectual property, and so forth. One can tell a great deal about the values and priorities of an organization based on its allocation of resources. For instance, an organization that balances shareholder returns with employee benefits and salary is different from an organization solely focused on maximizing shareholder returns. Likewise, an organization that invests in (and even looks for ways to profit from) recycling, green energy, and minimizing environmental impact displays its priorities and values in a different manner.

The key is planning and balance. While it is important to be generous in some circumstances, long-term financial viability is another priority and objective. Ensuring financial health and sustainability is essential and a solid starting point. Also, it is necessary to have clarity on the organizational mission and vision to ensure that the economic model is helping the organization achieve objectives.

Sustainable Learning and Development

Just because you are CEO, don't think you have landed. You must continually increase your learning, the way you think, and the way you approach the organization. I've never forgotten that.

— Indra Nooyi, former CEO of PepsiCo[36]

At first glance, it may seem odd to place the concept of learning in a section on sustainability, but it is a central element of ensuring that your organization is on the cutting edge of your industry and how it will interface with artificial intelligence, automation, sensor technology, virtual reality, and any number of other disruptive technologies. As you read this text, humans are on the cusp of a significant shift in machine learning and artificial intelligence (AI). Technology continues to permeate all aspects of organizational life. A few interesting facts to pique your interest:

- AI-driven Deep Genomics gets $180M to turn biology into informational medicines[37]
- Artificial intelligence has created its own movie trailer[38]
- Artificial intelligence has solved a 100-year-old biology problem[39]
- U.S. firefighters turn to AI to battle the blazes[40]
- Robots are performing surgery on animals with a high level of success[41]
- Harvard is working to develop an AI that is as fast as the human brain[42]
- Joby's electric flying taxi completes 150-mile flight[43]

What does all of this mean? Technology and capitalism have shifted many jobs to developing countries, but that was just the beginning. As technology continues to replace humans, your role as a manager or leader may become more and more in danger of being replaced. For instance, in large part of offshoring, digitization, and automation, more than 5 million manufacturing jobs were lost in the United States between 2000 and 2017.[44] This is only going to continue. As machines replace surgeons, attorneys,[45] and managers, how will you and your organization compete?

Bottom line, you, your team, and your organization need to be on the cutting edge of your industry and how it will interface with machine learning, autonomous vehicles, virtual reality, and robotics. Entire industries are being disrupted, and this reality will impact you in ways that can only be imagined. Futurists foresee an existence that sounds more like science fiction than fact.[46] What systems will you put in place that foster continuous learning for you and your team?

Leadership by Design

Design Principle: Weakest Link

Definition: The use of a weak or highly sensitive element that will fail in order to protect from or warn of further damage within a system.

In Other Words: Small failures can protect big systems.

For Example: A sprinkler system in a building or dormitory is designed to release water after something within the system breaks due to excessive heat but before a raging fire destroys everything.

For Leaders: Everyone is familiar with the cliché: A chain is only as strong as its weakest link. Knowing that organizations, teams, and industries are all part of a system—a chain, if you will—the weakest link represents the point of vulnerability, the place where the system could be broken or changed. There is always a weak link because elements are not uniform or equal. Identifying that weak link can be of great value, but what if you intentionally inserted a weak link as a warning (like when a fuse blows out and warns of a greater electrical malfunction)?

One way to use the weakest link in leadership is to reframe weakness as an acute sensitivity. Hire someone with high emotional intelligence and ask them to report on team dynamics. A concern from that person would serve as a warning that relationships need tending. Or identify the weakest point in the system and accommodate it as a learning tool. For example, interns or temporary workers may be the least competent and/or committed employees, but that perspective is advantageous as an early warning of miscommunication, lack of clarity, lack of transparency, or complacency. Those individuals will be the first to run to a competitor because they have the least to lose.

Think through "applying the weakest link principle:

1. identify how something might fail;
2. identify or define the weakest link in the system for that failure;
3. further weaken the weakest link and strengthen the other links as necessary to address the failure condition; and
4. ensure that the weakest link will only fail under the appropriate, predefined failure conditions."[47]

The weakest link is intended to deliberately fail to minimize damage. Use this concept to protect systems, facilitate change, and design the future.

Sustainable Results

Our 2021 strategy focuses on agility, optimism, innovation and meeting people where they are—consumers and employees alike. 2020 brought about some of our greatest challenges, but also some of our best examples of teamwork and creativity, and I couldn't be more proud of my team. As a leader, I'll push to maintain this momentum and new way of thinking to reach even more new and exciting milestones in 2021, in both our business and our culture.

— *Beth Ford, CEO of Land O' Lakes*[48]

Sustaining results is the ultimate goal that employees at Apple, Google, or any other successful organization seek. Many corporations come and go, but only a few have the longevity to succeed for decades amid multiple shifts (see IBM for an interesting case study). So, what are the ingredients of a winning culture? Exploring this topic at the individual and organizational levels is essential.

At the individual level, scholars have found that two components, thriving and learning (see the previous section), relate to employees with better performance, less burnout, and increased job satisfaction. Employees who thrive have a sense of vitality (e.g., enthusiasm, excitement, passion). They are intrinsically motivated, and as discussed in Chapter 7: Influence, Power, and Motivation, there is a sense that their work makes a difference. The second component, learning, means that thriving employees have the drive to learn and develop their knowledge, skills, and abilities.[49]

At an organizational level, what factors foster a culture that wins over time? According to *Harvard Business Review*, there are two distinctions: (1) "unique personality and soul based on shared values and heritage" and (2) "cultural norms and behaviors that translate the organization's unique personality and soul into 'customer-focused actions and bottom-line results.'"[50]

The authors also explore five key steps to instilling a winning culture, shown in Table 16.2.[51] While the steps in the table seem like common sense depending on the complexity of the organization, they can be challenging to implement. The good news is that for many of you reading this text, student organizations provide a practice field to work and achieve much of the content in the table.

TABLE 16.2 ■ Sustainable Results—Steps to a Winning Culture

Perform a culture audit and set new expectations	What aspects of the culture are healthy, core to the business, and critical drivers? What is missing?
Align the team	Is the senior team aligned with the vision and ready to adjust systems and old habits and build enthusiasm?
Focus on results and build accountability	Are key metrics clear and aligned, and is everyone driving toward the same vision?
Manage the drivers of culture	Are systems such as hiring, training, performance management, and incentives/rewards aligned with objectives?
Communicate and celebrate	Are organizational leaders communicating progress and celebrating wins (large and small)?

Source: Based on Meehan, P., Rigby, D., & Rogers, P. (2008). Creating and sustaining a winning culture. *Harvard Management Update.* Retrieved from https://hbr.org/2008/02/creating-and-sustaining-a-winn-1.

SUSTAINABLE YOU: MINDFULNESS AND PERSONAL GROWTH

LEARNING OBJECTIVE
16.5 Integrate mindful practices to sustain your personal growth.

Grit, in a word, is stamina. But it's not just stamina in your effort. It's also stamina in your direction, stamina in your interests. If you are working on different things but all of them very hard, you're not really going to get anywhere. You'll never become an expert.

—Angela Duckworth, author/scholar[52]

Finding your authentic voice and approach to leadership is an important first step. Many, however, believe their personal work ends after those initial efforts to grow and develop. How do you make personal development a systematic, sustainable, life-long process? In many ways, you are on your own when it comes to your continued learning and development, particularly once you exit formal education. Nevertheless, you have a great responsibility to ensure that you are in a constant state of growth and sensemaking or "a 'process' that includes the use of prior knowledge to assign meaning to new information."[53]

As you design your *process* for sustainable growth, two critical concepts should remain at the forefront of your thinking and enhance your activities—mindfulness and critical reflection. Ultimately, adding mindfulness and critical reflection to your plans for learning (as well as your daily activity) will build your resilience as an individual and a leader.

Leadership by Design

Design Principle: Exposure Effect[54]

Definition: Individuals tend to like and have a preference for stimuli that are familiar.[55]

In Other Words: The more you see/hear/interact with something, the more you like it.

For Example: When that new song comes out and you think, "Eh . . . it's ok." Then you hear it over and over and over and over . . . and soon, to your surprise, you like it. And then, even stranger, you hear it years later and fondly remember it as a favorite. Marketers know the exposure effect and replay songs frequently to increase exposure and thus listeners' sentiments.

For Leaders: Familiarity plays a role in appeal and acceptance—the more a leader is around and present, the more they will be liked. Of course, this is not automatic or assured. The exposure effect is most prevalent when the stimulus (leader in this case) is neutral and the exposure is subtle. Leaders can leverage the exposure effect to help reinforce and build commitment to the mission or vision. Do certain facets of your vision need greater buy-in and/or positive responses? In what ways can you increase exposure to that message? Be cautious—there is such a thing as overexposure, and that can lead to negative feelings or boredom.

As you design the future, what message do you as a leader need to really have followers know and love?

As described in Chapter 1, mindfulness simply means being aware of both your internal state and external context in the present moment (without evaluation). This habit of mind is critical

Chapter 16 • Systems and Sustainability **507**

because of the sheer number of stressors that anyone assuming a formal or informal position of leadership must endure. Whether it's rapid change, tough working conditions, interpersonal conflict, or chronic time stressors, leaders who are mindful and present have an opportunity to turn their present awareness into productive and appropriate action. For example, a leader mindful of her increasing level of frustration can pause, step away, and breathe rather than simply reacting in the moment. And according to at least one meta-analysis, there are a number of benefits of mindfulness-based programs, including a reduction in stress, burnout, and mental distress.[56]

Developing mindfulness requires intentional practice. Activities such as journaling, reflecting with mentors, and mobile applications such as *Calm* or *Headspace* can help develop this habit of mind. After all, "cultivating the ability to notice with curiosity, acceptance, and compassion the fullness of each moment"[57] may not come naturally to you and most of your peers. The reality is that there are a number of learning opportunities all around you that will help develop skills in this space. Learning opportunities may include short courses,[58] yoga,[59] meditation,[60] prayer,[61] or even body scan exercises.[62] While these practices may seem far-fetched or perhaps unrealistic, research suggests these and other techniques help leaders navigate the stressors inherent in leading others.

The second concept is **critical reflection**, which is the mental act of considering and modifying information and understanding, often replaying interactions to understand your behavior and the behavior of others. According to scholar Jon Wergin,[63] critical reflection is a learned skill, but like mindfulness, will require a habit of mind that is examining your actions and the result of your behavior. If you are practicing mindfulness and engaging in criticial reflection, you will develop a habit of mind that is in a continuous state of development.

Leaders seeking sustainable personal growth create external systems to help prompt, reinforce, and guide their development. For instance, you could secure a mentor or development coach who can help you identify areas for growth, potential steps forward, and the accountability needed to help you stay on track. You could also join a group or club that is designed to help you grow and develop (e.g., faith based, leadership oriented).

SUSTAINABLE LEADERSHIP—AUTHENTIC LEADERSHIP

LEARNING OBJECTIVE
16.6   Personalize the concept of authentic leadership.

This chapter on systems and sustainability and the entire textbook ends where it began—with the design of you. As discussed, leadership is the process of influencing others toward a common vision. An interesting nuance to the conversation about effective leadership is highlighted by George, Sims, McLean, and Mayer when they suggest that

> during the past 50 years, leadership scholars have conducted more than 1,000 studies in an attempt to determine the definitive styles, characteristics, or personality traits of great leaders. *None of these studies has produced a clear profile of the ideal leader* (emphasis added). Thank goodness. If scholars had produced a cookie-cutter leadership style, individuals would be forever trying to imitate it. They would make themselves into personae, not people, and others would see through them immediately.[64]

The reality is that you have to discover your personal, authentic, and unique approach to leadership, which will help you find your best fit. A sustainable approach to leadership likely has at least four primary ingredients—many of which are highlighted throughout this text. First, you are focused on the ultimate objective of *intervening skillfully*. The leader understands that as the players (followers, team members) and the context shift, so will the calculus for success. As a result, a skillful intervention in one setting or situation may not work in another. The sustainable leader is aware of this fundamental reality and adjusts and adapts.

A second attribute of the sustainable leader is an *awareness of default mindsets* (i.e., mental models and dispositions). Everyone reading (and working on) this book has defaults. In some contexts, defaults serve you beautifully; in many cases, they are the reason you have experienced success. A strong work ethic is a valuable default to have—but it can be taken to an extreme, become unhealthy, and create long-term problems with relationships, health, and identity. By intentionally choosing when to go with your defaults, you are more present and conscious of how you work, live, and play.

A third attribute of a sustainable leader is a *thriving and robust support network*. Sustainable leaders have a network of mentors, peers, and friends who will provide unfiltered feedback, guidance, and perspective. Leadership is difficult, and a sustainable leader has a strong supporting cast to help them stay on track, continuously grow, and adjust as needed.

Finally, a sustainable leader is an *authentic leader*. **Authentic leadership** is your unique, ethical, and honest way to help the work of the group move forward. While this text has been at the crossroads of leadership and design, it is a book about you, specifically how you design the many dimensions of you. Former Medtronic CEO and Harvard business professor Bill George suggests that "No one can be authentic by trying to imitate someone else."[65] Shamir and Eliam suggest four attributes of authentic leaders:

1. Authentic leaders do not fake their leadership. Authentic leaders are not playing a part outside of their true self. In other words, there is a high *person/role merger*, which means "they think of themselves in terms of that role and enact that role at all times, not only when they are officially in role."[66]

2. Authentic leaders do not take on a leadership role or engage in leadership activities for status, honor, or other personal rewards. Authentic leaders are working from a place where their central motivation is to help the movement, group, organization, or team.

3. Authentic leaders are originals, not copies. Authentic leaders are not working to copy or replicate another leader or their style and approach. They are comfortable *in their own skin* and understand their values, motivations, strengths, and areas for development.

4. Authentic leaders are leaders whose actions are based on their values and convictions. Authentic leaders are connected to a strong sense of mission and belief in the objective at hand. The objective aligns with their *actual* passions.[67]

The roots of authentic leadership stem from Greek philosophy (e.g., "To thine own self be true") and humanistic psychology.[68] And in many ways, this sums up the notion of authentic leadership (and this text). As an authentic leader, you must discover your unique way to help the work of the group move forward. Of course, this takes a great deal of self-exploration, and perhaps this text has provided you with some exciting ways to begin thinking about and exploring leadership. The reality is that each one of you must find your voice, and that process is a lifelong journey.

> ### Leadership by Design
>
> *Design Principle:* Storytelling (again)
>
> *Definition:* A method of creating imagery, emotions, and understanding of events through an interaction between a storyteller and an audience. The elements of story typically consist of setting, characters, plot, theme, and mood.
>
> *In Other Words:* Once upon a time . . . I worked with this team . . . with this organization . . . something really interesting happened . . . and we were awesome. Let's do it again.
>
>
> ©iStock.com/PeopleImages
>
> *For Example:* What is your story as a follower and as part of a great team?
>
> *For Leaders:* The story of sustainable organizations is one of intertwined logic and emotion. Create a strong foundation for your story using both. Winning hearts can pique interest, increase commitment, or help resolve a conflict. Using emotion shows how your idea will affect them personally. Appeal to logic while storytelling to overturn a past decision, address a complex problem, or gain the support of analytic, data-driven people. Design both the story and how you share the story.
>
> Legendary leaders and organizations make people feel wonderful, whether through their products or practices. Good stories become part of the listener and are remembered for a long, long time. What story will you design?

When you come into an organization, you bring with you an arcane potency, which stems, in part, from your uniqueness. That, in turn, is rooted in a complex mosaic of personal history that is original, unfathomable, inimitable. There has never been anyone quite like you, and there never will be. Consequently, you can contribute something to an endeavor that nobody else can. There is a power in your uniqueness—an inexplicable, unmeasurable power . . . a magic.

—*Gordon Mackenzie*

REFLECTION QUESTIONS

Design your future sustainable leadership. Take a moment (or much more) to consider your level of sustainable leadership by reflecting on and responding to the prompts that follow.

1. Can you think of a time when you have had to adjust and adapt to skillfully intervene and work with new followers?

2. List out some of your default mindsets. Then think about (and note) a couple of default mindsets that you most want, and why.

3. Do you have a thriving and robust support network? Map or list out that network, and then identify who you can count on for unfiltered guidance and feedback.

4. What about your leadership is authentic? How would you describe your unique approach to helping others move forward?

CHAPTER SUMMARY

This chapter focused on systems thinking, sustainability, and authentic leadership. Systems thinking is a core activity of leadership because, from a problem-solving perspective, leaders need to see the *whole* system to make decisions that are more integrated and fully account for the complexity involved.

Systems thinking is central to the success of leaders. Systems thinking, along with other components, can foster a learning organization. Likewise, the hope is that systems thinking will lead to sustainability.

Sustainability is defined as a sensible use of resources on many different dimensions. In fact, it is essential to think of sustainability as a system as well. It is likely that sustainable results are predicated on many different dimensions, such as ethical decision-making, environmental impact, creativity and innovation, fiscal responsibility, and more. Viewing these dimensions as a system is vital for long-term organizational health and wellness.

The chapter concludes with a discussion on the topic of authentic leadership, which means that you have discovered a style and approach to leadership that naturally aligns with your gifts, talents, passions, and values. Authentic leadership is not developed overnight—it is a long-term, lifelong endeavor that requires you to *know thyself* and ultimately prepare the next generation of leaders who follow.

KEY TERMS

Authentic leadership (p. 508)

Critical reflection (p. 507)

Generativity (p. 498)

Sustainability (p. 499)

System (p. 493)

Systems thinking (p. 493)

Chapter 16 • Systems and Sustainability   **511**

CORE™ ATTRIBUTE BUILDERS: BUILD NOW FOR FUTURE LEADERSHIP CHALLENGES

Attribute: Optimism

Builder: Read up on the GOOD news

There is a great deal of good being done to help foster sustainability across the globe. It is easy to focus on what is going wrong (and there are significant issues). However, there is good news as well. For instance, in the last 100 years, the number of people living in extreme poverty has decreased dramatically, literacy has increased, child mortality has decreased, and youth are more educated than ever before.[70] Another piece of good news is that the UN Global Compact proposes that business can be a "force for good," and its mission suggests that business "can take shared responsibility for achieving a better world."[71] The UN Global Compact has identified 17 Sustainable Development Goals to be achieved by 2030. In fact, more than 9000 companies and 3000 non-business organizations throughout the globe have committed. Each year, participants submit a communication on progress (COP) report. Organizations around the globe submit these reports and highlight the good occurring. They present an optimistic view of the efforts of millions of men and women. Look up some of your favorite organizations and see how they are contributing to the greater good. You can use your favorite search engine (search: UN Global Compact COP reports), and you will likely land on "The Communication on Progress (COP) in Brief" page. From there, you can view organizations (e.g., KPMG, Symantec, Royal Bank of Scotland, Intel, Dow Chemical, Accenture) participating at various levels.

SKILL BUILDER ACTIVITY

Leadership—Best Fit and Beliefs

As you reflect on everything you have explored in this textbook, it's useful to synthesize and refine who you are becoming as a leader. As you proceed in your journey, revisit and revise this document as you see fit. It will be inspiring to keep track of the continuously evolving picture of your best fit, your leadership beliefs, and how you will prepare for future challenges.

MY LEADERSHIP DESIGN™ BEGINS AND CONTINUES WITH THIS SUMMARY PAGE . . .

Reflect on and extract key insights about yourself that effectively sum up your current self-understanding of yourself as a leader and your best fit in a leadership context and process. There are three parts:

1. **Best Fit**

2. **Face the Future**

3. **Leadership Beliefs**

Be sure to revisit and reference past resources you found, self-assessments, and insightful wisdom from your leadership experiences and explorations. AND . . . from time to time . . . go back and consider HOW you can organize that information to make it most accessible to you for future use.

512   Module 5 ● Design the Future

WHAT IS YOUR BEST FIT?

Important Things I Know About Me as a Leader (What do I need to know and remember about myself?)	Important Things OTHERS Need to Know to Be Led by Me (What do followers need to know about me to successfully work with me?)

SUM IT UP (IN 3 SENTENCES OR LESS):

I lead best when:

HOW WILL YOU SUCCESSFULLY FACE THE FUTURE?

My Key Strengths, Skills, and Assets That Can Be Used to Address Future Challenges	What I Would Like to Develop to Be a Better Leader

* STAR (*) your top strengths, assets, and areas that you excel.

** CIRCLE (O) areas you want to work on developing right now . . . and make a plan to do so.

MY LEADERSHIP BELIEFS

Start noting your beliefs—what makes a great leader and great leadership? Be sure to add any clarifying notes, especially to single terms (like "honest").

The arrows in Figure 16.3 prompt you to summarize your beliefs into some important single statements representing your credo, your vision, and your mission as a leader.

What do I believe leaders need to know, do or be like?	What do I believe leadership should be like—for followers, for teams, for organizations?

Observing Leadership Theory in Action

Choose an organization to which you belong but are not in a formal leadership position. You might also engage in this activity with a small group.

Identify a meeting and/or event of the group where you are likely to observe the group's leader/s in action.

Chapter 16 ● Systems and Sustainability   **513**

FIGURE 16.3 ■ Summarize Your Beliefs in a Leadership Credo, Vision, and Mission

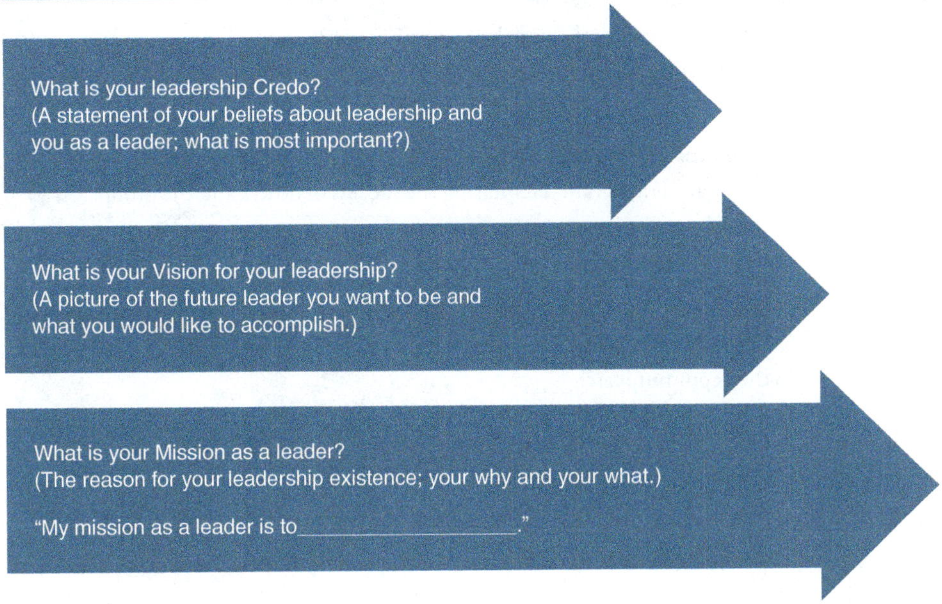

What is your leadership Credo?
(A statement of your beliefs about leadership and
you as a leader; what is most important?)

What is your Vision for your leadership?
(A picture of the future leader you want to be and
what you would like to accomplish.)

What is your Mission as a leader?
(The reason for your leadership existence; your why and your what.)

"My mission as a leader is to_____."

Attend the event and observe the leader and his or her interactions with followers. Specifically, observe each of the following items listed—prompting questions are provided to guide your thinking.

Take notes. From this experience, craft a one-page memo to the leader of the group you observed providing feedback as to what they did well and suggestions for making them more effective. (It is your decision as to whether you give the leader a copy of the memo.)

1. **Traits and Skills (Chapter 2)**
    Observe the leader.
    ● What traits and skills tend to be used?
    ● Which traits or skills seem to be effective, and how so?

2. **Situational (Chapter 9)**
    ● Is the leader more task or relationship focused?
    ● Does the leader adapt to the commitment and competence of the followers and move between support, coach, delegate, and direct?

3. **Path-Goal (Chapter 7)**
    Observe the relationship between the leader and each individual in the group.
    ● What does the leader use to influence?
    ● How do the followers respond?
    ● What motivates the followers?
    ● Does the leader remove barriers to their motivation?

4. **Leader-Member Exchange (Chapter 7)**
    Observe the relationship between the leader and each individual in the group.
    ● Does the leader give individualized consideration to each person?
    ● Does the leader appear to treat everyone equally?

5. **Transformational Leadership (Chapter 10)**

Again, observe the leader.

- Does the leader serve as a role model who inspires you?
- Does the leader stimulate your intellect?
- Does the leader attend to each person individually?

6. **The Vision–Servant Leadership (Chapter 13)**

- Does he or she act as a servant, facilitating the success of others and the group?
- Do they build community?
- Do you observe empathy?

7. **Group Dynamics**

Observe the dynamics of the group.

- How do they communicate?
- Are they open and honest with one another?
- Are they constructive? Critical? Overly polite?
- How does the group make decisions?
- How do they deal with conflict?

GLOSSARY

4Ps: This defines creativity: product, person, press, and process.

Achievement oriented: Leadership style in which the leader challenges others to work to the next level.

Active bystander: Recognizing and intervening when bias activity occurs using the following steps: (a) recognizing when an instance of bias occurs, (b) choosing to confront those situations, (c) taking action (including educating others and inviting them to try different approaches in the future), and (d) creating positive future patterns of thinking and acting.

Activism: Executing numerous direct, vigorous activities to bring about a change, generally social or political.

Adaptive challenges: Problems without a known solution; require collaboration and experimentation.

Adaptive cycles: Cycles that are natural to the evolution of living systems that occur at all levels of scale,

Adjourning: The last stage where the work of the group has concluded and the group members disband.

ADKAR model of change: This is a model of change starting with Awareness of a needed change, Desire to make the change, Knowledge about how to make the change, Ability to do so, and Reinforcement of the change once in place.

Advocacy: The process of recommending or supporting that change.

Agentic identity: Based on factors you share with others that reward you with unearned privileges based on membership in those groups.

Algorithmic problem: A problem with a well-defined set of rules or instructions for solving.

Altruism: Means that you should *love thy neighbor* and make decisions from a place of benefitting others.

Appreciative Inquiry: A method for facilitating organizational change the involves systematic discovery of what gives life to an organization or a community when it is most effective and most capable in economic, ecological terms.

Artifacts: Physical evidence (objects) that represent organizational values.

Authentic leadership: Your unique, ethical, and honest way to help the work of the group move forward.

Authority figure: An individual whose role provides them with formal power to determine the fate.

Autonomy: A source of motivation characterized by a feeling of ownership in how tasks are accomplished.

Availability heuristic: The ease with which you can bring to mind specific examples, which often results in erroneously reinforcing your beliefs.

Benchmarking: Evaluating ideas by comparison with a standard.

Bias: Your associations in favor of or against a person or group in society.

Blocks: The many things that stifle your creative thinking.

Both/And thinking: The mental habit of holistically analyzing problems or decisions to consider multiple perspectives, purposefully rejecting binary opposites in decision-making (either/or thinking).

Business model: Represents a company's rationale for how it creates value for customers, delivers its products to them, and captures value to make a profit.

Business model canvas: This is a tool that illustrates the nine key business components: (1) key partners, (2) key activities, (3) key resources, (4) value proposition, (5) customer relationships,

(6) channels, (7) customer segments, (8) cost structure, and (9) revenue.

Calculated risk-taking making: A decision that involves careful consideration of the possible outcomes.

Care: Acting in a manner that provides for and shows concern regarding another's needs and well-being.

Career pathing: A source of motivation characterized by having a clear sense for how you can progress and move forward in the organization.

Causal reasoning: A type of reasoning characterized by first setting a goal and then considering the means through which the goal can be accomplished.

Change: The process of becoming different yourself or fostering difference in other persons or things.

Change fatigue: A general state of disengagement from the change process due to natural cognitive, emotional, and social demands.

Character: The moral qualities of an individual.

Charisma: The personal quality that commands attention, respect, and attraction.

Charisms: Those skills or activities you love to do that feel like natural abilities.

Closure: Design principle—we tend to see complete figures even when part of the information is missing, which means what you do not show people, they will fill in the blanks on their own.

Code of ethics: Often a document that seeks to clarify right or wrong behavior in a profession or organization.

Collaboration: Two or more people working together to create or achieve greater success than can be achieved individually.

515

Community engagement: Where like-minded individuals come together to engage with and effect change in the local community.

Community solidarity: Unity (as in a group) that produces collegial interests, objectives, and points of view; refers to the ties in a society that bind people together.

Comparison: Design principle—to accurately understand and assess something, you must look at it next to things that relate.

Confidence: Latin root *con+fidere*, which means with intense trust—trust in yourself; the state of knowing you are capable and effective; as part of leadership CORE™, it is your ability to learn, adapt, and succeed.

Constructive dimension: Dimension of the brain that emphasizes your process of conceptualizing the world based on what you interact with in the world.

Convergent thinking: The mental process of finding a single best solution to a problem.

Creative confidence: Trust in yourself as a creative individual or a "natural ability to come up with new ideas and the courage to try them out."

Creativity: The personal capacities and process of generating a unique product that has value.

Credibility: The quality of being believed and, in practice, doing what you say you are going to do.

Crisis leadership: The ability to demonstrate courage and care during times of collective disruption.

Critical reflection: The mental act of considering and modifying information and understanding, often replaying interactions in an effort to understand your behavior and the behavior of others.

Crucible (of leadership): A difficult challenge that has the potential to transform your values, assumptions, and future capabilities as a leader.

Cultivating value-in-diversity: Behaviors positive and supportive of diversity that serve to establish and promote

perceptions and beliefs in the value of that diversity.

Culture: Shared values and assumptions by organizational (or group) members; the way we do things around here.

Customer discovery interviewing: Using a structured interview script to qualify an interviewee as a member of your assumed target segment and elicit beliefs and experiences relevant to the problem you are trying to solve and the solution you are working to develop.

Decide: The process of making a choice or determining a course of action.

Decision-action gap: That space between deciding what you *should* do and actually *doing it*, which exists when an individual or group knows what the correct course of action should be but struggles to make the *right* or *best* decision.

Decision criteria: Factors deemed important to consider in the process of choosing a course of action.

Decision-making: A specific process of choosing the best option.

Design principle: Rules that designers apply to help guide their process and enhance their product.

Design process: A general problem-solving process consisting of three major phases: understand, imagine, and implement; with iteration occurring throughout.

Design thinking: This is a cognitive approach to engaging problems that embodies a specific mindset that is explorative, user centered, divergent, multidisciplinary, integrative, and iterative.

Design thinking: This is a cognitive approach to engaging problems that embodies a specific mindset that is explorative, user-centered, divergent, multidisciplinary, integrative, and iterative.

Digital transformation: Comprises a broad array of activities and approaches that utilize digital technology to see, operate, and solve problems in new ways.

Dimensions of the brain: This is an organizational scheme for understanding and applying information about the brain to leadership activity. The six dimensions are the physiological dimension, emotional dimension, social dimension, reflective dimension, constructive dimension, and disposition al dimension.

Directive: Leadership style in which the leader provides guidance and psychological structure.

Disposition: Habits of mind often seen as tendencies or characteristics.

Dispositional dimension: Dimension of the brain that highlights habitual ways of processing information, also seen as mental habits that influence what individuals perceive and how they conceive information.

Divergent: Mindset of generating many, many ideas for a single problem.

Divergent: Mindset of generating many, many ideas for a single problem.

Diversity: Can be defined as a state characterized by the pursuit, presence, and appreciation of differences.

Ecocycle framework: Framework explains the movements and cycles in organizational systems, often used in planning and leading and comprising four main phases (birth, maturity, creative destruction, and renewal) cycling in an infinite loop.

Effectuation: A type of reasoning that starts with one's given resources that subsequently forge goals as the resources are applied.

Elaboration: The degree of detail in a given idea as a measure of creativity.

Emotional dimension: Dimension of the brain that influences how individuals see and react to situations and others based on feelings.

Emotional intelligence: A person's ability to know and regulate their own feelings, perceive and understand the feelings of others, and effectively work between their own and others' feelings.

Empathy: The ability to sense the feelings of others with the capacity to detect another's mindset.

Glossary **517**

Empowerment: A source of motivation characterized by feeling a sense of ownership/control and competence in your work.

Engagement: The degree of individual involvement, investment, and enthusiasm within and for a specific context or situation.

Entrepreneurial leadership: A unique set of concepts, mindsets, and activities used by leaders to identify opportunities, deepen understanding, and initiate and develop innovation.

Entrepreneurship: The process of pursuing opportunity through the conception, validation, and launch of new ideas into the marketplace.

Equality: Means everyone gets treated the same.

Equity: Is likewise a state but a state of just and fair systems of distributing benefits and burdens.

Essentialism: Flattening or limiting typically robust and intersectional social identities down to one or just a few characteristics.

Ethical perspectives: This describes five lenses through which to view ethical decisions, including utilitarianism, Kant's categorical imperative, justice as fairness, altruism, and pragmatism.

Ethics: An area of study that is concerned with codifying and defending right or wrong behavior in multiple contexts.

Evidence-based decision-making: Decisions are researched and made based on collected data rather than relying on your experience and expertise, personal observations, advice, hopes, or hunches.

Explicit bias: An awareness of your associations in favor or against a person or group.

Explorative: Mindset that assumes purposeful ambiguity and curiosity.

Explorative: Mindset that assumes purposeful ambiguity and curiosity.

Extrinsic motivation: Engaging in an activity because of external rewards for doing so.

Five Es: (1) Exhibit empathy by engaging in candid discussions, (2) engage digital transformation and competence, (3) empower an inclusive and collaborative work culture, (4) extend capacity with stretch assignments, (5) enrich the leadership capacity of others (social intelligence to bring out the best in your peers and the person leading you).

Fixed mindset: A state of mind wherein you see your abilities and capacity as a change agent as set traits—they are what they are.

Flexibility: The number of different answer categories comprising ideas as a measure of creativity.

Fluency: The total number of ideas generated as a measure of creativity.

Formal power: Legitimate power bestowed upon an individual who holds a position or role (e.g., judge, police officer).

Forming: The introductory stage of a group where members are getting to know one another and tend to act in very polite ways.

Founder's syndrome: An organizational disorder characterized by over-reliance on the charisma, involvement, and decisions of one or more founding members in place of mindful, collaborative, and strategic management and leadership.

Fragility: A state of perceiving and feeling threatened.

Freelance workers: An individual who desires to work for more than one employer on a part-time basis rather than full-time for only one organization.

Generativity: The process of guiding the next generation of individuals through purposefully crafting your own legacy.

Greater Purpose Statement (GPS): Identifies your driving reason for leading, merging what you love, are good at, the world you have chosen, and what that world needs.

Group: A collection of individuals who are coordinating their work for some reason or another.

Group/Team-level decision-making: Decisions made by a group/team.

Growth mindset: A state of mind wherein you believe that you can acquire and develop new abilities and that your capacity is only limited by your effort.

Harvesting diversity: Actively inviting members to offer their unique knowledge, skills, and abilities, as well as supporting the voicing of opinions and critical perspectives.

Heroes: Persons, alive or dead, real or imaginary, who possess characteristics that are highly prized in a culture and thus serve as models for behavior.

Heuristic problem: An open-ended problem with no specific formula for a solution, which thus needs a general set of guidelines to address.

Human capital: The value you bring from your knowledge, skills, experiences, and dispositions.

Human capital management (HCM): An employee-centered approach for assessing individual performance, predicting organizational results, and guiding the investments made in the area of human resources.

Ideation: The mental process of forming ideas.

Identity: The mental picture of yourself that you carry with and update as you change and grow.

Impact modelling: A general term for describing the decomposition of a new idea into constituent elements that are relevant to its viability.

Implicit bias: Automatic assumptions you believe to be true but which are not based upon facts.

Inclusion: Comprises the continuous process of individual consideration and welcome access to resources and opportunities.

Incubation: A purposeful stepping away from consciously focusing on the problem to allow unconscious processing and connections.

Individual-level decision-making: Decisions made by an individual.

Influence: The process of moving individuals or groups to a desired mindset, position, behavior.

Influence tactics: Actions designed to move others to a desired mindset; these include: rational persuasion, coalition, win-win, inspirational appeal, and ingratiation.

Informal power: Power derived from an individual characteristic, such as charisma, expertise, experience, wisdom, and so forth.

Ingratiation: An influence tactic characterized by increasing the level of positive feelings among the key decision makers.

Innovation: New things or methods that deliver value; the collaborative process of translating creative ideas into something of value.

Inquisitiveness: An inclination to ask questions, seek information, or otherwise inquire.

Inspirational appeal: An influence tactic characterized by aligning your proposed direction with the values, mission, and vision of the group or organization.

Integrative: Mindset of attending to and balancing multiple criteria, particularly viability, feasibility, and desirability.

Integrative: Mindset of attending to and balancing multiple criteria, particularly viability, feasibility, and desirability.

Integrity: Having strong moral character; assumes alignment of word to deed.

Intergroup dialogue (IGD): A communication technique that team leaders use to manage within-team and across-team interactions.

Intersectionality: Different identity elements are relevant all at the same time.

Intrapreneurship: Entrepreneurial behaviors within an existing organization, such as risk-taking and generating ideas.

Intrinsic motivation: Engaging in an activity for the inherent joy of the task.

Intuitive decision-making: Relies heavily on an individual or group's gut feeling, hunch, or intuition.

Invention: The creation of a new method, device, or process.

Iterate: The act of trying things out and improving the design based on feedback.

Iterative: Mindset of always seeing solutions in process—assessing and improving.

Iterative: Mindset of always seeing solutions in process—assessing and improving. Also, habits of mind (dispositions) that designers use to help enhance and guide their process.

Justice as fairness: Asserts that individuals in a free and democratic society should have equal access and opportunity to benefit from specific rights.

Kant's Categorical Imperative: Posits that an individual must do what is right at all costs.

Large-scale change: A more complex change process that requires integrating a strategic vision into change initiatives that redirect attention to entirely new processes, systems, or structures.

Lateral thinking: Attempting to look at a situation from a unique or unexpected point of view; having individuals step beyond the obvious solutions.

Laws: Rules developed by a social institution (e.g., state or nation) that govern correct behavior.

Lead a coalition: An influence tactic characterized by convening a group of like-minded people to convince decision makers.

Leadership capacity: Your fundamental attributes that can be applied to any leadership challenge in the future.

Leadership style: How a leader goes about addressing the four elements of defining the goal, clarifying the path, removing obstacles, and providing support. Styles include directive, supportive, participative, and achievement oriented.

Lean: An approach to organizational development that engages flexible, rapid methods to test and revise products and services before heavily investing.

Legitimate power: A source of power characterized by having actual authority over an individual or group.

Level 5 leadership: Leadership consisting of high-level resolve coupled with compelling personal humility.

Management: The process of organizing, controlling, and coordinating resources to achieve organizational value.

Manipulation: Similar to *influence* but often with more of a hidden or inauthentic intent.

Maslow's Hierarchy of Needs: This is a model of progressive categories of needs that drive human behavior. Four lower-order needs, which Maslow called deficiency needs, that must be satisfied (physiological—basics such as air, water, food; safety—from harm; belonging and love—relationships; esteem—esteem and respect from self and others) before moving up to the higher-level needs (cognitive, aesthetic, self-actualization, and transcendence).

Mental model: Your mental representation of things in the world—not just the picture in your head but how you understand things and even how you process information.

Metacognition: Thinking about your own thinking.

Mindfulness: The mental state of being in the present and in tune with all that is happening within yourself and in your immediate environment; being aware of the full, present moment, individuals, context, and/or situation.

Minimum viable product (MVP): The smallest, simplest thing you can build that conveys the product's value proposition to customers (and potentially captures value back).

Mission: The reason for an organization's existence.

Moral principles: Principles deemed *correct* or *incorrect* by individuals, groups, and societies.

Glossary **519**

Motivation: The internal desire for a person to act.

Multidisciplinary: Mindset that engages many minds and pursues multiple areas of expertise.

Multidisciplinary: Mindset that engages many minds and pursues multiple areas of expertise.

Nondecisions: Controversial issues or topics that have been consciously or unconsciously taken off the table by an individual or group.

Nonprofit organization: This is an organization that focuses on achieving a type of value different from financial. As an organization, they strive to achieve a cause or mission, funneling any financial profit back into serving the organization's efforts (versus paying investors or stockholders).

Norming: The third stage of group development where members have settled into roles and begin to establish the mission, purpose, and culture of the group.

Open-minded: The mindset of being receptive to new ideas and perspectives.

Opportunity recognition: Occurs when entrepreneurs become aware of a problem, dissatisfaction, or gap in current offerings that they find interesting and believe themselves capable of solving.

Oppression: Unjust treatment based upon inappropriate use of power.

Optimism: The ability and tendency to see the positive, both now and into the future.

Organizational climate: The recurring, often dynamic, patterns of behaviors, attitudes, and feelings that characterize what it is like to work within an organization.

Organizational culture: A way of life for a group of individuals that has been learned and developed over a period of time.

Organizational values: Generally emanating from founders, organizational

values guide the behavior of organizational members.

Originality: The total number of unique ideas as a measure of creativity.

Outmatched effort: A source of power characterized by consistently displaying superior effort.

Panarchy: These are the deep patterns that occur in the transformation cycles all human and natural systems go through. This specific cycle looks like an infinity loop, and it includes the following phases: exploitation, conservation, release, and reorganization.

Paradox mindset: Appreciating contradictions between opposing forces while valuing how they are mutually reinforcing.

Participative: Leadership style in which the leader provides involvement.

Performing: The fourth stage of group development where team members have settled into their roles and focus on the work at hand.

Perseverance: A steady persistence in a course of action in spite of unexpected delays.

Person: The knowledge, skills, and dispositions that support individual creative activity.

Personal identity: Parts of your identity that are individually unique to you.

Personal values: Beliefs or ideals that guide a person's behavior; what you find *personally* important or of some *worth*.

Perspective-making: Activity within a group whereby members share their individualized knowledge with one another, thereby raising collective knowing.

Perspective-taking: Activity whereby any community member attempts to see the world from someone else's point of view.

Physiological dimension: Dimension of the brain that recognizes there is a fundamental connection between your brain and your body.

Pivot: Changing an aspect of your idea, solution, or approach (or starting over) to reduce risk based on evidence and testing assumptions.

Positionality: The hidden influence of the unique constellation of agentic and targeted identities you embody.

Positive engagement: Your initiation and participation in ways that add value in a reflective and mindful manner, critically and carefully integrating new information into your understanding.

Practice: An activity used typically to maintain or improve one's performance.

Pragmatism: Engages any of the ethical perspectives to address ethical issues, understanding that no one perspective can be correct all of the time.

Press: The contextual variables that foster or inhibit creative thinking and behavior.

Privilege: Occurs when unearned power is unequally distributed by social structures and systems.

Proactive: Anticipating and preparing for a possible outcome.

Problem: A challenge or difficult matter of uncertain outcome.

Process: The steps of thinking and doing that maximize creative possibilities.

Process mapping: An activity where leaders and followers visually represent what an organization does, noting the flow of activities, decision points, roles, and any other variables involved in getting things done.

Product: The qualities and criteria that distinguish a solution as creative.

Project management: The application of knowledge, skills, tools, and techniques to a broad range of activities in order to meet the requirements of a particular project.

PsyCap: An individual's positive psychological state of development characterized by confidence, optimism, hope, and resilience.

Psychological safety: A source of motivation characterized by having trust in the organization, your supervisor, and your peers.

Purpose: The integration of your internal reasons for action and the external aim of your desired impact.

Radical empathy: The activation and expression of empathy that extends understanding another's experience such that it communicates authentic connection, support, and mutual influence.

Rational decision-making: Relies heavily on a logical process for the individual or group to make a decision.

Rational persuasion: An influence tactic characterized by sharing facts and using logic to persuade others.

Referent power: A source of power characterized by attracting others through your enthusiasm, energy, humor, and optimism.

Refining personal change capacity: Modest changes in your own behavior that people notice and at the same time convince them to follow your lead during the change process.

Reflective dimension: Dimension of the brain that is the capacity to consider and modify information and understanding.

Resilience: Latin root *resilire,* which means to spring back—your ability to withstand and recover from difficulties.

Rituals: Collective activities that are technically unnecessary to the achievement of desired ends but that within a culture are considered socially essential, keeping the individual bound within the norms of the collectivity.

Satisficing: A process of *satisfying* minimal criteria with a solution that will *suffice.*

Second-generation gender bias: Cultural, structural, and attitudinal beliefs and behaviors that exist to maintain the status quo and hold women back from ascending into leadership positions.

Servant leadership: A leadership approach that focuses first on others' needs, aspirations, and success.

Service: Action that is done for others—putting others' needs ahead of your own.

Service clubs: Organizations that usually were originally formed for social purposes that have evolved into making changes in the world.

Service learning: Campus-based volunteer opportunities that combine academic learning with principles of service to community.

Shadow experiences: Difficult experiences that influence how and what you perceive in the world, specifically the emotions and energies that inform your behavior in similar situations.

Shared accountability: Team members' focus on the work of and responsibility for the team, for the greater good of the organization.

Shared leadership: Where one individual takes a temporary leadership role on the team based on his or her area of interest and/or expertise.

Situational leadership: Behaviors utilized by leaders of an organization adjusting to fit the development level of the followers they are trying to influence.

Skills: What leaders can do—their competencies.

Social capital: The value created through common and stable individual relationships.

Social dimension: Dimension of the brain that focuses on the critical and inextricable role that others play in how you see and react to the world.

Social enrichment: The ability to get along well with others by getting them to collaborate and eventually partner with you for achieving a specific result.

Social entrepreneurship: The process of utilizing the marketplace to solve social problems (generally wicked social problems) in a novel manner.

Social identity: Human-made groupings based on shared characteristics (race, gender, ethnicity, sexual orientation, and religious affiliation).

Social impact model: A representation for the rationale for how a policy, program, project, or social venture creates value for beneficiaries, delivers the value to beneficiaries, and sustains its impact over time.

Social justice: (1) As a goal is the full and equitable participation of people from all social identity groups in a society that is mutually shaped to meet their needs; (2) as a process, it is being fair, democratic, participatory, respectful, and inclusive in the attainment of goals.

Societal cultures: Different cultures across nations, regions, or ethnicities.

Sources of motivation: These are the conditions that you design to alter someone's internal desire to act. Examples include empowerment, autonomy, career pathing, and psychological safety.

Sources of power: This is the specific origin of your capacity to influence others. Examples include referent, outmatched, and legitimate.

Spiritual capital: Individual dispositions that manifest as a sense of meaningfulness through (a) belief in something larger than self; (b) a sense of interconnectedness; (c) ethical and moral salience; (d) a call or drive to serve; and (e) the capability to transfer the latter conceptualizations into individual and organizational behaviors and ultimately added value.

stereotyping: Cognitive error wherein one incorrectly attributes to an entire group the characteristics of one or just a few of its members.

Stories: The words, gestures, pictures, and objects that carry often complex meanings, recognized as such only by those who share the culture.

Storming: The second stage of a group where members are vying for position in the group and attempt to establish their role in the group.

Strategic planning: The process by which an organization (a) clarifies (identify, develop, refine) values and vision; (b) translates those into goals; and then (c) creates action plans or strategies to achieve those goals.

Strengths-based leadership: Workers excelling in four specific domains: executing, influencing, relationship building, and strategic thinking.

Supportive: Leadership style in which the leader provides nurturance.

Sustainability: The ability to endure, specifically the process of using the resources of the present to ensure success in the future.

SWOT analysis: A strategic planning and decision-making tool used to evaluate the current strengths, weaknesses, opportunities, and threats relevant to an organization or specific situation that requires understanding.

Synergy: A group's energy where the sum of the energy of the group is greater than the combined output of each individual (the sum is greater than the total of the individual parts).

System: A group of interconnected, interdependent parts that make up a complex whole.

Systems thinking: A habit of mind (disposition) used to examine and understand the connections and interactions between individual parts making up a complex whole.

Targeted identity: Result in arbitrary challenges for belonging to certain groups.

Team: A collection of individuals with a collective goal.

Teaming: A temporary group put together to solve a problem, often with a diverse group of experts.

Team roles: The functions that each individual plays in the team (e.g., technical, interpersonal).

Technical problems: Challenges with a known solution.

Technology: The practical, material, and human application of scientific knowledge.

Tokenism: The act of viewing minoritized social identities as the representative for all people who share that minoritized identity and subsequently treating them as though their experiences are reflective of that identity.

Traits: Well-habituated, stable, and consistent personal characteristics.

Transactional leadership: A process whereby those in leadership roles directly supervise change by setting clear objectives and goals for followers as well as by using either punishments or rewards in order to encourage compliance with these goals.

Transformational leadership: A change process in which leaders and followers help each other advance to a higher level of morale and motivation.

T-shaped person: This is a metaphor for expertise within and across disciplines. The stem of the T represents an individual's depth of knowledge in their own field, while the cross of the T models an

individual's capacity to collaborate and work with other disciplines.

Tuckman's stages of group development: These stage include forming, storming, norming, performing, and adjourning.

User-centered: Mindset that focuses on the user and how they experience and feel.

User-centered: Mindset that focuses on the user and how they experience and feel.

Utilitarianism: Means that one should do the highest good for the most significant number of people.

Virtues: A continuum of traits, behaviors, and/or habits.

Vision: An aspirational image that provides short- and long-term direction for an organization and its members.

Volunteerism: Individual or group engagement with others and/or an organization for no compensation.

Vulnerability: The state of putting oneself in a position of emotional openness and at the risk of emotional exposure.

Wicked problem: A problem that is difficult or impossible to solve because of incomplete information, multiple perspectives, dynamic variables, and interconnections with other problems.

Win–win: An influence tactic characterized by helping others see how they will benefit from your idea or solution.

ENDNOTES

INTRODUCTION AND FOUNDATIONS

1. This concise definition is based off Northouse, P. (2019). *Leadership theory and practice* (8th ed.). SAGE. Northouse provides a clear, brief overview of the evolution of leadership definitions in Chapter 1. This definition may have origins with Seeman, M. (1960). *Social status and leadership*. Ohio State University, Bureau of Business Leadership; and later with Rauch, C., & Behling, O. (1984). Functionalism: Basis for an alternate approach to the study of leadership. In J. G. Hunt, D.-M. Hoskins, C. A. Schriesheim, & R. Stewart (Eds.), *Leaders and managers*. Pergamon.

2. Among the many resources listing definitions of leadership: http://www2.warwick.ac.uk/fac/sci/wmg/ftmsc/modules/modulelist/le/content_store_2012/leadership_definitions.doc

3. This is a real term describing problems that are difficult and likely impossible to solve because they are interconnected with other problems, have many competing and dynamic variables, and have many possible causes, and because of all this we have incomplete or contradictory knowledge. Wicked problems include things like poverty, homelessness, racism, wellness, and so forth. You should learn a bit more about wicked problems here: https://www.wickedproblems.com/1_wicked_problems.php

4. Ikonne, E. C. (2021). Why assigned leaders. In *Becoming a leader in product development* (pp. 1–26). Apress.

5. There is no single source that says leadership matters; rather, there are hundreds of specific studies across many fields of practice that describe successful organizations and the leadership activities that were critical to that success.

6. Keller, T. (1999). Images of the familiar: Individual differences and implicit leadership theories. *The Leadership Quarterly, 10*(4), 589–607.

7. Verlage, H., Rowold, J., & Schilling, J. (2012). Through different perspectives on leadership: Comparing the full range leadership theory to implicit leadership theories. *E Journal of Organizational Learning & Leadership, 10*(2), 68.

8. Lidwell, W., Holden, K., & Butler, J. (2010). *Universal principles of design, revised and updated: 125 Ways to enhance usability, influence perception, increase appeal, make better design decisions, and teach through design*. Rockport. http://universalprinciplesofdesign.com/books/

9. This table is a general summary and not intended as a review of research. However, as a start to exploring this topic further see: Catalyst, *Quick Take: Why Diversity and Inclusion Matter* (June 24, 2020). https://www.catalyst.org/research/why-diversity-and-inclusion-matter/; Eswaran, V. (2019, April 29). *The business case for diversity is now overwhelming*. World Economic Forum; Roberson, Q. M. (2019). Diversity in the workplace: A review, synthesis, and future research agenda. *Annual Review of Organizational Psychology and Organizational Behavior, 6*, 69–88.; Marder, A. (2017, September 18). *7 Studies that prove the value of diversity in the workplace*. Capterra. https://blog.capterra.com/7-studies-that-prove-the-value-of-diversity-in-the-workplace/

10. Kellerman, B. (2016). Leadership–It's a system, not a person! *Daedalus, 145*(3), 83–94.

11. Senge, P. M. (1994). *The fifth discipline fieldbook: Strategies and tools for building a learning organization*. Currency, Doubleday.

12. Cards developed by Middlebrooks, T. (2021). Self-published.

CHAPTER 1

1. Moore, C. (2021, March 17). What is mindfulness? Definition + benefits (Incl. Psychology). PositivePsychology.com. https://positivepsychology.com/what-is-mindfulness/

2. Good, D. J., Lyddy, C. J., Glomb, T. M., Bono, J. E., Brown, K. W., Duffy, M. K., Baer, R. A., Brewer, J. A., & Lazar, S. W. (2016). Contemplating mindfulness at work: An integrative review. *Journal of Management, 42*(1), 114–142. https://doi.org/10.1177/0149206315617003

3. Burns, J. M. (1978). *Leadership*. Harper & Row.

4. Burns, *Leadership*, p. 18.

5. Burns, *Leadership*, p. 4.

6. Burns, *Leadership*, p. 20.

7. Burns, *Leadership*, p. 43.

8. Burns, *Leadership*, p. 461.

9. Burns, *Leadership*, p. 460.

10. IIT Institute of Design, Capital One, Google, Ford, Philips, Salesforce, and VMLY&R. (2020, April 21). How design is helping

business leaders take innovation to the next level. *Fast Company*. https://www.fastcompany.com/90487468/how-design-is-helping-business-leaders-take-innovation-to-the-next-level?utm_source=postup&utm_medium=email&utm_campaign=_customposition=2&partner=newsletter&campaign_date=04212020?cid=search

11. For an early and concise conceptualization of this generalized design process, see: Dundon, E. (2002). *The seeds of innovation: Cultivating the synergy that fosters new ideas*. AMACOM.

12. Dell'Era, C., Magistretti, S., Cautela, C., Verganti, R., & Zurlo, F. (2020). Four kinds of design thinking: From ideating to making, engaging, and criticizing. *Creativity and Innovation Management, 29*(2), 324–344.

13. Liedtka, J. (2018). Why design thinking works. *Harvard Business Review, 96*(5), 72–79.

14. For a very interesting list of social innovatio projects using design thinking see: https://www.ideo.org/work

15. Brown, T., & Katz, B. (2019). *Change by design: How design thinking transforms organizations and inspires innovation* (Revised and updated). HarperBusiness, an imprint of HarperCollinsPublishers.

16. IDEO Design Thinking. (n.d.). Design thinking defined. https://designthinking.ideo.com/

17. Bruck, J., & Middlebrooks, A. (2010). Design-based learning for leadership. *Academic Exchange Quarterly, 14*(2), 17–22.

18. Lovett, J. (2018). *Original design overview*. http://www.johnlovett.com/test.htm

19. Jung, C. (1992). *C.G. Jung letters Vol. 1*. (G. Adler & A. Jaffe, Eds., R.F.C. Hull, trans., p. 33). Princeton University Press.

20. Luthans, F., Youssef, C. M., & Avolio, B. J. (2007). *Psychological capital: Developing the human competitive edge*. Oxford University Press.

21. Kong, F., Tsai, C.-H., Tsai, F.-S., Huang, W., & de la Cruz, S. (2018). Psychological capital research: A meta-analysis and implications for management sustainability. *Sustainability (Basel, Switzerland), 10*(10), 3457. https://doi.org/10.3390/su10103457

22. Schutte, N. S. (2014). The broaden and build process: Positive affect, ratio of positive to negative affect and general self-efficacy. *The Journal of Positive Psychology, 9*(1), 66–74. https://doi.org/10.1080/17439760.2013.841280

23. Nguyen, Q. (2016). Employee resilience and leadership styles: The moderating role of proactive personality and optimism. *New Zealand Journal of Psychology (Christchurch. 1983), 45*(2), 13–21.

24. Ackerman, C. E. (2021, February 12). What is self-confidence? + 9 ways to increase it. PositivePsychology.com. https://positivepsychology.com/self-confidence/

25. Confidence and optimism are positive emotions, and resilience is a positive resource; positive emotions and positive resources follow both of Barbara Fredrickson's theories: the broaden and build theory and the upward spiral theory of lifestyle change. Combined, the theories propose that experiencing positive emotions both increases our lens of perception to other positive resources and increases our likelihood of engaging in positive behaviors. See Fredrickson, B. L., & Joiner, T. (2018). Reflections on positive emotions and upward spirals. *Perspectives on Psychological Science, 13*(2), 194–199. https://doi.org/10.1177/1745691617692106

26. This outcome of leader confidence has been found in numerous studies, including Kilduff, G. J., & Galinsky, A. D. (2013). From the ephemeral to the enduring: How approach-oriented mindsets lead to greater status. *Journal of Personality and Social Psychology, 105*(5), 816–831. https://doi.org/10.1037/a0033667; Greenacre, L., Tung, N. M., & Chapman, T. (2014). Self confidence, and the ability to influence. *Academy of Marketing Studies Journal, 18*(2), 169–180; and DeCremer, D., & van Knippenberg, D. (2004). Leader self-sacrifice and leadership effectiveness: The moderating role of leader self-confidence. *Organizational Behavior and Human Decision Processes, 95*(2), 140–155.

27. Chen, Q., Kong, Y., Niu, J., Gao, W., Li, J., & Li, M. (2019). How leaders' psychological capital influence their followers' psychological capital: Social exchange or emotional contagion. *Frontiers in Psychology, 10*, 1578–1578. https://doi.org/10.3389/fpsyg.2019.01578

28. Kanter, R. (2011, April). Cultivate a culture of confidence. *Harvard Business Review*. https://hbr.org/2011/04/column-cultivate-a-culture-of-confidence

29. Ackerman, C. E. (2021, August 17). 12 tips for building self-confidence and self-belief. PositivePsychology.com. https://positivepsychology.com/self-confidence-self-belief/

30. Bandura, A. (1997). *Self-efficacy: The exercise of control*. Freeman.

31. Cuddy, A. (2012, June). *Your body language may shape who you are* [Video]. Ted Conferences. http://www.ted.com/talks/amy_cuddy_your_body_language_shapes_who_you_are

32. For example—Mindtools Content Team. (n.d.). *How self-confident are you?*https://www.mindtools.com/pages/article/newTCS_84.htm

33. Van Zant, A. B., & Moore, D. A. (2013). Avoiding the pitfalls of overconfidence while benefiting from the advantages of confidence. *California Management Review, 55*(2), 5–23.

34. Shipman, A. S., & Mumford, M. D. (2011). When confidence is detrimental: Influence of overconfidence on leadership

effectiveness. *The Leadership Quarterly, 22*(4), 649–665.

35. Cheng, J. T., Anderson, C., Tenney, E. R., Brion, S., Moore, D. A., & Logg, J. M. (2021). The social transmission of overconfidence. *Journal of Experimental Psychology. General, 150*(1), 157–186. https://doi.org/10.1037/xge0000787

36. Belmi, P., Neale, M. A., Reiff, D., & Ulfe, R. (2020). The social advantage of miscalibrated individuals: The relationship between social class and overconfidence and its implications for class-based inequality. *Journal of Personality and Social Psychology, 118*(2), 254–282. https://doi-org.tc.idm.oclc.org/10.1037/pspi0000187

37. Kouzes, J., & Posner, B. (2003). *Encouraging the heart: A leader's guide to rewarding and recognizing others.* Jossey-Bass.

38. Lounsbury, J. W., Sundstrom, E. D., Gibson, L. W., Loveland, J. M., & Drost, A. W. (2016, March). Core personality traits of managers. *Journal of Managerial Psychology, 31*(2), 434–450.

39. Carver. (2014). Dispositional optimism. *Trends in Cognitive Sciences, 18*(6), 293–299. https://doi.org/info:doi/

40. Chemers, M. M., Watson, C. B., & May, S. T. (2000, January). Dispositional affect and leadership effectiveness: A comparison of self-esteem, optimism, and efficacy. *Personality and Social Psychology Bulletin, 26*(3), 267–277.

41. Jimenez, W. P., Hu, X., Kenneally, C., & Wei, F. (2021). Do they see a half-full water cooler?: Relationships among group optimism composition, group performance, and cohesion. *Journal of Personnel Psychology, 20*(2), 75–83. https://doi.org/10.1027/1866-5888/a000271

42. Chowdhury, M. R. (2021, October 1). 11 optimism tools, examples and exercises to help improve your outlook. PositivePsychology.com. https://positivepsychology.com/optimism-tools-exercises-examples/

43. For those interested in digging deeper, research indicates that the process of springing or bouncing back from setbacks is not so straight-forward: Clark, J. N. (2021). Beyond "bouncing": Resilience as an expansion–contraction dynamic within a holonic frame. *International Studies Review, 23*(3), 556–579.

44. Edmondson, A. C. (2011, April 1). Strategies for learning from failure. *Harvard Business Review, 89*(4); Seligman, M. E. P. (1991). *Learned optimism.* A. A. Knopf; Seligman, M. E. P. (2011, January 1). Building resilience. *Harvard Business Review, 89*(4), 100–106.

45. Folkman, J. (2017, April 6). New research: 7 ways to become a more resilient leader. *Forbes.* https://www.forbes.com/sites/joefolkman/2017/04/06/new-research-7-ways-to-become-a-more-resilient-leader/?sh=6c762b717a0c

46. Birkinshaw, J., & Haas, M. (2016, January 1). Increase your return on failure. *Harvard Business Review, 94*(5), 88–93.

47. Sommer, S. A., Howell, J. M., & Hadley, C. N. (2016). Keeping positive and building strength: The role of affect and team leadership in developing resilience during an organizational crisis. *Group & Organization Management, 41*(2), 172–202.

48. Reid, J. (2008, May/June). The resilient leader: Why EQ matters. *Ivey Business Journal.* http://iveybusinessjournal.com/publication/the-resilient-leader-why-eq-matters/

49. Jiang, J. (n.d.). Rejection therapy. https://www.rejectiontherapy.com/100-days-of-rejection-therapy. You can also hear his experience at https://www.ted.com/talks/jia_jiang_what_i_learned_from_100_days_of_rejection

50. Motto, A. L., Seneca, & Campbell, R. (1970, January 1). Seneca, letters from a stoic: Epistulae morales ad lucilium. *The Classical World, 63*(5), 172.

51. Many resources are available providing suggestions for building resilience, including http://www.apa.org/helpcenter/road-resilience.aspx and https://www.mindtools.com/pages/article/resilience.htm.

52. Vonderlin, R., Biermann, M., Bohus, M., Lyssenko, L. (2020). Mindfulness-based programs in the workplace: A meta-analysis of randomized controlled trials. *Mindfulness, 11*, 1579–1598. https://doi.org/10.1007/s12671-020-01328-3

53. Martel, P., & Perkins, J. (2016, March). Building career resiliency: Hone your ability to grow from adversity. *Public Management, 98*(2), 6–9.

54. Salovey, P., & Mayer, J. D. (1990). Emotional intelligence. *Imagination, Cognition, and Personality, 9*(3), 185–211.

55. Bar-On, R. (2007). The Bar-On model of emotional intelligence: A valid, robust and applicable EI model. *Organisations & People, 14*, 27–34; Petrides, K. V., & Furnham, A. (2000). On the dimensional structure of emotional intelligence. *Personality and Individual Differences, 29*(2), 313–320.

56. Goleman, D., Boyatzis, R., & McKee, A. (2002). *Primal leadership: Realizing the power of emotional intelligence.* Harvard Business School Press.

57. Goleman, D. (2000). Emotional intelligence: Issues in paradigm building. In D. Goleman & C. Cherniss (Eds.), *The emotionally intelligent workplace: How to select for, measure, and improve emotional intelligence in individuals, groups, and organizations.* Jossey-Bass.

58. Mayer, J. D., Salovey, P., & Caruso, D. R. (2004). Emotional intelligence: Theory, findings, and implications. *Psychological Inquiry, 15*(3), 197–215.

59. Ramo, L. G., Saris, W. E., & Boyatzis, R. E. (2009). The impact of social and emotional competencies on effectiveness of Spanish executives. *Journal of Management Development, 28*(9), 771–793.

60. Boyatzis, R. E. (1999). From a presentation to the Linkage Conference on Emotional Intelligence, Chicago, IL, September 27, 1999. Cited in Cherniss, C. (1999). The business case for emotional intelligence. *Consortium for Research on Emotional Intelligence in Organizations, 4*, 1.

61. Hay/McBer Research and Innovation Group. (1997). This research was provided to Daniel Goleman and is reported in his book (Goleman, 1998). Cited in Cherniss, C. (1999). The business case for emotional intelligence. *Consortium for Research on Emotional Intelligence in Organizations, 4*, 2.

62. Nohe, C., Michaelis, B., Menges, J. I., Zhang, Z., & Sonntag, K. (2013, April). Charisma and organizational change: A multilevel study of perceived charisma, commitment to change, and team performance. *The Leadership Quarterly, 24*(2), 378–389.

63. Salzburg Global Seminar website. (n.d.). Upcoming programs. https://www.salzburgglobal.org/news/latest-news/article/are-we-becoming-disconnected-by-our-love-of-devices//.html/https://theworldunplugged.wordpress.com/about/#anchor1

64. Safian, R. (2013). *10 lessons for design-driven success.* http://www.fastcodesign.com/3016247/10-lessons-for-design-driven-success

65. Abate, A., Fitzgerald, D., Komatsuzaki, R., & Wieduwilt, U. (2019, October 22). Diversity and inclusion: What separates the best from the rest. *Russell Reynolds Insights.* https://www.russellreynolds.com/en/insights/reports-surveys/diversity-and-inclusion-what-separates-the-best-from-the-rest; And relative to corporate social responsibility, see the RSM US Middle Market Business Index Special Report on Corporate Social Responsibility, Diversity & Inclusion (Q4, 2018) https://rsmus.com/economics/rsm-middle-market-business-index-mmbi/corporate-social-responsibility-and-the-middle-market/diversity-and-inclusion-hand-in-hand-with-csr.html

66. Adams, M., & Bell, L. A. (2016). *Teaching for diversity and social justice* (3rd ed., p. 26). Routledge.

67. Allen, S. J., (Host). (2022, April 17). True belonging and dignity (No. Episode 119) [Audio podcast episode]. In *Phronesis: Practical wisdom for leaders.* https://practicalwisdom.buzzsprout.com/979897/10452334-ming-ka-chan-m-d-true-belonging-and-dignity

68. Dvornechcuck, A. (2022) Logo design process from start to finish. https://www.ebaqdesign.com/blog/logo-design-process

CHAPTER 2

1. Bennis, W., & Thomas, R. (2002). *Geeks and geezers.* HBS Press.

2. Bennis & Thomas, *Geeks and geezers*, p. 3.

3. Watts, L. L., Steele, L. M., & Mumford, M. D. (2019). Making sense of pragmatic and charismatic leadership stories: Effects on vision formation. *The Leadership Quarterly, 30*(2), 243–259.

4. Galbraith, J. K. (1971). A contemporary guide to economics, peace, and laughter. In A. D. Williams (Ed.), *Essays, Chapter 3: How Keynes came to America* (p. 50). Houghton Mifflin Company.

5. Bregman, P. (2015). Quash your bad habits by knowing what triggers them. *Forbes.* http://www.forbes.com/sites/peterbregman/2015/10/09/quash-your-bad-habits-by-knowing-what-triggers-them/#25f0429194f6

6. The Emotional Intelligence Network. (2016). http://www.6seconds.org/

7. Credit to Dr. Michael Dickmann, Emeritus Professor of Leadership for the Advancement of Learning and Service at Cardinal Stritch University.

8. Bransford, J., & National Research Council (U.S.). (2000). *How people learn: Brain, mind, experience, and school.* National Academy Press.

9. Resnick, B. (2020, June 22). "Realty" is constructed by your brain. Here's what that means, and why it matters. *Vox.* https://www.vox.com/science-and-health/20978285/optical-illusion-science-humility-reality-polarization

10. McKinsey & Company. (2021, May 24). Adam Grant on leadership, emotional intelligence, and the value of thinking like a scientist. *McKinsey Blog.* https://www.mckinsey.com/about-us/new-at-mckinsey-blog/adam-grant-on-modern-leadership

11. Collins, J. C. (2001). *Good to great: Why some companies make the leap—and others don't.* Harper Business.

12. Keating, K., Rosch, D., & Burgoon, L. (2014). Developmental readiness for leadership: The differential effects of leadership courses on creating "Ready, Willing, and Able" leaders. *Journal of Leadership Education, 13*(3), 1–16. https://doi.org/10.12806/V13/I3/R1

13. Swapp, B. (2018). But I'm an introvert: Extroverts and introverts can be effective leaders. *The Journal of Student Leadership, 2*(1), 15–20.

14. Cain, S. (2012). *Quiet: The power of introverts in a world that can't stop talking* (First). Crown.

15. Chiaburu, D. S., & Harrison, D. A. (2008). Do peers make the place? Conceptual synthesis and meta-analysis of coworker effects on perceptions, attitudes, OCBs, and performance. *Journal of Applied Psychology, 93*(5), 1082–1103. https://doi.org/10.1037/0021-9010.93.5.1082

16. Grant, A. (2015, September 4). Friends at work? Not so much. *New York Times*. https://www.nyti mes.com/2015/09/06/opinion/sun day/adam-grant-friends-at-work -not-so-much.html?_r=1

17. Riopel, L. (2021, April 16). The importance, benefits, and value of goal setting. *PositivePsychology. com*. https://positivepsychology.c om/benefits-goal-setting/

18. There are many definitions of vision, but this classic concise definition, along with an extensive explanation and toolkit relative to building shared visions, can be found in Senge, P. M. (1990). *The fifth discipline: The art and practice of the learning organization*. Doubleday/Currency.

19. Lidwell, W., Holden, K., & Butler, J. (2010). *Universal principles of design, revised and updated: 125 Ways to enhance usability, influence perception, increase appeal, make better design decisions, and teach through design*. Rockport Publishers. http://universalprinciplesofd esign.com/books/

20. Although leadership is exemplified and discussed all the way back to antiquity, possibly the two earliest published scholarly works directly focused on leadership are Terman, L. (1904). A preliminary study of the psychology and pedagogy of leadership. *Journal of Genetic Psychology, 11*, 413–451 and Mumford, E. (1909). *The origins of leadership* (Dissertation). University of Chicago.

21. Stogdill, R. M. (1974). *Handbook of leadership: A survey of the literature*. Free Press.

22. Northouse, P. G. (2019). *Leadership: Theory and practice* (8th ed.). SAGE.

23. Fuller, J. B., Patterson, C. E., Hester, K., & Stringer, D. Y. (1996). A quantitative review of research on charismatic leadership. *Psychological Reports, 78*(1), 271–287.

24. Zhang, X., Liang, L., Tian, G., & Tian, Y. (2020). Heroes or villains? The dark side of charismatic leadership and unethical pro-organizational behavior. *International Journal of Environmental Research and Public Health, 17*(15), 5546; Stadler, C., & Dyer, D. (2013, March 1). Why good leaders don't need charisma. *MIT Sloan Management Review, 54*(3), 95.

25. Tarakci, M., Greer, L. L., & Groenen, P. J. F. (2015, January 1). When does power disparity help or hurt group performance? *Journal of Applied Psychology, 101*(3), 415–429; Tasler, N. (2015, October 27). You don't need charisma to be an inspiring leader. *Harvard Business Review*.

26. Collins, J. (1997, October). *The death of the charismatic leader (And the birth of an architect)*. www.Jim collins.com

27. Katz, R. L. (1955, January/February). Skills of an effective administrator. *Harvard Business Review*, pp. 33–42.

28. Bolden, R., Gosling, J., Marturano, A., & Dennison, P. (2003). *A review of leadership theory and competency frameworks*. Edited version of a report for Chase Consulting and the Management Standards Centre. Centre for Leadership Studies, University of Exeter. http s://ore.exeter.ac.uk/repository/h andle/10036/17494

29. Kellerman, B. (2016). Leadership–It's a system, not a person! *Daedalus, 145*(3), 83–94.

30. Fayol, H. (1949). *General and industrial management*. Pitman.

31. Zaleznik, A. (2004, January). Managers and leaders: Are they different? *Harvard Business Review*. https://hbr.org/2004/01/ managers-and-leaders-are-they-different

32. Bennis, W. G. (1989). *On becoming a leader*. Addison-Wesley.

33. Yukl, G., & Lepsinger, R. (2005). Why integrating the leading and managing roles is essential for organizational effectiveness. *Organizational Dynamics, 34*(4), 361–375.

34. Yukl, G. (2012). Effective leadership behavior: What we know and what questions need more attention. *Academy of Management Perspectives, 26*(4), 66–85.

35. Bransford, J., & National Research Council (U.S.). (2000). *How people learn: Brain, mind, experience, and school*. National Academy Press.

36. Klein, G. A. (1999). *Sources of power: How people make decisions*. MIT Press.

37. Allen, S. J., & Middlebrooks, A. (2013, December 1). The challenge of educating leadership expertise. *Journal of Leadership Studies, 6*(4), 84–89.

38. Raffo, D., & Williams, R. (2018). Evaluating potential transformational leaders: Weighing charisma vs. credibility. *Strategy & Leadership, 46*(6), 28–34. https://doi.org/ 10.1108/SL-12-2017-0130

39. Kouzes, J. M., & Posner, B. Z. (2017). *The leadership challenge: How to make extraordinary things happen in organizations* (6th ed., p. 41). Wiley.

40. Kouzes & Posner, *The leadership challenge*, p. 41.

41. Kouzes & Posner, *The leadership challenge*, p. 29.

42. Goffee, R., & Jones, G. (2005, January 1). Why should anyone be led by you? *Harvard Business Review*, p. 1.

43. Lawrence-Lightfoot, S. (1999). *Respect: An exploration*. Perseus Books.

44. Ibarra, H., & Scoular, A. (2019, November-December). The leader as coach. *Harvard Business Review*. https://hbr.org/2019/11/th e-leader-as-coach

45. https://hbr.org/2004/01/manager s-and-leaders-are-they-different

46. Erikson, E. H. (1956). The problem of ego identity. *Journal of the American Psychoanalytic Association, 4*(1), 56–121.

47. Gardenswartz, L., & Rowe, A. (2009). The effective management of cultural diversity. In M. A. Moodian (Ed.), *Contemporary leadership and intercultural competence: Exploring the cross-cultural dynamics within organizations* (pp. 35–43). SAGE. https://doi.org/10.4135/9781452274942.n4; See https://www.gardenswartzrowe.com/why-g-r for a copy of the updated model.

48. Cho, S., Crenshaw, K. W., & McCall, L. (2013). Toward a field of intersectional studies: Theory, applications, and praxis. *Journal of Women in Culture and Society, 38*(4), 785–810. https://doi.org/10.1086/669608

49. Bandura, A. (2001). Social cognitive theory: An agentic perspective. *Annual Review of Psychology, 52*, 1–26.

50. Tatum, B. D. (2000). The complexity of identity: Who am I? In M. Adams, W. J. Blumenfeld, R. Castaneda, H. W. Hackman, M. L. Peters, & X. Zuniga (Eds.), *Readings for diversity and social justice* (pp. 9–14). Routledge.

51. Kezar, A., & Lester, J. (2010). Breaking the barriers of essentialism in leadership research: Positionality as a promising approach. *Feminist Formations, 22*(1), 163–185.

52. Dickens. (2017). Using gratitude to promote positive change: A series of meta-analyses investigating the effectiveness of gratitude interventions. *Basic and Applied Social Psychology, 39*(4), 193–208. https://doi.org/10.1080/01973533.2017.1323638

CHAPTER 3

1. Adam Grant. (n.d.). Give and take assessment. Adam Grant website. https://www.adamgrant.net/quizzes/give-and-take-quiz/

2. 16Personalities. (n.d.). Free personality test. 16Personalities website. https://www.16personalitie

s.com/free-personality-test; For an overview of the 16 Personality types see https://www.16personalities.com/personality-types

3. Chaleff, I. (2016). In praise of followership style assessments. *Journal of Leadership Studies, 10*(3), 45–48.

4. Burns, J. (1978). *Leadership.* Harper & Row.

5. Eurich, T. (2018). *Insight: How to succeed by seeing yourself clearly.* Pan Books.

6. Eurich, T. (2018, January 4). What self-awareness really is (and how to cultivate it). *Harvard Business Review.* http://https://hbr.org/2018/01/what-self-awareness-really-is-and-how-to-cultivate-it

7. Dweck, C. S. (2008). *Mindset: The new psychology of success.* Ballantine Books.

8. Tuff, K., Wojdak, J. M., & Fleming-Davies, A. (2018). *Cultivating your growth mindset.* National Professional Resources.

9. Davis, T. (2019, April 19). 15 ways to build a growth mindset. *Psychology Today.* https://www.psychologytoday.com/us/blog/click-here-happiness/201904/15-ways-build-growth-mindset

10. Pink, D. (2021). Pinkcast 4.13. This is how big time performers get the feedback they need. https://www.danpink.com/pinkcast/pinkcast-4-13-this-is-how-big-time-performers-get-the-feedback-they-need/

11. Kohlbacher, M., & Gruenwald S. (2011): Process orientation: Conceptualization and measurement. *Business Process Management Journal, 17*(2), 267–283.

12. Glavan, L. M., & Vukšić, V. B. (2017). Examining the impact of business process orientation on organizational performance: The case of Croatia. *Croatian Operational Research Review, 8*(1), 137–163. https://doi.org/10.17535/crorr.2017.0009

13. Jain, K. K., & Das, R. (2017). Risks of results oriented leadership: A perspective in need of a re-evaluation. *NHRD Network Journal, 10*(4), 104–110.

14. Blanchard, K. (2010, January 25). *Leading at a higher level. Peter Drucker Institute keynote speaker* [Video file]. https://www.youtube.com/watch?v=_hNYu4cdU2k

15. Buckingham, M., & Clifton, D. O. (2001). *Now, discover your strengths.* Free Press.

16. Strengths and their definitions loosely quoted from the Clifton StrengthsFinder measure, which can be found here: http://www.gallup.com/poll/166991/clifton-strengthsfinder-theme-descriptions-pdf.aspx; Students can take the measure (for a fee) here: https://www.gallupstrengthscenter.com/Purchase/en-US/Index/?utm_source=En_US&utm_medium=Ad&utm_campaign=SF2SiteAd

17. Ding, H., & Yu, E. (2020). Follower strengths-based leadership and follower innovative behavior: The roles of core self-evaluations and psychological well-being. *Journal of Work and Organizational Psychology, 36*(2), 36, 103–110. https://doi.org/10.5093/jwop2020a8; Ding, H., & Yu, E. (2021). How and when does follower strengths-based leadership contribute to follower work engagement? The roles of strengths use and core self-evaluation. *German Journal of Human Resource Management, 36*(2), 180–196. https://doi.org/10.1177/23970022211053284

18. Rath, T., & Conchie, B. (2009). *Strengths-based leadership: Great leaders, teams and why people follow.* Gallup Press.

19. Gallup, Inc. (2013). *State of the American workplace.* file:///C:/Users/tmidd/Downloads/State%20of%20the%20American%20Workplace%20Report%202013.pdf

20. Cross, N. (1982). Designerly ways of knowing. *Design Studies, 3*(4), 221–227; Cross, N. (2010, October

19–20). *Design thinking as a form of intelligence* (pp. 99–105). Proceedings of the 8th Design Thinking Research Symposium (DTRS8), Sydney, Australia.

21 Kimball, L. (2011). Rethinking design thinking. *Design and Culture, 3*(3), 285–306 (pp. 290–291). https://doi.org/10.2752/17547081 1X13071166525216

22 Kimball, Rethinking design thinking.

23 Micheli, P., Wilner, S. J., Bhatti, S. H., Mura, M., & Beverland, M. B. (2019). Doing design thinking: Conceptual review, synthesis, and research agenda. *Journal of Product Innovation Management, 36*(2), 124–148.

24 Brzozowski, L. (2015, August 4). Innovating a mature product—The Sealy Case. LinkedIn. https://www.linkedin.com/pulse/innovating-mature-product-sealy-case-len-brzozowski; Ketter, P. (2016, May). Design thinking: A company's DNA. *TD Magazine.* https://www.td.org/Publications/Magazines/TD/TD-Archive/2016/05/Design-Thinking-a-Companys-DNA

25 Wicked Problems. (n.d.). An introduction to wicked problems. https://www.wickedproblems.com/1_wicked_problems.php

26 Also referred to as the Conscious Competence Matrix or Learning Matrix; most attributed to Noel Burch at Gordon Training International, http://www.gordontraining.com/free-workplace-articles/learning-a-new-skill-is-easier-said-than-done/; and nicely explained here: Mind Tools Content Team. (n.d.). *The conscious competence ladder: Keeping going when learning gets tough.* https://www.mindtools.com/pages/article/newISS_96.htm

27 Harfort, T. (2011). *Trial and error and the God complex* [Video]. Ted Conferences. http://www.ted.com/talks/tim_harford/transcript?language=en

28 Schwartz, M. A. (2008, January 1). The importance of stupidity in scientific research. *Journal of Cell Science,121*(11), 1771.

29 Ibid, p. 1771.

30 Middlebrooks, A. (2016). Global leadership competencies: Inquisitiveness. In M. Mendenhall (Ed.), *International leadership: A reference guide.* Mission Bell Media.

31 Gregersen, H. (2016, April 1). When was the last time you asked, "Why are we doing it this way?" *Harvard Business Review.* https://hbr.org/2016/04/when-was-the-last-time-you-asked-why-are-we-doing-it-this-way

32 Smith, K. (2008). *How to be an explorer of the world: Portable life museum* (p. 5). Penguin.

33 Lucky Iron Firsh (n. d.). About us. Lucky Iron Fish website. http://www.luckyironfish.com/about-us

34 IDEO. (n.d.). *Design kit: The human-centered design toolkit.* https://www.ideo.com/post/design-kit; IDEO. (n.d.). *Method cards.* https://www.ideo.com/post/method-cards

35 IDEO. (n.d.). *Method cards.* https://www.ideo.com/work/method-cards

36 Fidelity. (2016, April 7). *Better quality of work life is worth a $7,600 pay cut for millennials.* https://www.fidelity.com/about-fidelity/individual-investing/better-quality-of-work-life-is-worth-pay-cut-for-millennials

37 Kolko, J. (2014). *Well-designed: How to use empathy to create products people love.* Harvard Business Review Press.

38 Turnali, K. (2016, January 17). Empathy, design thinking, and an obsession with customer-centric innovation. *Forbes.* http://www.forbes.com/sites/sap/2016/01/17/empathy-design-thinking-and-an-obsession-with-customer-centric-innovation/#5620a4c64285

39 Arghode, V., Lathan, A., Alagaraja, M., Rajaram, K., & McLean, G. N. (2021). Empathic organizational culture and leadership: Conceptualizing the framework. *European Journal of Training and Development*, ahead-of-print(ahead-of-print). https://doi.org/10.1108/EJTD-09-2020-0139

40 Wheatley, M. J. (n.d.). http://www.margaretwheatley.com/articles/listening healing.html

41 Linton, W. J. (1878). *Poetry of America.* George Bell & Sons.

42 Gershbein, D. (2014) *Extinction of the expert: How the knowledge economy is changing the innovation game.* http://daoofstrategy.blogspot.com/2014/08/succeeding-in-information-economy-as.html

43 Guest, D. (1991, September 17). The hunt is on for the Renaissance Man of computing. *The Independent.*

44 Bierema, L. L. (2019). Enhancing employability through developing T-shaped professionals. *New Directions for Adult and Continuing Education, 2019*(163), 67–81.; Demirkan, H., & Spohrer, J. (2015). T-shaped innovators: Identifying the right talent to support service innovation. *Research-Technology Management, 58*(5), 12–15.

45 Martin, R. L. (2009). *The opposable mind: How successful leaders win through integrative thinking* (p. 15). Harvard Business Press.; Also see Riel, J., & Martin, R. L. (2017). *Creating great choices: A leader's guide to integrative thinking.* Harvard Business Press.

46 Mack, T. (2015). Leadership in the future. In M. Sowcik, A. C. Andenoro, M. McNutt, & S. E. Murphy (Eds.), *Leadership 2050: Critical challenges, key contexts, and emerging trends* (pp. 9–22). Emerald.

47 Stahl, A. (2021, April 16). The future of offices and workspaces, post-pandemic. *Forbes.* https://www.forbes.com/sites/ashleystahl/2021/04/16/the-future-of-offices-and-workspaces-post-pandemic/?sh=75431f366442

48 Kearns, K. (2015). 9 great examples of crowdsourcing in the age

of empowered consumers. http://tweakyourbiz.com/marketing/2015/07/10/9-great-examples-crowdsourcing-age-empowered-consumers/

49 For one example of the many articles examining this trend, see Overstreet, K. (2021, May 1). The future of the workspace that isn't the workplace. *ArchDaily.* https://www.archdaily.com/960896/the-future-workspace-that-isnt-the-workplace

50 Colvin, G. (2015, July 23). Humans are underrated. *Fortune.* http://fortune.com/2015/07/23/humans-are-underrated/

51 Redman, P. (2013, October 7). Five essentials of strategic planning. *Stanford Social Innovation Review.* https://ssir.org/articles/entry/five_essentials_of_strategic_planning

52 For two recent examples, consider McCausland, T. (2021). Why innovation needs more diversity. *Research-Technology Management, 64*(2), 59–63.

53 Helbig, B. (2021, August 30). The best employers see the benefits of diversity, equity, inclusion. *The Atlanta Constitution.* https://www.ajc.com/top-workplaces/the-best-employers-see-the-benefits-of-diversity-equity-inclusion/NDFAKK25SFBWJAVJX6EYISMTUU/

54 Miller, J. (2021, February 18). For younger job seekers, diversity and inclusion in the workplace aren't a preference. They're a requirement. *The Washington Post.* https://www.washingtonpost.com/business/2021/02/18/millennial-genz-workplace-diversity-equity-inclusion/

55 Creary, S. J., Rothbard, N., & Scruggs, J. (2021). Improving workplace culture through evidence-based diversity, equity and inclusion practices. *PsyArXiv.* https://doi.org/10.31234/osf.io/8zgt9

56 Gassam, J. Z., & Salter, N. P. (2020). Considerations for hiring external consultants to deliver diversity trainings. *Consulting Psychology Journal: Practice and Research, 72*(4), 275-287. https://psycnet.apa.org/doi/10.1037/cpb0000170

57 Two examples of this include Comeaux, E. (2021, June 24). Doin' work: DEI implementation strategies for leadership teams. *Forbes.* https://www.forbes.com/sites/ediecomeaux/2021/06/24/doin-work-dei-implementation-strategies-for-leadership-teams/?sh=4089c6c07774; Cox, G., & Lancefield, D. (2021, May 19). 5 strategies to infuse D&I into your organization. *Harvard Business Review.* https://hbr.org/2021/05/5-strategies-to-infuse-di-into-your-organization

58 Staff. (2021, July 10). 5 powerful ways to take REAL action on DEI. *Center for Creative Leadership.* https://www.ccl.org/articles/leading-effectively-articles/5-powerful-ways-to-take-real-action-on-dei-diversity-equity-inclusion/

59 Vărzaru, A., Bocan, C., & Nicolescu, M. (2021). Rethinking corporate responsibility and sustainability in light of economic performance. *Sustainability, 13*(5), 2660. https://doi.org/10.3390/su13052660

60 Patagonia's Mission Statement. Retrieved August 9, 2021, from https://www.patagonia.com.au/pages/our-mission

61 Wilson, H. J., & Dougherty, P. R. (2018). Collaborative intelligence: Humans and AI are joining forces. *Harvard Business Review,* pp. 114–123.

62 McGowan, H. E. (2020, November 5). The Coronavirus ushers in the human capital era. *Forbes.* https://www.forbes.com/sites/heathermcgowan/2020/11/05/the-coronavirus-ushers-in-the-human-capital-era/?sh=25d8c84622dd

63 Buson, O. (2021). Artificial intelligence: Lates research and perspective on the implications of AI for human rights. *Business and Human Rights Resource Center.* http://www.business-humanrights.org

64 Gropius, W. (1925). *Internationale architektur.* Albert Langen Verlag.

65 Colvin, G. (2015, January 1). Humans are underrated. *Fortune, 172*(2), 34–43.

66 Bear, M. (2015). *Why empathy is the critical 21st century skill.* https://www.linkedin.com/pulse/20140424221331-1407199-why-empathy-is-the-critical-21st-century-skill/

67 Zenger, J., & Folkman, J. (2020, December 30). Research: Women are better leaders during a crisis. *Harvard Business Review.*

68 Pavlovich, K., & Krahnke, K. (2014). *Organizing through empathy.* Routledge.

69 Pashak, T. J., Conley, M. A., Whitney, D. J., Oswald, S. R., Heckroth, S. G., & Schumacher, E. M. (2018). Empathy diminishes prejudice: Active perspective-taking, regardless of target and mortality salience, decreases implicit racial bias. *Psychology, 9,* 1340–1356. https://doi.org/10.4236/psych.2018.96082

70 Stephan, W., & Finlay, K. (2001). Role of empathy in improving intergroup relations. *Journal of Social Issues, 55*(4), 729–743. And see: Ha, T. (2021, March 16). 5 exercises to help you build more empathy. *Ideas.TED.com.* https://ideas.ted.com/5-exercises-to-help-you-build-more-empathy/

71 Finnis, J. (2020, October 6). Why digitally literate leadership is so important right now. https://janefinnis.medium.com/why-digitally-literate-leadership-is-so-important-right-now-3c2d9b214dde

72 Gartner. (2021). The digital workplace reimagined. *A Deloitte Research Report.* https://www.gartner.com/technology/media-products/newsletters/Deloitte/1-27HTLMDE/index.html

73 Finnis, J., & Kennedy, A. (2020, July). The digital transformation agenda and GLAMS: A quick scan report for Europeana. https://pro

.europeana.eu/files/Europeana_ Professional/Publications/Digital%20transformation%20reports/ The%20digital%20transformation %20agenda%20and%20GLAMs% 20-%20Culture24%20findings%2 0and%20outcomes.pdf

74 Staff. (2019, December 20). Digital literacy the most important skill for leaders – Report. *Entrepreneur.* https://www.entrepreneur.com/article/344121#:~:text=Accor ding%20to%20the%20report%2C %20digital,important%20skill%2 0that%20leaders%20need.&text =Moreover%2C%20literacy%20in %20this%20space,on%20the%20 people%20around%20him

75 Siemans. (2021). MindSphere, the cloud-based, open IoT operating system. https://www.plm.automa tion.siemens.com/global/en/prod ucts/mindsphere/

76 Arghode, V., Lathan, A., Alagaraja, M., Rajaram, K., & McLean, G. (2021). Empathic organizational culture and leadership: Conceptualizing the framework. European Journal of Training and Development, 46(1/2), 239–256. https://doi .org/10.1108/EJTD-09-2020-0139 ISSN: 2046-9012

77 Kim, W. C., & Mauborgne, R. (2015). *Blue ocean strategy: How to create uncontested market space and make the competition irrelevant.* Harvard Business School.

78 Hightower, S. S. (2021, December 2021/January 2022). How Fizer is leading the way to create a more diverse, equitable, and inclusive workplace. *Forbes Magazine*, p. 38.

79 NBVC special report: Blue origin Crew launch into space. Retrieved August 11, 2021, from https://ww w.youtube.com/watch?v=4SSVr 3EKTlM

80 Clerkin, C. (2015). Creative leadership and social intelligence: The keys to leading in the digital age. In M. Sowcik, A. C. Andenoro, M. McNutt, & S. E. Murphy (Eds.), *Leadership 2050: Critical challenges, key contexts, and emerging trends* (pp. 175–187). Emerald.

81 See Wiest, B. (2018, March 13). 13 things socially intelligent leaders do differently. *Forbes.* https://ww w.forbes.com/sites/briannawies t/2018/03/13/13-things-socially-i ntelligent-leaders-do-differentl y/#40b32cdf4dbd for one of many examples of practical advice for social intelligence and leadership.

82 Goleman, D., & Boyatzis, R. (2008, January 1). Social intelligence and the biology of leadership. *Harvard Business Review,86*, 9.

83 Katou, A. A., Budhwar, P. S., & Patel, C. (2021). A trilogy of organizational ambidexterity: Leader's social intelligence, employee work engagement and environmental changes. *Journal of Business Research, 128*, 688–700. https ://doi.org/10.1016/j.jbusres.2020 .01.043

84 Liu, E. (2018). Embracing civic power. *Social Education*, 82(5), 251–254.

85 Liu, E. (2014, November). *How to understand power.* TED-Ed. https:/ /www.ted.com/talks/eric_liu_h ow_to_understand_power?lang uage=en

86 McIntosh, P. (1989, July/August). White privilege: Unpacking the invisible knapsack. *Peace and Freedom*, pp. 1–3.

87 Collins, J. (2001). *Good to great.* HarperCollins.

86. Reuters. (2016, January 26). *Comedian Carol Burnett 'gob-smacked' at SAG lifetime award.* http://www.reuters. com/article/us-awards-sag - carolburnett-idUSKCN0V4223

CHAPTER 4

1. Sinek, S. (2009). *Start with why: How great leaders inspire everyone to take action.* Penguin.

2. Hawken, P. (2021). Regeneration: Ending the climate crisis in one generation. https://www.penguin randomhouse.com/books/690153 /regeneration-by-paul-hawken/

3. Dhiman, S. (2017). Meaning & purpose in leadership: What are you willing to bet your life on? In *Holistic leadership.* Palgrave Macmillan. https://doi.org/10.1057/97 8-1-137-55571-7_8

4. Bergner, S., Kanape, A., & Rybnicek, R. (2019). Taking an interest in taking the lead: The influence of vocational interests, leadership experience and success on the motivation to lead. *Applied Psychology, 68*, 202–219. https://doi.or g/10.1111/apps.12150

5. For a deeper dive into the connection between leadership and purpose see, Kempster, S., Jackson, B., & Conroy, M. (2011). Leadership as purpose: Exploring the role of purpose in leadership practice. *Leadership, 7*(3), 317–334.

6. Rashid, R., & Brooks, A. C. (2021). How to identify what you enjoy. htt ps://www.theatlantic.com/podca sts/archive/2021/11/how-to-prior itize-joy-lorigottlieb-arthurbrook s-happiness-2021/620787/

7. See, for example, the Journal of Happiness Studies: https://www.s pringer.com/journal/10902

8. Frankl, V. E. (1985). *Man's search for meaning.* Simon and Schuster.

9. Frankl, *Man's search*, p. 86.

10. Sinek, S. (2009). *Start with why: How great leaders inspire everyone to take action.* Penguin.

11. Norman, D. (1988). *The design of everyday things.* Doubleday.

12. Harro, B. (2000a). The cycle of socialization. In M. Adams, W. J., Blumenfeld, R. Castañeda, H. W. Hackman, M. L. Peters, & X. Zuniga (Eds.), *Readings for diversity and social justice: An anthology on racism, sexism, anti-Semitism, heterosexism, classism, and ableism* (pp. 45–52). Routledge.

13. Pope, R. L., Reynolds, A. L., & Mueller, J. A. (2019). *Multicultural competence in student affairs: Advancing social justice and inclusion* (2nd ed.). Jossey-Bass.

14. Broido, E. M. (1997). *The development of social justice allies during college: A phenomenological investigation* (Publication No. 9817438) [Doctoral dissertation, The Pennsylvania State University]. ProQuest Dissertation Publishing.

15. Sleeter, C. E., & Carmona, J. F. (2017). *Un-standardizing curriculum: Multicultural teaching in the standards-based classroom* (2nd ed.). Teachers College Press.

16. Hurtado, S., Alvarez, C. L., Guillermo-Wann, C., Cuellar, M., & Arellano, L. (2012). A model for diverse learning environments. In *Higher education: Handbook of theory and research* (pp. 41–122). Springer.

17. Harro, B. (2000b). The cycle of liberation. In M. Adams, W. J., Blumenfeld, R. Castañeda, H. W. Hackman, M. L. Peters, & X. Zuniga (Eds.), *Readings for diversity and social justice: An anthology on racism, sexism, anti-Semitism, heterosexism, classism, and ableism* (pp. 463–469). Routledge.

18. Chin, J., & Trimble, J. (2015). *Diversity and leadership*. SAGE.

19. Hofstede, G., Hofstede, G. J., & Minkov, M. (2010). *Cultures and organizations: Software of the mind* (3rd ed.). McGraw-Hill.

20. McLaren, P. (2003). *Life in schools: An introduction to critical pedagogy in the foundation of education*. Allyn & Bacon.

21. Haslam, S. A., Reicher, S. D., & Platow, M. J. (2011). *The new psychology of leadership: Identity, influence, and power*. Psychology Press.

22. Chávez, A., & Sanlo, R. (Eds.). (2013). *Identity and leadership: Informing our lives, informing our practice*. NASPA.

23. Adapted by Nyasha M. Guramatunhu Cooper from Crosby, B., & Bryson, J. (2005). *Leadership for the common good: Tackling public problems in a shared-power world* (2nd ed.). Josey-Bass.

24. Personal correspondence (2021).

25. Note: Charisms, are special abilities, a special empowerment. These days we sometimes call them "superpowers." Whether extraordinary or ordinary, in the deepest sense of the word, one's charisms are given so that you can exercise them in the service of others. A charism is different from a natural or learned ability in the sense that when we use our charisms we feel it is something that we were always intended to do. In this sense, it can also be deeply connected with our faith or higher beliefs.

26. Quit your job and find your work. h ttps://www.youtube.com/watch?v =nXu7dDSflf8

27. Nakamura, J., & Csikszentmihalyi, M. (2014). The concept of flow. In *Flow and the foundations of positive psychology* (pp. 239–263). Springer.

28. Csikszentmihalyi, M., Montijo, M. N., & Mouton, A. R. (2018). Flow theory: Optimizing elite performance in the creative realm. In S. I. Pfeiffer, E. Shaunessy-Dedrick, & M. Foley-Nicpon (Eds.), *APA handbook of giftedness and talent* (pp. 215–229). American Psychological Association; Csikszentmihalyi, M. (1997). *Flow and the psychology of discovery and invention* (p. 39). HarperPerennial.

29. Peifer, C., & Wolters, G. (2021). Flow in the context of work. In C. Peifer & S. Engeser (Eds.), *Advances in flow research* (pp. 287–321). Springer. https://doi.or g/10.1007/978-3-030-53468-4_11

30. Barthelmäs, M., & Keller, J. (2021). Antecedents, boundary conditions and consequences of flow. In C. Peifer & S. Engeser (Eds.), *Advances in flow research* (pp. 71–107). Springer. https://doi. org/10.1007/978-3-030-53468 -4_3

31. Photographer Don Denton interviews T. J. Watt. (2011). Retrieved November 28, 2021, from http://d ondenton.ca/2011/01/11/tj-watt-i nterview/comment-page-1/

32. Badelt, B. (2021, November 26). Photographer of giant old-growth trees has 'best and worst job in the world.' *The Doc Project*. https: //www.cbc.ca/radio/docproject/p hotographer-of-giant-old-growth -trees-has-best-and-worst-job-i n-the-world-1.6251373

33. Photographer Don Denton interviews T. J. Watt. (2011). Retrieved November 28, 2021, from http://d ondenton.ca/2011/01/11/tj-watt-i nterview/comment-page-1/

34. You can watch his inspiring TED talk here: https://www.ted.com/t alks/bj_miller_what_really_ma tters_at_the_end_of_life?langu age=en

35. Palmer, P. J. (1999). *Let your life speak: Listening for the voice of vocation*. John Wiley & Sons.

36. Palmer, *Let your life speak*, page 2.

37. Father Richard Rohr offers a clear definition of "vocation"— "Vocation is one way in which we discover and grow into our "True Self." I'm not speaking so much about education, career, or livelihood, though in some cases they might overlap. In general, it is a Larger Life that somehow calls us forward (*vocatio* means "a call or summons" in Latin), more than we call it to us. We do not know its name yet, so how can we call it? If we engineer the process too much, we often mistake a security-based occupation for our soul's vocation." May 27, 2018. Retrieved November 28, 2021, from https://cac.org/let-your-life -speak-2018-05-27/

38. Millman, D. (2015). *The four purposes of life: Finding meaning and direction in a changing world* (p. 11). HJ Kramer.

39. Nepo, M. (2016). Understory. Quote excerpted from *The way under the way: The place of true meeting*. Sounds True.

40. Retrieved November 28, 2021, from https://www.youtube.com/w atch?v=sa1iS1MqUy4

41. Obama, B. (2020). My Eulogy for Congressman John Lewis. https://obama.medium.com/my-eulogy-for-congressman-john-lewis-101ea5eb49d1

42. Mathai, M. (2004, December 10). Nobel lecture. https://www.nobelprize.org/prizes/peace/2004/maathai/lecture/

43. Chan, K. Y., & Drasgow, F. (2001). Toward a theory of individual differences and leadership: Understanding the motivation to lead. *Journal of Applied Psychology, 86*(3), 481–498.

44. Chan & Drasgow, Toward a theory of individual differences,, p. 482.

45. Bergner, S., Kanape, A., & Rybnicek, R. (2019). Taking an interest in taking the lead: The influence of vocational interests, leadership experience, and success on the motivation to lead. *Applied Psychology, 68*(1), 202–219.

46. Aycan, Z., & Shelia, S. (2019). "Leadership? no, thanks!" a new construct: Worries about leadership. *European Management Review, 16*(1), 21–35.

47. United Nations. (2021). *The stainable development goals report*. https://unstats.un.org/sdgs/report/2021/The-Sustainable-Development-Goals-Report-2021.pdf

48. Consider Martin Seligman's very useful PERMA framework as a foundation for wellness, both achieving and facilitating. Positive emotions, engagement, relationships, meaning, and achievement. Seligman, M. (2011). *Flourish*. Free Press. And see Positive Psychology Center. (n.d.). PERMA theory of well-being and PERMA workshops. https://ppc.sas.upenn.edu/learn-more/perma-theory-well-being-and-perma-workshops

49. Livingston, R. W. (2021). *The conversation: How seeking and speaking the truth about racism can radically transform individuals and organizations: A science-based approach (First)* (p. 204). Currency.

50. Jacobs Foundation. (n.d.). Interview Nisha Ligon, Co-founder and CEO Ubongo. https://jacobsfoundation.org/en/interview-nisha-ligon-co-founder-and-ceo-ubongo/

51. Lionesses of Africa. (2021, June 13). Nisha Ligon, a social entrepreneur making an impact through adult edutainment. Retrieved November 27, 2021, from https://www.lionessesofafrica.com/blog/2021/6/13/nisha-ligon-a-social-entrepreneur-making-an-impact-through-edutainmentnbsp

52. Lidwell, W., Holden, K., & Butler, J. (2010). *The universal principles of design*. Rockport.

53. Aneel Chima - The role of deep purpose making in human flourishing. (2017). Retrieved December 05, 2021, from https://www.youtube.com/watch?v=smNrItEB1bk

54. Eiseley, L. C. (1969). *The unexpected universe*. Harcourt, Brace & World.

55. Ulrich, D., & Smallwood, N. (2007). *Leadership brand: Developing customer-focused leaders to drive performance and build lasting value*. Harvard Business School Press.

56. Bass, B., & Riggio, R. (2006). *Transformational leadership*. Lawrence Erlbaum.

57. Heifetz, R., Grashow, A., & Linsky, M. (2009). *The practice of adaptive leadership: Tools and tactics for changing your organization and your world*. Harvard Business School Press.

58. Aristotle. (2004). *Nicomachean ethics* (H. Tredennick, ed.). Penguin. 1097a30-34.

59. Aristotle, *Nicomachean*, 1098a18.

60. Pursuit of Happiness. (n.d.). *Aristotle: Pioneer of happiness*. https://www.pursuit-of-happiness.org/history-of-happiness/aristotle/

CHAPTER 5

1. Ryan's Well Foundation. (2021). *2020–2021 annual report*. https://www.ryanswell.ca/wp-content/uploads/2021/10/AGR-2020-2021-Updated.pdf

2. Ryan's Well Foundation. (2021). *2020–2021 annual report*. https://www.ryanswell.ca/wp-content/uploads/2021/10/AGR-2020-2021-Updated.pdf

3. Burns, J. M. (1978). *Leadership* (p. 455). Harper Torchbooks.

4. Ciulla, J. (2003). *The ethics of leadership* (p. xiv). Wadsworth/Thomson. https://scholarship.richmond.edu/cgi/viewcontent.cgi?article=1003&context=bookshelf

5. George, B. (2007). *True north* (p. 47). Wiley.

6. Fedor, L. (2020, December 8). Beth Ford: Transformative leadership during crises. *Twin Cities Business*. https://tcbmag.com/honors/beth-ford-transformative-leadership-during-crises/

7. Giles, S. (2016, March 15). The most important leadership competencies, according to leaders around the world. *Harvard Business Review*. https://hbr.org/2016/03/the-most-important-leadership-competencies-according-to-leaders-around-the-world

8. Brown, M. E., Treviño, L. K., & Harrison, D. A. (2005). Ethical leadership: A social learning perspective for construct development and testing. *Organizational Behavior and Human Decision Processes, 97*(2), 117–134.

9. United Nations. (1948). *The universal declaration of human rights*. http://www.un.org/en/universal-declaration-human-rights/

10. American Medical Association. (2016). *AMA code of medical ethics: AMA principles of medical ethics*. https://www.ama-assn.org/sites/default/files/media-browser/principles-of-medical-ethics.pdf

11. Hoban.org. (n.d.). *4 universal moral principles: Lessons of the ages*. https://www.hoban.org/s/1098/images/editor_documents/2009-10%20School%20Year/Bulgrin/4%20Basic%20Moral%20Principles.pdf?sessionid=f9e8cb31-22cc-4159-9676-b18595ccbc90&cc=1

12. Kinnier, R. T., Kernes, J. L., & Dautheribes, T. M. (2000). A short list of universal moral values. *Counseling & Values, 45*, 4–16.

13. King Jr., M. L. (1963, August 28). *I have a dream*. Lincoln Memorial, Washington, DC.

14. Akta Lakota Museum & Cultural Center. (n.d.). Seven Lakota values. https://aktalakota.stjo.org/lakota-culture/seven-lakota-values/

15. Government of Nunavut. (n.d.). Inuit societal values. https://www.gov.nu.ca/information/inuit-societal-values

16. Peterson, C., & Seligman, M. E. (2004). *Character strengths and virtues: A handbook and classification*. Oxford University Press.

17. Peterson & Seligman, *Character strengths*.

18. Singh, P., & Fenech, L. E. (Eds.) (2014). *The Oxford handbook of Sikh studies* (p. 240). Oxford University Press. ISBN 978-0-19-969930-8. https://books.google.com/books?id=8I0NAwAAQBAJ&pg=PA234

19. Alberta Regional Consortia. (n.d.). Seven sacred teachings. https://empoweringthespirit.ca/cultures-of-belonging/seven-grandfathers-teachings/

20. Joachim, H. H., & Rees, D. A. (1953). *Aristotle: The Nicomachean ethics*. Clarendon Press.

21. thirteenvirtues.com. (n.d.). thirteenvirtues website. http://www.thirteenvirtues.com

22. thirteenvirtues.com.

23. Lickona, T. (1993). *The return of character education*. http://www.ascd.org/publications/educational-leadership/nov93/vol51/num03/The-Return-of-Character-Education.aspx

24. Berkowitz, M. W. (2002). The science of character education. In W. Damon (Ed.), *Bringing in a new era in character education* (pp. 43–63, 55–56). Hoover Institution Press.

25. Berkowitz, "The science of character education."

26. Jeynes, W. H. (2019). A meta-analysis on the relationship between character education and student achievement and behavioral outcomes. *Education and Urban Society, 51*(1), 31, 33–71. https://doi.org/10.1177/0013124517747681 (p. 31)

27. Kuh, G. D., & Umbach, P. D. (2004). College and character: Insights from the National Survey of Student Engagement. *New Directions for Institutional Research, 2004*(122), 37–54.

28. Astin, H. S., & Antonio, A. L. (2004). The impact of college on character development. *New Directions for Institutional Research, 2004*(122), 55–64.

29. Berkowitz, M. W. (2002). The science of character education. In W. Damon (Ed.), *Bringing in a new era in character education* (pp. 43–63). Hoover Institution Press.

30. Berkowitz, "The science of character education."

31. Frost, N. (2021, April 24). New Zealand hosts 50000 fans in its largest concert since the pandemic began. *New York Times*. https://www.nytimes.com/2021/04/24/world/new-zealand-concert-covid.html

32. Ranson, B. (2020, June 29). Propositional density: More than just for design. Pt 1. https://www.linkedin.com/pulse/propositional-density-more-than-just-design-pt-1-bigi-ransom/

33. Knell, D. (2019, January 18). Propositional density: Meaning, motif, and the art of inception. https://bydavidknell.medium.com/propositional-density-meaning-motif-and-the-art-of-inception-a4b9c432b012

34. Stefaner, M. (2010, June 14). Propositional density in visualization. http://well-formed-data.net/archives/495/propositional-density-in-visualization

35. Center for Character and Leadership Development. (2011). *Developing leaders of character at the United States Air Force Academy—A conceptual framework*. Author.

36. Center for Character and Leadership Development. *Developing leaders of character*.

37. Schwartz, A. (2015, Summer). Inspiring and equipping students to be ethical leaders. *New Directions for Student Leadership, 2015*(146), 5–16.

38. Jones, T. (1991). Ethical decision-making by individuals in organizations: An issue contingent model. *Academy of Management Review, 16*(2), 366–395.

39. Bandura, A. (1999). Moral disengagement in the perpetration of inhumanities. *Personality and Social Psychology Review, 3*(3), 193–209.

40. Detert, J. R., Trevino, L. K., & Sweitzer, V. L. (2008). Moral disengagement in ethical decision making: A study of antecedents and outcomes. *Journal of Applied Psychology, 93*(2), 374–391, 374.

41. Hannah, S., Avolio, B., & May, D. (2011). Moral maturation and moral conation: A capacity approach to explaining moral thought and action. *Academy of Management Review, 36*(4), 663–685.

42. Schwartz, A. (2015, Summer). Inspiring and equipping students to be ethical leaders. *New Directions for Student Leadership, 2015*(146), 5–16.

43. Lipman-Blumen, J. (2005). The allure of toxic leaders: Why followers rarely escape their clutches. *Ivey Business Journal* (para. 9). http://iveybusinessjournal.com/publication/the-allure-of-toxic-leaders-why-followers-rarely-escape-their-clutches/

44. Lipman-Blumen. "The allure of toxic leaders."

45. Kellerman, B., & Pittinsky, T. L. (2020). *Leaders who lust: Power, money, sex, success, legitimacy, legacy.* Cambridge University Press.

46. Kellerman, B. (2008). *Followership: How followers are creating change and changing leaders.* Harvard Business School Press.

47. Hurwitz, M., & Hurwitz, S. (2015). *Leadership is half the story: A fresh look at followership, leadership, and collaboration.* University of Toronto Press.

48. Kelley, R. E. (1985). *The gold collar worker: Harnessing the brainpower of the new workforce.* Addison-Wesley.

49. Hollander, E. P. (2012). *Inclusive leadership: The essential leader-follower relationship* (p. 130). Routledge.

50. Chaleff, I. (2009). *The courageous follower: Standing up to & for our leaders* (3rd ed.). Berrett-Koehler.

51. Koonce, R. (2014). Introductory remarks. Proceedings of the 2014 International Followership Symposium, 16th Annual ILA Global Conference. *Journal of Leadership Education* (pp. 5–8). https://doi.org/10.12806/V13/I4/C2

52. Follett, M. P. (2013a). XII. Leader and expert. In H. C. Metcalf & L. Urwick (Eds.), *Dynamic administration: The collected papers of Mary Parker Follett* (pp. 247–269; 262). Martino Publishing.

53. Carsten, M. K., Harms, P., & Uhl-Bien, M. (2014). Exploring historical perspectives of followership: The need for an expanded view of followers and the follower role. In L. M. Lapierre & M. K. Carsten (Eds.), *Followership: What is it and why do people follow?* (pp. 3–25). Emerald. (p. 4).

54. I. Challeff, personal communication, January 19, 2016.

55. Carsten, M. K., Uhl-Bien, M., West, B. J., Patera, J. L., &

McGregor, R. (2010). Exploring social constructions of followership: A qualitative study. *The Leadership Quarterly, 21*(3), 543–562, 551.

56. Carsten, M. K., & Uhl-Bien, M. (2013). Ethical followership: An examination of followership beliefs and crimes of obedience. *Journal of Leadership & Organizational Studies, 20*(1), 49–61.

57. Kelley, R. E. (1988). In praise of followers. *Harvard Business Review, 66,* 142–148.

58. Chaleff, I. (2009). *The courageous follower: Standing up to & for our leaders.* Berrett-Koehler.

59. Graber, S. (2015, December 4). The two sides of employee engagement. *Harvard Business Review.* https://hbr.org/2015/12/the-two-sides-of-employee-engagement

60. Chaleff, I. (2021). Followership style. https://irachaleff.com/books/cf-the-book/

61. Kellerman, B. (2019). The future of followership. *Strategy & Leadership, 47*(5), 42–46. https://doi.org/10.1108/SL-07-2019-0109

62. Fabiano, S. (2021). *Lead and follow: The dance of inspired teamwork* (p. 19). Koehler Books.

63. Harro, B. (2000b). The cycle of liberation. In M. Adams, W. J., Blumenfeld, R. Castañeda, H. W. Hackman, M. L. Peters, & X. Zuniga (Eds.), *Readings for diversity and social justice: An anthology on racism, sexism, anti-Semitism, heterosexism, classism, and ableism* (pp. 463–469). Routledge.

64. Schwartz, A. (2015, Summer). Editor's notes. *New Directions for Student Leadership, 2015*(146), 5–16.

65. Gentile, M. C. (2017). Giving voice to values: A pedagogy for behavioral ethics. *Journal of Management Education, 41*(4), 469–479.

66. Gentile, M. C. (2017). Giving voice to values: A global partnership with UNGC PRME to transform management education. *The*

International Journal of Management Education, 15(2), 121–125.

67. Hannah, S., Avolio, B. J., & May, D. R. (2011). Moral maturation and moral conation: A capacity approach to explaining moral thought and action. *Academy of Management Review, 36*(4), 663–685.

68. Allen, S. J. (Host). (2021, August 19). Ethics is a team sport (No. 83). [audio podcast episode]. In *Phronesis: Practical wisdom for leaders.* https://practicalwisdom.buzzsprout.com/979897/9054989-dr-sean-hannah-ethics-is-a-team-sport

69. Lau, C. (2010). A step forward: Ethics education matters! *Journal of Business Ethics, 92*(4), 565–584.

70. Johnson, C. E. (2013). *Meeting the ethical challenges of leadership: Casting light or shadow.* SAGE.

71. Nash, L. (1981). Ethics without the sermon. *Harvard Business Review, 59,* 79–90.

72. Greenleaf, R. (2002). The servant as leader. In D. Kim (Ed.), *Foresight as the central ethic of leadership* (p. 1). The Greenleaf Center for Servant Leadership.

73. Hannah, S., Avolio, B. J., & May, D. R. (2011). Moral maturation and moral conation: A capacity approach to explaining moral thought and action. *Academy of Management Review, 36*(4), 663–685.

74. Allen, S. J. (Host). (2021, August 19). Dr. Craig Johnson - Casting Shadow or Light? (No. 12). [audio podcast episode]. In *Phronesis: Practical wisdom for leaders.* https://practicalwisdom.buzzsprout.com/979897/4550612-dr-craig-johnson-casting-shadow-or-light

CHAPTER 6

1. Nicholas, L. (2021, March 3). Meet the only black female CEO of a fortune 500 company. *Reader's*

Digest. https://www.rd.com/article/rosalind-brewer/

2. Ohnesorge, L. (2016). Report: IBM to sell significant stake in Lenovo. *Triangle Business Journal.* http://www.bizjournals.com/triangle/blog/techflash/2016/03/report-ibm-to-sell-significant-stake-in-lenovo.html

3. Krishna, A. (n.d.). https://www.ibm.com/about/arvind

4. Addady, M. (2016). Patagonia's donating all $10 million of its Black Friday sales to charity. *Fortune.* http://fortune.com/2016/11/29/black-friday-2016-patagonia/

5. Farra, E. (2021, November 9). Patagonia has a new mission to "Save Our Home Planet"—One of its first employees explains how they'll get it done. *Yahoo News.* https://www.yahoo.com/lifestyle/patagonia-mission-save-home-planet-171408290.html

6. Mumford, M. D., Zaccaro, S. J., Harding, F. D., Jacobs, T. O., & Fleishman, E. A. (2000). Leadership skills for a changing world: Solving complex social problems. *Leadership Quarterly, 11*(1), 11–35.

7. Blesch, C. (n.d.). Biomedical engineering student leads team to build a prosthesis for little girl's hand. *Rutgers School of Engineering.* http://soe.rutgers.edu/story/biomedical-engineering-student-leads-team-build-prosthesis-little-girl%E2%80%99s-hand (para. 2).

8. Marks, G. (2020, May 26). Why did this 17-year-old turn down $8 million for his coronavirus-tracking website? *Entrepreuner.com.* https://www.entrepreneur.com/article/350882

9. iGem. (n.d.). Welcome to iGem. *Internationally Genetically Engineered Machine Competition.* http://igem.org/Main_Page, para. 1.

10. Bender, J. (2015). How college students are advancing the fight against cancer. *From The Grapevine.* http://www.fromthegrapevine.com/innovation/how-college-st udents-are-advancing-fight-against-cancer#!

11. Bender, J. (2015), para. 3.

12. Lee, Y. N. (2021, May 20). New Zealand's economic recovery from Covid is 'a lot better than expected' says deputy prime minister. *CNBC.* https://www.cnbc.com/2021/05/20/new-zealand-budget-2021-economic-growth-covid-recovery-.html

13. Beaulne-Stuebing, L. (2021, June 10). UBC national forum aims to develop 'bold and concrete action' to address anti-Asian racism. *University Affairs.* https://www.universityaffairs.ca/news/news-article/ubc-national-forum-aims-to-develop-bold-and-concrete-action-to-address-anti-asian-racism/

14. Nutt, P. C. (2002). Selecting decision rules for crucial choices: An investigation of the Thompson framework. *The Journal of Applied Behavioral Science, 38*(1), 99–131.

15. Wansink, B., & Sobal, J. (2007). Mindless eating: The 200 daily food decisions we overlook. *Environment and Behavior, 39*(1), 106–123.

16. Singh, K. (2010). *Organizational behaviour: Text and cases.* Dorling Kindersley. Adapted from Maier, N. R. (1967). Assets and liabilities in group problem solving: The need for an integrative function. *Psychological Review, 74*(4), 239–249.

17. Center for Character and Leadership Development. (2011). *Developing leaders of character at the United States Air Force Academy—A conceptual framework.* Author; Simon, H. A. (1987). Making management decisions: The role of intuition and emotion. *The Academy of Management Executive (1987–1989), 1,* 57–64.

18. Miller, S. J., Hickson, D. J., & Wilson, D. C. (1999). Decision-making in organizations. In S. R. Clegg, C. Hardy, & W. R. Nord (Eds.), *Managing organizations: Current issue* (pp. 43–62). SAGE.

19. Simon, H. A. (1987). Making management decisions: The role of intuition and emotion. *The Academy of Management Executive (1987–1989), 1,* 57–64.

20. Hammond, J., Keeney, R., & Raiffa, H. (2002). *Smart choices: A practical guide to making better decisions.* Broadway Press.

21. Djulbegovic, B., Elqayam, S., & Dale, W. (2018). Rational decision making in medicine: Implications for overuse and underuse. *Journal of Evaluation in Clinical Practice, 24*(3), 655–665.

22. Doyle, J. (1999). Rational decision-making. In R. A. Wilson & F. C. Kiel (Eds.), *The MIT encyclopedia of the cognitive sciences* (pp. 701–703). The MIT Press; Simon, H. A. (1979). Rational decision-making in business organizations. *The American Economic Review, 69*(4), 493–513.

23. Parker, A. M., De Bruin, W. B., & Fischhoff, B. (2007). Maximizers versus satisficers: Decision-making styles, competence, and outcomes. *Judgment and Decision-Making, 2*(6), 342; Simon, H. A. (1959). Theories of decision-making in economics and behavioral science. *The American Economic Review, 49*(3), 253–283.

24. Dane, E., & Pratt, M. G. (2007). Exploring intuition and its role in managerial decision-making. *Academy of Management Review, 32*(1), 33–54. (p. 40).

25. Mui, C. (2011). Five dangerous lessons to learn from Steve Jobs. *Forbes.* http://www.forbes.com/sites/chunkamui/2011/10/17/five-dangerous-lessons-to-learn-from-steve-jobs/#1821263860da

26. Cohu, J. (2021). Pandemic demonstrates the necessity of intuitive decision-making skills. *Graziadio Business Review, 24*(2). https://gbr.pepperdine.edu/2021/07/intuitive-decision-making-skills/

27. Mintzberg, H., & Westley, F. (2001). Decision-making: It's not what you think. *MIT Sloan Management Review, 42*(3), 89.

28. Pink, D. (n.d.). Pinkcast 1.1: One question to help you make better decisions. https://www.danpink.com/pinkcast/episode-1/

29. Heifetz, R. A., & Linsky, M. (2002). *Leadership on the line: Staying alive through the dangers of leading.* Harvard Business School Press.

30. Trefis Team. (2014). How the fast casual segment is gaining market share in the restaurant industry. *Forbes.* http://www.forbes.com/sites/greatspeculations/2014/06/23/how-the-fast-casual-segment-is-gaining-market-share-in-the-restaurant-industry/#23f527a1d48f

31. Metcalf, H. C., & Urwick, L. (2004). *Dynamic administration: The collected papers of Mary Parker Follett.* Routledge.

32. Smith, W. K., & Lewis, M. (2022). *Both and thinking: Embracing creative tensions to solve your toughest problems.* Harvard Business School Press.

33. Schad, J., Lewis, M., Raisch, S., & Smith, W. (2016). Paradox research in management science: Looking back to move forward. *Academy of Management Annals, 10*(1), 5–64.

34. Miron-Spektor, E., Ingram, A. S., Keller, J., Smith, W. K., & Lewis, M. W. (2018). Microfoundations of organizational paradox: The Problem is how we think about the problem. *Academy of Management Journal, 61*(1), 26–45.

35. Andriopoulos, C., & Lewis, M. W. (2009). Exploitation-Exploration tensions and organizational ambidexterity: Managing paradoxes of innovation. *Organization Science, 20*(4), 696–717; Schad, J., Lewis, M., Raisch, S., & Smith, W. (2016). Paradox research in management science: Looking back to move forward. *Academy of Management Annals, 10*(1), 5–64; Smith, W. (2014). Dynamic decision making: A model of senior leaders managing strategic paradoxes. *Academy of Management Journal, 57*(6), 1592–1623.

36. See Brene Brown Podcast; https://brenebrown.com/podcast/brene-with-president-barack-obama-on-leadership-family-and-service/

37. See John McCain's *Final Letter to America*; Pascal (2018).

38. Hick's Law (Hick-Hyman Law). (n.d.). https://www.usability.gov/what-and-why/glossary/hicks-law-hick-hyman-law.html

39. Erffmeyer, E. S. (1983). *The Vroom-Yetton model of decision making: An empirical evaluation in applied settings.* Doctoral dissertation, Louisiana State University and Agricultural & Mechanical College.

40. Eisenhardt, K., & Zbaracki, M. (1992). Strategic decision-making. *Strategic Management Journal, 13,* 17–37; Mintzberg, H., Raisinghani, D., & Theoret, A. (1976). The structure of unstructured decisions. *Administrative Science Quarterly, 21,* 246–275; Simon, H. A. (1965). *The shape of automation.* Harper and Row.

41. Hammond, J., Keeney, R., & Raiffa, H. (2002). *Smart choices: A practical guide to making better decisions.* Broadway Press.

42. Beyth-Marom, R., Fischhoff, B., Quadrel, M. J., & Furby, L. (1991). Teaching adolescents decision making. In J. Baron & R. Brown (Eds.), *Teaching decision making to adolescents* (pp. 19–60). Erlbaum.

43. Guo, K. L. (2008). DECIDE: A decision-making model for more effective decision-making by health care managers. *The Health Care Manager, 27*(2), 118–127.

44. Kalbar, P. P., Karmakar, S., & Asolekar, S. R. (2012). Selection of an appropriate wastewater treatment technology: A scenario-based multiple-attribute decision-making approach. *Journal of Environmental Management, 113,* 158–169.

45. Saaty, T. L. (2008). Relative measurement and its generalization in decision-making: Why pairwise comparisons are central in mathematics for the measurement of intangible factors—The analytic hierarchy/network process. *RACSAM-Revista de la Real Academia de Ciencias Exactas, Fisicas y Naturales. Serie A: Matematicas, 102*(2), 251–318.

46. Henderson, D. R. (2008). *The concise encyclopedia of economics.* Liberty Fund.

47. Sinden, A. (2015). Formality and informality in cost-benefit analysis. *Utah Law Review, 2015*(1), 93.

48. Daniel, K. (2013). *Thinking, fast and slow.* Farrar, Straus and Giroux.

49. Kahneman, D., Sibony, O., & Sunstein, C. R. (2021). *Noise: A flaw in human judgment.* Little, Brown and Company.

50. Nickerson, R. S. (1998). Confirmation bias: A ubiquitous phenomenon in many guises. *Review of General Psychology, 2*(2), 175.

51. Cinelli, M., Morales, G. D. F., Galeazzi, A., Quattrociocchi, W., & Starnini, M. (2021). The echo chamber effect on social media. *Proceedings of the National Academy of Sciences, 118*(9), e2023301118.

52. Moravec, P., Minas, R., & Dennis, A. R. (2018). Fake news on social media: People believe what they want to believe when it makes no sense at all. *Kelley School of Business Research Paper, 18–87,* p. 36.

53. Snowden, D. J., & Boone, M. E. (2007). A leader's framework for decision-making. *Harvard Business Review, 85*(11), 68.

54. Esser, J. K. (1998). Alive and well after 25 years: A review of groupthink research. *Organizational Behavior and Human Decision Processes, 73*(2), 116–141. (p. 123).

55. McCauley, C. (1989). The nature of social influence in groupthink: Compliance and internalization. *Journal of Personality and Social Psychology*, *57*(2), 250–260.

56. Forsyth, D. R. (2020). Group-level resistance to health mandates during the COVID-19 pandemic: A groupthink approach. *Group Dynamics: Theory, Research, and Practice*, *24*(3), 139–152.

57. LeBoeuf, R. A., & Shafir, E. (2003). Deep thoughts and shallow frames: On the susceptibility to framing effects. *Journal of Behavioral Decision-Making*, *16*(2), 77–92.

58. Bolsen, T., Palm, R., & Kingsland, J. T. (2020). Framing the origins of COVID-19. *Science Communication*, *42*(5), 562–585.

59. Dunning, D., Griffin, D. W., Milojkovic, J. D., & Ross, L. (1990). The overconfidence effect in social prediction. *Journal of Personality and Social Psychology*, *58*(4), 568–581.

60. Herlina, H., Hadianto, B., Winarto, J., & Suwarno, N. A. N. (2020). The herding and overconfidence effect on the decision of individuals to invest stocks. *Journal of Economics and Business*, *3*(4), 12.

61. Guan, J., Lam, B. M., Lam, C. C., & Liu, M. (2021). CEO overconfidence and the level of short-selling activity. *Review of Quantitative Finance and Accounting*, *58*, 685–708, 1–24.

62. Parkinson, C. N. (1955). *Parkinson's law.* http://www.berglas.org/Articles/parkinsons_law.pdf

63. Newman, M. (2005). Congress opens hearings on steroid use in baseball. *The New York Times.* http://www.nytimes.com/learning/teachers/featured_articles/20050318friday.html

64. Alloy, L. B., & Abramson, L. Y. (1982). Learned helplessness, depression, and the illusion of control. *Journal of Personality and Social Psychology*, *42*(6), 1114–1116.

65. Langer, E. J. (1975). The illusion of control. *Journal of Personality and Social Psychology*, *32*(2), 311–328.

66. Meissner, P., & Wulf, T. (2017). The effect of cognitive diversity on the illusion of control bias in strategic decisions: An experimental investigation. *European Management Journal*, *35*(4), 430–439.

67. Kuhberger, A. (1998). A meta-analysis. *Organizational Behavior and Human Decision Processes*, *75*(1), 23–55.

68. Wu, Y., & Crocco, O. (2019). Critical reflection in leadership development. *Industrial and Commercial Training*, *51*(7/8), 409–420.

69. Loewenstein, G., & Lerner, J. S. (2003). The role of affect in decision-making. In R. Davidson, H. Goldsmith, & K. Scherer (Eds.), *Handbook of affective science*, (pp. 619–642). Oxford University Press; Simon, H. A. (1987). Making management decisions: The role of intuition and emotion. *The Academy of Management Executive (1987–1989)*, *1*, 57–64.

70. Heifetz, R. A., & Linsky, M. (2002). Leadership on the line. *Harvard Business Review*, p. 27.

71. Goleman, D. (2001). Emotional intelligence: Issues in paradigm building. In C. Cherniss & D. Goleman (Eds.), *The emotionally intelligent workplace: How to select for, measure, and improve emotional intelligence in individuals, groups, and organizations* (pp. 13–26). Jossey-Bass.

72. Van Boven, L., Loewenstein, G., Dunning, D., & Nordgren, L. F. (2013). Changing places: A dual judgment model of empathy gaps in emotional perspective taking. *Advances in Experimental Social Psychology*, *47*, 117–171. (p. 118).

73. Eisenhardt, K., & Zbaracki, M. (1992, Winter). Strategic decision-making. *Strategic Management Journal*, *13*, 17–37.

74. Klayman, J. (1995). Varieties of confirmation bias. *The Psychology of Learning and Motivation*, *32*, 385–418.

75. Sude, D. J., Pearson, G. D. H., & Knobloch-Westerwick, S. (2021). Self-expression is just a click away: Source interactivity impacts on confirmation bias and political attitudes. *Computers in Human Behavior*, *114*(2021), 1–11.

76. Jenkins, B. D., Le Grand, A. M., Neuschatz, J. S., Golding, J. M., Wetmore, S. A., & Price, J. L. (2021). Testing the forensic confirmation bias: How jailhouse informants violate evidentiary independence. *Journal of Police and Criminal Psychology*, *2021*, 1–13.

77. Rollwage, M., & Fleming, S. M. (2021). Confirmation bias is adaptive when coupled with efficient metacognition. *Philosophical Transactions of the Royal Society B*, *376*(1822), 1–8.

78. Folkes, V. S. (1998). The availability heuristic and perceived risk. *Journal of Consumer Research*, *15*, 13–23.

CHAPTER 7

1. Chaturvedi, S., Rizvi, I. A., & Pasipanodya, E. T. (2019). How can leaders make their followers to commit to the organization? The importance of influence tactics. *Global Business Review*, *20*(6), 1462–1474.

2. Chaney, M. (2015). Hazing on school campuses: What parents and students need to know. The Clay Center for Young Healthy Minds. http://www.mghclaycenter.org/parenting-concerns/young-adults/hazing-school-campuses-parents-students-need-know/

3. Allan, E. J. (2009). *Hazing in view: College students at risk: Initial findings from the National Study of Student Hazing.* Diane Publishing.

4. Chaney, Hazing on school campuses, para. 1.

5. About Us. Who we are. www.hazin gprevention.org

6. https://hazingprevention.org/

7. Harter, N. (2018, August 26). Personal correspondence.

8. Dugan, J. P. (2017). *Leadership theory: Cultivating critical perspectives*. Jossey-Bass.

9. House, R. J. (1996). Path-goal theory of leadership: Lessons, legacy, and a reformulated theory. *The Leadership Quarterly*, 7(3), 323–352.

10. Olowoselu, A., bin Mohamad, M., & Aboudahr, S. M. F. M. (2019). Path-goal theory and the application in educational management and leadership. *Education Quarterly Reviews*, 2(2), 448–455.

11. Northouse, P. G. (2021). *Leadership: Theory and practice* (9th ed.). SAGE.

12. Blanchard, K., Zigarmi, P., & Zigmari, D. (1985). *Leadership and the one minute manager*. Morrow.

13. Bosse, T., Duell, R., Memon, Z. A., Treur, J., & van der Wal, C. N. (2017). Computational model-based design of leadership support based on situational leadership theory. *Simulation*, 93(7), 605–617.

14. Higgins, C. A., Judge, T. A., & Ferris, G. R. (2003). Influence tactics and work outcomes: A meta-analysis. *Journal of Organizational Behavior*, 24(1), 89–106.

15. Reina, C. S., Rogers, K. M., Peterson, S. J., Byron, K., & Hom, P. W. (2018). Quitting the boss? The role of manager influence tactics and employee emotional engagement in voluntary turnover. *Journal of Leadership & Organizational Studies*, 25(1), 5–18.

16. Tufte, E. R., Goeler, N. H., & Benson, R. (1990). *Envisioning information* (Vol. 2). Graphics Press.

17. Heifetz, R. A. (2010). Adaptive work. *The Journal of Kansas Civic Leadership Development*, 2(1), 72–77. (p. 72).

18. Ford, J. (2013). Are you being influenced or manipulated? *Psychology Today*. https://www.psych ologytoday.com/blog/focus-forgi veness/201309/are-you-being-inf luenced-or-manipulated

19. Holroyd, J., Scaife, R., & Stafford, T. (2017). Responsibility for implicit bias. *Philosophy Compass*, 12(3), 1–13.

20. Project Implicit. (2011). *About us*. h ttps://implicit.harvard.edu/implic it/aboutus.html

21. Tenney, L. (2017). *Being an active bystander: Strategies for challenging the emergence of bias*. http://ki rwaninstitute.osu.edu/wp-conten t/uploads/2018/07/Being-an-Acti ve-Bystander-2017.pdf

22. Tost, L. P., Gino, F., & Larrick, R. P. (2013). When power makes others speechless: The negative impact of leader power on team performance. *Academy of Management Journal*, 56(5), 1465–1486.

23. Harford, T. (2011). Tim Harford: Trial, error and the God complex [video file]. TED. http://www.ted.c om/talks/tim_harford

24. Kotter, J. P., & Schlesinger, L. A. (1979, January 1). Choosing strategies for change. *Harvard Business Review*, 57, 106–114.

25. Kolb, D. (2021). Adaptive leadership: The case of Jacinda Ardern and New Zealand. *Academia Letters*, 2.

26. Allen, K. E., & Mease, W. P. (2001). *Optimizing energy: The theory of action energy*. https:// kathleenallen.net/wp-content/ uploads/2017/12/ILA-Energy-Handout.pdf

27. Soegaard, M. (2016). *Horror vacui: The fear of emptiness*. The Interaction Design Foundation. https:// www.interaction-design.org/ literature/article/horror-vacui-the-fear-of-emptiness.

28. Soegaard, M. (2016). Horror vacui: The fear of emptiness. *The Interaction Design Foundation*. https:// www.interaction-design.org/liter

ature/article/horror-vacui-the-fe ar-of-emptiness

29. https://www.youtube.com/watch ?v = e-ORhEE9VVg

30. Kozlowski, D., Hutchinson, M., Hurley, J., Rowley, J., & Sutherland, J. (2017). The role of emotion in clinical decision making: an integrative literature review. *BMC Medical Education*, 17(1), 1–13.

31. Cable, D. M., & Judge, T. A. (2003). Managers' upward influence tactic strategies: The role of manager personality and supervisor leadership style. *Journal of Organizational Behavior*, 24(2), 197–214.

32. Simpson, J. A., Farrell, A. K., Oriña, M. M., & Rothman, A. J. (2015). Power and social influence in relationships. In *APA handbook of personality and social psychology, Volume 3: Interpersonal relations*. (pp. 393–420); American Psychological Association. Simpson, J. A., Farrell, A. K., & Rothman, A. J. (2019). The dyadic power-social influence model extensions and future directions. In C. R. Agnew & J. J. Harman (Eds.), *Power in close relationships* (p. 86). Cambridge University Press.

33. Yukl, G., & Tracey, J. B. (1992). Consequences of influence tactics used with subordinates, peers, and the boss. *Journal of Applied Psychology*, 77(4), 525.

34. Closed Loop Partners. (2022). *Beyond the bag*. https://www.close dlooppartners.com/beyond-the -bag/

35. Yukl, G., Kennedy, J., Srinivas, E. S., Cheosakul, A., Peng, T. K., & Tata, J. (2001, August). Cross-cultural comparison of influence behaviour: A preliminary report. *Academy of Management Proceedings*, 2001(1), D1–D6.

36. Ohio Vax-A-Million Details Announced. (2021, May 17). https: //odh.ohio.gov/wps/portal/gov/od h/media-center/odh-news-releas es/odh-news-release-05-17-21

37. Chaturvedi, S., Rizvi, I. A., & Pasipanodya, E. T. (2019). How can

leaders make their followers to commit to the organization? The importance of influence tactics. *Global Business Review*, *20*(6), 1462–1474.

38. Falbe, C. M., & Yukl, G. (1992). Consequences for managers of using single influence tactics and combinations of tactics. *Academy of Management Journal*, *35*(3), 638–652.

39. Parsons, L. (2021, January 20). *Harvard Gazette*. Harvard alumna Amanda Gorman delivered a soaring inaugural poem. https://news.harvard.edu/gazette/story/2021/01/amanda-gormans-inauguration-poem-the-hill-we-climb/

40. Matsumoto, D., & Hwang, H. C. (2018). Social influence in investigative interviews: The effects of reciprocity. *Applied Cognitive Psychology*, *32*(2), 163–170.

41. Falbe, C. M., & Yukl, G. (1992). Consequences for managers of using single influence tactics and combinations of tactics. *Academy of Management Journal*, *35*(3), 638–652.

42. Goltz, S. M. (2020). On power and freedom: Extending the definition of coercion. *Perspectives on Behavior Science*, *43*(1), 137–156.

43. Yukl, G., & Tracey, J. B. (1992). Consequences of influence tactics used with subordinates, peers, and the boss. *Journal of Applied Psychology*, *77*(4), 525–535.

44. Riggio, R. (2009). Bosses from hell: A typology of bad leaders. *Psychology Today*. https://www.psychologytoday.com/blog/cutting-edge-leadership/200904/bosses-hell-typology-bad-leaders

45. Robertson, I. H. (2018). The winner effect—The neuropsychology of power. In P. Garrard (Ed.), *The leadership hubris epidemic* (pp. 57–66). Palgrave Macmillan.

46. For every child results. UNICEF. https://www.unicef.org/results

47. French, Jr., J. R. P., & Raven, B. (1959). The bases of social power. In D. Cartwright (Ed.), *Studies in social power* (pp. 150–167). Institute for Social Research.

48. Antonakis, J. (2017). Charisma and the "new leadership." In J. Antonakis & D. V. Day (Eds.), *The nature of leadership* (pp. 56–81). SAGE.

49. Mechanic, D. (1962). Sources of power of lower participants in complex organizations. *Administrative Science Quarterly*, *7*(3), 349–364.

50. Bonner, B. L., Soderberg, A. T., Meikle, N. L., & Overbeck, J. R. (2021). The effects of experience, expertise, reward power, and decision power in groups. *Group Dynamics: Theory, Research, and Practice*.

51. Bal, V., Campbell, M., Steed, J., & Meddings, K. (2008). The role of power in effective leadership. *Center for Creative Leadership*. http://insights.ccl.org/wp-content/uploads/2015/04/roleOfPower.pdf

52. Bal, Campbell, Steed, & Meddings, "The role of power in effective leadership."

53. Ibarra, H., & Hunter, M. L. (2007). How leaders create and use networks. https://hbr.org/2007/01/how-leaders-create-and-use-networks

54. Whetten, D. A., & Cameron, K. S. (2015). *Developing management skills* (9th ed.). Prentice Hall/Pearson.

55. French, J. R. P., Jr., & Raven, B. (1959). The bases of social power. In D. Cartwright (Ed.), *Studies in social power* (pp. 150–167). Institute for Social Research.

56. Ryan, R. M., & Deci, E. L. (2000). Intrinsic and extrinsic motivations: Classic definitions and new directions. *Contemporary Educational Psychology*, *25*(1), 54–67. (p. 54).

57. Deci, E. L. (1971). Effects of externally mediated rewards on intrinsic motivation. *Journal of Personality and Social Psychology*, *18*(1), 105.

58. Deci, E. L., Koestner, R., & Ryan, R. M. (1999). A meta-analytic review of experiments examining the effects of extrinsic rewards on intrinsic motivation. *Psychological Bulletin*, *125*(6), 627–628.

59. Cerasoli, C. P., Nicklin, J. M., & Ford, M. T. (2014). Intrinsic motivation and extrinsic incentives jointly predict performance: A 40-year meta-analysis. *Psychological Bulletin*, *140*(4), 1–20.

60. Chamorro-Premuzic, T. (2013, April 10). Does money really affect motivation? A review of the research. *Harvard Business Review Blog Network*. https://hbr.org/2013/04/does-money-really-affect-motiv; Judge, T. A., Piccolo, R. F., Podsakoff, N. P., Shaw, J. C., & Rich, B. L. (2010). The relationship between pay and job satisfaction: A meta-analysis of the literature. *Journal of Vocational Behavior*, *77*(2), 157–167; Katzenbach, J. R., & Khan, Z. (2010). Money is not the best motivator. *Forbes*. http://www.forbes.com/2010/04/06/money-motivation-pay-leadership-managing-employees.html

61. Coffee & Company. (2016, July 18). Starbucks expands health benefits for all eligible U.S. full- and part-time partners. *Starbucks Newsroom*. https://news.starbucks.com/press-releases/starbucks-expands-health-benefits

62. Baumgartner, N. (2020, April 8). Build a culture that aligns with people's values. *Harvard Business Review*. https://hbr.org/2020/04/build-a-culture-that-aligns-with-peoples-values

63. Michaelson, C. (2010). The importance of meaningful work. *MIT Sloan Management Review*. http://sloanreview.mit.edu/article/the-importance-of-meaningful-work/

64. Robbins, M. (2019). Why employees need both recognition and appreciation. *Harvard Business Review*. https://hbr.org/2019/11/why-employees-need-both-recognition-and-appreciation

65. Cacioppe, R. (1999). Using team-individual reward and recognition strategies to drive organizational success. *Leadership & Organization Development Journal, 20*(6), 322–331.

66. Sohail, M., & Malik, S. A. (2016). Impact of leader-follower interactions and employee satisfaction: Mediating effect of employee empowerment. *International Journal of Complexity in Leadership and Management, 3*(1–2), 85–100.

67. Conger, J. A., & Kanungo, R. N. (1988). The empowerment process: Integrating theory and practice. *Academy of Management Review, 13,* 471–482.

68. Gandhi, V., & Robison, J. (2021). The "great resignation" is the "great discontent." *Gallup.* https://www.gallup.com/workplace/351545/great-resignation-really-great-discontent.aspx

69. De Vito, L., Brown, A., Bannister, B., Cianci, M., & Mujtaba, B. G. (2018). Employee motivation based on the hierarchy of needs, expectancy and the two-factor theories applied with higher education employees. *International Journal of Advances in Management, Economics and Entrepreneurship, 3*(1), 20–32.

70. Herway, J. (2018). How to bring out the best in your people and company. *Gallup.* https://www.gallup.com/workplace/232958/bring-best-people-company.aspx

71. McClelland, D. C. (1961). *The achieving society.* Free Press.

72. Seifert, M., Brockner, J., Bianchi, E. C., & Moon, H. (2016). How workplace fairness affects employee commitment. *MIT Sloan Management Review, 57*(2), 15–17.

73. Mortensen, M., & Haas, M. (2021, February 24). Making the hybrid workplace fair. *Harvard Business Review.* https://hbr.org/2021/02/making-the-hybrid-workplace-fair

74. Hogg, M. A. (2001). A social identity theory of leadership. *Personality and Social Psychology Review, 5*(3), 184–200.

75. Hackman, J. R., & Oldham, G. R. (1976). Motivation through the design of work: Test of a theory. *Organizational Behavior and Human Performance, 16*(2), 250–279.

76. Hackman & Oldham, "Motivation through the design."

77. Barney, C. E., & Elias, S. M. (2010). Flex-time as a moderator of the job stress-work motivation relationship: A three nation investigation. *Personnel Review, 39*(4), 487–502.

78. DeSemt, A., Dowling, B., Mysore, M., & Reich A. (2021, July 9). *It's time for leaders to get real about hybrid.* McKinsey & Company. https://www.mckinsey.com/business-functions/people-and-organizational-performance/our-insights/its-time-for-leaders-to-get-real-about-hybrid

79. Smith, J., & Garriety, S. (2020). The art of flexibility: bridging five generations in the workforce. *Strategic HR Review, 19*(3), 107–110.

80. Edmondson, A. C. (2018). *The fearless organization: Creating psychological safety in the workplace for learning, innovation, and growth.* John Wiley & Sons.

81. Kouzes, J. M., & Posner, B. Z. (1987). *The leadership challenge: How to get extraordinary things done in organizations.* Jossey-Bass.

82. Graen, G. B., & Uhl-Bien, M. (1995). Relationship-based approach to leadership: Development of leader-member exchange (LMX) theory of leadership over 25 years: Applying a multi-level multi-domain perspective. *The Leadership Quarterly, 6*(2), 219–247; Uhl-Bien, M., & Maslyn, J. M. (2003, January 1). Reciprocity in manager-subordinate relationships: Components, configurations, and outcomes. *Journal of Management, 29*(4), 511–532.

83. Torka, N., Schyns, B., & Looise, J. K. (2010). Direct participation quality and organisational commitment: The role of leader-member exchange. *Employee Relations, 32*(4), 418–434.

84. Othman, R., Ee, F. F., & Shi, N. L. (2010). Understanding dysfunctional leader-member exchange: Antecedents and outcomes. *Leadership & Organization Development Journal, 31*(4), 337–350.

CHAPTER 8

1. World Economic Forum. (2020, October 20). The future of jobs. https://www.weforum.org/reports/the-future-of-jobs-report-2020

2. https://www.wurman.com/

3. https://www.design.upenn.edu/alumni/events/2015-lisa-roberts-david-seltzer-integrated-product-design-lecture-richard-saul-wurman

4. TED Conferences, LLC. (n.d.). *History of TED.* https://www.ted.com/about/our-organization/history-of-ted

5. https://www.ted.com/about/our-organization/history-of-ted

6. TED Staff. (2018, April 10). TED opens annual conference in Vancouver as media platform sees record global audience growth. *TEDBlog.* https://blog.ted.com/ted-opens-annual-conference-in-vancouver-as-media-platform-sees-record-global-audience-growth/

7. Wurman, R. S. (2009). *33: Understanding change & the change in understanding.* Greenway Communications.

8. Madjar, N., Greenberg, E., & Chen, Z. (2011). Factors for radical creativity, incremental creativity, and routine, noncreative performance. *Journal of Applied Psychology, 96*(4), 730–743.

9. Lee, Chang, J. Y., & Choi, J. N. (2017). Why reject creative ideas? Fear as a driver of implicit bias

against creativity. *Creativity Research Journal, 29*(3), 225–235. https://doi.org/10.1080/10400419.2017.1360061

10. May, M. (2016, April 14). Ideacide: The perils of self-censoring (and how you can stop it). *99u.* http://99u.com/articles/53751/ideacide-the-perils-of-self-censoring-and-how-you-can-stop-it

11. Olien, J. (2013, December 6). Inside the box: People don't actually like creativity. *Slate.* http://www.slate.com/articles/health_and_science/science/2013/12/creativity_is_rejected_teachers_and_bosses_don_t_value_out_of_the_box_thinking.html

12. Michalko, M. (2011). *Creative thinkering: Putting your imagination to work.* New World Library; Michalko, M. (2011, December 11). *The twelve things you are not taught in school about creative thinking.* http://creativethinking.net/the-twelve-things-you-are-not-taught-in-school-about-creative-thinking/#sthash.UJt7sQFv.dpbs

13. Gonzalez, C., Dana, J., Koshino, H., & Just, M. (2005, January 1). The framing effect and risky decisions: Examining cognitive functions with fMRI. *Journal of Economic Psychology, 26*(1), 1–20.

14. DiAngelo, R. (2018). *White fragility: Why it's so hard for white people to talk about racism.* Beacon Press.

15. Brown, B. (2012). *Daring greatly: How the courage to be vulnerable transforms the way we live, love, parent, and lead.* Gotham Books.

16. Holly, L. C., & Steiner, S. (2005). Safe space: Student perspectives on classroom environment. *Journal of Social Work Education, 41*(1), 49–61.

17. Arao, B., & Clemens, K. (2013). From safe spaces to brave spaces: A new way to frame dialogue around diversity and social justice. In L. M. Landreman (Ed.), *The art of effective facilitation: Reflections from social justice educators.* (pp. 135–150). Stylus.

18. Renner, F., Murphy, F. C, Ji, J. L., Manly, T., & Holmes, E. A. (2019). Mental imagery as a "motivational amplifier" to promote activities. *Behaviour Research and Therapy, 114,* 51–59. https://doi.org/10.1016/j.brat.2019.02.002

19. Brown, M. W., & Weisgard, L. (1949). *The important book.* Harper.

20. Drucker, P. F. (1963). *Managing for business effectiveness.* Harvard University.

21. For an overview of research connecting personality characteristics and traits to creativity, read among others: Runco, M. A. (2014). *Creativity: Theories and themes: Research, development, and practice* (2nd ed.). Elsevier Academic Press.

22. Guilford, J. P. (1960). *Alternate uses, Form A.* Sheridan Supply; Barron, F. (1963). *Creativity and psychological health.* Van Nostrand.

23. Loyd, S. (1976). *Sam Loyd's cyclopedia of 5000 puzzles, tricks and conundrums: With answers.* Pinnacle.

24. Vance, M., & Deacon, D. (1995). *Think out of the box.* Career Press.

25. Kelley, T., & Kelley, D. (2013). *Creative confidence: Unleashing the creative potential within us all.* Crown Business.

26. Kelley, T., & Kelley, D. (2012, December). Reclaim your creative confidence. *Harvard Business Review.* https://hbr.org/2012/12/reclaim-your-creative-confidence

27. Beghetto, R. A., Karwowski,. M., & Reiter-Palmon, R. (2021). Intellectual risk taking: A moderating link between creative confidence and creative behavior? *Psychology of Aesthetics, Creativity, and the Arts, 15*(4), 637–644. https://doi.org/10.1037/aca0000323

28. Wallas, G. (1926). *The art of thought.* Harcourt, Brace and Company.

29. Young, J. W. (1986). *A technique for producing ideas.* NTC Business Books.

30. Creating Innovative Thinkers. (n.d.). http://www.creativeeducationfoundation.org/

31. Osborn, A. F. (1952). *Wake up your mind: 101 ways to develop creativeness.* Scribner.

32. von Oech, R. (1983). *A whack on the side of the head: How to unlock your mind for innovation.* Warner Books; von Oech, R. (1986). *A kick in the seat of the pants: Using your explorer, artist, judge, & warrior to be more creative.* Perennial Library.

33. von Oech, R. (1986), p. 16.

34. Moaniba, I. M., Su, H. N., & Lee, P. C. (2018). Knowledge recombination and technological innovation: The important role of cross-disciplinary knowledge. *Innovation: Organization & Management, 20*(4), 326–352. https://www.tandfonline.com/doi/abs/10.1080/14479338.2018.1478735

35. Afeyan, N., & Pisano, G. P. (2021). What evolution can teach us about innovation. *Harvard Business Review.* https://hbr.org/2021/09/what-evolution-can-teach-us-about-innovation

36. Johnson, S. (2010, July). Where good ideas come from. *TED Global 2010.* http://www.ted.com/talks/steven_johnson_where_good_ideas_come_from/transcript?language=en; Johnson, S. (2010). *Where good ideas come from: The natural history of innovation.* Riverhead Books.

37. Osborn, A. F. (1963). *Applied imagination: Principles and procedures of creative problem-solving.* Scribner.

38. Eberle, B. (1996). *Scamper: Games for imagination development.* Prufrock Press.

39. Thanks to Nat Measely and the Fun Dept for this example, which they use to create fun *deliveries.*

40. Stafford, C. O., & Howard, S. G. (Hosts). (2020, January 14).

Creative confidence podcast [Audio podcast episode]. In *Generating Better Ideas: Brendan Boyle*. IDEOU. https://open.spotify.com/episode/6NSt7MJIQqVeCX2vPPMuq0?si=107e340e91aa4696

41. Brown, T. (2008). Tales of creativity and play. *TED*. http://www.ted.com/talks/tim_brown_on_creativity_and_play

42. Ahmed, W. (December 18, 2021). Ismail al-Jazari: the Muslim Inventor who may have inspired Leonardo da Vinci. *Europeana*. https://www.europeana.eu/en/blog/ismail-al-jazari-the-muslim-inventor-who-may-have-inspired-leonardo-da-vinci

43. Lupton, E., & Lipps, A. (Eds.). (2018). *The senses: Design beyond vision*. Chronicle Books.

44. The Biomimicry Institute—Inspiring Sustainable Innovation. (n.d.). https://biomimicry.org/

45. The Biomimicry Institute. (n.d.). *Biomimicry 101, biomimicry examples*. https://biomimicry.org/biomimicry-examples/#.WAqWx4WcHIU

46. Culatta, R. (n.d.). Iterative design. *Instructionaldesign.org*. http://www.instructionaldesign.org/models/iterative_design.html

47. Yu, X., Li, D., Tsai, C.-H., & Wang, C. (2019), The role of psychological capital in employee creativity. *Career Development International*, *24*(5), 420–437. https://doi.org/10.1108/CDI-04-2018-0103

48. von Oech, R. (1986). *A kick in the seat of the pants: Using your explorer, artist, judge, & warrior to be more creative* (p. 143). Perennial Library.

CHAPTER 9

1. Nayal, P., Pandey, N., & Paul, J. (2021). Covid-19 pandemic and consumer-employee-organization wellbeing: A dynamic capability theory approach. *Journal of Consumer Affairs*. Online ahead of print.

2. Keen, P. K., Gilkey, R., & Baker, E. L. (2020). Crisis leadership—from the Haiti earthquake to the COVID pandemic. *Journal of Public Health Management and Practice*, *26*(5), 503–505.

3. Kouzes, J., & Posner, B. (2012). *The leadership challenge* (5th ed.). Jossey-Bass.

4. Boland, Jr., R. J., & Tenkasi, R. V. (1995). Perspective making and perspective taking in communities of knowing. *Organizational Science*, *6*(4), 350–372.

5. Kanter, R. M. (1977). *Men and women of the corporation*. Basic Books.; Kanter, R. M. (1977b). Some effects of proportion on group life: Skewed sex ratios and responses to token women. *American Journal of Sociology*, *82*, 965–990.

6. Holgersson, C., & Romani, L. (2020). Tokenism revisited: When organizational culture challenges masculine norms, the experience of token is transformed. *European Management Review*, *17*(3), 649–661.

7. Adichie, C. N. [TEDGlobal 2009]. (2009, July). The Danger of a Single Story. [Video]. *TED*. https://www.ted.com/talks/chimamanda_ngozi_adichie_the_danger_of_a_single_story?language=en

8. Framework based on Dickmann, M., & Stanford-Blair, N. (2003). *Mindful leadership: A brain-based framework*. Corwin.

9. This activity was brilliantly conceived and executed by Dr. Michael Dickmann, Professor Emeritus at Cardinal Stritch University. Many others in this chapter were inspired by the latter.

10. Specifically, there are 43 quintillion variations of the Rubik's cube—that is 43,252,003,274,489,856,000.

11. Robinson, K. (2006). Do schools kill creativity? http://www.ted.com/talks/ken_robinson_says_schools_kill_creativity/transcript?language=en

12. National Institute of Mental Health. (n.d.). *5 things you should know about stress*. http://www.nimh.nih.gov/health/publications/stress/index.shtml; Sanders, L. (2014). New evidence that chronic stress predisposes brain to mental illness. *Berkeley News*. http://news.berkeley.edu/2014/02/11/chronic-stress-predisposes-brain-to-mental-illness/

13. Arvay, C. G. (2018). *The biophilia effect: A scientific and spiritual exploration of the healing bond between humans and nature*. Sounds True.

14. Zhong, W., Schröder, T., & Bekkering, J. (2021). Biophilic design in architecture and its contributions to health, well-being, and sustainability: A critical review. *Frontiers of Architectural Research*, *11*(1), 114–141.

15. Salingaros, N. A. (2019). The biophilic healing index predicts effects of the built environment on our wellbeing. *Journal of Biourbanism*, *8*(1/2019), 13–34.

16. Hähn, N., Essah, E., & Blanusa, T. (2021). Biophilic design and office planting: a case study of effects on perceived health, well-being and performance metrics in the workplace. *Intelligent Buildings International*, *13*(4), 241–260.

17. Consortium for Research on Emotional Intelligence in Organizations. (n.d.). *Welcome to the Emotional Intelligence Consortium website*. http://eiconsortium.org/; Six Seconds. (n.d.). The case for emotional intelligence. *Six Seconds*. http://www.6seconds.org/case/

18. Aristotle; Nicomachean Ethics; Book II, 1109.a27.

19. Galbraith, J. K. (1971). *A contemporary guide to economics, peace, and laughter*. Houghton Mifflin.

20. For a very comprehensive dive into this work, see: http://www.pz

.harvard.edu/resources/thinking-dispositions

21. Tishman, S., Perkins, D. N., & Jay, E. (1995). *The thinking classroom: Learning and teaching in a culture of thinking*. Allyn & Bacon.

22. The application ideas are only the beginning—see Dickmann, M., & Stanford-Blair, N. (Eds.) (2002). *Connecting leadership to the brain* (pp. 196–211). Corwin for many more specific ideas.

23. Bushe, G. R. (2012). Appreciative inquiry: Theory and critique. In D. Boje, B. Burnes, & J. Hassard (Eds.), *The Routledge companion to organizational change* (pp. 87–103). Routledge.

24. Smith, J. (2013). 20 people skills you need to succeed at work. *Forbes*. http://www.forbes.com/sites/jacquelynsmith/2013/11/15/the-20-people-skills-you-need-to-succeed-at-work/2/#6da3723

25. Hinchcliffe, D. (2013). Today's enterprise collaboration landscape: Cloudy, social, mobile. *ZDNet*. http://www.zdnet.com/article/todays-enterprise-collaboration-landscape-cloudy-social-mobile/

26. Catalyst. (2020, October). *Women in the workforce: United States (Quick Take)*. https://www.catalyst.org/research/women-in-the-workforce-united-states/; U.S. Department of Education, National Center for Education Statistics. (2020). *Degrees conferred by postsecondary institutions, by level of degree and sex of student: 1869-20 through 2029-30. Digest of Education Statistics*. National Center for Education Statistics, Institute of Education Sciences, U.S. Department of Education. https://nces.ed.gov/programs/digest/d20/tables/dt20_318.10.asp

27. Ely, R. J., Ibarra, H., & Kolb, D. M. (2011). Taking gender into account: Theory and design for women's leadership development programs [Special Issue]. *Academy of Management Learning & Education, 10*(3), 474–493.;

Bureau of Labor Statistics. (2021). *Employed persons by detailed occupation, sex, race, and Hispanic or Latino ethnicity*. Current Population Survey. https://www.bls.gov/cps/cpsaat11.htm

28. DeFrank-Cole, L., & Tan, S. J. (2022). *Women and leadership: Journey toward equity*. SAGE.

29. DeFrank-Cole & Tan, *Women and leadership*.

30. Eagly, A. J., Johannesen-Schmidt, M. C., & van Engen, M. L. (2003). Transformational, transactional, and laissez-faire leadership styles: A meta-analysis comparing women and men. *Psychological Bulletin, 129*(4), 569–591.

31. Eagly, A. H., Karau, S. J., & Makhijani, M. G. (1995). Gender and the effectiveness of leaders: A meta-analysis. *Psychological Bulletin, 117*(1), 125–145.; Zenger, J. & Folkman, J. (2019, June). Research: Women score higher than men in most leadership skills. *Harvard Business Review*. https://hbr.org/2019/06/research-women-score-higher-than-men-in-most-leadership-skills

32. Ibarra, H., Ely, R., & Kolb, D. (2013, September). Women rising: The unseen barriers. *Harvard Business Review, 3*, 4–8.

33. Eagly, A. H., & Karau, S. J. (2002). Role congruity theory of prejudice toward female leaders. *Psychological Review, 109*(3), 573–598; Heilman, M. E. (2001). Description and prescription: How gender stereotypes prevent women's ascent up the organizational ladder. *Journal of Social Issues, 57*(4), 657–674.

34. Diehl, A. B., & Dzubinski, L. M. (2016). Making the invisible visible: A cross-sector analysis of gender-based leadership barriers. *Human Resource Development Quarterly, 27*(2), 181–206. https://doi.org/10.1002/hrdq.21248; Offermann, L. R., & Coats, M. R. (2018). Implicit theories of leadership: Stability and change over two decades. *The Leadership Quarterly*,

29(4), 513–522. https://doi.org/10.1016/j.leaqua.2017.12.003

35. U.S. Bureau of Labor Statistics. (2021). America time use survey. https://www.bls.gov/news.release/atus.nr0.htm

36. DeFrank-Cole, L., & Tan, S. J. (2022). *Women and leadership: Journey toward equity*. SAGE; Hoyt, C. L. (2010). Women, men, and leadership: Exploring the gender gap at the top. *Social and Personality Psychology Compass, 4*(7), 484–498.

37. Eagly, A. H., Diekman, A. B., Johnnesen-Schmidt, M. C., & Koenig, A. M. (2004). Gender gaps in sociopolitical attitudes: A social psychological analysis. *Journal of Personality and Social Psychology, 87*(6), 796–816. https://doi.org/ 0.1037/0022-3514.87.6.796; Eagly, A., Kinahan, M., & Bosak, J. (2018). *Where and why do women lead: Leadership for the public good versus private profit*. Presentation at the Society for Industrial and Organizational Psychology Conference, Chicago, IL.

38. Gallup.com. What is employee engagement and how do you improve it? https://www.gallup.com/workplace/285674/improve-employee-engagement-workplace.aspx#ite-357473

39. Kanter, R. (2013). Three things that actually motivate employees. *Harvard Business Review*. https://hbr.org/2013/10/three-things-that-actually-motivate-employees

40. Friedman, R. (October 21, 2021). 5 Things high-performing teams do differently. *Harvard Business Review*. https://hbr.org/2021/10/5-things-high-performing-teams-do-differently

41. Zaleznik, A. (1977). Manager and leaders: are they different? *Harvard Business Review, 55*, 67–78.

42. Rost, J. C. (1998). Leadership and management. In G. R. Hickman (Ed.), *Leading organizations: Perspectives for a new era* (pp. 97–114). SAGE.

43. See as one example, Longmuir, F. (2021). Leading in lockdown: Community, communication and compassion in response to the COVID-19 crisis. *Educational Management Administration & Leadership*.

44. Eldor, L. (2018). Public service sector: The compassionate workplace—The effect of compassion and stress on employee engagement, burnout, and performance. *Journal of Public Administration Research and Theory, 28*(1), 86–103.

45. Kirby, J. N., Tellegen, C. L., & Steindl, S. R. (2017). A meta-analysis of compassion-based interventions: Current state of knowledge and future directions. *Behavior Therapy, 48*, 778–792.

46. Lefebvre, J. I., Montani, F., & Courcy, F. (2020). Self-compassion and resilience at work: A practice-oriented review. *Advances in Developing Human Resources, 22*(4), 437–452.

47. Fernandez, R., & Stern, S. (2020, November 9). Self-Compassion will make you a better leader. *Harvard Business Review*.

48. Houston, E. (2021, August 13). 12 Best Compassion training exercises & activities. *PositivePsychology.com*. https://positivepsychology.com/compassion-training/

49. Collins, J. (2011). *Great by choice*. HarperCollins.

50. Gavin, M. (2019, January 15). 4 Examples of business analytics in action. *Harvard Business School Online*. https://online.hbs.edu/blog/post/business-analytics-examples

51. Innovation and creativity—A culture of its own. https://quickbooks.intuit.com/in/resources/the-next-mile/innovation-and-creativity-a-culture-of-its-own/

52. Grenny, J., Ptterson, K., McMillan, R., Switzler, A., & Gregory, E. (2021). *Crucial conversations: Tools for talking when stakes are high* (3rd ed). McGraw-Hill Education.

53. Conger, J., & Benjamin, B. (1999). *Building leaders: How successful companies develop the next generation*. Jossey-Bass.

54. Senik, S. (2009). How great leaders inspire action. *TED*. https://www.ted.com/talks/simon_sinek_how_great_leaders_inspire_action?language=en

55. Annual Report. (2014). *What is a benefit corporation?* https://bcorporation.net/about-b-corps

56. Krueger, K. (2016, April 12). Freelance workers are the new HR disruptors, Deloitte Human Capital Trends 2016. *LinkedIn*. https://www.linkedin.com/pulse/freelance-workers-new-hr-disruptors-deloitte-human-capital-krueger-6123247708862959616

57. Fuller, J., Raman, M., Bailey, A., & Vaduganathan, N. (2020). Rethinking the on-demand workforce. *Harvard Business Review, 98*(6), 96–103.

58. Senge, P. (2006). *The fifth discipline: The art and practices of a learning organization*. Crown Business Publishers.

59. Buckley, P., Viechnicki, P., & Barua, A. (2016). A new understanding of Millennials: Generational differences reexamined. *Deloitte Insights*. https://www2.deloitte.com/insights/us/en/economy/issues-by-the-numbers/understanding-millennials-generational-differences.html

60. Blanchard, K., Hersey, P., & Johnson, D. (2012). *Management of organizational behavior*. Pearson-Prentice Hall.

61. Blanchard & Johnson, *Management of organizational behavior*.

62. Fernandez, C. F., & Vecchio, R. P. (1997). Situational leadership theory revisited: A test of an across-jobs perspective. *The Leadership Quarterly,8*(1), 67–84.

63. Anderson, M. (2015, October 29). Technology device ownership: 2015. *Pew Research Center*. http://www.pewintern et.org/2015/10/29/technology-device-ownership-2015/

64. Porter, L., & McLaughlin, G. (2006). Leadership and the organizational context: Like the weather? *The Leadership Quarterly, 17*(6), 559–576.

65. McLaughlin, D. (2016). Developing an attractive work cultures is key to performance. *Smart Business Online*. http://www.sbnonline.com/article/126024/

CHAPTER 10

1. Donaldson, K. (2011). 40 under 40: Krista Donaldson. *Silicon Valley Business Journal*. http://www.bizjournals.com/sanjose/news/2011/11/28/40-under-40-krista-donaldson.html

2. Smith, C. (2019). What is change management? The three levels of change. https://change.walkme.com/what-is-change-management-the-three-levels-of-change/

3. Kübler-Ross, E. (1969). *On death and dying*. Touchstone.

4. Danes, S. (1993). Change: Loss, opportunity, and resilience. *University of Minnesota Extension*. https://conservancy.umn.edu/bitstream/handle/11299/118663/1/Danes.pdf

5. Prochaska, J. O., Redding, C. A., & Evers, K. (2002). The transtheoretical model and stages of change. In K. Glanz, B. K. Rimer, & F. M. Lewis (Eds.), *Health behavior and health education: Theory, research, and practice* (3rd ed.). Jossey-Bass.

6. Helsloot, I., Boin, A., Jacobs, B., & Comfort, L. K. (2012). *Megacrises: Understanding the prospects, nature, characteristics, and the effects of cataclysmic events*. Charles C. Thomas; Also see Perrow, C. (1984). *Normal accidents*. Basic Books.

7. Gigliotti, R. A. (2019). *Crisis leadership in higher education: Theory*

and practice. Rutgers University Press.

8. Seeger, M. W., & Ulmer, R. R. (2001). Virtuous responses to organizational crisis: Aaron Feuerstein and Milt Cole. *Journal of Business Ethics, 31*(4), 369–376.

9. Koehn, N. (2018). *Forged in crisis: The making of five courageous leaders*. Scribner.

10. Ulmer, R. R., Sellnow, T. L., & Seeger, M. W. (2018). *Effective crisis communication: Moving from crisis to opportunity* (4th ed.). SAGE.

11. Goodstein, L., & Burke, W. (1991). Creating successful organization change. *Organizational Dynamics, 19*(4), 5–17.

12. Odumeru, J. A., & Ogbonna, I. G. (2013). Transformational vs. transactional leadership theories: Evidence in the literature. *International Review of Management and Business Research, 2*(2), 355–361.

13. Burns, J. M. (1978). *Leadership*. Harper & Row.

14. Maslow, A. H. (1943). A theory of human motivation. *Psychological Review, 50*, 370–396.

15. Bass, B. M., & Avolio, B. J. (1994). *Improving organizational effectiveness through transformational leadership*. SAGE.

16. Bass & Avolio, *Improving organizational effectiveness*.

17. Bass & Avolio, *Improving organizational effectiveness*.

18. ProSci. (2005). *Change management toolkit: Using Prosci's ADKAR model for managing the people side of change*. Author. Also see https://www.prosci.com/adkar

19. Lieberman, M. (2013). *Social: Why our brains are wired to connect*. Crown Publishers.

20. Aiken, C., & Keller, S. (2009, April). The irrational side of change management. *McKinsey Quarterly*. https://www.mckinsey.com/business-functions/organization/our-insights/the-irrational-side-of-change-management

21. http://www.get2test.net/index.html#academic; Courtney, H., Lovallo, D., & Clarke, C. (2013, November). Deciding how to decide. *Harvard Business Review*. https://hbr.org/2013/11/deciding-how-to-decide

22. Beaudan, E. (2006, January/February). Making change last: How to get beyond change fatigue. *IVEY Business Journal*. https://ivey-businessjournal.com/publication/making-change-last-how-to-get-beyond-change-fatigue/

23. Higgs, M., & Rowland, D. (2011). What does it take to implement change successfully? A study of the behaviors of successful change leaders. *Journal of Applied Behavioral Science, 47*(3), 309–335.

24. Kotter, J. (2007, July). Leading change: Why transformational efforts fail. *Harvard Business Review*, pp. 59–67.

25. Fullan, M. (1982). *The meaning of educational change*. Teachers College Press; Fullan, M., & Stiegelbauer, S. (1991). *The new meaning of educational change* (2nd ed.). Teachers College Press; Miles, M. B., & American Educational Research Association. (1986). *Implementing change, toward a data-based theory*. Teach'em.

26. Ewenstein, B., Smith, W., & Sologar, A. (2015, July). Changing change management. *McKinsey & Company*. http://www.mckinsey.com/global-themes/leadership/changing-change-management

27. Gladwell, M. (2000). *The tipping point: How little things can make a big difference*. Little, Brown and Company.

28. Heath, C., & Heath, D. (2007). *Made to stick: Why some ideas survive and others die*. Random House.

29. Kotter, J. P. (1996). *Leading change*. Harvard Business School Press.

30. Sloane, P. (2006). *The leader's guide to lateral thinking skills: Unlocking the creativity and innovation in you and your team*. Kogan Page.

31. Ewenstein, B., Smith, W., & Sologar, A. (2015). Changing change management. *McKinsey & Company*. http://www.mckinsey.com/global-themes/leadership/changing-change-management

32. Kerzner, H. (2009). *Project management: A systems approach to planning, scheduling and controlling*. John Wiley.

33. Kerzner, *Project management*.

34. Carroll, J. M. (1983). Presentation and form in user interface architecture. *Byte, 8*(12), 113–122; Carroll, J. M., & Carrithers, C. (1984). Blocking learner error states in a training-wheels system. *Human Factors, 26*(4), 377–389.

35. Tierney, P. (1988). Work relations as a precursor to a psychological climate for change: The role of work group supervisors and peers. *Journal of Organizational Change Management, 12*(2), 120–133.

36. Lynch, P. (2010). 7 ways to achieve lasting behavioral change. *Business Alignment Strategies, Inc.* http://www.businessalignment-strategies.com/articles/behavioral-change.php

37. Quinn, R., & Cameron, K. (2019). Positive organizational scholarship and agents of change. In A. B. Shani & D. A. Noumair (Eds.), *Research in organizational change and development* (pp. 31–57). https://doi.org/10.1108/S0897-301620190000027004

38. Shenberger, M. A., & Guthrie, K. L. (2021). Leader activists. In K. L. Guthrie & V. S. Chunoo (Eds.), *Shifting the mindset: Socially just leadership education* (pp. 191–203). Information Age Publishing.

39. Anthony, M., Jr. (2018). Intersecting activism and social justice in leadership education. In K. L.

Guthrie & V. S. Chunoo (Eds.), *Changing the narrative: Socially just leadership education* (pp. 41–56). Information Age Publishing.

CHAPTER 11

1. Endangered Alphabets Project. (n.d.). Endangered alphabets website. http://www.endangeredalphabets.com/

2. Endangered Alphabets. (n.d.). *Why we care.* http://www.endangeredalphabets.com/about-us/why-we-care/

3. Hall, E. T. (1981). *Beyond culture.* Anchor Books.

4. Cameron, K. S., & Quinn, R. E. (2011). *Diagnosing and changing organizational culture: Based on the competing values framework* (3rd ed.). Jossey-Bass.

5. Bersin, J. (2015, July/August). The new culture wars: Becoming irresistible through year-round engagement. *HR Professional, 32*(5), 33–34.

6. Bremer, M. (2015, August 28). Edgar Schein on culture. *Leadership & Change.* https://www.leadershipandchangemagazine.com/edgar-schein-on-culture/

7. *Forbes.* (2022, August 10). Meet the world's best management consultant firms, *Forbes* online. https://www.forbes.com/best-employers/#30ad7d61461b

100 Best Companies to Work For | Fortunehttps://fortune.com › best-companies

8. Comparably. (n.d.). Best company culture 2021. Comparably website. https://www.comparably.com/news/best-company-culture-2021

9. Schein, E. H. (2004). Organizational climate and culture. In G. R. Goethals, G. J. Sorenson, & J. M. Burns (Eds.), *Encyclopedia of leadership* (pp. 1113–1117). SAGE.

10. O. C. Tanner. (n.d.). How does leadership influence organizational culture. O. C. Tanner website. https:/ /www.octanner.com/insights/articles/2019/10/23/how_does_leadership_.html

11. Deal, T. E., & Kennedy, A. A. (2000). *Corporate cultures: The rites and rituals of corporate life.* Perseus Books.

12. Schein, E. H. (2010). *Organizational culture and leadership.* John Wiley.

13. Janicijevic, N. (2011). Methodological approaches in the research of organizational culture. *Economic Annals, 56*(189), 69–99.

14. Cronin, T. E., & Genovese, M. A. (2012). *Leadership matters: Unleashing the power of paradox.* Paradigm Publishers.

15. Hofstede, G., Hofstede, G. J., & Minkov, M. (2010). *Cultures and organizations: Software of the mind: Intercultural cooperation and its importance for survival* (p. 6). McGraw-Hill.

16. Hall, E. T. (1989). *Beyond culture.* Random House.

17. Hall, *Beyond culture.*

18. Reiche, S. (2017). Globalization backlash: How to stay grounded. *Harvard Business Review, 35,* 33–38

19. House, R. J., Hanges, P. J., Javidan, M., Dorfman, P. W., & Gupta, V. (2004). *Culture, leadership and organizations: The GLOBE study of 62 societies.* SAGE.

20. House, Hanges, Javidan, Dorfman, & Gupta, *Culture leadership and organizations,* p. 17–18.

21. Solomon, C. M., & Schell, M. S. (2009). *Managing across cultures.* McGraw-Hill.

22. Ulrich, D. (2019). Changing facets of leadership in East Asia: Globalization, innovation and performance in Japan, South Korea and China. *Asia Pacific Business Review, 25*(2), 159–160.

23. McCauley, C. D., & Palus, C. J. (2020). Developing the theory and practice of leadership development: A relational view. *The Leadership Quarterly, 32*(5), 101456

24. U.S. News Staff (2021, May 18). Top 10 countries for technological expertise, ranked by perception. https://www.usnews.com/news/best-countries/slideshows/top-10-countries-for-technological-expertise-ranked-by-perception

25. Meyer, E. (2014). *The culture map: Breaking through the invisible boundaries of global business.* Public Affairs.

26. Watanabe, R., & Watanabe, R. (2022). Kabuki leadership: Cultivating adaptive leadership in a hierarchical collectivist culture in Japan. In M. Raei & H. T. Rasmussen (Eds.) *Adaptive leadership in a global economy.* Routledge.

27. Guo, S. (2018). The review of the implicit followership theories (IFTs). *Psychology, 9*(4), 623–632.

28. Sugimoto, Y. (2021). *An introduction to Japanese society.* Cambridge University Press.

29. Vandenbroucke, G. (2018). Comparing Japan's lost decade with the U.S. great recession. *Economic Synopses,* (3), 1–2.

30. Rowley, C., Oh, I., & Jang, W. (2019). New perspectives on East Asian leadership in the age of globalization: Local grounding and historical comparisons in the Asia Pacific region. *Asia Pacific Business Review, 25*(2), 307–315.

31. George, B. (2003). *Authentic leadership: Rediscovering the secrets to creating lasting value.* Jossey-Bass.

32. Bennis, W., & Goldsmith, J. (2010). *Learning to lead: A workbook on becoming a leader* (4th ed.). Basic Books.

33. Fairholm, M. R. (2013). *Putting your values to work: Becoming the leader others want to follow.* Praeger.

34. Cameron, K. S., & Quinn, R. E. (2011). *Diagnosing and changing organizational culture: Based on the competing values framework.* Jossey-Bass.

35. Cronin, T. E., & Genovese, M. A. (2012). *Leadership matters: Unleashing the power of paradox*. Paradigm Publishers.

34. WarbyParker.

36. Bennis, W. (2009). *On becoming a leader*. Perseus Book Group.

37. Warby Parker. (n.d.). *2021 Impact report*. https://www.warbyparker.com/assets/img/impact-report/Impact-Report-2021-v2.pdf

38. Google. (n.d.). *Ten things we know to be true*. https://www.google.com/about/philosophy.html

39. Thomas, J. (2022, April 19). How the pandemic can change the workplace culture for the better. *Strategy&*. https://www.strategyand.pwc.com/m1/en/articles/2020/how-the-pandemic-can-change-workplace-culture-for-the-better.html

40. Chatman, J., & Gino, F. (2020, August 17). Don't let the Pandemic sink your company culture. *Harvard Business Review*. https://hbr.org/2020/08/dont-let-the-pandemic-sink-your-company-culture

41. Meyer, E. (2014). *The culture map: Decoding how people think, lead, and get things done across cultures*. Public Affairs.

42. Cawsey, T. F., Desza, G., & Ingols, C. (2016). *Organizational change: An action-oriented toolkit*. SAGE.

43. Kotter, J. P. (2012). *Leading change*. Harvard Business Review Press.

44. Bennis, W. (2009). *On becoming a leader*. Perseus Book Group.

45. Stavros, J. M., Godwin, L. N., & Cooperrider, D. L. (2015, January 1). Appreciative inquiry: Organization development and the strengths revolution. In W. Rothwell, J. Stavros, & R. Sullivan (Eds.), *Practicing organization development: Leading transformation and change* (4th ed., pp. 96–116). Wiley; More information on AI can be found at https://www.centerforappreciativeinquiry.net/

and https://appreciativeinquiry.champlain.edu/

46. Whitney, D., & Trosten-Bloom, A. (2010). *The power of appreciative inquiry: A practical guide to positive change*. Berrett-Koehler.

47. Heath, C., & Heath, D. (2007). *Made to stick: Why some ideas survive and others die* (p. 145). Random House.

48. Heath & Heath, *Made to stick*, p. 144.

49. Frog Design. (n.d.). *We are a global design, innovation and strategy firm*. http://www.frog design.com/work/frog-collective-action-toolkit.html

50. Drucker, P. F., & Drucker, P. F. (2010). *The five most important questions self-assessment tool: Participant workbook*. Jossey-Bass.

51. Drucker, P. F. (2016). *The Peter F. Drucker reader: Selected articles from the father of modern management thinking*. Harvard Business School Press.

52. Hurson, T. (2008). *Think better (your company's future depends on it—and so does yours): An innovator's guide to productive thinking*. McGraw-Hill.

53. Kotter, J. P. (2012). *Leading change*. Harvard Business Review Press.

CHAPTER 12

1. Iny, D. (2016, March). 10 habits of successfully remote teams. *Inc.com*. http://www.inc.com/danny-iny/10-habits-of-highly-successful-remote-teams.html

2. Iny, "10 habits."

3. Iny, "10 habits," para. 9.

4. Bennis, W. (1997, December 1). The secrets of great groups. *Leader to Leader, 3*, 29–33. (p. 29)

5. Bennis, "The secrets of great groups," p. 29.

6. Doyle, A. (2022, March 7). Important teamwork skills that employers value. https://www.thebalancecareers.com/list-of-teamwork-skills-2063773

7. Boss, J. (2016, July). Accelerate your understanding of teams with these 3 facts. *Forbes.com*. http://www.forbes.com/sites/jeffboss/2016/07/25/accelerate-your-understanding-of-teams-with-these-3-facts/#4c533f6a44ed

8. Boss, "Accelerate your understanding."

9. Chiu, C-Y., Owens, B.P., & Tesluk, P.E. (2016). Initiating and utilizing shared leadership in teams: The role of leader humility, team proactive personality, and team performance capability. *Journal of Applied Psychology, 101*(12), 1705–1720.

10. Ziegert, J. C., & Fudy, S. B. (2021). Integrating formal and shared leadership: The moderating influence of role ambiguity on innovation. *Journal of Business and Psychology, 36*, 969–984.

11. Ziegert & Fudy, "Integrating formal and shared leadership."

12. Shumpter, J. (2016, March). Team spirit. *The Economist*. http://www.economist.com/news/business-and-finance/21694962-managing-them-hard-businesses-are-embracing-idea-working-teams

13. Pollack, L. (2021). Recalculating: Navigating your career through the changing world of work. *Harper Business*; And summarized findings in the blog post: Silver linings: How great companies were able to thrive during the pandemic. https://lindseypollak.com/great-companies-successful-during-pandemic/

14. Rolls, J. (2021). Self-management: A 21st century panacea? *Organization Development Journal, 39*(3), 67–80.

15. Mutha, P., & Srivastava, M. (2021). Engaging virtual teams: Do leadership & trust matter? *Indian*

Journal of Industrial Relations,
56(4), 732–737.

16. Garro-Abarca, V., Palos-Sanchez, P., & Aguayo-Camacho, M. (2021). Virtual teams in times of pandemic: factors that influence performance. *Frontiers in Psychology, 12*, 232.

17. Mutha, P., & Srivastava, M. (2021). Decoding leadership to leverage employee engagement in virtual teams. *International Journal of Organizational Analysis.*

18. Satell, G., & Windschitl, C. (2021, May 11). High-performing teams start with a culture of shared values. *Harvard Business Review.* hrb.org/2021/05/high-performing-teams-start-with-a-culture-of-shared-values

19. Prossack, A. (2021, January 31). 5 key characteristics of high performing teams. *Forbes.* http://www.forbes.com/sites/ashiraprossack1/2021/0131/5-key-characteristics-of-high-performing-teams/?sh=d42efa0351d0

20. Blinn, C. (1996). Developing high performance teams. *Online, 20*(6), 56.

21. Indeed Editorial Team. (2021, June 24). Indeed.com. 10 Group roles for workplace teams (with examples). https://www.indeed.com/career-advice/career-development/group-roles

22. Hackman, J. R. (2010). Leading teams: Imperatives for leaders. In G. R. Hickman (Ed.), *Leading organizations: Perspectives for a new era* (2nd ed.). SAGE.

23. Larson, C. E., & LaFasto, F. M. J. (1989). *Teamwork: What must go right, what can go wrong.* SAGE.

24. Silva, R. (2016, June 24). Management and good leadership a process to build high-performance teams. *LinkedIn.* https://www.linkedin.com/pulse/management-good-leadership-process-build-teams-ricardo-antonio-silva

25. Crawford, B. (2016, January). Developing an all-star leadership team. *AboutLeaders.* http://aboutleaders.com/developing-star-leadership-team

26. Dahl, D. (2019, November 19). AmericanExpress.com. 9 ways to help your team lead more effectively. https://www.americanexpress.com/en-us/business/trends-and-insights/articles/9-ways-to-help-lead-your-team-more-effectively/

27. Katzenback, J. R., & Smith, D. K. (2003). *The wisdom of teams.* HarperCollins.

28. Indeed Editorial Team. (2021, November 25). 7 characteristics of effective teams (with benefits and tips). https://www.indeed.com/career-advice/career-development/characteristics-of-effective-teams

29. Bassi, L., & McMurrer, D. (2007, January 1). Maximizing your return on people. *Harvard Business Review, 85*(3), 115–123.

30. Willis Towers. (n.d.). *U.S. workers say performance management doesn't make the grade.* https://www.towerswatson.com/en/Insights/Newsletters/Americas/Insider/2004/us-workers-say-performance-management-doesnt-make-the-grade

31. Shumpter, J. (2016, March). Team spirit. *The Economist.* http://www.economist.com/news/business-and-finance/21694962-managing-them-hard-businesses-are-embracing-idea-working-teams

32. Dessel, A., Rogge, M. E., & Garlington, S. B. (2006). Using intergroup dialogue to promote social justice and change. *Social Work, 51*(4), 304–315.

33. Zuniga, X., & Nagda, B. A. (2001). Design considerations in intergroup dialogue. In D. Schoem & S. Hurtado (Eds.), *Intergroup dialogue: Deliberative democracy in school, college, community, and workplace* (pp. 306-327). The University of Michigan Press.

34. Tuckman, B. W. (1965). Developmental sequence in small groups. *Psychological Bulletin, 63*(6), 384–399.

35. Tuckman, B. W., & Jensen, M. A. C. (1977). Stages of small-group development revisited. *Group & Organization Studies, 2*(4), 419–427.

36. Tuckman & Jensen, "Stages of small-group development."

37. Larson, C. E., & LaFasto, F. M. J. (1989). *Teamwork: What must go right, what can go wrong.* SAGE.

38. Bennis, W. (1997). The secrets of great groups. *Leader to Leader, 3,* 29–33.

39. LeadershipNow. (2021, January 4). Teams that work. https://www.leadershipnow.com/leadingblog/2021/01/teams_that_work.html

40. Larson, C. E., & LaFasto, F. M. J. (1989). *Teamwork: What must go right, what can go wrong.* SAGE.

41. Shapiro, M. (2015). *HBR guide to leading teams.* Harvard Business School Publishing Corp.

42. Gallup Strengths Center. (2016). https://www.gallupstrengthscenter.com/

43. Parisi-Carew, E. (2015, September 23). 8 reasons why teams fail. *LeadChange* https://leadchangegroup.com/8-reasons-why-teams-fail/

44. Harvey, J. (1974). The Abilene paradox: The management of agreement. *Organizational Dynamics, 3*(1), 63–80.

45. Janis, I. L. (1971). Groupthink. *Psychology Today, 5*(6), 84–90.

46. Janis, I. L. (1973, September 1). Groupthink and group dynamics: A social psychological analysis of defective policy decisions. *Policy Studies Journal, 2*(1), 19–25.

47. Lencioni, P. (2002). *The five dysfunctions of a team: A leadership fable.* Jossey-Bass.

48. Lencioni, *The five dysfunctions,* p. 189.

49. Forbest Coaches Council. (2016, August 26). 14 warning signs that your team is nearing dysfunction.

https://www.forbes.com/sites/forbescoachescouncil/2016/08/26/14-warning-signs-that-your-team-is-nearing-dysfunction/?sh=41a79b276bd5

50. Edmondson, A. C. (2012). Teamwork on the fly. *Harvard Business Review, 9*(4), 72–80.

51. Boss, J. (2016, July). Accelerate your understanding of teams with these 3 facts. *Forbes.com.* http://www.forbes.com/sites/jeffboss/2016/07/25/accelerate-your-understanding-of-teams-with-these-3-facts/#4c533f6a44ed

52. Nelson, B. (1994). *1001 ways to reward employees.* Workman Publication.

53. This idea was contributed by David Rosch during the 2014 Great Ideas Share and Teach Forum at the International Leadership Association Conference in San Diego, CA.

CHAPTER 13

1. Brown, C. (2014, September 30). *Toyota awards $25,000 to Camden Sophisticated Sisters Drill Team.* BLACK ENTERPRISE website. https://www.blackenterprise.com/toyota-awards-25000-to-sophisticated-sisters-drill-team/; Bush, D. (2013, February 19). *Tawanda Jones: Mother, friend and mentor to youth of Camden, N.J.* https://whyy.org/articles/tawanda-jones-mother-friend-and-mentor-to-youth-of-camden-nj/; Burling, S. (2013, April 13). Trying out for Camden's Sophisticated Sisters. *The Philadelphia Inquirer.* http://www.lexisnexis.com; Griffith, J. (2013, June 29). Changing lives for Camden kids: Drill team provides stability through dance, discipline. NJ.com. http://www.nj.com/news/index.ssf/2013/06/camden_drill_team_sophisticated_sisters.html; WYSK. (2013, May 2). Tawanda Jones is turning the city of Camden around one kid at a time. *Women You Should Know.* http://www.womenyoushouldk

now.net/tawanda-jones-is-turning-the-city-of-camden-around-one-kid-at-a-time/

2. Scudamore, B. (2015, December 5). 3 tips to create a workplace culture that employees love. Forbes.com. https://www.forbes.com/sites/brianscudamore/2015/12/05/creating-culture-its-all-about-people/#1eb65c667ad5

3. Cole, M. B. (2015, April 21). A culture of care, without compromise. *Stanford Social Innovation Review.* https://ssir.org/articles/entry/a_culture_of_care_without_compromise

4. Burns, J. M. (1978). *Leadership.* Harper & Row.

5. Willoughby, A. (2014, March 31). How to create a workplace people love coming to. FastCompany.com. https://www.fastcompany.com/3028368/how-to-create-a-workplace-people-love-coming-to

6. Shamir, B., & Eilam, G. (2005). "What's your story?" A life-stories approach to authentic leadership development. *The Leadership Quarterly, 16*(3), 395–417.

7. Younger, H. (2021, Fall). The art of caring leadership: How leading with heart uplifts teams and organizations. *Leader to Leader, 102,* 8–13

8. Brower, T. (2021, September 19). Empathy is the most important leadership skill according to research. Forbes. https://www.forbes.com/sites/tracybrower/2021/09/19/empathy-is-the-most-important-leadership-skill-according-to-research/?sh=1c2849483dc5

9. Kislik, L. (2002, May 5). How to be a compassionate manager in a heartless organization. *Harvard Business Review.*

10. TED. (2010, June 11). Brene Brown: The power of vulnerability [Video]. YouTube, https://www.youtube.com/watch?v=iCvmsMzlF7o

11. Nair, L. (2021, December 5). The soft stuff is the hard stuff: Leaders must show vulnerability in uncertain times. Fortune.com.

12. Nair, "The soft stuff."

13. Lowinger, J. (2021). The importance of showing vulnerability as a leader. *Mind Strength Method.* https://drjodie.com.au/blog/the-importance-of-showing-vulnerability-as-a-leader#:~:text=Being%20vulnerable%20as%20a%20leader,become%20more%20involved%20and%20invested

14. Indeed. (n.d.). *7 examples of vulnerable leadership.* https://www.google.com/search?q=7+examples+of+vulnerable+leadership&oq=7+examples+of+vulnerable+leadership&aqs=chrome.0.69i59j69i60l3.10417j0j4&sourceid=chrome&ie=UTF-8

15. Indeed, *7 examples.*

16. Elzinga, D. (n.d.). Brene Brown: Vulnerability in leadership. http:cultureamp.com/blog/brene-brown-vulnerability-in-leadership

17. Maslow, A. H. (1943). A theory of human motivation. *Psychology Review, 50*(4), 370–396.

18. Maslow, A. H. (1968). *Toward a psychology of being.* Van Nostrand Reinhold.

19. Maslow, A. H. (1943). A theory of human motivation. *Psychology Review, 50*(4), 370–396.

20. Maslow, A. H. (1969). The farther reaches of human nature. *Journal of Transpersonal Psychology, 1*(1), 1–9.

21. Maslow, "The farther reaches," pp. 1–9.

22. Northouse, P. G. (2016). *Leadership: Theory and practice.* SAGE.

23. Kouzes, J. M., & Posner, B. Z. (1987). *The leadership challenge: How to get extraordinary things done in organizations.* Jossey-Bass.

24. Great Place to Work. (n.d.). Current best workplaces for women list. https://www.greatplacetowork.com/best-workplaces/giving-back/2017

25. Greenleaf, R. K. (1977). *Servant leadership: A journey into the nature of legitimate power and greatness.* Paulist Press.

26. Greenleaf, Servant leadership, pp. 13–14.

27. Spears, L. C. (2010). Character and servant leadership: Ten characteristics of effective caring leaders. *The Journal of Virtues & Leadership, 1*(1), 25–30. https://www.regent.edu/acad/global/publications/jvl/vol1_iss1/Spears_Final.pdf

28. Spears, "Character and servant leadership," p. 27.

29. Focht, A., & Ponton, M. (2015). Identifying primary characteristics of servant leadership: Delphi study. *International Journal of Leadership Studies, 9*(1), 44–61.

30. Barbuto, J. E., & Wheeler, D. W. (2006). Scale development and construct clarification of servant leadership. *Group & Organization Management, 31*(3), 300–326.

31. Ignore Gravity. (2019). *Empathetic organization.* https://www.empathic-organization

32. The World Economic Forum. (2016). 10 Companies that are great at empathy. Retrieved July 10, 2022, from https://www.weforum.org/agenda/2016/11/empathy-index-business/

33. Batsios, N. (2019, January 16). The servant as leader. *Agile Coach.* https//www.medium.com/agileactors/the-servant-as-actor-fdabakd40ae97

34. Chaudhry, A., Xiaoyun, C., Liden, R.c., Point, S., & Vidyarthi, P. R. (2021). A meta-review of servant leadership: Construct, correlates, and the process. *Journal of Comparative International Management, 24*(2), 59–99.

35. Marabella, S. D. (2014). Serving our employees and volunteers: Teaching, mentoring, and spirit-building in the workplace. *Leader to Leader, 74,* 7–12.

36. Walker, C. A. (2015). New managers need a philosophy about how they'll lead. *Harvard Business Review.* https://hbr.org/2015/09/new-managers-need-a-philosophy-about-how-theyll-lead (para. 3)

37. Collins, J. (2001). *Good to great: Why some companies make the leap and others don't.* HarperCollins.

38. Sipe, J. W., & Frick, D. M. (2015). *Seven pillars of servant leadership: Practicing the wisdom of leading by serving.* Paulist Press.

39. Coetzer, M. (2020, July 14) The rise of servant organizations. Forbes. https://www.forbes.com/sites/forbescoachescouncil/2020/07/14/the-rise-of-servant-organizations/?sh=74aa23253b5f

40. Lichtenwalner, B. (2017, April 20). Servant leadership companies [Web post]. http://modernservantleader.com/featured/servant-leadership-companies-list/

41. Rima, S. D. (2013). *Spiritual capital: A moral core for social and economic justice.* Gower.

42. Middlebrooks, A., & Noghiu, A. (2010). Leadership and spiritual capital: Exploring the link between individual service disposition and organizational value. *International Journal of Leadership Studies, 6*(1), 67–85.

43. Bagwell, L. S., & Bernheim, B. D. (1996). Veblen effects in a theory of conspicuous consumption. *The American Economic Review, 86*(3), 349–373.

44. Jordan, J. V., & Schwartz, H. L. (2018). Radical empathy in teaching. In H. L. Schwartz & J. Snyder-Duch (Eds.), *New Directions for teaching & learning: No. 153. Teaching and emotion* (pp. 27–28). Jossey-Bass.

45. Schlossberg, N. K. (1989). Marginality and mattering: Key issues in building community. In D. C. Roberts (Ed.), *New Directions for Student Services: No. 48. Designing campus activities to foster a sense of community* (pp. 5–15). Jossey-Bass.

46. Scudamore, B. (2015, December 5). 3 tips to create a workplace culture that employees love. Forbes.com. https://www.forbes.com/sites/brianscudamore/2015/12/05/creating-culture-its-all-about-people/#1eb65c667ad5

47. Kouzes, J. M., & Posner, B. Z. (2012). *The leadership challenge: How to make extraordinary things happen in organizations* (5th ed.). Wiley.

48. Kouzes, J. M., & Posner, B. Z. (2011). *Encouraging the heart workbook.* Wiley.

49. Komives, S. R., & Wagner, W. (2017). *Leadership for a better world: Understanding the social change model of leadership development.* John Wiley.

50. Austin, H. S., & Austin, A. W. (1996). *A social change model of leadership development guidebook.* Higher Education Research Institute, University of California, Los Angeles.

51. Austin & Austin, *A social change model.*

52. Soria, K. M., & Mitchell, T. D. (2016). *Civic engagement and community service at research universities: Engaging undergraduates for social justice, social change and responsible citizenship.* Palgrave Macmillan.

53.

54. Service Learning Collective. (2015, Feb. 14). Advanced service-learning toolkit. http://compact.org/initiatives/service-learning/

55. Sarikas, C. (2015, October 10). 129 great examples of community service projects [Web log post]. *PrepScholar.* http://blog.prepscholar.com/129-examples-of-community-service-projects

56. Corporation for National and Community Service. (2016, November 15). New report: Service unites Americans; Volunteers give service worth $184 billion. ht

tps://www.nationalservice.gov/n
ews room/press-releases/2016/
new-report-service-unites-
americans-volunteers-give-
service-worth-184

57. Higher Education Research Institute. (2017). College senior survey. *HERI*. https://heri.ucla.edu/co
llege-senior-survey/

58. Bengtson, B. (2020, December
18). Reimagine your corporate
volunteer program. *Harvard Business Review*. https://hbr.org/2020
/12/reimagine-your-corporate-vo
lunteer-program

59. Bengston, "Reimagine your corporate volunteer program."

60. Rotary website. https://www.rota
ry.org/

61. Kiwanis website. http://www.kiwa
nis.org/

62. Lions Club website. http://www.li
onsclubs.org/

63. Willoughby, A. (2014, March 31).
How to create a workplace people
love coming to. Fast Company. htt
ps://www.fastcompany.com/3028
368/how-to-create-a-workplace
-people-love-coming-to

CHAPTER 14

1. Washington Post Live. (2021,
March 1). Transcript: Race in
America: Mae Jemison, MD.
Retrieved from https://www.
washingtonpost.c
om/washington-post-live/2021/0
3/01/transcript-race-america-m
ae-jemison-md/

2. Durant, W. & Durant, A. (n.d.). Tak
e the next giant leap forward. 100
Year Starship website. https://100
yss.org/mission/purpose

3. Mayer, M. (2006). Ideas come from
everywhere. Stanford University
eCorner. http://ecorner.stanford.
edu/videos/1524/Ideas-Come-Fr
om-Everywhere

4. Mayer, "Ideas come from
everywhere."

5. Zhuo, J. (2016). Solve only real
problems. Stanford University
eCorner. http://ecorner.stanford.
edu/videos/4697/Solve-Only-Rea
l-Problems

6. Chen, J. (2016). Choose to see
beauty. Stanford University
eCorner. http://ecorner.stanford.
edu/videos/4674/Choose-to-See
-Beauty

7. University of Notre Dame. (2017).
Necessity is indeed mother
of invention, regardless of
resources, study shows. Science-
Daily. www.sciencedaily.com/rele
ases/2017/09/170928121659.htm

8. Keeley, L., Walters, H., Pikkel,
R., & Quinn, B. (2013). *Ten types of
innovation: The discipline of building breakthroughs* (pp. 6–7). Wiley;
For an overview and examples of
the ten types of innovation see htt
ps://doblin.com/ten-types

9. Keely, Walters, Pikkel, & Quinn,
Ten types, p. 13.

10. A downloadable TUBRIC template
can be found at the Buck Institute
for Education at http://www.bie.or
g

11. From the model introduced in
Keeley, et al. (2013). *Ten types of
innovation: The discipline of building breakthroughs*. Wiley.

12. Gray, D., Brown, S., & Macanufo,
J. (2010). *Gamestorming: A playbook for innovators, rulebreakers,
and changemakers*. O'Reilly Media.
http://gamestorming.co
m/games-for- decision-making/
how-now-wow-matrix/

13. Capatina, A., Bleoju, G., Matos,
F., Vairinhos, V. (2017). Leveraging intellectual capital through
Lewin's Force Field Analysis: The
case of software development
companies. *Journal of Innovation &
Knowledge, 2*(3), 125–133. https://
doi.org/10.1016/j.jik.2016.07.001

14. Beghetto, R. A. (2016a). *Big wins,
small steps: How to lead for and with
creativity*. Corwin.

15. Beghetto, R. A. (2007). Ideational
code-switching: Walking the
talk about supporting student

creativity in the classroom.
Roeper Review, 29, 265–270;
Beghetto, R. A., & Kaufman, J.
C. (2007). Toward a broader con-
ception of creativity: A case for
mini-c creativity. *Psychology of
Aesthetics, Creativity, and the Arts,
1*, 73–79.

16. Kaufman, J. C., & Beghetto, R. A.
(2009). Beyond big and little: The
Four C Model of creativity. *Review
of General Psychology, 13*, 1–12.

17. Beghetto, R. A. (2013). *Killing ideas
softly? The promise and perils of
creativity in the classroom*. Information Age Publishing.

18. Beghetto, R. A. (2016b). Leveraging micro-opportunities to
address macroproblems: Toward
an unshakeable sense of possibility thinking. In D. Ambrose & R. J.
Sternberg (Eds.), *Creative intelligence in the 21st century: Grappling
with enormous problems and huge
opportunities*. Sense.

19. Beghetto, "Leveraging
micro-opportunities."

20. Du, X., Zhang, H., Zhang, S.,
Zhang, A., & Chen, B. (2021).
Creativity and leadership in the
creative industry: A study from
the perspective of social norms.
Frontiers in Psychology, 12, 1087.

21. Sawyer, K. (2017). *Group genius:
The creative power of collaboration*.
Basic Books.

22. Leroy, H., Buengeler, C., Vees-
traeten, M., Shemla, M., & Hoever,
I. J. (2021). Fostering team creativity through team-focused
inclusion: The role of leader harvesting the benefits of diversity
and cultivating value-in-diversity
beliefs. *Group & Organization Management, 0*(0), 1–42.

23. Shore, L. M., Randel, A. E., Chung,
B. G., Dean, M. A., Ehrhart, K. H.,
& Singh, G. (2011). Inclusion and
diversity in work groups: A review
and model for future research.
Journal of Management, 37(4),
1262–1289.

24. Leroy, H., Buengeler, C., Vees-
traeten, M., Shemla, M., & Hoever,

I. J. (2021). Fostering team creativity through team-focused inclusion: The role of leader harvesting the benefits of diversity and cultivating value-in-diversity beliefs. *Group & Organization Management, 0*(0), 1–42.

25. Newman, A., Donohue, R., & Eva, N. (2017). Psychological safety: A systematic review of the literature. *Human Resource Management Review, 27*(3), 521–535.

26. Huang, L., Krasikova, D. V., & Liu, D. (2016). I can do it, so can you: The role of leader creative self-efficacy in facilitating follower creativity. *Organizational Behavior and Human Decision Processes, 132*, 49–62.

27. Andersson, M., Moen, O., & Brett, P.O. (2020). The organizational climate for psychological safety: Associations with SMEs' innovation capabilities and innovation performance. *Journal of Engineering and Technology Management, 55*, 101554. https://www.sciencedirect.com/science/article/abs/pii/S0923474820300023

28. For more information on mental models, see https://mentalmodels.princeton.edu/about/what-are-mental-models/

29. Goh, C. (May 16, 2016). How to apply mindfulness to the creative process. *Mindful.org*. https://www.mindful.org/apply-mindfulness-creative-process/#:~:text=Preparation%3A%20Mindfulness%20meditation%20boosts%20divergent,higher%20quality%20initial%20rough%20ideas

30. For a review of this work and future directions, see Jia, X., Li, W., & Cao, L. (2019). The role of metacognitive components in creative thinking. *Frontiers in Psychology, 10*, 2404.

31. Oppezzo, M., & Schwartz, D. L. (2014). Give your ideas some legs: The positive effect of walking on creative thinking. *Journal of experimental psychology: learning, memory, and cognition, 40*(4), 1142.

32. Waruwu, H., Asbari, M., Purwanto, A., Nugroho, Y., Fikri, M., Fauji, A., Shobihi, A., Hulu, P., Sudiyono, R., Agistiawati, E., & Dewi, W. (2020). The role of transformational leadership, organizational learning and structure on innovation capacity: Evidence from Indonesia private schools. *EduPsyCouns: Journal of Education, Psychology and Counseling, 2*(1), 378–397. https://ummaspul.e-journal.id/Edupsycouns/article/view/499; Shah, S. H. A., Sultana, A., Gul, A., Sajjad, S., Aziz, S., Basit, A., & Qadir, A. (2020). Transformational leadership influence on innovation directly and indirectly through affective commitment in hotel industry of Malaysia. *International Review of Management and Marketing, 10*(6), 22–28. https://ideas.repec.org/a/eco/journ3/2020-06-3.html; Khalili, A. (2016, January 1). Linking transformational leadership, creativity, innovation, and innovation-supportive climate. *Management Decision, 54*(9), 2277–2293.

33. Boies, K., Fiset, J., & Gill, H. (2015). Communication and trust are key: Unlocking the relationship between leadership and team performance and creativity. *The leadership quarterly, 26*(6), 1080–1094.

34. Henker, N., Sonnentag, S., & Unger, D. (2015, June 1). Transformational leadership and employee creativity: The mediating role of promotion focus and creative process engagement. *Journal of Business and Psychology, 30*(2), 235–247.

35. Jyoti, J., & Dev, M. (2015, January 5). The impact of transformational leadership on employee creativity: The role of learning orientation. *Journal of Asia Business Studies, 9*(1), 78–98.

36. Hyypia, M., & Parjanen, S. (2013, May 6). Boosting creativity with transformational leadership in fuzzy front-end innovation processes. *Interdisciplinary Journal of Information, Knowledge, and Management, 8*, 21–41.

37. Eisenbeiss, S. A., & Boerner, S. (2013, March 1). A double-edged sword: Transformational leadership and individual creativity. *British Journal of Management, 24*(1), 54–68.

38. OPENIDEO website. (n.d.). https://openideo.com/

CHAPTER 15

1. Godin, S. (2014, March 25). The debilitating myth of musical chairs. *Seth's Blog.* http://sethgodin.typepad.com/seths_blog/2014/03/the-debilitating-myth-of-musical-chairs.html

2. Mochari, I. (2016, March 23). Why half of the S&P 500 companies will be replaced in the next decade. *Inc. Magazine.* http://www.inc.com/ilan-mochari/innosight-sp-500-new-companies.html; Also see http://www.wipo.int/portal/en/;http://www.singularity.com/charts/page17.html

3. World Economic Forum. (2020). *The future of jobs report 2020.* https://www3.weforum.org/docs/WEF_Future_of_Jobs_2020.pdf

4. Word Economic Forum, *The future of jobs report.*

5. Cultural India. (n.d.). Ashoka. https://www.culturalindia.net/indian-history/ancient-india/ashoka.html

6. Aggarwal, M. (nd). Ashoka's policy of dhamma: History of India. https://www.historydiscussion.net/religion/ashokas-policy-of-dhamma-history-of-india/614

7. Ashoka, Everyone a Change Maker. (2019). *Leading social entrepreneurs.* https://www.ashoka.org/sites/default/files/2021-04/2019_LSE_Cover_Web_031221_small_0.pdf

8. Neck, H. M., Neck, C. P., & Murray, E. L. (2019). *Entrepreneurship: The practice and mindset.* Sage.

9. Sobel, R. S. (2008). Entrepreneurship. *The Library of Economics and Liberty.* http://www.econlib.org

/library/Enc/Entrepreneurship .html; for the earliest mentions of entrepreneur, see Cantillon, R. (1756). *Essai sur la nature du commerce en général: Traduit de l'anglois*. F. Gyles.

10. Aulet, B. (2013). *Disciplined entrepreneurship: 24 steps to a successful startup*. John Wiley. Additional current information can be found at: https://www.d-eship.com/ and in this video: http://www.prweb.com/releases/2013/8/prweb11023086.htm

11. Deutsch, W. (2018, August 13). What great entrepreneurs, salespeople, and business leaders have in common. *Chicago Booth Review*. https://www.chicagobooth.edu/review/what-great-entrepreneurs-salespeople-and-business-leaders-have-common

12. Greenberg, D., McKone-Sweet, K., & Wilson, H. J. (2011). *The new entrepreneurial leader: Developing leaders who shape social and economic opportunity*. Berrett-Koehler.

13. There have been many editions and translations of Say's original work first published in 1800 in Paris. The latest, in English, is Say, J. B., Quddus, M., & Rashid, S. (2017). *A treatise on political economy*. Cosimo Classics.

14. Greenberg, D., McKone-Sweet, K., & Wilson, H. J. (2011). *The new entrepreneurial leader: Developing leaders who shape social and economic opportunity*. Berrett-Koehler.

15. Butler, T. (2017, March). Hiring an entrepreneurial leader. *Harvard Business Review*. https://hbr.org/2017/03/hiring-an-entrepreneurial-leader

16. Jobs, S., & Silicon Valley Historical Association. (2013). *Steve Jobs: Visionary entrepreneur*. Silicon Valley Historical Association.

17. Dweck, C. S. (2008). *Mindset: The new psychology of success*. Ballantine Books.

18. Yeager, D. S., & Dweck, C. S. (2020). What can be learned from growth mindset controversies? *American Psychologist, 75*(9), 1269–1284. https://doi.org/10.1037/amp0000794

19. IDEO. (2003, November). *Method cards*. https://www.ideo.com/work/method-cards

20. Korte, R., Smith, K. A., & Li, C. Q. (2018). The role of empathy in entrepreneurship: A core competency of the entrepreneurial mindset. *Advances in Engineering Education, 7*(1), n1.

21. Maeda, J. (2006). *The laws of simplicity*. MIT Press.

22. Selway, J. (2013, March 5). The complexity of simplicity. *UXMag.com*. http://uxmag.com/articles/the-complexity-of-simplicity

23. Sarasvathy, S. D. (2009). *Effectuation: Elements of entrepreneurial expertise*. Edward Elgar.

24. Society for Effectual Action. (n.d.). *Effectuation 101*. http://www.effectuation.org/?page_id=207

25. Sarasvathy, S. D. (2001). Effectual reasoning in expert entrepreneurial decisions: Existence and bounds [ENT D1–D6]. Paper presented at the meeting of the *Academy of Management 2001 Meeting Best Paper Proceedings*.

26. Masterson, M. (2007). *Ready, fire, aim: Zero to $100 million in no time flat*. John Wiley.

27. Friedlander, A. (2016). *A misfit entrepreneur's guide to building a business your way*. Rosabella Consulting.

28. Gunderson, L. H., & Holling, C. S. (2002). *Panarchy: Understanding transformations in human and natural systems*. Island Press.

29. Bower, J. L., & Christensen, C. M. (1995). Disruptive technologies: Catching the wave. *Harvard Business Review, 73*(1), 43–53; Kiuchi, T., & Shireman, B. (2002). *What we learned in the rainforest: Business lessons from nature*. Berrett-Koehler.

30. Hurst, D. K. (2012). *The new ecology of leadership: Business mastery in a chaotic world*. Columbia University Press.

31. Lipmanowicz, H., & McCandless, K. (2013). *The surprising power of liberating structures: Simple rules to unleash a culture of innovation*. Liberating Structures Press.

32. Dufays, F. (2018). Exploring the drivers of tensions in social innovation management in the context of social entrepreneurial teams. *Management Decision, 57*(6), 1344–1361.

33. For an overview of the state of the field, see Gupta, P., Chauhan, S., Paul, J., & Jaiswal, M. P. (2020). Social entrepreneurship research: A review and future research agenda. *Journal of Business Research, 113*, 209–229.; and Bansal, S., Garg, I., & Sharma, G. D. (2019). Social entrepreneurship as a path for social change and driver of sustainable development: A systematic review and research agenda. *Sustainability, 11*(4), 1091.

34. Bedi, H. S., & Yadav, M. N. (2019). Social entrepreneurship: A conceptual clarity. *Our Heritage, 67*(10), 1006–1016.

35. Aziz, A. (2020, March 7). The power of purpose: The business case for purpose (All The Data You Were Looking For). *Forbes*. https://www.forbes.com/sites/afdhelaziz/2020/03/07/the-power-of-purpose-the-business-case-for-purpose-all-the-data-you-were-looking-for-pt-2/?sh=60c34b483cf7

36. Kannampuzha, M., & Hockerts, K. (2019). Organizational social entrepreneurship: Scale development and validation. *Social Enterprise Journal, 15*(3), 290–319

37. Aziz, A. (2020, March 7). The power of purpose: The business case for purpose (All The Data You Were Looking For). *Forbes*. https://www.forbes.com/sites/afdhelaziz/2020/03/07/the-power-of-purpose-the-business-case-for-purp

ose-all-the-data-you-were-looki ng-for-pt-2/?sh=60c34b483cf7

38. Blank, S. (2013). *Four steps to the epiphany*. K&S Ranch.

39. Osterwalder, A., & Pigneur, Y. (2010). *Business model generation: A handbook for visionaries, game changers, and challengers*. John Wiley.

40. Maurya, A. (2012). *Running lean: Iterate from Plan A to a plan that works*. O'Reilly Media.

41. Ries, E. (2011). *The lean startup: How today's entrepreneurs use continuous innovation to create radically successful businesses*. Crown Business.

42. Godin, S. (2016, December 6). The other person is always right. *Seth's Blog*. http://sethgodin.type pad.com/seths_blog/2016/12/th e-other-person-is-always-righ t.html

43. Fitzpatrick R (2013) The Mom Test. Foundercentric.com, p. 12.

44. York, J. M. (2019). Practical skills to get the most from customer interviews for entrepreneurs and startups. *Archives of Business Administration and Management, 2*, 126.

45. Middlebrooks, A. (2016). The paradox of serious fun. In R. A. Beghetto & B. Sriraman (Eds.), *Creative contradictions in education: Cross disciplinary paradoxes and perspectives* (pp. 265–280). Springer-Verlag.

46. Fluegge-Woolf, E. R. (2014). Play hard, work hard. *Management Research Review, 37*(8), 682.

47. Measley, N., & Gianoulis, N. (2015). *Playing it forward: The definitive "how to" model for creating a winning workplace culture*. The Fun Dept.

48. Good, V., Hughes, D. E. & Wang, H. (2022). More than money: Establishing the importance of a sense of purpose for salespeople. *Journal of the Academy of Marking Science, 50*, 272–295. https://doi.o rg/10.1007/s11747-021-00795-x

49. Pink, D. (2009). *Drive: The surprising truth about what motivates us*. Riverhead Books.

50. Tushman, M. L., Smith, W. K., & Binns, A. (2011). The ambidextrous CEO. *Harvard Business Review, 89*(6), 74–81.

51. Freeman, D., & Siegfried, R. L. (2015). Entrepreneurial leadership in the context of company startup and growth. *Journal of Leadership Studies, 8*(4), 35–39.

52. Carasco-Saul, M., Kim, W., & Kim, T. (2015). Leadership and employee engagement: Proposing research agendas through a review of literature. *Human Resource Development Review, 14*(1), 38–63.

53. Jin, M., McDonald, B., & Park, J. (2016). Followership and job satisfaction in the public sector: The moderating role of perceived supervisor support and performance-oriented culture. *International Journal of Public Sector Management, 29*(3), 218–237.

54. Gallup. (n.d.). *Gallup employee engagement center*. https://q12.gal lup.com/

55. Gallup. (n.d.). *State of the American manager*. http://www.gallup.com/ services/182138/state-american -manager.aspx

56. Aon Hewitt. (2015, June). *Say, stay, or strive? Unleash the engagement outcome you need*. http://www.aon .com/attachments/human-capita l-consulting/2015-Drivers-of-Say -Stay-Strive.pdf

57. Seppala, E., & Cameron, K. (2015, December 1). Proof that positive work cultures are more productive. *Harvard Business Review*. http s://hbr.org/2015/12/proof-that-p ositive-work-cultures-are-more -productive

58. Johnson, C. (1955). *Harold and the purple crayon*. HarperCollins.

59. For a great example of this, check out: The social graph: The journey from Francis to Bono, in Baehr, E., & Loomis, E. (2015). *Get backed: Craft your story, build the perfect pitch deck, and launch the venture of your dreams*. Harvard Business Review Press.

CHAPTER 16

1. Global Ranking. (n.d.). Market Capitalization of Unilever (UL). htt ps://companiesmarketcap.com/u nilever/marketcap/

2. *Fortune*. (n.d.). World's Most Admired Companies. https://fortu ne.com/worlds-most-admired-c ompanies/2021/search/?orderi ng=asc

3. Unilever. (n.d.). Climate action: Strategy and goals. https://www. unilever.com/planet-and-socie ty/climate-action/strategy-and -goals/

4. Unilever. (n.d.). Our position on. ht tps://www.unilever.com/planet-a nd-society/our-position-on/

5. Unilever. (2020). *Basis of preparation 2020: Uniliver sustainable living plan progress summary*. https://as sets.unilever.com/files/92ui5egz/ production/e4aa61b4fa7970c7a3f 43a62c825366babd6c693.pdf/Uni lever-basis-of-preperation-susta inability-2020.pdf

6. Unilever. (2020). *DJSI Industry Leader Report | 2020*. https://port al.csa.spglobal.com/survey/docu ments/DJSI_IndustryLeader_CO S_2020.pdf

7. Hall, S. (2020, March 16). Ex-Unilever CEO Paul Polman on creating a sustainable and diverse business

8. Allen, S. J. (Host). (2021, August 19). Helle Bank Jorgensen - Stewards of the Future (No. 82). [audio podcast episode]. In *Phronesis: Practical wisom for leaders*. https: //practicalwisdom.buzzsprout.co m/979897/9028478-helle-bank-jo rgensen-stewards-of-the-future

9. The Deming Institute. (n.d.). Deming Institute website. https://demi ng.org/quotes/10141/

10. Every leader should be familiar with Deming's 14 Points for

management success, found in Deming, W. E. (2018). *Out of the crisis*. MIT press. These insights and more resources can be found at https://deming.org/explore/fourteen-points/

11. Bellinger, G. (2004). Archetypes. *Systems Thinking*. http://www.systems-thinking.org/arch/arch.htm

12. Reeves, M., Levin, S., Fink, T., & Levina, A. (2020). Taming complexity. *Harvard Business Review*, *98*(1), 112–121.

13. Snowden, D. J., & Boone, M. E. (2007, November). A leader's framework for decision making: Wise executives tailor their approach to fit the complexity of the circumstances they face. *Harvard Business Review*, *85*(11). https://hbr.org/2007/11/a-leaders-framework-for-decision-making

14. Gleick, J. (1987). *Chaos: Making a new science*. Penguin Books; Taleb, N. N. (2007). *The Black Swan: The impact of highly improbable fragility*. Random House.

15. Allen, K. E., & Mease, W. P. (2001). Energy optimization and the role of the leader. (p. 2), http://www.kathleenallen.net/index.php/writings/leadership-change/24-ila-energy-opt-2/file

16. Savitz, A. W. (2013). *The triple bottom line: How today's best-run companies are achieving economic, social, and environmental success—and how you can too*. Jossey-Bass.

17. Senge, P. (2006). *The fifth discipline: The art and science of the learning organization* (p. 3). Currency Doubleday.

18. Batchelder, J. M. (2021). *Latin* college student leadership meaning-making through generativity as cultural capital* (Publication No. 28317939) [Doctoral dissertation, The Florida State University]. ProQuest Dissertations Publishing.

19. Komives, S. R., Owen, J. E., Longerbeam, S. D., Mainella, F. C., & Osteen, L. (2005). Developing a leadership identity: A grounded theory. *Journal of College Student Development, 46*(6), 593–611.

20. Hastings, L. J. & Sunderman, H.M. (2019). Generativity and socially responsible leadership among college student leaders who mentor. *Journal of Leadership Education, 18*(3), 1–14.; Hastings, L. J., Griesen, J. V., Hoover, R. E., Creswell, J. W., & Dlugosh, L. L. (2015). Generativity in college students: Comparing and explaining the impact of mentoring. *Journal of College Student Development, 56*(7), 651–669. https://doi.org/10.1353/csd.2015.0070

21. United Nations. (n.d.). *Our common future*, Chapter 2: *Towards sustainable development*. http://www.un-documents.net/ocf-02.htm#III

22 Harper, J. (2016, April 15). 10 Inspiring quotes that define workplace culture: Positive workplace quotes. https://www.thehrdigest.com/10-inspiring-quotes-define-workplace-culture/

23. McGregor, J. (2016). The biggest "gift" Steve Jobs gave Apple CEO Tim Cook before he died. *Washington Post*. https://www.washingtonpost.com/news/on-leadership/wp/2016/08/16/the-biggest-gift-steve-jobs-gave-apple-ceo-tim-cook-before-he-died/

24. Allworth, J., Wessel, M., & Wheeler, R. (2011). Why Apple doesn't need Steve Jobs. *Harvard Business Review*. https://hbr.org/2011/08/why-apple-doesnt-need-steve-jo

25. Larkins, A. (2021, July 7). Apple Stock—Apple shares continue to climb as Tim Cook approaches 10th anniversary as CEO. https://fintechzoom.com/fintech_news_apple-stock/apple-stock-apple-shares-continue-to-climb-as-tim-cook-approaches-10th-anniversary-as-ceo/

26. Lantry, L. (2016, March 8). Who's your favorite eco-heroine? Sierra magazine website. https://www.sierraclub.org/sierra/2016-2-march-april/green-life/whos-your-favorite-eco-heroine

27. Farber, M. (2016). Patagonia is donating all its Black Friday sales to charity. *Fortune*. http://fortune.com/2016/11/22/black-friday-2016-patagonia-sales/

28. Patagonia. (2016). *Patagonia's mission statement*. http://www.patagonia.com/company-info.html

29. Toward a zero waste future. Wal-Mart Stores, Inc.: *2016 Global Responsibility Report*. https://cdn.corporate.walmart.com/a4/32/d7eb7ffa416c951694eb95099953/grr-12-zero-waste-future.pdf

30. CEO magazine. (2019, June 4). Exclusive interview with Brené Brown. https://www.theceomagazine.com/lifestyle/interview/brene-brown/

31. Hill, L., Brandeau, G., Truelove, E., & Lineback, K. (2015). The capabilities your organization needs to sustain innovation. *Harvard Business Review*, para. 18. https://hbr.org/2015/01/the-capabilities-your-organization-needs-to-sustain-innovation

32. Hill, L., Brandeau, G., Truelove, E., & Lineback, K. (2015). The capabilities your organization needs to sustain innovation. *Harvard Business Review*. https://hbr.org/2015/01/the-capabilities-your-organization-needs-to-sustain-innovation

33. Fisk, P. (n.d.). Mary Barra: Reinventing GM for an electric future. https://www.peterfisk.com/leader/mary-barra-2/

34. Egan, M. (2016). 5,300 Wells Fargo employees fired over 2 million phony accounts. *CNN Money*, para. 3. http://money.cnn.com/2016/09/08/investing/wells-fargo-created-phony-accounts-bank-fees/

35. Parsons, S. (2013, April 3). Lord Nicholas Stern identifies 3 obstacles to international climate action. World Resources Institute website. https://www.wri.org/insights/lord-nicholas-stern-identif

ies-3-obstacles-international-climate-action

36. Shandrow, K. L. (2016, August 16). Inspiring quotes from 10 visionary business leaders who changed everything. Entrepreneur website. https://www.entrepreneur.com/slideshow/280879

37. Vinluan, F. (2021, July 28). AI-driven Deep Genomics gets $180M to turn biology into informational medicines. *MedCity News*. https://medcitynews.com/2021/07/ai-driven-deep-genomics-gets-180m-to-turn-biology-into-informational-medicines/

38. 20th Century Fox. (2016, August 31). Morgan: IBM creates first movie trailer by AI [HD]. *YouTube*. https://www.youtube.com/watch?v=gJEzuYynaiw

39. Herkewitz, W. (2015). A computer just solved this 100-year-old biology problem. *Popular Mechanics*. http://www.popularmechanics.com/science/a15886/computer-scientific-theory

40. Asher-Schapiro, A. (2021, July 23). US firefighters turn to AI to battle the blazes. *The Christian Science Monitor*. https://www.csmonitor.com/Environment/2021/0723/US-firefighters-turn-to-AI-to-battle-the-blazes

41. Strickland, E. (2016, May 4). Autonomous robot surgeon bests humans in world first. *Spectrum*. http://spectrum.ieee.org/the-human-os/robotics/medical-robots/autonomous-robot-surgeon-bests-human-surgeons-in-world-first

42. Pascual, K. (2016, January 27). Harvard to develop AI that works as fast as human brain. *Tech Times*. http://www.techtimes.com/articles/127773/20160127/harvard-to-develop-ai-that-works-as-fast-as-human-brain.htm

43. Dumas, B. (2021, July 27). Joby's electric flying taxi completes 150-mile flight. *Fox Business*. https://www.foxbusiness.com/technology/joby-electric-flying-taxi-completes-150-mile-flight

44. Abel J. R. & Deitz R. (2019, February 6). Where are manufacturing jobs coming back? *Liberty Street Economics*. https://libertystreeteconomics.newyorkfed.org/2019/02/where-are-manufacturing-jobs-coming-back.html

45. Chowdhry, A. (2016, May 17). Law firm Baker Hostetler hires a "digital attorney" named ROSS. Forbes. http://www.forbes.com/sites/amitchowdhry/2016/05/17/law-firm-bakerhostetler-hires-a-digital-attorney-named-ross/#717cbe221caa

46. Diamandis, P. (2015, January 26). Ray Kurzweil's mind-boggling predictions for the next 25 years. *Singularity Hub*. http://singularityhub.com/2015/01/26/ray-kurzweils-mind-boggling-predictions-for-the-next-25-years/; Galeon, D. (2016). AI will colonize the galaxy by the 2050s, according to the "father of deep learning." *Futurism*. https://futurism.com/ai-will-colonize-the-galaxy-by-the-2050s-according-to-the-father-of-deep-learning/

47. Lidwell, W., Holden, K., Butler, J., & Elam, K. (2010). *Universal principles of design: 125 ways to enhance usability, influence perception, increase appeal, make better design decisions, and teach through design*. Rockport Publishers.

48. Brinded L. (2021, January 13) Land O'Lakes CEO on making history as the first openly gay woman to run a Fortune 500 firm. Yahoo! finance. https://finance.yahoo.com/news/land-o-lakes-ceo-beth-lord-interview-first-openly-gay-women-to-run-fortune-500-company-000116132.html

49. Spreitzer, G., & Porath, C. (2012). Creating sustainable performance. *Harvard Business Review*, *90*(1), 92–99.

50. Meehan, P., Rigby, D., & Rogers, P. (2008, February 27). Creating and sustaining a winning culture. *Harvard Business Review*. https://hbr.org/2008/02/creating-and-sustaining-a-winn-1

51. Meehan, Rigby, & Rogers, "Creating and sustaining."

52. Martin, R. [host]. (2016, May 1). Forget talent, success comes from "grit." [audio podcast]. In *Weekend Edition Sunday*. NPR. https://www.npr.org/2016/05/01/476346709/forget-talent-success-comes-from-grit

53. Schwandt, D. R. (2005). When managers become philosophers: Integrating learning with sense-making. *Academy of Management Journal*, *4*(2), 176–192.

54. Zajonc, R. B. (1968, January 1). Attitudinal effects of mere exposure. *Journal of Personality and Social Psychology*, *9*(2), 1–27.

55. Fournier, G. (2016). Mere exposure effect. *Psych Central*. http://psychcentral.com/encyclopedia/mere-exposure-effect/

56. Vonderlin, R., Biermann, M., Bohus, M., & Lyssenko, L. (2020). Mindfulness-based programs in the workplace: A meta-analysis of randomized controlled trials. *Mindfulness*, *11*(7), 1579–1598.

57. Rogers, H. B. (2013). Koru: Teaching mindfulness to emerging adults. *New Directions for Teaching and Learning*, *2013*(134), 73–81.

58. Rogers, H. B. (2013). Koru: Teaching mindfulness to emerging adults. *New Directions for Teaching and Learning*, *2013*(134), 73–81.

59. Call, D., Miron, L., & Orcutt, H. (2014). Effectiveness of brief mindfulness techniques in reducing symptoms of anxiety and stress. *Mindfulness*, *5*(6), 658–668.

60. Jha, A. P., Krompinger, J., & Baime, M. J. (2007). Mindfulness training modifies subsystems of attention. *Cognitive, Affective, & Behavioral Neuroscience*, *7*(2), 109–119.

61. Blanton, P. G. (2011). The other mindful practice: Centering prayer & psychotherapy. *Pastoral Psychology*, *60*(1), 133–147.

62. Call, D., Miron, L., & Orcutt, H. (2014). Effectiveness of brief mindfulness techniques in reducing symptoms of anxiety and stress. *Mindfulness, 5*(6), 658–668.

63. Wergin, J. F. (2019). *Deep learning in a disorienting world*. Cambridge University Press.

64. George, B., Sims, P., McLean, A. N., & Mayer, D. (2007). Discovering your authentic leadership. *Harvard Business Review, 85*(2), 129.

65. George, Sims, McLean, & Mayer, Discovering your authentic leadership, p. 129.

66. Shamir, B., & Eilam, G. (2005). What's your story? A life-stories approach to authentic leadership development. *The Leadership Quarterly, 16*(3), 395–417.

67. Shamir, B., & Eilam, G. (2005). What's your story? A life-stories approach to authentic leadership development. *The Leadership Quarterly, 16*(3), 395–417.

68. Avolio, B. J., & Gardner, W. L. (2005). Authentic leadership development: Getting to the root of positive forms of leadership. *The Leadership Quarterly, 16*(3), 315–338.

69. Mackenzie, G. (1998). *Orbiting the giant hairball: A corporate fool's guide to surviving with grace*. Viking.

70. Roser, M. (2016). The short history of global living conditions and why it matters that we know it. *Our World in Data*. https://ourworldind ata.org/a-history-of-global-living -conditions-in-5-charts/

71. United Nations Global Compact. (n.d.). *Who we are*. https://www.un globalcompact.org/what-is-gc/ mission

INDEX

action plans, 122, 192, 254, 356, 358, 362, 383
Assessing Leadership Challenges, 27, 29, 32, 34–35
attentive leadership, 376, 378, 382, 393
authentic leadership, 402, 489, 507–8, 510

behaviors, leader's, 55, 167, 169
beneficiaries, 466, 476, 478
best practices, 53, 117, 357, 476, 487, 495–96
brain, 53–56, 243–44, 247, 260, 262, 273, 276–85, 303, 429, 431, 449–51, 453, 455, 457
brainstorming, 93, 100, 194–95, 202, 207, 256–58, 267
brainstorming rules, 256–57, 268
building community, 128, 170–71, 409, 422–23
business model, 473–74, 477, 485
business model canvas, 477–78, 485, 487–88

change, 26–27, 30, 51–52, 66–69, 74, 80–81, 101–2, 116, 125–28, 203, 274–75, 292, 305, 307–17, 319–33, 354–56, 415–16, 442–44, 468, 494–95
    successful, 321, 328, 330–31, 356
change agents, 82, 310, 321, 328, 332
change efforts, 324, 329, 331, 355–56
change fatigue, 321, 330–31
change process, 296, 310–11, 313–14, 316–26, 328, 330–33, 356, 402, 429
changing, 19–20, 52, 55, 101–2, 106, 283, 285, 289, 307, 309, 313–14, 317, 320
characteristics of culture, 337, 341, 343
characteristics of servant leadership, 409, 422, 424
Charisms and Flow Questions, 131–32, 139
climate of innovation, 449–50, 452–53
code of ethics, 154–55, 176
collaborative process, 102, 431, 434, 436–38, 457

collaborative work culture, 109–11, 116
common purpose, 167–68, 302, 370, 372–73, 376–77, 380, 415–16
community engagement, 124, 419, 422
community members, 275, 339, 365, 449, 457
community service, 400, 419–20
confident, 24–28, 41, 58, 66, 267, 269, 298, 314, 458
Confident leaders, 26, 28, 61, 63
constructive dimension, 283, 303, 451–52
context and culture, 252, 363, 468
convergent thinking, 253, 268, 439, 441, 457, 501
core values, 104, 155, 315, 317, 342, 351, 359, 370, 501
    organization's, 104, 311, 317
Creating a Culture, 431, 444, 447–48
creative confidence, 239, 245–46, 249–51, 270, 432, 451
creative ideas, 19, 242–43, 246, 252, 254, 351, 431, 433, 435–39, 456, 459
creative individuals, 250, 432, 444, 447, 456
creative problem-solving, 86, 95, 244, 246, 252, 255
creative problem-solving processes, 18–19, 45, 237, 253, 255, 266, 269, 359
creative process, 252, 254, 258, 270–71, 416, 438, 447, 453, 456
Creative products, 248–49, 270
creative work, 131, 242, 453–54
creativity, 93, 237, 239–71, 429, 431–32, 434–39, 441, 445–56, 458–59, 465, 480–81, 499, 501
creativity and innovation, 114, 245, 435–36, 448, 451–52, 459, 510
Credible leaders, 71–73
crisis leadership, 315–16, 331
cultural differences, 113, 340, 345–46, 375
cultural values, 104, 340, 343–44, 352, 364
culture
    caring, 399, 401–2, 412
    organization's, 104, 111, 317, 338, 341, 348, 355, 449–50

culture of care, 399, 402, 407, 412–13, 421–22, 475
Culture of Innovation, 110, 252, 260, 269, 429, 431–59, 462, 501
customer segments, 477–78, 487

decision-action gap, 163, 171, 175–76, 186, 188
decision and process, 192, 197, 206
decision criteria, 185, 194–95, 206
decision-making process, 179, 186, 191, 193, 195, 201, 203, 221, 231, 301, 347
decisions, making, 181–82, 184–85, 190, 234, 294, 298, 482
definition of leadership, 51, 57, 62–63, 166, 184, 203, 211, 307, 372, 407
design, relationship, 117, 209, 233
Design Culture, 15, 49, 79, 335, 337, 352, 359, 363, 369, 457, 461
Design Culture and Community, 338–426
designers, 18–23, 38–40, 51, 85, 260–61, 283, 309, 415, 432, 434, 467
design framework, 20, 211, 331, 467
designing, 15–16, 18, 20–22, 24, 36–39, 47–124, 126, 170–72, 233, 273–74, 285–86, 289–91, 325–27, 329–32, 380, 400–427, 429, 432–33, 450, 483
designing culture, 109, 217, 233, 353–54, 359
designing leadership relationships, 147, 199, 214, 233, 273, 276
designing relationships, 62, 122, 143, 163, 206, 233–34, 279, 281, 310
Design Leadership Relationships, 98, 147, 150–236
Design Leadership Self, 47, 50–146
Design Model, 15, 49, 79, 121, 149, 181, 209, 239, 273, 307, 337
Design Others' Success, 15, 49, 79, 121, 149, 181, 239–40, 242–304, 307–8, 310–32, 337
Design Principle, 15, 18, 22–24, 39–40, 196, 200, 290, 301–2, 323, 380, 452, 454, 467, 504, 506
design process, 15, 18–20, 39–40, 44–45, 86, 88–89, 319, 438, 447, 467

559

design relationships, 15, 49, 79, 104, 121, 144, 149, 209–10, 233, 235, 239
design success, 15, 49, 79, 121, 171, 181, 369, 376, 378, 393, 399
Design thinkers, 86, 92, 324
design thinking, 15, 18, 20–21, 39–40, 79–80, 85–88, 90, 97–98, 101, 115–17, 324, 326, 447–48, 465, 467
design-thinking, 21, 92, 95, 98, 117–18
Design Thinking Disposition, 21, 92, 97, 101, 256
design-thinking dispositions, 21, 86–87, 89, 98, 117, 431, 444, 447–48, 456
differences, individual, 103, 170, 384, 392, 397
Discovering Leadership, 16–44
divergent thinking, 92–93, 95, 249–51, 253, 255–56, 266, 268, 438, 441, 458, 471
drivers of innovation, 435–36, 456

effective leadership, 63, 65–66, 70, 82, 87, 112, 149–50, 210, 212, 284, 315, 346, 348–49
Effective teams, 369, 372–73, 376–77, 387, 393
employees, engaged, 84, 289, 483
employers, 91, 110, 296, 317, 373, 421
empowerment, 230, 232, 235, 352, 370, 375, 411, 423, 468
entrepreneurial leaders, 429, 461–62, 466–67, 469, 479–80, 482–85
Entrepreneurial Leadership, 429, 462–63, 465–87
entrepreneurial process, 461, 464, 466, 473, 476, 479–80, 482, 485
entrepreneurs, 30, 124, 333, 436, 462, 464–68, 470–72, 474–76, 478, 480, 485–86
entrepreneurship, 461–62, 464–67, 469, 477, 480, 485
environmental sustainability, 407, 500–501
Ethical Actions, 147, 149–79, 502
ethical challenges of leadership, 149, 161, 174
ethical issues, 118, 149, 151, 162–63, 488
ethical leadership, 149, 154, 171–72, 176
Exemplary Leadership, 209, 233, 281
expert leader, 60, 69–70, 75

fixed mindset, 82, 117, 468
Flow Questions, 131–32, 139
followers, individual, 60, 234, 324, 414
followership, 149–51, 167–69, 382
framework, 15, 36, 39, 68–69, 75, 83, 172, 277, 286, 294, 296
framework for leadership success, 15–45

generating ideas, 93, 100, 250, 255, 257, 262, 267–68, 281, 433, 439, 448
GPS (Greater Purpose Statement), 121–22, 140–43, 434
Greater Purpose Statement. See GPS
great leaders, 16, 50, 189, 507, 512
group, diverse, 95, 380, 392, 448
group development, 369, 383–84, 394
group members, 40, 44, 151, 195, 202, 204, 207, 217, 375, 382–83, 390
group move, 207, 383, 508
group of individuals, 43, 95, 109, 141, 155, 186, 219, 373, 393
group projects, 86, 158, 162, 203, 207, 234, 371
groups and teams, 276, 371, 373
groupthink, 169, 199, 205, 389–90
growth mindset, 79, 82–83, 116–17, 273, 289, 292–93, 295, 468, 485, 493

habits, design-thinking, 21, 98, 271
HCM (HUMAN CAPITAL MANAGEMENT), 378–79, 394
help individuals, 111, 192, 287
HUMAN CAPITAL MANAGEMENT. See HCM

idea-generating techniques, 95, 237, 239, 255–56, 264, 266–67, 269–71, 359, 453
individual and organizational levels, 320, 456, 505
individual behavior, 276, 335, 342, 405
individual change, 308, 310, 330
individual consideration, 36, 141, 402, 455
individuals and groups, 181, 186, 200, 205, 245, 357, 451, 497
individuals and teams, 20, 431–32, 438, 449, 455
individuals work, 22, 84, 284, 383, 453
individual values, 343, 402, 415–16, 442
influence followers, 62, 102, 216, 221
influence strategies, 220–21, 235

influence tactics, 210, 212, 218–19, 221, 235
influencing, 38–39, 50–51, 59–64, 75, 150–51, 209, 214–17, 219–20, 273, 280, 285, 372, 465–66, 481, 493–94
innovation for individuals and teams, 431, 449, 455
innovation process, 19, 45, 302, 431, 437, 441, 444
innovative efforts, 310–11, 317
innovative ideas, 45, 85, 93–94, 98, 218, 240, 319, 321, 326, 442, 449
Innovative leaders, 434, 456, 462
innovative organizations, 239, 456, 475
integrative thinking, 95–97
intrinsic motivation, 227–28, 235–36, 318

launch of new ideas, 464–65, 469, 485
leader and follower, 54, 60–62, 166, 234
leader/group, 168, 204–5
leaders
    aspiring, 41, 55–56, 58, 411
    individual, 30, 50, 58, 83, 255
    organizational, 105, 112, 161, 320, 349, 351, 355, 373, 377, 409, 448
    student, 165–66, 194
    successful, 52, 59, 84, 96
    toxic, 165–66, 169
    transformational, 318–19, 330
leaders and followers, 17, 62, 84, 118, 167, 169, 171, 275, 280, 318, 326–27
leaders and leadership, 16, 47, 49, 54, 56, 63, 66, 71, 74–75, 77, 128
leaders and members, 195, 353–54, 382
leaders and team members, 374, 383, 386
leadership, 15–18, 20–24, 35–40, 47–80, 101–8, 110–12, 114–17, 121–26, 135–38, 141–45, 149–51, 165–77, 181–85, 209–12, 287–89, 291–94, 345–49, 409–13, 498–501, 506–13
    innovative, 20, 245–46, 437
    toxic, 165–66, 168, 172, 177
leadership actions, 168, 277, 318
leadership activities, 16, 49, 58, 75, 136, 143, 234, 279, 367, 402, 508
leadership and management, 69, 75, 125, 291–92, 421
leadership and management practices, 292, 299, 302
Leadership Behavior, 69, 166, 213, 300, 349

Index **561**

leadership brand, 143–45, 294
Leadership by Design, 22, 196, 200, 214, 323, 326, 411, 414, 452, 454, 504, 506, 509
Leadership by Design Model, 15, 49, 79, 121, 149, 181, 209, 239, 273, 307, 337
leadership capacity, 16, 21, 40, 47, 52, 79–119
Leadership Challenges, 35, 40, 76, 145–46, 233, 235, 365, 394–95, 407, 422–23, 457, 482, 485–86
leadership CORE, 25, 39, 273
leadership design, 38, 60, 153, 163, 307, 481, 511
leadership development, 58, 82, 134, 415, 422, 499
leadership experiences, 28, 52, 418, 511
leadership models, 51, 68, 407
leadership positions, 16, 38, 51, 57, 62, 65, 125, 135, 145, 288–89, 298
leadership practices, 129, 216, 233, 273–74, 285, 292–93, 295, 302–3, 345, 347, 387
    effective, 22, 273, 275, 281
leadership problems, 69, 247, 258
leadership process, 61, 96, 176, 416, 449
leadership purpose, 132, 136, 141
leadership relationships, 60, 92, 116, 128–29, 228, 429, 481
leadership roles, 73–74, 84–85, 101, 109, 111–13, 274, 291–92, 296–98, 300, 302, 307, 309, 316–19, 328, 373
leadership style, 105, 126, 144, 191, 207, 209, 212–13, 235, 274, 301, 309
leadership success, 15–45, 79, 81, 115, 140, 151, 410, 455
leadership work, 32, 185, 198, 211
leaders influence, 59, 214–15, 493
leader's work, 149, 181, 210
leading change, 307, 310, 318, 321, 331–32
learning leadership, 51–53, 62, 116–17, 122
learning organization, 296, 298, 489, 497–98, 510
legitimate power, 215, 226–27, 235
levels, organizational, 125, 320, 330, 348, 456, 502, 505
levels of change, 307, 309, 322
life, organizational, 151, 162, 217, 224, 408, 493, 503

management practices, 296, 298–99, 302, 429
meeting, 99, 107, 186, 193, 198, 201–2, 204, 276, 279–82, 371, 395–97, 452–54

next, 198, 202, 258
members
    individual, 29, 373, 409
    organizational, 109, 351, 355, 357, 359, 364, 498
mindfulness, 16, 32, 40, 54–55, 465, 506–7
Minimum viable product. *See* MVP
MVP (Minimum viable product), 478–79, 485, 488

network, 95, 102, 225, 227, 286, 288–89, 311, 438, 440, 508, 510
next time, 58, 167, 171, 197, 301, 469
nonprofit organization, 308–9, 418, 422

organizational change, 316, 320, 354–56
organizational culture, 109–10, 288, 292, 324, 328, 337, 340–43, 345, 348–52, 354–55, 364, 500, 502
organizational goals, 116, 191, 369, 407
organizational structures, 36, 72, 102, 106, 189, 353, 411, 475
organizational success, 36, 61, 213, 225, 240, 349, 358, 363, 393, 400, 455
organizational values, 111, 116, 163, 291, 317, 326, 337–38, 342, 348–49, 364, 447
organizations design, 122, 337, 351
organization's values, 311, 348–49, 351, 364
original ideas, 362, 441–43

peer groups, 203, 222, 225
personal appeal, 220–21, 324
personal leadership brand, 73, 143–44
personal values, 71, 113, 154–55, 159–60, 176, 337, 344, 348–49, 408
plants, 441–42, 445, 500
positionality, 74, 76, 128–29
problems, 18–22, 86–89, 92–93, 99–100, 184–88, 191–97, 204–7, 237, 242–54, 256–60, 262–64, 266–68, 270–71, 372, 389, 432–34, 436–39, 450–51, 468–71, 493–95
    engaging, 21, 85, 447, 467
    new, 246, 447, 452
    single, 21, 87, 89, 92–93, 101, 250, 256, 270, 441, 448
problem-solving, 93, 99–100, 106, 181, 185, 193, 237, 239–71, 357, 359, 372–73, 376, 378
problem-solving process, 19, 97, 100, 185, 268, 372
problem statement, 195, 198, 437
process-orientation, 79, 82–83, 116

radical empathy, 399, 412, 422
real world, 37, 62–63
relationships, quality, 112–13, 311
research-based, 421, 425–26
resistance to change, 319–20, 328, 330
reward power, 222–23, 227

sense of purpose, 125, 133, 407
servant leaders, 408–10, 422–23
servant leadership, 156, 399, 403, 407–10, 422–23, 514
service learning, 418–19, 421–22, 427
shadow experiences, 121, 133–35, 141–43
shared leadership, 373, 389, 393–94
shared values, 104, 109, 340, 345, 355, 379, 415, 500, 505
Situational Leadership, 300, 302–3
social change, 133, 288, 382, 475
    positive, 135, 415, 417
Social Change Model, 399, 413, 416, 419
social dimension, 278, 281, 303, 450–51
social identities, 74–76, 114, 127, 246, 275–76, 498
societal cultures, 103, 343, 353, 364
solutions, 19–20, 87–89, 92, 97–100, 191–92, 219, 221, 244–45, 247–49, 251, 254–55, 260, 325–26, 372, 436–37, 450–51, 478–79, 487–88, 494–95, 501–2
sources of motivation, 227–32, 235, 411
sources of power, 70, 209, 212, 222–25, 227–28, 235
stages of development, 383–85, 394, 470
state, emotional, 26, 32–33, 91
strategic planning, 68, 102, 247, 358–59, 361–64, 474
student experience, 149, 151, 175
success
    designing, 217, 285, 323
    individual, 141, 170, 355, 393
    organization's, 218, 363, 366, 413, 432–33
success of leaders, 489, 493, 510
support change, 310, 327–28
sustainable leadership, 489, 498, 507, 510
systems, organizational, 329, 474, 493, 496
systems thinking, 489, 493–94, 497–98, 510

table, 34–35, 65–66, 69–70, 72, 98–100, 131–32, 191–92, 204–5, 213–15, 227–28, 253–54, 258–60, 265–68, 283–84, 376, 413–15, 447–48, 450–54, 469–70, 505
Team leaders, 374, 381, 385, 449

team leadership, 369–70, 382, 385–86, 393–94
teams, 89–91, 109–12, 123, 167–69, 182–84, 186–88, 190–92, 198, 200–203, 224–25, 230, 234, 252, 315–16, 356–58, 369–95, 441–44, 449–55, 502, 504–5
  great, 28, 242, 369, 375, 377, 379, 382, 395, 509
  innovative, 431, 448, 501
  successful, 152, 374, 386
teamwork, 83, 167, 347, 349, 366, 369, 372, 392, 397, 437, 465
technical problems, 181, 188, 206
traits, 28, 38, 59, 63, 65–66, 68, 70–71, 75–76, 154, 159, 513
traits and skills, 54, 66–67, 71, 81, 513
transformational leadership, 141, 318, 331, 402, 455–56, 514

unique ideas, 70, 243, 250, 255, 432, 439, 462
Utilizing Change Processes Effectively, 237, 309–33

values, high, 177–78, 200, 412
values and ethical actions, 147, 151–79, 502
virtual teams, 370–71, 375, 380–81
virtues, 50, 150, 154–60, 165, 172–73, 175–76, 178, 403
vision
  organizational, 62, 293, 379
  organization's, 341, 350, 364, 402
vulnerability, 58, 239, 245–46, 270, 382, 392, 403–4, 413, 422, 504

wicked problems, 86–87, 117, 247
work culture, 104, 112, 279, 292, 294, 296, 328, 366
workers, 74, 108, 110–11, 230, 298, 302, 408, 410, 440
workforce, 110–11, 287–88, 294, 296, 298, 319, 322, 340, 409, 462
working environment, 102, 110, 286, 294, 303, 450
work life, 108, 116, 316
workplace, 84, 101–4, 106–7, 109, 112, 287–88, 314, 316, 399, 402–4, 407, 447, 449
work processes, 300–301, 375
world influences, 55–56, 135